The British Isles

Atlantic Ocean

Shetland Islands

W0110347

Orkney Islands

The Hebrides

Scotland

• Inverness

• Aberdeen

▲ *Ben Nevis*

The United Kingdom of Great Britain and Northern Ireland (UK)

● **Edinburgh**

Glasgow

Isle of Arran

North Sea

Northern Ireland

● **Belfast**

Hadrian's Wall

Vindolanda • ● Newcastle upon Tyne

● Durham

River Wear

Lake District

• Rievaulx

■ **Dublin**

Republic of Ireland

• Ennis

The Isle of Man

Irish Sea

Liverpool ● • Manchester

England

Bethesda • • • River Dee
Caernafon • • Llangollen • Whitchurch
Mount Snowdon ▲ • Chirk • Ellesmere

• Birmingham

• Cambridge

Wales

River Towy

• Oxford

■ **London**

Bristol • *River Thames*

Cardiff ●

• Bath

● Glastonbury

Celtic Sea

Portsmouth • • Brighton
• Hastings
The Solent

Devon •

English Channel   **France**

Plymouth •

■ capital cities of the UK and the Republic of Ireland
● capital cities of the countries
● important cities/places in On Track 1–6

0   50   100 miles

0   100 km

westermann

On Track ◀◀◀

Englisch für Gymnasien
Ausgabe Bayern

6

von:

David Baker

Lucy Buxton

Jon Hird

Claudia Maria Hugo

Fiona MacKenzie

Adrian Tennant

Agnes Tennant

Patricia Wedler

Story von Marcus Sedgwick mit
  Illustrationen von Pete Williamson

herausgegeben von:

Helga Holtkamp

Begleitmaterialien zum Lehrwerk:

Workbook ISBN 978-3-14-040826-4
Medienpaket ISBN 978-3-14-062678-1
Schulaufgabentrainer ISBN 978-3-14-040896-7

BiBox – Digitale Unterrichtsmaterialien
Nähere Informationen unter www.bibox.schule

Vokabel-Apps sind online erhältlich.

© 2023 Westermann Bildungsmedien Verlag GmbH, Georg-Westermann-Allee 66, 38104 Braunschweig
www.westermann.de

Das Werk und seine Teile sind urheberrechtlich geschützt. Jede Nutzung in anderen als den gesetzlich zugelassenen bzw. vertraglich zugestandenen Fällen bedarf der vorherigen schriftlichen Einwilligung des Verlages.

Die enthaltenen Links verweisen auf digitale Inhalte, die der Verlag bei verlagsseitigen Angeboten in eigener Verantwortung zur Verfügung stellt. Links auf Angebote Dritter wurden nach den gleichen Qualitätskriterien wie die verlagsseitigen Angebote ausgewählt und bei Erstellung des Lernmittels sorgfältig geprüft. Für spätere Änderungen der verknüpften Inhalte kann keine Verantwortung übernommen werden.

Druck A[1] / Jahr 2023
Alle Drucke der Serie A sind inhaltlich unverändert.

Beratung durch: Claudia Maria Hugo (Lindau), Günter Fischer (Mitwitz),
Friedrich Frenzel (Bad Neustadt an der Saale), Dr. Jürgen Kurtz (Gießen), Dr. Mario Oesterreicher (Nürnberg),
Christian Schulze (Lindau), Eva Maria Veitenhansl (München), Juliane Lobischer (Berlin),
Alexa Bradbury (Paderborn)

Lektorat: Christine House
Redaktion: Julia Huneke, Dr. Martin Walter
Umschlaggestaltung: Detlef Möller, Paderborn
Coverfoto vorne: © SergeBertasiusPhotography / Shutterstock.com. Edinburgh city centre at night
Coverfoto hinten: © Molchanov, Dmitry / Shutterstock.com
Druck und Bindung: Westermann Druck GmbH, Georg-Westermann-Allee 66, 38104 Braunschweig

ISBN 978-3-14-**040806**-6

How to use this book

On Track 6 starts with a *Welcome* double-page spread. Then there are three regular workshops and one extra workshop on projects and skills. Every regular workshop has the same three parts. Parts one and two teach you new things, and part three helps you practise what you have learned. The activities and exercises have numbers and letters. Sometimes they have symbols, too.

Here is an explanation of the symbols:

Symbols in *On Track 6*

audio	🔊 14))	Listen to a dialogue, a text, song or story.
video	🎞 2	Watch a film.
partner work	👥	Work with a partner.
group work	👥	Work with two or more partners.
mediation	M	Help an English person to understand German or a German person to understand English.
revision	*	Grammar revision
step 1, 2, 3, …	S1	Activities with this symbol help you with a more complex task – step by step.
grammar	→ G2	There is more information about this grammar point in the *Appendix*.
webcode		There is a webcode on the left-hand page of every workshop. This webcode helps you to find all the audio and video material. You will also find transcripts of the audios and videos as well as solutions to the activities on the *Review* pages.
First track	≫≫	Do the First track exercises on **pages 145–151**.

Vocabulary in *On Track 6*

In *On Track 6* you will encounter many original and authentic texts from all kinds of sources: from books, newspaper and website articles as well as videos and podcasts. These text types contain a lot of individual vocabulary that you do not have to learn to use actively, but need to know to understand the text. As before, in *On Track 6* we have put them in **grey** in the *Appendix*. But we have also put a lot of words in **grey** that are similar in German and English (and not false friends). Any word, however, whether **receptive** or **productive** can be found in the two dictionaries at the end of the book.

How to use the webcodes

A webcode is like a small website. All the *On Track* audio and video material that you need for class or homework is here: www.westermann.de/webcodes. There is also extra material. You can listen and watch online or download everything. Type in the code for the workshop (**WES-40806-001**) without the @ and click "Aufrufen". There is your page for *Workshop 1*. There are webcodes in your workbook, too.

These are the webcodes in *On Track 6*:

Welcome:	@ WES-40806-000	Workshop 2: @ WES-40806-002	Workshop 4: @ WES-40806-004
Workshop 1:	@ WES-40806-001	Workshop 3: @ WES-40806-003	

Contents

Page	Workshop and topic	Communication
10	**Welcome to *On Track 6*: Living in a changing world**	
12	**Workshop 1: Scotland — Land of the Brave**	
14	**Planning an expedition** Talking about planning an expedition	Read a text. Explain the meaning of words. Listen to a conversation. Make notes about photos. Watch a video and correct statements.
18	**A brief history of Scotland** Talking about Scottish history and historical figures	Listen to a radio programme. Match words to their definitions. Read a text. Carry out some research about a film or TV series. Prepare and give a presentation.
24	**Method coach: Recognizing text types**	
25	**Workshop task: Writing different texts**	
26	**The sounds of Scotland** Talking about Scottish music	Listen to a conversation. Summarize a text. Write an email. Make notes. Write a review.
30	**Scottish politics** Talking about Scottish politics	Read a text. Watch a video. List arguments. Listen to an interview. Write a blog post. Research a Scottish author.
36	**Method coach: Preparing to write a persuasive text**	
37	**Workshop task: Writing a persuasive text**	
38	**More practice**	
40	**Mediation**	
42	**Ready for Workshop 2?** (Review)	
44	**Reading: Poems and songs: Robert Burns, Jackie Kay, Runrig**	
48	**Cudweed and the Bagpipes: ONE** (Reading for fun)	
52	**Workshop 2: America — Land of Dreams**	
54	**Slavery and the American Civil War** Talking about American history	Compare photos. Listen to a radio documentary. Make notes about an article. Listen to a conversation. Comment on quotes. Write a biography.

PART 1

PART 2

PART 3

PART 1

Vocabulary	Grammar	Skills focus	
trips and expeditions, awards, outdoors, linguistics, Scottish Gaelic	Past progressive (G 1)* Present perfect (G 1)* Simple past (G 1)*	listening and viewing	
history, clans and crofters, legends and myths, linguistics, presentations	Past perfect (G 1)*	speaking	
artists and bands, musical traditions, folk music, music reviews	Adjectives, adverbs and adverbials (G 5)*	writing	
politics and parties, voting, elections, referendums, blogs, novels		reading	
slavery, Civil War, historical figures, monuments	Passive (G 2)*	writing	

* grammar revision

Page	Workshop and topic	Communication
58	**The Civil Rights Movement** Talking about civil rights	Watch a video. Write a short text. Prepare a presentation. Comment on quotes. Read an article. Describe posters. Match words and phrases to definitions.
64 65	**Method coach: Looking at extracts from a novel** **Workshop task: Analysing extracts from a novel**	
66	**Blues and Motown** Talking about black music	Listen to a conversation. Read an article. Present a short talk about a musical genre. Comment on quotes. Watch a video. Discuss rhetorical techniques.
70	**Black Lives Matter movement** Talking about protests	Read an article. Listen to a podcast. Do some research about famous Black Americans. Hold a class debate.
76 77	**Method coach: Looking at the lyrics of a song** **Workshop task: Analysing the lyrics of a song**	
78	**More practice**	
80	**Mediation**	
82	**Ready for Workshop 3?** (Review)	
84	**Reading: Novel and film review: Harper Lee, *Green Book* review**	
88	**Cudweed and the Bagpipes: TWO** (Reading for fun)	

Page	**Workshop 3: My generation**	Communication
92	**Workshop 3: My generation**	
94	**Youth culture** Talking about youth culture(s)	Read an article. Write a short text about teenage life. Listen to a conversation. Talk about teenage language. Watch a video.
98	**Gaming culture** Talking about gaming	Describe a picture. Listen to a conversation. Hold a debate. Read an article. Hold a presentation and give feedback.
104 105	**Method coach: How to assess texts** **Workshop task: Assessing claims**	
106	**Digitalization** Talking about data literacy and media use	Comment on a quote. Read an article. Make a poster about media use. Summarize a conversation. Describe pictures. Write an argumentative essay.

PART 1   PART 2   PART 3   PART 1   PART 2

Contents

Vocabulary	Grammar	Skills focus
political activism, historical figures, racial segregation, discrimination, political organizations	Passive (G 2)*	reading
(evolution of) musical genres, artists and bands, African American vernacular, speeches		listening and viewing
protests, counterculture, social media, historical figures	Reported speech (G 4)*	speaking
social groups, teenage language, past experiences and expectations		listening and viewing
gaming, fashion, tatoos, subcultures, historical figures	Conditional sentences (G 3)*	speaking
working and living online, digital literacy, tentative language, social media, digital detox		writing

* grammar revision

Page	Workshop and topic	Communication

PART 2

| 110 | **Social issues**
Talking about social issues and Gen Z | Read an article.
Watch a video.
Create a questionnaire.
Make notes on and discuss an article.
Write a letter to the editor.
Find definitions. |

| 116 | **Method coach: Critical thinking** | |
| 117 | **Workshop task: Reporting on fake news** | |

PART 3

118	**More practice**	
120	**Mediation**	
122	**Ready for the next level?** (Review)	
124	**Reading: Short story and drama excerpt: Vesna Main, Craig Taylor**	
128	**Cudweed and the Bagpipes: THREE** (Reading for fun)	

132	**Workshop 4: Projects and skills**	
134	**Text types (1): Text analysis**	
136	**Text types (2): Grammar and style**	
138	**Planning your presentation**	
141	**Brushing up your dictionary skills**	
142	**Presentations: Structuring and giving presentations**	
144	**Giving feedback**	

| 145 | **First track** (language help) | |

152	**Appendix**	
152	**Grammatical terms**	
154	**Grammar**	
168	**Irregular verbs**	
171	**Vocabulary**	
237	**Dictionary: English – German**	
293	**Dictionary: German – English**	
335	**Dictionary: Names**	
338	**Acknowledgements**	

Vocabulary	Grammar	Skills focus
Gen Z, challenges, positive/negative adjectives, protests, (history of) teenagers	Adjectives, adverbs and adverbials (G 5)*	reading

* grammar revision

@ WES-40806-000

Welcome to *On Track 6*

Living in a changing world

 Welcome to year 10.
In *On Track 6*, we will be looking at such diverse topics as Scotland, Black history, music and growing up in different cultures. Do the quiz and and find out what you already know about these topics.

1. Which of these statements is correct?
   A Scotland is part of the United Kingdom.
   B The population of Scotland is a quarter of the population of England.
   C The capital of Scotland is Glasgow.

2. In which of these battles did the Scots defeat the English?
   A Battle of Falkirk
   B Battle of Bannockburn
   C Battle of Dornock

3. Which of these statements is correct?
   A Black History month is in February in every country that celebrates it.
   B Black History month is in February in both the USA and UK.
   C Black History month is celebrated in a different month in the USA and UK.

4. What was the reason for the American Civil War?
   A To end slavery.
   B To save the Union.
   C To gain independence.

5. Which of these musical genres is usually associated with rebellious youth?
   A Blues
   B New Wave
   C Rock 'n' roll

6. Which social issue is this picture connected to?

 Listen and check your answers to the quiz.

In many of the topics in *On Track 6*, we look at how the world has changed in the last couple of centuries and at prominent figures involved in these changes. Read the quotes about changing the world. Which one do you like the most? Think of reasons for your answer.

> *What you do makes a difference, and you have to decide what kind of difference you want to make.*

Jane Goodall (English primatologist)

> *Yesterday I was clever, so I wanted to change the world. Today I am wise, so I am changing myself.*

Rumi (13th century Persian Poet)

> *Change is the law of life, and those who look only to the past and present are certain to miss the future.*

John F. Kennedy (US President from 1961–1963)

> *If you can't fly, then run. If you can't run, then walk. If you can't walk, then crawl. But whatever you do, you have to keep moving forward.*

Martin Luther King Jr. (American civil rights activist)

> *I alone cannot change the world, but I can cast a stone across the water to create many ripples.*

Mother Teresa (Albanian-Indian nun and missionary)

 Tell the other students in the group which quote you like and why. Try to persuade your group that the quote you picked is the best one.

> *Education is the most powerful weapon which you can use to change the world.*

Nelson Mandela (South African revolutionary and politician)

 Listen to four teenagers talking about different topics and complete the tasks.

1 State the topic that each teenager talks about.
2 Explain what Brendan means by 'I'll give anything a go'. And what does Paige mean by 'is close to my heart'?
3 Discuss the points each teenager makes about their topic.

Workshop 1

Scotland – Land of the Brave

Scotland is part of the United Kingdom and has a ninety-six-mile land border with England to the south. The capital city is Edinburgh, although Glasgow is the largest city. With a population of just 5.3 million, fewer live there than in London, so there is lots of wide, open space. Amazingly, Scotland has over 6,000 miles of coast and if you add the islands this almost doubles. There are four distinct regions in Scotland: the Borders, the Central Belt, the Highlands and the Islands.

Describe what you see in the photos. What do you think is the link to Scotland? Say which photo you like the best and give reasons.

Listen to the news items, then match the information to the photos A – E.

Choose two news items that interest you. Listen again and note down at least four facts. Then do some research about one of the stories.

Work with a partner. Tell each other the information you found out about the story.

Look at the facts in the *Did you know …?* box.
Explain which one surprised you the most and why.

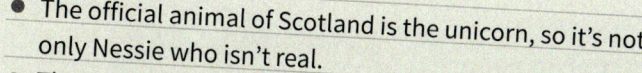

Did you know …?
- The official animal of Scotland is the unicorn, so it's not only Nessie who isn't real.
- There are more people with red hair as a proportion of the population in Scotland than anywhere else in the world.
- The shortest commercial flight is between Westray and Papa Westray in the Orkney Islands. It takes two minutes!
- There are more than 30,000 freshwater lochs throughout the country.

Scotland is often referred to as 'Land of the Brave'. This name is closely linked to the song 'Scotland the Brave'. Read the text and explain the connection.

4)) Then listen to a recording of the two most popular songs mentioned. Explain which of the two you prefer and why.

Traditional Scottish bagpipe music is like the essence of this small country in a sound.

So, you might think this soul-stirring piece would be the ideal national anthem for a country whose history is so full of fearless warriors, bloody battles and passionate loyalties […].

[…] The lyrics for 'Scotland the Brave' were written in 1951 by the multi-talented Cliff Hanley (he was a journalist, author, songwriter, public speaker and more).

Cliff was a Glaswegian (born in Glasgow) and this piece was originally only intended to be sung at a musical performance at Glasgow's Empire Theatre.

But it immediately touched the hearts and souls of the Scottish people and became hugely popular. […] It did have a rival for the affection of the people though – another piece of traditional Scottish music, 'The Flower of Scotland' which was traditionally sung at rugby matches and at other celebrations such as Burns' Night and St. Andrews' Night. As there was no official Scottish national anthem, in 2006 an online voting system was set up through the website of the Royal Scottish National Orchestra that allowed the Scottish people to vote for one of four popular Scottish songs. The winner would become the national anthem. The songs in question were 'Scotland The Brave', 'The Flower of Scotland', 'Highland Cathedral' and 'Scots Wha Hae'.

'The Flower of Scotland' was the clear winner with 41 % of the votes, and 'Scotland The Brave' came in second with 29 % but is so well-loved that it is still thought of as the 'unofficial' national anthem of Scotland.

Source (abbreviated): "Scotland The Brave", MyWay LLC, 2010, https://www.scottish-at-heart.com/scotland-the-brave.html [08.07.2022]

PART 1

PART 2

PART 3

Planning an expedition

1* The Duke of Edinburgh's Award

a The students from Hill End School in Durham have completed both the Bronze and Silver Awards of the Duke of Edinburgh's Award. Now they are preparing for the Gold Award. Read the extracts from the website. The extracts cover three topics. Decide what the three topics are and label the parts, then check with a partner.

The Duke of Edinburgh's Award

1 The Duke of Edinburgh first underlined{considered}[1] the idea of a national programme to support young people's
5 development in the autumn of 1954, at the request of his inspiring former headmaster Kurt Hahn, who [...] believed that young people have more courage, more strength and more compassion than they know. He underlined{felt}[2] that, if properly supported and challenged,
10 these qualities underlined{could be developed}[3] for the good of young people and the communities in which they lived.
2 Although initially only available to boys aged between 14 and 18, there was great demand for a similar programme for girls. In 1959, a girls' programme underlined{was
15 launched}[4] and, at the same time, the DofE formally became a charitable trust. [...] In the 1970s, the DofE began to partner with businesses to help young people who were at work, in training or job hunting. [...] Today, the Award forms a core part of many apprenticeships and
20 training schemes in the UK, and employers underlined{are actively looking for}[5] DofE Award holders when recruiting, citing the important skills of teamwork, resilience and confidence the Award provides. [...] Participation in the Award underlined{has grown}[6] every year since
25 inception. By 2017, over six million people underlined{had taken part}[7] in DofE programmes in the UK, with over eight million worldwide. [...] Throughout the UK, over 300,000 people underlined{are taking part}[8] in DofE programmes at any one time.
3 By 1971, the DofE underlined{was operating}[9] in 31 countries,
30 increasing to 48 countries by 1989 as it spread beyond the boundaries of the Commonwealth. The expansion led to the creation of The Duke of Edinburgh's International Award Foundation in 1988, which underlined{has made}[10] programmes available to young people in more
35 than 140 countries.

Source (abbreviated and adapted): "The Duke of Edinburgh's Award", The Royal Household, Crown Copyright, https://www.royal.uk/duke-edinburghs-award [08.07.2022]

🔊)) Words and phrases

to accommodate	to provide with a space to stay
boundary	border
compassion	a strong feeling of sympathy

CULTURE CORNER

The Duke of Edinburgh's Award (DofE) is an awards programme for young people that was founded in the United Kingdom in 1956 by His Royal Highness, Prince Philip, the Duke of Edinburgh (1921 – 2021).

b Read the extracts again. Look at the underlined verbs and decide which tense they are in: past passive, past perfect, past progressive, present perfect, present progressive, simple past. Check your answers with a partner.

> **Remember:**
> - We use the simple past to talk about something that happened in the past and we know when.
> - We use the present progressive form to talk about something that is happening now or over a period of time.
> - We use the present perfect to talk about something in the past which is connected with, or has consequences in the present. We also use it to talk about an experience (or lack of experience) in the past when we don't know the exact time.
> - We use the past perfect to show one event happened before another in the past.
> - We use the passive in different tenses when we focus on the action and not on who does the action.

2 The awards.
Look at the table describing the three awards. List all the similarities and differences.

	Bronze	Silver	Gold
Volunteering	3 months	6 months	12 months
Physical	3 months	3 or 6 months	6 or 12 months
Skills	3 months	3 or 6 months	6 or 12 months
Expedition	2 days, 1 night	3 days, 2 nights	4 days, 3 nights
Residential	--	--	5 days, 4 nights
Starting age	9+	10+	16+

Must be completed by the participant's 25th birthday.

inception	the beginning of an official organization or activity
resilience	the ability to be happy or successful again after sth. bad has happened

3 **The sections**

a Choose a section of the awards (volunteering, physical, skills, expedition or residential) and do some research about the activities participants can do and how they are assessed.

b Share your findings.

4 **Planning the trip**

a The students are making plans for their Gold expedition. Listen to the first part of their conversation and do the tasks.

1 Summarize what they discuss.
2 Outline the criteria the students need to consider to make the right choice.
3 Explain what the next step is.

b Listen to the second part of the conversation. Explain which of the four regions do you think the students will choose and why.

CULTURE CORNER

The text about Mar Lodge includes places names that are particularly Scottish:
- **blair** – a meadow or field
- **atholl** – a line dividing different areas
- **glen** – a valley

You find more Scottish words in the vocabulary box on page 175.

---

5 **Mar Lodge.** Read the article that David found about Mar Lodge and complete the tasks.

1 List the reasons why Mar Lodge is a suitable place to do the expedition part of the DofE Award.
2 Explain why you need to be able to use a map and compass to find your way.
3 State why it is necessary to contact Mar Lodge before you go there.

Mar Lodge – Duke of Edinburgh Award

Looking for somewhere to do your expedition part of your Duke of Edinburgh Gold Award?
5 Then look no further than Mar Lodge. There are fifteen Munros (mountains over 3,000 feet) on the

10 estate, including four out of five of the highest mountains in the UK. Head north to walk through Larig Ghru, a 19-mile-long mountain pass, or south through Glen Tilt to reach Blair Atholl. Both routes offer the type of challenges you are expected to cope with during the Gold Award. The landscape is varied, you'll find
15 heathered moors, ragged peaks, rolling glens, wild rivers, just to name a few features. There are mountain bothies on the estate around natural water sources and of course ample opportunity for wild camping. There is no waymarking anywhere as nature is fiercely protected. You'll definitely need to practise your
20 navigation and map reading skills as you won't get a mobile signal for your phone or GPS. If you decide to come to Mar Lodge for your award, contact us first as we can only accommodate one DofE group at a time and we also need to notify mountain rescue, just in case.

---

6 **It's your turn: Think about the DofE Award.** Choose one of the options and make notes. Work in groups. If you worked on option A, share your experiences. If you worked on option B, present your ideas.

A	**B**
If you have participated in a similar programme for young people: - Describe the programme (who / what / where / why?). - Describe your personal experience / involvement / achievements. - List the short and long-term benefits of the programme (both personal and wider).	If you haven't participated in a similar programme yet: - State what kind of programme you would mostly be interested in. - Design the structure, content and length of the programme. Use the table on page 14 as an example for your design. - Explain who would benefit from the programme and what you would personally get out of it.

Grammar and structures (revision)

Past progressive → G1
I **was researching** the islands.

Present perfect → G1
I**'ve been** to Scotland a couple of times.

Simple past → G1
I really **enjoyed** when we did the Silver Award last year.

@ WES-40806-001

→ Workbook, page 10

PRACTICE A

PART 1

PART 2

PART 3

1　**a** Read what Helen, a participant of the DofE Award, wrote about her experience.

p. 145 Complete the text with the correct form of the verbs from the box. Be careful as some are negative and one is passive.

> be (2x) ■ be able to ■ do ■ encounter ■ enjoy ■ feel ■ go into ■ have ■
> know ■ make ■ reach ■ see ■ tell ■ use ■ walk ■ want ■ wear

While on my Gold DofE expedition, we ‗1‗ [up a mountain] when we ‗2‗ some horrendous weather – with the heavens opening and fog coming down thick (pretty typical weather for July!). The path ‗3‗ very
5 boggy and one of the walkers in my group managed to slip off some stepping-stones straight into the bog in a very comedic manner. She ‗4‗ pull herself out and I attempted to traverse the same route before ending up waist deep in the bog myself – ruining the pair of socks
10 I ‗5‗ on my hands having failed to pack any gloves. Covered in bog, I ‗6‗ too bright myself but my teammate came off worse and actually ‗7‗ medical shock.
Though we ‗8‗ exactly where we ‗9‗ on the map, with the heavy fog we ‗10‗ where we needed to go next and we ‗11‗ to get caught wandering off the path given the condition of my teammate.
15 We ended up pitching two tents which the five of us squeezed into, changing into dry clothes and trying to get warm while also ‗12‗ contact with base camp to organize a rescue party. [...] It was dark by the time our rescue party ‗13‗ us and we then ‗14‗ pack our tents away by torchlight before hiking down the side of the mountain to find a clearing in a forest to do a second night of wild camping [...]. [...] Though [we were all] pretty miserable at the time, we all ‗15‗ looking back
20 on the adventure and it helped us to develop resilience in the face of adversity. Our DofE assessor ‗16‗ us we ‗17‗ exactly the right thing given the circumstances we [had] faced and apparently we ‗18‗ as an example in the years since: so much so that our group is slightly legendary at our school!

Source (abbreviated and adapted): Helen Sheppard, The Duke of Edinburgh's Award, 2021,
https://www.dofe.org/memories/stories/helen-sheppard/ [08.07.2022]

b Read the story again and work on the tasks.

1 Describe Helen's reaction when one of the group slipped into the bog.
2 Explain why she was lucky compared to her teammate.
3 Comment on the actions the group took after the incident.

 c Discuss how you would have felt as part of the group. Give reasons for your answers.

2　**a** When the students are camping for their Gold Award, they meet some young people. Listen to the conversation and do the tasks.

1 Outline were the young people come from and what is different about JT.
2 Interpret what Kirsty means by 'south of the border'.

b Listen to the conversation and explain the meaning of these words and expressions.

● bonnie
● wee
● to bag a Munro
● dreich

))) **Words and phrases**

bog　　　　　an area of soft wet ground
to pitch　　　to put up a tent
to traverse　to move or travel through an area

@ WES-40806-001

→ Workbook, page 11   **LISTENING AND VIEWING PRACTICE**

1 Look at the photos and make notes on what you can see and what the photos tell you about Scotland. Then compare your ideas with a partner.

A

B

C

D

2 Watch the video about Scottish Gaelic and decide whether the statements are true or false. Correct the false statements.

1 English has always been the most widely spoken language in Scotland.

2 Lots of place names in Scotland originate from Gaelic.

3 Ballachulish is a village in the Scottish Highlands.

4 Scottish Gaelic is only linked to Irish Gaelic and Welsh.

5 The language came across from Ireland in the 8th century A.D.

6 The Education Act of 1872 made Gaelic the official language in schools.

7 There are place names in New Zealand, Canada and the USA which originally come from Gaelic.

8 All the events at the Royal National Mod are held in Gaelic.

3 Watch the video again and make notes about the topics on the right. Then compare with a partner.

4 Watch the last part of the video again (5:13 to 6:02). Explain what these Gaelic phrases mean.

- place names
- origins of Scottish Gaelic
- influences on languages spoken in Scotland
- culture and traditions
- films, TV programmes and video games

Madainn mhath   *Feasgar math*   *Ciamar a tha sibh?*

The gu math, tapadh leibh   *Mar sin leibh*

5 Explain the purpose of the video. If you were making a video about Germany, what would you include in it? Give reasons for your choices. Share your ideas with the class.

Old town hall in Bamberg

Apartments in Munich

A brief history of Scotland

1 **Fact or fiction?**

a Look at the two film stills and describe the people you see. Find out whether they were real or not.

Mel Gibson as William Wallace in *Braveheart*

Saoirse Ronan as Mary Queen of Scots

b Listen to a radio programme and do the tasks.

1 Explain what the radio programme is about.
2 Comment on the speaker's view of the film *Braveheart*.
3 List the inaccuracies in *Braveheart*.
4 Illustrate how the film about Mary Queen of Scots is fiction not fact.
5 Explain how *Macbeth* by Shakespeare isn't factual.
6 Discuss why films and plays might not always stick to the facts.

c Listen again and find words in the interview to match these definitions.

1 well-known
2 not true
3 see or notice something
4 to represent someone in a particular way in a film, play or book
5 the freedom to include things in a story that aren't actually true

---

124 AD 1

Scotland's recorded history began with the arrival of the Romans. Despite building two impressive fortifications the Romans never truly conquered Caledonia. Unable to defeat the Caledonians and Picts, the Romans eventually withdrew and over time retreated away from Britain.

800 AD 2

Around 800 AD the Vikings began crossing the treacherous North Sea from Norway and Denmark to trade and settle in Scotland. While Vikings began to settle in the west, the Picts were forging a new kingdom: the Kingdom of Alba.

1297 3

In 1297, Edward's army planned to cross the River Forth at Stirling Bridge; the Scots seized the opportunity to attack at the crossing of the River Forth, the Stirling Bridge, forcing the English army to retreat. It was here that one of Scotland's most famous figures, William Wallace, earned his place in the history books forever.

1306 4

Unrest continued into the 14th century when Robert the Bruce took the throne and was crowned king. Fighting continued until 1314 at the Battle of Bannockburn, where Robert the Bruce and his army defeated Edward II, a major turning point in his rule.

1542 5

Mary was just six days old when her father, James V died and she was crowned Queen of Scots. Later Elizabeth I imprisoned Mary and, after almost 19 years of captivity, had her executed at Fotheringhay Castle in Northamptonshire in 1587.

1603 6

James VI became King of Scotland at the age of just 13 months in 1567. When Elizabeth I died with no children he became James VI of Scotland and James I of England – a historic move that's now known as the Union of the Crowns.

1707 7

In 1707 The Act of Union brought Scotland even closer to Britain by creating a single Parliament of the United Kingdom of Great Britain at the Palace of Westminster.

1746 8

The Battle of Culloden in 1746 was the final Jacobite rising and the last battle fought on British soil. After defeat at the battle, Bonnie Prince Charlie fled. He was helped to escape to Skye by Flora Macdonald.

Source (abbreviated and adapted): "History", Brand Scotland, https://www.scotland.org/about-scotland/history-timeline [08.07.2022]

Words and phrases

to **flee**	to escape by running away, especially because of fear or danger
to **huddle**	sitting close together
kelp	a large brown plant that grows in the sea and is sometimes used in food, medicines or as a fertilizer

PART 1

PART 2

PART 3

2 **A timeline of Scottish history**

a Bex has always been interested in history. After returning from Scotland, she finds out more about Scottish history. Read the brief history of Scotland (timeline on **page 18**) and complete it using the headings from the box.

> Arrival of the Vikings ■ Battle of Stirling Bridge ■ Bonnie Prince Charlie ■ Mary Queen of Scots ■ Robert the Bruce crowned ■ The Act of Union ■ The Roman Empire ■ The union of the crowns

p. 145 **b** Choose one of the people mentioned in the text and carry out some research. Make notes about what you find out and put together a short (3-minute) presentation.

 c Give your talk to your group. Answer any questions and listen to their feedback.

> **TIP**
>
> Giving feedback (more tips on pp. 139/140)
> *Your presentation was interesting but …*
> *Could you tell me more about …?*
> *I didn't really understand …*
> *I would have liked to know more about …*
> *I didn't know …, so that was interesting.*

3 **Clans and crofters.** Bex finds a short podcast about another part of Scottish history. Listen and complete the tasks.

12))

1 Explain why clan systems were common in the Scottish Highlands.
2 Outline the structure of the clan system.
3 Describe how the English rulers tried to break up the clan system.
4 Speculate why many landlords paid for crofters to emigrate.

4* **A crofter's life**

a Read a text that retells the story of a young girl whose parents were crofters. Complete the diary with the correct form of the verbs.

> So, we **1** (*arrive*) in America last week after we **2** (*spend*) thirty-five days on a boat. My parents were crofters in the Scottish Highlands as their **ancestors** **3** (*be*) for centuries. Life **4** (*become*) too hard, so we ended up
> 5 **emigrating**. Although I **5** (*not go*) to school by the time I was a teenager, I **6** (*learn*) to read and write a bit and I hope that will help me find a job and help my family survive. I'll have to get used to everything here as it's so different to back home. Before we emigrated, I **7** (*spend*) my whole
> 10 life living on crofts. By the time we left, I **8** (*live*) in three different places. Each time we **9** (*move*), life got more and more difficult. Last year the potato harvest **10** (*be*) terrible, worse than it **11** (*ever be*)! We were really frightened that we would **starve**. I **12** (*start*) to notice
> 15 that every evening before bed my parents would **huddle** by the fireplace whispering. Now I know they were talking about leaving for America and how to pay the **passage** to get here.
> We **13** (*find out*) that our passage **14** (*pay for*) paid for
> 20 by the landlord as it **15** (*not be*) as expensive as helping us out with money to stay on the croft. Nobody knew how long the **famine** was going to last, so it was cheaper just to **get rid of** us!

b Look at the **bold** words in the text. Try to work out the meaning from the context. If you are not sure, check in a monolingual dictionary.

> **Remember:**
> We use the past perfect to talk about an event which happened before another event in the past.
> *We **had lived** on another croft before we moved here and life was tough, …*
> *The potato harvest was terrible last year, worse than it **had** ever **been** before!*

5 **It's your turn: How accurate is it?** In the radio interview in **1**, the professor explained how films and plays about famous people from Scotland are often inaccurate. Do some research about a film or TV series about Scottish history and find out how accurate it is. You can pick one of these examples: *Outlander, Outlaw King, Mary Queen of Scots*. Present your findings to your group. Find tips on **pp. 105** and **140**.

Grammar and structures

Past perfect (revision) → G1
We **had lived** on another croft before we moved here.

PART 1

1 **a** Look at the pictures from the DofE expedition. Discuss what you think happened, then listen to an extract from Bex's expedition diary and check your ideas.

 A
 B
 C
 D
E

b Listen to the story again and complete the tasks.

1 Explain why the teenagers didn't get to bed until very late.
2 Describe what happened to Deepak.

3 List the signs in Deepak's behaviour that show he has a problem.
4 Speculate about what the group will do after they had found out why Deepak's mood has changed.

c Write the ending of the story in your exercise book.

PART 2

2 One evening during the expedition David read a book about Scottish legends.
Read three extracts and decide whether the sentences are true, false or not in the text.

Robert the Bruce was born in 1274 at Lochmaben, where he was knight and lord of Annandale. In 1306, he was crowned King of Scotland and he tried to free the country from English rule. Unfortunately, that
5 same year he was defeated in battle and had to go into hiding. Legend has it that while he was hiding in a cave in the Western Isles he watched a spider building a web in the entrance of the cave. However, partly because of the windy weather the web kept on being
10 destroyed. Against all odds the spider finally managed to succeed. Robert the Bruce was inspired by the spider's efforts and decided to carry on fighting the English. He is said to have told his men: 'If at first you don't succeed, try, try and try again!'

15 Another legend, which is known around the world, is about Nessie, or the Loch Ness Monster. Legend has it that a 'monster' lives in Loch Ness. This legend is more than 1,500 years old … so a very old monster! In 1934, a doctor from London took a photo that has become
20 almost as famous as Nessie herself. Since then many more photographs have been produced supposedly showing the Loch Ness Monster. Many of these have

been shown to be hoaxes and yet the legend continues. Whether or not it is true, it has made Loch Ness one of the most popular tourist attractions in
25 Scotland with thousands of people visiting and hoping to catch a glimpse of Nessie.

A different legend is one connected to the Corryvreckan whirlpool. Unlike the other two legends there is no disputing that the whirlpool actually exists.
30 Located between the islands of Jura and Scarba off the west coast of Scotland, the whirlpool is actually the third largest in the world. According to legends the Norse king Breacan wanted to marry a local princess. In an attempt to impress her father he sailed close to
35 the whirlpool and then anchored his boat using three different ropes. The first of these was made from hemp, the second from wool and the third from the hair of a maiden. It was said that the purity of the maiden's hair would make the rope unbreakable.
40 However, first the hemp rope snapped, then the one made from wool and finally the one made from hair. The boat was dragged under and the king had to be rescued by the one surviving crew member.

PART 3

1 Robert the Bruce beat the English Army in 1306.
2 Robert the Bruce hid in a cave with some of his men.
3 The Robert the Bruce legend is about not giving up.
4 The legend of the Loch Ness Monster started in 1934.
5 Some of the photos taken of Nessie are believed to be authentic.
6 The Corryvreckan whirlpool is one of the biggest in the world.
7 One of Breacan's ropes was made with hair from a Scottish princess.
8 After he survived, Breacan married the princess.

→ Workbook, pages 14/15   **PRACTICE B**

3 **a** Bex heard about a famous female Scottish explorer – Isobel Wylie Hutchison.
Complete the text about her with the correct form of the verbs in brackets.

Born at Carlowrie Castle in West Lothian, Isobel Wylie Hutchison answered a soul-felt urge ___1___ (*explore*) the lands of the Arctic. In the 1920s, at a time when women ___2___ (*expect*) to immerse themselves in home life, she defied convention and ___3___ (*wander*) at will around Iceland and Greenland, ___4___ (*stay*) with local people and immersing herself in their culture.
She then ___5___ (*take*) herself to Alaska, sailing around the Aleutian Islands and voyaging into the high Arctic with the help of rugged fur-trappers and traders who ___6___ (*become*) lifelong friends.
Isobel's twin passions ___7___ (*be*) botany and adventure: she travelled on impulse, following her heart and later ___8___ (*write*) about her experiences with energy and passion. Sweeping over the sparkling ice by dog sled and warming herself in candlelit igloos at night, Isobel is likely ___9___ (*be*) the first woman ___10___ (*cross*) from Alaska to Arctic Canada at Demarcation Point.

Source (adapted): Jo Woolf, "Compulsive explorers: five Scots who stepped off the map into the unknown", history Scotland, 03.08.2017, https://www.historyscotland.com/history/compulsive-explorers-five-scots-who-stepped-off-the-map-into-the/ [12.07.2022]

b Read the text again and do the tasks.

1 Discuss what the writer means by the phrase 'she defied convention'.
2 Comment on the adventures described by the writer.

4 The students also found a brochure with some information about Scots.
Read the extract and complete the tasks.

Scots is one of three native languages spoken in Scotland today, the others are English and Scottish Gaelic. A national census from 2011 confirmed that over one and a half million people in Scotland identified themselves as Scots speakers. This means that about one third of the Scottish population belong to this language group which is the country's second largest after English.
5 Scots originated with the languages brought over by the Angles when they arrived in Britain in about 600 AD. During the Middle Ages, it grew apart from its sister tongue which was spoken in England.
Scots is the name for four Scottish dialects: Insular, which is spoken in the Orkney and Shetland Islands; Northern – spoken in the Highlands; Central, which you'll hear from Glasgow all the way across to the East coast; and Southern – spoken in the Borders. Of course, within these four main dialects, you'll hear lots of
10 variations, not just in the accent, but in the words used. For example, a cheeky child in Aberdeen is an 'ill-trickit bairn', but in Glasgow they say 'gallus wean'.

1 Explain why Scots and English are called sister tongues.
2 Speculate why there are four dialects and so many variations in such a small country.

5 Read and listen to an extract from a conversation between Kirsty and Rab and match the numbered words and phrases with the standard English ones in the box. The context will help you. Compare your answers with a partner.

cold ■ doesn't ■ don't know
■ food ■ get away ■ little ■ potatoes ■
swim ■ tasty ■ tomorrow ■ you

Kirsty	Do you want some more scran (1)?
Rab	I dinnae ken (2). I'm not too hungry, but maybe a wee (3) bit.
Kirsty	Here yer (4) are.
Rab	It's tidy (5) scran. Did you cook it?
Kirsty	Aye. I'm glad you like it.
Rab	Who dinnae (6) like tatties (7)?
Kirsty	What are yer doing th'morra (8)?
Rab	I'm going for a dook (9) in the loch.
Kirsty	Awa (10)! It'll be really cauld (11).

1 a The final requirement of the expedition part of the Duke of Edinburgh's Award is that the participants give a joint presentation about their experiences. The Durham students are discussing how to put together their presentation. Copy the items of the plan of action in your exercise book in the order you expect them to be mentioned. Then listen and check.

b Think of the procedure you use when preparing for a presentation. Make notes of the differences and compare them with a partner.

Plan of action:
- select the relevant documents
- collate the relevant documents
- choose from the personal accounts
- rehearse the presentation
- add pictures, drawings
- set the deadline
- decide on individual topics
- work on your allocated part

2 The group collects information for their presentation. Read each piece (A – G) and match them to the topics.

Topics

camping ■ geographical features ■ itinerary (2x) ■ leadership ■ fauna and flora (2x)

PART 3

A

Date	What you did	Hours	Initials
???	Cover route from Coylumbridge via Lairig Ghru to Corrour Bothy	8	???
???	On route observation of vegetation (photos)	As above	???
???	On route observation of wildlife (photos)	As above	???

B We planned to set off early as even though the route didn't seem to be difficult, we wanted to get to the top of the Cairngorm mountains before it became too hot. Of course, Bex misplaced her sunglasses and everyone was scrambling around for ages looking for them.

C David appointed himself to take charge on the first day and insisted that he had studied the map before and everything was in his head. Ha ha! I wonder why we got lost then, again and again ... (He could have paid attention to the signposts ...). We teased him so much, he'll never live it off ... and we'll never ever believe what he says again, I promise!

D The Cairngorms contains the finest collection of different landforms outside arctic Canada — from granite tors to 'leavings' from ice age glaciers. It also includes a rare kind of pinewood found only in Scotland and Norway.

E A wide variety of shrubs and plants. Examples: common juniper and whortleberry (shrubby plants). Other examples: orchids, in lots of different colours and bearberries that are favoured by polar bears in the summer months.

F Throughout our walk, we came in contact with many animals such as a heard of red deer, red squirrels, a golden eagle (actually we saw 7 of them!). And, of course, several grouse which Bex insisted were in fact turkeys. Even Deepak, who had researched the wildlife way before the expedition, couldn't convince her otherwise.

G On the grounds of Corrour Bothy. Gained permission to use the site to put up our tents but needed to agree to comply with the code of conduct. It meant that we had to make sure we hadn't left any rubbish behind when we left and there was no trace of us being there at all. May supervised us and she was so bossy that I almost fell out with her.

3 The extracts in **2** are from different sources. Match each of them to the source below and explain which features helped you to decide. The word cloud on the right shows some examples of such features.
Then discuss your ideas with a partner.

p. 146

- personal blog / diary
- logbook
- encyclopaedia / fact sheet

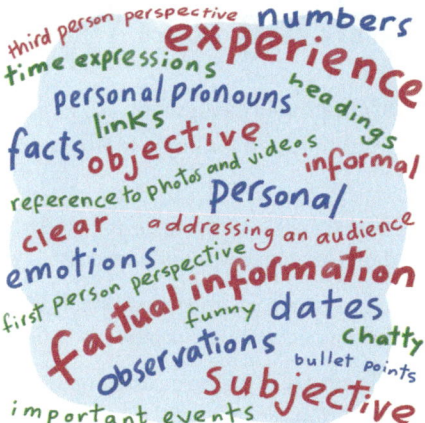

4 a Listen to Deepak and Bex discussing how to use the different notes for the presentation. Make a list of techniques and features Deepak mentions. Is there anything else you would add to the list?

16

b Now listen to two extracts from the presentation the group put together and identify which pieces of information from **2** they have used.

17

c Compare the topics and the presentation sections. Discuss with a partner what changes have been made and why.

5 a Make a presentation of 3 – 4 minutes. Think of an expedition or excursion you went on. Follow these steps and if you need more help, see **pp. 135 (3), 142/143**.

1　Think about how you introduce your topic.
2　When you talk about an event, organize the content in chronological order.
3　When you describe something, use a variety of adjectives and adverbs.
4　You may want to make notes, but do not write out the whole presentation.
5　Use neutral language. Humour and colloquial expressions are fine as long as they are not offensive.
6　When you give your presentation, speak clearly and make eye contact with your audience.

b Student A: Give your presentation.
Student B: Give feedback to your partner. Use the list in **a** for your feedback. Make sure it is balanced, constructive and includes concrete examples and suggestions. Then swap roles. On **p. 144** you find more tips on giving constructive feedback.

> **Useful phrases for a presentation**
> - *I'd like to begin with … / First, I'll …*
> - *Next, I … / Then, we'd like to …*
> - *On this slide, you can see …*
> - *My next slide focusses on …*
> - *Here is some background information about …*
> - *I'd like to finish by …*
> - *I'm sure you have many questions …*
> - *Thank you for your attention.*

@ WES-40806-001

→ Workbook, page 17 **METHOD COACH**

Recognizing text types

PART 1

PART 2

PART 3

S1 **Identifying basic categories.** Read about four common text types and match the names in the box to the descriptions below.

> descriptive ■ informative ■
> instructive ■ persuasive

> **1** texts tell you how to do something: a recipe or how to install a new device. You use verbs such as *must / must not* in direct language without unnecessary words. There are often diagrams or numbered points.
>
> **2** texts help you to picture what is being described: characters in a story or emotions in song lyrics. You use adjectives, adverbs and comparisons, appealing to the readers' senses to describe how something sounds, feels etc.
>
> **3** texts try to make you do something: an advert wanting you to buy something or a letter from a charity asking for support. You can use emotive or amusing language, repetitions, exclamations, and rhetorical questions.
>
> **4** texts aim to advise or tell you about something: health advice on a notice board or information about an event on a website. You use facts, giving information clearly and without repetition.

S2 **Communication purposes**

a Copy and complete the table in your exercise book with the following text types according to their different communicative aims.

b Check with a partner. Give reasons for your choices. Think of examples you've read to support your choices.

> advert ■ blog ■ brochure ■ charity appeal ■
> email ■ fictional story ■ graphic novel ■
> information leaflet ■ letter ■ manual ■
> newspaper or magazine article ■ recipe ■
> review ■ song lyrics ■ summary ■ textbook

Inform	Instruct	Persuade	Describe
???	???	???	???

S3 **Where does it go?**

a Match each sentence to one of the four types.

1 The forest path was thick with autumn leaves that crackled and spiralled away under her boots, which felt as heavy as her heart.
2 Line and grease the cake tin and pre-heat the oven to 160 degrees.
3 Don't miss this chance of a lifetime! A luxurious world cruise could be yours – why delay?
4 The figure approaching her was a tall thin man whose prominent cheek bones resembled the blades of a knife.
5 Separate the egg yolk from the white before mixing the dry ingredients.
6 Building works will continue to affect the upper school timetable.
7 Her lips moved in a silent prayer: could she dare to hope that he had come back for her?

8 Please avoid all construction areas and observe health and safety notices.
9 Relax on a sunny deck between thrilling trips to the world's most exciting cities – what's not to like?!
10 During the renovations, the science lab will be temporarily relocated to Block F.
11 One third of the flour can be replaced with ground almonds if preferred.
12 So why delay? Sign up today!

b Put the matching sentences together to make a mini-text for each text type.

c Choose two mini-texts and add a sentence to each. It can be in any position in the text.

 d Read and listen to the new texts. Discuss which ones you think are the best and explain why.

@ WES-40806-001

→ Workbook, page 17   **WORKSHOP TASK**

Writing different texts

S1 **Looking at different text types.**
Read the text and answer the questions.

Edinburgh Castle is one of the oldest fortified places in Europe.
5 Built on a 350-million-year-old volcanic rock, this castle has a long, rich history as a royal residence, military garrison,
10 prison and fortress. The castle is now a world-famous visitor attraction and an iconic part of the Old and New Towns of Edinburgh World Heritage Site.
The castle has a complex building
15 history. The oldest part, St Margaret's Chapel, dates from the 12th century. The Great Hall was erected by James IV around 1510, the Half Moon Battery by the Regent Morton in the late 16th
20 century, and the Scottish National War Memorial after the First World War. A small water fountain, known as the 'Witches Well', marks the spot where hundreds of women suspected of bein
25 witches were burnt between the 15th and 18th centuries.
Today, the castle houses the Honours (Crown Jewels) of Scotland, the Stone of Destiny, the famous 15th century gun
30 Mons Meg, the One o'clock Gun and the National War Museum of Scotland.

1 What do you think the purpose of this text is?
2 Where might you find this text?
3 Think of at least two things the text does not tell you about Edinburgh Castle.

S2 **Analyse a text.** Look at the layout and photo and read this text, then answer the questions.

Duncan Hotel: your perfect location!

You will not find a better place to stay! Situated in the heart of the Grassmarket looking onto Edinburgh Castle this Old Town family hotel is the perfect place to stay to immerse yourself in all the capital has to offer. Awe-inspiring views,
5 a relaxing pool and top attractions just a short stroll away make this place a dream destination for your stay.

Perfect facilities!
With a wide range of different rooms whatever your need is you'll find the perfect setting. Whether you need a
10 spacious family room with facilities for children or a single one if you are a lone traveller, each room offers a walk-in shower, free toiletries, high-speed WiFi and complimentary snacks and drinks. And if you want to chill out after a busy day, you can take a dip in our swimming pool, relax in the
15 sauna or squeeze in a work-out in our fully equipped gym.

Eat and drink!
Whether you want to enjoy a leisurely in-room breakfast, a light bite at the bar, our chefs offer you exquisite Scottish dishes or prepare meals for your dietary requirements.

20 **Stay, save and explore!**
Watch out for our unique offers – from reduced prices to vouchers for city events – you are certain to find something that makes your stay cheaper, memorable and more enjoyable.

25 *'I was here for 4 nights with a castle view room and had a lovely time. The staff were always welcoming and very friendly. The breakfast was lovely with high quality ingredients and lots of choice. Would recommend this hotel for your stay in Edinburgh.'*

1 What text type is it? How do you know?
2 What words are repeated most often and why?
3 In what way is the final paragraph different?

S3 **Write your own text.** Prepare to write a short text about a popular tourist site. If you need help, you find more support in your students' book: on writing persuasive texts (**pp. 37, 136/137**), assessing and citing sources (**pp. 105, 140**).

- You are going to write an introduction of 30 – 50 words to a persuasive text. Decide on a place you want to write about and think about how you might persuade someone to go there.
- Research the place you've chosen and find an appropriate photo.
- Make notes on the structure of your text: you will need a good, catchy title and a short opening paragraph clearly indicating the purpose of your text.

The sounds of Scotland

1 **Scottish music.** The following pictures show different Scottish musicians. Collect the ideas you have about Scottish music.

2 **Sounds strange!** May is listening to some music. Listen to her conversation with Deepak and complete the sentences.

1 The music May is listening to is …
2 The video Kirsty sent May was …
3 The dance moves on the video …

4 Deepak finds the music …
5 Deepak thinks the name cèilidh is …

3 **The cèilidh.** Deepak carries out some research about the cèilidh. Read the information he found and put it into the correct order to make a text.

The origin of cèilidh goes back centuries. It came about from the need for socializing. In the eighteenth century, Scottish towns or rural habitats didn't offer many opportunities for entertainment. …

A In larger communities these social gatherings grew bigger and were usually held in halls. It's worth mentioning that cèilidh is known and practised in Ireland as well.

B To some extent it is similar to formal Scottish country dancing, but it is easier and greatly resembles the well-known barn dances. Nowadays, cèilidhs are common on celebratory occasions such as birthday parties and, naturally, at weddings.

C At the end of the working day, there were therefore impromptu gatherings in homes where neighbours got together to share songs, music, poetry and storytelling around the fire.

D Often the band will call out dance instructions or there might be dance callers who teach the steps. The cèilidh dance is all inclusive – most age groups and levels of ability can join in and dance along to the catchy tunes that vary from high energy dances to slower waltzes.

E This is reflected in the term, as the name 'cèilidh' comes from Gaelic and means 'a visit'.

F These days the main element of the cèilidh is generally dancing. The cèilidh band usually consists of two to six players who play an assortment of different instruments.

18 **Words and phrases**

assortment a mixed collection of things or people   **distinction** difference or contrast   **to retain** to keep

PART 1

PART 2

PART 3

4* **Kirsty's email**

a Kirsty writes an email to May. Read the email, then do the tasks.

> Hi May,
>
> I'm glad you liked the video of my brother's wedding. It was an amazing experience, although I'd been to some fantastic cèilidhs before. In fact,
> 5 my aunt always has a cèilidh on her birthday and they are usually really good fun.
> Anyway, you'll never believe it, but one of the musicians was a former band member of the Bay City Rollers, one of Scotland's most famous
> 10 bands. In the 1970s, they were everywhere and my grandma loved them! IMHO they were pretty tacky. ☺
> I'm seriously into a band called Admiral Fallow. They play modern folk music, and I feel great
> 15 when I listen to them. I've seen them live at least 13 times and I've got all their records. Last year, I saw them play on a number of occasions and each time they just blew me away. Have you heard of them? You should come up and
> 20 visit and we can go and see them together. I'll check when they're playing again and let you know.
>
> XXX
>
> Kirsty

1 List the main points of the email.

2 Explain the following expressions: 'IMHO', 'pretty tacky', 'into a band', 'blew me away'.

b List all of the adverbs and adverbials in the email and match them to the categories in the box below. ≫≫
p. 146

> **Remember:**
> We use adjectives
> - to describe nouns: *It was an **amazing** experience. The experience was **amazing**.*
> - after certain verbs: *I feel **great** when I listen to them.*
>
> An adverb can modify other words or clauses. An adverbial is a part of a sentence and can consist of a single word or several words. It functions like an adverb. We use both in a number of ways:
> - time: ***Last year** I saw them play on four occasions.*
> - frequency: *I have **often** been to concerts by Admiral Fallow.*
> - manner: *We were **happily** singing along.*
> - degree: *They were **rather** well known.*

5 **Scottish folk music. Student A:** Read text A. **Student B:** Read text B. Work in pairs and summarize the main points of your text. Then create one text about Scottish folk music.

> **A** Scotland is known for is its traditional folk music. Widely recognized all over the world, it hasn't lost its popularity. Despite the fact that today Scotland is a truly multicultural society, Scottish music has managed to retain many of its
> 5 traditional aspects. However, folk music in Scotland is far from being uniform – it can be said that it is one of the most varied forms of all folk music in the world. There is a clear distinction between the different types of music due to the geographical locations, historical events and the industry
> 10 ordinary people work in.

> **B** Scottish folk music seems to differ somewhat from region to region. In the Shetland and Orkney Isles you may detect the influence of Norwegian music, the songs are in English and are frequently accompanied by the
> 5 fiddle. Move to the Highlands and you hear Gaelic, with bagpipes in the background. In the past, the songs and music had to be learned by heart, sung from memory and passed on from generation to generation. In the Lowlands and the Border regions, the songs are sung in
> 10 Scots or English and their style resembles English music.

6* **It's your turn: My music.** Write an email (150 words) to
≫≫ someone you recently met describing the music you
p. 146 like. Use adverbs, adverbials and adjectives to make your email interesting.

Grammar and structures (revision)

Adjectives → G5

It was an **amazing** experience …

… one of the musicians was a **former** band member of the Bay City Rollers

Adverbs → G5

… my aunt **always** has one for her birthday and they are **usually** really great fun.

Adverbials → G5

Last year I saw them play on twelve occasions …

→ Workbook, page 20

PRACTICE A

PART 1

1 **a** After talking to May, Deepak carried out some research about Scottish music for a presentation.
20)) Listen and decide whether these sentences true or false. Correct the false statements.

1 *Scots Wha Hae* is a song written by Robert Burns.
2 Burns wrote the majority of songs in 'A select Collection of Scottish Airs for the Voice'.
3 You won't hear pipers in Modern Scottish bands.

20)) **b** Listen again and make notes. What does Deepak say about the following?

● Robert Burns   ● songs from the border region   ● songs about work   ● modern music

PART 2

2 **a** Read the text and complete it with the correct form of the words in the box.
With some words, you need to decide whether you need an adverb. There are two words
you don't need.

> always ■ certain ■ definite ■ generous ■ great ■ important ■
> particular ■ social ■ unique ■ usual

Attending a Scottish cèilidh is a ⬛**1** experience. A cèilidh is a traditional
Gaelic ⬛**2** gathering, and they still take place today, ⬛**3** in the more
isolated, Northern communities, where they are still an ⬛**4** institution.
They ⬛**5** involve Gaelic folk music and dancing. In the old days,
5 cèilidhs were the only form of entertainment, so they also included lots
of storytelling and singing. They were also a place where people who
didn't usually meet could get together and exchange news. There is no
dress code, but wearing a kilt is ⬛**6** appreciated. Cèilidhs are ⬛**7**
good fun, so if you get the chance to go to one, grab it. You'll have a really
10 ⬛**8** time and you'll be able to learn some traditional Scottish dances.

b Read the extract again and work on the tasks.

1 Describe what you would experience at a modern cèilidh.
2 Explain how cèilidhs have changed over the years.

PART 3

3 Complete the email from May with the correct form of the words in the
box and the correct form of the verbs in brackets.

> awful ■ really
> ■ serious ■ usual

Hi Kirsty,

I ⬛**1** (*never, hear*) of the Bay City Rollers until you mentioned them in your email, so I ⬛**2** (*go*) online to see if I
could find anything about them. I watched a couple of videos and I agree with you, they are pretty ⬛**3** ! ☺
How many records did they sell? And, ⬛**4** , did your gran really like them? Please don't tell her what I said.
I ⬛**5** (*watch*) a couple of Admiral Fallow songs and that's much more my kind of music.
Also, I ⬛**6** (*speak*) to my parents about coming up to visit you and they both think it would be fine. Why don't you
talk to your parents and let me know? Of course, it ⬛**7** (*not, be*) during term time as my parents would never let me
miss any school. Next week we have exams. I'm not looking forward to them, even though I ⬛**8** do quite well. When
do you have exams in Scotland? I know it's not the same as it is down here, but I ⬛**9** don't know much about it.
If you don't want to write about exams, I ⬛**10** (*understand*).

May xxx

@ WES-40806-001

→ Workbook, page 21   **WRITING PRACTICE**

1 **a** Make a list of the information that you would expect to find in a music review. Then read the review and check your ideas.

Tonight at The Soup Kitchen, Admiral Fallow arrive ahead of album number three *Tiny Rewards*, due to be released at the end of May. The intention of this short, three-date tour is to
5 air a set list of new tracks for the first time, allowing the six-piece Glasgow outfit to practise their arrangements, keeping the fans happy by complementing all of this with a few old favourites as well […].
10 The show is a sell-out, which is significant, and it immediately improves upon my previous Admiral Fallow experience during the *Tree Bursts in Snow* tour. The band were musically thrilling that night in the Sugarmill, but the
15 audience […] was particularly underwhelming and the atmosphere was certainly lacking. Tonight is a different kettle of fish, however, and […] there was definitely an eager sense of anticipation enhancing the already intimate

surroundings that The Soup Kitchen offers. […] 20 It was an absolute joy when the band opened with 'Salt' to see the stage bathed in wonderful colour and this continued throughout the evening, ultimately contributing to a genuinely unique Soup Kitchen experience. […] 25
This first song establishes the dynamic of the evening pretty quickly. The new material possesses a metronomic quality, but suddenly catches you by surprise as changes of pace are unexpectedly introduced. […] We're back on 30 familiar ground with the next track 'Subbuteo' from their first album *Boots Met My Face*. Perhaps their most popular song, it prompts a very respectful and subtle contribution from the crowd, who sing along quietly […]. It's a 35 wonderful moment and one that underlines the affection for the song. […]
The band follow this with further emotional, expressive material from the forthcoming album. 'Liquor and Milk', 'Holding the Strings', 40 'Carousel' and 'Easy as Breathing' all sound extremely positive, but the band's [taste] for visual songwriting means the material is often the kind which grows on you the more you listen. […] 45

Source (abbreviated and adapted): Iain Fox, "Concert review: Admiral Fallow at The Soup Kitchen – Manchester", AMBY, 13.03.2015, https://amusicblogyea. com/2015/03/13/concert-review-photos-admiral-fallow-the-soup-kitchen-manchester/ [12.07.2022]

b Read the review again and make notes on the following information.

1 a description leading up to the concert
2 names of some of the songs played
3 name of the artist / band
4 name of the venue
5 personal feelings
6 the audience
7 time and date
8 type of music

c Find words and expressions in the review that match these definitions.

1 an organization or group
2 not causing someone to feel any excitement
3 changes the situation completely
4 a feeling of excitement about something that's going to happen in the near future
5 full of energy
6 a regular rhythm or beat to a piece of music
7 not loud or obvious in any way
8 happening soon

2 **a** Think of a concert you've seen in the past (live or online). Make notes about the elements listed in **1b**.

b Look at the adjectives and adverbs used in the music review about the Admiral Fallow concert. Write down five more adjectives and adverbs that could be used in a music review.

c Use your notes to write a review. Write between 180 and 200 words. Remember to use adjectives and adverbs to give your review some colour.

PART 1

PART 2

PART 3

Scottish politics

1 **A brief history**

a After the students get back to Durham, Deepak wants to find out more about Scotland.
He finds an article about Scottish politics. Read it, then complete the sentences below.

A brief history of Scottish politics

The existence of a Scottish parliament can be
traced back to the 13th century. In fact, for
about 400 years Scotland was an independent
kingdom. It was only in 1707, with the Acts of
5 Union, that Scotland started to be ruled from
London.

Then, for almost 300 years, Scotland had no
parliament of its own. In 1997 there was a
referendum and the **electorate** voted for a
10 **devolved** administration. The new Scottish
parliament was responsible for health, education, justice, rural affairs, economic development and
transport, but not taxes. However, by 2007, the government did have an annual **budget** of £27
billion. That compared to a budget of £587 billion for the Westminster government.

For the first few years, from 1999 until 2007, the Scottish parliament was led by the Labour Party.
15 However, in 2007 there was a big **shift** and the Scottish National Party won the most seats. One of
the main policies of the SNP was to call for Scottish **independence** from the UK. On September 18,
2014, the people of Scotland voted on the question: 'Should Scotland be an independent country?'
44.7 % voted 'Yes' and 55.3 % 'No'. Voters were told it was 'a once in a generation **referendum**',
however, by 2020 there were calls for a second referendum after the UK voted to leave the EU in
20 what was known as 'Brexit'.

1   From the 13th century until the Act of Union in 1707 Scotland was …

2   Some areas like health, education and economic development became …

3   Until 2007, the Labour Party …   4   On September 18, 2014, 55 % of Scottish voters …

5   After Brexit, …

b Use the context to work out and explain the meaning of the words and phrases in blue.

2 **Indyref2.** Deepak finds a video online about a proposed second Scottish independence
referendum (for which you will often hear the abbreviation 'Indyref2'). Watch it and do the tasks.

1   Note down how many seats there are in the Scottish Parliament.
2   Explain why Nicola Sturgeon says that there is a mandate for independence.
3   Outline her argument for another referendum.
4   State what she says about the government in Westminster.

3 **Scottish independence**

a After watching the video, Deepak reads a blog that mentions some of the arguments for and against independence. Collect them in two lists.

For and against
by Rab Macintosh

In the first Scottish independence referendum I wasn't able to vote as I was too young. However, I do remember the debates that took
5 place before the referendum, especially as my mum voted 'Yes' and my dad voted 'No'! You can imagine what our house was like before and after the referendum! Anyway, if we do have a second referendum, I want to know what I'm voting for, so I've looked at
10 some of the arguments for and against.
1 All the revenue from oil in the North Sea would belong to Scotland and it would be able to spend it for the benefit of the population.
2 At the moment, the UK's nuclear weapons are kept on submarines based in Scotland. The SNP are against nuclear weapons, so if
15 Scotland became independent, these would need to be moved out of Scotland.
3 International power. As a small independent country, how much say would Scotland have on international decisions? Probably not a lot!
20 **4** Now Scotland, as part of the UK, has left the EU. Would the new independent country apply to rejoin? What would the requirements be?
5 Scotland would be in complete control of its political future. At the moment there are 59 MPs in Westminster representing
25 Scottish constituencies. This is from a total of 650, meaning decisions about Scotland are made by politicians from England!
6 What currency do we use? If we carry on using the pound sterling, what will that mean? If we need a new currency, what happens?
7 What will happen to the economy? In Scotland we don't have a lot
30 of industry, and the ones we do have are either a lot smaller than in the past (ship building) or are likely to shrink in the future (North Sea Oil).

b Discuss which arguments you think are the strongest. Which ones do you identify with?

CULTURE CORNER

Margaret Thatcher became Leader of the Conservative Party in 1979. She was then elected Prime Minister, the first female to hold that position in Britain. She won three elections and was Prime Minister for 11 years before she resigned in 1990. During her time in office she was a controversial figure. She cut social welfare programmes, reduced the power of trade unions, and privatized many state-run industries.

4 **A strong leader.** Read the text about Nicola Sturgeon and complete the tasks.

Who is Nicola Sturgeon? A profile of the SNP leader

Born in the North Ayrshire town of Irvine in 1970, Nicola Sturgeon became an SNP member at the tender age of 16, having been
5 inspired by […] Margaret Thatcher! She told BBC Radio Four's Women's Hour: 'Thatcher was prime minister, the economy wasn't in great shape, lots of
10 people around me were looking at a life or an immediate future of unemployment and I think that certainly gave me a strong sense of social justice and, at that stage, a strong feeling that it was wrong for Scotland to be governed by a Tory government that we hadn't
15 elected.' […]
[After losing the 2014 Independence Referendum, Alex Salmond, leader of the SNP, stepped down and was replaced by Nicola Sturgeon.] […] The party had already been the biggest kid on the block in Scottish politics […] but
20 with Ms Sturgeon at the helm the party truly became an electoral juggernaut, starting with the 2015 general election […] taking 56 of the 59 seats in Scotland. […]
The UK's exit from the EU presented the SNP with an opportunity, as well as a challenge […]. The SNP's 2016
25 manifesto […] had raised the possibility of Scotland taking a fresh look at going its own way if voters north of the border backed 'Remain', while the UK as a whole voted to leave the EU. That is, of course, exactly what happened. […]

Source (abbreviated and adapted): Philip Sim, "Who is Nicola Sturgeon? A profile of the SNP leader", BBC News, 26.05.2017, https://www.bbc.co.uk/news/uk-scotland-25333635 [12.07.2022]

1 Analyse what inspired Nicola Sturgeon to become a politician.
2 Explain what is meant by the phrase 'the biggest kid on the block' (l. 20).
3 Discuss why the UK leaving the EU might present the SNP with both an opportunity and a challenge.

5 **It's your turn: Voting for the first time**

p. 146
a In the Scottish independence referendum, people of 16 and 17 were given the vote for the first time. Carry out some research and find out what people thought about giving young voters a voice. Make notes about some of the arguments both in favour and against the idea. (**pp. 105, 139/140**)

b What's your opinion on giving young people the vote? Share the information you found out with the rest of your group and have a discussion.

PART 1

PART 2

PART 3

a Look at the photos. What is the connection between the photos and the topic of Scottish politics? Discuss your ideas with a partner.

🔊21 **b** Listen to the interview and check your ideas.

🔊21 **c** Listen again and complete the tasks.

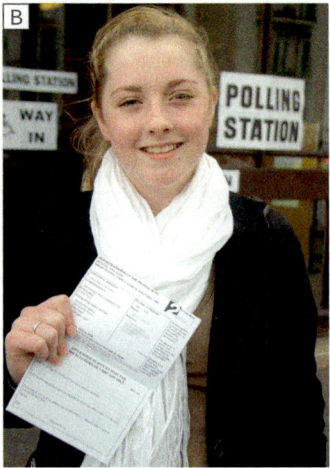

1 Describe why the 2014 Scottish referendum was different from other votes.
2 State why the arguments put forward weren't always simple.
3 Comment on the high turnout for the referendum.
4 Explain what is meant by the word 'scaremongering'.

a Read an article about young people and politics. Find out the meaning of the <u>underlined</u> words and phrases. Check your ideas with a partner.

How involved are Scottish youngsters in politics? The 2014 Independence vote could be viewed as <u>a turning point</u> that mobilized young people as this was the first occasion when 16- to 17-year-olds were allowed to vote. <u>Prior to</u> the vote, these youngsters had proved that they didn't <u>take this opportunity lightly</u>, did their research, contributed to the national debate and were <u>hands-on</u> supporters of political organizations
5 representing their views. This enthusiasm hasn't <u>worn off</u> since the referendum but has resulted in a larger <u>cohort</u> of young people who are at the <u>forefront</u> of today's Scottish politics. We interviewed some young people a few years after the Independence Referendum in 2014. Here's what they had to say:

Erin: 'I am fighting against the view society has of young people. When I tell people that I spend my
10 weekends working for my party, they are like "why aren't you going out drinking and acting like a normal teenager?"'

Ross: 'I remember back in 2014 having to search on the Internet to find out what a referendum was [...]. Fast
15 forward a couple of years – I am an SNP member.'

Jack: 'My family and friends were all voting 'Yes', but my view was completely different. I knew I was in the minority but held my ground. I did a lot of research to argue my side. Everyone kind of respected me for it.'

20 Tom: 'I find it annoying when people say that we are lazy and apathetic – it's completely untrue.'

Amy: 'I want to be involved in politics – not just for young people but for everyone. You should understand that we are the adults of tomorrow.'

Miriam: 'I was initially sceptical about independence. 25 The debates we had at uni made me question my <u>assumptions</u> and it's through those conversations that I began to support Scottish independence. That's how my involvement with the SNP began.'

Stewart: 'It was definitely the referendum that turned 30 me into a bit of <u>a political animal</u>. Engaging with folks who had a different ideology <u>spurred</u> me to dig deep – and I am still there.'

Callum: 'One of my best friends I've known since we were 5 was an <u>ardent</u> supporter of independence. 35 After several bottles of wine and screaming matches, I knew I had to be on the side I believe in. I joined the Labour Party …'

Scott: 'I was <u>crushed</u> by the result. But I joined the Greens the day after because I wanted to turn my 40 disappointment into positive action.'

b Read the article again. Match the statements to the correct person / people.

1   … and … tried to find out about the issues in the referendum.
2   … became interested in politics because of the referendum.
3   … thinks it's important for young people to be involved in politics as it's about their future.
4   … volunteered during the lead up to the referendum.
5   … voted differently from the rest of his / her family.
6   … was upset by the outcome of the referendum.
7   … was involved in some big arguments about Scottish Independence with a close friend.
8   … wasn't happy with the way a lot of people viewed teenagers.
9   … changed his / her mind because of discussions.

3 In her blog, Kirsty wrote an entry about her brother's wedding. Read her post and complete it with the adverbs and adverbials from the box. There are two that you don't need.

p. 147

> easily ■ enthusiastically ■ for a few hours ■ for the party ■ in a long time ■
> incredibly ■ late into the night ■ luckily ■ probably ■ quite ■ recently ■
> unfortunately

Hi guys!
I am sorry I haven't posted anything for a while, but I have a good excuse. My brother got married!
You can imagine how **1** busy I was with the preparations. But now that it's over, I thought I would
share the best moments with you. Click on this link to the video about the wedding. It was **2** the
5 best evening I've had **3** . There was so much food and the music was great.
My parents had rented the village hall **4** and there were more than a hundred guests. Everyone
was dancing **5** and **6** everyone let their hair down. The band was **7** good, although the
fiddle player could have been better. **8** , I didn't have to go to school the next day, because we
danced **9** . I'll **10** have a cèilidh for my eighteenth birthday. What do you think? How would you
10 celebrate your 18th? Send me your comments, ideas …
Kirsty

4   **a** In another blog post, Kirsty wrote about her favourite music. Write a post about the type of music you like. Use the notes to structure it. Include adjectives and adverbials (five each). Write 180 words. You can find help on **pp. 37** (*TIP*), **135 (3)**.

- type of music
- why you like it
- how / when introduced to it?
- how often / where listen to it?
- your friends' opinion

b Swap your texts and suggest ways to improve them. On **p. 144** you find tips on giving constructive feedback.

PART 1

PART 2

PART 3

1 Val McDermid is a contemporary Scottish author who specializes in crime fiction. In her book, *My Scotland*, she takes the reader through landscapes she's known all her life and shows how she has used them in some in some of her books. Read the extract and put the examples from *Killing the Shadows* (**p. 35**, A – C) in the correct places in the text.

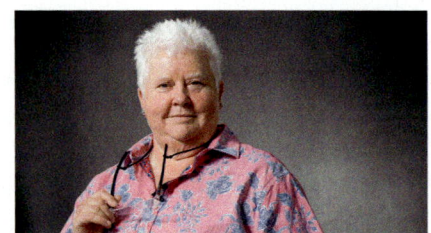

My protagonist in *Killing the Shadows* is Dr Fiona Cameron, a geographic data analyst who sometimes places her profiling expertise at the <u>disposal</u> of the police. She's eventually invited to examine the cases of the dead writers, which takes her to Edinburgh, the home of the first victim. I let her stay in Channings Hotel, where I'd regularly been made welcome as a guest of the Edinburgh International Book Festival. And I gave her a room with a view:

Fettes College, Edinburgh

| 1 |

Because a sense of place is about more than description. It's about the responses of characters to their surroundings. So talking about place also includes politics, economics, romance, history, pain and many other matters.
There will be more about Edinburgh later, so for now, let's leave Fiona walking back to her hotel late at night.

| 2 |

Later, the story takes Fiona into the Highlands, to the eastern side of the watershed in the <u>sprawling</u> county of Sutherland. I was seventeen when I first experienced this part of the country. I was having an adventure in the summer between school and university. I was travelling across to the west coast on a Post Bus, which is exactly what it sounds like. It's a minibus run by Royal Mail that carries passengers and delivers letters and parcels along the way. I'd been <u>lulled</u> by the familiarity of gently rolling fields, so similar to the fertile heart of Fife. Then suddenly, everything changed. How Fiona tells it is how I experienced it, too:

| 3 |

Source: from *My Scotland* by Val McDermid, Sphere: London, 2019. Source of extracts on p. 35: from *Killing the Shadows* by Val McDermid, HarperCollins: New York, 2001.

2 **a** Look at the underlined words in the text above and in the examples A – C on **page 35**. Explain their meaning. If needed, use a monolingual dictionary. If a word has more than one meaning, decide which one fits the context best.

  b Compare your explanations with a partner and make sentences containing these words.

3 **a** McDermid writes: 'So talking about place also includes politics, economics, romance, history, pain and many other matters'. Read the extract again and identify where these elements are incorporated in her descriptions.

  b Compare and discuss your findings.

A Then she was driving along the narrow inlet of the Kyle of Sutherland, the dark water lined with heavy conifer forests, making somehow <u>sinister</u> the sunlit route into the
5 wilderness that spread out ahead of her. As she turned up the River Shin towards Lairg, she could see she was entering the north-west Highlands proper, with sudden <u>vistas</u> opening ahead of rounded hills brown with
10 heather, their rocky outcroppings grey and random. <u>Scattered</u> in the landscape were the ruined walls of croft houses, often just a pair of <u>battered</u> gable ends left standing. This was the landscape of the Highland Clearances,
15 that brutal depopulation of the countryside where crofters had been driven off their land by rich landowners eager to make the easier money that came with rearing Cheviot sheep. Now the fragments of their homes were the
20 only sign that this had been the starting point for the Highland diaspora that had colonized the British Empire …

B Through the smirr of rain, she could see the steely ribbon of the Firth of Forth. Over on her left, a vast <u>looming</u> Gothic pile with an intimidating spire dominated the streets spread below her. 'What's that building?' she asked
5 the porter just as he was leaving.
'That's Fettes College,' he said. 'Where Tony Blair went.'
It explained a lot, she thought.

C She was almost the only person on the streets. She turned on to the Dean Bridge, enjoying the <u>spectacle</u> of walking above tree-top level, with random blocks of light from the New Town tenements glowing pale yellow
5 through the <u>insubstantial</u> mist.

CULTURE CORNER

Tony Blair (*1953), British politician who served as Prime Minister of the UK from 1997 to 2007 and Leader of the Labour Party from 1994 to 2007.

---

4   **a** Read the texts about three contemporary Scottish writers, then decide which author's work you would like to read. Give reasons for your choice.

Ali Smith
Winner of the 2015 Bailey's Women's Prize for Fiction and the Costa Novel Award […], Ali Smith has been showing her unique creativity for many years with her many acclaimed short story collections and novels. In her recent works, the *Seasonal Quartet*, readers were treated to something rarely seen since Charles Dickens: novels engaging with events as they unfolded –
5 including Brexit, migration and climate change. With *Companion Piece* (2022), Smith takes another bracing dive into the waters of British society, finding humour, empathy and clarity in the hue and cry all around us.

Louise Welsh
Louise Welsh established herself in the literary crime scene with her successful debut novel *The*
10 *Cutting Room* (2002), which won [several awards]. The novel follows a Glaswegian auctioneer as he investigates the truth of a disturbing collection of photographs found in the house of a dead man. Her last two novels, *A Lovely Way to Burn* (2014) and *Death is a Welcome Guest* (2015), are parts of the *Plagues* Trilogy, set in an imaginary Britain that has been destroyed by a deadly disease.

James Robertson
15 James Robertson's work includes both historical novels and [ones] set in present-day Scotland. His widely praised novel *And the Land Lay Still* (2010), presents a panoramic and insightful exploration of Scottish society during the second half of the 20th century following the lives of many different characters from different backgrounds and periods whose stories are intertwined. Published a few years before the independence referendum, the novel provides an insight on
20 how the independence movement and leftwing politics gained strength in Scotland. Robertson has also written several short story and poetry collections.

Source (abbreviated and adapted): ll. 1-3, 9-21: Helena Fornells, Culture Trip, 27.10.2017, https://theculturetrip.com/europe/united-kingdom/scotland/articles/10-contemporary-scottish-writers-you-need-to-know/ [12.07.2022]

  b Do further research on your preferred author, their publications and share your findings.
(*TIPs* on **pp. 105, 140**)

Preparing to write a persuasive text

S1 **Studying texts.** You are going to study two texts on the same subject. Read the title and the first paragraph of each. Write down how you know which is text is an informative one and which a persuasive text.

A **Tackling health and environmental issues connected to poor diet is imperative in Scotland**

After smoking, Scottish eating habits are the second most important cause of the nation's poor health. The average Scottish diet is low in cereals, vegetables and fruit but high in confectionery, fatty meat products, sweet and salty snacks, cakes and excessive amounts of sugary drinks and alcohol.

B **Meat: to eat or not to eat?**

Would you call it a caring world in which animals suffer a horrible death to satisfy an eating preference? Reliable scientific studies show that cattle, pigs and chickens suffer. **They can feel stress, they can feel pain and they can feel fear.** I strongly believe that it is cruel and unethical to kill animals for food. In my opinion, veganism is the best way to eat. Here are my reasons.

S2 **Analysing texts**

a The remaining three paragraphs of A and of B are mixed up. Read each paragraph and decide if it comes from the informative text or from the persuasive one. Give a reason for every choice.

---

1 The current dietary habits have an adverse effect not only on the nation's health but on the environment, too. The ecological footprint of the average Scottish diet is high, mainly because of the excessive meat consumption. This high footprint of meat is due to the large area of land needed for animal grazing and animal feed.

2 Not only is veganism good for you, it's good for your planet. Much of the world's deforestation has happened, **with catastrophic consequences**, because forests have been slashed and burnt to create pasture for cattle. Gas emissions further endanger our environment. **Can we really go on this way?**

3 Finally, to return to the animals. **I am absolutely positive** that raising animals in captivity is cruel. **Don't be fooled by fake statistics.** Most meat comes from farming methods where animals live in filthy, overcrowded spaces. I truly think that if most compassionate people **saw pigs with their tails cut off**, chickens with their beaks removed or cows with horns and tails cut off with no painkillers, they would never eat meat again.

4 A healthy diet based on the recommendation above provides all the nutrients that are essential for avoiding disease and for achieving general well-being. Several governmental organizations are working alongside charities, the food and drink as well as hospitality sectors to change eating habits. Fortunately, there are already positive signs as the number of Scots adopting a vegan diet has surged in recent years. In 2013, Glasgow was named the vegan capital of the UK, and veganism is becoming more and more widespread.

5 Calculations show that a diet based on healthy eating recommendations has a lower footprint than the current average. Eating mainly fruit, vegetables and wholegrain foods, and moderate amounts of meat, dairy and eggs is not only good for the Scottish people but also better for the environment.

6 Veganism is good for you. **Meat eaters may argue** that meat is the best source of protein. **However**, a vegan diet **gives you the complete nutrition you need and deserve**. Non-meat sources of iron like leafy greens and beans contain better iron than red meat, for example.

---

b Talk about the choices you made above and together put the paragraphs in the correct order to complete texts A and B.

S3 **Persuasive techniques.** Copy the table with the different persuasive techniques. Look at the **purple** expressions and decide which type the examples belong to.

Technique	Examples from the text	Technique	Examples from the text
Personal opinion	???	Repetition	???
Emotive language	???	Imperatives	???
Rhetorical questions	???	Exaggeration	???
Counterarguments	???	Complimenting	???

PART 1

PART 2

PART 3

→ Workbook, page 28   **WORKSHOP TASK**

Writing a persuasive text

S1   **Identifying techniques.** Read an informative text about keeping fit and getting exercise. Which of the following techniques do you find? Give examples.

> counterarguments ■ dates ■
> emotive language ■ examples ■ facts ■
> repetition ■ statistics ■ warnings

Benefits of exercise

Experts recommend that teenagers get 60 minutes or more of moderate to vigorous physical activity each day. Here are some of the reasons:
Exercise benefits every part of the body, including the
5 mind. Exercising causes the body to make chemicals that can help a person feel good and sleep better. It can also help some people who have mild depression and low self-esteem. Plus, exercise can give
10 people a sense of accomplishment.
Exercise helps people lose weight and lowers the risk of some diseases, including obesity, type 2 diabetes and high blood pressure. Exercise can
15 help a person age well. This may not seem important now, but your body will thank you later. For example, osteoporosis (a weakening of the bones) can be a problem as people get older. Weight-bearing exercise – like jumping, running, or
20 brisk walking – can help keep bones strong. The three parts of a balanced exercise routine are: aerobic exercise, strength training and flexibility training.

Aerobic exercise
Aerobic exercise is any type of exercise that gets the
25 heart pumping and gets you breathing harder. Your heart and lungs get stronger and are better at getting oxygen (in the form of oxygen-carrying blood cells) to all parts of your body.
If you play team sports, you're probably getting at least 60 minutes or more of moderate to vigorous activity on
30 practice days. Some team sports give you a great aerobic exercise, as do biking, running, swimming, dancing, inline skating, tennis, cross-country skiing, hiking, and walking quickly.
35

Strength training
Strong muscles support your joints and help prevent injuries. You don't have to lift weights to make your muscles and bones stronger. Different
40 types of exercise strengthen different muscle groups, for example: for arms, rowing or cross-country skiing; for strong legs, running, biking, rowing, or skating; for core strength, rowing, yoga or pilates, planks and crunches.
45

Flexibility training
Being flexible helps improve a person's sports performance. Dance or martial arts require great flexibility as do karate, ballet, gymnastics, and yoga. Stretching after your workout will also help you improve your
50 flexibility.

S2   **Persuading a friend.** Imagine you have a friend who hates every form of exercise – a real couch potato. Rewrite the text in **S1** with the purpose of persuading your friend to try exercising.

S3   **Write a new text**

a   Write a persuasive text of about 180 words on one of the following topics or a topic of your choice. Find more tips on **pp. 136/137**.

- Young people need screen time.
- The voting age should be lowered to 16.
- Every teenager should do a social year.

b   Share your text in class and read your classmates' texts. Give constructive feedback (tips on **p. 144**). Is the purpose of the text clear to the reader? Are you persuaded?

TIP

- Think of a good title.
- Make your opinion clear in the introduction.
- Find strong supporting evidence.
- Use paragraphs for arguments and counterarguments.
- Use strong and emotive language but never become aggressive or sarcastic.
- For persuasive texts use the present tense.

You can use **emphatic comparatives**: *much stronger, far more beneficial, …*
Show reasons and causes by using **conjunctions**: *for that reason, so, therefore, as a result, …*
Linking adverbials will help structure your persuasive argument: *in the first place, next, finally, …*
Counterarguments can anticipate opposition: *some may argue that … but …; contrary to …; despite what some people say, …*

PART 1

PART 2

PART 3

1 David was too lazy to write his diary entry every evening during the expedition, so he left it until the last night and made some mistakes. Decide whether the <u>underlined</u> words and phrases are correct or wrong. Correct the wrong ones.

Day 1

Everyone agreed with my suggestion to go to the Highlands and we travelled up in the school mini-bus overnight. <u>It's a quite long journey</u>[1] so it took six hours. By the time we <u>arrived</u>[2], everyone <u>were</u>[3] tired. Not a great way to start a four-day hike! After having arrived, we had a safety briefing, pitched our tents and tried to get a <u>good nights sleep</u>[4].

Day 2

What is it with Bex? She knows <u>I've planned</u>[5] this for weeks and know the route inside out. In the end, we let Deepak navigate as we all have to take turns as leaders, so I <u>lead</u>[6] for most of tomorrow.

Day 3

What a great evening! We met another group, from Aberdeen. They were doing their Gold Award, too. We <u>chatted hours</u>[7] so we didn't get a lot of sleep. We <u>set of</u>[8] a bit late, and unfortunately we got lost and everyone blamed me, <u>than</u>[9], then they all started laughing! As if they could have done better.

Day 4

<u>It's raining</u>[10] the whole time and Bex hasn't stopped complaining. This is <u>probably</u>[11] the last time <u>I'm camping</u>[12] with her. Today was definitely the coldest day, and the others were worried it might snow. At least it is the last leg, and we all know we will be sleeping in proper beds <u>when we will finally</u>[13] get home.

---

2 **a** Bex found a website with some interesting facts about Scotland. Complete the text with the correct form of the verbs in brackets and the words from the box.

> handful ▪ notorious ▪ red ▪
> shortest ▪ tallest ▪ twisted

Cool facts about Scotland

Most countries have a national animal. The USA ▮1▮ (*have*) two: the bald eagle and the bison. For Germany it's the black eagle, while for Scotland it's an animal that ▮2▮ (*not exist*): the unicorn!

Everyone ▮3▮ (*hear*) of Niagara Falls on the border between Canada and the USA, but Scotland ▮4▮ (*be*) home to the ▮5▮ waterfall in the UK at 658 feet, which is three times the height of Niagara!

Scotland is also home to the oldest tree in Europe – a ▮6▮ yew tree, called the Fortingall Yew, that people say ▮7▮ (*be around*) for between 3,000 and 9,000 years!

There are almost 800 islands dotted around the coast of Scotland, but only 130 ▮8▮ (*inhabit*) and on some there are just a ▮9▮ of people.

If you travel to the islands by plane, you might want to experience the world's ▮10▮ commercial flight from Westray to Papa Westray

in the Orkney islands – the flight takes just two minutes. Or fly to Barra and ▮11▮ (*land*) on one of the world's last beach runways!

In the Outer Hebrides, you could ▮12▮ (*visit*) Calanais Standing Stones, one of the most complete stone circles anywhere in Europe. The stones are believed to ▮13▮ (*erect*) around 2,900 BC.

Edinburgh, the capital city, ▮14▮ (*build*) on seven hills – just like Rome – and has more listed buildings than anywhere else in the world. It was also the first city in the world to have its own fire brigade.

Around 13% of Scots have ▮15▮ hair, far more than the average around the world, which stands at just 2%. It is thought that this is a legacy of Viking ancestry.

The raincoat ▮16▮ (*invent*) in Scotland by a man called Charles Macintosh, who ▮17▮ (*be born*) in Glasgow. Of course, it wasn't a bad idea given how much it rains in Scotland. Some people even refer to raincoats as Macs!

As a land full of myths and legends it's little surprise that a small town in Scotland, Bonnybridge, is ▮18▮ for UFO sightings with more than 300 reported every year.

---

 b Which of these facts do you think is the most interesting? Give reasons for your choice and try to convince other students to agree with you.

3 Listen to an extract from a radio programme about Scottish myths and legends, then work on the tasks.

1 State what makes Fingal's Cave special.
2 Explain why Finn McCool built the Giant's Causeway.
3 Describe what inspired Pink Floyd and Mendelssohn Bartholdy.

4 Deepak is sending a letter with photos from the Duke of Edinburgh Gold Expedition to his great-grandmother back in Agra. Use the illustrations to write his letter (200 words). Remember to use the correct tenses.

5 Deepak wrote a short text about the DoE expedition. Complete the text with the words and phrases in the box. There are three extra words or phrases.

> at the time ■ beautiful ■ extreme ■ five days ago ■ fortunately ■ in India ■ in the end ■ on the last morning ■ pleasant ■ rational ■ sentimental ■ serious ■ unluckily ■ usually

For me the DoE experience wasn't very 1 . 2 I managed to forget my water bottle. Now, I know that doesn't sound very 3 , but 4 it felt like the end of the world. I'm 5 thought of as 6 , so such a reaction seems rather 7 . What people don't know is that it was a present from my aunt 8 , so it has 8 value to me. 10 , the others were willing to go back with me and look for it, so everything turned out all right 11 .

1 Isle of Arran

a Du planst einen gemeinsamen Urlaub mit deinem finnischen Austauschpartner Kimi. Ihr wollt zwei Wochen in Schottland verbringen. Eure Flüge nach Glasgow sind bereits gebucht. Nun plant ihr euer Ausflugsprogramm. Heute bist du zufällig auf einen Podcast über die schottische Insel Arran gestoßen. Du schlägst Kimi in einer E-Mail auf Englisch vor, Arran zu besuchen. Hör dir zunächst den Podcast an und beschreibe die Lage der Insel. Du erklärst, warum man Arran als kleine Ausgabe von Schottland bezeichnen kann. Du nennst außerdem drei Orte, die du auf Arran gern besuchen würdest und erzählst, was es dort zu erleben oder zu sehen gibt.

b Du schickst Kimi eine Sprachnachricht, in der du erklärst, wie ihr nach Arran reisen und wie ihr euch vor Ort fortbewegen könnt. Beschreibe ihm die für euch einfachste Verbindung nach Arran. Benutze dazu die folgenden Informationen und mache dir Notizen, bevor du die Nachricht aufnimmst.

REISEN AUF ARRAN

Anreise

Caledonian MacBrayne (CalMac) betreibt zwei Autofähr-Verbindungen zur Insel. Die Verbindung von Ardrossan[1] nach Brodick[2]
5 ist die beliebtere der beiden Routen und sorgt für die Anbindung der Insel an die Region Ayrshire[3] auf dem Festland. Ardrossan ist nur 45 Minuten von Glasgow entfernt und man kann es entweder mit
10 dem Auto oder dem öffentlichen Nahverkehr erreichen. Lochranza[4] im Norden der Insel verfügt über eine Fährverbindung nach Claonaig[5], einem kleinen Hafen auf der Kintyre[6]-Halbinsel in
15 Argyll[7].

Außerdem ist es günstig

Die Fährverbindung von Ardrossan nach Brodick ist eine von verschiedenen schottischen CalMac-Routen, für die die
20 Preise aufgrund des Road Equivalent Tariffs (RET) Programms, das bei den Gebühren angewendet wurde, reduziert wurden. Dadurch ist ein Fährticket recht preiswert.

Von A nach B kommen

25 Das Straßennetz führt um die Küste der Insel herum und eine Straße teilt die Insel sozusagen in zwei Teile – sie ist auf der Insel als ‚the String' bekannt. Einige der Straßen sind einspurig und es gibt viele Einbuchtungen, um aneinander vorbeizufahren. Es gibt drei Haupt-Busstrecken, die den Norden und Süden Arrans sowie den ‚String' anfahren und die entsprechend der Fahrpläne der Fähren verkehren. Im Sommer werden durch saisonale Busunternehmen zusätzliche Touren
30 angeboten: Eine tolle Gelegenheit, die Sehenswürdigkeiten zu erkunden.

Quelle: "Die Isle of Arran: Reisen auf Arran", VisitScotland 2022, https://www.visitscotland.com/de-de/destinations-maps/arran/ [12.07.2022]

[1] **Ardrossan** [ɑːrˈdrɒsən] – [2] **Brodick** [ˈbrɒdɪk] – [3] **Ayrshire** [ˈeəʃə] – [4] **Lochranza** [lɒkˈrɑnzə] – [5] **Claonaig** [ˈkløːnɛk] – [6] **Kintyre** [kinˈtaɪr] – [7] **Argyll** [ɑːrˈgaɪl]

c Dein finnischer Austauschpartner Kimi ist begeistert von deiner Idee und hat bei weiteren Recherchen herausgefunden, dass Arran eine Tochterinsel hat, Holy Isle. Kimi hat dir den folgenden Reisebericht über diese Tochterinsel geschickt. Auf Deutsch erzählst du einem Freund oder einer Freundin, was Holy Isle besonders macht und erklärst, warum gerade Hobbyfotograf Kimi diese Insel gerne besuchen möchte.

The Holy Isle – Arran [...]

Holy Isle is located close to the eastern shore of the Isle of Arran on Scotland's west coast. This small (one square mile) island has a rich religious history dating back hundreds of
5 years and the tradition of quiet seclusion continues to this day thanks to the Centre for World Peace and Health located on the western edge of the isle.

Visitors are welcome to walk around and
10 enjoy the landscape on the many paths that circle Holy Isle and there are some beautiful views across Arran and the Firth of Clyde [...]. [...]

Holy Isle isn't exactly big but it's a fascinating
15 place and I have to say it was the highlight of my last trip to Arran. [...]

The island has a spiritual history dating back at least 600 years, and you'll find religious remnants all along the western side including a spring that's reputed to have healing powers, and a hermit cave where the 6th-century monk St. Molaise lived.
20 The spiritual tradition continues to this day with the Centre for World Peace and Health Buddhist community that offers residential courses and retreats at a large, converted farmhouse near the ferry jetty, as well as a closed retreat on the southern point of the island.

Although Holy Isle is privately owned, it's still possible to visit it as a tourist via the ferry from Lamlash Bay, or you could do what I did and kayak out there. Both options are good fun although if you can, I
25 definitely recommend sailing out there in a kayak as the views are fantastic.

The stretch of water between Lamlash Bay and Holy Isle is sheltered so you won't have to worry about rough seas (most of the time) and the water is beautifully clean. Expect to see lots of fish, jellyfish and marine plant life as you paddle around the bay. [...]

There are a couple of rules once you get on Holy Isle which must be observed, the first of which is no
30 littering and the second is no overnight camping. That's completely fair in my opinion as the community has worked long and hard to promote the island as a wildlife reserve and they've gone to great lengths to promote nature with a native tree planting programme on Holy Isle's northern edge.

The only other request is that day visitors stick to the main paths which is
35 partly due to the conservation aspect, partly to do with respecting the Buddhists and partly for your own safety when you climb the 1,000-foot Mullach Mor hill in the island's centre. [...]

From the jetty on the Lamlash Bay side, you'll see the retreat is decorated with Tibetan flags and artworks and you might see the occasional monk working.
40 The mix of the traditional Scottish farmhouse and the Buddhist decorations makes for a great photo opportunity, but in the spirit of giving the residents their privacy, it would be a good idea not to spend too long there. [...]

Don't be surprised if you stumble across a few curious animals during your walk as there are herds of wild Eriskay ponies, Saanen goats and Soay sheep
45 meandering about. The goats seem to enjoy the beaches while the ponies can be found wandering through the bracken, so wherever you go you're guaranteed to pass them at some point. [...]

Quelle (gekürzt): Craig Neil, "Holy Isle Visitor Guide", Out About Scotland 2022, https://outaboutscotland.com/holy-isle-arran/ [12.07.2022]

Ready for Workshop 2?

1 a Choose two of these photos. List five facts for each
one, then share them with a partner.

A

B

C

D

b Choose one of the topics from this workshop (*Duke of Edinburgh's Award, the history of Scotland,
Scottish music,* or *Scottish politics*) and give a short (3-minute) talk to the rest of the class.

2 a Read another entry from May's DofE diary
and complete it with the correct form of the
verbs in brackets and the words from the box.

> chatting ■ hard ■ lurking ■
> mythical ■ stunning

b Read May's diary entry again and
complete the tasks.

1 Comment on why May says the day
was both the best and the worst.
2 Discuss whether you would be
interested in taking the DofE Gold
Award based on everything you have
read or heard.

For me the third day was both the best and the worst of the
expedition. I ▮1▮ (*wake up*) early, before the others had ▮2▮
(*even, stir*). I unzipped the front of the tent and poked my head
out, the mist ▮3▮ (*lift off*) the loch and it was like waking up to
a ▮4▮ world. I shivered, not from cold, but from the fear there
might be a monster ▮5▮ in the loch.
We ▮6▮ (*go*) to bed late the night after meeting with a group
from Aberdeen. We ▮7▮ (*sit*) around ▮8▮, wrapped in our
sleeping bags against the cold. After a late breakfast, we set off,
the going was ▮9▮, but the worst thing was how tired I ▮10▮
(*feel*) – and I'm sure it was the same for the others. In fact, I think
Bex ▮11▮ (*be*) so tired that she couldn't even ▮12▮ (*complain*)
about the rain! The landscape was ▮13▮, but I think I was
beyond enjoying it. The focus was on putting one foot in front of
the other and ▮14▮ (*not fall over*), which happened to Deepak
twice! Anyway, that's what the DofE Gold Award is all about ☺.

3 **a** Deepak found a text about the Edinburgh Fringe. Complete it with the phrases from the box. There are two you don't need.

> the whole city becomes the venue ■ visitors come from around the world ■ the festival is a place for everyone ■ the city is a riot of colour ■ hoping for the chance of the experience of a lifetime ■ only the best artists are invited ■ Here are just some of the incredible artists ■ for three weeks in August

The Edinburgh Festival Fringe is the single greatest celebration of arts and culture in the world. Every year, ▢1, Edinburgh hosts an explosion of creative energy like nowhere else.
From big names in entertainment to the most obscure acts from around
5 the globe, ▢2. The Fringe is open-access, meaning that anyone with an act who can find a venue is welcome. In fact, for the Fringe ▢3 and many places are open round the clock. The Fringe includes theatre, comedy, dance, cabaret, circus skills, music, spoken word and lots more. So, for these three weeks ▢4, noise and excitement. You often hear
10 regular festival goers say 'I saw them before they became famous.' ▢5 who had their breakthrough at the Fringe: Billy Connolly, Rowan Atkinson, Robin Williams and the New Zealand amusing comedy band Flight of the Concords.
The only downside is that finding accommodation can be a challenge
15 with thousands of people flocking to the city ▢6.

b Find words or expressions in the text that match these definitions.

1 a place which provides the space for a special event
2 to provide everything for a special event
3 not known to many people

4 twenty-four hours a day
5 important in the development of someone
6 the main disadvantage of a situation

4 David asks Bex about the book she's reading. Listen and do the tasks.

🔊 24

1 Explain what a Selkie is.
2 State what David compares Selkies to.

3 Comment on David's reaction to the story.
4 Discuss the possible purpose of the story.

5 Complete the text about Kelpies with the correct form of the verbs in brackets.

In April 2014, two 30-metre-high statues ▢1 (*unveil*) in Falkirk, Scotland. The two statues appear to be horse heads, but are in fact Kelpies, a mythical Scottish creature.
One story tells of how a Kelpie ▢2 (*capture*) a family of children.
5 The family lived near a loch inhabited by a Kelpie. One day the children ▢3 (*play*) near the water when the Kelpie tried to get them into the water. When the last child climbed onto the Kelpie's back, nine of the children ▢4 (*already, trap*). Like his brothers and sisters before him his hands ▢5 (*become*) stuck to the neck of the Kelpie. To escape the young boy cut off his finger and
10 managed to get away. There ▢6 (*be*) many such stories about Kelpies over the centuries.
In all the stories Kelpies are seen as frightening creatures that are similar in many ways to mermaids. The legends surrounding Kelpies were so important to Scottish folklore that even Robert Burns ▢7 (*write*) a poem about them.

Poems and songs

Robert Burns.

[25] **Address to a Haggis (1786) (Scots)**

Fair fa' your honest, sonsie face,
Great chieftain o the puddin'-race!
Aboon them a' ye tak your place,
Painch, tripe, or thairm:
5 Weel are ye wordy o' a grace
As lang's my arm.

The groaning trencher there ye fill,
Your hurdies like a distant hill,
Your pin wad help to mend a mill
10 In time o need,
While thro your pores the dews distil
Like amber bead.

His knife see rustic Labour dight,
An cut you up wi ready slight,
15 Trenching your gushing entrails bright,
Like onie ditch;
And then, O what a glorious sight,
Warm-reekin, rich!

Then, horn for horn, they stretch an strive:
20 Deil tak the hindmost, on they drive,
Till a' their weel-swall'd kytes belyve
Are bent like drums;
The auld Guidman, maist like to rive,
'Bethankit' hums.

25 Is there that owre his French ragout,
Or olio that wad staw a sow,
Or fricassee wad mak her spew
Wi perfect scunner,
Looks down wi sneering, scornfu view
30 On sic a dinner?

Poor devil! see him owre his trash,
As feckless as a wither'd rash,
His spindle shank a guid whip-lash,
His nieve a nit;
35 Thro bloody flood or field to dash,
O how unfit!

But mark the Rustic, haggis-fed,
The trembling earth resounds his tread,
Clap in his walie nieve a blade,
40 He'll make it whissle;
An legs an arms, an heads will sned,
Like taps o thrissle.

Robert Burns.

[26] **Address to a Haggis (1786) (English)**

Good luck to you and your honest, plump face,
Great chieftain[1] of the sausage race!
Above them all you take your place,
Stomach, tripe[2], or intestines[3]:
5 Well are you worthy of a grace
As long as my arm.

The groaning trencher[4] there you fill,
Your buttocks like a distant hill,
Your pin would help to mend a mill
10 In time of need,
While through your pores the dews[5] distill[6]
Like amber bead[7].

His knife see rustic Labour wipe,
And cut you up with ready slight,
15 Trenching your gushing[8] entrails[9] bright,
Like any ditch[10];
And then, O what a glorious sight,
Warm steaming, rich!

Then spoon for spoon, the stretch and strive:
20 Devil take the hindmost[11], on they drive,
Till all their well swollen bellies by-and-by
Are bent like drums[12];
Then old head of the table, most like to burst,
'The grace!' hums.

25 Is there that over his French ragout,
Or olio[13] that would sicken a sow,
Or fricassee would make her vomit
With perfect disgust,
Looks down with sneering[14], scornful[15] view
30 On such a dinner?

Poor devil! see him over his trash,
As feeble[16] as a withered rush,
His thin legs a good whip-lash[17],
His fist a nut;
35 Through bloody flood or field to dash,
O how unfit.

But mark the Rustic, haggis-fed,
The trembling earth resounds his tread[18],
Clap in his ample[19] fist a blade,
40 He'll make it whistle;
And legs, and arms, and heads will cut off
Like the heads of thistles[20].

---

[1] **chieftain** a chief of a tribe or clan – [2] **tripe** stomach tissue – [3] **intestines** Gedärme – [4] **trencher** a wooden plate – [5] **dew** Tau – [6] **to distill** here: to flow out – [7] **bead** pearl – [8] **to gush** herausspritzen – [9] **entrails** Eingeweide – [10] **ditch** Graben – [11] **the hindmost** the last – [12] **drum** a large, cylindrical wooden container – [13] **olio** smell – [14] **sneering** höhnisch – [15] **scornful** spöttisch – [16] **feeble** weak, inadequate – [17] **whip-lash** Peitschenhieb – [18] **tread** step – [19] **ample** reichlich, hinreichend – [20] **thistle** Distel, die Nationalblume Schottlands

Ye Pow'rs, wha mak mankind your care,	You powers, who make mankind your care,
And dish them out their bill o fare,	And dish them out their bill of fare[21],
45 Auld Scotland wants nae skinking ware	45 Old Scotland wants no watery stuff,
That jaups in luggies:	That splashes in small wooden dishes;
But, if ye wish her gratefu prayer,	But if you wish her grateful prayer,
Gie her a Haggis	Give her a Haggis!

Robert Burns is widely regarded as the national poet of Scotland who wrote poems and songs – mainly in Scots but also in English. He was also famous for his rebellion against orthodox religion and morality. His poems often celebrated aspects of Scottish culture and life. His best known song is the traditional 'Auld Lang Syne' which is usually sung on New Year's Eve. To commemorate Burns' contribution to Scottish culture, Scotland celebrates an annual 'Burns Night' on his birthday on January 25. People usually have a supper with traditional Scottish food, like haggis, and say poems of his work. Burns' 'Address to a Haggis' is usually the first poem to be recited, while the haggis is brought to the table, often accompanied with a slow hand clap. When the line 'an cut you up wi' ready slight' is reached, the haggis is cut with a sharp knife.

Robert Burns (1759 – 1796)

CULTURE CORNER

Haggis is the national dish of Scotland. It is a type of pudding made from the liver, heart, and lungs of a sheep (or other animal), minced and mixed with beef or mutton fat, oatmeal and seasoned with onion, cayenne pepper, and other spices. The mixture is packed into a sheep's stomach and boiled.

A 10-step poetry analysis

First steps

1. Try to express the impression that reading the poem has made on you and write down some key words or phrases for the main idea(s) you associate with the text.
2. Note words and phrases you remember word for word.
3. Is there a personal message for you in the text? Does it appeal to your senses? What can you hear, see, taste and feel?

Analysis

4. Check unknown words in order to understand their literal meaning as a basis for interpretation. It is important to be aware that words in poetry often convey images or metaphors, so sometimes the literal meaning is not what the writer intended to express.
5. Point out formal aspects, e. g. structure (stanza), rhyme scheme, …
6. Define stylistic devices, explain their function in the text and the effect on the reader (see box on **pages 204/205**).
7. Analyse figurative language and motifs (see box on **pages 204/205**).
8. Research the poet's personal background (biography) and find out any facts that might have influenced his or her way of seeing and writing about the world.

Summary

9. Sum up your results to write a critical evaluation of the poem.
10. Say the lines again aloud and try to memorize the first stanza and the last (or an adequate number of lines if there is no division into stanzas). If you want to, you can learn the complete poem by heart.

---

[21] **bill of fare** menu

1 Analysis

a To understand and interpret the poem, you can follow the 10-step poetry analysis scheme (**p. 45**). Then, work on these tasks.

1 Check the Scottish vocabulary Kay uses and find English equivalents.
2 Identity, home and displacement are tightly connected with language. Analyse the influence using national (regional) language has on someone's identity.
3 Consider Kay's upbringing and examine her reasons for using Scottish vocabulary.
4 Explain the difference between dialect and sociolect.

b In the first verse of the poem, the writer talks about how she lost her Scots words when she moved to England. Summarize what Kay wants to convey in the second and third verse.

2 Creative tasks

a Discuss your experiences with poetry with a partner. Think about the following questions.

1 Can you remember the last poem you read? What was it about?
2 Is poetry difficult to understand, more difficult than a story?
3 Can words in a poem tell you more or less about a subject than a novel or some search results on the internet?
4 What is the intention of a poet / a poem?
5 Do you like poetry? Why or why not?

b Identify the images in the **quotation** below and explain their literal meaning first, then analyse their metaphorical quality. Then, give a definition of this stylistic device.

Poetry is a life-cherishing force.
For poems are not words, after
all, but fires for the cold, ropes
let down to the lost, something
as necessary as bread in the
pockets of the hungry.

Mary Oliver, *A Poetry Handbook*

c Write a text of about 120 words and evaluate the **quotation**. Focus on whether you agree or disagree and give reasons.

d Write an acrostic. Either find single items or phrases that match the letter or make complete sentences to express your ideas about poetry.

Jackie Kay (*1961) was born to a Scottish mother and Nigerian father in Edinburgh and was adopted as a baby by the Kay family from Glasgow.
Both parents were politically active, her father worked full-time for the Communist Party of Great Britain, and her mother was the Scottish secretary of the Campaign for Nuclear Disarmament.
Her unconventional origin and upbringing is reflected in her poetry. She has also published novels and plays, several collections of short stories as well as work for radio and theatre and writing for children, both fiction and poetry. In March 2016, Kay was appointed the Makar or National Poet for Scotland for a five-year term.

27)) Jackie Kay, 'Old Tongue' (2005)

When I was eight, I was forced south.
Not long after, when I opened
my mouth, a strange thing happened.
I lost my Scottish accent.
5 Words fell off my tongue:
eedyit, dreich, wabbit, crabbit
stummer, teuchter, heidbanger,
so you are, so am ur, see you, see ma ma,
shut yer geggie or I'll gie you the malkie!

10 My own vowels started to stretch like my bones
and I turned my back on Scotland.
Words disappeared in the dead of night,
new words marched in: ghastly, awful,
quite dreadful, *scones* said like *stones.*
15 *Pokey hats* into ice cream cones.
Oh where did all my words go –
my old words, my lost words?
Did you ever feel sad when you lost a word,
did you ever try and call it back
20 like calling in the sea?
If I could have found my words wandering,
I swear I would have taken them in,
swallowed them whole, knocked them back.

Out in the English soil, my old words
25 buried themselves. It made my mother's blood boil.
I cried one day with the wrong sound in my mouth.
I wanted them back; I wanted my old accent back,
my old tongue. My dour soor Scottish tongue.
Sing-songy. I wanted to *gie it laldie.*

Source: from *Life Mask* by Jackie Kay, Bloodaxe Books: Hexham, 2005, p. 50.

Runrig, 'Loch Lomond' (1979)

By yon bonnie banks and by yon bonnie braes
Where the sun shines bright on Loch Lomond
Where me and my true love spent many happy days
On the bonnie, bonnie banks of Loch Lomond

5 T'was there that we parted in yon shady glen
On the steep, steep sides of Ben Lomond
Where in purple hue the Highland hills we view
And the moon glints out in the gloaming

Chorus:
10 You'll take the high road and I'll take the low road
And I'll be in Scotland afore ye
Where me and my true love will never meet again
On the bonnie, bonnie banks of Loch Lomond

Where wildflowers spring and the wee birdies sing
15 On the steep, steep side of Ben Lomond
But the broken heart it kens nae second spring
Though resigned we may be while we're greetin'

Chorus (2x)

On the bonnie, bonnie banks (repeated)

Text, 00: MacDonald, Calum / MacDonald, Rory / Jones, Malcolm
Elwyn / Munro, Donald / Cherns, Richard Frederic / Harley,
Christopher James / Bayne, Iain
Copyright: BMG Rights Management UK Ltd/BMG Rights
Management GmbH, Berlin

Runrig were a Scottish Celtic rock band from the Isle of Skye named after a traditional Scottish practice of farming land (*run rig*). The band was active between 1973 and 2018. They released 14 studio albums, with a number of their songs sung in Scottish Gaelic. Their version of the Scottish traditional song 'The Bonnie Banks o' Loch Lomond' has become the band's as well as the Scottish rugby and the Scottish football teams' unofficial anthem.

CULTURE CORNER

'The Bonnie Banks of Loch Lomond' or simply 'Lomond' is a traditional Scottish folk song, first published in *Vocal Melodies of Scotland* in 1841. Loch Lomond is Scotland's and Great Britain's largest lake (36.4 km long). Its waters contain 22 islands and it is a popular leisure location.

1 **Listen to the song.** Describe the impressions you had while listening and make a list of the emotions and pictures the song triggers in your head.

2 **Looking at language.** Identify the Scottish Gaelic vocabulary. You have come across most of these words in this workshop. Translate the lyrics into modern English. You find help on **page 181**.

3 **Explain the lyrics**

a Interpret the communicative situation between the speaker and the addressee. How is their relationship described? Give reasons for your choice and evidence from the lyrics.

b Now read about two possible interpretations of the song. Discuss what you think is the most plausible and give reasons for your choice.

A lot of interpretations are connected to the Jacobite uprising in 1745. Scotland was ruled by an English king, when the Scottish, who were called Jacobites – referring to the Latin
5 name for their last king James – rebelled against the English and were defeated. It is said that the song is sung by the lover of a captured Jacobite rebel who was waiting to be executed in London after a show trial. The
10 heads of the executed men were set upon poles and exhibited in all of the towns between London and Edinburgh in a procession along the 'high road' (the most important road), while the relatives of the rebels walked back
15 along the 'low road' (the normal road for peasants and commoners).

Another interpretation of the 'low road' is that it refers to the traditional underground route taken by the 'fairies' who transport the soul of a Scot who died in a foreign land – here
5 England – back to his homeland. Connected to this is an interpretation that claims that the two people in the song are both soldiers. The English would find two brothers or friends and tell them that they could choose who would
10 die and who would live. The singer is therefore telling his friend that they will both go back to Scotland, but he will go on the 'low road' or that of the dead and be home first. This is supported by him singing that he will never
15 meet his love again in the real, on Loch Lomond.

Marcus Sedgwick
Cudweed and the Bagpipes

ONE

Flying upside down is something I don't do very often. When I was younger, I used to do it a lot (mostly to show off[1] to young lady ravens). But these days I find that flying upside down leads to all
5 sorts of problems, most of which end up with me having one wing in a bandage for a few weeks. However, as this story about Cudweed and the bagpipes starts, I was flying upside down, outside
10 the castle. Not only that, but I was flying upside down holding a letter in my beak, also upside down, so that Cudweed could read it. Because he was also upside down.
15 He was at that moment dangling from a long rope, that was wrapped around his ankle. He was slowly revolving[2], just as you imagine a fourteen-year-old
20 boy would slowly revolve when hanging from the battlements[3] of the castle by a single rope wrapped around his ankle. Now, maybe I started this story in
25 the wrong place, and I should go back a little, to the reason why Cudweed was hanging by a rope from the battlements. It all began one morning when Valevine seemed very grumpy, during breakfast. He is often grumpy over
30 breakfast, for example, when he hasn't slept well, but this morning there was something more seriously wrong. He was looking through his diary, counting on his fingers and, it seemed, doing some calculations.
35 'Blast[4]!' he said, finally. 'What is it?' asked Solstice. (I should mention that Solstice is now away at university but had just come back for the Easter holidays. So, everything was just like old times, which is to say; total chaos.)

40 'Bad news, I'm afraid,' her father said. Cudweed immediately looked worried. 'Bad news?' he asked. 'News? The bad kind? Bad?' 'I'm afraid so, my boy,' Valevine said. He looked deadly serious. 'It's time to clean the windows.'
45 'What windows?' asked Solstice.
'The windows of the castle, obviously,' Valevine said. 'But we don't clean the castle windows!' said Cudweed.
50 'Yes, we do! Every ten years, on May the 23rd. Whether they need doing or not.' 'They need doing!' said Minty, who had been silent up to now. 'Look at
55 them! They're so dirty you can barely see out of them!' 'But I don't remember doing them before,' said Solstice. 'Well, for one thing, we used to pay
60 someone else to do them,' Minty explained. 'But we decided to save the money. And for another thing, you would have been very young the last time. But if ten years have passed, then it's
65 time to do them ourselves.' 'Yes, dear,' said Valevine. He looked at Solstice and Cudweed. 'So, who's going to do the outside?' 'The *what*?' asked Cudweed.
So that was how it had started, with a long argument
70 about whether it would be Solstice or Cudweed who would abseil on a rope down the walls of the castle to do the outside of the windows that did not open. It was a very long argument, during which I hid, and I only came out when it turned out that they had
75 decided to toss a coin. Cudweed lost. And so there he was, abseiling down the outside of the castle walls, with a bucket of hot water in one hand.

---

[1] **to show off** [ʃəʊ ɒf] angeben – [2] **to revolve** [rɪˈvɒlv] sich drehen – [3] **battlements** [ˈbætlmənts] Zinnen – [4] **Blast**! [blɑːst] *ugs.* So ein Mist!

I sat on the top of the East Tower and watched the
80 whole thing.
I did not expect it to end well.
But in fact, it didn't even *start* well.
Cudweed looked nervous. Anxious. To be honest he
looked terrified. He had just made it to his first
85 window when Solstice stuck her head out of the
window next to him, one that did open, and shouted,
'how's it going?'
Well, that was enough for Cudweed to drop the
bucket, which fell a few hundred metres to the rocks
90 below the castle wall and smashed[5] into tiny pieces.
He screamed, and started trying to climb back up,
frantically. I have no idea how he managed it, but in
his desperation[6], he somehow succeeded in letting
the rope slip from his waist and get tangled around[7]
95 his ankle. So, there he was; hanging upside down
with just the rope around one ankle, way above the
ground and with nothing else to save him.
At that moment, Valevine poked his head out[8] of the
window next to Solstice.
100 'Spot of bother[9], eh?'
Cudweed screamed again, for about five minutes.
Then he took a deep breath and then he shouted,
'Get me out of here!'
Now, the next thing that happened was Minty, who
105 poked her head out of a third window, and said,
'Cudweed, stop messing around when you should be
cleaning windows. Anyway, you have an important
letter.'
She was waving the letter in her hand, and she
110 clearly expected him to read it, there and then.
'Now?' cried Cudweed.
'Yes, now!' said Minty. 'It's very important.'
'I'm a bit busy,' said Cudweed.
'Stop making excuses[10]!' said Minty. 'You always
115 make excuses.'
Now personally, I thought that Cudweed had a point,
but Minty would not be stopped.
She saw that she was too far away to hand the letter
to Cudweed, so she had me fly over, and take it from
120 her. Then I had to fly upside down so Cudweed could
read it.
And he did, eventually, and that involved some very
clever flying from me, not only upside down, but
hovering[11] in front of Cudweed's face for long
125 enough for him to take the whole thing in[12].

Finally, when he had read it, he was not happy.
He took an even deeper breath and then he shouted
'Get me out of here!' so loud, and so crossly, that
everyone did what they should have done in the first
130 place, and rushed up to the rooftops[13] to haul[14]
Cudweed back up to safety.
'What is it?' asked Solstice once Cudweed was safe
again and everyone had got their breath back.
Cudweed showed the letter to everyone.
135 'I have to do work experience!!' he said. 'It's an official
letter. It says that although I have been home-
schooled, I still have to go and do work experience
somewhere. Real work! In a real company!'
'Well, what's so bad about that?' asked Solstice.
140 'I don't want to!' cried Cudweed.
'Ah,' said Solstice. 'That is a problem. I see.'
'No, you don't see,' Cudweed said, 'it's *even worse*
than that!'
At this point he glared at[15] his parents.
145 'I would have had a free choice of places to go, but ...'

'But ...?' asked Solstice, who was also looking at her
parents as if she knew what Cudweed was about to
say.
'Apparently, this letter is a final warning. They sent
150 five other letters over the last four months,
explaining what I needed to do. And what I needed to
do was choose from a long list of the places I could
go to.'

---

[5] **to smash** [smæʃ] zeschmettern; zerschlagen – [6] **desperation** [ˌdespəˈreɪʃən] Verzweiflung – [7] **to get tangled around** [get ˈtæŋgəld əˈraʊnd] sich in etw. /
um etw. wickeln; verwicklen – [8] **to poke out** [pəʊk aʊt] aus etw. herausschauen – [9] **spot of bother** [spɒt əv ˈbɒðə] in Schwierigkeiten – [10] **to make excuses**
[meɪk ɪkˈskjuːsɪz] Ausflüchte machen; Ausreden haben – [11] **to hover** [ˈhɒvə] schweben – [12] **to take sth. in** [teɪk ˈsʌmθɪŋ ɪn] etw. aufnehmen; etw. verstehen –
[13] **rooftop** [ˈruːftɒp] Dach – [14] **to haul** [hɔːl] ziehen – [15] **to glare at sb.** [gleə ət ˈsʌmbɒdi] jdn. zornig anstarren

'Do you know what happened to those letters,
155 Father? Mother?' asked Solstice, who knew *perfectly
well* what had happened to those letters.
'Well, we have to light the fires in the castle with
something,' said Valevine, looking very
uncomfortable.
160 'I thought so,' said Cudweed. 'So now there is just a
choice of three things left.'
He did not look happy, and when he read from the
letter, we saw why.
'One! I can go to a factory at the docks where they
165 turn the insides[16] of fish into dog food.'
'Oh,' said Solstice, looking ill.
'Two! I can go to a university department where they
are running ten boring experiments into the most
boring jobs of all time, and study what makes them
170 boring by doing the boring jobs.'
'Ah,' said Valevine. 'Eeee. Oh.'
'Or, three!' said Cudweed, 'I can go to a tiny place in
the very far north of Scotland and learn how to make
bagpipes!'
175 'Hmm,' said Minty, 'which one are you going to
choose?'
'Well, it will have to be the bagpipes, won't it?' said
Cudweed, looking very cross.
'It doesn't sound so bad, does it?' said Solstice.
180 'Scotland might be fun.'
'Scotland will be cold and wet,' Cudweed said. 'I know
it will.'
'Making bagpipes might be fun,' Minty added.
'No it won't,' said Cudweed, firmly.
185 'Why not?' asked Valevine. 'It could be a useful thing
to learn.'
'Useful?!' cried Cudweed, looking angrier than ever.
'Anyway, I don't want to. For one thing, bagpipes
sound like someone is strangling[17] a cat. No, that's
190 wrong, two cats. And for another thing, it's cruel!'
'Cruel?' asked Minty, 'How is it cruel?'
'You know how they make bagpipes?' Cudweed asked.
Everyone shook their heads.
'Well, it's obvious, isn't it?' Cudweed said. 'You only
195 have to look at them! Obviously, you just take a sheep,
and turn it inside out. Then you drill some holes in
one of its legs and blow. That's why they make such
an awful sound – it's the dead sheep screaming.'
Everyone stared at Cudweed.
200 'I'm not sure that's how you make bagpipes,' said
Solstice. 'In fact, I'm pretty sure it isn't.'

'It is,' said Cudweed, 'and it's cruel. Not only to the
sheep, but to everyone who has to listen to the things
afterwards.'
205 'I really think you might be wrong,' said Solstice.
'Well,' said Minty, 'it looks like you're going to have
the chance to find out, doesn't it?'
'Unless you prefer the job at the fish factory?' asked
Valevine, 'Or the boring research into boring things?'
210 Cudweed didn't even bother replying to this
suggestion from his father, and he stomped off to his
room, explaining that he was going to start packing,
because he had to leave in two days' time, and that
he was going to spend most of his time
215 experimenting with putting different things in his
ears to try to block out the sound of the bagpipes.
I felt really sorry for him, and I tried to cheer him up
by sitting in his room with him while he put various
things in his ears, like socks, pasta and the stalks[18] of
220 large flowers, with the flowers still attached. Having

---

[16] **insides** [ɪnˈsaɪdz] Innereien – [17] **to strangle** [ˈstræŋgl] erdrosseln; ersticken – [18] **stalk** [stɔːk] Stängel – [19] **hi-fi (high fidelity)** [ˈhaɪ faɪ] Hi-Fi-Anlage;
Stereoanlage

put something in his ears, he would then play music as loud as he could on his hi-fi[19], and then he'd shake his head sadly, because nothing he tried blocked the sound out completely.

225 But he was so unhappy, I didn't want to leave him, and I made myself comfortable on a pile of his clothes while he went on trying to find the perfect earplugs[20]. Two days later, Cudweed sat on a train, heading north to Scotland. Solstice, Minty and Valevine had

230 taken him to the station with his two suitcases and put him on board. The train rattled[21] along at high speed, and as it went, the weather got worse. It got colder and colder, and then it started raining, and it was hard to believe it was May.

235 How do I know this?
Well, that is very simple.
I had spent a long time sitting with Cudweed in his room while he put things in his ears. I didn't want to leave him because he looked so miserable, but

240 eventually, as he worked on long into the night, I had fallen asleep on the pile of clothes on his bed.
And the next thing I knew, I woke up in a small dark place that smelled of socks, and it didn't take me long to work out what had happened – Cudweed had

245 packed me in one of his suitcases!
I'd squawked and squawked but although Cudweed heard me and quickly let me out, I already knew that

it was too late, because I could feel the rocking[22] of the train and hear the noise of the wheels on the tracks[23].

250 'Ark!' I cried.
'Edgar!' said Cudweed, 'I'm so pleased to see you! And I'm very glad you didn't die in my suitcase.'
So was I. I mean, the lack of air was one thing, the smell of the socks was even more dangerous ...

255 'Are you coming with me?' asked Cudweed.
'Kaork!' I said.
'Or maybe it was just an accident[24]? Maybe you want to fly home?'
'Kraaark,' I said.

260 Cudweed looked out of the window, and saw the name of a small railway station flying by.
'Erm, we're a long way into Scotland already,' he said.
'Sorry. I mean, you don't have to come with me, only ...'

265 Now, I *could* have climbed out of the window and flown home. It wasn't that far, not for a strong raven like me.
But there were two things that stopped me.
First, it was raining, and I *really* hate flying in the

270 rain.
And second, there was Cudweed's face.
He was looking at me with hope and sadness all mixed together, and I knew I could not leave him to face the bagpipes alone.

---

[20] **earplugs** ['ɪəplʌgz] Ohrenstöpsel – [21] **to rattle** ['rætl] rattern – [22] **to rock** [rɒk] *hier:* schaukeln – [23] **(train) tracks** [træks] Bahnschienen – [24] **accident** ['æksɪdənt] Versehen

America – Land of Dreams

Look at the photos and read the captions. Describe what you can see in each photo. What do you know about the different people and events? Make notes.

Martin Luther King Jr., Washington 1963, about to deliver his 'I have a dream' speech

Barack Obama, 44th president of the USA (born 1961)

Selma to Montgomery March, Alabama, 1965

Aretha Franklin (1942 – 2018)

American Civil War (1861 – 1865)

Muhammad Ali, triple world heavyweight champion (1942 – 2016)

Rosa Parks (1913 – 2005) on a bus after segregation laws were scrapped

30)) Listen to three students giving short presentations about some of these people or events. Copy the chart into your exercise book and make notes of the most important facts.

Name of person / event	Date(s)	Summary
???	???	???
???	???	???
???	???	???

30)) Listen again. Each student thought the person or event they were describing was the most important. From the presentations who or what do you think has had the greatest impact on the USA? Give reasons for your choice.

Slavery and the American Civil War

1 Slavery and the American Civil War

a The students from Rochester are doing a school history project about slavery and the American Civil War. Look at the pictures and describe what you can see.

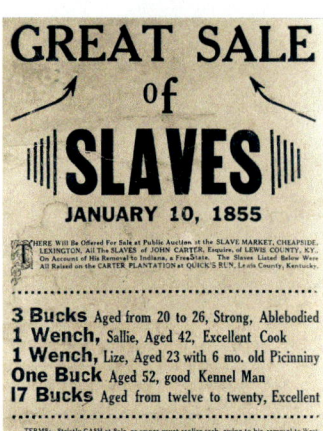

GREAT SALE of SLAVES JANUARY 10, 1855

b You are going to listen to a radio documentary about slavery in the USA. Before you listen, think about what you may hear. Note down your ideas.

32)) **c** Listen and complete the tasks.

1 Describe in what ways slaves were seen as property.
2 Explain why slavery was so important to the South.
3 Explain what impact the American Civil War had on slavery and on American society.
4 Outline who Frederick Douglass was.
5 Interpret why the speaker says: 'It is an uncomfortable subject for many Americans'.
6 Comment on how the speaker deals with the topic. Is he subjective / objective / factual? Does he express his personal opinion?

2 A brief history of slavery in the USA

a Chris has found a short article about slavery and the Civil War. Read the article and make notes about …

- the first slaves in the US,
- why slavery was important to the South,
- reasons for the Civil War.

A brief history of slavery in the USA

Many Americans' introduction to US history is the arrival of 102 passengers on the Mayflower in 1620. But a year earlier, 20 **enslaved** Africans were brought to the British colonies against their will […]. [T]he
5 captives who landed in Virginia are believed to be the first slaves to arrive into what would become the United States 150 years later […].
Slavery **flourished** initially in the tobacco fields of Virginia, Maryland and North Carolina. In the
10 tobacco-producing areas of those states, slaves **constituted** more than 50% of the population by 1776. Slavery then spread to the rice plantations further south […].
The British-operated slave trade across the Atlantic was
15 one of the biggest businesses of the 18th century. Approximately 600,000 of the 10 million African slaves made their way into the American colonies before the slave trade – not slavery – was banned by Congress in 1808. By 1860, though, the US recorded nearly 4 million
20 enslaved black people – 13% of the population […]. Eight of the first 12 US presidents were slave owners […]. According to Abraham Lincoln, the Civil War was fought to keep America whole, and not for the **abolition** of slavery – at least initially. Southern states
25 said they wanted **to secede** to protect states' rights, but they were really fighting to keep people enslaved. Lincoln took on the fight for the freedom of slaves, [as it has been suggested by some historians], because he was worried the British would support […] and
30 recognize the South as a separate **entity**. [So, for Lincoln the war was more about protecting the Union than ending slavery.] […]

Source (abbreviated and adapted): https://www. theguardian.com/news/2019/aug/15/400-years-since-slavery-timeline

b Look at the **bold** words. Each choose three and work out the meaning from the context. Then explain the meaning to a partner.
p. 147

31)) **Words and phrases**

to **compromise**	to make an agreement with someone else where both sides give up some things they want	**outcry**	a reaction of anger or strong protest
		paramount	more important than anything else
enamored	liking something a lot	**plantation**	a large area of land, especially in a hot country, where crops such as coffee, sugar and cotton are grown

c Complete the Remember box.

Remember:
- We use the passive when we are more interested in [1] than [2] does the action. *20 enslaved Africans **were brought** to the colonies.*
- When we want to know who carried out [3], we use 'by' + the [4] or organization: *… the slave trade … was banned **by** Congress in 1808.*
- We form the passive with 'be' + [5]:
  *… the civil war **was fought** to keep America whole …* (simple past)
  *… it **has been suggested** …* (present perfect)

CULTURE CORNER

The **Confederate States** of America was an attempt by 11 southern states to secede from the Union in 1860. It was made up of states that were pro-slavery. Led by Jefferson Davis, it existed for four years before being defeated in the Civil War.

3* **The Lincoln Memorial.** Complete the text with the correct form of the verbs in brackets.

The Lincoln Memorial stands at the west end of the National Mall as a [...] monument to the 16th President. The memorial [1] (*design*) by Henry Bacon [and [2] (*base on*) ancient Greek temples. It [3] (*surround*) by
5 36 fluted Doric columns, one for each of the thirty-six states in the Union at the time of Lincoln's death, and two columns at the entrance]. There are carved inscriptions of Lincoln's second Inaugural Address and
10 his Gettysburg Address [in the north and south side chambers. In the central hall is the solitary figure of Lincoln sitting and thinking.] The statue [4] (*carve*) in four years by the Piccirilli
15 brothers under the supervision of the sculptor, Daniel Chester French. The statue of Lincoln is 19 feet high and weighs 175
20 tons. The original plan was for the statue to be only ten feet high, but this [5] (*change*) so that the figure of Lincoln would not be
25 dwarfed by the size of the chamber. A commission to plan a monument [6] (*propose*) in 1867, shortly after Lincoln's death. [However, this first] project was never started for lack of funds. [In 1910, a bill [7] (*approve*)
30 by Congress to construct the current memorial which [8] (*can see*) by the public.] The Memorial [9] (*visit*) by millions of visitors each year and is the site of many large public gatherings and protests.

IN THIS TEMPLE
AS IN THE HEARTS OF THE PEOPLE
FOR WHOM HE SAVED THE UNION
THE MEMORY OF ABRAHAM LINCOLN
IS ENSHRINED FOREVER

Source (abbreviated and adpated): https://sites.google.com/a/pvlearners.net/dsms-wa-dc/lincoln-memorial

4 The origins

33)) **a** Ava asks Chris what he found out when he did research about the American Civil War. Listen to the conversation, take notes to complete the sentences, then check with a partner.

1 It's a myth that Lincoln …
2 History might have been very different if …
3 By the early 1800s, …

b Look at these two lines from the conversation. Discuss how you can decide whether something you read on the internet is true or not.

Chris   Yes, I found a copy of the letter on the internet. I copied that line as I think it's important to be factually correct.
Ava   We've been told that because of all the fake news around nowadays.

5 **It's your turn: Slavery.** Read these quotes about slavery. As a group, discuss what each one means. Then choose one or two that you think are the most powerful. Give reasons for your choice.

1 *Those who deny freedom to others deserve it not for themselves.*
Abraham Lincoln (1809 – 1865)
2 *Slavery has never been abolished from America's way of thinking.*
Nina Simone (Singer, 1933 – 2003)
3 *I did not know I was a slave until I found out I couldn't do the things I wanted.*
Frederick Douglass (1818 – 1889)
4 *Whenever I hear anyone arguing for slavery, I feel a strong impulse to see it tried on him personally.* Abraham Lincoln (1809 – 1865)

Grammar and structures

Passive (revision) → G2
20 enslaved Africans **were brought** to the British Colonies …
… as it **has been suggested** by some historians …

WES-40806-002

→ Workbook, page 40

PRACTICE A

PART 1

1* Ava and Chris continue talking about slavery and the Civil War. Complete their conversation, then listen and check.

34
p. 147

abolish ▪ defend ▪ hit ▪ involve ▪ kill ▪ organize ▪ pass ▪ practice ▪ prevent ▪ pull down ▪ reflect ▪ remove

A. So, let me get this right. The slave trade __1__ in 1808, but slavery was still legal.

C. Yes, even after 1808 slavery __2__ by people in the South as a 'Positive Good'.

5 A. That just sounds crazy …

C. Yes, to us, but segregation __3__ in the South even in the middle of the 20th century. In fact, the debate still goes on …

A. What do you mean?

10 C. Today, many African Americans __4__ from voting in elections.

A. But how? Doesn't everyone of the age of 18 have the right to vote?

C. Sure, but many voters __5__ from the voting registers. After the 2016 election, several states

15 __6__ in voter suppression, efforts that include additional obstacles to registration, the prevention of early voting and stricter voter identification requirements. And it's the African Americans that __7__ the hardest. 20

A. That's terrible.

C. Yes, and there are other signs that the mentality of many people in the southern states hasn't changed much. We can still find a lot of statues in the South of Confederate 25 heroes like General Lee.

A. I thought all of them __8__ a long time ago?

C. No, in fact in 2017 a march __9__ in protest against the removal of a statue in Charlottesville in South Carolina and a man 30 __10__. And laws __11__ in some states making it illegal to remove them.

A. We have to hope that as people's attitude is changing, this __12__ in the legislation.

PART 2

PART 3

2 Read the article about Confederate statues and match these headings to paragraphs A–F. There are two more than you need.

1 Confederate monuments are in every town of the USA

2 From the late 1900 to the middle of the 20th century

3 The largest project

4 The latest developments

5 Turning to other symbols

6 Twenty percent of all monuments were gradually removed

7 Who financed the monuments?

8 White women are represented on many statues.

3 Discuss whether controversial historical statues should be destroyed, moved to a museum or left where they are.

Up or down?

A While every statue in every town has a different origin, taken together, the roughly 700 Confederate monuments in the United States tell a national story. […] The vast 5 majority of [the statues] were built between the 1890s and 1950s […]. […] These monuments tended to glorify leaders of the Confederacy like General Robert E. Lee or former President of the Confederacy Jefferson Davis […]. [All of those monuments were there to teach values to people, which is 10 why they put them in the city squares and in front of state buildings.] […]

B White women were instrumental in raising funds to build these Confederate monuments. The *United Daughters of the Confederacy*, founded in the 1890s, was probably the most important and influential group […].

15 **C** In fact, the group was responsible for creating what is basically the Mount Rushmore of the Confederacy: a gigantic stone carving of Davis, Lee and Jackson in Stone Mountain, Georgia. Its production began in the 1910s, and it was completed in the 1960s.

D By then, the construction of new Confederate 20 monuments had begun to taper off, but the backlash to the Civil Rights Movement was spreading Confederate symbols in other ways: in 1956, Georgia redesigned its state flag to include the Confederate battle flag; and in 1962, South Carolina placed the flag atop its capitol building. […]

E Protesters and city officials have gradually taken 25 down statues in multiple towns and cities. [A]s of February 2019, at least 138 Confederate symbols had been removed from public spaces since 2015.

F More statues were targeted following protests over the police killing of George Floyd, a black man in Minneapolis, on May 25, 2020. On June 9, 2020, protesters toppled a statue of Confederate President 30 Jefferson Davis in Richmond, Virginia. And on September 8, 2021, a 12-ton statue of Confederate Gen. Robert E. Lee was removed more than 130 years after it was installed in Richmond – a former capital of the Confederacy.

Source (abbreviated and adapted): https://www.history.com/news/how-the-u-s-got-so-many-confederate-monuments

1 **a Think:** What information is included in a person's biography? Think about important dates and the person's achievements. Make notes.

b Pair: Work with a partner and compare your ideas.

c Share: Share your ideas as a group and try to come up with a definitive list of essential elements for a biography.

2 **a** Read the biography of Abraham Lincoln and put the paragraphs in the correct order.

A Lincoln was the 16th president of the United States and one of the great American leaders. His presidency was dominated by the American Civil War.

B In the effort to win the war, Lincoln assumed more power than any president before him, declaring martial law and suspending legal rights. He had difficulty finding effective generals to lead the Union armies until the appointment of Ulysses S. Grant as overall commander in 1864.

C In 1864, Lincoln stood for re-election and won. In his second inaugural address, he was conciliatory towards the southern states.

D Abraham Lincoln was born on 12 February 1809 near Hodgenville, Kentucky. He was brought up in Kentucky, Indiana and Illinois. His parents were poor pioneers and Lincoln was largely self-educated. In 1836, he qualified as a lawyer and went to work in a law practice in Springfield, Illinois. He sat in the state legislature from 1834 to 1842 and in 1846 was elected to Congress, representing the Whig Party for a term. In 1856, he joined the new Republican Party and in 1860 he was asked to run as their presidential candidate.

E In the presidential campaign, Lincoln made his opposition to slavery very clear. His victory provoked a crisis, with many southerners fearing that he would attempt to abolish slavery in the South. Seven southern states left the Union to form the Confederate States of America, also known as the Confederacy. Four more joined later. Lincoln vowed to preserve the Union even if it meant war.

F Fighting broke out in April 1861. Lincoln always defined the Civil War as a struggle to save the Union, but in January 1863 he nonetheless issued the Emancipation Proclamation, which freed all slaves in areas still under Confederate control. This was an important symbolic gesture that identified the Union's struggle as a war to end slavery.

G On 19 November 1863, Lincoln delivered his famous Gettysburg Address at the dedication of a cemetery at the site of the Battle of Gettysburg, a decisive Union victory that had taken place earlier in the year.

H On 9 April 1865, the Confederate general Robert E. Lee surrendered, effectively ending the war. It had lasted for more than four years and 600,000 Americans had died. Less than a week later, Lincoln was shot while attending a performance at Ford's Theatre in Washington D.C. and died the next morning, 15 April 1865. His assassin, John Wilkes Booth, was a strong supporter of the Confederacy.

Source (paragraphs jumbled up): "Abraham Lincoln (1809-1865)", BBC History, 2014, https://www.bbc.co.uk/history/historic_figures/lincoln_abraham.shtml [08.07.2022]

b Compare the order of your paragraphs. Then read the text again and check your ideas for **1**.

3 **a** Choose one of the people connected to slavery or the American Civil War. Do some further research and use the notes to write a biography of 220–220 words (*TIPs* on **pp. 105, 140**).

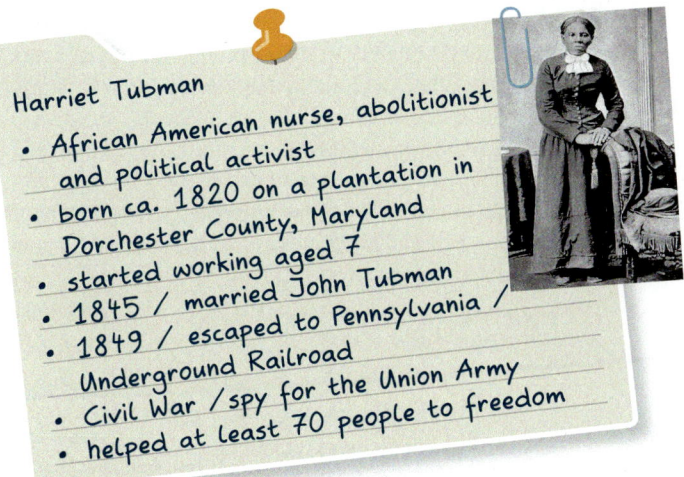

Harriet Tubman
• African American nurse, abolitionist and political activist
• born ca. 1820 on a plantation in Dorchester County, Maryland
• started working aged 7
• 1845 / married John Tubman
• 1849 / escaped to Pennsylvania / Underground Railroad
• Civil War / spy for the Union Army
• helped at least 70 people to freedom

Frederick Douglass
• African American abolitionist and social reformer
• born ca. 1818 / plantation in Dorchester County, Maryland
• born into slavery / raise grandmother
• learn read and write in secret
• escape in Sep. 1838 via ship and train
• joined American Anti-Slavery society
• 1845 / publish autobiography
• most photographed man of the 19th c.

b Swap your text with a partner. Give each other feedback on how to improve them.

The Civil Rights Movement

1 The Civil Rights Movement

 a Watch the video about the Civil Rights Movement and match the dates in the box to the four topics.

 b Watch the video again and make notes about the four topics in **a**. Then compare your notes.

> 1955 ■ 1964 ■ mid-20th century ■ 1963

> The start of the Civil Rights Movement
> ■ Rosa Parks ■ Dr Martin Luther King Jr.
> ■ President Lyndon Johnson

2 What happened?

 a Listen to the conversation between the students. Say what each person is researching.

 b Listen again and complete the sentences.

1 Mitch is confused about …
2 The date of Martin Luther King day …
3 Previous research gives the idea …
4 Kelly's pleased with her assignment …
5 Mitch made a connection between …

3 Martin Luther King Jr

a Mitch reads an article about Martin Luther King Jr. Complete it with the phrases below.

A which helped bring about such landmark legislation as the Civil Rights Act

B the economically disadvantaged

C a wave of riots swept major cities across the country

D it is widely regarded as a watershed moment in the history of the American Civil Rights Movement

E was assassinated

F including members of the King family

G was held on August 28

H known as the 'I Have a Dream' speech

I who a century earlier had brought down the institution of slavery in the United States

J who played a key role in the American Civil Rights Movement

Martin Luther King Jr. was a social activist and Baptist minister ▢1 from the mid-1950s until his assassination in 1968. King sought equality and human rights for African Americans, ▢2 and all victims of injustice through
5 peaceful protest. He was the driving force behind watershed events such as the Montgomery Bus Boycott and the 1963 March on Washington, ▢3 and the Voting Rights Act. King was awarded the Nobel Peace Prize in 1964 and is remembered each year on Martin Luther King, Jr. Day, a U.S.
10 federal holiday since 1986. […] [I]n 1957, he and other civil rights activists – most of them fellow ministers – founded the Southern Christian Leadership Conference (SCLC), a group committed to achieving full equality for African Americans through nonviolent protest. […] During a
15 month-long trip to India in 1959, he had the opportunity to meet family members and followers of Gandhi, the man he described in his autobiography as 'the guiding light of our technique of nonviolent social change.' [...] [The March on Washington] ▢4 and attended by some 200,000 to
20 300,000 participants, ▢5 and a factor in the passage of the Civil Rights Act of 1964.
The March on Washington culminated in King's most famous address, ▢6, a spirited call for peace and equality that many consider a masterpiece of rhetoric.
25 Standing on the steps of the Lincoln Memorial – a monument to the president ▢7 – he shared his vision of a future in which 'this nation will rise up and live out the true meaning of its creed: "We hold these truths to be self-evident, that all men are created equal."' […]
30 On the evening of April 4, 1968, Martin Luther King ▢8. He was fatally shot while standing on the balcony of a motel in Memphis, where he had traveled to support a sanitation workers' strike. In the wake of his death, ▢9, while President Johnson declared a national day of mourning.
35 James Earl Ray, an escaped convict and known racist, pleaded guilty […] and was sentenced to 99 years in prison. He later recanted his confession and gained some unlikely advocates, ▢10, before his death in 1998. […]

Source (abbreviated): https://www.history.com/topics/black-history/martin-luther-king-jr

Words and phrases

to assassinate	to murder a famous person, particularly for political reasons	**fervor**	very strong feelings about something
to culminate	to end with a particular result or at a particular time	**limelight**	the center of public attention
		to stoke	to make people feel something more strongly
		watershed	an event or a period of time that marks an important change

b Read the text again and complete the sentences.

1 King's main aim was to …
2 King's effort was recognized when …
3 The highlight of the March on Washington …
4 A national day of mourning was declared …
5 The purpose of King's trip to Memphis was …

CULTURE CORNER

In 1943, 12 years earlier, Rosa Parks had first clashed with bus driver James Blake. Parks stepped onto his very crowded bus on a chilly day, paid her fare at the front, then resisted the rule in place for Black people to disembark and re-enter through the back door. She stood her ground until Blake pulled her coat sleeve, enraged, to demand her cooperation. Parks left the bus rather than give in.

4 **A hero.** Ava made some notes about Rosa Parks. Use them to write a short text (120 words) about her.

- Thursday, December 1, 1955
- Rosa Parks / bus / home from work
- Refused / give up seat
- Arrested / two police officers
- Blacks / boycotted bus / support Parks
- Parks / $10 fine
- November 13, 1956 / Supreme Court ruled / segregation unconstitutional
- Moved from Montgomery to Detroit
- Died / 92 / October 24, 2005

5 It's your turn: A presentation

a Look at these images connected to the Civil Rights Movement. Describe what you see in the pictures.

p. 148

b Work with a partner and discuss the significance or importance of the person or event for the Civil Rights Movement. The words in the word cloud can help you.

c With your partner, choose on of the people or events and write notes for a short presentation. (Tips on **pp. 139/140, 22/23, 142/143**.)

d Hold your presentation and ask the other students to give feedback (see **page 144**).

Grammar and structures

Passive (revision) → G2

Martin Luther King day **is celebrated** on … The march on Washington **was held** on August 28 …

PART 1

PART 2

PART 3

1 **a** Read the quotes and make notes about their meaning. Then discuss your ideas with a partner.

> *If you are neutral in situations of injustice, you have chosen the side of the oppressor. If an elephant has its foot on the tail of a mouse, and you say that you are neutral, the mouse will not appreciate your neutrality.*

Archbishop Desmond Tutu (1931 – 2021)

> *One has a moral responsibility to disobey unjust laws.*

Martin Luther King Jr. (1929 – 1968)

> *A man who stands for nothing will fall for anything.*

Malcolm X (1925 – 1965)

b Read this quote from Malcolm X. Discuss how his approach to civil rights differed from that advocated by Martin Luther King Jr.

> *Concerning nonviolence, it is criminal to teach a man not to defend himself when he is the constant victim of brutal attacks.*

2 **a** Before you read the article about Malcolm X, another leader of the Civil Rights Movement, write down what you would like to find out.

b Read the article, find the following words and choose the correct meaning.

1 to urge
  a to show that you support an idea with what you say or do
  b to say that something is important in a particular situation
  c to add the most recent information to something

2 stance
  a a determined attempt to oppose someone or something you consider to be wrong
  b a way of standing or holding your body
  c an attitude about an issue that you state clearly

3 rejection
  a a return to your previous character or behaviour
  b when someone accepts that something unpleasant will happen and they cannot change it
  c a refusal to accept, approve or support something

4 to foreshadow
  a to show or give a warning that something will happen in the future
  b to be forced to give up a right or a benefit because of something you did
  c to decide not to do or have something

Malcolm X

Malcolm X was an African American leader in the Civil Rights Movement, minister and supporter of Black nationalism. He urged his fellow Black Americans to protect themselves against white aggression 'by any
5 means necessary,' a stance that often put him at odds with the nonviolent teachings of Martin Luther King Jr. His charisma and oratory skills helped him achieve national prominence in the Nation of Islam, a belief system that merged Islam with Black nationalism. After Malcolm X's
10 assassination in 1965, his bestselling book, *The Autobiography of Malcolm X*, popularized his ideas and inspired the Black Power movement.
Malcolm X was born Malcolm Little in 1925, in Omaha, Nebraska. […] The family moved to Lansing, Michigan
15 after the Ku Klux Klan made threats against them, though the family continued to face threats in their new home. […]
Though highly intelligent and a good student, he dropped out of school following eighth grade. He began wearing
20 zoot suits[1], dealing drugs and earned the nickname 'Detroit Red.' At 21, he went to prison for larceny[2].
It was in jail that Malcolm X first encountered the teachings of Elijah Muhammad, head of the Lost-Found Nation of Islam, or Black Muslims, a Black nationalist
25 group that identified white people as the devil. Soon after, Malcolm adopted the last name 'X' to represent his rejection of his 'slave' name[3].
Malcolm was released from prison after serving six years and went on to become the minister of Mosque No. 7 in
30 Harlem, where his oratory skills and sermons in favor of self-defense gained the organization new admirers: The Nation of Islam grew from 400 members in 1952 to 40,000 members by 1960. His admirers included celebrities like Muhammad Ali, who became close friends
35 with Malcolm X before the two had a falling out. […]

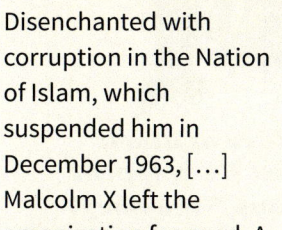

Disenchanted with corruption in the Nation of Islam, which suspended him in December 1963, […] Malcolm X left the organization for good. A few months later, he traveled to Mecca, where he underwent a spiritual transformation: 'The true brotherhood I had seen had influenced me to recognize 45 that anger can blind human vision,' he wrote. Malcolm X returned to America with a new name: El-Hajj Malik El-Shabazz.

In June 1964, he founded the Organization of Afro-American Unity, which identified racism, and not the 50 white race, as the enemy of justice. […] Malcolm X was assassinated by a Black Muslim[4] at an Organization of Afro-American Unity rally in the Audubon Ballroom in New York City on February 21, 1965. Malcolm X had predicted that he would be more important in death than 55 in life, and had even foreshadowed his early demise in his book, *The Autobiography of Malcolm X*. […]

The book and Malcolm X's life have inspired numerous film adaptations, most famously Spike Lee's 1992 film *Malcolm X* starring Denzel Washington. Malcolm X is 60 buried in Ferncliff Cemetery, New York.

Source (abbreviated): https://www.history.com/topics/black-history/malcolm-x

---

[1] **zoot suit** a type of suit that uses a lot of cloth, popular from the mid-1930s and often associated with African-American men
[2] **larceny** a legal term for theft of someone's property
[3] **slave name** the name given to slaves by their owners
[4] Thomas Hagan, who thought that Malcolm X had betrayed the movement.

CULTURE CORNER

The Lost-Found Nation of Islam, often known just as Nation of Islam (NOI) was founded in 1933 by Wallace D. Fard (Wali Fard Mohammad) in Detroit, Michigan and assisted by his deputy Elijah Mohammad, who soon took over the leadership. Nation of Islam believed it was time for black people to take back control, drop their 'slave names' and even create a separate black nation in the southern states of Georgia, Alabama, and Mississippi.

---

3 **a** Look at these sentences and say whether they are true for Martin Luther King, Malcolm X or both of them. If you don't know the answers, read the text on **page 58** again.

1 He was a Christian and a minister of the church.
2 He changed his name because he considered his original name to be a slave name.
3 He was an excellent speaker.
4 He was murdered at a rally.
5 When he was young, he became a criminal.
6 He went on a trip to India to learn from another great leader.

b Read the quote by Martin Luther King, which he wrote in a telegram to Malcolm X's wife after Malcolm's death. Explain the expression 'eye to eye'. Then assess to which degree Martin Luther King agreed with Malcolm X on race issues.

> *While we did not always see eye to eye on methods to solve the race problem, I always had a deep affection for Malcolm and felt that he had a great ability to put his finger on the existence and root of the problem.*

4 **a** With a partner, discuss which questions from **3a** you could find answers to.

b Read the article again and complete the tasks.

1 Explain why Malcolm X became such an important leader in the Civil Rights Movement in the 1950s and 1960s.
2 Evaluate in what way Malcolm X's childhood influenced his beliefs later on in life.
3 Explain why he changed his name twice.
4 Find out why Malcolm X and Muhammad Ali fell out.
5 Assess what Malcolm X meant by 'racism, not the white race, was the enemy of justice'.

1 Look at the posters from the Black Panther Party. Comment on style and their meaning and interpret their message.

2 **a** Read Ava's text about the Black Panther Party and complete the tasks.

[The Black Panther Party was one of the most divisive organizations to emerge during the Civil Rights Movement in the USA. Founded in 1966 in Oakland California by two young political activists, Huey Newton and Bobby Searle, it became possibly the era's most influential militant black power organizations.] Like Malcolm X, the Black Panthers believed that nonviolent protests could not truly liberate black
5 Americans or give them power over their own lives. They linked the African American liberation movement with liberation movements in Africa and Southeast Asia.
Its members confronted politicians, challenged the police, and protected black citizens from brutality. [The founders were particularly] disappointed in the failure of the civil rights movement to improve the condition of Blacks outside the South. They saw brutality against civil rights protesters as part of a long
10 tradition of police violence and state oppression. Rather than integrating American society, members wanted to change it fundamentally. For them, black power was a global revolution.
[While I understand why the Black Panther Party was popular with many poor, disenfranchised African Americans, I don't feel that the often overt call for violence was right or that it furthered their cause. Of course, many of the Black Panther members would say that peaceful protests had been met with violence
15 from both the police and some members of society and that they had the right to 'fight fire with fire.'
In addition, there was another side to the Black Panther Party which was extremely positive. The party's community service programs – called 'survival programs' – provided food, clothing, and transportation and clearly benefited many of the poorest in the community.] Local chapters of the Panthers, often led by women, focused attention on community 'survival programs.' They organized a free breakfast program for
20 20,000 children each day as well as a free food program for families and the elderly. They sponsored schools, legal aid offices, clothing distribution, local transportation, and health clinics […] in several cities.
[…] Among the organization initiatives, they campaigned for prison reform, held voter registration drives, […] opened free health clinics in a dozen cities serving thousands who could not afford it, and created Freedom Schools in nine cities, including the noteworthy Oakland Community School, led by Ericka
25 Huggins from 1973 to 1981.
Women made up about half of the Panther membership and often held leadership roles. Vanetta Molson directed Seattle's survival programs. Lynn French in Chicago and Audre Dunham in Boston were inspirational local leaders. Elaine Brown became the national chairwoman in 1972. Still, the organization's members struggled to overcome gender inequality.
30 [To sum up, the Black Panther Party, while advocating violent protest also did a lot for many communities across the USA. In my opinion, the organization was a product of its time. It is not difficult to understand why Newton and Searle felt they had little alternative. However, this does not mean that I personally advocate the use of violence, but I do have some empathy. In addition, I feel that the good the Black Panther Party did outweighs the negative aspects.]

Source of ll. 4–11, 18–29 (abbreviated and adapted): https://nmaahc.si.edu/blog-post/black-panther-party-challenging-police-and-promoting-social-change

1 Summarize what the Black Panther Party did between 1966 and 1981.
2 State how the Black Panther Party views were similar to those of Malcolm X.
3 Explain how some members of the party justified the use of violence.
4 Comment on Ava's statement 'While I understand …' (ll. 12–13).

b Find words or phrases in the text which match the definitions.

p. 148

1 causing people to be split into groups that disagree with or oppose each other
2 to free a person or a country from the control of somebody else
3 cruel and unfair treatment of people, especially by not giving them the same freedom and rights as other people
4 to take away somebody's rights, especially the right to vote
5 to have a helpful and useful effect
6 an organized effort by a group of people to achieve something
7 to support something publicly
8 important or interesting
9 to be greater or more important than something else

3 The Ten-Point Program was a list of demands that the founders of the Black Panther organization drew up originally in 1966. Read this extract from the updated, 1972 version of the program and complete the tasks.

1. We want freedom. We want power to determine the destiny of our Black and oppressed communities.
2. We want full employment for our people.
3. We want an end to the robbery by the capitalist of our Black and oppressed communities.
4. We want decent housing, fit for the shelter of human beings.
5. We want education for our people that exposes the true nature of this decadent American society. We want education that teaches us our true history and our role in the present-day society.
6. We want completely free health care for all Black and oppressed people.
7. We want an immediate end to police brutality and murder of Black people, other people of color, all oppressed people inside the United States.
8. We want an immediate end to all wars of aggression.
9. We want freedom for all Black and poor oppressed people now held in U.S. federal, state, county, city and military prisons and jails. We want trials by a jury of peers for all persons charged with so-called crimes under the laws of this country.
10. We want land, bread, housing, education, clothing, justice, peace and people's community control of modern technology.

Source (abbreviated): https://archive.org/details/Blackpntrs10Pnt

1 Examine and evaluate the demands made in the document.
2 Speculate how American government and establishment (the dominant class in American society) reacted to this document.
3 Discuss to what extent this is a 'revolutionary' document.

Looking at extracts from a novel

S1 Literary terms. Match the terms with their definitions.

1 using the same expressions more than once
2 who tells the story (not the author)
3 when and where the story takes place
4 the main subject of a book or story
5 words beginning with the same letter
6 the perspective from which the story is told
7 one of the main characters in the story
8 the storyline and how it develops

> alliteration ■ narrator ■ plot ■
> point of view ■ protagonist ■ repetition ■
> setting ■ theme

S2 Harper Lee. Read about Harper Lee's novel *To Kill a Mockingbird*. **Student A:** Do some research about the plot of the novel. **Student B:** Find factual information about the Great Depression. Share your findings with your partner.

In To Kill a Mockingbird *Harper Lee tells the story of Scout Finch (the narrator), a young girl growing up in a small (fictional) Alabama town in the 1930s, during the Great Depression.*

S3 Making notes. Read these extracts from *To Kill a Mockingbird*. Study the examples of how to make notes when analysing an extract (from this novel). Then answer these questions: What does Atticus want to instil in the children with the mockingbird example? What makes Calpurnia's warning controversial?

> **TIP**
>
> **Identifying literary devices**
> Writers use language (words, imagery, dialogue) and structure (how a text is put together) to create their stories, characters and themes. When we analyse literary texts we try to explain the purpose of literary devices – how writers make language choices, and the effect their words have on the reader. When identifying literary devices, try to relate them to a character, a main theme or the setting.

> **Literary devices often found in literary texts**
> - alliteration   - allusion
> - climax   - imagery
> - irony   - metaphor
> - parallelism   - personification
> - register   - repetition
> - rhetorical question - symbol
>
> You already know some of these devices from **On Track 5** (students' book 5, p. 153).

Extract A: Atticus teaches his son, Jem, the moral responsibility of using an air rifle.

Atticus said to Jem one day, '… Shoot all the bluejays you want, if you can hit 'em, but remember it's a sin to kill a mockingbird.' That was the only time I ever heard Atticus say it was a sin to do something, and I asked Miss Maudie about it. 'Your father's right,' she said. 'Mockingbirds don't do one thing except make music for us to enjoy. They don't eat up people's gardens, don't nest in corn cribs, they don't do one thing but sing their hearts out for us. That's why it's a sin to kill a mockingbird.'

- allowing the children to call the father by his first name is a sign of Atticus treating his children as equal
- strong warning, unusual from Atticus
- Scout wants a second opinion from a neighbour
- to introduce repetition
- using repetition to give emphasis
- another example of repetition
- double negative, emphatic use

Extract B: Calpurnia, the black housekeeper in the Finch household, scolds Scout for mocking a boy from her school for his lack of table manners.

'Don't matter who they are, anybody sets foot in this house's yo' comp'ny, and don't you let me catch you remarkin' on their ways like you was so high and mighty! Yo' folks might be better'n the Cunninghams but it don't count for nothin' the way you're disgracin' 'em.'

- everyone should be treated the same way
- Calpurnia reverts to the use of 'negro language' as she is outraged
- colloquial, intimate address but shows that Calpurnia doesn't regard herself as part of the family
- used for emphasis

S4 Answer the question. What do these extracts tell you about the children's relationship to their father and other adults around them? Use the notes to help you.

Analysing extracts from a novel

S1 **Annotating an extract.** Read two extracts illustrating the prevailing racism in town, preceding the Tom Robinson trial. Study the notes on the <u>underlined</u> phrases in Extract C and make a copy of Extract D for your own notes. What impression does the conversation in extract C give you about the relationship between Atticus and Scout?

Extract C:

> 'Do you defend niggers, Atticus?' I asked him that evening.
> 'Of course I do. Don't say nigger, Scout. That's common.'
> ''s what everybody at school says.'
> 'From now on it'll be everybody less one –'
> 'Well if you don't want me to grow up talkin' that way, why do you send me to school?'

- Scout uses the derogative, racist term naturallyw
- simple but strong, straightforward answer
- Atticus avoids using the term 'racist' instead hints to their stand in the community, how their values, morals are different
- Scout defends herself, she is one of the school community
- a gentle but firm warning, worded as a statement in third person
- Scout challenges Atticus – reference to her dislike of school

Extract D:

> 'This case, Tom Robinson's case, is something that goes to the essence of a man's conscience – Scout, I couldn't go to church and worship God if I didn't try to help that man.' 'Atticus, you must be wrong ...' 'How's that?' 'Well, most folks seem to think that, they're right and you're wrong ...' 'They're certainly entitled to think that, and they're entitled to full respect for their options,' said Atticus, 'but before I can live with other folks I've got to live with myself. The one thing that doesn't abide by majority rule is a person's conscience.'

> **TIP**
>
> **Annotating an extract**
> First read the extract to get a sense of its purpose and meaning. On your next read-through, annotate – comment on – interesting words and phrases. If there is a specific question, annotate the extract to support your answer, keeping the question in mind as you do this. Highlight or underline key parts of the text to use in your answer. Always link a feature to its effect: what is the author trying to convey here? Think about the following:
> - the narrative voice
> - how characters are presented
> - the main themes of the extract
> - what literary devices are used
> Remember to use the correct literary terms.

Source of extracts A – D: from *To Kill a Mockingbird* by Harper Lee, 114th edition, Grand Central Publishing: Boston, New York, 1982, pp. 119, 33, 99, 139/140.

How does Atticus's explanation help Scout find the right moral stand in the mixed and complex community she is growing up in?

S2 **Complete the sentences.**

1 Scout uses the term 'nigger' because …
2 With the words 'that's common', the author conveys …
3 The purpose of the conversation in extract C from Scout's point of view is to …, while for Atticus …
4 Atticus's explanation of his decision to defend a black man is an example of how the author uses …
5 The reason Scout challenges Atticus's stand is that …
6 The detailed explanation Atticus gives to Scout shows …

> **Useful phrases to analyse an extract:**
> *The purpose of this extract is …*
> *It's written from the point of view of …*
> *The conflict / tension arises when …*
> *This is a typical example (of) …*

S3   **Your choice.** Go to the webcode and annotate one of the extracts from the novel. What does the author want to convey and how does she do it? Share your notes with a partner and discuss your analysis.

Blues and Motown

1 You've got the blues!

a Listen to the conversation between Chris and Kelly. Note down dates and explain why they are important.

b Listen again and complete the summary.

Blind Willie McTell  musician, who ⬛2⬛ before Kelly's father was born. Bob Dylan, who ⬛3⬛ for literature, ⬛4⬛ a song about Blind Willie McTell. Kelly ⬛5⬛ to the song, but Chris thinks she ⬛6⬛ Motown songs.

Blind Willie McTell (1901 – 1959)

2 The Motown story

a After Chris has played Kelly some Motown music, he lends her an article about it. Read it and complete the tasks.

A brief history of Motown

On 12 January 1959, the music sensation that changed America – and the world beyond it – was set in motion. Detroit-born 29-year-old Berry Gordy founded Tamla Records with an $800 loan from his family's [...] savings. By the following year, he'd merge this into the Motown Record Corporation: an independent empire that would seal its genuinely iconic status, introducing legends including The Jackson 5; Diana Ross and **The Supremes**; Stevie Wonder; Smokey Robinson; Marvin Gaye; Martha and The Vandellas; The Commodores and many others among its hundreds of signings. [...]

The 'Motown Sound' is unmistakeable for its glorious melodies and killer hooks [...]. Motown's name was rooted in industry and community: a nod to the 'Motor Town' nickname of its native city. Prior to founding the label, Gordy had also worked on production lines at the Lincoln-Mercury car plant. He set up the label's base in a modest two-storey house at 2648 West Grand Boulevard, also known as **Hitsville USA**. [...]

Before Motown, Gordy had signed deals for two singles by rising R&B stars The Miracles, featuring a young Smokey Robinson – only to receive a royalty cheque for just $3.19. Robinson reportedly told Gordy: 'You might as well start your own record label; I don't think you could do any worse than this'. [...] The Miracles would become Motown's first million-selling recording artists. [...]

Motown was also powerfully significant as a black-owned corporation employing multi-racial staff within its label teams; in an era when America was undeniably divided and the mainstream was an exclusionary zone (in 1967, the Detroit riots also erupted in response to police raids in black neighborhoods), Hitsville produced music as a vital, unifying life force. [...]

In the early 1970s, the corporation also shifted its HQ to LA (and began to produce some of its most innovative classics, including Marvin Gaye's *What's Going On?* and Stevie Wonder's *Innervisions* albums), although Detroit's original Hitsville building remains its spiritual home today, as the Motown Museum. [...]

Source (abbreviated): https://www.bbc.com/culture/article/20190109-motown-the-music-that-changed-america

1 State how the label got its name.
2 Assess the importance of the comment made to Gordy by Smokey Robinson.
3 Explain how Motown differed from other record companies and what made it successful.

b Read the article again. Work out the meaning of the underlined words and phrases from the context.

c Compare your definitions with a partner. Then check using a monolingual dictionary.

37)) Words and phrases

gloomy	sad and without hope
to merge	to combine two or more things to make one thing
royalty cheque	money paid based on the number of sales of sth., e.g. a record
stricken	seriously affected by an unpleasant feeling or a difficult situation
up your street	sth. a person would like or prefer

3 **All blue!** Chris finds a podcast about blues music. Read the tasks
39 before listening. Then listen and make notes.

1 Outline the origins of the blues.
2 Explain the phrase 'having the blues'.
3 Describe how urban blues started.

B.B. King (1925 – 2015)

4 **Black music**

a Kelly asks Chris to give her more information about different types of music
associated with black musicians. Match the types of music to the definitions.

funk ■ gospel ■ grime ■ hip-hop ■ R'n'B ■ soul

b Find words in the texts that match these definitions.

p. 148

Rihanna (born 1988)

A This genre of music originated in the late 1960s in
African American communities. Musicians combined
elements of jazz and soul to create a new sound.
There was more emphasis on bass and drums to
make something that was more danceable.

James Brown (1933 – 2006)

C A genre of music which emerged
in the late 1970s. It was
popularized by DJs and black
urban performers. The most
important feature of this style is
the rapid, and often slangy, vocals.

B This style of music became popular in
the 1940s and 50s when blues musicians
turned to electric instruments and tried
to play more upbeat, faster songs. Many
artists also included soul music in their
repertoire.

1 a style, especially in the arts, that involves a particular set of
  characteristics
2 to join or mix together to make a single thing
3 a particular importance or attention that is given to something
4 all the music that you can perform or play
5 to appear by coming out of something else
6 a strong feeling of wanting or wishing for something

D This genre of music has its
roots in gospel singing and
developed in the 1950s and
1960s. It often deals with
topics of desire, hardship and
romance and is characterized
by an emphasis on vocals and
a passionate delivery of songs.

40 **c** Listen to the extracts of the four genres and match each one to
the correct definition.

5 **It's your turn: Your favourite music**

a Choose one of the genres of music from **4** or another you like and collect information about the
following: history, musical style (e. g. instruments or rhythms), topics, famous artists. Also take
into account its impact on society. Tips on collecting ideas and notes on **pp. 139/140**.

b Find photos and songs that illustrate your genre. Prepare a poster and present it in class.
The others give feedback. Tips on giving constructuive feedback on **p. 144**.

@ WES-40806-002

→ Workbook, page 51   **PRACTICE A**

PART 1

1 Listen to a conversation between Chris and Kelly and do the tasks.

🔊 41

1 Explain why Chris is upset.
2 Compare the different attitudes of Chris and Kelly to the use of Black English.
3 Discuss whose attitude / opinion you agree with and give reasons why.

> **CULTURE CORNER**
>
> **Cultural appropriation** is the unacknowledged or inappropriate adoption of the customs, practices, ideas, etc. of one people or society by members of another and typically more dominant people or society.

PART 2

2 **a** After their conversation, Chris sends Kelly an article to read. Make notes about the most important information.

[...] AAVE [African American Vernacular English] is a dialect of English spoken by many African Americans and some black Canadians. It has its own grammatical structures, vocabulary, and accents, which makes it just as valid a variant of English as British English.

5 Black people are still the targets of systemic racism in North America and around the world. Simply being identified as black can negatively affect access to employment, housing, health care, education, and fair treatment by law enforcement. [...] When black people use AAVE [...] they can be [...] seen as uneducated or illiterate.

10 The continued systemic oppression of black people is why the blending of black slang into mainstream language is seen as appropriation and exploitation, rather than appreciation and shared cultural mixing. Where it's risky for black people to use their own dialect, non-black people can pick and choose terms and use them to sound 'cool.' [...] Before words like 'bae' and 'on fleek' go viral on social media and are adopted by the non-black masses, they're

15 considered improper, and the black people who coined the terms and use them in everyday ways lose out on opportunities because of how they're perceived. Yet, companies constantly profit off of black slang after these words hit the mainstream, and black people rarely ever get credit for it. [...]

Source (abbreviated): https://www.huffingtonpost.ca/2018/12/30/2018-slang-words-appropriation_a_23629985/

PART 3

b Compare your notes. Did you have the same key points? Outline the argument the article presents and consider whether the writer makes a valid point or not. Think of examples of similar phenomena – regional or social varieties – in German.

3 Kelly and Chris have another conversation about Black English. Listen and complete the tasks.

🔊 42

1 How does Chris explain the following sentences?
She the one.
I don't have none.
He be workin'.
2 Explain why Chris mentions Shakespeare.
3 Analyse how Kelly's opinion changes during the conversation.
4 Comment on the comparison Chris makes between AAVE and other forms of English.

4 **a** **Think:** Read the quotes and comment on the use of AAVE.

> *When words from marginalized communities enter the mainstream, we should elevate the voices of their creators, instead of just taking their words.*

> *The point is, AAVE, when used by African American people, is often associated with 'undesirable' parts of society like poverty, drugs, violence, and gangs. But when corporations or white people use it, they are co-opting its 'cool' potential for their own gain [...].*

b **Pair:** Discuss your ideas with a partner.

c **Share:** Do you think it's okay for white people to use Black English? Give reasons for your answers.

1   **a** As part of a school project on how to give a great speech, Ava starts by making a mind map of what she thinks is important. Make a mind map with your ideas. Then compare and collate your ideas with a partner. Find tips on collating ideas on **pp. 139/140**.

b Ava then reads some tips from a website. Match the headings to the information.

> capture people with a story ■ connect with your audience ■ ensure your speech has a point ■
> focus on good structure ■ have the right tone for your message ■
> leave your audience wanting more ■ practise and revise

1

Your audience is giving you their time, so make sure you're not wasting it. Nearly everyone has heard a speech and walked away wondering what it was really about. Don't make this mistake.

2

Although you're the one giving the speech, you have to think of it as more of a conversation. You can also use eye contact and gestures. Use language your audience feels comfortable with.

3

Don't talk down to your audience. Whether your aim is to challenge, entertain, motivate or inform, you must think about how you say things, not just what you say.

4

Your speech needs a clear beginning, middle and end. Don't just dive into a topic. Start by giving your main points and letting the audience know how you'll arrange your speech.

5

People react to stories, they grab attention. They're not only a great way to start a speech, but can be used to illustrate a point and appeal to the emotions of your audience.

6

Don't go in cold. You need to rehearse what you are going to say and refine it so that it has the impact you want it to.

7

Too many speakers talk for too long. Keep your speech a bit on the shorter side so you don't bore your audience.

---

2   **a** Ava watches a video about Barack Obama giving what has been described as one of the greatest speeches ever given by a politician. Watch the video. Which of the points from the tips do the commentators also make?

b Ava made a list of techniques she noticed while watching the video. Look at her list and with a partner find out at what stage in the speech they are used.

- repetition
- contrast
- inclusive pronouns
- key words / phrases
- storytelling
- jokes
- personal examples
- dynamic body language

c Discuss what effects these techniques have in the speech.

Black Lives Matter movement

1 **Introduction.** Describe and analyse the two photos. Which one would you use to illustrate an article about the Black Lives Matter movement?

2 **Black Lives Matter**

a Ava saw a news story on TV about Black Lives Matter protests. She became interested in the issues , so looked for articles on the internet. Read one of the articles she found. Who are the following people?

- Alicia Garza
- George Zimmerman
- Trayvon Martin
- George Floyd
- Kamala Harris

The year 2020 will be remembered for a lot of things – not least the rise of the Black Lives Matter movement around the world

The organization has led huge street rallies and high-profile campaigns against racism and police brutality. […] [The Black Lives Matter movement was started in the US by three women – Alicia Garza, Patrisse
5 Cullors and Opal Tometi –] after the not guilty verdict against George Zimmerman, who shot dead unarmed black teenager Trayvon Martin. 'Black people alongside our allies stood up to change the course of history and we won,' said Alicia Garza.
10 Protests erupted again this year after the killing of George Floyd, who died in May after a police officer knelt on his neck during his arrest in Minneapolis.
'Black Lives Matter, after seven years, is now really in the DNA and the muscle memory of this country,' said Garza.
15 'We all have watched how our community members, our family members, are being murdered on camera.'
[Garza added that the media continually focused on the wrong issues:] 'Over and over again, the burden of responsibility for violence gets placed at our feet, but
20 nobody talks about the violence that our communities

are experiencing both at the hands of government neglect, but also at the hands of police officers.' […]
The BLM trio welcomed [the election of] Kamala Harris, who has made history as the first female, first black and first Asian-American US vice-president […]. But they said 25 they would lobby for her to be not just a 'symbol but a fighter for our communities.' […]
Describing how its role has changed this year, Garza said BLM was increasingly making connection across the world, including elevating the #EndSars protests against 30 police violence in Nigeria. 'We are transforming politics as we know it but we are very focused on transforming power, the way that it operates, and making sure there is more power in the hands of more people,' she said.
Patrisse Cullors said the achievements of BLM in 2020 35 would go down in the history books. 'What I'm excited about is that my child gets to say that his mom, alongside other fierce black women, did everything that she could, and we could, to make this place better for us.' […] 40

Source (abbreviated and adapted): https://www.bbc.co.uk/news/world-us-canada-55106268

b Complete the tasks.

1 State the reasons the three women started the Black Lives Matter movement.

2 Assess the importance of the BLM movement according to the information in the article.

3 Reflect on the quote from Patrisse Cullors at the end of the article.

43)) Words and phrases

to **affiliate**	to link a group, a company or an organization very closely with another, larger one
controversy	public discussion and argument about sth. that many people strongly disagree about, think is bad, or are shocked by
to **elevate**	to give sb. or sth. a higher position or rank, often higher than they deserve

to **erupt**	to start happening suddenly and violently
to **lobby**	to try to influence a politician or a government in order to pass or change a law
to **spark**	to cause sth. to start or develop, particularly suddenly

3 **Taking the knee!** Mitch, who is very interested in American football, is listening to a podcast about a famous player, Colin Kaepernick. Listen to the podcast and work on the tasks.

1 Describe what Colin Kaepernick did.
2 Explain why he took this action and why it was seen as controversial.
3 Find out what happened to Kaepernick in the end.

Remember:
● We use reported speech to talk about what other people say.
*Kaepernick said that he **had thought** about going public with his feelings for a while …*
Here is what he actually said:
*'I **thought** about going public with my feelings for a while …'*
● When reporting what is said, we move the tense of the verb one step back:
thought – had thought
● However, there are exceptions to this rule. So, for example, if something is not about a concrete event and will still be true in the present or future, we do not backshift:
*Kaepernick said that he was aware of what he was doing and that **he knows** it will not sit well with a lot of people …*
● Be careful: pronouns may also change, e. g. *my* changes to *his.*

4* **An interview.** Complete the summary of an interview with Colin Kaepernick.

p. 148

In an interview, Colin Kaepernick said he ▢**1** going to stand up to show pride in a flag for a country that ▢**2** black people and people of color. His coach was ▢**3** about Colin's decision and ▢**4** that it wasn't ▢**5** right to tell Colin not to do something. Later on in the interview, Kaepernick said he ▢**6** about going public with his feelings for a while, but that he ▢**7** that he needed to understand the situation better. He ▢**8** the interviewer that he ▢**9** his feelings with his family before deciding to take the action he had.

5 **It's your turn: About recent protests**

a Look at the pictures and think about recent protests. The following questions might help you come up with ideas for a discussion.

● Would you support any of these issues? Why (not)?
● Would you go on a march?
● Are there other issues you feel strongly about?
● Do you feel protests are effective? Why (not)?
● If not, what other means are there to initiate change?

b Discuss your ideas in a group.

Grammar and structures

Reported speech (revision) → G4
Kaepernick **said** that he **had thought** about going public …
He **said** that he **wasn't going to stand up** to show pride in a flag for a country that oppressed black people …

PART 1

PART 2

PART 3

1 a Look at the picture of Ava and Mitch. What do you think Mitch is doing? Discuss your ideas with your partner. Then listen and check.

🔊 45

🔊 45 **b** Listen again and complete the tasks.

1 Comment on Ava's views about the news on social media.
2 Make a list of five different sources of the news. Which are the most reliable? Why?

2 a What other words could you add to the mind map? Draw your own. More tips on mind maps on pp. 139/140.

b Read the article about social media and politics. Match the missing headings to the correct **sections** (A – D). There is one extra heading.

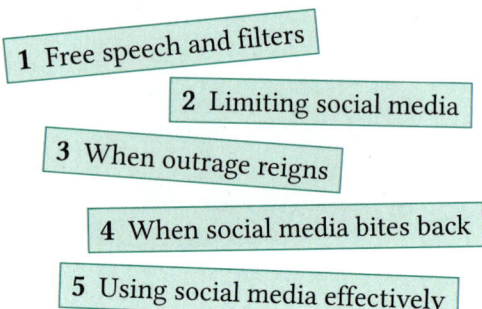

1 Free speech and filters
2 Limiting social media
3 When outrage reigns
4 When social media bites back
5 Using social media effectively

Social media help
but in this politic

> **A**

[...] Love him or hate him, for years former President Donald Trump has been one of the most effective politicians on social media.
5 '   1   ' said Michael Humphrey, an assistant professor at the journalism and media communication department at Colorado State University. [...] With so many politicians now using social media to communicate with their constituents, Humphrey believes this is the most
10 engaged people have ever been in national politics. [...]
'   2   and, I think, for some it's hard to determine what's reality, what's true and what's fact,' Senator Rhonda Fields said. Unlike life offline, social media also allows users to filter their content so they only see,
15 read and interact with content from a similar viewpoint. The phenomenon is known as an echo chamber.

> **B**

[...] The way people talk to one another has also changed; the anonymity social media sites created allowed for the
20 advent of internet trolls, keyboard warriors, [haters] and more. [...] '   3   ' said Senator Dominick Moreno. [Adding] '   4   '
The most salacious the story, the more views; the more views, the more eyes on advertising; the more advertising,
25 the more revenue for the company.
'   5   We like things that get us riled up, that shock us and, unfortunately, what that means is that reporters are attracted to talking about it and people are attracted to sharing it on social media, and it's a perpetual
30 cycle of outrage,' said Sage Naumann, the communications director for the Colorado Senate Republicans. [...]

c In the article there are some **direct quotes** from different people. Here is what they said in reported speech (a – g). Complete the gaps 1 to 7 with what each person actually said.

a Senator Moreno said that you could say hurtful things with little to no consequences.
b Sen. Rhonda Fields added she thought social media had helped fuel the misinformation and lies ...
c Michael Humphrey said he wasn't sure anybody had used social media to the extent Trump had done.

bring people together,
climate it's tearing us apart

C

After the 2016 election, social media companies started to take large steps to crack down on trolls, bots, foreign influence and misinformation campaigns plaguing their sites. [...] After the insurrection of the U.S. Capitol in January 2021, [some platforms] cracked down even more on false information and users who were either perpetuating false information or encouraging violence. '   6   , and I think it became impossible after the events of Jan. 6,' said Brian Keegan, [an assistant professor at the department of information science at the University of Colorado at Boulder]. Afterward, Keegan believes tech companies started to do some serious soul-searching about the role their platforms played in condoning the insurrection and took steps to deter further violence. [...]

35
40
45

D

Over the years, Congress has held numerous hearings about the increasing role social media plays in the daily lives of Americans and how much power these companies should be afforded. [...] '   7   ' Humphrey said. 'We are going to have to start talking about this in reasonable and balanced ways to figure [...] the way that we let a democracy get onto the social media platforms.' For now though, it's up to social media giants to implement their own best practices in who they allow to use their platforms, what they allow to be said and how they play a role in the country's political divide.

50
55
60

Source (abbreviated and adapted): https://www.thedenverchannel.com/news/360/social-media-helps-bring-people-together-but-in-this-political-climate-its-tearing-us-apart

3 **a** **Think:** Read this quote from Karen North, a professor of digital social media. Make notes about your opinion of the quote.

> *People unfortunately don't realize how vulnerable they are to being manipulated. It's very hard to think about a time when we come back to people hear the news, think about the news, and talk to people, instead of finding out about the news from someone who is an opinion leader first. And so if that is our future, we need to educate people that the news you are reading may be an opinion and not news.*

b **Pair:** Work with a partner and discuss the meaning and consequences of the quote. Also take into account the illustration below. Suggest three or four ways people can be 'educated'.

c **Share:** Discuss how you could create a school campaign to educate other students about the accuracy or inaccuracy of news stories.

d Sage Naumann responded by saying that we were addicted to outrage nowadays.

e Humphrey told us that the tech companies had become so powerful and that now they really were part of the establishment.

f He also added that he thought social media had had a huge impact on people's dialogue and that it hadn't been for the better.

g Brian Keegan said he thought social media platforms wanted to ignore, deny or diminish the linkage for a really long time.

1 Look at these four photos. Say what you know about each of the people.

Colin Kaepernick

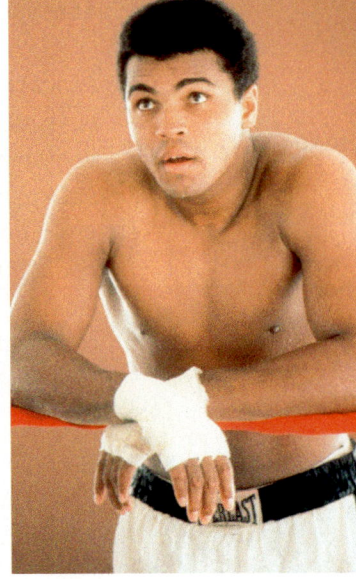
Muhammad Ali

Jesse Owens

Barack Obama

2 **a** Listen to the conversation between Ava and Chris. Who does Chris think is the greatest black American ever?

b Read these sentences and phrases from the conversation. Who is Chris talking about in each one?

> Rosa Parks ■ Martin Luther King Jr. ■ Jack Johnson ■ Jesse Owens

1 … instrumental in the Civil Rights Movement.
2 … won four gold medals at the Olympic Games.
3 … didn't seek out fame.
4 … overcame discrimination in the US.
5 … was just an ordinary citizen.
6 … faced a lot of discrimination.

→ Workbook, page 57   **SPEAKING PRACTICE**

3 Here is some brief information about four other black Americans who are often considered 'great'. Choose one, or one of the other people from this workshop, and carry out some research. Make notes about what you find out. (*TIPs* on **pp. 105, 140**.)

Maya Angelou
- Author whose autobiography *I know why the caged bird sings* tells the story of how racism affects a young girl growing up.
- Worked closely with Martin Luther King Jr. to end segregation.
- Her books have been considered a defense and celebration of black culture.

Jackie Robinson
- First black American to play for a major league baseball team.
- Played for the Brooklyn Dodgers from 1947 until 1956.
- Was voted Most Valuable Player (MVP) in 1949 and was part of the championship winning team in 1955.

Toni Morrison
- Author whose influential novels, e. g. *The Bluest Eye* and *Beloved*, deal with racism and the Black American experience.
- Was awarded the Nobel Prize in Literature (1993) and the Presidential Medal of Freedom (2012).

Ruby Bridges
- At age 6, Bridges embarked on a historic walk to school as the first African-American student to integrate the all-white William Frantz Elementary School in Louisiana.
- She ate lunch alone and sometimes played with her teacher at recess, but she never missed a day of school that year.
- In 1999, she established 'The Ruby Bridges Foundation' to promote tolerance and create change through education.

4 a Which black personality would you have liked to meet and why? Make a list of the reasons.

b Read the *TIP* and phrases in the box below and hold a class debate. Convince the class about your choice of personality. If you need help, you find tips for collecting ideas and notes on **pp. 139/141**.

TIP

When you present your viewpoint:
- Structure it clearly.
- Give reasons. Your reasons should be logical, specific and convincing (use comparison, contrast and cause-effect structures).
- Avoid emotive language.
- Support your reasons: use explanations, examples and facts.

When you argue against somebody's viewpoint / argument:
- Counter-arguments should be factual and supported effectively.
- Show respect for the different opinion.

Phrases to use in a debate
- *The main reason I consider / opt for … the most + adj; the greatest + noun is because …*
- *In support of my choice, I want to / I'd like to …*
- *In my opinion, …*
- *It's important to consider …*
- *We cannot ignore the fact that …*
- *While I see / accept your opinion/ argument, let me point out that / draw attention to the fact that …*
- *Can you explain why …?*
- *All things considered, I believe / feel / am convinced that …*

→ Workbook, page 58   **METHOD COACH**

Looking at the lyrics of a song

PART 1

PART 2

PART 3

S1 **Key words.** Look at these words from a song by singer-songwriter John Legend. What can you remember about these words in connection to the Civil Rights Movement in the USA?

> Rosa   Martin Luther King Jr.   Selma

S2 **Literary devices.** Match the literary devices in the box to the definitions.

> alliteration ■ allusion ■ imagery
> ■ internal or end rhyme ■ metaphor
> ■ personification ■ point of view

1 words that give sensory impressions
2 the perspective from which the story is told
3 a figure of speech that makes comparison between two unlike things
4 repetition of a consonant / vowel sound at the beginning of a word
5 words that sound similar
6 the use of human characteristics to describe animals, objects or ideas
7 a reference to a well-known literary work

S3 **Read the lyrics.** List all the words you don't know. With a partner, find the meanings of the words you don't know.

CULTURE CORNER

Ferguson is a small town in Missouri, USA. In August 2014, it made international news after protests turned violent. The protests took place the day after the fatal shooting of Michael Brown by a police officer. This was one of the first incidents that led to the Black Lives movement in the USA.

John Legend, Glory (2014)

(Chorus:)
One day when the glory comes
It will be ours, it will be ours
Oh one day when the war is won
5 We will be sure, we will be sure
Oh glory (glory, glory)
Oh (glory, glory)

Hands to the Heavens, no man, no weapon
Formed against, yes glory is destined
10 Every day women and men become legends
Sins that go against our skin become blessings
The movement is a rhythm to us
Freedom is like religion to us
Justice is juxtapositionin' us
15 Justice for all just ain't specific enough
One son died, his spirit is revisitin' us
Truant livin' livin' in us, resistance is us
That's why Rosa sat on the bus
That's why we walk through Ferguson with our hands up
20 When it go down we woman and man up
They say, 'Stay down', and we stand up
Shots, we on the ground, the camera panned up
King pointed to the mountain top and we ran up

Chorus

25 Now the war is not over, victory isn't won
And we'll fight on to the finish, then when it's all done
We'll cry glory, oh glory (glory, glory)
Oh (glory, glory)
We'll cry glory, oh glory (glory, glory)
30 Oh (glory, glory)

Selma's now for every man, woman and child
Even Jesus got his crown in front of a crowd
They marched with the torch, we gon' run with it now
Never look back, we done gone hundreds of miles
35 From dark roads he rose, to become a hero
Facin' the league of justice, his power was the people
Enemy is lethal, a king became regal
Saw the face of Jim Crow under a bald eagle
The biggest weapon is to stay peaceful
40 We sing, our music is the cuts that we bleed through
Somewhere in the dream we had an epiphany
Now we right the wrongs in history
No one can win the war individually
It takes the wisdom of the elders and young people's energy
45 Welcome to the story we call victory
The comin' of the Lord, my eyes have seen the glory

Chorus

When the war is won, when it's all said and done
We'll cry glory (glory, glory)
50 Oh (glory, glory)

Text, (OT): Legend, John / Lynn, Lonnie / Smith, Che
Copyright: BMG Rights Management GmbH, Berlin

Analysing the lyrics of a song

S1 **Meaning.** Read the lyrics again and complete the tasks.

1 The title of the song is repeated several times in the song. What is its meaning and what significance does it have?
2 Describe the main theme of 'Glory' in your own words.
3 Explain the connection between the events in Ferguson and those in Selma.
4 Give examples of repetition and explain why Legend uses it in the song.
5 Point out how Legend uses music metaphors to connect the song's message with the topic of the Civil Rights Movement.
6 Explain how the lyrics convey the need for solidarity.

S2 **Listen to the song.** Talk about how listening to the song adds to your understanding of the lyrics, then do the tasks.

47))

1 Contrast the way the verses and the chorus are sung.
2 Put the lyrics of the song into the context of the Civil Rights Movement.
3 Explain the meaning of the lines 'Somewhere in the dream we had an epiphany.'
4 Comment on the words of the chorus.

S3 **Write a short analysis.** Use the useful phrases and the literary terms you have learned to analyse the song. Support your analysis with quotes from the song where relevant.
Explain the effects of the devices used to illustrate the following:

• The attitude of the people vs. the reality they face
• The role of the narrator

> **Useful phrases to analyse song lyrics**
> *The purpose of this song is to convey /*
> *depict …*
> *The songwriter …*
> *… uses … in order to evoke / portray …*
> *… contrasts sth. with …*
> *… appeals to the reader's emotions by …*
> *… makes use of …*
> *The rhythm reflects / suggests …*
> *The word … is a clue to …*
> *The idea is presented / expressed /*
> *illustrated by …*

S4 **Further analysis.** Choose one of the tasks below and write at least 300 words taking into account what you have learned about the analysis of novels and songs. Support your analysis with quotes from the novel and song where relevant.

• Black lives is a defining theme in *To Kill a Mockingbird* and in the song 'Glory'. Describe how they each utilize this historical / economical period to convey their message.
• Outline the main themes in both the novel and the song. Comment on which had the more powerful effect on you and explain why.
• Compare and contrast the writers' use of literary devices. What do they tell you about their attitude to the themes of their work?

1 a Ava has come across an article on the internet. Read it and put the headings in the correct place. There's one heading you don't need.

> How is it celebrated? ■ What is the origin of Juneteenth? ■
> How did it become a federal law? ■ What is different this year?

Juneteenth: What is the newest US holiday …?

Last year, President Joe Biden signed the Juneteenth National Independence Day Act, which establishes a
5 holiday that commemorates the end of slavery in the US. So what is Juneteenth and how did it become a holiday?

A

10 On 19 June 1865 – months after the northern US states had defeated the South in [a civil war fought over slavery] – enslaved African Americans in Galveston, Texas, ⬛**1** (*tell*) they were free. […] The day became known as Juneteenth, a word created by joining the words 'June' and 'nineteenth'
15 together. […] The liberation of enslaved people in Texas came more than two and half years after President Abraham Lincoln issued the Emancipation Proclamation, declaring all enslaved people in the rebellious states to be free.
The declaration by General Grainger to bring the Emancipation
20 Proclamation into effect in Texas ⬛**2** (*see*) by many as the end of slavery.

B

[Already 49 states and Washington DC formally recognise Juneteenth as a state or ceremonial holiday. South Dakota is the last remaining state.] When he was senator of Illinois, Barack
25 Obama co-sponsored legislation to make Juneteenth a national holiday, but the law ⬛**3** (*never pass*) – even after he became president.
[The US House of Representatives backed the legislation by 415-14, a day after it was unanimously approved by the
30 Senate.] With the signature of President Biden, it became law. It is the first new federal holiday since Martin Luther King Jr. Day ⬛**4** (*establish*) in 1983. […]

C

The ending of slavery did not do away with racism, and in the
35 years after so-called Jim Crow laws ⬛**5** (*create*) to separate black people from white society and limit their civil rights. The legacy of those laws ⬛**6** (*still dismantle*).
The deaths of George Floyd, Breonna Taylor and other African Americans at the hands of police have [led to] anti-racism
40 protests [by followers of the Black Lives Matter movement]. It also comes as a fierce cultural debate rages over the history of slavery and how it should ⬛**7** (*teach*) in American schools.

Source (abbreviated and adapted): "Juneteenth: What is the newest US holiday and how is it celebrated?", BBC News, 13.06.2022, https://www.bbc.com/news/world-us-canada-57515192 [21.07.2022]

b Read the article again and complete it with the correct form of the verbs in brackets.

2 Chris and Ava talk about Black Lives Matter. Read their conversation and report what is said in the <u>underlined</u> sentences.

C. Have you heard? Black Lives Matter has been nominated for the Nobel Peace Prize. I am so excited!

A. I saw it online, the internet is full of this story. There are several interviews with Petter Eide, a member of the Norwegian parliament, who made the nomination.

C. Yes, and he's had controversial responses to the nomination. When asked about his choice, he told a CBC interviewer that (1) <u>'I believe that BLM today represents the strongest global force or global movement to fight racial injustice.'</u>

A. I saw that! The interviewer really challenged him pointing out that the BLM movement is not exactly peaceful.

C. Do you remember how he responded? He said that (2) <u>'I'm quite convinced that BLM is a peaceful organization.'</u> And he added that (3) <u>'We found studies showing more than 90% of the demonstrations in the US were peaceful.</u>

<u>Most incidents of violence were based on either aggressive police behavior or counter-demonstrations.'</u>

A. Didn't he also say (4) <u>'If you go back 55 years in time, when Martin Luther King received the Peace Prize, exactly the same argument came up. This is nothing new. People that are against those movements will argue in that direction.'</u>

C. For me his most convincing argument was when he pointed out that (5) <u>'For the Nobel Prize Committee, it is not unusual to link a fight for [racial] justice with peace. There will be no peace without justice.'</u>

A. He came across as very passionate in that interview. But I think he is a realist at the same time. Do you remember how he concluded the discussion? He said that (6) <u>'It's a long shot to see them receive the prize, but it's quite important that we spark this discussion. That in itself is a contribution.'</u>

→ Workbook, pages 59–61   **MORE PRACTICE**

3 **a** Lots of teenagers have participated in or even organized BLM protests in the USA. Make a list of the reasons why you think young people might feel the need to be part of the movement.

b Read what some of the teenagers said. Check how many reasons from your list they mention.

1 *At the end of the day, whether I sit at home or I'm on the front lines, I could be killed just for the color of my skin …. If anything were to happen to me, I would want it to be for a righteous cause.*

Nupol Kiazolu, 19

2 *I have a voice, … I have things that I want to say, and I would feel wrong if I didn't put my part into this.*

Dario Rossin, 17

3 *… the movement is about spreading joy through the pain that people are feeling as they fight for justice ….*

Alexandre Beamon, 15

4 *We felt a need to help spread awareness …. All lives matter regardless of skin color, but specifically black lives because of the injustices they face.*

Veronikka Kew, 16

5 *As teens, we are tired of waking up and seeing another innocent person being slain in broad daylight …. As teens, we are desensitized to death because we see videos of black people being killed in broad daylight circulating on social media platforms. As teens, we feel like we cannot make a difference in this world, but we must.*

Zee Thomas, 18

6 *It's your brothers and sisters. It's people in your community, people you know who are feeling oppressed …. Their moms and dads are getting killed because of their skin color, because people are afraid of them.*

Emma Smith, 17

7 *We wanted to create something that would be even more of an inspiration especially for teens because it shows other teens that you can do anything ….*

Jade Fuller, 15

c Discuss what would make you participate in or organize a protest. Whose reason is the closest to yours?

4 **a** **Think:** Read the facts about Barack Obama and do some research. Which ones are incorrect?

b **Pair:** Discuss what you found out with a partner. Then agree on the most interesting. Give reasons for your choice.

c **Share:** Tell the class which fact you and your partner found the most interesting and why.

> **Did you know that…?**
> - Barack Obama, the 45th president of the US, was the second president to be born outside mainland America. He was born in Hawaii.
> - he was only the 8th president to be left-handed.
> - in 2007, he won his first Grammy for the best spoken-word album, for the audiobook version of *The Audacity of Hope*. Other nominees in the same category included former presidents Bill Clinton and Jimmy Carter.
> - in 2012, Obama became the first US president to officially sanction same-sex marriage.
> - Obama's childhood nickname was 'Barry'.
> - he hasn't liked coffee since working in a coffee shop as a teenager.
> - he collects *Superman* and *Conan the Barbarian* comics.
> - Obama had the tennis court at the White House turned into a basketball court.

5 Choose one of these famous black Americans. Do some further research and use the notes to write a summary of their life and achievements. *TIPs* on **pp. 105, 140.**

Prince (1958–2016)
- born Prince Rogers Nelson / Minneapolis, Minnesota
- begin play / piano / aged 7
- one of the first black artists on MTV
- first hit 'Little Red Corvette' (1983)
- 1993 / change name to symbol
- often / play all instruments himself
- songs / love, desire, sexuality
- has his own shade of purple

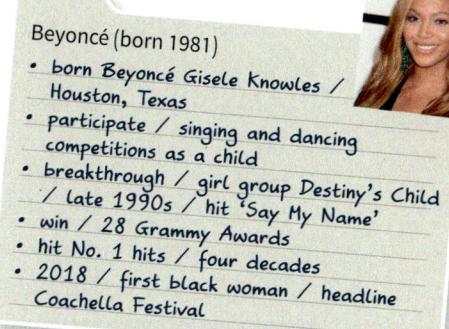

Beyoncé (born 1981)
- born Beyoncé Gisele Knowles / Houston, Texas
- participate / singing and dancing competitions as a child
- breakthrough / girl group Destiny's Child / late 1990s / hit 'Say My Name'
- win / 28 Grammy Awards
- hit No. 1 hits / four decades
- 2018 / first black woman / headline Coachella Festival

1 Young people fighting racism

a Im Englischunterricht beschäftigt ihr euch mit verschiedenen Aktionen und Initiativen gegen Rassismus. Du bereitest einen kurzen Vortrag auf Englisch über die "Afro Jugend München" vor und bist auf folgenden Zeitungsartikel gestoßen. Mache dir zunächst Notizen. Halte dann einen kurzen Vortrag auf Englisch, in dem du Lise-Christine Kobla Mendama vorstellst und erläuterst, was die AJM ist.

Bitte zuhören

Ihre Wurzeln, ihre Herkunft, ihre Hautfarbe: Die „Afro Jugend München" tanzt, macht Fotoshootings und diskutiert über Rassismus

Sie reckt ihre rechte Faust in die Höhe. Lise-Christine
5 Kobla Mendama, 19, genannt Lizzy, steht im Juni dieses Jahres auf dem Münchner Königsplatz. 25 000 Menschen haben sich hier versammelt. Sie sind dem Aufruf zu einer Demonstration unter dem Motto „Silent Protest – Nein zu Rassismus" gefolgt. Lizzy ist nicht Teil dieser
10 Menge. Sie steht auf der Bühne. Am Mikrofon. „Keiner, der schwarz geboren ist, kann was dafür. Aber auch niemand, der privilegiert geboren ist, kann was dafür. Das ist nicht das Problem. Das Problem sind die Menschen, die ihre Privilegien nicht nutzen, um
15 Menschen, die unterdrückt werden, zu helfen", sagt sie mit fester Stimme. Die Menge applaudiert. Lizzy wirkt älter, als sie ist. Sie spricht selbstsicher und sprüht vor Energie und Tatendrang. Sie sagt selbst, ihr Terminkalender sei stets gefüllt: Lizzy ist Model, Sängerin, Poetry-Slammerin, Influencerin und Aktivistin. Zudem studiert sie Ägyptologie an der LMU und arbeitet nebenbei als Finanzberaterin. Lizzy verfolgt ein Ziel: „Ich möchte eine erfolgreiche schwarze Frau sein, um in der Welt etwas zu
20 verändern", sagt sie.
Ein Miniatur-Afrika aus Gold. Es hängt an einer filigranen Kette um ihren Hals. Hin und wieder wandert ihre Hand an den kleinen Anhänger. So als würde sie sich versichern wollen, dass er noch da ist. „Die Kette bedeutet mir alles, weil ich Afrika immer bei meinem Herzen trage. Ich hatte sie eine Zeitlang verloren, da ging es mir echt schlecht", sagt Lizzy. Sie ist Sprecherin und Mitinitiatorin bei
25 „Afro Jugend München", kurz AJM. Anfang Oktober sitzt sie zusammen mit zwei weiteren Mitgliedern, Akin Laja, 21 und Patricia Balzer, 23, in einem Café am Rotkreuzplatz und spricht über die Anfänge dieser Jugendinitiative, unvergessene Events, sowie das turbulente Jahr 2020. Die AJM – das sind junge Münchner von 13 bis einschließlich 25 Jahren, die sich unabhängig von ihrer Nationalität und Herkunft mit ihren afrikanischen Wurzeln verbunden fühlen. Der Jugendinitiative von und für
30 junge Menschen geht es darum, Begegnungs- und Austauschort zu sein. Es geht darum, sich kreativ zusammenzutun und Events auf die Beine zu stellen: Fotoshootings, Modeschauen, Partys, Konzerte, Reisen oder Diskussionen. Die Aufmerksamkeit liegt dabei auch auf dem, was sie alle verbindet: ihre Wurzeln, ihre Herkunft, ihre Hautfarbe. Und deshalb geht es bei der Afro Jugend München unweigerlich auch um Erfahrungen mit Rassismus, um Toleranz, um „Black Lives Matter". [...]
35 Akin und Lizzy kennen sich bereits seit circa zehn Jahren. Den Anstoß zur AJM gab ein Treffen, das Akins Mutter organisierte. Sie regte 2013 eine Gesprächsrunde an, bei der die anwesenden Jugendlichen darüber reden sollten, wie Afrika in ihren Geschichts- und Erdkundebüchern dargestellt wird. „Ich fand es sofort schön, schwarze Jugendliche zu treffen, die mir einerseits ähnlich waren, aber ich andererseits auch durch den Multikulturalismus einiges Neues lernen konnte", sagt Akin, der im
40 fünften Semester Psychologie studiert. Von 2014 an trafen sich zwölf dieser Jugendlichen auf eigene Faust wieder und gründeten dann die „Afro Jugend München". [...]

5   **b** Dein Englischlehrer ist begeistert von deinem Vortrag. Er bittet dich, für eine englischsprachige Sonderausgabe eurer Schülerzeitung einen Artikel über Rassismus zu schreiben. Du bist auf den folgenden Film gestoßen, in dem du weitere Informationen über Lizzy und AJM gefunden hast. Erläutere auf Englisch, was man unter diesem Begriff versteht, welche Formen von Rassismus es gibt und von welchen persönlichen Erfahrungen Lizzy berichtet.

2   **Talking about youth organizations**

a Deine englische Austauschpartnerin weiß von deinem Vortrag und hat deinen Artikel für die Schülerzeitung gelesen. Sie erzählt dir, dass es bei ihr ähnliche Gruppierungen wie die Afro Jugend München gibt. Sie schickt dir einen Link zu Informationen über die *UK Youth*. Lies den Artikel und mach dir Notizen. Dann fasse den Artikel auf Deutsch in ca. 120 Wörtern zusammen.

#YoungAndBlack: Raising Voices for Change Youth Voice Campaign Launched

[…] Organizations have come together to launch the #YoungAndBlack campaign. A space to share, listen and learn from the experiences of young Black people. […]

Collectively, we have been inundated with heartfelt cries and appeals from young Black people right
5 across Britain who feel they don't have the opportunity or even the right to share their thoughts and experiences on racism in the UK and beyond.
They see organizations and individuals grappling with whether they should make formal 'statements' to categorically denounce the brutal murder of a Black man that has flooded our screens. They hear the debates suggesting that racial inequality isn't a problem in Britain, and they are confounded.
10 We also hear from young people of all races who want to have the space to understand the experiences of their Black peers, space to discuss race and discuss what needs to change to create a just society, equal for all. While many organizations remain silent, young Black people are left devastated, feeling abandoned and unseen.
We recognize the power of storytelling to create empathy and change. We recognize that being seen
15 and heard is required to achieve justice. True system change will only come when we are able to discuss the role race plays in all parts of our society. […]
Through an online campaign […] we seek to truly illuminate and create safe spaces for young Black people to share stories, connect and highlight their personal experiences of being #YoungAndBlack in Britain. But this isn't about one race talking to itself. We believe that true social cohesion starts with
20 real understanding. That journey starts with active listening. Let's boldly work together to foster more understanding as we amplify young Black experiences in Britain.

Call to action:

- Organizers are now asking young Black people, students, youth organizations, celebrities, professionals and more, to use the campaign hashtag to create and share short stories on social
25 media, reflecting on what it means to be #YoungAndBlack in Britain today.
- We are calling on youth organizations, schools, media and brands to offer their platforms and create the space to listen to young Black people as they share their stories. […]

Quellen (gekürzt): https://jungeleute.sueddeutsche.de/bitte-zuhoeren/#more-4540 (S. 80); https://www.ukyouth.org/2020/06/youngandblack-raising-voices-for-change-youth-voice-campaign-launched (S. 81)

b Erstelle eine Präsentation auf Englisch, in der du die Ideen und Ziele der beiden Organisationen vorstellst.

Ready for Workshop 3?

a Listen to the radio podcast about Lincoln and complete the tasks.

1 Outline the different narratives that are presented in the podcast.

2 Explain which of the stories has some basis and can be considered true.

3 Comment on what Lincoln wrote to the *New York Tribune* in 1862.

b Match the words from the podcast to the definitions. Check your answers using a monolingual dictionary.

1	dispel	**2**	contentious	**3**	enigmatic
4	barely	**5**	affectionately	**6**	avail
7	determine	**8**	perpetuate		

a by the smallest amount, only just

b causing, involving or likely to cause disagreement or argument

c in a way that shows liking or love

d mysterious and impossible to understand completely

e to cause something to continue

f to discover the facts or the truth about something

g to remove fears, doubts and false ideas, usually by proving them wrong or unnecessary

h use, advantage or purpose

2 a Read the interview and match the questions to the responses (A – D). There is one extra question that you don't need.

1 How has Black music impacted social movements?

2 What impact has the Black community had on American music?

3 Why do you think Black music has been so influential?

4 What one fact about the American music industry often flies under the radar?

5 Where do you see the future of Black music going?

Many of your Top 40 favorites were created by Black songwriters

By Maya Eaglin

Music and the performing arts have not only entertained the masses; they have also served to
5 document history […]. Time and time again, Black musicians mirror what's going on in the world through their music
10 […]. Sidney Madden is a co-host of NPR's podcast 'Louder Than a Riot,' which **1** the intersections of music and culture. Her expertise as a music journalist gives a glance into how Black culture **2** the music and
15 entertainment industry as a whole.

'Every genre that **3** from America has Black roots associated with it, from rock 'n' roll to blues to disco,' Madden said. 'The fingerprints of Black creators are all over what makes American music so unique.' […]

20 **A**

Sidney Madden: […] The fabric of what American society is socially, economically, industrially – it wouldn't be what it is without Black people. And you can see that especially when it comes to music.

25 **B**

Madden: Theft of Black creativity is something that is in the bedrock of American society. […] You could think of Elvis and where he **4** a lot of his stage presence from, [his bravado and conviction], even some of the storytelling in
30 his music – it **5** directly from Black descendants like Chuck Berry. Even if you look on the pop charts right now, so many artists who **6** titans of the game right now wouldn't be anything and they wouldn't have a song to string together if it **7** for their Black writers. […]

35 **C**

Madden: As we say on our podcast, 'Louder Than a Riot,' all hip-hop is protest music, right? […] I think with the watershed moment we **8** last year that's continuing to permeate with the Black Lives Matter movement in
40 America and globally, more people **9** that there would be nothing, there would be no soundtrack to the protest, without Black music. […]

D

Madden: I see the future of Black music going where Black
45 people are going, and that's limitless. The more we use our voice to talk about things that matter, things that need **10** […] these are the things that need to be improved in our community, because if it's going to be improved in our community, it's going to be improved in America as a
50 whole. That's where we're going. We're going to more positions of power, influence and applicable change.

Source (abbreviated and adapted): https://www.nbcnews.com/news/nbcblk/soundtrack-history-how-black-music-has-shaped-american-culture-through-n1258474

p. 149

b Complete the article with the correct form of the verbs from the box (1 – 10).

> be ■ be born ■ change ■ consider ■ focus on ■ have ■ influence ■ see ■ steal ■ take

c Read the article again. Explain why some people might see this interview as controversial.

3 Read these quotes about the abolition of slavery and the Civil Rights Movement. Choose two to explain. Then, discuss which of the quotes you find the most interesting / controversial.

> *If there is no struggle, there is no progress.*

Frederick Douglass

> *Differences of race, nationality or religion should not be used to deny any human being citizenship rights or privileges.*

Rosa Parks

> *There is no noise as powerful as the sound of the marching feet of a determined people.*

Martin Luther King Jr.

> *To sin by silence when they should protest makes cowards of men.*

Abraham Lincoln

> *You can't separate peace from freedom because no one can be at peace unless he has freedom.*

Malcolm X

4 **a** Complete the short news article with the correct form of the words from the box.

> arrest ■ compare ■ double ■ estimate ■ protest ■ stark ■ storm ■ treat

Numbers show a ⬛1 difference between arrests made at Black Lives Matter protest and arrests at Capitol Hill

On January 6, 2021, when Congress was certifying Joe Biden as the next president of the United States, supporters of Donald Trump ⬛2 the Capitol Building in Washington D.C. 52 people were ⬛3, while four people died in or around the grounds, among them a woman who was shot and died in hospital later.
In ⬛4, on June 1, 2020 alone more than 280 people were arrested in Washington D.C. for taking part in ⬛5 in support of Black Lives Matter. The Washington Post reports, that an ⬛6 14,000 people were arrested as part of anti-racism protests in all of the US in 2020. Marcia Fudge, a Congresswoman of the Democrats said, 'There is a ⬛7 standard, without a doubt…' between how the police ⬛8 protesters of Black Lives Matter in the summer of 2020 and supporters of Donald Trump at the Capitol Building.

b Discuss why there was such a difference in the number of arrests made at the different protests.

5 Choose one personality from the workshop and write a short essay (120–160 words). Include the following aspects.

- relevant personal information (background, family, education, etc.)
- the era the person lived in (political, socio-economical characteristics)
- their achievement (why they are considered great, what distinguishes them from others)

Harper Lee, *To Kill a Mockingbird* (1960), Chapter 20

ALL MEN ARE CREATED EQUAL.

 A cartoon

a Describe and interpret the cartoon. Take into account what historic event / document it refers to and consider its impact.

b Discuss to what extent it can be linked to recent political movements that seek to highlight racial tensions.

2 **The novel.** Read the excerpt from *To Kill a Mockingbird*, then work on the tasks.

1 Sum up the line of arguments Atticus Finch follows to prove Tom Robinson's innocence and point out what has (really) happened.

2 There is an unspoken but widely accepted code of conduct in the Southern US states in the 1960s. Examine what Mayella Ewell's behaviour reveals about this code and analyse the consequences for its members, both black and white.

 3 Find out about the origin of Atticus's name and discuss how its meaning contributes to the court scene.

4 The idea of being equal or being different is decisive for the understanding of the extract. Elaborate on this and explain the functions of the Supreme Court as an element of the American system of government.

'Gentlemen,' he said. Jem and I again looked at each other: Atticus might have said, 'Scout.' His voice had lost its aridity[1], its detachment[2], and he was talking to the jury as if they were folks on the post office corner.

'Gentlemen,' he was saying, 'I shall be brief, but I would like to use my remaining time with you to
5 remind you that this case is not a difficult one, it requires no minute sifting[3] of complicated facts, but it does require you to be sure beyond all reasonable doubt as to the guilt of the defendant. To begin with, this case should never have come to trial. This case is as simple as black and white.

'The state has not produced one iota[4] of medical evidence to the effect that the crime Tom Robinson is charged with ever took place. It has relied instead upon the testimony[5] of two witnesses whose evidence
10 has not only been called into serious question on cross-examination[6], but has been flatly contradicted by the defendant. The defendant is not guilty, but somebody in this courtroom is.

'I have nothing but pity in my heart for the chief witness for the state, but my pity does not extend so far as to her putting a man's life at stake[7], which she has done in an effort to get rid of her own guilt.

'I say guilt, gentlemen, because it was guilt that motivated her. She has committed no crime, she has
15 merely broken a rigid[8] and time-honored code of our society, a code so severe that whoever breaks it is hounded[9] from our midst as unfit to live with. She is the victim of cruel poverty and ignorance, but I cannot pity her: she is white. She knew full well the enormity of her offense[10], but because her desires were stronger than the code she was breaking, she persisted in breaking it. She persisted, and her subsequent reaction is something that all of us have known at one time or another. She did something
20 every child has done – she tried to put the evidence of her offense away from her. But in this case she was

---

[1] **aridity** *here:* excitement – [2] **detachment** the state of not being emotionally involved into sth. – [3] **to sift** to examine information, e. g. in documents –
[4] **iota** a tiny amount of – [5] **testimony** proof that sth. is true – [6] **cross-examination** a way of asking questions in court, usually about sth. that has been
said before – [7] **to put at stake** to risk – [8] **rigid** strict – [9] **to hound** to persecute sb. – [10] **offense** anything illegal; crime

no child hiding stolen contraband[11]: she struck out at her victim – of necessity she must put him away from her – he must be removed from her presence, from this world. She must destroy the evidence of her offense.

'What was the evidence of her offense? Tom Robinson, a human being. She must put Tom Robinson away
25 from her. Tom Robinson was her daily reminder of what she did. What did she do? She tempted[12] a Negro.

'She was white, and she tempted a Negro. She did something that in our society is unspeakable: she kissed a black man. Not an old Uncle, but a strong young Negro man. No code mattered to her before she broke it, but it came crashing down on her afterwards.

30 'Her father saw it, and the defendant has testified[13] as to his remarks. What did her father do? We don't know, but there is circumstantial evidence[14] to indicate that Mayella Ewell was beaten savagely by someone who led almost exclusively with his left. We do know in part what Mr. Ewell did: he did what any God-fearing, persevering[15], respectable white man would do under the circumstances – he swore out a warrant[16], no doubt signing it with his left hand, and Tom Robinson now sits before you, having taken
35 the oath with the only good hand he possesses – his right hand.

'And so a quiet, respectable, humble[17] Negro who had the unmitigated[18] temerity[19] to "feel sorry" for a white woman has had to put his word against two white people's. I need not remind you of their appearance and conduct[20] on the stand – you saw them for yourselves. The witnesses for the state, with the exception of the sheriff of Maycomb County, have presented themselves to you gentlemen, to this
40 court, in the cynical confidence that their testimony would not be doubted, confident that you gentlemen would go along with them on the assumption – the evil assumption – that all Negroes lie, that all Negroes are basically immoral beings, that all Negro men are not to be trusted around our women, an assumption one associates with minds of their calibre.

'Which, gentlemen, we know is in itself a lie as black as Tom Robinson's skin, a lie I do not have to point
45 out to you. You know the truth, and the truth is this: some Negroes lie, some Negroes are immoral, some Negro men are not to be trusted around women – black or white. But this is a truth that applies to the human race and to no particular race of men. There is not a person in this courtroom who has never told a lie, who has never done an immoral thing, and there is no man living who has never looked upon a woman without desire.'

50 Atticus paused and took out his handkerchief. Then he took off his glasses and wiped them, and we saw another 'first': we had never seen him sweat – he was one of those men whose faces never perspired[21], but now it was shining tan.

'One more thing, gentlemen, before I quit. Thomas Jefferson once said that all men are created equal, a phrase that the Yankees[22] and the distaff side[23] of the Executive branch in Washington are fond of
55 hurling[24] at us. There is a tendency in this year of grace, 1935, for certain people to use this phrase out of context, to satisfy all conditions. The most ridiculous example I can think of is that the people who run public education promote the stupid and idle[25] along with the industrious[26] – because all men are created equal, educators will gravely tell you, the children left behind suffer terrible feelings of inferiority. We know all men are not created equal in the sense some people would have us believe – some people are
60 smarter than others, some people have more opportunity because they're born with it, some men make

---

[11] **contraband** goods that have been brought into a country illegally, e. g. by smugglers – [12] **to tempt** to make sb. want to have sth. – [13] **to testify** to speak seriously about something, especially in a law court, or to give or provide proof – [14] **circumstantial evidence** not proven but based on sth. that seems to be true – [15] **persevering** continuing firmly, not giving up in spite of difficulties – [16] **warrant** a legal document, e.g. a warrant for arrest – [17] **humble** respectful; modest; decent – [18] **unmitigated** complete; full – [19] **temerity** self-confidence, usually displayed in an exaggerated way – [20] **conduct** behaviour –
[21] **to perspire** to sweat – [22] **Yankee** sb. from the Northern states of the USA – [23] **the distaff side** *here:* women – [24] **to hurl** to throw with a lot of power –
[25] **idle** lazy – [26] **industrious** busy

more money than others, some ladies make better cakes than others – some people are born gifted beyond the normal scope of most men.

'But there is one way in this country in which all men are created equal – there is one human institution that makes a pauper[27] the equal of a Rockefeller, the stupid man the equal of an Einstein, and the ignorant
65 man the equal of any college president. That institution, gentlemen, is a court. It can be the Supreme Court of the United States or the humblest J.P. court[28] in the land, or this honorable court which you serve. Our courts have their faults, as does any human institution, but in this country our courts are the great levelers[29], and in our courts all men are created equal.

'I'm no idealist to believe firmly in the integrity of our courts and in the jury system – that is no ideal to
70 me, it is a living, working reality. Gentlemen, a court is no better than each man of you sitting before me on this jury. A court is only as sound[30] as its jury, and a jury is only as sound as the men who make it up. I am confident that you gentlemen will review without passion the evidence you have heard, come to a decision, and restore this defendant to his family. In the name of God, do your duty.'

Atticus's voice had dropped, and as he turned away from the jury he said something I did not catch.
75 He said it more to himself than to the court. I punched Jem. 'What'd he say?'

'"In the name of God, believe him," I think that's what he said.'

Source: from *To Kill a Mockingbird* by Harper Lee, 114th edition, Grand Central Publishing: Boston, New York, 1982, pp. 271–275.

---

3 **Looking at details.** Read the extract again and work on the tasks.

1 Collect words and phrases connected to law and the court and arrange them in a mind map. Take into consideration their hierarchical structure. If you need help, you find more support on **pp. 139/141** (mind maps, collating ideas) and **pp. 64/65**, **123** (analysing literature)

2 Describe the atmosphere in the court room in general and Atticus Finch's emotional state in particular.

3 Illustrate four examples of rhetoric devices that Atticus uses in his plea.

4 Analyse the narrator's point of view and its effect on the reader. Show how it supports the message the author wants to convey.

Film review: Green Book

1 **Before you read.** Make a mind map.
With a partner, collect aspects that you think belong in a film review.

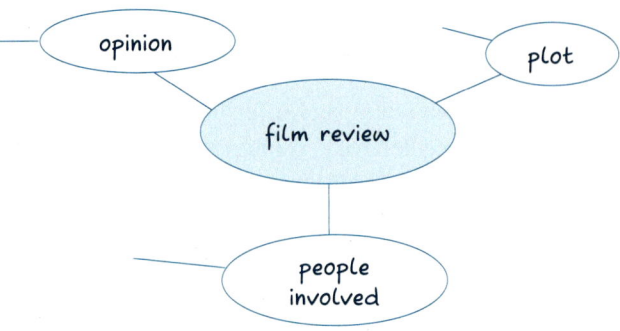

CULTURE CORNER

The Green Book or *The Negro Motorist Green Book* was a travel guide that was published between 1936 and 1967. It listed businesses, workshops and restaurants that would accept African American drivers. It was compiled by Victor Hugo Green (1892-1960), a black postman from Harlem, New York City. By 1940 it had tripled in length and by 1947 it contained more than 80 pages.

---

[27] **pauper** poor – [28] **J.P. court** Justice of the Peace court; a court with little authority – [29] **leveler** sth. that makes people seem equal – [30] **sound** (*adj.*) reasonable; sensible; reliable

2 The film review

a Now read the review and look at the different paragraphs. Decide what aspects they address and match them to the words and phrases from the box. There are two you don't need.

> awards ■ background information ■ cast ■ length ■ personal opinion ■ production ■ scene description ■ summary

b Use your list from **1** and check which elements in **2a** you included in your list. What aspect surprised you?

c A film review uses specific vocabulary. From the context, work out the meaning of the underlined words.

3 Write your own film review. Choose a film that you have seen recently and write a review (200 words). The phrases in the box can help you.

Film review: Useful phrases

Actors
- XY's performance is apealing / convincing ...
- ... gives the part much personality.

Genre
- action film, comedy, drama, thriller, ...

Plot/Story
- The story is amusing / confusing / entertaining / exciting / thrilling / unrealistic ...
- The scene in which ... happens, is full of tension / builds up tension

Opinion
- I thought the film was great / fantastic / OK / a must-see
- It is a worthwile watch ...
- I highly / strongly recommend this film ...

Soundtrack
- The music conveys a melancholy / happy / dramatic atmopshere ...

Green Book review – a bumpy ride through the deep south

Mahershala Ali plays a jazz musician who confronts the racism of his driver, played by Viggo Mortensen, in a warm but tentative real-life story.

Mahershala Ali and Viggo Mortensen are two
5 excellent actors outclassing[1] their material in this amiable, feelgood entertainment, inspired by[2] a true story. Mortensen plays Tony Vallelonga, a 1960s nightclub bouncer from New York who got a job as personal driver and minder to African-American jazz
10 musician Don Shirley (Ali) on a tour through the Jim Crow south – armed with *The Green Book*, a guide to hotels and restaurants hospitable to black people.

The movie, in fact, has its own green book, negotiating[3] subjects and areas where it needs to
15 tread carefully. Class and race aren't the only issues – there is also sexual identity, which the film touches on once and then moves on without the principals ever saying another word about it.

In real life, Tony became a show business figure,
20 acting in *Goodfellas* and *The Sopranos*; he died in 2013 and his son Nick is this film's producer and co-screenwriter[4], with Peter Farrelly directing. It's a standard-issue heartwarmer, a liberal white/black tale like *Driving Miss Daisy* or the recent *The Upside*.
25 (There are some eerily close resemblances to the latter film, including a moment in which the servant must teach the master about Aretha Franklin.)

Tony's job is to cure Don of his snobbery and emotional frigidity, and Don must cure Tony of his
30 racism and ignorance – although this half of the equation is fudged. In an initial scene, Tony puts a couple of glasses in the bin because his wife has let two black workmen drink out of them. But the level of fanatical racism this implies pretty much vanishes
35 when Tony meets Don. So their road trip to self-discovery begins, and we hold our breath for when the white good-ol'-boy racists inevitably show up, or for when Shirley wishes to use the white bathroom at those grand places where he has been booked to
40 play. Vallelonga's nickname is 'Tony Lip'; he tells Shirley this is because of his reputation as a bullshitter. [...]

Well, it's a handsomely made and watchable picture and there is a real warmth in Ali and Mortensen's
45 performances.

Source (abbreviated): https://www.theguardian.com/film/2019/jan/30/green-book-review-mahershala-ali-viggo-mortensen-peter-farrelly

49)) Marcus Sedgwick

Cudweed and the Bagpipes

TWO

The next morning was very different.
It was bright and sunny, but still, I did not
fly home to Castle Otherhand.
Why? I will explain …

5 We had arrived late in the evening, in the
middle of a heavy thunderstorm, in a
remote corner of northern Scotland. Don't
ask me where, all I can say is that the train
station was smaller than the train itself,

10 and that wasn't even the end of our
journey. We had to take a taxi for forty-five
minutes across the rainswept[1] landscape,
which was mountains and moorland[2], and
all looking very bleak.

15 The taxi driver took us to a pub which was
also the local B&B[3], where we were told Cudweed
would be staying during his work experience. At the
back of the pub, across a courtyard[4], were some
stables that had been converted[5] to bedrooms. The

20 pub and the B&B were run by a lady called Sheila,
who seemed happy to see Cudweed but less happy to
see me.
'Is that thing yours?' asked Sheila, squinting[6] at me.
'He's not a thing, he's a raven,' said Cudweed. 'And

25 no, he's not mine. He doesn't belong to me. He's my
friend.'
'Oh,' said Sheila. Then she squinted some more at me.
'Just see he doesn't, you know … make … a mess.'
'Kraak!' I said, because that was very rude. I am a

30 very well-behaved raven and do not make messes of
any kind, never mind[7] the kind of 'mess' she was
thinking about.
After that, Cudweed ate the last of the sandwiches
he'd been given for the train ride, and I ate nothing,

35 and I sulked[8] about that a lot.

Then we went to sleep, listening to the rain get
heavier and heavier. And heavier.
But when we woke up the next morning, it was bright
and sunny. It was warm, in fact, almost hot, and the
40 sun was drying the roofs and the courtyard quickly.
There was steam rising from the cobblestones[9] and the
last traces of a gentle mist were quickly disappearing.
After our miserable arrival the night before, it all
seemed a little bit better.
45 We realized that we had overslept, Cudweed was
supposed to[10] be at the bagpipe factory by nine and it
was already a quarter to nine. But he insisted[11] we
had breakfast before setting out.
'That's funny,' said Cudweed as we walked across to
50 the pub.
He was pointing to the sign of the pub, which
showed its name – The Ugly Sheep, with a picture
that showed, yes, a sheep that was indeed very ugly.
'Kork!' I said to Cudweed, ignoring the pub sign.
55 'Yes, Edgar,' Cudweed said, 'I will make sure you get
some breakfast.'

---

[1] **rainswept** ['reɪnswept] regengepeitscht – [2] **moorland** ['mʊələnd] Moorland; Sumpfland – [3] **B&B (Bed and Breakfast)** [ˌbiː ənd 'biː] Übernachtung mit Frühstück – [4] **courtyard** ['kɔːtjɑːd] Hof; Innenhof – [5] **to convert sth. into** [kən'vɜːt 'sʌmθɪŋ 'ɪntə] etw. umbauen in – [6] **to squint at sb.** [skwɪnt ət 'sʌmbədi] einen Blick auf jdn. / etw. werfen – [7] **never mind** ['nevə maɪnd] geschweige denn; von … gar nicht erst zu reden – [8] **to sulk** [sʌlk] schmollen – [9] **cobblestone** ['kɒblstəʊn] Kopfstein; Pflasterstein – [10] **to be supposed to do** [bi sə'pəʊzd tə duː] etw. tun sollen – [11] **to insist** [ɪn'sɪst] bestehen auf – [12] **to set out** [set aʊt] aufbrechen

After breakfast, we set out for[12] the factory, following the instructions that Sheila had given us. It was very simple; it was just a five-minute walk along the road, with high mountains to one side of us and a loch on the other, and we were there.

Now, I had been planning on getting Cudweed to the door of the factory, and then setting off home, but when we got there ... well, I'll come to that.

The first thing was that Cudweed met the owner of the factory. He came outside to meet us and, since it was such a lovely morning, we stood there enjoying the sunshine.

His name was Hamish and he appeared to be very old. In fact, I would have been surprised if he was anything less than 108, but despite being more wrinkled[13] than a walnut[14], he was very quick and very sharp[15].

He looked at Cudweed and me and then he said, 'You're late! And you didn't say you were bringing a raven with you.'

'It was an accident,' explained Cudweed.

'How do you accidentally bring a raven with you?' asked Hamish, and then he waved his hand. 'Actually, I can guess ... Is he staying?'

'Yes,' said Cudweed.

'Kraak,' I said at the same time, but I was also impressed that Hamish knew I was a raven. Most people usually just say 'bird,' or 'thing', or, if I'm lucky, 'crow'.

Then we met the other two students who had come to learn how to make bagpipes.

First, there was Andrew; he was a Scottish boy with a big smile on his face almost all the time it seemed.

'Hello, birdy,' he said to me, and I said, 'rork,' very crossly, but Andrew didn't notice I was cross and just kept on smiling.

Andrew explained that he had come to learn how to make bagpipes because he had found out that his great-grandfather used to make them, but the family had forgotten. So now he wanted to restore the tradition.

Then there was Wiebke. She was a German student and had come all the way from Germany to learn about Scottish bagpipes. And she was doing that because her family made German bagpipes. She explained that in Germany a bagpipe was a little different and was called a Dudelsack, and she had come to learn all about the Scottish version.

Then everyone looked at Cudweed and asked why he had come.

Cudweed shrugged and said, 'I didn't want to turn fish guts[16] into dog food.'

No one said anything to that.

After a long pause, however, Hamish looked at me and said, 'So you'll be wanting to meet Catriona?'

'Kork?' I said, because I had no idea what he was talking about.

'Of course you do,' said Hamish, 'don't be shy.'

'Rarark,' I said, and I was just thinking to myself, why does he think I want to meet anyone? And why does he think I might be shy?

And then he whistled[17] and a moment later a bird flew around the corner of the factory building and landed on Hamish's shoulder.

Not just any bird, but a raven.

A lady raven.

In fact, a very beautiful lady raven.

---

[13] **wrinkled** ['rɪŋkld] faltig; runzlig – [14] **walnut** ['wɔːlnʌt] Walnuss – [15] **sharp** [ʃɑːp] hier: scharfsinnig – [16] **guts** [gʌts] Eingeweide – [17] **to whistle** ['wɪsl] pfeifen

And my tiny heart gave a little extra
125 thump and I decided there and then
that it might be a good idea to stay
and watch over Cudweed, for a
while. Just to be sure. You know?
I opened my beak to say something
130 to her, but a strange thing happened.
I couldn't think of anything to say!
And before I could think again, she
looked at me strangely, and flew
away …
135 For the rest of the day Cudweed
started to learn about bagpipes.
To start with, he was very nervous,
and it was obvious why.
On the hill behind the factory were some fields, and
140 in the fields, there were a lot of sheep.
Hamish took everyone into the workshop and started
explaining all about the history of the bagpipe. But
Cudweed wasn't listening.
All he could do was stare out of the window, at the
145 sheep. He looked nervous and sad all at once.
'Are you listening?' asked Hamish after a while, and
Cudweed turned his attention back to what Hamish
was saying.
But five minutes later he was just staring out of the
150 window at the sheep again, and Hamish had to stop
and get Cudweed to listen again.
This happened three more times until finally Hamish
lost his patience[18].
'Cudweed! Young man! What is so interesting about
155 the sheep?'
Cudweed looked really upset.
He stared at the floor for a long time and finally he
mumbled[19] something.

'What?' asked Hamish. 'Speak up!'
160 'I don't want to kill a sheep,' he said.
'What?!' cried Andrew and Wiebke.
'Why do you think you have to kill a sheep?' asked
Hamish.
Cudweed stared at him and his bottom lip was
165 wobbling, and he looked as if he might cry.
'Because that's what bagpipes are made from – you
take a sheep and turn it inside out and drill[20] holes in
its leg bones. Don't you?'
Hamish was staring at Cudweed.
170 He stared at him for about thirty seconds, and then
he burst out[21] laughing.
'We don't kill sheep to make bagpipes!' he said,
wiping a tear from his eye.
Now Cudweed looked very embarrassed, and he still
175 looked like he might cry.
'Oh, now, I'm sorry for laughing,' said Hamish. 'But
your face! You don't need to worry – those sheep out
there are nothing to do with our bagpipes!'
Wiebke raised her head and smiled at Cudweed.
180 'In a way, you were right to worry,' she said, 'because
in the old days we used to make the bag from animal
skins. Or the bladders[22] of goats; things like that. So it
wasn't such a crazy thing to think. Nowadays we use
modern fabrics[23]. Isn't that right, Hamish?'
185 She smiled at Cudweed and Cudweed looked much
happier. He smiled back.
'Is, is that true?' he asked.
'Yes,' Hamish said, 'that is true. I shouldn't have
laughed at you. We used to use animal skins, but now
190 we use artificial fabric – it's much cheaper, easier to
work with, and more flexible. So that's what you'll be
working with. Not the bladders of dead cows.'

---

[18] **patience** ['peɪʃns] Geduld – [19] **to mumble** ['mʌmbəl] murmeln; nuscheln – [20] **to drill** [drɪl] bohren – [21] **to burst out** [bɜːst aʊt] losplatzen; herausplatzen –
[22] **bladder** ['blædə] Blase – [23] **fabric** ['fæbrɪk] Stoff – [24] **to get to sb.** [get tə 'sʌmbədi] jdn. in Mitleidenschaft ziehen

some rolls, some dive bombs, and some combination tricks.

230 I was showing off, I know it, but I couldn't think of a better way to get her attention. Sadly, none of it seemed to be working, and I was just flying upside down again, and looking backwards to see if I had got her attention, when I flew into the wall of the

235 bagpipe factory, with a smack[27].

Now, all this talk about bladders was getting to me[24] and I decided I needed to go and find a nice quiet

195 spot in the corner of the field to let nature take its course. If you know what I mean.

It was a lovely morning. So when I had finished doing what I needed to do, I decided not to hurry back inside to the workshop. I could already hear the

200 sound of drills[25] and saws[26] from inside, so I knew they were making progress. I thought I would leave Cudweed to get on with it; I had been thinking only very recently that it's about time Cudweed started to look after himself a bit more.

205 I mean, I know it's hard for Cudweed. He worries about everything but he's a teenager now and very soon he won't even be a teenager anymore, he'll be an adult. And all that happens very fast, so this work experience seemed like the perfect chance for him to

210 a) stop worrying about everything all the time and b) learn to do something by himself, without me or Solstice always nearby to help.

And all of this had absolutely nothing to do with the fact that just as I was crossing the field, I saw

215 Catriona fly by a little way ahead of me.

She hadn't seen me, or, if she had, she was pretending not to.

Now, it's been a long time since I was 'romantically involved' with anyone (raven or any other creature

220 for that matter), but I had to admit, there was something about Catriona that made me want to spend some time with her.

But the first thing was to get her attention, because so far, she hadn't even said 'krurk' to me.

225 So that was how, for the second time in a few days, I found myself flying upside down, in an attempt to attract Catriona's attention. I flew upside down, did

And that was where I was sitting in a daze[28] when Cudweed came out of the factory.

It was lunchtime, which ought to have made him happy, but he looked upset again.

240 'Korork?' I asked.

'No!' said Cudweed. 'I mean, yes, I am getting on okay. I have cut a piece of wood that will be the "chanter" – that's the bit with the holes that you use to make the notes – and it is going well.'

245 'Ark?' I said.

'Yes, but I just found something out. Hamish said that we will spend the month making and learning how to play the bagpipes, and then at the end we will all play one simple piece we have learned. And then he

250 told us the date that will happen. May 26th!'

'Rark!' I exclaimed.

'I know!' said Cudweed. 'My birthday! In all the fuss[29] about coming here, I wasn't thinking that far ahead. It will be my birthday while I am here! I won't

255 be at home with everyone! It's awful!'

And with that poor Cudweed stomped off to find some lunch, and I watched as he started to work his way through a huge plate of sandwiches, very grumpily.

---

[25] **drill** [drɪl] Bohrer – [26] **saw** [sɔː] Säge – [27] **smack** [smæk] Knall – [28] **in a daze** [ɪn ə ˈdeɪz] benommen; betäubt – [29] **fuss** [fʌs] Aufregung

Workshop 3

My generation

 Look at the pictures, then discuss what each one shows about young people and what matters to them.

E

F

🔊 50))) Listen to a radio programme about young people today and note down the pictures in the order the guest talks about them.

🔊 50))) Listen again and complete the tasks.

1 Describe how Dr Spellman shows that teenagers today are health conscious.
2 Explain how Dr Spellman thinks teenagers today are similar to previous generations of teenagers.
3 Reflect on what Dr Spellman says about teenagers and technology.
4 Discuss the claim that young people as well as adults spend a lot of time online. Support your arguments.
5 Comment on the importance of social issues for teenagers today.

👥 Interview your classmates and collect ideas about what is important to them. Use your results to find out about teenage issues and design a survey. Find tips on collating ideas on **pages 139/140**.

Present your surveys and give each other feedback. On **page 144** you find tips on giving constructive feedback.

Youth culture

PART 1

1 **Paige's question.**
Read the message Paige sent to Aimee and complete the tasks.

> Hi Aimee.
> Just a quick message. I watched a TV programme over here with my dad – all about youth culture and now he wants me to explain what our culture is! OMG!! Any ideas? ✔

1 Explain why Paige texts Aimee.
2 Speculate on how she will reply.

2 **Youth culture**

a Discuss what you understand by the term 'youth culture' and make notes.

b Read an article from an American dictionary website outlining their idea of youth culture. Compare the ideas in the article to yours.

c Read the article again and complete the tasks.

1 Summarize the key areas the writer has included to illustrate youth culture.
2 Outline and draw comparisons between different generations the writer describes.
3 Find arguments that support or contradict Erikson's point.
4 Comment on the examples of youth culture the writer has highlighted.
5 Look at the words in bold and find more examples. Explain what they tell you about the author's attitude.

3 **Aimee's reply.**
Read Aimee's reply to Paige and explain why this is (not) the kind of reply you thought Paige would get.

> Hi Paige,
> What a weird message?! I chatted to a few people about your question. Holly said if she were you, she'd ask him what he did when he was young. My mum thinks the only thing that's changed since she was young is how addicted our generation is to their smartphones. I pointed out that when she was young, they didn't exist! And Brendan said that he has more in common with a 16-year-old in Brazil than with his parents! Here's a link to an article I found … ✔

What i

Common youth culture examples

The term 'youth culture' refers to the ways that teenagers conduct their lives. Youth culture can pertain to interests, styles, behaviors, music, beliefs, vocabulary, clothes, sports and dating. The concept behind youth culture is that adolescents are a subculture with norms [...], behaviors, and values that differ from the main culture of older generations within society [...]. There are many examples of youth culture and subcultures in society.

10 **Personal appearance** is one of the most visible indicators of teen culture …
- Twenty-first century youth **seem to have** a 'less is more mindset,' focusing on low maintenance hairstyles and minimal makeup, if any. Fashions **tend to be** casual [...].
15
- The [...] culture of the 1980s was much more high maintenance, with youth emphasizing perfect makeup and spending hours with curling irons and hot rollers. [...]
20
- In the turbulent 1960s, a desire for civil rights and freedom from tyranny impacted fashion. Short skirts and fringed jackets were popular among hippies and freedom fighters alike.

Youth culture can also be seen in terms of the type of
25 **entertainment** that is popular among young people.
- Modern youth **tend to connect** with peers digitally, spending hours interacting with friends via social media sites, whereas previous generations spent hours talking on the phone.
30
- Video games have become important to many teens. Teens today **often spend** hours playing online games, forming bonds with gamers that they get to know in the virtual world. [...]
- As kids move into adolescence, their entertainment
35 preferences often change. For example, youth **may start to prefer** comic books over novels and children's stories.

Each generation of youth tends to engage in a bit of **rebellion** [...].

Words and phrases

aloofness	unfriendly behaviour that shows a lack of interest in other people	**to pertain**	to exist or apply in a particular situation or at a particular time
cutting	missing or not attending	**turbulent**	causing trouble, arguments, or violence
		tyranny	unfair or cruel use of power or authority

youth culture?

- For modern teens, environmental responsibility is a major emphasis. Many teens commit to minimizing their environmental impact and speak out to encourage others to do so. 40
- Youth in the 21st century tend to be quicker to speak out and mobilize against injustice and in favor of inclusiveness than previous generations. [...] 45
- For rebellious youth, behaviors such as cutting school or even low-grade criminal activity can be an attempt to assert independence and non-conformity.

For each generation of youth, **peer pressure** can have a very powerful impact on behavior. Youth sometimes change their perceptions or behaviors as a way of fitting in with other people in their age group [...]. 50

- Depending on the behaviors of their peer group members, youth may change the way they treat others, either by showing greater kindness or perhaps more aloofness. 55
- The desire to fit in can also impact teens' academic performance. Making similar grades to one's peers is a way that teens can conform to the expectations of their peer groups. 60

Understanding youth culture

Specifically defining what youth culture is can be a bit difficult because it is a moving target. Each generation will have its own unique youth culture [...], though it's important to avoid stereotyping people based on their generation. [...] 65

- Psychologists such as Erik Erikson theorize that the primary goal in the developmental stage of adolescence is to answer the question, 'Who am I?' This being the case, it is natural to assume that in determining one's identity, one would seek others within the same age group to grow and learn together and understand the social norms and values of society. [...] 70

Source (abbreviated): Mary Gormandy White, "Examples of Youth Culture: Trends of the Past & Today", LoveToKnow Media, 2022, https://examples.yourdictionary.com/examples-of-youth-culture.html [12.07.2022]

---

4 **Around the world.** Paige asks a question online about what it's like being a teenager and gets these replies. Read them and do the tasks.

 I'm Alina and I live in Sao Paulo in Brazil. I guess I'm a typical teen here as I love dancing, especially samba. We have lots of parties and festivals, so there are lots of opportunities to do what I love. When I'm not dancing, I enjoy watching *telenovelas*, these are soap operas, 5 and then we get together and chat about the latest episodes.

 I'm Somchai and I live in Chang Mai in Thailand. Most of my time is spent at school and we even stay on for after school clubs. I'm really into breakdancing and often go to the park with friends to show off our latest moves. 10 I also go to the park most evenings to practise Tai Chi. When I'm not at school or in the park then I enjoy hanging out in internet cafés, meeting new people and playing games online.

 My name's Kojo and I'm from Ghana. Life as a teenager here is complicated. We see lots of western 15 culture on TV, but we are also influenced by Ghanaian traditions. So, one game I like to play with my friends is called Oware, which is an ancient board game played by two players and 48 seeds or nuts. The aim is to capture more seeds than your opponent. After school and at weekends I'm expected to 20 help out at home, so I don't have as much time as I'd like to hang out with my friends.

 Hi, I'm Adam and I live in Prague in the Czech Republic. I think I'm a typical Czech teenager. I enjoy going to the movies, watching TV and hanging out in 25 cafés. I also play hockey and volleyball in the summer. Although I spend a lot of time with my friends, most evenings I sit together with my family in the kitchen talking about daily life. My grandma and grandpa live with us, so it's an extended family.

1 List what the teenagers have in common and where they differ.
2 Write a short text about being a German teenager (about 80 words). Write about yourself or an invented character.

5 **It's your turn: Rebellious youth.** Read this quote from singer John Lydon (formerly Johnny Rotten of the Sex Pistols). What's your opinion?

Listen, you know this: If there's not a rebellious youth culture, there's no culture at all. It's absolutely essential. It is the future. This is what we're supposed to do as a species, is advance ideas.

The Sex Pistols, Britain's most influential punk group was formed in 1975 and disbanded in 2008

PART 1

PART 2

PART 3

1   **a**   **Think:** One very important component of youth culture is language. When you hear youth language, what do you associate it with? What features can you think of? Make notes.

b   **Pair:** Compare your ideas.

c   **Share:** Share your ideas with the class.

2   Listen to Aimee and her mum, Gwen, talking about teenage language. Then complete the tasks.

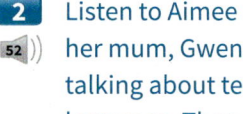
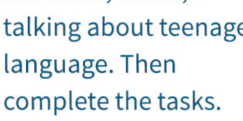

1   Give an example of slang Aimee's mum doesn't understand.

2   Explain why Aimee says, 'I can't tell you!'

3   Comment on Aimee's opinion that things were the same when her mum was young.

3   **a**   Look at the heading of the article Aimee shared with her mum. What kind of information do you think you will be given? Read the article, look up words you don't understand and check your ideas.

b   Read the article again and complete the tasks.

1   In your own words, summarize the results of the study and how it was undertaken.

2   Explain why the statement 'Teenagers are ruining language' has been successfully debunked by the study.

3   Explain why the results of the study did or didn't surprise you. Give reasons for your opinion.

4   Work in groups and discuss the following questions.

1   What slang terms are popular with your group of friends in Germany?

2   Are there any slang terms in use that you don't really understand?

3   Do you agree that youth language is a natural way language changes?

Teenagers' role in language change is overstated, linguistics research finds

If you're too 'basic' to 'YOLO' or think that slang is never 'on fleek,' fear not: How teenagers speak 'IRL' is not ruining the English language, according to Kansas State University linguistics research.

In fact, teenagers may not be causing language change the way that we
5 typically think, said Mary Kohn, assistant professor of English. Kohn studies language variation and how language changes over time. Kohn's latest research found that teenagers are not solely causing language change. Rather, language changes occur throughout a lifetime and not just during the teenage years.

10 'Our research has shown teens are being dynamic with language, but not necessarily in a consistent way,' Kohn said. 'We aren't eliminating the possibility that teenagers are driving sound change, but we might be grossly overstating the role of teenagers.'

Kohn found there was not a consistent language path that a person took
15 from childhood through adolescence and into adulthood. Language change is more individualistic and varies for each person, she said.

'Very commonly, people think that teenagers are ruining language because they are texting or using shorthand or slang,' Kohn said. 'But our language is constantly developing and changing and becoming what it needs to be
20 for the generation who is speaking it. As a linguist, I find this really exciting because it shows me that our language is alive.'

Kohn used [...] a database that followed 67 children from infancy to their early 20s. The database includes audio and interview recordings from nearly every year of the children's lives and also has recordings of family
25 members, friends and teachers – all valuable information for understanding how language changes as individuals grow up, Kohn said. Using this database, Kohn studied sound waves – a precise measurement of how people pronounce words. She focused on 20 individuals during four different time periods: fourth grade, eighth grade, tenth grade and
30 post-high school at age 20. Kohn measured pronunciations to see if the participants dramatically changed during the teenage years. [...] 'The teenager subgroup did not stand out as a group from the rest of the subgroups, meaning there was nothing special about being a teenager,' Kohn said. 'Just because you are a teenager doesn't mean you will change
35 your language. Perhaps our stereotypes about how teenagers speak are often based on subgroups of teenagers that stand out to us as most distinct. We notice the kids who make bold fashion statements, so we also might notice the kids who are making dramatic linguistic changes.'

Other subgroups experience language change, Kohn said, and she
40 suggests that sources of language change may happen in younger children. Children turn away from adult influence when they get to school, which may be the crucial point when language starts to shift. During high school, teenagers often explore their own identities and may again choose to change their pronunciations and use language as a part of
45 their identities. When these teens grow up and graduate from college or get a job, they may change their language again to sound more professional and meet the demands of their jobs and pressures of the workplace, Kohn said.

'All languages, throughout history, change as generations grow up and
50 move through life,' Kohn said. 'As long as there are people who are living and breathing and speaking, we're going to invent new words. We're going to invent new ways of speaking.'

Kohn recently published the research in a monograph, *The way I communicate changes but how I speak don't.* The research was a
55 collaboration with researchers at North Carolina State University, including Walt Wolfrom, Janneke Van Hofwegen, Charlie Farington and Jennifer Renn.

Source: Kansas State University. "Teenagers' role in language change is overstated, linguistics research finds." ScienceDaily. ScienceDaily, 14 January 2016. <www.sciencedaily.com/releases/2016/01/ 160114122029.htm>.[27.09.2022]

→ Workbook, page 71   **LISTENING AND VIEWING PRACTICE**

1 Look at the photos from a video where five young people speak about what it is like to be a teenager. In groups, discuss what the adjectives express in this context and why the teenagers chose these particular ones.

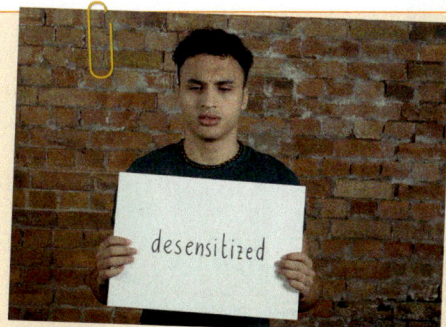

2 **a Think:** Watch the video with the sound off. Make notes about what you see. Focus on the speakers' body language. What does it reveal to you?

 b Pair: Compare your notes. Do you agree?

 c Share: Share your ideas about the video.

3 **a** Now watch the video, but this time with the sound on. Were your ideas correct?

b Watch again and complete the tasks.

1 List the topics that the teenagers talk about.
2 State which of the teenagers has a positive outlook.
3 Explain why Emma has two opposing adjectives.
4 Assess why Rob feels frustrated.

4 Look at these words from the video.

- **Student A:** Check the meaning of the words in list A.
- **Student B:** Check the meaning of the words in list B.

Use a monolingual dictionary. Explain your words to your partner.

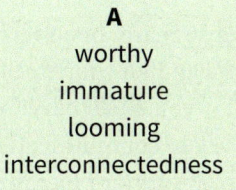

A	B
worthy	get to grips
immature	moulds
looming	glorifies
interconnectedness	obtainable

5 **a** Which of the teenagers from the video can you identify with best?
What do you have in common? Explain the similiarites to a partner. Give reasons for your choice.

b How would you answer the questions in the video and what adjectives would you choose? Why?

 c Discuss your ideas together.

Gaming culture

PART 1

PART 2

PART 3

1 **Video games.** Look at the photos and describe what the people are doing. What kind of games could they be playing?

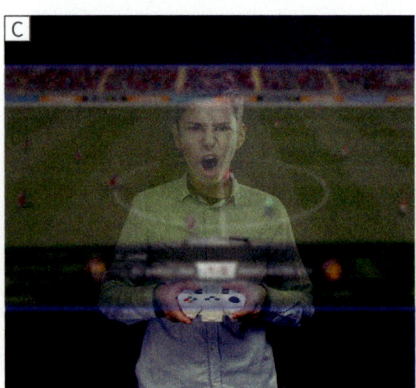

2 **Turn the clock back!** Listen to the conversation between Aimee's mother Gwen and Aimee's uncle Craig and complete the tasks.

54))

1 Outline what Craig says about online and video gaming.
2 Explain why Gwen is not worried about Aimee's health.
3 Comment on Gwen's statement 'You seem to have changed your tune since we started speaking ...'

3 **An argument.** Complete the conversation between Aimee and Liam with the correct form of the verbs in brackets to make conditional sentences.

p. 149

A. What's up, Liam? Why are you looking so upset?
L. If I ▌1▐ (*tell*) you, you ▌2▐ (*laugh*). I've just had an argument with my parents.
A. Wow! What was the argument about?
L. Online gaming. More specifically about how much time I spend on playing games.
A. They think it's too much. Am I right?
L. Yes. In their opinion if I ▌3▐ (*not, spend*) hours on gaming, I ▌4▐ (*be*) more sociable.
A. If I ▌5▐ (*know*) you were going to discuss your gaming habits, I ▌6▐ (*help*) you.
L. How?
A. There are so many benefits to gaming.
L. Do you mean like cooperation?
A. Yes. And if you ▌7▐ (*play*) with others, you ▌8▐ (*develop*) communication skills and will get better at forward planning, too.

L. I guess that's true. And if I ▌9▐ (*not, play*) with others I ▌10▐ (*not, be*) such a good team player.
A. Don't push it, Liam! By the way, do you remember that environmental game I showed you?
L. Yes. What about it?
A. If I ▌11▐ (*not, play*) that game, I ▌12▐ (*not, learn*) problem-solving strategies and ▌13▐ (*not, get*) top marks in my science test.
L. Oh, ... that's a persuasive argument. If I ▌14▐ (*talk*) to you earlier, I ▌15▐ (*argue*) my case better. But my parents were right about one thing.
A. What's that?
L. If I ▌16▐ (*not, spend*) so much time in front of the screen, I ▌17▐ (*not, be*) tired all of the time.

53)) **Words and phrases**

to take the torch   to take over, to continue

4 Youth and gaming

a Read the article and complete the tasks.

1 Summarize the information in the text about Gen Z and video and online gaming.
2 Explain the importance of Gen Z to the industry.

b Student A: Look at the first four underlined words and work out the meaning from the context.
Student B: Work out the meaning of the other underlined words. Explain the words to each other.

Remember:

- We use conditional sentences type I to talk about things that are possible in the future, but not definite.
  *If I **interrupt** her now, she**'ll lose** her score.*
- We use conditional sentences type II for situations or events which are unlikely, imaginary or possible, but not very likely in the present and future.
  *If she **spent** too long online, I **would talk** to her about it.*
- We use conditional sentences type III for events in the past which did not happen.
  *If I **hadn't played** games, I **wouldn't have become** interested in how these games were designed.*
- We can also use modal verbs in conditional sentences.
  *If I **could** turn the clock back, I **would** use the gaming skills to help with my career.*
- For some situations we can create mixed conditional sentences.
  *If I**'d realized** how many skills I learned, I **would** probably **be** in a different job.*
  (past condition: *if*-clause type III; present result: type II verb in the main clause)

How Generation Z has taken the lead in the video game industry

A new era of gaming is underway, with those born in the late '90s looking to take the torch from previous generations. Anyone born after 1996 belongs to Generation Z, a diverse cohort that may well become the most educated generation
5 to date. They are digital natives who communicate primarily through social media and texts, and they spend much more time on the internet compared to previous generations. When it comes to this time online, Gen-Zers are arguably more tech-savvy and thus have higher standards.
10 Starting with the commercial birth of gaming back in the 1950s, the industry has bloomed to become one of the most profitable sectors in entertainment. Over the past few years, it has been thoroughly revolutionized. [...] Internet services have become easily accessible, and computer processors
15 have significantly evolved, providing excellent speed for more demanding games.
Many game developers are focusing on building new games around local traditions, culture and folklore to attract this new generation. Gen Z wants to create a sense of belonging.
20 They want to connect with like-minded people across the globe, and realize that being a gamer is a great way to socialize. Plus, the most recognized gamers also earn revenue through live streams [...]. Gen Z has helped with the evolution of competitive gaming, better known as esports.
25 [...] Developers [...] help build communities and generate revenue while doing what this generation loves the most. Gen Z wants to learn and innovate – they are ready to adapt and change and also value creativity. [...]
The growth in technologies like 3D graphics, improved AI and
30 VR has led to the further development of growth within the video game industry. With these innovations, Gen Z players get more realistic simulations and can connect to other players in a better way. The industry's future will depend on the continued creation of unique experiences and growth
35 within the aforementioned categories for sustained success with Gen Z. [...]

Source (abbreviated): https://www.entrepreneur.com/article/402181

5 It's your turn: A debate

a Get together in groups.
- **Group A:** You think online and video gaming has lots of benefits.
- **Group B:** You think the negative aspects of online and video gaming outweigh the benefits.

Make a mind map of the arguments. Think about the arguments the other side will put forward and come up with counterarguments. (*TIP* on **p. 75**)

b Hold the debate. Your teacher will be the chair. (*Phrases* on **p. 75**)

Grammar and structures

Conditionals (revision) → G3

If I **interrupt** her now, she**'ll lose** her score.
If she **spent** too long online, I **would talk** to her about it.
If I **hadn't played** games, I **wouldn't have become** interested in how these games were designed.

If I **could** turn the clock back, I **would** use the gaming skills to help with my career.

1 Aimee is chatting with her sister Holly. Complete the conversation with the prompts. In some cases, you have to use conditional sentences.

Aimee Hi sis! What r u doing this weekend?
Holly weather | nice | hang out | friends | local park.
Aimee What | do | rain?
Holly go | window-shopping.
Aimee I bet | buy something.
Holly Sure. If | see something | like and | not too expensive | get it. What about u?
Aimee Relaxing. I'm so tired.

Holly That's because you went out last night.
Aimee Yeah, and | if not | not see Hive Society.
Holly U know what mum | say | she find out u went to a concert?
Aimee She | unless u tell her.
Holly Okay, but as long as u | not say anything about that tattoo I got.
Aimee Deal.

2
a Aimee found an article about tattoos. Complete the article with the correct form of the verbs in brackets and the prepositions in the box.

p. 150

| among ■ at ■ from ■ in ■ of |
| ■ on ■ towards ■ with |

While tattoos have been an important part of many cultures, particularly those of Pacific Islanders, the tradition in the West is quite different. If you trace the history of tattoos in Europe, you __1__ (*see*) that the first
5 ones were linked to sailors returning from voyages. Common tattoos featured stars, anchors and even birds. If you __2__ (*ask*) a sailor about the meaning of their tattoo a century ago, you were likely to have been told that they were a form __1__ protection.
10 __2__ the start of the twentieth century tattoos started to become popular __3__ the elite. In fact, Winston Churchill's mother had a tattoo of a snake around her wrist. This craze didn't last long, and tattoos soon went out of fashion.
15 Fifty years later and tattoos became seen as a sign of rebellion. In fact, the negative attitude __4__ tattoos meant that if you decided to get one you often had it placed somewhere it was unlikely to be seen because of the clothes you wore. If you had a tattoo that was
20 visible, you __4__ (*often, find*) it difficult to get a job. However, __5__ the 1970s onwards tattoos started to become more mainstream. By the twenty-first century it was not unusual to find someone with a tattoo. A survey in 2015 found that one __6__ five people in the UK had a
25 tattoo, with almost half of all millennials __5__ (*admit*) to having at least one.
Tattoos seem to be particularly popular __7__ groups that can be very influential such as pop stars and footballers.

30 We asked some people about getting tattoos. Here are some of the things they said:

Amy (33) 'When I told my mum I was going to get a tattoo she looked horrified. Remember, if you get one
35 done now it __6__ (*be*) difficult to get rid of it later', she said. 'If I __7__ (*listen*) to her, I __8__ (*not worry*) so much about it later. I was only 18 at the time and had the name of my boyfriend and a heart tattooed on my
40 arm. Of course, a few weeks later we split up, but his name remained as a reminder.'

Megan (21) 'I was only 17 when I decided I wanted a tattoo. Of course, I had to wait a year as you have to be
45 18 in the UK before you can get one. On my birthday I went to a local artist. Now I have over twenty and I __9__ (*definitely get*) more.'

Marcus (19) 'A lot of my friends have
50 tattoos, but I don't think I'll have one despite the peer pressure. If you __10__ (*get*) one when you are young, it might look good. But I don't think tattoos look good __8__ older people, especially if
55 you put on weight and your skin stretches!'

b Read the article again and complete the tasks.

1 State how the attitude to tattoos has changed over time.
2 Explain why having a tattoo when you are young might not be a good idea.
3 Comment on why more and more young people are getting tattoos.

3 **a** Read the article about teenage fashion in the 2010s and look at the photo. Check that you understand everything, and complete the tasks.

Teenage fashion: What's cool now?

They say if you want to feel young, you should spend time with young people. Rubbish. I've just spent a day with four teenagers, and I feel about 95. There is nothing like discovering exactly how ancient you appear to the
5 youth of today to put paid to fanciful notions that one is still – as we said in my day – down with the kids. Example. I asked Will Spratley, 15-year-old music and drama enthusiast, whose style he admired. He pulled out an old copy of NME[1], and flicked to an article about
10 Gorillaz. 'I think Damon Albarn looks good,' he said. And then he added, helpfully, 'He was the lead singer of Blur.' Thanks for the tip, son. Ouch. […]
Teenagers have their own vocabulary, their own jokes, their own heroes. They scorn our rules, but police their
15 own society with exacting systems of etiquette […]. At the nub of teenage rebellion is their compulsion to flaunt their differences. […]
How do the teenagers of today want to dress? To find out, we asked four teenagers – 13-year-old Marla, and
20 15-year-olds Grace, Will and Ryan […]. […] The first surprise was the almost complete absence of trends. […]. Neither are they particularly interested in what celebrities are wearing […]. Ryan wore a T-shirt with a motif of gunmen against a peace sign – 'it's by Banksy.
25 He's an artist. It's against war and stuff' – which he said was his current favourite piece of clothing, along with a pair of bright yellow [sneakers]. […]
The girls […] mesh clothes with music. Grace Horigan, 15, who came to our shoot after sitting two GCSE exams that day, had chosen a day outfit 'for a festival' – high-
30 waisted denim shorts, flowing white top, boots, feather necklace – while Marla, who has wanted to be in a band 'since about year two' is the lead singer and guitarist in a

band, Forever Making History, who recently played their first pub gig. She is comfortable on stage, but wrinkles her nose and shakes her hair over her face when I ask her how she would define her own style. 'Um. Indie, I guess. Rock.' […]
Grace and her friends pool their clothes. 'We lay them out on a bed, talk about who's already worn what, who wants to wear what, and everyone shares. We borrow my older sister's clothes, too.' […]
And do you know what? Sometimes parents are, like, really unfair. Marla's mum, for instance, won't let her wear short skirts. When you say short, I ask, what do you mean exactly? She points to a spot about half a centimetre below her knicker line, but gives me such a heartfelt can-you-believe-how-unfair-she-is look that I can't bring myself to tell her that her mum has a point. 'And then,' Marla continues, 'when it's cold she sometimes literally makes me wear a jacket!' Imagine. […]

_____
[1] NME = New Musical Express, a popular British music magazine

Source (abbreviated): https://www.theguardian.com/lifeandstyle/2010/jul/16/teenage-fashion-style

1 List the influences on the clothes teenagers wear.
2 Compare yourself to the young people shown in the picture and interviewed in the article.
3 Assess whether this kind of article could still be written today.
4 Comment on the writer's view that spending time with young people makes you feel young is rubbish.

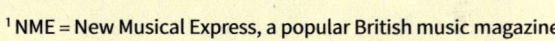

b Read the article again. Choose the best option for each of the expressions.

1 Down with the kids. (l. 6)
  a You don't like young people.
  b You understand what young people are like.
  c You like the same things as young people.

2 … their compulsion to flaunt their differences. (ll. 16f)
  a … the pressure to show they are different.
  b … the need to show they are not the same.
  c … the need to show off.

3 … the almost complete absence of trends. (l. 21)
  a There are no trends that everyone follows.
  b There are some favourite trends.
  c There is almost no difference to the trends.

4 Grace and her friends pool their clothes. (l. 39)
  a They buy their clothes together.
  b They share their clothes.
  c They wash their clothes a lot.

1 **a** At school, Aimee, Paige and Liam were given an assignment. They have to answer the question: 'If you could live in a different time, when would it be?' and then give a presentation. Look at the photos and describe what you can see. If you're unsure, do some research.

1920s

1960s

1990s

b Speculate which decades the students will choose. Give reasons for your answer.

🔊 55 **c** Listen and see if you guessed correctly. Which pictures do you think each of the students used to illustrate their presentation?

2 **a** Choose one of the people in the
p. 150 pictures. Carry out some research and
make notes about what they contributed
to the decade(s) they represent.
Why did they become famous?
Find tips on assessing and citing sources
on **pp. 105, 140**.

The Beatles (1960s)

J.K. Rowling (1990s / 2000s)

Greta Thunberg (2010s / 2020s)

 b Tell a partner about your research.

---

3 **a** If you could choose a decade
to live in, when would it be?
It doesn't have to be one of the
above. Carry out some research
and make some notes.
Put together a three-minute-
presentation. Include pictures
to illustrate your presentation.

> **Useful phrases**
> *If I could choose a decade to live in, it would be …*
> *I'd love to have been alive in …*
> *Imagine living in the …*
> *In my opinion, …*
> *I think …*
> *The … was the decade when …*

b Work in groups and give your presentation. Make notes and give the presenters in your group
feedback about their presentation. Say what you liked as well as what could be improved and
how. You can use the table below. You find more tips on giving feedback on **p. 144**.

	Suggestions
Delivery (body language, eye contact, speed, …)	???
Communication (vocabulary, style, …)	???
Visuals (slides, illustrations, …)	???

→ Workbook, page 77

METHOD COACH

@ WES-40806-003

How to assess texts

S1 **Classify a text**

a Read the two texts and decide what the purpose of each one is. Here are some tips to help you:
- For text A list those words that trigger emotions.
- For text B consider how the information is presented (e. g. use of tenses, choice of vocabulary, etc.).
- For both texts: What are the authors' intentions? How does the text make you feel?

Give reasons for your answers.

A

Feel great in second-hand clothes

If you are like us, you care about the environment, you care about the future of our planet. At the same time, you are fashion conscious and passionate about new clothes. But the pleasure of purchasing a new item of clothing makes you feel guilty as you are aware of the harm the making of your shiny new outfit caused the environment. Does this sound familiar to you?

5 There is a solution: make second-hand your first choice! In our shop we only sell pre-loved items, unique and vintage pieces and even designer items at affordable prices. Our motto is: fashion is eternal, fashion is affordable, fashion is sustainable, fashion is guilt-free.
Find your gem and make it your own! Our staff are at hand to advise you whatever your needs.
And it gets even better. Do you need a glamorous outfit for a special occasion? Find your perfect piece,
10 reserve it and rent it for the day. No more discarded bundle at the back of your wardrobe gathering dust and no unwanted dent in your bank balance either.
Come and see us! Join our ever-growing customer base of like-minded people.
Do what is right and feel good about it!

Mark & Billie

B

Fashion is one of the largest consumer goods industries in the world and one of the most contaminating. The fashion business model that comes out with new trends every month and the idea of buying and throwing away
5 clothes is creating a terrible impact on the planet in terms of natural resources consumption, energy and emissions. According to a 2019 report by the University of Washington, the textile industry is responsible for about one-fifth of global water pollution. And this is only
10 one aspect of all the negative impacts clothes manufacturing from new natural or synthetic material has on our environment. Many leading textile brands are already tackling this issue. Using recycled materials, which currently stands at 65% of all production, the
15 sector will prevent 2.8 billion tonnes of carbon dioxide being emitted by 2050. This example shows that the valuable habit of recycling clothes can be extremely beneficial in the long run. If we, consumers get into the habit of recycling our clothes instead of throwing them
20 away, there will be real benefits to our world. To name a few, there will be saving up on water consumption, our carbon footprint will be reduced, and we'll achieve a more balanced biodiversity. We do this together, because there is no Planet B.

---

b With a partner, each choose a different text and look up the words you don't know.
Explain the meaning of the new words to your partner.

S2 **Questions about texts.** Look at the questions and try to answer them for your text. Are there any questions that are not relevant to your text? If so, why not? Compare your findings.

1 What is the main point of this text?
2 Who wrote it?
3 Why was it written?
4 When was it written?
5 Has the context changed since it was written?
6 Is the evidence supported?
7 How did the authors come to their conclusions?
8 Do you agree with the conclusions?
9 What does this add to our knowledge?
10 Why is it useful?

Assessing claims

 S1 **Looking at statistics**

 a You are going to watch the animated film *When can you trust statistics?* What do you know about the source? Do you think it is reliable?

b Choose the correct options, then compare your answers with a partner. Watch again and explain why the wrong options are false.

1 One approach to statistics is to say that
   a 98% of them are lies.
   b they're all untrustworthy.
   c you're a fool to believe them.

2 The three Cs of data wisdom are
   a be calm, check claims and be careful.
   b stay calm, get context and be careful.
   c be careful, get context and be clear.

3 When a claim has had an emotional effect on you,
   a think about your reaction before you share it.
   b analyse the data and then share it.
   c think about how others might react before you share it.

4 In the example about the NHS savings, the important question is how
   a many people are overweight in the UK.
   b much money is saved by how many people.
   c significant £100 million is over five years.

5 Statistics cannot teach us anything unless
   a we use them to fight our battles.
   b they help to confirm our beliefs.
   c they inspire us to ask questions.

6 While not accepting statistical claims at face value, we should
   a not dismiss them out of hand either.
   b stay cautious of those we agree with.
   c ask if the figures are increasing or decreasing.

TIP

Assessing sources for academic purposes will also help you assess real-life situations.
When you have to make choices or form an opinion, whether at school or in everyday life, you need to be well informed. An interested mindset will help you ask yourself the right questions when you're looking for information.
● Is this the right source? Is it reliable? Can I check it?
● Do any of the claims make me suspicious?
● Is this information relevant for me at this moment?
● Is it possible to consider the claim from a different angle?

S2 **Drawing conclusions from statistics**

 a Study a statement a business school in Spain published in 2019 relating to the performance of students at a final exam for an English language degree. In what way is the percentage of girls who took the exam presented differently and what is the effect?

> 8% of girls who took the exam failed to receive top points. Meanwhile 58% of boys who took the exam received grades between A and C.

b Look at the statistics reported in the UK in September 2019. Do you find these statistics comprehensive enough? Give reasons for your answer.

> **The proportion of young people in England going to university has passed the symbolic 50% mark for the first time**
> Figures from the Department for Education, for 2017–18, show 50.2% of people going into higher education. The figures are higher for women, where 57% are going to university.
> The annual statistics on entry to higher education show the proportion of people set to go to university before the age of 30.

56 **c** Listen to an expert analysing the report. Copy the headings and make notes while listening.

The data provided in the report tells you	The data does not give information about
???	???

d Compare your notes. Discuss whether the analysis has changed your reaction to the report. Give reasons.

 S3 **Writing your assessment.** Find a headline, tweet or post that offers a claim based on statistics.
Do some research by checking the sources and studying the figures. Write your evaluation and share it with a partner. (See *TIP* on citing sources on **p. 140**.)

Digitalization

1 **The power of the internet.** Read the quote about the internet. With a partner, talk about whether you agree with it or not. Discuss where people could be disadvantaged. Give reasons for your answers.

> The internet has changed everything. We expect to know everything instantly. If you don't understand digital communication, you're at a disadvantage.

Bob Parsons (*1950, American entrepreneur)

2 **Digital inequality**

a Read the article about young people and inequality in the digital world. Outline the three key areas of data literacy.

Not all young people are 'digital natives' – inequality hugely limits experiences of technology

There is a belief that younger people are fully engaged with the digital world, [but data literacy is not uniformly high among younger people, as is often assumed]. Instead, some young people have very low levels of data literacy.
5 We are concerned that widespread perceptions of 'digital natives' lead people to believe that digital media use is constant across certain ages or generations, and that all members of this generation have similar experiences of technology. This could not be further from the truth. [...]
10 [Digital technology users of all ages can be divided into five groups.] These are extensive political; extensive; general; limited; and social and media users. Both types of extensive users have a high probability of engaging with the online world, with one being likely to carry out political action
15 online. General users have a moderate level of online engagement, but don't tend to use social media. Limited users have a low probability of engaging with any digital systems. [...]
The 'social and media' group is young – most are under 25 –
20 and mainly makes use of social media, entertainment media [...] and games. They sound like your archetypal 'digital natives'. In fact, they are one of the groups [...] that appear to lack critical thinking skills and knowledge about the digital world.
25 By contrast, the two extensive groups also contain young people, aged between 16 and 25. However, these younger people [...] show far higher data and digital literacy.

Understanding data

[There are] three key areas of data literacy. These are data
30 thinking, data doing, and data participation.
'Data thinking' covers critical skills – being able to assess and check data in the online environment. For example, this includes being able to understand how social media companies might use information about us and thinking
35 about the reliability of information we find online.

'Data doing' focuses on practical skills involving data handling and data management. For example, it might cover social media users being able to identify and highlight the source of the information they share with others. Or it might involve identifying reliable data from the internet that will 40 help you in your everyday life.
'Data participation' covers our shared experience of digital society. Examples might include a person who actively contributes to online forums or helps others to engage with digital systems. [S]ocial and media users have much lower 45 levels of data thinking, doing and participating than all other groups [except for] limited users. [...] The social and media users show some of the lowest understanding of how their data is shared and used to create value. Compared to other groups, they have the lowest levels of concern about how 50 online platforms operate, [e.g. they are happy to be targeted with advertising, or trust online retailers with their data]. [...]

Other inequalities

[R]esearch also shows how digital inequalities correspond with other key elements of economic, social and cultural 55 inequality. As well as being young, 'social and media users' are very likely to have left education at 16–18 with basic [...] qualifications. They are often lower skilled and in lower-income work or unemployed. [...]
On the surface, they might look like the archetypal 'digital 60 natives': young people deeply engaged with social and entertainment media, and with their smartphone to hand all the time. But our social and media users are a group marked by narrow and limited digital media use and a lack of data literacy. [...] Aspects of social inequality such as education 65 and social class have a huge impact on how we experience digital technologies. They affect the skills we acquire and our ability to think critically about the systems, platforms, data, information and content we encounter.

Source (abbreviated and adapted): https://theconversation.com/not-all-young-people-are-digital-natives-inequality-hugely-limits-experiences-of-technology-133102

57)) **Words and phrases**

archetypal	having all the qualities that make sth./sb. typical of a particular kind of person or thing
competency	the ability to do sth. well
to encounter	to come across or find

b Read the following statements and decide whether they are true, false or not in the text. Correct the false statements.

1 The term 'digital natives' is widely applied to the young generation as they are competent users of technology.
2 General users do not use social media at all.
3 Overuse of social media is dangerous and harmful to the user.
4 It is only the 'social and media' group that doesn't know anything about how the digital world works.
5 Users who are classified as belonging to the two extensive groups have the same level of data and digital literacy.
6 'Social and media' users do not care about how their data is used for advertising or are happy to share their personal details with online retailers.
7 People who are not 'digital natives' are more likely to be unemployed.
8 Economic, social and cultural inequalities in society are on par with digital inequality.

3 Quotes

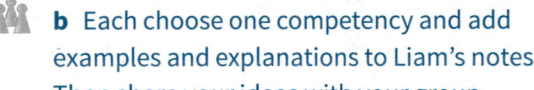

a Read these quotes from the article. With a partner, discuss the purpose of the underlined words and expressions. Consider what would happen if you left them out. Decide whether the writer expresses indisputable facts, a degree of possibility or an opinion.

- '*General users [...] don't tend to use social media.*'
- '"*Social and media users*" *are very likely to have left education at 16 – 18 with basic [...] qualifications. They are often lower skilled and in lower-income work or unemployed.*'

b Skim the article and find other examples of tentative (cautious) language.

c Check with your partner and discuss the author's reasons for using them.

> **TIP**
>
> **Tentative (cautious) language** is used when the writer wants to express an idea that is not 100% factual, when there is a possibility of uncertainty or when the claim they make is an opinion rather than a fact.

4 Digital literacy

a Liam researched digital literacy skills. He made notes about what each competency entails. Read them and match each to an expression in the box. Check with a partner.

> collaboration and creativity ■
> communication and netiquette ■
> critical thinking ■ digital culture ■
> finding information ■ functional skills ■
> online safety skills

> 1 Master how to search for accurate and reliable information.
> 2 Analyse and evaluate information.
> 3 Identify potential risks and be conscious of personal security.
> 4 Know how to operate your device effectively.
> 5 Show respect for different, culturally diverse online communities.
> 6 Participate in collaborative learning, teamwork.
> 7 Make sure that you are comfortable with what you share; think about the risks.

b Each choose one competency and add examples and explanations to Liam's notes. Then share your ideas with your group.

5 It's your turn: Make a poster about media use

a Look at the tips about social media use. Analyze the message, think about how you would answer the questions and give examples of how you apply these principles to your social media activity.

b Discuss what else you could add to these questions and principles.

c Create a poster using your ideas from **b**.

> **Before you like, post, or share something on social media …**
>
> **T Is it True?**
> **H Is it Helpful?**
> **I Is it Inspiring?**
> **N Is it Necessary?**
> **K Is it Kind?**

→ Workbook, page 80   **PRACTICE A**

1 Read the beginning of a conversation between Brendan and Aimee and summarize in your own words what they are talking about.

Brendan   Hey, watch where you are going! You almost knocked me over!

Aimee   Oh, hi … Sorry, I didn't see you.

Brendan   Of course not – you can't peel your eyes off your phone. What's so important?

Aimee   This invitation to join this online gaming community. Have you seen it? It's right up your street. But the places are limited so you need to accept it like right now.

Brendan   OK, I might have a look this evening.

Aimee   What do you mean this evening? Why not now?

Brendan   I don't have my phone on me.

Aimee   You don't have your phone on you? That's not like you … What's happened? You've never left the house without your phone before.

Brendan   True, but that's going to change now. You see, my mum had a long talk to me about my excessive phone use, and I must admit she was right.

Aimee   Don't tell me you've decided to go cold turkey? I could never do that …

Brendan   No, not at all. I am still using my phone or laptop, but I'm on a kind of digital detox. And before you ask me, the rules are self-imposed, noone forced them on me. Do you want to hear what they are?

Aimee   Sure, I'm intrigued.

Brendan   OK. So my rule number one is …

2 p. 151

a List three rules you would follow if trying a digital detox. Give reasons for your ideas. Then listen to Brendan and compare your ideas to his.

b Complete the tasks.

1 Do you have the same rules as Brendan?
2 Are there any rules you have come up with that are different from Brendan's?
3 Discuss why Brendan is so committed to a digital detox.
4 Comment on the issues raised by Brendan.

3 To convince Aimee, Brendan showed her his mum's research on the excessive use of digital devices. Read and discuss it with a partner.

1. In a poll conducted by the organization Common Sense Media, 50% of teens reported that they felt that they were addicted to their mobile devices.
A whopping 78% of the teen respondents said that they checked their devices hourly. […]
2. One study conducted by researchers in Sweden found that heavy technology use among young adults was linked to sleeping problems, depressive symptoms, and increased stress levels. […]
3. Researchers have also found that in-bed electronic social media use has adverse effects on sleep and mood. […] The results found that using social media when you are in bed at night increases the likelihood of anxiety, insomnia, and shorter sleep duration.
4. A study […] found that heavy daily technology use was associated with an increased risk for mental health problems among adolescents.

Source (abbreviated and adapted): Kendra Cherry, Claudia Chaves, "What Is a Digital Detox?", verywellmind.com, 19.11.2020, https://www.verywellmind.com/why-and-how-to-do-a-digital-detox-4771321 [12.07.2022]

4 Design a poster to encourage young people to do a digital detox.

How to do a digital detox?
The dos and the don'ts

@ WES-40806-003

1 **a Think:** Look at the photos and note down as many advantages and disadvantages of digital technology as you can think of. What do you think about the situations in the pictures below? Add them to your list.

b Pair: Compare your ideas with a partner. What are your thoughts about the pictures?

c Share: Two pairs get together in a group. Share the advantages and disadvantages you and your partner came up with and agree on the most important and the most dangerous.

2 Read this news story and discuss what role technology played in the incident.

A woman in Australia fell off a cliff to her death on Saturday after trying to take a photo at the precarious location. Rosy Loomba, 38, was with her husband and child when the accident occurred […].
5 Police said Loomba climbed past safety barriers and warning signs, to pose on a rock for a photo when she tripped over the edge, falling more than 80 meters […] down the cliff face […].
In the aftermath, authorities reminded the public to
10 pay attention to safety signs and guidelines, and that no photo is worth a person's life.
'We can't rope off every part of Victoria,' said Police Minister Lisa Neville. 'People have to take responsibility.'

Source (abbreviated and adapted): Jessie Yeung, "Australian woman dies trying to take photo at edge of 262-foot cliff", CNN travel, 14.12.2020, https://edition.cnn.com/travel/article/australia-selfie-woman-death-intl-hnk-scli/index.html [12.07.2022]

3 Read the *TIPs* below and on **p. 75**, then write an argumentative essay (200 – 250 words) about the advantages and disadvantages of digital technology.

TIP

Writing an argumentative essay
● Organize your essay: write an introduction, clear paragraphs in the main body anda conclusion.
● Try to engage your readers by addressing them directly. You could also:
  – reference a recent newspaper article
  – use a quote
  – include interesting facts and figures
  – include a personal anecdote.
● In your introduction, outline the topic and how you will organize your essay.
● Structure your paragraphs clearly. Write the thesis, then present the arguments and give examples.
● Make sure your essay is balanced. You can say which arguments you find more convincing in the conclusion, but in the body of the essay you need to stay neutral. You shouldn't take sides.

Social issues

1 **The biggest challenges of recent years**

a Read the list below and make notes on three issues that have had an impact on your life. Rank them in order of importance. If necessary, add to the list.

- extensive use of social media
- racism / Black Lives Matter
- body image / mental health
- elections / politics
- veganism
- climate change / natural disasters
- global pandemic
- gender / identity issues
- immigration
- globalization

 b Compare why you chose the items on your list. As a group, agree on the three most common issues.

2 **Gen Z.** Read the article about Generation Z and do the tasks.

1 Identify what the biggest concern of this generation is. Support your answer with examples from the article.
2 Analyse the use of adjectives with positive and negative connotations in the first paragraph. Discuss whether you personally agree with this description or not.
 3 List the issues the article mentions and evaluate their relevance to your life. Share your ideas and give reasons for them.

Gender fluid, hyper-stressed, politicall[...] What do we know[...]

Today's youngest generation [...], born after 2000, are connected yet isolated, savvy but anxious, indulged yet stressed. They have grown up with social media, a constant proliferation of information on a fully
5 mobile internet [...]. [...] Connectivity permeates their lives – from friendships to relationships, news, entertainment, shopping – and has transformed how they interact. [...]
Young people are also reported to have a much more
10 fluid sense of sexual identity and gender. [...] [They are perceived to be more racially tolerant, more receptive to immigrants, and more accepting of non-traditional families than any generation before them.]
15 One of the starkest markers of Gen Z to date is the sharp rise in reported mental health issues. [...] [W]hen it comes to low self-esteem, a lot of young people are putting that down to concerns about education, their future and the online world, [which
20 is] with them 24/7. Every time they switch on their phones they are getting messages about parties they have not been invited to, or they are seeing photos of their friends doing things, or their whole self-worth is based on how many likes they are getting [...]. It
25 absolutely permeates their sense of self-wort[h.] [...] Generation Z's wider political engagement is going through a period of transformation. [...] While most of Generation Z are still too young to vote, their focus has shifted away from party politics to single-topic
30 issues such as feminism or climate change; much of the civic engagement and organizing they do takes place on social media rather than through traditional political structures. [...]

TIP

Adjectives with positive and negative connotations
Connotation is an idea or a feeling a word evokes. For example, 'connected' triggers a positive feeling – the adjective has a positive connotation, meanwhile 'lonely' is more associated with negative feelings, hence it has a negative connotation.

---

59)) **Words and phrases**

aspiration	a strong desire to achieve sth.		
civic	relating to the people living in a town or city	**to permeate**	to be present in every part of sth.
fluid	likely to change	**proliferation**	a sudden increase in the amount of sth.
to indulge	to let sb. do or have whatever they want	**receptive**	willing to consider new ideas or listen to sb. else's opinions

PART 1   PART 2   PART 3

engaged, connected but lonely: about modern teens?

The feelings of social isolation reported by many teenagers can be hard for older people to understand. [T]here is a perception that this generation should be the happiest and the most content because they have got so much connectivity, across the world, and so much information at their fingertips. [...] But that connectivity is actually disconnecting people from real friendships and the opportunity to enjoy the world together. It is creating absolutely unrealistic ideals that young people cannot get t[o.] [...]
The contradictions of connectivity are the real challenge for Generation Z and for society at large. In many ways, they already appear more responsible than their predecessors – more politically engaged and eager to reframe perspectives on sexual orientation and gender, while demanding action on the issues of mental health, education, equality and racism. As they emerge into adulthood, we will see what world they make.

35

40

45

50

Sources: https://www.theguardian.com/lifeandstyle/2016/dec/10/
generation-z-latest-data-teens; https://www.canr.msu.edu/news/
millennials_todays_teen_and_young_adult_population

CULTURE CORNER

Generation Z refers to people born between 1997 and 2012. What makes this generation different from the ones before is that they were born into a digital world. Rather than having to learn to use digital devices and social media, it has been a part of their lives from the start. Kids born after 2012 are called Generation Alpha. They are the first generation who have entirely grown up with smart technology and streaming services.

3 **Life as we'd known it came to a halt**

a You are going to watch a video from 2021 about how the Corona pandemic has changed American teenagers' lives. Before you watch, list all the issues you expect the young people to talk about.

8 **b** Watch the video and make notes about what they say about
● their feelings,
● how they were affected by the pandemic,
● what they will do once the pandemic is over.

8 **c** Watch the video again and add to your notes. Then work in groups and compare your notes. Decide if the comments were mostly positive or negative.

d Choose the comment from each section that is the closest to yours. Share with your group and give reasons for your choices.

4 **The future for me**

a Think about your aims, plans and dreams. Write notes for each heading. You find tips for collecting ideas and notes on **pages 139/140**.

Personal aspirations	The world around me
???	???

b Compare with a partner. What are the similarities or differences?

5 **It's your turn: An interview.**

You are going to interview five people about their past year. Use these questions to create your own questionnaire in your group and give reasons for your choices.

1 What was the biggest challenge in their life in the past year?

2 What did they achieve/accomplish and what are they proud of?

3 What would they do differently if they could?

4 Which event in Germany/in the world had an impact on their lives?

1 Skim the three article excerpts about different teen issues and match them to the headlines.

Understanding gender these days is way over my head – but my teen girls are helping me get there

What we understand about young people's motivations

It's never been easy being a teenager. But is this now a generation in crisis?

1

Young people are demanding change. In the last few days, young Indigenous activists and their supporters [...] led waves of protest across the country. For some young people, climate change is urgent. For others, gun violence is a crisis. From truth and reconciliation to inclusion and diversity and
5 mental health, young people are bringing awareness to societal crises and making headlines along the way. [...]
[Y]oung people do share a concern for the future and their contribution to it. Our research shows that young people between the ages of 14 and 29 show levels of [...] motivation that is as high or even higher than adults.

2

[Youth unemployment is more than 13%, the cost of higher education is rapidly rising, a drought of affordable housing coupled with low pay is keeping many young people sealed
5 under the parental roof and trapped in what one report called 'suspended adulthood'. The ubiquity of the internet and social media, with its [...] body shaming and cyberbullying, is encroaching on their well-being, while a
10 relentless focus on academic high-achieving is turning up the pressure in the classroom. Youth, traditionally thought of as the most enviable time of life, can now look like a deeply challenging and sometimes unpleasant time of
15 life. [...]
[Julia Britton, a leading consultant child and adolescent psychotherapist,] says, 'I look at myself as a teenager in the 1970s and so many issues were [already] around [...] but there are
20 many differences, too. The context certainly is different. I think there are far more pressures educationally, more sense that it's all hinged on one exam, and certainly teachers are hugely concerned about the mental distress they are
25 seeing.' [...]

3

I am a mom living in London, [Ontario in Canada], and I have two teen girls. [...] My children are advocates and they are very into social justice. [...] They are accepting, tolerant and caring young people. They have a huge variety of
5 friendships with a diverse group of young people who identify as straight, lesbian, bisexual, gay, trans, queer and non-binary. These days, it's increasingly apparent that gender is a much more fluid concept.
My teenagers are also at an age and stage where they
10 question a lot of things. Which means they also hold me to a higher standard sometimes.
Our conversations sometimes go like this:

Teen: *I was talking with X because we have a project due. X is trans/poly-sexual/transitioning/non-binary.*
15 **Me:** *[...] I don't even know what polysexual is. Explain that to me, please.*
Teen: *It means X is attracted to many genders.*
Me: *OK.*

At this point, I'm slowly processing what I've been told.

20 **Teen:** *Mom, there are at least 63 different genders.*
Me: *63?*

I then sit with a puzzled look on my face, and make a mental note to [look up] how many different gender and sexual identities there are later. [...]

25 Teen leaves my office.
[I sit] questioning and trying to process this new-to-me information. I pride myself on striving to use inclusive language in many areas of life. [...] I work hard on biting my tongue when I want to say: 'How is that even possible?
30 When I was your age there were only two genders.' [...]

2 **a** Choose one article and make notes about its content. Use a dictionary to check unknown vocabulary if necessary. You find a bilingual dictionary at the end of your students' book.

b Get together with two people who have chosen a different article from yours. Explain why you have chosen your article, then discuss which one you find the most interesting or thought-provoking. Which one is closest to your views?

3 Listen to Aimee and Liam talking and do the tasks.

1 Describe how Aimee feels and explain the reason.
2 Explain why Liam is surprised by Aimee's reaction.
3 Assess whether the solution Liam suggests is a good idea or not.
4 State how you would feel if your parents behaved like Aimee's mum.

4 **a** Read the email Aimee's mum sent to the local newspaper. List the issues she writes about.

b Compare your lists and discuss which issue(s) apply to you and how you protect yourself online.

5 **a** Write a letter to the editor with your views about teenagers and online security. Write about 200 – 250 words.

p. 151

b Exchange letters and compare the views you and your partner included.

Sources (p. 112, abbreviated and adapted): https://theconversation.com/what-we-dont-understand-about-young-peoples-motivations-129058 (1); https://www.theguardian.com/society/2016/sep/24/teenagers-generation-in-crisis (2); https://www.cbc.ca/parents/learning/view/understanding-gender-in-2019-is-way-over-my-head-but-my-teen-girls-are-help

Dear Editor,

In response to your question, as to whether or not teenagers care about online privacy, I'd like to share my thoughts with you and other readers. Watching my teenage daughter interacting online is like watching a horror
5 movie. I often look at her social media accounts and see photos of her and her friends, tags identifying the people in the photos, random comments from people I've never heard of and I doubt she has either!
Her generation might be digital natives, but when it comes to online security they seem to be clueless. I saw a survey a few months ago, which said that
10 91% of 12–17-year-olds post photos of themselves, so my daughter certainly isn't alone. 91% are also happy to post their name, 82% their birthday, 71% where they live and the school they go to, 53% their email address and even 20% are okay posting their mobile phone number. Have they never heard of identity theft?
15 Even when there are stories in the news about people not getting hired or losing their job because of something they wrote or posted online when they were younger, my daughter just shrugs and says, 'Well, they were silly, weren't they?' It's as if she feels she's immune to the same thing happening to her.
20 When I explained how many of the big social media companies collect data on her and her friends, she looked at me and said, 'So what? As long as I don't have to pay to use the site …' It's shocking! Then there are those targeted adverts. It's like water off a duck's back. I know they influence her as she often buys products she could only have seen advertised online.
25 The strange thing is that she's recently 'blocked' me from seeing some of her social media platforms. How can she be worried about her mum seeing the things she posts and not concerned about strangers or the long-term impact this might have on her future? It just doesn't make sense to me.

Gwen Jones-Gordon

1 Look at this sentence from an article called 'A brief history of teenagers.' Discuss why you think the writer says that the teenager is an invention of the 20th century.

> *The teenager is one of the more unusual inventions of the 20th century.*

2 Complete the text with the phrases below. There are two you don't need.

1 and that money would come from two principal sources

2 and the brands they follow

3 But are they really so different?

4 but a first date once meant an introductory chat

5 but only recently did it occur to anybody that this was a special thing

6 but the word didn't stick

7 but the meaning is quite clear.

8 parents gradually had fewer children and spent more per child

9 either earned or taken from their parents

10 especially those with power and money

11 compulsory public education for kids

12 understanding teenagers has never been easy

A brief history of teenagers

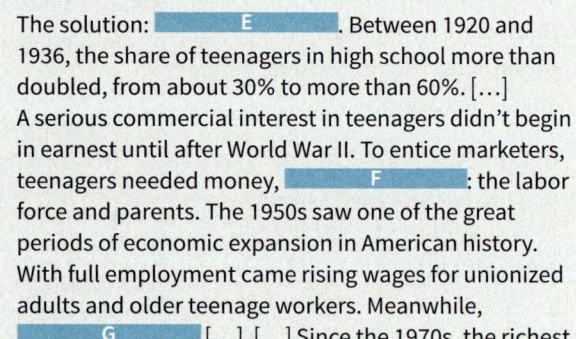

The teenager is one of the more unusual inventions of the 20th century. Humans have been turning 13 for tens of thousands of years, ⸺ A ⸺, or that the bridge between childhood and adulthood deserved its own name. The term *teen-ager* dates back to the early 1900s, ⸺ B ⸺. Even until World War II, there are hardly any instances of teenagers in the popular press. In the last few decades, however, the national media has nurtured a growing obsession with teenagers [...]. The press exhaustively tracks the apps young people use, the music they listen to, ⸺ C ⸺. [...] If most ancient cultures were gerontocratic, ruled by the old, modern culture is fully teenocratic, governed by the tastes of young people, with old fogies forever playing catch-up.

The teenager emerged in the middle of the 20th century thanks to the confluence of three trends in education, economics, and technology. High schools gave young people a place to build a separate culture outside the watchful eye of family. Rapid growth gave them income, ⸺ D ⸺. Cars (and, later, another mobile technology) gave them independence.

As the US economy shifted from a more localized agrarian society to a mass-production machine, families relocated closer to cities, and – at least initially – many sent their children to work in the factories. This triggered a countermovement to prevent kids from being forced to toil in mills.

The solution: ⸺ E ⸺. Between 1920 and 1936, the share of teenagers in high school more than doubled, from about 30% to more than 60%. [...] A serious commercial interest in teenagers didn't begin in earnest until after World War II. To entice marketers, teenagers needed money, ⸺ F ⸺: the labor force and parents. The 1950s saw one of the great periods of economic expansion in American history. With full employment came rising wages for unionized adults and older teenage workers. Meanwhile, ⸺ G ⸺ [...]. [...] Since the 1970s, the richest 20% of US households have more than doubled their spending on childhood 'enrichment,' such as summer camps, sports, and tutors. [...] It might be a horrifying consideration for today's singles, ⸺ H ⸺ in the living room with a girl's parents. This might have been followed by a deliciously awkward family dinner. But cars emancipated romance from the stilted small talk of the family parlor. Just about everything a modern single person considers to be a 'date' was made possible, or permissible, by the invention and normalization of car-driven romance. The fear that young men and fast cars were upending romantic norms was widespread. [...]

The last 60 years have made teenagers separate. ⸺ I ⸺ Or are teens just like adults – but with less money, fewer responsibilities, and no mortgage? [...] For adults, ⸺ J ⸺, the rules are what keep you safe. When you're young, every rule is illegitimate until proven otherwise. It is precisely because they have so little to lose from the way things are that young people will continue to be the inexhaustible motor of culture.

Source (abbreviated): https://www.saturdayeveningpost.com/2018/02/brief-history-teenagers/

PART 1 PART 2 PART 3

→ Workbook, pages 86/87 **READING PRACTICE**

3 **a** Choose one picture and describe how it relates to the text.

b Write a caption for each picture linking it to the text.

4 **a** Look at these words from the article and choose the correct meaning for the context.

1 nurtured (l. 15)
   a take care of something
   b help develop and grow
   c look after

2 exhaustively tracks (l. 16)
   a comes up with a complete list
   b quickly comes up with a list
   c lists the most common

3 confluence (l. 23)
   a where certain areas are important
   b increased importance
   c when two or more things come together

4 triggered (l. 33)
   a to cause someone to have a particular feeling or memory
   b to make something happen
   c to make someone say or do something unusual

5 toil (l. 34)
   a to work very hard doing a difficult or tiring job
   b to spend time in a dangerous place
   c to move from one place to another

6 entice (l. 39)
   a to lead someone into a trap
   b to provide someone with false hope
   c to persuade someone to do something

7 unionized (l. 43)
   a working together
   b being a member of a trade union
   c working for a trade union

8 upending (l. 58)
   a to make something more typical
   b to increase something
   c to completely change something

9 mortgage (l. 63)
   a a legal agreement where a bank lends you money to buy a house
   b a permanent place where you work for your whole life
   c a set of tasks that have to be completed by a certain time

b Read the text again and do the tasks.

1 Describe in your own words what is meant by 'old fogies' (l. 20).
2 Explain why companies began to be interested in targeting teenagers in the 1950s.
3 Analyse the importance of compulsory education in the development of teenagers.

5 Get together in groups and work on the tasks.
   ● **Group A:** Speculate why parents began to have fewer children in the 1950s.
   ● **Group B:** Illustrate what a first date could have looked like in the 1960s.

→ Workbook, page 88 **METHOD COACH**

Critical thinking

S1 **Reaching accurate conclusions**

a Think about what you understand by the term 'critical thinking'. In a group, make notes and give reasons for your choices. (Tips on **pp. 139/140**)

b You are going to read why critical thinking is important. Skim the text below and choose the correct heading for each paragraph.

1 Make up your own mind
2 What, where, when, who, why, how?
3 Key skill in all disciplines
4 Justify your assessment

A

What does being critical mean? It does not just mean finding fault. It means assessing evidence from a variety of sources and making reasoned
5 conclusions. As a result of your analysis, you may decide that a particular piece of evidence is not robust, or that you disagree with the conclusion. You should, however, be able to state why you have come to this view and incorporate this into
10 a bigger picture.

B

Being critical goes beyond describing what you have heard in class or what you have read. It involves synthesizing, analysing and evaluating
15 what you have learned to develop your own argument or position. Thinking about a topic in an objective and critical way will help you identify the different arguments.

C

20 Critical thinking is essential in all subjects and fields – in science and engineering, as well as the arts and humanities. The types of evidence used to develop arguments may be very different, but the processes and techniques are similar. Critical
25 thinking is required for pre-university, undergraduate and postgraduate levels of study.

D

Purposeful reading can help with critical thinking because it encourages you to read actively rather
30 than passively. When you read, ask yourself questions about what you are reading and make notes to record your views. Recognizing weaknesses or negative points in an argument will help you evaluate its strength or validity.

---

c Read the article again and compare the notes you made in **a** with the ideas in the article. Write down elements you didn't have in your notes.

S2 **Acquiring data wisdom**

 a Read some advice about data wisdom and complete it with the words in the box. Then listen and check your answers.

> agree ■ balanced ■ empathy ■ evaluate ■
> ■ indisputable ■ motives ■ original ■
> prejudices ■ reject ■ reliable

Getting data savvy

We are fortunate to live in a world where there is so much information and knowledge available to us in the easiest way possible. However, not everything out there is ▮1▮,
and that's where some strategies for data wisdom come
5 in. Asking questions about a claim, the right questions, will help you to ▮2▮ arguments, to step back and get different perspectives.
There are certain things to avoid and the first is what is called confirmation bias. This is when you automatically
10 ▮3▮ with statements or claims because they match your own opinion. Here, the strategy is to be actively willing to change your mind. Remember, if you are not prepared to be wrong, you will never come up with anything ▮4▮.
Beware of algorithms in social media platforms. These
15 are a way of sorting preferences based on your online activities. They can be very useful in matching the best content for your interests. However, they can also feed into your preconceptions and ▮5▮ and confirm what you thought you already knew. Even something that seems
20 totally true can have shades of meaning. In other words, what seems like an ▮6▮ fact can be more nuanced than you think.
Having intellectual ▮7▮ can have very successful results when you are thinking something out. Putting yourself in
25 other people's shoes and really trying to understand their point of view can lead to a much more ▮8▮ reaction, even if, in the end, you still agree to differ.
Another key strategy in data wisdom is of course to check your sources. Critical thinking depends on being aware of
30 ulterior ▮9▮. Does the person or organization making the claim have a vested interest? This may be as simple as trying to sell you something, but can also be used in social engineering, [for example] by swaying your voting choices in a government election. And finally, avoid
35 dismissing an argument based on the person who is making it. As a teenager, you will often have heard: You're too young to understand. Equally, teenagers may ▮10▮ a claim or an argument presented by a parent or teacher with: You're too old to understand. Listen to what is being
40 said without judging it on a preconception.

---

b Check if you use any of the above strategies. Say why you find them useful and describe how you use them. Then consider the ones you don't use and think about why not, and why you should use them. Discuss with a partner.

Reporting on fake news

S1 Bad influence(rs)?

a Read Aimee and Liam's conversation about influencers who give their followers bad advice and summarize what they are saying.

Liam   I watched a documentary last night about this awful person – she made a fortune by claiming she had cured herself of cancer. Pretending to be ill – I mean, who does that?

Aimee   That's incredible. Why did she do it?

Liam   She was a wellness blogger with, would you believe, over two million followers. She was selling a diet, a diet book, an app, a lifestyle basically. And sharing photos of herself looking A-MA-ZING … beautiful, slim, gorgeous hair, really healthy …

Aimee   But it's easy enough to do that with photo editing software, isn't it?

Liam   Yeah, but it's very convincing.

Aimee   Plus there are algorithms that suggest content – all you have to do is like a single post. I've done it myself: just liking a fitness programme prompted all sorts of slimming content to pop up – tips, diet pills and even body sculpting. It's insane.

Liam   What's worse in this case, some genuinely sick people chose to stop traditional medical treatments because they wanted to believe they could heal their conditions naturally. And she was everywhere, in magazines, in the news, on people's phones.

Aimee   Hmm, so I guess they trusted her. How did they find out she was a fake?

Liam   She lied about donating some of her book and app sales to charity. A journalist started digging and found out the truth.

Aimee   The moral of that is: don't believe everything you read.

b Collect similar examples of harmful advice given by influencers that you have come across and make a list. Discuss the different cases considering the following points:

- What made the bloggers and their posts successful?
- If they had any similarities, what were they?
- What were the bloggers' ulterior motives?

> **TIP**
>
> **How to spot fake news online**
> - **Check the source:** Does the website look real? If you aren't sure, click on the 'About' page and look for a clear description of the organization.
> - **Spot fake photos:** Are they altered or taken from an unrelated site? Use a tool like a reverse image search to show you if the same image is used elsewhere.
> - **Check if the story is in other places:** Look on news sites that you know and trust to confirm it's not fake.
> - **Look for other signs** such as ALL CAPS and lots of ads that pop up when you click on a link.
> - **False hopes:** If the news offers you hope for an easy solution to a problem you have, check it out carefully. If it sounds too good to be true, it probably isn't true.

c Discuss how you would advise a friend who was being influenced by a blogger you think is giving them bad advice.

S2 Finding a controversial report

a Find an article, a blog or report that makes a strong claim about one of the following topics. Choose a topic of your own if you prefer.

1 University education makes you a better citizen
2 Flying and driving less will stop global warming
3 Police 'stop and search' increasing for Black youth
4 Listening to classical music makes you smarter
5 Young people have no interest in politics

b Copy the article that you've found and highlight anything that you feel is controversial, or which makes you doubt its accuracy. Make notes, using the tips on critical thinking and identifying fake news.

S3 An analysis.
Write a short analysis of the report and outline what is good or bad about the claim. Describe how it can or cannot be verified and share your analysis in class. Write at least 200 words.

1 **a** Look at these photos which are connected to the topics of this workshop. What can you remember about them? Choose one and put together a two-minute presentation. (Tips on **pp. 22/23, 142/143**)

b Give your presentation. The others in your group should give feedback. (Tips on **p. 144**)

2 Brendan decides to write some advice and information about digitalization and digital detox.
Read the start of each sentence and complete each one with an appropriate ending.
Then compare your sentences with a partner.

p. 151

1 If your eyes hurt, …
2 If you suffer from FOMO, …
3 If you can't get to sleep at night, …
4 If I hadn't been born in the 21st century, …
5 If I didn't have internet access at home, …
6 If a new app is released, …

3 Listen to a podcast about gangs and gang culture in the USA and complete the tasks.

1 State what inspired the podcast.
2 Explain in what way gangs have changed over the decades.
3 Assess the impact the internet has had on gang life.

4 a Aimee has found a blog about how to be a happy, positive teenager. Match the headings to each paragraph.

> Believe in yourself ■ Be positive ■ Find a hobby ■ Goal ■
> Happiness & support ■ Keep motivated ■ Push yourself ■
> Routine ■ Stop comparing yourself

Staying positive

1

[It] is important, not just for teens but for anyone [...]. Exams, peer pressure and personal stresses can really put a toll on your life, so you need to make sure you have a clear mindset. A lot of people think positivity just means happiness, but it doesn't. It means looking at your situation and turning it at a different angle.

2

[T]o lead a positive life, you need [this]. You need to be able to know what is happening next. Perhaps you will wake up and get ready the same way each day or go for a run after school; things like this will help more than you think.

3

[T]o keep yourself positive you need to be surrounded by a happy support network. [...] You need people to be there for you, and people to support your decisions.

4

[I]f you take your situation and think about what you could gain from it, it will help you! Set a goal, try and take down the barriers that are in your way.

5

[...] To be honest, in everyday life I'm not the most motivated person [...]. [...] If someone asks me to do something, I don't respond quickly if I don't feel like completing the task... I hope I'm not alone. [But I am working on it.]

6

[I] have realized that the more stuff which I have going on which I enjoy doing, the more I get done in day-to-day life. It's like your brain almost wants you to get stuff out of the way to get on with what you love.

7

It might not be easy, but just telling yourself that you have to do what you have to do, can really help. [...] Reward yourself afterwards.

8

[This] is especially hard as a teen. Through the exam period you can feel like you have completely failed if you don't get the results you were hoping for. [...] [Y]ou can just feel so down in the dumps, it's not fun at all. [...] Being proud of who you are and what you believe in is admirable if you forget about what other people say.

9

[...] Looking at other people [...] has no relevancy as to where you are now personally. Just because someone might have X, Y, Z, doesn't mean they don't have the A, B, C that you have, too. We all have our own goals and our own barriers, so you have to realize that this little journey you are on is bound to be different.

Source (abbreviated and adapted): https://tollydollyposhfashion.com/ultimate-guide-teenager-2-0/

b Do you agree with the author's ideas? Is there any other advice you could add on how to stay positive?

 c Work in groups of three. Divide the text so that each group member has three different sections. Add your own ideas to each paragraph, then discuss your ideas in your group.

5  **Japan's new human beings.** Aimee finds an interesting video on the internet and sends it to Paige. Watch it and complete the tasks.

9

1 Look up the meaning of the expressions 'cheek to jowl' and 'the straight-laced'.
2 Describe how, according to the speaker, foreign influences have impacted Japanese teenagers. Comment on this trend.
3 Analyse why this generation is often referred to as 'The New Human Beings'.
4 Evaluate the speaker's assertion that these kids are just as dedicated as their parents.

1 German culture

Die Schülerinnen und Schüler eurer amerikanischen Partnerschule wollen einen Blog über deutsche Kultur starten. Sie haben dich als Gastblogger(in) eingeladen, drei kurze Beiträge zu schreiben. Im ersten erklärst du, wie die Deutschen von ihren Nachbarn gesehen werden, und was ihre Eigenwahrnehmung ist. Im zweiten Blogeintrag definierst du den Begriff „Hotel Mama" und gehst dabei auf den Unterschied zwischen jungen Männern und Frauen und mögliche Gründe dafür ein. Dein dritter Blogbeitrag handelt von der Bedeutung und dem Ursprung des Wortes „Spießer". Benutze das Transkript eines Interviews und die beiden Artikel für deine Blogbeiträge.

SPRECHER: Wie leben die Deutschen, und wie sind sie wirklich?

NINA: Hallo! Wir sind Nina …

DAVID: … und David vom Deutschlandlabor. Wir
5 beantworten Fragen zu Deutschland und den Deutschen.

NINA: Heute geht es um das Thema „Mentalität". Wie sind die Deutschen?

DAVID: Und gibt es typisch deutsche Eigenschaften?

10 SPRECHER: Im Ausland gelten die Deutschen oft als pünktlich, fleißig, ordentlich und humorlos. Dieses alte Bild von den Deutschen hat sich bis heute an vielen Orten der Welt gehalten. Aber aktuelle internationale Studien zeigen, dass es in vielen Ländern heute ein
15 positives Bild von Deutschland und den Deutschen gibt. Doch wie sehen sich die Deutschen selbst?

DAVID: Wie sind die Deutschen?

PERSONEN AUF DER STRASSE:
Ehrlich.
20 Gewissenhaft.
Kalt, diszipliniert.
Strebsam, fleißig.
Sparsam.
Höflich, nett, ordentlich, fleißig.
25 Auch hilfsbereit.
Wir werden auch immer weltoffener.
Die Deutschen versuchen immer alles ganz genau zu machen, alles ganz präzise zu gestalten. […]

SPRECHER: Es gibt etwa 80 Millionen Deutsche, und die
30 sind natürlich nicht alle gleich. Aber es gibt Unterschiede zwischen verschiedenen Kulturen, die zu Problemen führen können. Kommunikationsexperte Wolfgang Jockusch bereitet Mitarbeiter aus anderen Ländern auf die Arbeit in Deutschland vor.

35 NINA: Herr Jockusch, Sie kennen die Deutschen ganz gut, hab ich gehört. Wie sind wir Deutschen denn?

WOLFGANG JOCKUSCH: Das kommt darauf an, wen man fragt. Viele halten uns zum Beispiel für die besonders pünktlichen Leute. Ja, also Deutschland und
40 Pünktlichkeit und Ordnung und Zuverlässigkeit, das wird immer sehr gerne miteinander verbunden. […] Also, ich glaube, was ganz typisch deutsch ist, ist unsere direkte Kommunikation. Die Deutschen lieben es, auf den Punkt zu kommen.

45 NINA: Ich höre so oft, dass wir Deutschen so fleißig sind. Ist das richtig?

WOLFGANG JOCKUSCH: Fleiß hat sicherlich auch einen hohen Stellenwert für die Deutschen. Man kann Kulturen danach vergleichen, ob sie sich eher über
50 Leistung orientieren und Wettbewerb oder auf der anderen Seite Harmonie … Wenn ich daraus einen Vergleich mache, dann ist die deutsche Kultur sicherlich eine, die sehr auf Leistung und Wettbewerb orientiert ist.

55 SPRECHER: Oft sagt man, die Deutschen halten sich an Regeln und Verbote, wie auf diesen Schildern. Heute sollen David und Nina ein paar neue Regeln finden […]

PERSONEN AUF
DER STRASSE: […]
60 Du musst anfangen, laut zu singen, wenn dich irgendetwas nervt! Nicht immer so
65 unter Zeitdruck sein, sondern einfach mal die Sachen ein bisschen ruhiger angehen!
70 Du musst viel mehr lachen! Du sollst keine Currywurst essen! Du darfst keine weißen Tennissocken in Sandalen tragen! Du musst gar nix!
75 Du musst das Leben mehr genießen! Du musst freundlich sein, wenn du möchtest, dass auch andere zu dir freundlich sind.

DAVID: Die Deutschen sagen über die Deutschen, dass sie ordentlich, diszipliniert und genau sind. Sie haben
80 viele Regeln und sind oft sehr direkt, wenn sie ihre Meinung sagen.

NINA: Ich finde es ja gut, wenn man direkt und ehrlich ist.

DAVID: Ich auch! Du bist ein bisschen dicker geworden.

85 NINA: Was?

DAVID: Ich bin nur direkt und ehrlich.

NINA: Sehr witzig!

Viele 25-Jährige wohnen daheim – Hotel Mama bleibt beliebt

In Deutschland wohnen viele junge Erwachsene noch bei ihren Eltern. Dabei halten es die jungen Männer länger aus, als die jungen Frauen.

Mehr als jeder vierte junge Erwachsene wohnt in Deutschland mit 25 Jahren noch bei den Eltern. Dabei bleiben Söhne länger zuhause als Töchter, wie das Statistische Bundesamt an
5 diesem Mittwoch in Wiesbaden mitteilte. 34 Prozent der 25-jährigen Männer lebten 2019 noch im Elternhaus, bei den Töchtern waren es 21 Prozent.

Mädchen ziehen schneller aus

Der Unterschied zwischen den Geschlechtern bleibt auch in höherem Alter bestehen: Mit 30 Jahren wohnten noch 13 Prozent der ledigen Söhne im Elternhaushalt, aber nur fünf Prozent der Töchter. Der Jugendforscher Klaus Hurrelmann sieht darin
10 einen Beleg, „dass die Emanzipation der Männer ins Stocken geraten ist". Auch Untersuchungen wie die Shell Jugendstudie belegten diesen Trend, sagte er der Deutschen Presse-Agentur. „Um das 20. Lebensjahr herum geht die Schere auseinander."
Jugendforscher Klaus Hurrelmann: „Die jungen Frauen erzielen die besseren Bildungsergebnisse. Sie sind agiler im Umgang mit ihren Lebensherausforderungen. Sie sind selbstständiger und selbstbewusster und wollen sich deswegen früher von ihren Eltern lösen." Bei jungen Männern sei eher der gegenteilige Trend zu beobachten:
15 **Jugendforscher Klaus Hurrelmann:** „Sie (die jungen Männer) genießen das Hotel Mama so lange sie können. Das ist angenehm, das ist bequem. Sie wollen in Deckung bleiben, so lange es geht."
Dass Männer so spät von zu Hause ausziehen, ist für Hurrelmann „auch ein Zeichen von Irritation, dass Frauen so stark sind".

Kaum Veränderungen zu beobachten

Im Durchschnitt checkten Söhne 2019 mit 24,4 Jahren aus dem Hotel Mama aus, Töchter mit 22,9 Jahren. In Summe ist die
20 Tendenz leicht fallend: Nach Angaben des Statistischen Amtes der Europäischen Union (Eurostat) sank das geschätzte durchschnittliche Alter beim Auszug in Deutschland zwischen 2010 und 2019 von 24,1 auf 23,7 Jahre.
„Das Auszugsverhalten junger Menschen hat sich in den vergangenen 20 Jahren kaum verändert", berichteten die Statistiker mit Blick auf die Zeitreihe: Im Jahr 2000 lebten rund 30 Prozent der 25-Jährigen mit ihren Eltern unter einem Dach, 2019 waren es – beide Geschlechter zusammengerechnet – 28 Prozent. [...]

Wann gilt jemand als spießig?

[...] Die Definition des Spießers

Abwertend meint man mit Spießer eine Person, die durch ein starkes Bedürfnis nach sozialer Sicherheit charakterisiert ist. Außerdem hegt sie eine Abneigung
5 gegen Veränderungen der gewohnten Lebensumgebung und ist geistlich unbeweglich sowie überaus konform mit gesellschaftlichen Normen. Gemeint sind also engstirnige Menschen, die viel Wert auf geordnete Lebensverhältnisse legen und sich anders lebenden Personen gegenüber recht
10 intolerant verhalten.
Der Begriff gilt seit dem 19. Jahrhundert als Kurzwort für die sogenannten Spießbürger. Vermutlich geht die allgemeine Bezeichnung auf das Mittelalter zurück. Dort wohnten Bürger in der Stadt, die diese mit dem Spieß als
15 Waffe verteidigten. [...]

Was genau bedeutet es, „spießig" zu sein?

Was bedeutet es überhaupt, „spießig" zu sein? Grundsätzlich ist das Urteil eher subjektiv. Und nicht zu verleugnen ist, dass dieser Begriff eher negativ behaftet
20 ist. [...] Außerdem halten sich „Spießer" irgendwie immer an Regeln und sind übervorsichtig. Wenig Spontanität und ein hohes Sicherheitsbedürfnis stehen an oberster Stelle. Ob das wirklich negativ ist oder nicht, liegt ebenfalls im Auge des Betrachters.

Anzeichen dafür, dass Sie so werden, wie Ihre „spießigen" Eltern

25 [...] Beispiele, die als Anzeichen fürs Spießer-Dasein gelten.
1. Sie sind ständig müde und müssen das auch jeden wissen lassen.
2. Sie schalten beim Feiern jetzt einen Gang zurück und eskalieren nicht, damit Sie am Montagmorgen bloß nicht verkatert auf der Arbeit erscheinen
3. „Früher war alles besser" zählt nun zu Ihren Lieblingssätzen?
4. Sie ziehen praktische und sichere Kleidung einem perfekten Style vor? Fahrradhelme stehen nun auch ganz oben auf der Fahrrad-Tagesordnung.
5. Sie bekommen keine Trends mehr mit und verbringen jeden Abend mit „Netflix and Chill."
6. Ihre aktuelle Bettwäsche wird ins Farbschema integriert und jede Woche putzen Sie Ihr Auto.
7. Sie planen heute schon, was Sie morgen kochen werden.
8. Sie beschweren sich beim Vermieter wegen der lauten Kinder und der wilden Partys.
9. Sonntagabend schauen Sie Tatort mit Ihrem Liebsten.
10. 22 Uhr ist die neue Schlafenszeit.
11. Ihre Wohnung ist keine Jugendherberge mehr.
12. Sie erkennen nun den „guten" Wein.
13. Sie regen sich übers Wetter auf.
14. Das Grüne in Ihrem Fenstersims ist nun eine Orchidee und auch andere Pflanzen finden in Ihrer Wohnung Platz.

Quellen (gekürzt): https://learngerman.dw.com/de/16-mentalit%C3%A4t/l-18945073/lm# (S. 120); zdf.de Nachrichten: Panorama: „Viele 25-Jährge wohnen daheim: Hotel Mama bleibt beliebt", 05.08.2020, https://www.zdf.de/nachrichten/panorama/kinder-wohnen-100.html; https://www.blog.de/wann-gilt-jemand-als-spiessig/#die-definition-des-spiessers

Ready for the next level?

1 **a** Think about the different topics in the workshop and choose the one you liked the most. Create a mind map with your topic in the middle and fill it with the relevant vocabulary.

b Find a partner with the same topic and compare your mind maps. Combine the two to make a more comprehensive one. Find tips on collating ideas on **pp. 139/140**.

c Find pairs who have chosen a different topic and present your mind maps. Make notes and ask more detailed questions about each other's topic.

2 Read the information, then follow the instructions.

1 On a card, write three adjectives that could describe a young person's state of mind. Label your list, but do not use your name.
2 Collect the cards and shuffle them.
3 Pick a card. Make sure it's not yours. Choose one of the adjectives and think of what advice you could give to the writer.
4 Write a text (about 100 words) about what you would do if you were feeling that way. Use the same label for your text as on the card.
5 Display your text in the classroom. Find the one that is for you and read it.

Being a teenager in the 21st century is challenging. While there are immense advantages to benefit from, being bombarded by the never-ending flow of news, social media posts and adverts makes it hard to stay calm and focused on what matters – school, family, friends and, most importantly, yourself.

3 Listen to a radio interview with Alexandra Belman, a psychologist specializing in adolescent behaviour. 63)) As you listen, choose the correct ending to complete the sentences.

1 The expert Alexandra Belman …
 a focuses on theoretical research in teenage behaviour.
 b helps teenagers with behavioural problems.
 c uses her expertise to help both parents and teenagers.

2 According to Nicky, the interviewer, …
 a parents understand their teenage children because they remember being young.
 b parents question their ability to remember their teenage years.
 c parents find it challenging to understand their teenage children.

3 Being a teenager …
 a is different now than it was in earlier decades.
 b means that you go through the same experiences regardless when you live.
 c is challenging, because their parents don't understand them.

4 The reason youth culture exists is because …
 a it helps teenagers to resolve conflicts with the parents.
 b it's how teenagers shape their identities.
 c teenagers distance themselves from their parents' culture.

5 Eric Erikson called the conflict teenagers go through …
 a identity crisis.
 b development in the life cycle.
 c conflict resolution.

6 Peter Blos describes the process teenagers go through …
 a the same way as Erikson does.
 b differently to Erikson's interpretation.
 c as a possible stage in teenagers' lives.

7 The outcome of this exploratory stage …
  a is likely to be identical for all teenagers.
  b can be different for teenagers.
  c is what Erikson calls 'Identity Achievement'.

8 During the socialization process, teenagers …
  a look outside the family to help them form their identities.
  b seek out peers who have the same values as them.
  c rely on trends to determine the youth culture they want.

4 **a** Read the text about Louis Braille, a famous teen inventor and complete it with the correct form of the verbs from the box.

adapt ■ adopt ■ award ■ be (2x) ■ become ■ develop ■ die ■ invent ■ lose ■ spread ■ start ■ use

Famous teens in history: Louis Braille, the inventor

Braille ▮1▮ born in Coupvray, France, on 4 January, 1809. Due to an accident, he ▮2▮ his sight at the age of three. He was ten years old when he ▮3▮ a scholarship to France's prestigious Royal Institute for Blind Youth in Paris. At the time the system of reading was pretty basic, just raised letters on a
5 page. […] [Although the Institute had access to a dot-based code system which ▮4▮ by the military for communication in the dark, it was complicated and slow to use. Using this idea, Braille ▮5▮ working on a new code that ▮6▮ quicker and more efficient.] By the time he was 15, Braille's new system was basically complete. […]
10 Braille is not a language, it's a system of writing, which means it ▮7▮ to different languages. Braille codes ▮8▮ for maths and scientific formulae. [He also] ▮9▮ a system for writing music, too. […] Braille's system ▮10▮ (not) by the Royal Institute
15 until 1854, two years after Braille ▮11▮. The system soon ▮12▮ the method of choice among blind French-speakers, and by the 1880s ▮13▮ to virtually every school for the blind in the world.

Sources (abbreviated and adapted): ll. 4-13: "The incredible story of the boy who invented Braille", BBC Ideas, 22.06.2019, https://www.youtube.com/watch?v=o9BOQ6IpTSE [12.07.2022]; ll. 14-18: Linda Cerce, "Inventor Louis Braille touched lives with literacy", NJ State Library: TBBC Blog, 04.02.2022, https://www.njstatelib.org/inventor-louis-braille-touched-lives-with-literacy/ [12.07.2022]

b Research another famous teen. You can choose another inventor, an actor, a singer or an activist like Kenidra Woods. Make notes and then give a short presentation. (Tips on **pp. 22/23, 105, 142/143.**)

5 Brainstorm what defines your generation. Think of music, fashion, the use of social media, etc. Then write an essay (200 words) with the title: 'My generation'. Swap your essay with a partner and give each other feedback to improve your work. If you need help, you find more support in your student's book: tips on collecting notes and ideas (**pp. 139/140**), writing an argumentative essay (*TIP* on **p. 109**), giving constructive feedback (**p. 144**).

p. 151

Short story: Vesna Main, 'A Hair Clasp' (2018)

1 Before you read

a The story is called 'A Hair Clasp'. Have a look at picture A and describe the object in as much detail as possible.

b With a partner, collect ideas as to when and why somebody would wear such a piece of jewellery.

c The first sentence of the story reads: 'We went swimming, my daughter and I'. Look at picture B and describe the scene (place, people, atmosphere, emotions, etc.).

> Vesna Main is a Croatian writer, was born in Zagreb and is living in London and France. She studied comparative literature and holds a PhD from the Shakespeare Institute in Birmingham. She has worked as a journalist, teacher and has also been a lecturer at universities in Nigeria and the UK. She published two novels, *A Woman with No Clothes On* (2008) and *The Reader the Writer* (2015), and a collection of short stories.

We went swimming, my daughter and I. She was twenty and a good swimmer. I didn't need to keep an eye on her. I read on the beach while she went into the sea. From time to time, I lifted
5 my eyes from my book and looked at her. She would smile and raise an arm, as if in greeting. Or perhaps she wanted to say, 'Look at me,' as children often do, seeking recognition[1] even when they are past their childhood. The last
10 time I saw her, the waves had grown and the choppy sea tossed her around playfully. One moment she was hidden under the foamy[2] whiteness, another moment she was riding the crest[3] of the waves, shimmering against the glistening[4] surface of the water. I smiled and 15 thought how much I loved her. This happy young woman. I wanted to shout how lovely she looked, but there was no point as my voice would have been lost in the crushing power of the sea. So I greeted her with my hand up in the 20 air and went back to my reading. The next time I looked up, I couldn't see her. I saw other swimmers, a dozen of them, enjoying the waves. I wanted to see her smiling and communicating her pleasure to me so I climbed 25 a bridge next to where they were swimming.

---

[1] **recognition** *hier:* attention – [2] **foamy** of a mass of small bubbles on the surface of a liquid – [3] **crest** the highest point of a wave – [4] **glistening** shining with reflecting light

I still couldn't spot her. A thought crossed my mind that she may have drowned. I have always been a worrier but sometimes your worst fears come true. I looked harder, I moved around the bridge but I still couldn't see her. My chest tightened[5] with fear. Was this really happening? Then I noticed a beautiful hair clasp, an antique piece that someone must have left there or, more likely, lost. The piece was lying on top of a stone pillar that formed part of the banister[6] of the bridge. Cupping[7] it in the palm of my hand, I caressed the pearly section held by its silver frame. The intricacy[8] of its craft and the smoothness of the object charmed[9] me. As I turned it around, sunshine played hide and seek[10] on its surface. I would have loved to have it but the find was too valuable not to report. But something told me that I had the right to keep it. I clutched[11] it firmly and walked home alone. I will be careful never to lose it.

from: Vesna Main, *Temptation: A User's Guide*, Salt Publishing: London, 2018, pp. 33f.

2 Grasping the story

a Read the story carefully, then summarize it in two to three sentences.

b With a partner, discuss your impression of the story. Do you like it? Why / Why not?

c Choose one sentence that strikes you most and explain why.

3 Close reading

a Read ll. 1 – 21. Compare the story to your description of picture B. Contrast the scenes by finding similarities and differences.

b Look at the *TIP* box, then read ll. 21 – 42. Divide the story into different parts. Take into account the way the narrator uses tension to play with the reader's attention until the very end.

c Point out three literary devices in the text and examine their effect.

d Analyse the narrator's point of view.

e Interpret the message the author wants to convey.

> **TIP**
>
> Every story has a 'story arc', that means the path the story follows. Usually, it provides a beginning, a middle and ending of the story.
> - **Exposition:** This is the reader's introduction to the story. The exposition offers background information about the main character(s), the setting, and time period.
> - **Rising action:** This is when conflict begins to develop. It is usually a series of events that put the main events of the story in motion.
> - **Climax:** This is the highest point of tension and usually the point with the greatest intensity in a story.
> - **Falling action:** The falling action is the opposite of the rising action, i. e. all the events that happen after the climax and lead the readers to the solution.
> - **Resolution:** This is the ending or conclusion of the story. It can be happy or tragic, depending on the genre.

4 Further activities

a A short story usually has an open or a surprise ending. Read ll. 42 – 46, then, with a partner, share ideas for a follow up of the story. Make notes and present your ideas to your class. (Tips on **pp. 139/140, 22/23, 142/143.**)

b Write a diary entry (180 words) and reflect on what has happened. Decide which perspective you want to take – that of the parent or that of the daughter, who – in this case – has survived.

c Pay special attention to the vocabulary. Collect adjectives and verbs from the story that describe objects in detail and the atmosphere.

---

[5] **to tighten** to become tense and stiff – [6] **banister** a row of wooden posts with a bar along the top – [7] **to cup** to form a cup with your hands – [8] **intricacy** the state of containing a large number of details – [9] **to charm** to please or delight, e. g. through attraction – [10] **to play hide and seek** a children's game in which one player shuts their eyes while the others hide, and then goes to look for them – [11] **to clutch** to grasp or hold sth. tightly

Drama: Craig Taylor, *Play no. 14* (2009)

1   **Before you read**

a Look at the photos and describe what you see. What situations are the people in?
Make a list of words and expressions that you associate with the police.

b Compare your list with a partner and sort your words and expressions into positive and
negative aspects.

2   **The play.** Read the play on your own, then do a roleplay in class.

> Craig Taylor (* 1976) in Edmonton, Canada, is a journalist who is currently living in London. He writes for several British
> and Canadian newspapers and magazines. His *One Million Tiny Plays about Britain* were originally published by *The
> Guardian*. They are a collection of everyday conversations taking place all around Britain.

*(Two police officers have stopped a young man on
his bicycle in Kennington, south London)*

Police 1   We'd probably let you go if you hadn't
lied.

5 Man   I never lied.

Police 2   What colour was it?

Man   Fine, then. Red, then.

Police 1   Why did you say it was amber?

Man   Because it was amber.

10 Police 2   Then how did we both see you cycle
through a red light?

Man   You think I know that? Maybe you
don't see colour so well. Maybe I look
white to you.

15 Police 2   You don't look white to us. (*pause*)

Police 1   Nice bicycle.

Man   Yeah, it is.

Police 1   A little small for you.

Police 2   You didn't want to buy a proper sized
one? 20

Police 1   When you went to the shop?

Police 2   When did you buy that bicycle, Derek?

Man   I never bought it.

Police 2   Really? You never bought it?

Police 1   That's surprising. 25

Man   Because it's my brother's.

Police 2   He likes pink bikes, does he, Derek?
Small bikes, Derek?

Man   Why you calling me that? It's not my
name. 30

Police 2   What's your name?

Man   It's … you know.

Police 1	No, we don't know.
Man	It's Chilly.
35 Police 2	That's not what it says on your driving licence.
Police 1	Why does it say Derek?
Police 2	What's Chilly? Is that your hip hop name?
40 Man	It's my name.
Police 1	Your gangsta name?
Man	It's my name.
Police 1	Do you know what my hip hop name would be? Bizzy.
45 Police 2	Why's that?
Police 1	Because I get busy. I'm generally a busy person.
Police 2	See, we both like hip hop.

Police 1	Respect. (*pause*)
Police 2	So is it Chilly, Derek?	50
Police 1	Put on a jumper.
Police 2	If you're Chilly. (*pause*)
Man	Does that mean I can go?
Police 1	You listen to 50 Cent, Derek?
Man	No.	55
Police 1	What are you listening to? Those are some pretty nice headphones.
Police 2	They must be your brother's too?
Man	They're mine.
Police 2	Like the bike.	60
Police 1	Now, when I ask you what colour that light was what are you going to say? Chilly?
Man	Amber. Whatever. (*pause*) Red.

from: *One Million Tiny Plays About Britain* by Craig Taylor, Bloomsbury Publishing: London, 2009, Kindle version.

3 **Reading for gist**

a Describe where the scene takes place and describe the situation, summarizing what the three people are talking about.

b Explain who the characters in the dialogue are and their relationship to each other.

4 **Reading for detail.** Read the text again and do the tasks.

1 Look at lines 1 – 11 of the play and describe the structure of the sentences. Is there anything unusual?
2 Identify the stylistic devices used and explain what function they have in this text.
3 Examine what roles the issues of colour and hip-hop play in this microdrama.
4 Compare the structure of this microdrama with what you know about the structure of a short story and that of a classical play.

5 **Literary analysis.** Using your findings from tasks **3** and **4**, write an analysis of the play (200 words).

> **TIP**
>
> Some key terms for analysing dramatic texts:
> Find more information and terms on **pp. 64, 125** (*TIP*) and in the **Vocabulary Appendix**.
> - **comedy:** play with a happy ending
> - **tragedy:** play with a sad ending
> - **act and scenes:** the formal structure of a play; each act usually consists of one or more scenes
> - **playwright:** the author of a play
> - **pun:** a play with words
> - **properties ('props'):** items used by actors on stage
> - **stage directions:** what the author wants the actors to do on stage
> - **register:** a particular type of language used in a specific situation or for a specific purpose
> - **comic relief:** a means of including humorous elements in the plot, often to relieve tension. It can be an amusing scene or character, a comic remark or incident.

🔊)) 64 Marcus Sedgwick

Cudweed and the Bagpipes

THREE

A couple of weeks passed, and we settled into a routine. Every day Cudweed and I would leave the Ugly Sheep after breakfast and go along to the factory. It was always my favourite time, because
5 after that first day when we arrived in the thunderstorm, the weather had been lovely; not what I was expecting from Scotland at all. And it was always really nice to fly along beside the loch on the way, while Cudweed stomped[1] along the road.
10 Everything was very beautiful indeed and I decided that I liked Scotland a lot. And then there was the
15 other reason why I enjoyed the morning journey to the factory – namely that every morning Catriona was sitting on a fence post[2]
20 at the end of the lane that led up to the factory.

Now, usually, she flew off as soon as she saw us coming, and I wondered if she was very shy, or if she had really already decided not to talk to me for some
25 reason or other. But one morning she didn't fly away and we actually spoke.
'Kork?' I said, and she said, 'Ark-ark.'
So naturally, I said, 'Kronk.'
She looked at me and tipped her head[3] on one side.
30 Then she said, 'Rork' and flew off.
So that was that, and at least it was a start, but I knew no more about her than before, really.
And Cudweed, meanwhile, was very unhappy.
The good news was that it turned out he was very
35 good at making bagpipes. He had a natural talent for cutting and sawing and drilling things.
It was as if he was born to make bagpipes – he did everything really, really well. When Hamish explained something to the three students, Cudweed would
40 understand it immediately and do it perfectly. In fact, he was so good that he was better than Andrew, whose ancestors had made bagpipes, and he was even better than Wiebke, who had already been helping to make the German version of bagpipes for a while.
45 Everyone watched Cudweed with admiration[4] as he rapidly completed his first set of bagpipes and, though he couldn't play a note on them when Hamish gave them a try, he announced that he was impressed.
50 So you might have thought that all this would make Cudweed happy – he was getting on very well with Andrew. Andrew told us that his favourite hobby was rock climbing, and he pointed at a vertical[5] cliff that was on the other side of the valley, near the Ugly
55 Sheep.
'I'd love to climb that!' Andrew said, and Cudweed stared at the cliff and just looked rather ill. I think he was remembering the window cleaning at the castle. Cudweed was also getting on very well with Wiebke.
60 It turned out that both Andrew and Wiebke were also staying at the Ugly Sheep – we just didn't meet them on that first morning because we were late to the factory. And, after a few days, I realized that Cudweed liked Wiebke in the same way that I liked Catriona. It
65 seemed to make him happy to be making friends, and he was great at learning how to make bagpipes.
But!
But he was still worrying.
He was worrying because he wasn't going to be at
70 home for his birthday, and the thing with Cudweed has always been that he worries SO MUCH.
I sat down with him one day.
We were back at the Ugly Sheep, after a hard day's work. Well, it had been a hard day for Cudweed
75 – who had had to do the trickiest part of making bagpipes; putting the whole thing together. This was

---

[1] **to stomp** [stɒmp] stapfen; stampfen – [2] **(fence) post** [pəʊst] (Zaun-)Pfahl – [3] **to tip one's head** [tɪp wʌnz 'hed] seinen Kopf neigen – [4] **admiration** [ˌædməˈreɪʃən] Bewunderung – [5] **vertical** [ˈvɜːtɪkl] vertikal; senkrecht

his second set and when he had finished, Hamish had declared that it was even better than Cudweed's first attempt.

80 'In fact,' Hamish said, 'this is good enough to go in a shop and be sold. I am really impressed!'

But the fact that Hamish was impressed did not cheer Cudweed up. He was still upset about his birthday.

'Rerk,' I said to him.

85 'I know, Edgar,' he replied. 'But I just can't help it.'

'Kraaark,' I suggested. 'Konk?'

'I know. Solstice always says the same thing. She says once I worry about one thing, I start worrying about *everything*.'

90 'Rork-rork,' I pointed out.

'I know. I'm really good at making bagpipes. And I think Wiebke is really nice; and Andrew makes me laugh, but I can't stop worrying anyway! And then I worry that I'm worrying!'

95 I pecked his head in case it would help him to stop worrying. It didn't.

'And now,' said Cudweed, 'I have to play a tune on the bagpipes at a little party in two weeks' time and I can't play a single note yet. I'll be awful. Everyone

100 will laugh.'

I thought about this and I decided that it was time for Cudweed to stop worrying about everything. I thought that maybe the best thing to do would be to leave him here alone, so he would have to just cope

105 by himself. But every time I thought that, Catriona would fly past in the distance and I would change my mind. But at least, he could do something about learning to play the bagpipes.

'Kronk,' I told him. 'Ark, ark, awwwwwk. Rerk.'

110 He looked at me.

'Do you think she would?'

'Rork!' I said.

'Then okay,' he said, 'I will. I'll ask Wiebke to give me some really easy lessons and learn to play one simple

115 tune on my bagpipes.'

'Rurk!' I said, because it was great to see him looking a bit happier.

'I'll ask her tomorrow in fact!' and he even smiled.

So there was Cudweed looking a little happier, but just at that moment, Catriona flew by, as if she was

120 in a hurry, and my little heart jumped for a moment, and then sank sadly back down again.

The second half of Cudweed's work experience rushed by.

125 He had texted Solstice to tell her how upset he was that he would not be at home for his birthday, and she told him not to worry. She said they were sending his presents to him at the Ugly Sheep, and that he ought to look forward to having a birthday somewhere new

130 for once. (And in a very special place.)

Cudweed meanwhile worked on his third set of bagpipes, which was impressive, because Andrew and Wiebke were still finishing their first ones. Hamish said that if Cudweed wanted to actually come and

135 work for him for real when he grew up, he would be very welcome, because he had never seen anyone who was so good at making bagpipes with so little experience.

And when he wasn't working on making his bagpipes,

140 he was learning how to play them. He had asked Wiebke if she could teach him something simple to play, because he was really not very good at playing the instrument. Andrew was there and he asked if she would help him, too, because he was also having

145 trouble. And Wiebke had agreed, so now, every lunchtime, the three of them took their sandwiches out into the field behind the factory and Wiebke showed them the basics; blowing into the bag to keep air in it, squeezing it gently to send air down the

150 chanter, and then she taught them a simple tune each.

So all that was going well, but still Cudweed worried.

He worried that he wasn't good enough.

He worried that he would make a fool of himself at the concert.

155 He worried that he worried.

There was someone else who was worried that he wasn't good enough: me.

---

6 **appealing** [ə'pi:lɪŋ] attraktiv

I wondered what it was. I had tried to speak to
Catriona every day, and the more I tried, the less it
160 seemed she wanted to have to do with me.
Every day I flew upside down, or sang a raven song,
or generally tried to look cute and appealing[6], but
eventually I had to accept that she just wasn't
interested in me. It made me very sad because I had
165 been happy being a single raven for a very long time.
And now I had suddenly seen another raven I liked
and thought it would be nice to spend time with her,
but she didn't want to spend time with me …
But then, one afternoon, I found out why.
170 I saw Catriona hurrying across the valley, with half a
dead rabbit in her beak, and I thought I would try
one last time to chat to her, so I followed …

She flew a long way, and I flapped along behind and
did my best to keep up, but she was very fast and
175 agile as she flew up the mountainside, to her nest,
I assumed[7].
And I was right, she was flying home, and when I got
there, I saw something I hadn't expected.
There was a nest and in the nest were three baby
180 ravens, to whom she was busy feeding the mouse.
Well, I hadn't expected that.
'Kork!' I said, by way of hello, and when she turned
and saw me, she said, 'kork'.
And then, finally, we had a proper chat.
185 I asked who the baby ravens were, and she explained
that they were hers. And I asked where their father
was and she explained that he had been struck by[8]
lightning a few months before and now she was left
to bring them up all by herself, which was why she
190 was so busy all of the time.
'Kark,' I said, and that was just to say that I was sorry
to hear about her husband, and I understood that
things were difficult for her. And that I would leave
her to get on with looking after the babies.

195 'Rark,' she said, which was her way of saying that
she thought I was a nice raven and she was sorry not
to have more time to spend with me, but that was
how it was.
So I left her in peace feeling sorry for her, and for her
200 husband who had been fried[9]. No raven deserves
such an end. …
Then it was May 26th.
It had come around so suddenly; Cudweed's birthday
and the day of the party to celebrate the end of the
205 work experience. Just as Solstice had promised, there
was a pile[10] of presents waiting for Cudweed at
breakfast time, and he opened them all, and I was
pleased with him, because he actually managed to
enjoy himself a little. Finally, he's growing up, I
210 thought!
But he was still worried about the concert. Hamish
had said he was inviting 'one or two people', but in
the end there was a group of forty or so local people
who had come to hear the three students each play a
215 tune on their new bagpipes.
Andrew went first, and he was very good.
Everyone clapped and cheered.
Then Wiebke went second, and she was incredible.
She played traditional German tunes and some
220 Scottish ones too, and everyone clapped and cheered
even more. Then it was Cudweed's turn, and he was
very, very nervous, so nervous he made two attempts
at starting his tune, but on the third go, he got it
right, and although it was simple, everyone was
225 really pleased and clapped and cheered for him, too.
When it was over, I flew over to him and pecked him
on his head, just to congratulate him and because I
wanted to point something out to him.
'Rurk,' I said, and he said, 'Edgar, what is it? You
230 mustn't worry about me so much, I am fine.'
But he hadn't seen what I had seen, so I pecked him
again, from behind, and when he turned around, he
found himself face to face with the family; Solstice,
and his mother and father, and even the twins.
235 'What are you doing here?' he asked, looking
surprised.
'Oh, Cudweed!' said Minty. 'You're so clever to play
that tune!'
'You heard it?' he asked.
240 'Yes, we sneaked in[11] at the back,' said Solstice. 'We
wanted to surprise you!'
'They told us you made the bagpipes, too,' said
Valevine. 'Is that true?'

---

[7] to **assume** [əˈsjuːm] annehmen – [8] **to be struck by** [biː ˈstrʌk baɪ] von etw. getroffen werden – [9] **to fry** [fraɪ] braten – [10] **pile** [paɪl] Stapel – [11] **to sneak in**
[ˈsniːk ɪn] sich hineinschleichen

'Yes, in fact I have made three sets,' said Cudweed.

245 'Wow,' said Solstice. 'My little brother is growing up!'

'Finally,' muttered[12] Valevine, and I thought that was mean, so I pecked him, hard.

And while he was trying to fight me off and getting cross, Wiebke came over, and Cudweed said, 'Family, 250 can I introduce you to my friend, Wiebke? She is German and she would like to come and stay with us in the castle during the summer. I assume that is fine with you all?'

And then everyone stared at Cudweed, open 255 mouthed, because he had never sounded so mature[13] before in his whole life.

'Er, yes, of course, dear. Wiebke, how nice to meet you,' said Minty.

'Also, our friend Andrew has invited Wiebke and me 260 to go rock climbing in a few days' time, and I would like to go.'

Everyone stared at Cudweed *again*, because we were all thinking about the fuss with the window cleaning at the castle, which had gone very badly.

265 'I know what you're thinking,' Cudweed said. 'But that accident with the window cleaning wasn't my fault. If you three hadn't surprised me and been shouting at me and getting me to read things, it might have gone a lot better. So, I would like to go 270 rock climbing to find out.'

Everyone stared at Cudweed so hard that I thought their eyeballs might fall out. But they didn't.

So, a few days later, Cudweed and Wiebke went rock climbing with Andrew and, do you know what?

275 Everything went *absolutely perfectly*.

I sat with the rest of the family as we watched them climbing up the side of a rock face in the valley near the Ugly Sheep, and I knew that Cudweed had finally started to grow up and look after himself. But the 280 main thing that seemed to have changed was this; he was worrying about things a whole lot less.

And that would be nice for everyone. But I realized something for me, too. Cudweed had given me an idea. If he could invite Wiebke to stay with us at the 285 castle, in the summer, there was nothing to stop me coming to Scotland from time to time to see a certain lady raven, and maybe even help her look after her baby ravens a little. From time to time.

So as Cudweed reached the top of a cliff face, I flew 290 up to congratulate him, with a loud 'kork!', because I was very proud of him, and then I set off for the mountainside, to see what Catriona thought about my idea …

(And do you know what? She said yes.)

⇒ THE END ⇐

---

[12] **to mutter** [ˈmʌtə] murmeln – [13] **mature** [məˈtʃʊə] erwachsen

Projects and skills

1 At the end of this workshop, you will give a presentation.

- Choose one of the **topic areas** given below and respond to one of the propositions (**1.**, **2.**) given for that topic area.
- For the proposition chosen, you must decide whether to agree, disagree or take a neutral stance towards it.
- You can choose the form your presentation takes. For example, it could be a talk, an article, a blog, a video or a mixture of media.
- Your presentation must show confident use of the skills which you will be practising during the workshop.
- You may cover similar ground to the texts in this workshop, but you must also do independent research, and provide references for your sources.

Propositions

Climate and sustainability

1. Individuals cannot affect climate change: the responsibility lies with governments and big companies.
2. Achieving net zero carbon emissions by 2050 is impossible.

Media and communication

1. Social media does more harm than good.
2. Modern means of communicating are faster than what came before, but they aren't better.

2 Read the following extracts and note down which key words you would use to summarize the topic in each extract. The first key word has been **highlighted** for you.

1 Air **pollution** is choking our cities and causing a global health crisis. Most pollution on our roads comes from burning fossil fuels, and in the UK the main culprit is diesel-using cars and vans.

2 [This] is thought to affect around 5% of young people and has been described as more addictive than cigarettes and alcohol.

3 The rise of smartphones and tablets means children's relationships are now increasingly conducted online, and they are navigating new friendships often unchaperoned and hidden from view. In the playground or the living room at home, as adults we can observe how children are interacting with each other – and step in if we see anything concerning. In a world of 24-hour connectivity, these protections don't exist online.

4 Honey isn't the only thing bees give us. They also provide us with food by pollinating a huge range of crops, not to mention wild plants. But, like many other parts of the natural world, bees are at risk and the way we produce our food is to blame.

5 The trend over the last decade has been for increasing internet use among the older population. However, a substantial group – including the majority of those age 75 and over – are not online.

6 Soy beans are an excellent source of protein [...] [but] the agricultural industry has also become reliant on these beans for animal feed. [T]he drive to produce greater amounts of cheap meat and dairy is accelerating climate change and destroying forests.

7 New levels of connectivity + technology are further compounding + causing new exclusions. These often reflect, reproduce + amplify divides which exist between socio economic classification, ethnicity, + gender to name but a few.

Sources of texts 1 – 6 (abbreviated and adapted): see text credits

3 Match the definitions with words from the texts. Which of these words could be useful in your presentation?
Is there other vocabulary you would include?
Explain your answers.

1 to fill a space so as to make movement difficult or impossible
2 capable of making someone form a habit
3 not supervised
4 dependent on
5 to make the negative aspects of something worse
6 to add detail

4 Divide your group into two subgroups. Group A watches video 10 and group B watches video 11. Do the tasks.

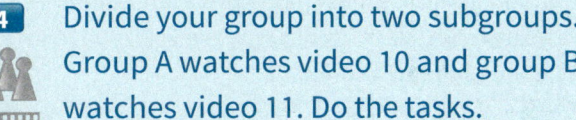
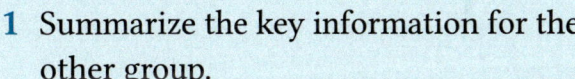

1 Summarize the key information for the other group.
2 Explain how well the video fits with the propositions.
3 Say how well you think the presenter conveys the information.

In-depth

Climate and sustainability. Find out what is meant by 'the just transition' and explain whether you think it is important and why.

Media and communication. Find relevant articles or discussions in your usual source of news. What are people's current interests? Are their interests the same as or different from yours? Why do you think this is?

Text types (1): Text analysis

1 **Text types**

a Read the text about an organization called the Climate Group and do the tasks.
Decide which of the two statements characterizes the Climate Group better.

1 It's a company that collects accurate information about environmental problems.
2 It's an organization that campaigns to improve the environment.

b Which words and expressions in the texts helped you to decide? Give line numbers.

The Climate Group

A We're an international non-profit founded in 2003, with offices in London, New York, New Delhi, Amsterdam and Beijing.

B [Since 2003,] we've grown our network to
5 include over 500 multinational businesses in 175 markets worldwide. [...]

C Science says that we must cap global warming at 1.5°C to avoid the disastrous effects of climate change. To be in with a fighting chance
10 at doing this, we must halve global emissions in the next ten years – that's why the 2020s have to be the Climate Decade.

D **Our mission** is to drive climate action. Fast.

E **Our goal** is for a world of net zero carbon emissions by 2050, with greater prosperity for all.

F 15 **We make it happen:** we convince, challenge and help organizations to make commitments, then turn them into action.
We multiply it: we build and run networks. We join up organizations to unlock the power of collective action that shares the same ambitions and creates influence.
We shout about it: we share what we achieve together to show more organizations what they could do.

G 20 **Scale:** we power large networks and hold each organization accountable.
Speed: we focus on action now – not action tomorrow.

H **We work with** leaders and decision makers from business and government because they shape the market frameworks that can help the
25 world achieve net zero emissions by 2050. They have the tools and influence to make it possible in the time we have left.

I **Our work is focused on systems** with the highest emissions and where our networks have
30 the greatest opportunity to drive change. They include energy, transport, built environment and industry. [...]

Source (abbreviated and adapted): https://theclimategroup.prod.acquia-sites.com/about-us

2 **Vocabulary: Persuasive language**

a Look at these words and phrases from the text. Would you use them in …
- a simple, factual description of a problem?
- a description to persuade people that a problem is urgent?

1 we must cap global warming (ll. 7f.)
2 the disastrous effects of climate change (ll. 8f.)
3 the 2020s have to be the Climate Decade (ll. 11f.)
4 Our mission is to drive climate action. Fast. (l. 13)
5 We make it happen (l. 15)
6 We shout about it (l. 19)
7 Speed: we focus on action now – not action tomorrow. (l. 21)
8 to make it possible in the time we have left (ll. 26f.)

b Practise saying the expressions in **a** aloud.

3 **Planning: Structuring presentations around key questions.**
Match the questions to the paragraphs in the text in 1 (A – I).

1 How big are we? Where do we work?
2 How will we know when we have succeeded?
3 In what specific areas do we work?
4 What does our organization do to help the environment?
5 What is good about the way we do our work? What makes us different?
6 What is the problem we are trying to solve?
7 What kind of organization are we? Where are we based?
8 What was our organization created to do?
9 Who helps us with our work?

> **TIP**
>
> Writing questions is often a good way to structure a text. First, think about all the questions that someone might ask you (or that you would like them to ask you). Then answer those questions in your presentation.

4 **In-depth**

Look at the 17 sustainable development goals. Choose one goal and search for a campaign that deals with the goal you have chosen. Find some expressions that are important for this campaign and make a list of keywords.
Decide which ones might be useful for your presentation on the proposition you have chosen (p. 132).

SUSTAINABLE DEVELOPMENT GOALS

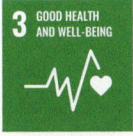

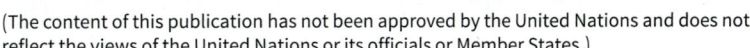

(The content of this publication has not been approved by the United Nations and does not reflect the views of the United Nations or its officials or Member States.)

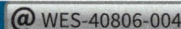

Text types (2): Grammar and style

 1 Planning: Writing for a specific audience.

Read texts A and B and answer these questions.

1 Who do you think wrote them and why?
2 Who are they written for?
3 What are the most important differences between them?
4 How does the language used in them vary?

2 Persuasive and explanatory texts: Grammar and language features

a Here are some ways writers and speakers use language to describe a problem and explain how to deal with it. Which of these techniques (1 – 10) are used in Text A and which in Text B?

1 Repeating the same word or phrase
2 Using contracted forms to make the tone friendly
3 Using *must* to say that something is urgent and has to happen
4 Using *people* or *you/your* to give general advice
5 Using phrases such as *A good way of …* and *It's OK to …*, to show that you are giving advice (and not telling people what to do)
6 Using short sentences for emphasis
7 Using uncontracted forms to make the tone serious
8 Using *we/our* to get the reader / listener to agree with the argument
9 Using modal forms *might, can, could* to make a suggestion less strong
10 Writing text that could easily be read aloud as part of a speech to an audience

b List the examples of the language types in **a** (1 – 10) that you can find in the two texts. One example is given below.

1 Repeating the same word or phrase:

Text A: Now is the moment to … (ll. 14 + 16)

Text A

This is our darkest hour. […]

Biodiversity is being annihilated around the world. Our seas are poisoned, acidic and rising. Flooding and desertification will render vast
5 tracts of land uninhabitable and lead to mass migration.

Our air is so toxic that the United Kingdom is breaking the law. It harms the unborn whilst causing tens of thousands to die. The breakdown
10 of our climate has begun. There will be more wildfires, unpredictable super-storms, increasing famine and untold drought as food supplies and fresh water disappear. […]

Now is the moment to step up. To participate. To
15 refuse to be a bystander.

Now is the moment to begin building a world where love, care and freedom are prioritized. […]

All institutions must communicate the danger we are in. We must be clear about the extreme
20 cascading risks humanity now faces, the injustice this represents, its historic roots, and the urgent need for rapid political, social and economic change. […]

Where we need to be better, we will do what is
25 required. We stand with people of colour, we stand with the trans community, we stand with women, we stand with disabled people, we stand with the Global Majority. We stand with all who are oppressed by our toxic system. […]

Sources (abbreviated): ll. 1-13: from *This Is Not a Drill: An Extinction Rebellion Handbook*, Penguin: London, 2019. Google Books; ll. 4-29: https://extinctionrebellion.uk/2022/01/23/xr-uk-strategy-2022/

Text B

[…] There are lots of benefits to keeping in touch with your friends on social media apps […] – it's been useful during the pandemic or other times when people can't meet up in person. There are
5 some problems with only talking to friends online though, misunderstandings can easily happen, especially if it's just by chat and not video or voice calls. […]

A good way of not getting involved in any social
10 media drama is to try and encourage people to meet in person, where it's safe and possible, or to at least talk in a group call or video chat. This helps people to remember that everyone there is a real person and what they say has
15 consequences. This might not always be possible, but if people see each other in person more often, it can help stop drama before it happens.

If drama does happen, it's okay to just not get
20 involved. One of the good things about group chats is you don't have to respond to anything you don't want to. You can also still talk to people individually if you want to, without having to reply in the main chat. By not getting
25 involved you can let people know you're uncomfortable with drama and won't be taking any sides. […]

Source (abbreviated): https://www.childline.org.uk/get-support/ask-sam/bullying-abuse-and-safety-asksam/social-media-drama/

---

3 'The rule of three'

a Read the text in the box below and find four examples of 'the rule of three' in text A. Do you think this is a good strategy? Why / Why not? Find some other examples of it online.

> Text A uses a presenting strategy called 'the rule of three' (or 'triples'). This is when speakers or writers use a list of three words or expressions. The idea behind it is that a group of three items is more memorable than one item (or another number of items).

b As well as the grammar and language features listed above, persuasive texts often involve
- **emotive language** (vocabulary used to make the reader / listener feel a certain emotion) and
- **hyperbole** (exaggerated language that is used to have an effect on the reader / listener). Are there examples of these in text A?

4 **In-depth**

Look at the propositions again and choose the final topic of your presentation. Then decide on the format of your presentation (written or spoken, for a website or podcast or for a live audience).

Propositions

Climate and sustainability
1. Individuals cannot affect climate change: the responsibility lies with governments and big companies.
2. Achieving net zero carbon emissions by 2050 is impossible.

Media and communication
1. Social media does more harm than good.
2. Modern means of communicating are faster than what came before, but they aren't better.

Planning your presentation

1 **Research: Using your sources**

a Read the texts and do the following tasks.

1 Read the three texts about an innovation which addresses environmental problems and explain where you think the texts come from:

a an abstract introducing an exhibitor at an exhibition for scientists

b a popular science website aimed at the general public

c a university website aimed at all university members, not just scientists

2 Evaluate whether these sources are trustworthy and if you can trust each of them equally. Explain why or why not.

3 Assess if there is enough information for you to write an article about robot bees. If not, explain what else you would like to know.

b Find two more sources of information about robot bees which you trust and which give you the information you want. Explain why you have chosen them and what kind of sources provide useful information when researching online.

2 **Groundbreakers?**

a Here are some inventions which address environmental problems in sustainable and innovative ways. Research one of them, bearing in mind these questions:

● Can you find reliable sources of information in more than one place about this invention?

● Are there positive and negative opinions?

● Are there other similar inventions?

● Are the brand names strong and clear

1 The Seabin

2 Groasis Waterboxx

3 Zéphyr Solar balloon

4 AirCarbon plastic

5 Eka1 and Eka2 seeds

6 Demetra

b Present your findings in a two-minute talk to the class.

Text A ▫▫✕

These Robot Bees Might Save Us From The Bee-Pocalypse

The B-Droid is coming to take real bees' jobs – and that might be exactly what we need.

Without bees, plants go un-pollinated, and eventually we starve. Usually in bleak future scenarios, it's the robots that are causing

5 all the problems, but today the bees are dying with no machine interference. Instead, it's a robot that may save us from their demise: the B-Droid. It's a robotic bee that can buzz between flowers and pollinate plants. And the biggest winner might be the bees, because – if the robot-bees are successful – real bees

10 won't need to be transported all over the world to pollinate commercial crops. They can stay at home and relax. [...]

Text B ▫▫✕

B-Droid – a robot that's busy as a bee

[...] For a number of years, there have been mass deaths of bees worldwide. Environmental pollution, fungi, viruses or parasites might be to blame. Also, bees don't travel long distances well. In

5 the United States they are transported hundreds of kilometres and, after several days of pollination, they die of fatigue. The effects of such a situation may be direr than we all think. It's estimated that a third of all agricultural crops and approximately 90% of plants growing in the wild require pollination, and bees

10 are the main pollinators. [Our scientists] have decided to rise to the challenge and build a robot for pollinating. [...]

Text C ▫▫✕

Could the flying B-Droid help bees with pollination?

[...] Based on the data indicated by a user, the system plans its own operation process and then executes it. This autonomous device finds flowers (recognition), locates them, (positioning

5 system) collects their pollen and transports it to other flowers of the same species (mechanical system). It navigates itself upon the data gathered by a visual system (computer vision) and controls its own actions with a real-time computer system (control system and software). The system is made in two

10 versions – flying and driving (on-ground mobile device). [...]

Sources of texts A – C (abbreviated and adapted): Charlie Sorrel, Fast Company, 14.12.2016, https://www.fastcompany.com/3066318/these-robot-bees-might-save-us-from-the-bee-pocalypse; Warsaw University of Technology, 02.12.2016, https://www.pw.edu.pl/engpw/Research/Business-Innovations-Technology-BIT-of-WUT/B-Droid-a-robot-that-s-busy-as-a-bee; Rafal Dalewski, "B-Droid", SciTech Poland, 2017, http://scitechpoland.com/portfolio/b-droid/ [12.07.2022]

3 Ways of collating ideas

a Everyone needs to find a method to bring together facts, information, ideas and opinions in a way that best helps them to shape a coherent conclusion in written or spoken form. Use mind maps if you find they work for you, but consider these other methods, too. Read the texts, then rank these four methods in your order of preference. Explain your choices.

The mind mash

'Download' all your ideas on a topic onto one sheet of paper – A4 is best for small or standard size handwriting or use A3
5 paper if your handwriting is large. Just keep writing and don't try to organize your notes at all. After you have written down every point, large or small, circle them to divide one from another. Then
10 use different coloured highlighter pens to link ideas. Soon you will have a visual representation of how to organize your ideas about the topic into your presentation. You can then give each
15 highlighter colour a number to show the order in which you're going to present your ideas.
Variation: This method works well for a group, too: fasten an A1 sheet of paper to
20 a large table and sit around it as a group to write your notes. Your first task after every point has been written down and circled is to identify and delete duplications before using highlighters.

Sticky notes shuffling

25 Use multicoloured sticky notes and an A2 or A3 piece of paper. Secure the paper to a wall. Write your ideas / opinions / information / key points onto separate sticky notes. Transfer these to your blank
30 paper. You can then position your keynotes in groups and move them around until you are satisfied with the organization. With this method of collating ideas, it's easy to come back to
35 your wall over a number of days as your planning crystallizes.

+ see next page!

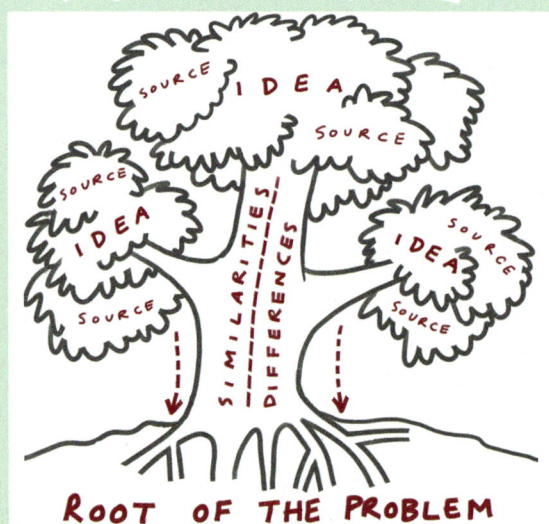

Tree to root

This method helps you to explore a problem by starting with lots of information and gradually digging down to get to the root of the problem.

40 Start at the top of the tree by doing lots of research and grouping together lists of sources and information as the branches and leaves. In the trunk of the tree, explore the similarities and differences in the sources and information you
45 have. At ground level, consider what you know now. Then finish by reaching the root of the problem.

Root to tree

This method starts by exploring exactly what you want to know before finding out information. Write an idea or a question at the root of your tree   50 then work your way up, first breaking your ideas into mini-ideas or smaller questions at ground level. Then, in the trunk of your tree identify where you will look for relevant information. At the top of the tree, do your targeted research to create the   55 sturdy tree branches and finally make smaller branches and leaves with notes of sources, proof or evidence to back up what you want to say.

b Research one of these innovations, collating your information and ideas using one of the methods described in **a**.

- edible cutlery
- converting fog into drinking water
- fabric created from coffee grounds
- an ethical smartphone
- a vegan water bottle

c Write a short article about your chosen innovation showing that you have found reliable sources of information. See the *TIP* on citing your sources.

4 In-depth

Investigate these other methods of collating ideas, and try them out if you find them interesting:

- cluster diagramming
- fishbone diagram
- Venn diagram
- rich pictures or doodles
- the five 'whys'
- causal loop diagramming

> **TIP**
>
> **Citing print sources:** Provide: the name of the authors; the title of the work; the publisher and the year of publication; the page number (if the information can be located on a particular page or if directly quoted); for example:
> Karskens, Grace, *The Rocks*, Melbourne University Press, Carlton (1997), p. 87.
>
> **Citing electronic or online sources:** As a rule, provide as much information as possible concerning authorship, location and availability. These sources require similar information to print sources. However, in some cases extra information may be required: the page, paragraph or section number – what you cite will depend on the information available as many sources don't have pages; the format of the source accessed, e. g. e-book, podcast, etc.; an access date for online sources, that is, identify when a source was viewed or downloaded; and the location, e. g. a database or web address; for example:
> UK Youth homepage: 'About us', copyright UK Youth 2020, last accessed 18th Feb 2022, https://www.ukyouth.org/about-us/.

@ WES-40806-004

Brushing up your dictionary skills

1 A game with a serious purpose

a Look at the different elements of the dictionary entry for 'bluff' and try to remember them.

> **bluff**[1] / blʌf / *noun* (*no plural*) an attempt to make somebody believe you will do something or that you know something: *There was a great bit in the film when the actor said, 'I'm going to push you in the river' to the bad guy but he didn't. It was just a bluff.*
>
> **bluff**[2] / blʌf / *verb* (**bluffs, bluffing, bluffed**) to try to make somebody believe you will do something or that you know something: *I don't think he's going to push him in the river – he's just bluffing.*

b Read the rules and make sure that you understand them. Clarify any questions you might have with a partner or your teacher.

The Rules

1 Your team chooses three unknown English words from a dictionary.
2 Tell the teacher your team's three words.
3 In your team, write three definitions (a, b and c) for each word – only one of which is correct.
4 Each team reads out its three words and three definitions. The other teams note down which defintion they think is correct.
5 For every correct definition, a team gets one point; for every incorrect definition a minus point. (So a team can have a 'minus' score!)
6 The team with the highest number of points wins.

2 Play 'Who's bluffing?'. Read the *TIP*, write your definitions, and play the game.

> **TIP**
>
> You must make the other teams believe your definitions. So:
> 1 Give the correct pronunciation(s) of the word using IPA if possible.
> 2 Say what part of speech your word is and give the correct kind of definition.
> 3 Include multiple meanings.
> 4 Include provenance for the words.
> 5 Give plausible example sentences.

Presentations

1 **Structuring and giving presentations**

a Read the advice. Do you agree with it? Why or why not?

HOW TO PREPARE AND WRITE A PRESENTATION

Preparation for the presentation
1. Decide on whether you are going to agree or disagree with the statement.
2. Think of personal examples from your life or your friends' lives to support your opinion.
3. Do research: find evidence to support our opinion. Also try to find evidence against your opinion.
4. Decide on what the main parts of your argument are and what order to present them in.

Introduction to the presentation
5. Introduce yourself.
6. Explain why you chose the subject and why you think it is important.
7. Make your personal opinion clear – say whether you agree or disagree with the statement.
8. Summarize what you are going to talk about and in what order.

Body of the presentation
9. Present the arguments that support your opinion one by one.
10. For each argument, give evidence that supports it.
11. Describe arguments that go against your opinion and then explain why you think they are wrong.
12. Use strong language when you think a problem is urgent or serious.

Conclusion to the presentation
13. Make it clear that you have come to the end of your presentation.
14. Summarize the main points of your arguments again.
15. Thank the audience for listening and ask for questions.

b The advice in **a** is for a spoken presentation. How would you change it for a written presentation? Give reasons.

2 **Preparing**

a Watch a presentation. In what ways has the presenter followed the advice (5 – 15) in **1a**?

> **TIP**
>
> Notice **how the speaker asks for questions** at the end. If you ask, 'Does anyone have any questions?' it's embarrassing for the speaker and the audience if there aren't any. But if you say, 'I'm sure you have lots of questions for me …', it sounds more confident, and this should encourage the audience to start asking questions.

b Match the expressions from Dr Hilton's presentation with the pieces of advice (5 – 15) in **1a**.
Which piece of advice has she **not** followed?

a For example, we know that … ■ Here are some figures which show …

b Good afternoon, my name is …

c I have a professional interest in this subject, as I … ■ I also have a very personal
interest, because I …

d In this presentation, I'll … ■ First, I'll … ■ Then, I'll ■ After that … ■ I'll finish by …

e My own view is that …

f Of course, I have to accept that not everyone agrees with me. It's true that …

g So, my final point is …

h Thank you everyone for listening to my presentation. I'm sure you will have lots of
questions for me and I'd be very happy to answer them.

i The first point I want to make is ■ My second / third point is …

j … then we will see enormous problems ■ … then there will be a huge crisis

c Think about the advice when preparing your own presentation.
Which pieces of advice will you follow? What language will you use?

- -

3 **Giving a presentation.** There are a lot of things to remember
and check when you prepare for, rehearse, and give a
presentation. Use your preferred method of collating ideas
(from **pages 139/140**) to do your planning. Here is one way of
doing it, using a mind map.

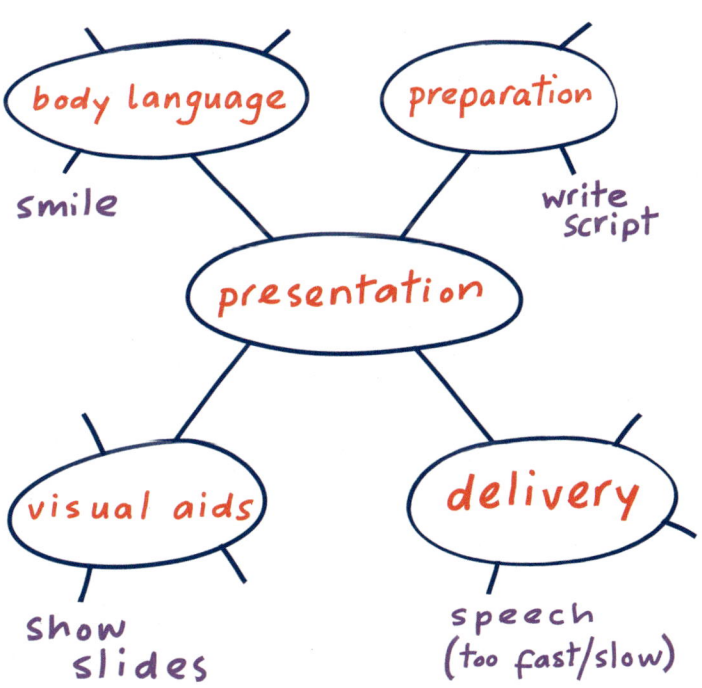

@ WES-40806-004

Giving feedback

1 **Feedback and its importance.** Use these prompts and your own ideas to write a short explanation of what feedback is and what is important when you give feedback.

2 **Preparing to give feedback.** Watch the video and make notes of points, both positive and negative, that you'd like to make to the presenter. Remember to think about her body language and her visual aids as well as what she says, how well she expresses it and organizes it.

3 **Giving feedback.** Write a paragraph of constructive criticism for the presenter of the video or record yourself giving oral feedback. Use your notes from **2** and choose ways of talking about positive and negative points from the box.

> **TIP**
>
> When you want to give **constructive criticism** clearly, don't use a positive comment followed by a negative introduced by 'but'. People tend to hear the positive comment but not the more important negative comment which follows it. You sound polite but you are giving a confusing message. For example, the sentence 'Your body language was really good, but maybe you could gesticulate a bit less' would be more clearly expressed by 'I think your points would come across more clearly if you gesticulated a bit less. Otherwise, your body language was really good.'

Useful phrases: Talking about a presentation

Positive points
- *I thought ... was very effective.*
- *... interested me / fascinated me because ...*
- *I was impressed that you ...*
- *Several times, I recognized that you ...*
- *What I really liked / loved about your presentation / article was that ...*
- *I particularly liked the way you ...*
- *What I liked most was ...*
- *My favourite part was ... because ...*

Negative points and suggestions
- *I wonder if the slide on ... was clear enough.*
- *When you presented ..., I noticed that ...*
- *I think it would be worth mentioning / clarifying ...*
- *When I listened to your introduction / conclusion, I didn't really see what you meant by ...*
- *I couldn't quite understand why ... / the point you were making about ...*
- *Have you considered ...?*
- *I suggest that you think about adding / leaving out ...*
- *It might make a difference if you ...*
- *It might be helpful if you ...*

>>> First track

1 **a** Read what Helen, a participant of the
p.16 DofE Award, wrote about her experience.
Complete the text with the correct form of
the verbs in brackets.

While on my Gold DofE expedition, we
[1] (*walk*) [up a mountain] when we
[2] (*encounter*) some horrendous
weather – with the heavens opening and
5 fog coming down thick (pretty typical
weather for July!). The path [3] (*be*)
very boggy and one of the walkers in my
group managed to slip off some stepping-
stones straight into the bog in a very
10 comedic manner. She [4] (*be able to*) pull
herself out and I attempted to traverse the
same route before ending up waist deep
in the bog myself – ruining the pair of
socks I [5] (*wear*) on my hands having
15 failed to pack any gloves. Covered in bog,
I [6] (*not feel*) too bright myself but my
teammate came off worse and actually
[7] (*go into*) medical shock.
Though we [8] (*see*) exactly where we
20 [9] (*be*) on the map, with the heavy fog
we [10] (*not know*) where we needed to
go next and we [11] (*not want*) to get
caught wandering off the path given the
condition of my teammate. We ended up
25 pitching two tents which the five of us
squeezed into, changing into dry clothes
and trying to get warm while also
[12] (*make*) contact with base camp to
organize a rescue party. […] It was dark
30 by the time our rescue party [13] (*reach*)
us and we then [14] (*have to*) pack our
tents away by torchlight before hiking
down the side of the mountain to find a
clearing in a forest to do a second night
35 of wild camping […]. […] Though [we
were all] pretty miserable at the time, we
all [15] (*enjoy*) looking back on the
adventure and it helped us to develop
resilience in the face of adversity. Our
40 DofE assessor [16] (*tell*) we [17] (*do*)
exactly the right thing given the

circumstances we [had] faced and apparently
we [18] (*be used*) as an example in the years
since: so much so that our group is slightly
45 legendary at our school!

Source (abbreviated and adapted): Helen Sheppard, The Duke of
Edinburgh's Award, 2021, https://www.dofe.org/memories/stories/
helen-sheppard/ [08.07.2022]

2 **b** Choose one of these people mentioned in the
p.19 text for a talk. Use the information in the text, the
notes below and any other facts you find.

Mary Queen of Scots
- 8 December 1542 – 8 February 1587
- Queen of Scotland from 14 December 1542 – 24 July 1567
- married three times
- spent her youth in France, first husband King Francis II of France
- returned to Scotland after the death of her first husband, married Lord Darnley
- had a son who later became James VI of Scotland
- Darnley was killed; Mary married Earl of Bothwell, the man thought to be behind Darnley's murder
- Bothwell had so many enemies – Mary was forced to give up the throne
- escaped to England, imprisoned by her cousin Queen Elizabeth I who later had her executed

Bonny Prince Charlie
- 31 December 1720 – 31 January 1788
- also known as 'The Young Pretender' – he claimed to have rights to the thrones of England, Scotland and Ireland
- led the unsuccessful Jacobite revolution of 1745 – 1746
- escaped from Scotland by ship to France
- wandered around Europe but failed to find supporters
- settled in Rome where he lived until his death
- became a national hero of Scotland and the topic of many ballads and legends

3 The extracts in **2** are from different sources. Which ones? First look at the 'odd one out' task below.

p. 23 Decide which word or phrase doesn't match the source on the left. Where does it belong? Once you have the typical features of each source, say where the extracts in **2** are from. Then discuss your ideas with a partner.

- personal blog / diary: chatty – emotions – objective – personal
- logbook: experience – dates – informal – time expressions
- encyclopaedia / fact sheet: clear – factual information – important events – subjective

4 **b** Match the highlighted adverbs and adverbials

p. 27 in the email to the categories in the Remember box.

Hi May,

I'm glad you liked the video of my brother's wedding. It was an amazing experience, although I'd been to some fantastic cèilidhs before. In fact,
5 my aunt always has a cèilidh on her birthday and they are usually really good fun.
Anyway, you'll never believe it, but one of the musicians was a former band member of the Bay City Rollers, one of Scotland's most famous
10 bands. In the 1970s, they were everywhere and my grandma loved them! IMHO they were pretty tacky. ☺
I'm seriously into a band called Admiral Fallow. They play modern folk music, and I feel great
15 when I listen to them. I've seen them live at least 13 times and I've got all their records. Last year, I saw them play on a number of occasions and each time they just blew me away. Have you heard of them? You should come up and
20 visit and we can go and see them together. I'll check when they're playing again and let you know.

XXX

Kirsty

---

6 **It's your turn: My music.** Write an email (150

p. 27 words) to someone you recently met describing the music you like. Use some of the adverbs, adverbials and adjectives below to make your email more interesting.

- adverbs: always, extremely, just, luckily, never, really, recently, unfortunately
- adverbials: a few days / weeks ago, in the 1990s, last week / month, many / several times
- adjectives: amazing, awesome, cool, fantastic, great, wonderful

5 **a** In the Scottish independence referendum,

p. 31 people of 16 and 17 were given the vote for the first time. Decide if these statements are for or against giving young voters a voice.

A They have no experience of the real world. How can they know what is best for them and for Scotland?

B Issues like health affect everyone – whatever age you are.

C We've held debates at school to discuss independence. Our students are probably better informed than many adults.

D If we're old enough to get married, we're old enough to vote!

E Giving young people the right to vote, won't boost political engagement.

F Lowering the voting age will encourage young people to take responsibility for their own futures.

G Most young people I know will just go along with what their friends do. They don't have their own opinion.

H 18 is the norm in most democracies. 16 and 17-year-olds are still too immature for such a responsibility.

3 In her blog, Kirsty wrote an entry about her
p. 33 brother's wedding. Choose the correct adverbs to complete her post.

Hi guys!
I am sorry I haven't posted anything for a while, but I have a good excuse. My brother got married! You can imagine how **1** (**incredibly /**
5 **probably / quite**) busy I was with the preparations. But now that it's over, I thought I would share the best moments with you. Click on this link to the video about the wedding. It was **2** (**easily / luckily / recently**) the best
10 evening I've had **3** (**for a few hours / in a long time / probably**). There was so much food and the music was great.
My parents had rented the village hall **4** (**for the party / in a long time / luckily**) and there
15 were more than a hundred guests. Everyone was dancing **5** (**easily / enthusiastically / luckily**) and **6** (**for a few hours / for the party / unfortunately**) everyone let their hair down. The band was **7** (**incredibly / probably / quite**)
20 good, although the fiddle player could have been better. **8** (**Luckily / Recently / Unfortunately**), I didn't have to go to school the next day, because we danced **9** (**enthusiastically / late into the night / recently**).
25 I'll **10** (**easily / probably / recently**) have a cèilidh for my eighteenth birthday. What do you think? How would you celebrate your 18th? Send me your comments, ideas …
Kirsty

---

2 **b** Match the **bold** words in the text to the correct
p. 54 meaning below. Then check with a partner.

- **a** develop and grow
- **b** formal ending of a practice or system
- **c** formally become a separate part of sth.
- **d** make up
- **e** taken as a slave
- **f** unit or part, *here*: state

---

1 Ava and Chris continue talking about slavery and
p. 56 the Civil War. Complete their conversation with the verbs in brackets in the correct form. Then listen and check.

A. So, let me get this right. The slave trade **1** (*abolish*) in 1808, but slavery was still legal.

C. Yes, even after 1808 slavery **2** (*defend*) by people in the South as a 'Positive Good'.

A. That just sounds crazy …

C. Yes, to us, but segregation **3** (*practice*) in the South even in the middle of the 20th century. In fact, the debate still goes on …

A. What do you mean?

C. Today, many African Americans **4** (*prevent*) from voting in elections.

A. But how? Doesn't everyone of the age of 18 have the right to vote?

C. Sure, but many voters **5** (*remove*) from the voting registers. After the 2016 election, several states **6** (*involve*) in voter suppression, efforts that include additional obstacles to registration, the prevention of early voting and stricter voter identification requirements. And it's the African Americans that **7** (*hit*) the hardest.

A. That's terrible.

C. Yes, and there are other signs that the mentality of many people in the southern states hasn't changed much. We can still find a lot of statues in the South of Confederate heroes like General Lee.

A. I thought all of them **8** (*pull down*) a long time ago?

C. No, in fact in 2017 a march **9** (*organize*) in protest against the removal of a statue in Charlottesville in South Carolina and a man **10** (*kill*). And laws **11** (*pass*) in some states making it illegal to remove them.

A. We have to hope that as people's attitude is changing, this **12** (*reflect*) in the legislation.

5 b Work with a partner and discuss the significance or importance of the person or event for the Civil Rights Movement. The words in the word cloud can help you. Use these phrases to give your opinion.

p. 59

I (really) think …
I (strongly) believe …
In my opinion, …
From my point of view, …
I don't agree with you about …
I'm not convinced that …
As I see it …
I base my argument on …
First …, second …, third …

2 b Find words or phrases in the text which match the definitions.

p. 63

brutality ■ community service program ■ disenfranchise ■ divisive ■ further ■ liberate ■ noteworthy ■ outweigh ■ sponsor

1 causing people to be split into groups that disagree with or oppose each other
2 to free a person or a country from the control of somebody else
3 cruel and unfair treatment of people, especially by not giving them the same freedom and rights as other people
4 to take away somebody's rights, especially the right to vote
5 to have a helpful and useful effect
6 an organized effort by a group of people to achieve something
7 to support something publicly
8 important or interesting
9 to be greater or more important than something else

4 b Which of these words from the texts match the definitions?

p. 67

combine ■ emerge ■ emphasis ■ genre ■ passionate ■ repertoire

1 a style, especially in the arts, that involves a particular set of characteristics
2 to join or mix together to make a single thing
3 a particular importance or attention that is given to something
4 all the music that you can perform or play
5 to appear by coming out of something else
6 a strong feeling of wanting or wishing for something

4 An interview. Choose the correct verb forms to complete the summary of an interview with Colin Kaepernick.

p. 71

In an interview, Colin Kaepernick said he **isn't standing up / wasn't going to stand up / hasn't stood up** (1) to show pride in a flag for a country that **is oppressing / is going to oppress / oppressed** (2) black people and people of color. His coach **asked / is asked / was asked** (3) about Colin's decision and **added / was added / has added** (4) that it wasn't **my / her / his** (5) right to tell Colin not to do something. Later on in the interview, Kaepernick said he **thinks / has thought / had thought** (6) about going public with his feelings for a while, but that he **feels / felt / fell** that (7) that he needed to understand the situation better. He **explained / said / told** (8) the interviewer that he **discusses / has discussed / had discussed** (9) his feelings with his family before deciding to take the action he had.

2 **b** Complete the article with the correct form of
p. 83 the verbs in brackets.

Many of your Top 40 favorites were created by Black songwriters

By Maya Eaglin

Music and the performing arts have not only
entertained the masses; they have also served to
document history […]. Time and time again, Black
musicians mirror what's going on in the world through
5 their music […]. Sidney Madden is a co-host of NPR's
podcast 'Louder Than a Riot,' which ___1___ (*focus on*) the
intersections of music and culture. Her expertise as a
music journalist gives a glance into how Black culture
___2___ (*influence*) the music and entertainment industry
10 as a whole.

'Every genre that ___3___ (*be born*) from America has
Black roots associated with it, from rock 'n' roll to blues
to disco,' Madden said. 'The fingerprints of Black
creators are all over what makes American music so
15 unique.' […]

A

Sidney Madden: […] The fabric of what American
society is socially, economically, industrially – it
wouldn't be what it is without Black people. And you
20 can see that especially when it comes to music.

B

Madden: Theft of Black creativity is something that is in
the bedrock of American society. […] You could think of
Elvis and where he ___4___ (*take*) a lot of his stage
presence from, [his bravado and conviction], even some
25 of the storytelling in his music – it ___5___ (*steal*) directly
from Black descendants like Chuck Berry. Even if you
look on the pop charts right now, so many artists who
___6___ (*consider*) titans of the game right now wouldn't
be anything and they wouldn't have a song to string
30 together if it ___7___ (*be*) for their Black writers. […]

C

Madden: As we say on our podcast, 'Louder Than a
Riot,' all hip-hop is protest music, right? […] I think with
35 the watershed moment we ___8___ (*have*) last year that's
continuing to permeate with the Black Lives Matter
movement in America and globally, more people ___9___
(*see*) that there would be nothing, there would be no
soundtrack to the protest, without Black music. […]

D
40
Madden: I see the future of Black music going where
Black people are going, and that's limitless. The more
we use our voice to talk about things that matter, things
that need ___10___ (*change*) […] these are the things that
45 need to be improved in our community, because if it's
going to be improved in our community, it's going to be
improved in America as a whole. That's where we're
going. We're going to more positions of power,
influence and applicable change.

Source (abbreviated and adapted): https://www.nbcnews.com/
news/nbcblk/soundtrack-history-how-black-music-has-shaped-
american-culture-through-n1258474

3 **An argument.** Complete the conversation
p. 98 between Aimee and Liam with the correct form of
the verbs in brackets to make conditional
sentences. The words in blue will help you.

A. What's up, Liam? Why are you looking so
upset?

L. If I **told** you, you ___1___ (*laugh*). I've just had
an argument with my parents.

A. Wow! What was the argument about?

L. Online gaming. More specifically about how
much time I spend on playing games.

A. They think it's too much. Am I right?

L. Yes. In their opinion if I ___2___ (*not, spend*)
hours on gaming, I **would be** more sociable.

A. If I ___3___ (*know*) you were going to discuss
your gaming habits, I **would have helped**
you.

L. How?

A. There are so many benefits to gaming.

L. Do you mean like cooperation?

A. Yes. And if you **play** with others, you ___4___
(*develop*) communication skills and will get
better at forward planning, too.

L. I guess that's true. And if I **didn't play** with
others I ___5___ (*not, be*) such a good team
player.

A. Don't push it, Liam! By the way, do you
remember that environmental game I
showed you?

L. Yes. What about it?

A. If I **hadn't played** that game, I ___6___ (*not,
learn*) problem-solving strategies and ___7___
(*not, get*) top marks in my science test.

L. Oh, … that's a persuasive argument. If I ___8___
(*talk*) to you earlier, I **would have argued**
my case better. But my parents were right
about one thing.

A. What's that?

L. If I ___9___ (*not, spend*) so much time in front
of the screen, I **wouldn't be** tired all of the
time.

2 **a** Aimee found an article about tattoos. Complete the article with the correct form of the
p. 100 verbs in brackets and the correct preposition.

While tattoos have been an important part of many cultures, particularly those of Pacific Islanders, the tradition in the West is quite different. If you trace the history of tattoos in Europe, you ▮1▮ (see) that the first
5 ones were linked to sailors returning from voyages. Common tattoos featured stars, anchors and even birds. If you ▮2▮ (ask) a sailor about the meaning of their tattoo a century ago, you were likely to have been told that they were a form **at / from / of** protection.
10 **At / In / With** the start of the twentieth century tattoos started to become popular **among / in / of** the elite. In fact, Winston Churchill's mother had a tattoo of a snake around her wrist. This craze didn't last long, and tattoos soon went out of fashion.
15 Fifty years later and tattoos became seen as a sign of rebellion. In fact, the negative attitude **at / of / towards** tattoos meant that if you decided to get one you often had it placed somewhere it was unlikely to be seen because of the clothes you wore. If you had a tattoo that
20 was visible, you ▮4▮ (often, find) it difficult to get a job. However, **among / from / in** the 1970s onwards tattoos started to become more mainstream. By the twenty-first century it was not unusual to find someone with a tattoo. A survey in 2015 found that one **among / from /
25 in** five people in the UK had a tattoo, with almost half of all millennials ▮5▮ (admit) to having at least one. Tattoos seem to be particularly popular **at / in / with** groups that can be very influential such as pop stars and footballers.

30 We asked some people about getting tattoos. Here are some of the things they said:

Amy (33) 'When I told my mum I was going to get a tattoo she looked horrified. Remember, if you get one
35 done now it ▮6▮ (be) difficult to get rid of it later', she said. 'If I ▮7▮ (listen) to her, I ▮8▮ (not worry) so much about it later. I was only 18 at the time and had the name of my boyfriend and a heart tattooed on my
40 arm. Of course, a few weeks later we split up, but his name remained as a reminder.'

Megan (21) 'I was only 17 when I decided I wanted a tattoo. Of course, I had to wait a year as you have to be
45 18 in the UK before you can get one. On my birthday I went to a local artist. Now I have over twenty and I ▮9▮ (definitely get) more.'

Marcus (19) 'A lot of my friends have
50 tattoos, but I don't think I'll have one despite the peer pressure. If you ▮10▮ (get) one when you are young, it might look good. But I don't think tattoos look good **at / in / on** older people,
55 especially if you put on weight and your skin stretches!'

---

2 **a** Choose one of the people in the pictures. Look
p. 103 at the notes below about their lives. Do some more research and find out what they contributed to the decade(s) they represent. Write a short text (100 words) and explain why they became famous.

J.K. Rowling

· born 31 July 1965 as Joanne Rowling
· writes under two pen names.
  J. K. Rowling and Robert Galbraith
· author of Harry Potter series
· got the idea for the Harry Potter books on a delayed train in 1990
· 12 publishers rejected her first book
· sold more than 500 million copies of her books
· books and movies popular with children and adults
· first person to become a billionaire by just being an author

Greta Thunberg
· born in Sweden on 3 January 2003; diagnosed with Asperger syndrome, a kind of autism
· became a climate activist when she was 12 or 13
· 2018: during the election, she started a strike in front of the Swedish parliament
· continued striking on Fridays; inspired others to do the same
· founder of Fridays for Future movement
· spoken at many international events; well known for her direct speaking manner
· criticizes world leaders for failing to address the climate crisis
· speeches published in a book 'No One is Too Small to Make a Difference'

The Beatles
· 1960: founded in Liverpool, England
· members: John Lennon, Paul McCartney, George Harrison, Ringo Starr
· for many they were the most successful and influential pop group ever
· main songwriters: Lennon and McCartney
· 1962: first single 'Love Me Do'
· by 1964: world stars; excitement caused by the band was known as 'Beatlemania'
· 1970: Beatles broke up, but all continued their music careers
· 1980: John Lennon was murdered in New York; 2001 George Harrison died

2 **a** Think about when and why you and your friends use your phones. The list below will help you. Then list three rules you would follow if trying a digital detox. Give reasons for your choices. Then listen to Brendan and compare your ideas to his.

58

p.108

- text friends
- follow what others are doing
- contact parents if I'm late
- school group chat for projects
- check facts for homework
- check bus / train times
- play games
- watch the news online

5 **a** Write a letter to the editor with your views about teenagers and online security.
p.113 Write about 200 – 250 words. Use these ideas to help you.

> **Beginning**
> - Say why you are writing – refer to the email Aimee's mother wrote.
>
> **Middle**
> - Outline whether you agree or disagree with her opinion that teenagers 'seem to be clueless' when it comes to online security.
> - Give reasons to back up your opinion; include examples.
>
> **End**
> - Summarize your opinion in one or two sentences.
> - Ask other readers how they feel.

2 Brendan decides to write some advice and
p.118 information about digitalization and digital detox. Match the start of each sentence with an appropriate ending. Then compare your sentences with a partner.

1 If your eyes hurt, …
2 If you suffer from FOMO, …
3 If you can't get to sleep at night, …
4 If I hadn't been born in the 21st century, …
5 If I didn't have internet access at home, …
6 If a new app is released, …

a ask yourself what you will really miss if you switch your phone off.
b reduce the time you spend looking at your phone or screen.
c it would be very difficult to lead a 'normal' life.
d switch off your phone at least two hours before you go to bed.
e I would have had less technology to help me in my daily life.
f I will download it if I think it's useful.

5 Brainstorm what defines your generation. Copy
p.123 and complete the mind map below. Then write an essay (200 words) with the title: 'My generation'. Swap your essay with a partner and give each other feedback to improve your work.

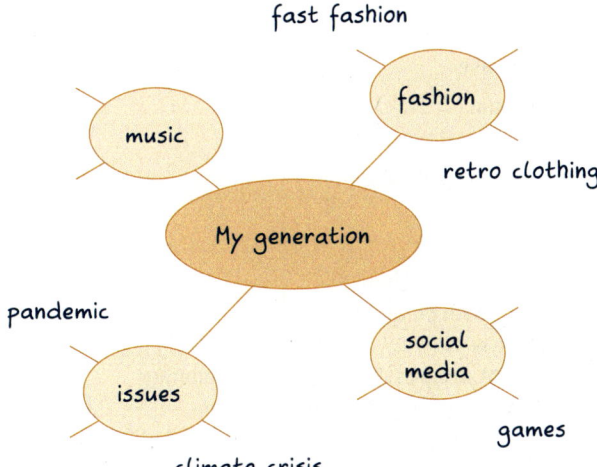

fast fashion

fashion

music

retro clothing

My generation

pandemic

social media

issues

games

climate crisis

Appendix
Grammatical terms

Here are some of the most important **grammatical terms** in English:

active	aktiv
adjective	Adjektiv; Eigenschaftswort
adverb	Adverb (Wortart); Umstandswort
adverb of frequency	Adverb der Häufigkeit
adverb of manner	Adverb der Art und Weise
adverb of place	Adverb des Ortes
adverb of time	Adverb der Zeit
adverbial	adverbiale Bestimmung (Satzglied); Umstandsangabe
article	Artikel
definite article	bestimmter Artikel
indefinite article	unbestimmter Artikel
aspect	Aspekt
auxiliary	Hilfsverb
clause	Teilsatz
adverbial clause	Adverbialsatz
comment clause	nicht notwendiger Relativsatz, der sich auf den gesamten Satz bezieht
contact clause	notwendiger Relativsatz ohne Relativpronomen
if-clause	Bedingungssatz; Konditionalis
main clause	Hauptsatz
relative clause	Relativsatz
defining relative clause	notwendiger Relativsatz
non-defining relative clause	nicht notwendiger Relativsatz
subordinate clause (of time)	Temporalsatz
comparative	Komparativ; Vergleichsform
conditional	Konditionalis; Konditionalsatz
conditional type I, II, III, mixed	Konditionalsatz Typ I, II, II, gemischt
demonstrative determiner	Demonstrativbegleiter
future	Futur; Zukunft
future perfect	Futur II
future progressive	Verlaufsform des Futur
future with *going to*	Futur mit *going to*
future with *will*	Futur mit *will*
present progressive with future meaning	Verlaufsform des Präsens mit Zukunftsbezug
simple present with future meaning	einfache Form des Präsens mit Zukunftsbezug
gerund	Gerundium
imperative	Imperativ; Befehlsform
infinitive	Infinitiv; Grundform
to–infinitive	*to*-Infinitiv
modal	Modalverb
modal substitute	Ersatzform eines Modalverbs
negative	negativ; verneinend
noun	Substantiv; Nomen
countable noun	zählbares Substantiv
uncountable noun	nicht zählbares Substantiv

object
   direct object
   indirect object
	Objekt
	   direktes Objekt
	   indirektes Objekt

participle
   participle construction
   past participle
   perfect participle
   present participle
	Partizip
	   Partizipialkonstruktion
	   Partizip Perfekt
	   having + Partizip Perfekt
	   Partizip Präsens

passive
   by-agent
	Passiv
	   Handelnde(r) im Passivsatz

past
   simple past
   past progressive
	Präteritum; Vergangenheit
	   einfache Form der Vergangenheit
	   Verlaufsform der Vergangenheit

past perfect
   past perfect (simple)
   past perfect progressive
	Plusquamperfekt
	   einfache Form des Plusquamperfekts
	   Verlaufsform des Plusquamperfekts

plural	Plural; Mehrzahl
positive	positiv; bejaht
possessive *'s*	*s*-Genitiv
possessive determiner	Possessivbegleiter

preposition
   preposition of place
   preposition of time
	Präposition
	   Präposition des Ortes
	   Präposition der Zeit

present
   simple present
   present progressive
	Präsens; Gegenwart
	   einfache Form des Präsens
	   Verlaufsform des Präsens

present perfect
   present perfect (simple)
   present perfect progressive
	Perfekt
	   einfache Form des Perfekt
	   Verlaufsform des Perfekt

pronoun
   indefinite pronoun
   interrogative pronoun
   object pronoun
   personal pronoun
   possessive pronoun
   reciprocal pronoun
   reflexive pronoun
   relative pronoun
   subject pronoun
	Pronomen
	   Indefinitpronomen; unbestimmtes Pronomen
	   Interrogativpronomen; Fragepronomen
	   Objektpronomen
	   Personalpronomen
	   Possessivpronomen; besitzanzeigendes Pronomen
	   Reziprokpronomen
	   Reflexivpronomen
	   Relativpronomen
	   Subjektpronomen

prop word *one/ones*	Stützwort *one/ones*
quantifier	Numeral; Zahlwort

question
   question tag
	Frage
	   Frageanhängsel; Bestätigungsfrage

reported speech
   backshift
	indirekte Rede
	   Rücksetzung der Zeitform um eine Stufe

singular	Singular; Einzahl
statement	Aussagesatz
subject	Subjekt
superlative	Superlativ
tense	Zeitform

verb
   irregular verb
   regular verb
	Verb; Tätigkeitswort
	   unregelmäßiges Verb
	   regelmäßiges Verb

word order	Wortstellung

Grammar

Do you have a question about grammar?
The **grammar appendix** explains all the grammar that you have revised in this book.

G 1	Tenses (revision)	WS 1
G 2	Passive (revision)	WS 2
G 3	Conditional sentences (revision)	WS 3
G 4	Reported speech (revision)	WS 2
G 5	Adjectives, adverbs and adverbials (revision)	WS 1

G 1 Tenses (revision)

Present tenses

Simple present

- The simple present is the infinitive of the verb without *to*. For the third person singular *(he / she / it)* we add *-s*.
  We make negatives and questions with a form of *do* – except when the question word is the subject of the sentence (see example below).
  *She **wants** to read the book.*
  *They **don't go** to the cinema very often.* • *He **doesn't live** here anymore.*
  *Who **does** this dog **belong** to?* • ***Don't** you **like** this movie?* • *Who **are** you?*

- We use the simple present to talk about something that happens all the time or that is always true.
  *My mum **works** as a nurse.* • *I **love** my dog.*
  *We normally **watch** football on Saturday afternoon.*

Present progressive

- We form the present progressive with *am / are / is + -ing*. We form the negative with *am not / aren't / isn't + -ing*.
  *They**'re playing** tennis now.*

- We use the present progressive to talk about what is happening now while we are speaking.
  *We **aren't eating** lunch at the moment.*
  ***Are** you **reading** the newspaper or can I have it?*

- Some verbs do not have a progressive form, for example *know, like, want* or *understand*.

Past tenses

Simple past

- With regular verbs, we add *-ed* to the infinitive of the verb to make the simple past. We form the negative with *didn't* and questions with *did*.
  *The **played** a concert in Glasgow yesterday.*

- Some verbs don't add *-ed* in the simple past. They are irregular (see the list on pages **163/164**).
  *We **went** to the beach yesterday.* NOT *We ~~goed~~ to the beach yesterday.*
  *He **sent** me an email an hour ago.* NOT *He ~~sended~~ me an email an hour ago.*

- We use the simple past to talk about things that happened at a time in the past. We often use expressions of time like *yesterday, last Thursday, two months ago,* etc.
  *We **stayed** in Scotland for two weeks last summer.*
  *The Angles **arrived** in Britain in about 600 AD.*
  *The slaves **didn't have** control over their own bodies.*
  *What similarities **did** you **find**?*

Past progressive

- We form the past progressive with *was / were + -ing*. We form the negative with *wasn't / weren't + -ing*. For questions, we put the subject between *was / were* and the *-ing* form.
  *My parents met when they **were living** in Edinburgh.*
  *Sorry, I **wasn't listening**. What did you say?*
  ***Were** the others **waiting** when you arrived?*

- We often use the past progressive together with the simple past to give background information.
  *It **was raining** when I got up.*
  *While we **were cycling** home from training last week, I had an accident and fell off my bike.*
  *Jack went home from school early yesterday because he **wasn't feeling** well.*
  *What **were** you **doing** when I saw you in town last Saturday?*

+ see next page!

Present perfect

- We form the present perfect with *has/have* and the past participle. We form the negative with *hasn't/haven't* and the past participle. For questions, we put the subject between *has/have* and past participle.
  She **has called** several times. • I **haven't seen** Chloe in school today.
  Have you **watched** the programme on slavery in the US?

- We use the present perfect in two main ways.
  – To talk about something in the past which is connected with or has consequences in the present. We often use the present perfect in this way with *yet* and *already*.
  I've already **booked** the tickets. • I **haven't seen** the exhibition yet.
  Has she **given** her presentation yet?
  – To talk about something that started in the past and continues now. We often use the present perfect in this way with *for* and *since*.
  He's **lived** in this house for ten years. • We've **been** friends since we were seven.

Present perfect progressive

- We form the present perfect progressive with *has/have + been + -ing*. We form the negative with *hasn't/haven't + been + -ing*. For questions, we put the subject between *has/have* and *been*.
  I've **been playing** the guitar for three years/since I was 11.
  We **haven't been playing** very well since our trainer left.
  How long **have** you **been learning** English?

- We often use the present perfect progressive to talk about an action or a situation which started in the past and continues to the present. We use it with *for*, *since* and *all* as well as in questions with *How long*.
  I've **been living** here for years/since 20... • The kids **have been playing** in the garden all afternoon.
  Sorry, I'm late. – Don't worry. We **haven't been waiting** long.
  How long **have** you **been working** here?

Past perfect

- We form the past perfect with *had* and the past participle. We form the negative with *hadn't* and the past participle. For questions, we put the subject between *had* and the past participle.
  I was late and the exam **had** already **started**. • He **hadn't told** me he was Meg's friend.
  Which travel guide **had** they **checked** before they started on the route?

- We use the past perfect to show that one event happened before another one in the past. We use the past perfect for the event that happened first and the simple past for the more recent event. We often use sequence adverbs such as *when*, *before*, *after* and *until* to link the two events.
  After we **had spent** 35 days on a boat, we **arrived** in America.
  We **had hoped** to reach this place sooner, but the bad weather **slowed** us down.
  The boy **had** just **had** his 8th birthday when he **fell** and **died**.

- We also use the past perfect to show that something happened before a time in the past.
  We'd **travelled** over 200 miles by 12 o'clock. • I **hadn't met** him before the concert last June.

Past perfect progressive

- We form the past perfect progressive with *had + been + -ing*. We form the negative with *hadn't + been + -ing*. For questions, we put the subject between *had* and *been*.
  We'd **been playing** for 20 minutes when it started to rain.
  I **hadn't been waiting** for long when the bus came.
  Had you **been looking for** an internship for long before you got one?

- We use the past perfect progressive to focus on the length of the earlier action and to show that it was in progress before the second action started.
  I'd **been playing** rugby for three years when I became captain.
  We **hadn't been driving** for long when dad realized that he didn't have his phone.
  How long **had** the others **been waiting** when you finally arrived?

Ways of expressing the future

<u>*Will* future</u>

- We form the *will* future with *will* + the infinitive of the verb without *to*. The verb form always stays the same. For negatives we use *won't*. For questions we put the subject between *will* and the infinitive of the verb without *to*.
  They **won't be** on time. • **Will** he **arrive** today?

- We use *will* to offer or promise to do something for somebody.
  I'll help you with your homework this evening.
  There isn't any milk in the fridge. – Don't worry. I **won't forget** *to buy some this afternoon.*

- We use *will* when we decide to do something spontaneously while we are speaking.
  You look hungry. We'll buy a sandwich. • *I'm so tired, I* **won't stay up** *much longer.*

- We use *will* for predictions that are based on personal feeling or opinion.
  You'll love it in Scotland! • *It* **won't take** *long.* • *It'll take you longer than you think.*

<u>*Going to* future</u>

- We form the *going to* future with a form of *be* + *going to* + the infinitive of the verb without *to*. We make negatives with a negative form of *be*. For questions we put the subject between the form of *be* and *going to*.
  I'm not going to do the internship at my mother's office. • *She's not going to win the race.*
  Are *you* **going to start** *at a new school in September?*

- We use *be going to* for decisions and future plans that were made before the time of speaking.
  I'm going to join the school drama club next term.
  We're going to book our train tickets at the weekend.

- We use *be going to* for predictions that are based on present evidence. In other words, there is something in the present that indicates something in the future.
  Look at the traffic. We're going to be late. • *It looks like it's going to be a lovely day.*

<u>The simple present</u>

- We use the simple present with a to talk about future events when the statements are based on present facts, and when these facts are something fixed like a timetable, schedule or calendar. We use it with an expression of time.
  The bus leaves at 6.30, please hurry up. • *The football match starts at three o'clock on Sunday.*

<u>Present progressive</u>

- We use the present progressive, often with a future meaning, to talk about future arrangements. Typically, we use it with an expression of time.
  Next week, I'm seeing my cousin to discuss my internship.
  We're meeting at the pizzeria this evening. • *When are Isabella and Gabriel going to the US?*

<u>Future perfect</u>

- We form the future perfect with *will have* + past participle. We make negatives with **won't**. For questions we put the subject between *will* and *have*. We often use the future perfect with **by**.
  Will *you* **have had** *dinner* **by** *8.30?*

- We use the future perfect to talk about something already completed by a point in the future.
  The apprenticeship starts in September. I'll have finished my A-levels by then.

- We can use the future perfect to talk about something not completed by a point in the future.
  I'm afraid I won't have finished my report by Friday.
  I won't have had time to do much research before the interview.

+ see next page!

Future progressive

- We form the future progressive with *will be + -ing*.
  *Next year most of my friends **will be doing** an apprenticeship.*

- We use the future progressive for an action in progress at a specific time in the future.
  *Hopefully **by** September I'**ll be working** somewhere in the US or Canada.*
  *This time tomorrow, I'**ll be having** my interview.*
  *At 3 o'clock, we'**ll be driving** to the airport.*

! In **German** we often use different tenses to express the same meaning as in English. This is true for ways of expressing the future as well as the past.

*I'**m going to meet** Ava after school.*	*Ich **treffe** Ava nach der Schule. (Absicht)*
*I'**m meeting** Ava after school.*	*Ich **treffe** Ava nach der Schule. (Vereinbarung)*
*I think, we'**ll meet** after school, or tomorrow.*	*Wir **treffen** uns nach der Schule, nehme ich an.*
*We'**ve been discussing** the issue for ages.*	*Wir **diskutieren** das Thema seit Jahren.*
*I **went** to see my gran yesterday.*	*Ich **habe** gestern meine Oma **besucht**.*

The passive (all tenses) (also see → G2)

- We form the passive with *be* in the appropriate tense + past participle.

  Simple present (*am/is/are* + **past participle**)
  *The internet **is used** by billions of people every day.* • *Today, most goods **are paid for** electronically.*

  Simple past (*was/were* + **past participle**)
  *The March on Washington **was held** on August 28, 1963.*
  *Both Martin Luther King Jr. and Malcolm X **were assassinated** in the 1960s.*

  Present perfect (*has been/have been* + **past participle**)
  *Gwen **has been hired** by a fashion company.*
  *Musical genres and fashion **have been linked** to young people since the 1920s.*

  Will (*will be* + **past participle**)
  *What kind of information do you think you **will be given**?* • *Many jobs **will be lost**.*

  Modal verbs (*can be/might be/had to be* + **past participle**)
  *Stories **can be used** to illustrate a point and appeal to the emotions of your audience.*
  *The new website **might be launched** soon.*
  *Until the early 20th century, all household chores **had to be done** by hand.*

- We use the passive in different tenses when we focus on the action and not on who does the action.

G 2   Passive (revision)

<u>Form</u>

- We form the passive with the appropriate form of *be* + past participle.
  'Scotland the Brave' **is** so **well-loved** *that it* **is** still **thought of** *as the 'unofficial' national anthem of Scotland.*
  Many photographs supposedly showing the Loch Ness Monster **have been shown** *to be hoaxes.*
  Hundreds of women **were burnt** *for being suspected of being witches.*
  The year 2020 **will be remembered** *for the rise of the Black Lives Matter movement.*

- We form a question by putting the subject after the auxiliary verb *be* or between the auxiliaries if there are two of them.
  When **was** *Edinburgh Castle* **built**? • **Has** *the World Cup ever* **been held** *in Scotland?*
  What time **will** *we* **be collected** *from the hotel?*

- When a verb is followed by a preposition, the preposition stays in the same position in the passive.
  We can make sure the place **is looked after**.
  At the hotel, all diets **are catered for**.

- When a verb has two objects, the passive sentence can begin with either the direct or the indirect object. The direct object is usually a thing and the indirect object is usually a person. When we begin with the direct object, we use the preposition *to* or *for* before the indirect object.
  The land **was given back to the original owners**. OR *The original owners* **were given back** *the land.*
  Four seats **were saved for us**. OR *We* **were saved** *four seats.*

- Verbs that take two objects include:
  ask • buy • find • get • give • lend • make • offer • pay • promise • sell • send • show • teach • tell

<u>Use</u>

- We often use the passive when we do not mention who does an action, as we are more interested in what happens than who does the action. This is usually because who does the action is obvious, unknown or not important. The passive also means we can avoid using vague subjects like *someone, people* and *they*.
  During the Middle Ages Scots grew apart from its sister tongue which **was spoken** *in England.*
  'The Flower of Scotland' **was** *traditionally* **sung** *at rugby matches.*

- However, we can use the passive with *by* to say who does the action. This is often when we give new information about an existing topic. The passive enables us to put the existing information first and the new information second.
  Bonnie Prince Charlie **was helped** *to escape to Skye* **by Flora Macdonald**.
  Our passage **was paid for by the landlord**.

- We use *be* + past participle after modal verbs.
  Explain which of the stories **can be considered** *true.*
  You **won't be contacted** *unless you give us permission.*

- We use the passive infinitive *to be* + past participle after verbs that are normally followed by *to*-infinitive (e. g. *allow, ask, expect, hope, like, need, want*).
  Copy the items in your exercise book in the order you **expect** *them* **to be mentioned**.
  Racism is a topic that **needs to be addressed**.

- When we use the passive in a relative clause, we can sometimes omit the relative pronoun and *be*.
  There are some amazing carvings (which are) **made** *from wood, ivory and sandstone.*
  I took part in a sponsored run for a charity (which is) **called** *ResCom.*

G 3 Conditional sentences (revision)

Workshop 3

G 3.1 Summary

Workshop 3

There are three types of conditional sentences, as well as mixed types (→ G3.5).

Conditional sentences type I → G3.2
if-clause: **simple present**   main clause: *will* + **infinitive**
If I go to China,   *I will visit the Great Wall.*
(= It's likely or possible that I'll visit China.)

Conditional sentences type II → G3.3
if-clause: **simple past**   main clause: *would* (*'d*) + **infinitive** (conditional)
If I went to China,   *I would visit the Great Wall.*
(= It's not very likely that I'll visit China.)

Conditional sentences type III → G3.4
if-clause: **past perfect**   main clause: *would* (*'d*) + *have* + **past participle** (conditional perfect)
If I had gone to China in 2019, I would have visited the Great Wall.
If I'd gone to China in 2019,   I'd have visited the Great Wall.
(= I had a chance to go to China in the past, but I didn't go.)

❗ In conditional sentences, the *if*-clause can come first or second. If it comes first, we need to use a **comma** between *if*-clause and main clause (see examples above). But if it comes second, there is **no comma** between main clause and *if*-clause, e.g.: *I will visit the Great Wall if I go to China.*

G 3.2 Conditional sentences type I (revision)

Workshop 3

Form:
- In conditional sentences type I: The verb which follows *if* is in the simple present. The verb in the main clause is *will* (or *'ll*) + infinitive (without *to*).

- For negative conditional sentences type I, we use *do/does not/don't/doesn't* + infinitive in the *if*-clause and *will not/won't* + infinitive in the main clause.
  if-clause: *do/does not/don't/doesn't* + **infinitive**   main clause: *will not/won't* + **infinitive**
  If she doesn't come soon,   *we won't have time to finish our homework.*

- For conditional type I questions, we use *will* in the main clause.
  If you have time, will you watch a movie with me?
  Will you watch a movie with me if you have time?

We use conditional sentences type I:
- to say that something will happen after something else has happened first.
  if-clause: **simple present**   main clause: *will/won't* + **infinitive**
  If Bex comes to my house this evening,   *we'll do our homework together.*

- to say that something is possible.
  if-clause: **simple present**   main clause: *can* + **infinitive**
  If we have time after our homework,   *we can watch a movie.*

- to tell someone to do (or not to do) something.
  if-clause: **simple present**   main clause: (*don't* +) **infinitive**
  If Bex is late,   *please tell her I'm in my room.*
  If we are busy,   *please don't ask us any questions.*

+ see next page!

- We can use *when* to talk about something we are sure will happen.
  ***When** Jeff goes home, I will phone my grandma.* (= I know that Jeff will go home.)

- We use *if* to talk about something we are not sure will happen.
  ***If** Jeff goes home late, I'll phone my grandma tomorrow.* (= I don't know what time Jeff will go home.)

! We use sentences with *if* or *when* + the simple present in both parts to say something is always true.
*If/When you **travel** alone, you **have to** be careful.*

G 3.3 Conditional sentences type II (revision)   Workshop 3

Form:

- In conditional sentences type II: The verb which follows *if* is in the simple past. The verb in the main clause is *would* (or *'d*) + infinitive (without *to*). We call this the conditional (mode).

- For negative conditional sentences type II, we use *did not/didn't* + infinitive in the *if*-clause and *would not/wouldn't* + infinitive (conditional) in the main clause.
  ***if*-clause: *did not/didn't* + infinitive**   **main clause: *would not/wouldn't* + infinitive (conditional)**
  *If I **didn't have** a nice voice,*   *I **wouldn't sing** in the school choir.*

- For conditional type II questions, we use *would* in the main clause.
  *If you **had** six months' holiday, where **would** you **go**?*
  *Where **would** you **go** if you **had** six months' holiday?*

We use conditional sentences type II:

- to talk about things that are possible, but that are not likely to happen.
  ***if*-clause: simple past**   **main clause: *would* + infinitive (conditional)**
  *If I **went** to Edinburgh,*   *I **would visit** the castle.*
  (= I don't think I'll go to Edinburgh, but it is possible.)

- We use the simple past in the *if*-clause in conditional sentences type II, but we are still talking about the future.
  *If I **played** the violin, I'd join the school orchestra.* (= I don't play the violin.)

- We use *If I were …* in a conditional sentence type II *if*-clause. It means the same as *If I was …*, but it is more formal.
  ***If I were** you, I'd buy that jacket.*

- We can use *could* or *might* instead of *would* in conditional sentences type II.
  *If we had enough time, we **could go** to the art market. (= We probably won't have enough time.)*
  *If we went to the art market, we **might find** a nice picture. (= Perhaps we would find a nice picture.)*

G 3.4   Conditional sentences type III (revision) Workshop 3

Form:

- In conditional sentences type III: The verb which follows *if* is in the past perfect. The verb in the main clause is *would + have* + past participle. We call this the conditional perfect (mode).

  if-clause: **past perfect**   main clause: *would / 'd + have* + **past participle**
                                           (conditional perfect)

  *If I **had brought** my camera to the party,   I **would have taken** lots of pictures.*

- For negative conditional sentences type III, we use *had not / hadn't* + infinitive in the *if*-clause and *would not have / wouldn't have* + past participle (conditional perfect) in the main clause.

  if-clause: **past perfect**   main clause: *would not / wouldn't* + *have* + **past participle**
                                           (conditional perfect)

  *If I **hadn't come** to the party,   I **wouldn't have met** you.*

- For conditional type III questions, we use *would … have* + past participle (conditional perfect) in the main clause.

  *If she **had remembered** her purse, **would** she **have bought** the coat?*
  ***Would** she **have bought** the coat if she **had remembered** her purse?*

- In short form conditional sentences type III, we use ***'d*** instead of ***had*** (in the *if*-clause) and instead of ***would*** in the main clause.

  *If I**'d** taken my camera to the party, I**'d** have taken lots of pictures.*
   = ***had***   = ***would***

- We can use *could have* and *might have* instead of *would have*.
  *If I had studied harder, I **could / might have** passed my exams.*

We use conditional sentences type III:

- to talk about things that did **not** happen in the past.
  *If they **had known** that the hotel was so far from the station, they **would have come** by taxi. They **wouldn't have walked**.*
  (= But they didn't know it was far from the station, so they walked.)

G 3.5   Mixed types of conditional sentences (revision) Workshop 3

In a mixed conditional sentence:

- we can use a conditional sentence type II *if*-clause (past) and a conditional sentence type III verb in the main clause (conditional perfect).

  *If I still **lived** in England,   I **would have played** in the match yesterday.*

  PRESENT CONDITION   →   **PAST RESULT**

- we can use a conditional sentence type III *if*-clause (past perfect) and a conditional sentence type II verb in the main clause (conditional).

  *If my dad **hadn't got** a new job,   I **wouldn't live** in Germany now.*

  PAST CONDITION   →   **PRESENT RESULT**

G 4 Reported speech (revision) Workshop 2

G 4.1 Reported speech in statements and questions in the present, present perfect and future (revision) Workshop 2

We sometimes report a person's exact words or the general idea.

Statements:
- We can use *say* and *tell* to report what someone says.
  *He **says** that he loves the area.*
  *Thomas **tells** me that you're going back to the UK.*

- We can use *that* after *say* and *tell*. There is no rule about *that* and it is usually personal choice.
  *She **says** she's not hungry.*   OR   *She **says that** she's not hungry.*

- We use an indirect object (e. g. *me, us*) after *tell*.
  *He tells **me** they are hoping to set off at about 6.30.*

- As well as *say* and *tell*, we can use reporting verbs such as *admit, agree, assure, claim, deny, inform, suggest, think*, etc.
  *He **admits** he's wrong.*
  *She **agrees** it's a good idea.*

- When we use reporting verbs in the present, the present perfect or the future, we generally keep the information we are reporting in the same tense as the original comment. This is usually to show that something is still true, relevant or important.
  *I**'ll be** home in ten minutes.* → *She says she**'ll be** home in ten minutes.*
  *It**'s** Jenna's birthday today.* → *Alice tells me it**'s** your birthday today.*
  *I think Sam **left** about an hour ago.* → *He thinks that Sam **left** about an hour ago.*
  *We**'re going** to the beach.* → *Luke says they**'re going** to the beach.*

- We sometimes need to change pronouns *(we → they)* and other words such as
  here → there, etc.
  *I've lived **here** since I was 13.* → *He says he's lived **there** since **he** was 13.*

Questions:
- We can report a question with verbs such as *ask, want to know* and *wonder*.
  Fred: 'Is everything OK?' → *Fred**'s asking** if everything is OK.*
  David: 'When are we leaving?' → *David **wants to know** when we're leaving.*
  Jessica: 'Where are we going next?' → *She**'s wondering** where we are going next.*

- For a *yes/no*-question (without a question word) we use *if* or *whether*.
  *He **is asking** me **if** I know his brother.*
  *Olga **has asked** me **whether** I can give her a surfing lesson.*

- The word order is different from direct questions but the same as in statements.
  *'Where **does he live**?'* → *She wants to know where **he lives**.*
  *'When **are we leaving**?'* → *He keeps asking when **we're leaving**.*
  NOT ~~She's wants to know where does he live.~~ • ~~He keeps asking when are we leaving.~~

G 4.2   Reported speech in statements and questions in the past and in requests, offers, orders and advice (revision)   Workshop 2

Statements and questions

When reporting speech, we often use the past tense forms *said, told, asked, wanted to know, was wondering, assured, admitted, denied, explained, suggested, promised,* etc. We usually 'backshift' the tense (move the tense one step back in time) in the statement, comment or question we are reporting.

- **present tense**   →   **past tense**
  'I **work** in Glasgow.'   She told me she **worked** in Glasgow.
  'What's wrong with you?'   Keira asked Fred what **was** wrong with him.
  'OK, I admit I'**m** wrong.'   He admitted he **was** wrong.

- **past tense / present perfect**   →   **past perfect**
  'I **didn't want** to go.'   She explained she **hadn't wanted** to go.
  'We'**ve** just **arrived**.'   He said they'**d** just **arrived**.

- **will**   **would**
  'I'**ll call** you later.'   She promised she'**d call** me later.

- **can**   **could**
  'I **can't find** it.'   He admitted he **couldn't find** it.

- **must**   **had to**
  'We **must leave** now.'   She said they **had to leave**.

We sometimes use the past tense forms of reporting verbs such as *said, told, asked, wanted to know, was wondering,* etc. and do not change the tense of the reported sentence. This is usually to show that a statement or information is still true, relevant or important.
'Sam **left** about a hour ago.' → He said that Sam **left** about an hour ago.
'I'**ll** be home in ten minutes.' → She said she'**ll** be home in ten minutes.
'Where'**s** Jamie **going**?' → She was wondering where Jamie'**s going**.

Requests, offers, orders and advice

- We can report a request with verbs such as *asked* and *want* + indirect object + *to*-infinitive.
  'Can you wait here?' → She asked **us to wait** here.
  'Could you repeat the question?' → She wanted **me to repeat** the question.

- We can report an offer with *offer* + *to*-infinitive.
  'I can give you a lift if you like.' → Maria offered **to give** us a lift.
  'I'll help you if you like.' → He offered **to help** us.

- We can report an order or advice with *told* + indirect object + (*not*) + *to*-infinitive.
  'You should apologize to them.' → She told me **to apologize** to them.
  'Don't be late again.' → He told me **not to be** late again.

We can also use the present tense of the reporting verbs:
Gareth **wants** me **to help** him.
She'**s asking** us **to wait** here.
Petra'**s offering to give** us a lift.
The life guard **is telling** us **not to swim** here.

⚠ Note that, in English, we don't use a comma after the reporting verb. In **German**, there is a comma. Another important difference between English and German is that, in **German**, we use the *Konjunktiv*.
Fred's asking if everything is OK.   Fred fragt**,** ob alles in Ordnung **sei**.
She said (that) she wouldn't tell her mum.   Sie sagte**,** dass sie es **nicht** ihrer Mutter **erzähle**.

G 4.3 Changes to adverbs of time and place in reported speech (revision)

Workshop 2

When we are reporting and use a reporting verb in the past, we need to change adverbs of time and place.
'I saw Anders **yesterday**.' → She mentioned she'd seen Anders **the day before**.
'I'll call you **next week**.' → She said she'd call me **the following week**.
'This is the first time I've been **here**.' → He said it was the first time he'd been **there**.

Common changes include:
yesterday → the day before
tomorrow → the next day / the day after
last weekend / week / month / year → the weekend / week / month / year before
next weekend / week / month / year → the following weekend / week / month / year
here → there

G 5 Adjectives, adverbs and adverbials (revision)

Workshop 1

G 5.1 Adjectives

Workshop 1

We use adjectives to give information about the quality of a thing, a person, or an event, or to specify a thing as distinct from another thing.

Adjectives can be used to modify a noun (attributive function). They appear between the determiner (for example: a / an, the, or zero article) and the noun.
We had done exactly the **right** thing given the circumstances we faced.

Adjectives can also be used in predicative function, as a subject complement or an object complement.
Explain how Macbeth by Shakespeare isn't factual. • Everything is so different to back home.
I find it annoying when people say that we are lazy and apathetic.

Adjectives can be used with very to intensify them.
During the 1940s and 1950s, city blues was **very popular** in black clubs and bars.

Adjectives can be used in comparative and superlative forms, see G5.3 .

G 5.2 Adverbs and adverbials (revision)

Workshop 1

An **adverbial** modifies a word or a part of a sentence. It can be one word (an **adverb**) or more words (a phrase). We use adverbials in a number of ways.

- **Adverbials of place** tell us where something happens.
  Liam thinks we presented everything too seriously **at the assembly**.
  We went **to Oxford** on Friday. We were **there** for a few hours.
  In the science room, a group of students were sitting and standing around.

  Adverbials of place generally go after the verb and its object. However, you can sometimes put them at the beginning of the sentence.

- **Adverbials of time** tell us when or how long something happens.
  We went to Oxford **on Friday**. We were there **for a few hours**.
  I bought a new computer **last week**.
  Last term, we did something called an environmental review.

+ see next page!

Adverbials of time generally go after the verb and its object. However, you can sometimes put them at the beginning of the sentence.
Already, *just* and *recently* generally go immediately before the main verb. However, you can also put *already* and *recently* at the end of the sentence.
*Doesn't the school **already** have a compost bin?*
*I've **just** finished my assignment.*
*I spoke to Jeff **recently**.*

- **Adverbials of manner** tell us how something happens.
*Liam thinks we presented everything **too seriously** at the assembly.*
*A group of students were sitting and standing around, chatting **noisily**.*
*You'll **easily** pass the exam.*

Adverbials of manner generally go after the verb and its object. However, they can sometimes go before the main verb.

- **Adverbials of frequency** tell us how frequently something happens.
*I **always** cycle to work. I **never** drive or get the bus.*
*There is **usually** a meeting **every week**.*

Adverbials of frequency generally go before the main verb but after the verb *be*. Frequency phrases (for example *every week*, *once a year*) generally go at the end of the sentence.

- **Adverbials of certainty** tell us how certain we are about something.
***Maybe** he's right.*
***Perhaps** our presentation was quite good in the end.*
*We will **probably** have a meeting next week.*

Adverbials of certainty often go at the beginning of the sentence, but they can go in a range of positions.

- **Adverbials of degree** tell us the degree or strength of something.
*That's a **very** good idea.*
*The meeting was **quite** useful.*
*He can draw **really** well.*

Adverbials of degree generally go directly before the word they modify.

- **Comment adverbials** tell us how the speaker feels about the whole sentence.
***Unfortunately**, too much paper and plastic is landing in the rubbish bin.*
*We know where to start, **luckily**.*

Comment adverbials generally go at the beginning of the sentence. They can sometimes go at the end of the sentence.

G 5.3 Comparative and superlative adjectives: form

Workshop 1

For most adjectives, we add *-er* to make comparative adjectives and *the ... -est* to make superlative adjectives.
*near – near**er** – **the near**est*

! For adjectives that end in *e*, we add *-r* or *-st*: *nice – nicer – the nicest*

For adjectives that end in *y*, we change the *y* to *i*, so we add *-ier* or the *-iest*: *happy – happier – the happiest*

For adjectives that end in one **vowel** and one **consonant**, we double the **consonant**:
big – bigger – the biggest

We don't use *the* before comparatives and we don't use *as* after comparatives.
*Your ice cream is bigger **than** mine.* NOT ~~...bigger than the mine~~ OR ~~bigger as mine.~~

For long adjectives (three syllables or more), we use *more* for comparative adjectives and *the most* for superlative adjectives.
interesting – **more** *interesting* – **the most** *interesting*

! For many two-syllable adjectives, we can use either *-er* and *-est* **or** *more* and *the most*.

We use *-er* and *-est* with adjectives that end in *-y* or the sounds [ə] and [l]:
easier, the easiest • *cleverer, the cleverest* • *simpler, the simplest* NOT ~~more easy …~~

We use *more* and *the most* with adjectives that end in *-ful*, *-less*, and *-ing*:
the most careful • *the most useless* • *the most boring* NOT ~~the carefullest …~~

The adjectives *good* and *bad* are irregular: *good – better – the best* • *bad – worse – the worst*

We can use *one of the* before superlative adjectives to talk about a member of a group. When we use *one of the*, we make the noun plural.
She's **one of the cleverest** *students in the class.*

We make comparisons like this:

Comparative + *than*	not as + adjective + as
She's **taller than** *me.*	*I'm* **not as tall as** *her.*
He's **more careful than** *me.*	*I'm not* **as careful as** *him.*

G 5.4 Comparative and superlative adverbs: form   Workshop 1

For adverbs with one syllable, we add *-er* for comparative adverbs and *the …-est* for superlative adverbs.
For adverbs with two or more syllables, we add *more* for comparative adverbs and *the most* for superlative adverbs.

	comparative	superlative
fast	fast**er**	**the** fast**est**
hard	hard**er**	**the** hard**est**
high	high**er**	**the** high**est**

	comparative	superlative
quietly	**more** quietly	**the most** quietly
carefully	**more** carefully	**the most** carefully
noisily	**more** noisily	**the most** noisily

Some adverbs are irregular:

	comparative	superlative
well	better	the best
badly	worse	the worst

Irregular verbs

infinitive	simple past	past participle	German
to **arise** [əˈraɪz]	**arose** [əˈrəʊz]	**arisen** [əˈrɪzən]	entstehen
to **be**	**was / were**	**been**	sein
to **beat**	**beat**	**beaten**	schlagen
to **become**	**became**	**become**	werden
to **begin**	**began**	**begun**	beginnen, anfangen
to **bet**	**bet**	**bet**	wetten
to **bite** [baɪt]	**bit** [bɪt]	**bitten** [ˈbɪtn]	beißen
to **bleed** [bliːd]	**bled** [bled]	**bled** [bled]	bluten
to **blow**	**blew**	**blown**	blasen
to **break**	**broke**	**broken**	brechen
to **bring**	**brought**	**brought**	bringen
to **build**	**built**	**built**	bauen
to **burn**	**burnt / burned**	**burnt / burned**	(ver)brennen
to **burst**	**burst**	**burst**	platzen
to **buy**	**bought**	**bought**	kaufen
to **catch**	**caught**	**caught**	fangen
to **choose** [tʃuːz]	**chose** [tʃəʊz]	**chosen** [ˈtʃəʊzən]	auswählen
to **come**	**came**	**come**	kommen
to **cost**	**cost**	**cost**	kosten
to **cut**	**cut**	**cut**	schneiden
to **deal** [diːl]	**dealt** [delt]	**dealt** [delt]	handeln
to **dig**	**dug**	**dug**	graben
to **do** [duː]	**did** [dɪd]	**done** [dʌn]	machen, tun
to **draw**	**drew**	**drawn**	zeichnen
to **dream** [driːm]	**dreamt** [dremt] / **dreamed** [driːmd]	**dreamt** [dremt] / **dreamed** [driːmd]	träumen

infinitive	simple past	past participle	German
to **drink**	**drank**	**drunk**	trinken
to **drive** [draɪv]	**drove** [drəʊv]	**driven** [ˈdrɪvən]	fahren
to **eat** [iːt]	**ate** [et, eɪt]	**eaten** [ˈiːtn]	essen
to **fall**	**fell**	**fallen**	fallen, stürzen
to **feed** [fiːd]	**fed** [fed]	**fed** [fed]	füttern
to **feel** [fiːl]	**felt** [felt]	**felt** [felt]	(sich) fühlen, spüren
to **fight**	**fought**	**fought**	kämpfen
to **find**	**found**	**found**	finden
to **fly**	**flew**	**flown**	fliegen
to **forget**	**forgot**	**forgotten**	vergessen
to **forgive**	**forgave**	**forgiven**	vergeben
to **freeze**	**froze**	**frozen**	frieren
to **get**	**got**	**got / gotten (AE)**	bekommen, holen
to **give**	**gave**	**given**	geben, schenken
to **go** [gəʊ]	**went** [went]	**gone** [gɒn]	gehen, fahren
to **grow** [grəʊ]	**grew** [gruː]	**grown** [grəʊn]	wachsen, anbauen
to **hang**	**hung**	**hung**	hängen
to **have (got)**	**had**	**had**	haben
to **hear** [hɪə]	**heard** [hɜːd]	**heard** [hɜːd]	hören
to **hide** [haɪd]	**hid** [hɪd]	**hidden** [hɪdn]	(sich) verstecken
to **hit**	**hit**	**hit**	schlagen
to **hold**	**held**	**held**	halten
to **hurt**	**hurt**	**hurt**	wehtun

infinitive	simple past	past participle	German
to **keep** [ki:p]	**kept** [kept]	**kept** [kept]	(be)halten
to **kneel** [ni:l]	**knelt** [nelt]	**knelt** [nelt]	knien
to **know** [nəʊ]	**knew** [nju:]	**known** [nəʊn]	wissen, kennen
to **lead** [li:d]	**led** [led]	**led** [led]	führen
to **learn**	**learnt / learned**	**learnt / learned**	lernen
to **leave** [li:v]	**left** [left]	**left** [left]	verlassen
to **lend**	**lent**	**lent**	leihen
to **let**	**let**	**let**	lassen
to **lie**	**lay**	**lain**	liegen
to **light** [laɪt]	**lit** [lɪt] / **lighted** [ˈlaɪtɪd]	**lit** [lɪt] / **lighted** [ˈlaɪtɪd]	anzünden, anmachen
to **lose** [lu:z]	**lost** [lɒst]	**lost** [lɒst]	verlieren
to **make**	**made**	**made**	machen, herstellen
to **mean** [mi:n]	**meant** [ment]	**meant** [ment]	bedeuten
to **meet** [mi:t]	**met** [met]	**met** [met]	(sich) treffen, kennen-lernen
to **mow**	**mowed**	**mown / mowed**	mähen
to **pay**	**paid**	**paid**	bezahlen
to **put**	**put**	**put**	stellen
to **quit**	**quit**	**quit**	aufhören
to **read** [ri:d]	**read** [red]	**read** [red]	lesen
to **rebuild**	**rebuilt**	**rebuilt**	wieder aufbauen
to **rewrite** [ˌri:ˈraɪt]	**rewrote** [ˌri:ˈrəʊt]	**rewritten** [ˌri:ˈrɪtn]	umschreiben
to **ride** [raɪd]	**rode** [rəʊd]	**ridden** [ˈrɪdn]	fahren, reiten
to **ring**	**rang**	**rung**	klingeln, anrufen

infinitive	simple past	past participle	German
to **rise** [raɪz]	**rose** [rəʊz]	**risen** [ˈrɪzən]	ansteigen, (sich) erheben
to **run**	**ran**	**run**	laufen, rennen, leiten
to **say** [seɪ]	**said** [sed]	**said** [sed]	sagen
to **see**	**saw**	**seen**	sehen
to **sell**	**sold**	**sold**	verkaufen
to **send**	**sent**	**sent**	schicken
to **set**	**set**	**set**	setzen, stellen, legen
to **shake**	**shook**	**shaken**	schütteln
to **shine** [ʃaɪn]	**shone** [ʃɒn]	**shone** [ʃɒn]	scheinen
to **shoot** [ʃu:t]	**shot** [ʃɒt]	**shot** [ʃɒt]	schießen
to **show**	**showed**	**shown / showed**	zeigen
to **shrink**	**shrank**	**shrunk**	schrumpfen
to **sing**	**sang**	**sung**	singen
to **sink**	**sank**	**sunk**	sinken
to **sit**	**sat**	**sat**	sitzen
to **slay** [sleɪ]	**slew** [slu:]	**slain** [sleɪn]	töten; schlachten
to **sleep** [sli:p]	**slept** [slept]	**slept** [slept]	schlafen
to **smell**	**smelt / smelled**	**smelt / smelled**	riechen
to **speak** [spi:k]	**spoke** [spəʊk]	**spoken** [ˈspəʊkən]	sprechen
to **spend**	**spent**	**spent**	verbringen, ausgeben
to **split**	**split**	**split**	sich trennen
to **spoil**	**spoilt**	**spoilt**	verderben
to **spread**	**spread**	**spread**	sich ausbreiten, etw. verteilen

infinitive	simple past	past participle	German
to **stand**	**stood**	**stood**	stehen
to **steal**	**stole**	**stolen**	stehlen
to **stick**	**stuck**	**stuck**	kleben
to **sting**	**stung**	**stung**	stechen
to **strike**	**struck**	**struck**	zuschlagen; treffen
to **strive** [straɪv]	**strove** [strəʊv]	**striven** [ˈstrɪvən]	sich bemühen
to **swim**	**swam**	**swum**	schwimmen
to **take**	**took**	**taken**	nehmen, dauern
to **teach** [tiːtʃ]	**taught** [tɔːt]	**taught** [tɔːt]	unterrichten
to **tear** [teə]	**tore** [tɔː]	**torn** [tɔːn]	reißen

infinitive	simple past	past participle	German
to **tell**	**told**	**told**	sagen, erzählen
to **think**	**thought**	**thought**	denken, glauben
to **throw**	**threw**	**thrown**	werfen
to **understand**	**understood**	**understood**	verstehen
to **wake up**	**woke up**	**woken up**	aufwachen
to **wear** [weə]	**wore** [wɔː]	**worn** [wɔːn]	tragen
to **weave**	**wove**	**woven**	weben
to **win** [wɪn]	**won** [wʌn]	**won** [wʌn]	gewinnen
to **withdraw**	**withdrew**	**withdrawn**	sich zurückziehen
to **write** [raɪt]	**wrote** [rəʊt]	**written** [ˈrɪtn]	schreiben

Vocabulary

Here are all the words from the workshops. They are in the same order as in the workshop.

There is the page number and the activity.

A ▢ at the side is for words from the listening text. A ▢ is for words from videos.

Words in **grey** are important for one text or they are culture-specific. You don't have to be able to use them actively and you can always find them in the dictionary list at the end of the book

The phonetic transcription in the Vocabulary and in the Dictionary [ ] tells you how you say a word in British English.

The example sentence shows you how we use a word.
= shows words with the same meaning
≠ shows words with the opposite meaning

! shows words with the same meaning in French, Latin or Spanish or it gives other interesting information about the word.

When you work with the *Vocabulary*, cover the German, look at the English word and the example and say the German word. You can also cover the German and the example sentences to practise the English.

page	exercise	**Welcome Workshop**		
10		to **defeat** [dɪˈfiːt]	*In which of these battles did the Scots defeat the English?*	besiegen
		civil [ˈsɪvl]	*What was the reason for the American Civil War?*	Bürger…; bürgerlich
		slavery [ˈsleɪvəri]	*You are going to listen to a radio documentary about slavery.*	Sklaverei
		rebellious [rɪˈbeljəs]	*Which of these musical genres is associated with rebellious youth?* **!** *Lat. 'rebellis; -e'*	rebellisch; rebellierend
		blues [bluːz]	*Although the blues evolved in the US south, it has lots of musical influences from Africa.*	Blues
		wave [weɪv]	*A wave of riots swept major cities across the country.*	Welle
		to **abolish** [əˈbɒlɪʃ]	*The slave trade was abolished in 1808, but slavery was still legal.* **!** *Fr. 'abolir'; Sp. 'abolir'*	abschaffen
		racism [ˈreɪsɪzəm]	*Can you think of any recent controversies in Germany connected to racism or racist language?*	Rassismus
11		**primatologist** [ˈpraɪmətɒlədʒɪst]	*The primatologist won an award for her research with monkeys.*	Primatenforscher(in)
		wise [waɪz]	*My mother is wise and gives good advice.*	weise; klug
		ripple [ˈrɪpl]	*I alone cannot change the world, but I can cast a stone across the water to create many ripples.*	Welle; Kräuselung
		to **pick** [pɪk]	*Try to persuade your group that the quote you picked is the best one.*	auswählen
		referendum [ˌrefəˈrendəm]	*Personally, if I got the chance to vote in a new referendum I'd vote 'yes'.*	Referendum; Volksabstimmung

page	exercise	**Welcome Workshop**		
		momentous [məˈmentəs]	*I was much too young at the time to vote, but it was a momentous event in recent history.*	bedeutsam; folgenschwer
		jazz [dʒæz]	*Musicians combined elements of jazz and soul to create a new sound.*	Jazz
		grunge [grʌndʒ]	*I'll probably give any music a go, but I do find metal and grunge just a little bit too loud and not to my taste.*	Grunge
		to tend to [tend tə]	*Teenagers across the world tend to be far more similar than they are to their parents' generation.*	zu etwas neigen
		to nag [næg]	*My dad nags me for spending too much time on my smartphone without asking me what I'm doing.*	an jemandem herumnörgeln

page 12	exercise	**Workshop 1**		
		to embed [ɪmˈbed]	*Scotland embedded LGBTI teaching across the curriculum.*	einbetten; verankern
		rationale [ˌræʃəˈnɑːl]	*The rationale for investing more in education is clear.*	Begründung
		subsequently [ˈsʌbsɪkwəntli]	*She won the award and subsequently got a scholarship to study.*	folglich; darauf folgend
		to attempt [əˈtempt]	*You should attempt to get better results.*	versuchen
		suicide [ˈsuːɪsaɪd]	*Too many teens are depressed and attempt suicide!* ❗ *Lat. 'suicidium, -i'; Fr. 'suicide' (m.)*	Suizid; Selbstmord
		proactively [ˌprəʊˈæktɪvli]	*The Scottish government should be applauded for proactively looking to address social issues.*	proaktiv
		demise [dɪˈmaɪz]	*The demise of tropical coral reefs shows the threat of climate change.*	Niedergang
		coral [ˈkɒrəl]	*Tropical coral reefs are dying.*	Korallen...
		to symbolize [ˈsɪmbəlaɪz]	*The demise of tropical coral reefs symbolizes the threat of climate change.*	symbolisieren
		offshore [ˌɒfˈʃɔːr]	*Not far offshore in western Scotland you can find vast reefs.*	küstennah; offshore
		calcified [ˈkælsɪfaɪd]	*In the reefs there are calcified organisms like mussels.*	verkalkt
		seaweed [ˈsiːwiːd]	*The reefs are formed by cold-water coral and calcified seaweed.*	Seetang
		biodiverse [ˌbaɪəʊdaɪˈvɜːs]	*Coral reefs are some of the most biodiverse ecosystems on the planet.*	artenreich
		ecosystem [ˈiːkəʊsɪstəm]	*Marine ecosystems are also important habitats.*	Ökosystem
		scallop [ˈskɒləp]	*Cold-water coral reefs provide a home to species like scallops and catsharks.*	Kammmuschel; Jakobsmuschel

page   exercise

Workshop 1		
catshark [kætʃɑːk]	*Catsharks live in cold water reefs.*	Katzenhai
to **erase** [ɪˈreɪz]	*We need to learn from the past, not erase it.*	auslöschen
loch [lɒk, lɒx]	*In recent years scientists have been analysing water from Loch Ness for DNA.*	Loch; See
to **surface** [ˈsɜːfɪs]	*The most likely candidate for Nessie that has surfaced in media reporting of the research is a giant eel.*	auftauchen
eel [iːl]	*Eel DNA was detected at many locations in Loch Ness.*	Aal
to **sample** [ˈsɑːmpl]	*Eel DNA was detected at almost every location sampled in Loch Ness.*	probieren; eine Probe nehmen
catfish [ˈkætfɪʃ]	*Shark, catfish and sturgeon are all fish.*	Wels
exotic [ɪɡˈzɒtɪk]	⚠ *Fr. 'exotique'; Sp. 'exotico'*	exotisch
at least [ət liːst]	*Think of at least two things the text does not tell you about Edinburgh.*	mindestens
to **debunk** [diːˈbʌŋk]	*Another idea that has been debunked is that climate change is natural.*	widerlegen; entlarven
bagpipe [ˈbæɡpaɪp]	*Another myth that has recently been debunked is the idea that bagpipes are particularly Scottish.*	Dudelsack
tartan [ˈtɑːtn]	*My grandmother wears tartan skirts.*	Tartan; Schottenstoff
wail [weɪl]	*In Edinburgh I often hear the familiar wail of bagpipes.*	Klagen, Jammern, Klagelaut
unpalatable [ʌnˈpælətəbl]	*Some people find meat unpalatable.*	ungenießbar
bound: to be bound [biː baʊnd]**, was, been** [wəz, biːn]	*If you go to the mall you're bound to spend money.*	etwas zwangsläufig tun
walker [ˈwɔːkər]	*Some walkers set themselves the challenge of climbing each of the 282 Munros.*	Wanderer; Wanderin
formidable [fəˈmɪdəbl]	*These keen walkers have set themselves some formidable challenges.*	beachtlich; gewaltig
summit [ˈsʌmɪt]	*Our challenge is to reach the summit of the mountain.* ⚠ *Lat. 'summitas, -is' (f.)*	Gipfel
disposable [dɪˈspəʊzəbl]	*What is your disposable income?*	verfügbar
to **value** [ˈvæljuː]	*Many UK residents are valuing the relatively low costs of hillwalking.*	wertschätzen
staycation [ˌsteɪˈkeɪʃn]	*People are enjoying staycations as a way of saving money.*	Ferien zuhause
hillwalking [ˈhɪlwɔːkɪŋ]	*Hillwalking is a low cost activity to do on holiday.*	Wandern
gear [ɡɪər]	*We got hiking gear for our trip.*	Ausrüstung
achievable [əˈtʃiːvəbl]	*My own view is that Net Zero is achievable and desirable, but there will be problems along the way.*	erreichbar

page	exercise	**Workshop 1**		
		aching [ˈeɪkɪŋ]	*After a day of hard work you need to relax your aching muscles.*	schmerzend; schmerzhaft
		to **recuperate** [rɪˈkjuːpəreɪt]	*After the long hike, you'll want to sleep in your own bed and let your aching muscles recuperate.*	sich erholen
		to **nurture** [ˈnɜːtʃə]	*Our botanical creams work to revive, nurture, restore and protect.*	pflegen; fördern
		to **flourish** [ˈflʌrɪʃ]	*There is a flourishing network of long-distance footpaths.*	(auf)blühen; gedeihen
		footpath [ˈfʊtpɑːθ]	*We walked along the footpath to the next town.*	Fußweg; Pfad
		halo [ˈheɪləʊ]	*The footpaths produced a 'halo effect' around mountain-based activities.*	Strahlenkranz
13		**unicorn** [ˈjuːnɪkɔːn]	*The official animal of Scotland is the unicorn, so it's not only Nessie who isn't real.*	Einhorn
		freshwater [ˈfreʃwɔːtə]	*There are more than 30,000 freshwater lochs throughout the country.*	Süßwasser
		essence [ˈesns]	*Traditional Scottish bagpipe music is the essence of this country in a sound.* **⚠** *Sp. 'esencia' (f.)*	Wesen; Wesentliche
		fearless [ˈfɪələs]	*The history of our country is full of stories about fearless warriors.*	furchtlos
		bloody [ˈblʌdi]	*They fought bloody battles.*	blutig
		loyalty [ˈlɔɪəlti]	*Scottish history is full of bloody battles and passionate loyalties.*	Loyalität; Treue
		lyrics [ˈlɪrɪks]	*Traditional songs were handed down and old lyrics were often turned into new ones.*	Liedtext
		rival [ˈraɪvl]	*He had a rival for the place on the team.*	Rivale; Rivalin
		affection [əˈfekʃn]	*It's a wonderful moment and one that underlines the affection for the song.*	Zuneigung
		bare [beə]	*He spent a night on the bare mountainside*	nackt; kahl
		to **hark** [hɑːk]		*altmodisch für:* (zu)hören
		to **leap** [liːp]	*During their walks, they leaped over a lot of streams*	springen; (an)steigen
		to **tower** [ˈtaʊə]	*The towering walls of the Acropolis are a spectacular sight.*	ragen; sich erheben
		gallant [ˈgælənt]	*The team made a gallant effort to win the game, although they were the underdogs.*	furchtlos; höflich
		standard [ˈstændəd]	*The Royal Standard is the flag used by the monarch of the United Kingdom.*	Flagge; Fahne

page	exercise	**Workshop 1**		
		endeavour [ɪnˈdevə]	*You must make an endeavour to work harder.*	Bemühen; Anstrengung
		misty [ˈmɪsti]	*It can become quite misty in the Highlands.*	neblig; dunstig
		purple [ˈpɜːpl]	*Purple is often associated with royalty.*	lila; violett
		staunch [stɔːntʃ]	*He is a staunch supporter of Scottish independence.*	standhaft; treu
		fair [feə]	*Kathleen has dark hair and fair skin.*	schön
		maiden [ˈmeɪdn]	*= a young woman that is not married*	Maid (*altmodisch*); unverheiratete Frau
		sunlit [ˈsʌnlɪt]	*Tom enjoys walking through the sunlit streets in the afternoon.*	sonnenbestrahlt
		to **yearn for sth./so.** [jɜːn fə]	*I've always yearned to go to a rock festival.*	nach etw./jmd. verlangen; schmachten
		to **beam** [biːm]	*My brother beamed with joy at the sight of his new sneakers.*	strahlen; glänzen
		to **long for sth./so.** [lɒŋ fə]	*Helen longed for a new adventure, so she quit her job.*	sich nach etw./jmd. sehnen
14	1a	**courage** [ˈkʌrɪdʒ]	*Young people today will need courage to deal with growing environmental problems.*	Mut
		compassion [kəmˈpæʃn]	*He believed that young people have more courage, more strength and more compassion than they realize.*	Mitgefühl; Anteilnahme
		charitable [ˈtʃærətəbl]	❗ *Fr. 'charitable'*	Wohltätigkeits...
		scheme [skiːm]	*The award forms a core part of many apprenticeships and training schemes in the UK.*	Programm
		holder [ˈhəʊldə]	*The award holders were listed in the newspaper.*	Träger(in), Halter(in)
		to **recruit** [rɪˈkruːt]	*Our company is recruiting new employees.*	einstellen; rekrutieren
		resilience [rɪˈzɪliəns]	*We all look back on the adventure and how it helped us to develop resilience in the face of adversity.*	Widerstandsfähigkeit
		inception [ɪnˈsepʃn]	*Participation in the award has grown every year since inception.*	Einführung
		boundary [ˈbaʊndri]	*I set boundaries to my digital activities.*	Grenze
15	4a	**posh** [pɒʃ]	*The hike is much easier with all of your posh gear.*	schick; nobel
		afield [əˈfiːld]	*I've been thinking we should go further afield on this hiking trip.*	draußen
		gentle [ˈdʒentl]	*I'm surprised as I always think of you as being so kind and gentle.*	sanft

page	exercise	Workshop 1		
		stroll [strəʊl]	Awe-inspiring views, a relaxing pool and top attractions are just a short stroll away.	Spaziergang
		terrain [təˈreɪn]	The terrain isn't particularly difficult to walk. ❗ Fr. 'terrain' (f.); Sp. 'terreno' (m.)	Gelände
		civilization [ˌsɪvəlaɪˈzeɪʃn]	We like to hike rough terrain and be cut off from civilization.	Zivilisation
		to rely on [rɪˈlaɪ]	We all rely far too much on mobile phones.	sich verlassen auf
	4b	**rugged** [ˈrʌgɪd]	We need something rugged so that it's challenging.	rau; schroff
	5	**estate** [ɪˈsteɪt]	There is a large house and a lake on the estate.	Anwesen
		heathered [ˈheðəd]	The landscape is varied, you'll find heathered moors and wild rivers.	mit Heide bewachsen
		ragged [ˈrægɪd]	The landscape is beautiful, with rolling hills and ragged peaks in the distance.	zerklüftet
		ample [ˈæmpl]	In the forests there is ample opportunity for wild camping.	ausreichend
		waymarking [ˈweɪmɑːkɪŋ]	There is no waymarking anywhere here in order to protect nature.	Wegmarkierung
		fiercely [ˈfɪəsli]	There is no waymarking anywhere as nature is fiercely protected.	heftig; verbissen
		navigation [ˌnævɪˈgeɪʃn]	❗ Lat. 'navigare (-o, -avi, -atum)' = to go by ship; Fr. 'navigation' (f.); Sp. 'navegación' (f.)	Navigation
		to accommodate [əˈkɒmədeɪt]	If you decide to visit our hotel, contact us first as we can only accommodate one group at a time.	unterbringen
		to notify [ˈnəʊtɪfaɪ]	If hikers don't return on time we notify mountain rescue.	benachrichtigen
16	1a	**horrendous** [həˈrendəs]	We had horrendous weather on holiday.	schrecklich
		heaven [ˈhevn]	The heavens are opening up and the rain is coming down.	Himmel
		fog [fɒg]	The heavy fog made the path difficult to see.	Nebel
		boggy [ˈbɒgi]	The path was very wet and boggy.	matschig
		stepping-stone [ˈstepɪŋ stəʊn]	One of the walkers in my group managed to slip off some stepping-stones straight into the water.	Trittstein
		bog [bɒg]	I slipped and ended up in the bog.	Sumpf; Moor
		to traverse [trəˈvɜːs]	I attempted to traverse the same route she had taken before ending up in the bog myself.	durchqueren
		waist [weɪst]	I slipped and fell to my waist in the bog.	Taille

page	exercise			
		Workshop 1		
		to **wander** ['wɒndə]	Don't wander off the path or you might get lost in the forest.	wandern
		to **pitch** [pɪtʃ]	We ended up pitching two tents that the five of us squeezed into.	aufstellen
		torchlight ['tɔːtʃlaɪt]	It was dark by the time our rescue party found us and we had to pack our tents away by torchlight.	Fackelschein; Taschenlampenlicht
		clearing ['klɪərɪŋ]	We found a clearing in the forest to camp in.	Lichtung
		adversity [əd'vɜːsəti]	Though we were all miserable at the time, we developed resilience in the face of adversity.	Widrigkeit
		assessor [ə'sesə]	❗ Lat. 'assessor, -is' (m.)	Gutacher(in); Bewerter(in)
		legendary ['ledʒəndri]	He is a legendary artist: generations have listened to his music.	legendär
	2	**rig** [rɪg]	Her dad works on the rigs, so they live in Aberdeen.	Bohrinsel
		dull [dʌl]	We had a very dull evening.	öde; langweilig
		gloomy ['gluːmi]	The expression 'having the blues' means you are feeling gloomy.	trübe; schlechtgelaunt
17		to **originate** [ə'rɪdʒɪneɪt]	Lots of place names in Scotland originate from Gaelic.	stammen
	2	to **boast** [bəʊst]	My culture proudly boasts ancient myths and legends.	sich rühmen
		to **entwine** [ɪn'twaɪn]	The town proudly boasts ancient myths and legends entwined into vibrant modern culture.	verflechten
		unbeknownst [ˌʌnbɪ'nəʊnst]	Unbeknownst to most, Scotland's most commonly spoken language wasn't always English.	unbekannt
		whilst [waɪlst]	Whilst you're in Scotland, be sure to go listen to traditional music.	wenn
		to **weave** [wiːv], **wove, woven** [wəʊv, 'wəʊvən]	Gaelic is woven into everyday life and culture in Scotland.	weben
		to **stem from** [stem frəm]	Our culture stems from a long and colourful history.	von etwas kommen
		fitting ['fɪtɪŋ]	Milo is a very fitting name for such a cute puppy.	passend
		abbey ['æbi]	The building of abbeys on the borders and coast meant other languages became more dominant.	Kloster
		lowland ['ləʊlənd]	The growth of industry in many lowland towns and villages meant other languages became more dominant.	Ebene
		legislation [ˌledʒɪs'leɪʃn]	We hope that as people's attitudes are changing this will be reflected in the legislation. ❗ Lat. 'lex, legis' (f.) = law	Gesetzgebung

page	exercise	**Workshop 1**		
		sole [səʊl]	English was the sole language taught in schools following the Education Act. ⚠ Fr. 'seul'; Sp. 'solo'	einzig
		to result [rɪˈzʌlt]	The law resulted in many children who spoke Gaelic being forced to attend school in English.	resultieren; als Ergebnis haben
		ultimately [ˈʌltɪmətli]	The law that required children to speak English in school ultimately led to the Gaelic language primarily being used at home.	schlussendlich
		landlordism [ˈlændlɔːdˈɪzəm]	People in Highland communities were forced off their land by famine, landlordism and economic decline.	Großgrundbesitzertum
		remnant [ˈremnənt]	You can see remnants of Gaelic in countries with immigrant pasts.	Überrest
		to reverberate [rɪˈvɜːbəreɪt]	Lower frequencies reverberate longer than higher frequencies.	nachhallen
		handwoven [hændˈwəʊvn]	The jacket is made from handwoven cloth.	handgewebt
		tweed [twiːd]	The tweed jacket makes me itch.	Tweed(stoff)
		spirited [ˈspɪrɪtɪd]	Despite many challenges over time, Gaelic and its spirited culture has survived.	lebendig
		odds [ɒdz]	Against all odds they finally managed to succeed.	Chancen; Widrigkeiten
		to soak up [səʊk]	In Scotland you can soak up a welcoming atmosphere, history and Gaelic culture.	aufsaugen
		blockbuster [ˈblɒkbʌstə]	One blockbuster that everybody remembers was The Lion King.	Blockbuster; Hit
		to grace [greɪs]	The party was graced by film stars.	zieren; schmücken
		bard [bɑːd]	Shakespeare is one of the best-known bards in the world.	Barde
		mythical [ˈmɪθɪkl]	The stories draw on legends to create a mythical world. ⚠ Fr. 'mythique'; Sp. 'mítico'	mystisch; geheimnisvoll
		whisky [ˈwɪski]	The word 'whisky' is short for the Gaelic word that means 'water of life'. ⚠ 'whiskey' (in Ireland and the US)	Whisky
		to charm [tʃɑːm]	We were charmed by his good manners.	einnehmen; bezaubern
		to exchange [ɪksˈtʃeɪndʒ]	Let's exchange addresses.	austauschen
		pleasantry [ˈplezntri]	When people meet they exchange a few pleasantries.	Nettigkeit
		to immerse [ɪˈmɜːs]	There are plenty of ways to immerse yourself in a language and its culture.	eintauchen
18	1b	**renowned** [rɪˈnaʊnd]	On today's programme we're talking to renowned Scottish historians.	renommiert; berühmt

page	exercise	Workshop 1		
		fake [feɪk]	*The topic of the programme is the problem with fake news.*	falsch; fake
		to portray [pɔːˈtreɪ]	*The movie portrays Mary and Queen Elizabeth as friends, but they were rivals from the start.*	darstellen; porträtieren
		artistic [ɑːˈtɪstɪk]	*My mum is a painter and other people in my family are artistic, too.*	künstlerisch
		cold-blooded [ˌkəʊld ˈblʌdɪd]	*It's true that he killed a king, but it wasn't cold-blooded murder, it was during a battle.*	kaltblütig
	2a	**fortification** [ˌfɔːtɪfɪˈkeɪʃn]	*Despite building two impressive fortifications the Romans never truly conquered Caledonia.*	Festung
		to withdraw [wɪðˈdrɔː], **withdrew, withdrawn** [wɪðˈdruː, wɪðˈdrɔːn]	*The Romans had to withdraw because they were loosing.*	sich zurückziehen
		to retreat [rɪˈtriːt]	*The Romans withdrew and over time retreated away from Britain.*	zurückweichen
		treacherous [ˈtretʃərəs]	*Vikings crossed the treacherous North Sea and settled in Scotland.*	verräterisch; tückisch
		to forge [fɔːdʒ]	*Ancient people forged the kingdom of Alba.*	schmieden
		to seize [siːz]	*The Scots seized the opportunity to attack at the crossing of the River Forth.*	ergreifen
		unrest [ʌnˈrest]	*There are periods of civil unrest in the USA.*	Unruhe(n)
		to imprison [ɪmˈprɪzn]	*Elizabeth I imprisoned Mary and later had her executed.*	einsperren
		captivity [kæpˈtɪvəti]	*I am absolutely positive that raising animals in captivity is cruel.* ⊞ *Fr. 'captivité' (f.)*	Gefangenschaft
19	3	**to strike** [straɪk], **struck, struck** [strʌk, strʌk]	*When famine struck, many people left the land to work in factories.*	zuschlagen; treffen
		landlord [ˈlændlɔːd]	*Many landlords paid for the farmers on their land to emigrate.*	Grundbesitzer; Verpächter
	4a	**croft** [krɒft]	*We didn't have a farm, only a small croft.*	Kate; kleiner Hof
		to huddle [ˈhʌdl]	*After the kids went to sleep the parents huddled by the fireplace and talked in low voices.*	hocken
		to whisper [ˈwɪspə]	*At night my parents would huddle by the fireplace whispering.*	flüstern
		passage [ˈpæsɪdʒ]	*We didn't have to pay for the passage to America.* ⊞ *Fr. 'passage' (f.), Sp. 'pasaje' (m.)*	Überfahrt; Passage
		to get rid of [get rɪd əv], **got, got** [gɒt, gɒt]	*Landlords wanted to get rid of the crofters so they could use the land themselves.*	loswerden

page	exercise	Workshop 1		
20	1a	**to dust** [dʌst]	*He stood up and dusted himself off.*	abstauben
		to drag [dræg]	*The child was dragging his feet and looking back at the playground.*	schleppen
		to confront [kənˈfrʌnt]	*They confronted him about the missing things.*	konfrontieren; entgegentreten
		to blurt [blɜːt]	*He can't keep a secret. He blurts everything out immediately.*	herausplatzen
	2	**knight** [naɪt]	*Robert the Bruce was knight and lord of Annandale.*	Ritter
		supposedly [səˈpəʊzɪdli]	*Many photographs have been produced supposedly showing the Loch Ness Monster.*	angeblich
		hoax [həʊks]	*Many of the stories have been shown to be hoaxes and yet the legends continue.*	Falschmeldung; Schwindel
		whirlpool [ˈwɜːlpuːl]	*It can be dangerous if you get too close to a whirlpool.*	Strudel
		unlike [ˌʌnˈlaɪk]	*The brothers are very unlike each other.*	anders als
		to dispute [dɪˈspjuːt]	*Unlike the other two legends there is no disputing that the earth is not flat!*	bestreiten; anfechten
		hemp [hemp]	*The rope made from hemp wasn't as strong as the one made from wool.*	Hanf
		maiden [ˈmeɪdn]	*Maiden is an old word for a girl.*	Maid; Jungfer
		purity [ˈpjʊərəti]	🅱 *Lat. 'purus, - a, -um' = pure*	Reinheit
		unbreakable [ʌnˈbreɪkəbl]	*It was said that the purity of the maiden's hair would make the rope unbreakable.*	unzerbrechlich
21	3a	**to defy** [dɪˈfaɪ]	*They defied all the common rules.*	trotzen; sich widersetzen
		convention [kənˈvenʃn]	*She defied convention in her culture and went to university.*	Konvention
		urge [ɜːdʒ]	*You have to resist the urge to check what others post on social media.*	Drang
		to voyage [ˈvɔɪɪdʒ]	*Someday I hope to voyage around the world.* = *travel*	reisen
		trapper [ˈtræpə]	*The fur trappers lead the group up the mountain.*	Fallensteller(in)
		trader [ˈtreɪdə]	*They voyaged into the Arctic with the help of trappers and traders.*	Händler(in)
		lifelong [ˈlaɪflɒŋ]	*They met in kindergarten and became lifelong friends.*	lebenslang
		botany [ˈbɒtəni]	*Isobel loves botany and travel, so she often visits places with forests and gardens.*	Pflanzenkunde
		impulse [ˈɪmpʌls]	*She travelled on impulse when she had the time and the money.*	Impuls; Anstoß

page	exercise	**Workshop 1**		
	4	**variation** [ˌveəriˈeɪʃn]	❗ *Lat. 'variatio, -nis' (f.);* *Fr. 'variation' (f.);* *Sp. 'variedad' (f.)*	Variation; Abwechslung

Scottish words

atholl [ˈæθə]	*a line dividing different areas* – Grenze	
Awa! [əˈwɑː]	*Get away!* – Ach, hör doch auf!	
aye [aɪ]	*yes* – ja	
blair [bleə]	*a meadow or field* – Wiese, Feld	
bonny / bonnie [ˈbɒnɪ]	*beautiful* – schön	
bothy [ˈbɒθɪ]	*a basic shelter (in the Highlands) that can be used by anyone* – Schutzhütte	
cauld [kɑːl(d)]	*cold* – kalt	
clan [klan]	*a social and political unit bearing a common name from (a supposed) ancestor and united under a chief* – Clan, Stamm, Sippe	
croft [krɒft]	*an area of land used to grow crops* – kleiner Bauernhof	
crofter [ˈkrɒftə]	*one who has tenure and use of a croft, typically as a tenant farmer* – Pächter und Bewohner eines *crofts*	
dinnae [dɪˈnə]	*do / does not (dae = to do, daes = does)*	
douk [duk]	*swim* – Bad	
dreich [drɪç]	*dull or gloomy weather* – trübes, tristes Wetter	
glen [glɛn]	*a valley* – Tal	
hame [heːm]	*home* – Zuhause	
ken [kɛn]	*to know* – wissen	
loch [lɒk, lɒx]	*a lake or fjord* – See, Meeresarm	
munro [ˈmənrəʊ]	*a mountain that is more than 3,000 feet (914 metres) high* – Berg von mind. 914m Höhe	
to bag a munro	*to climb a Scottish mountain that is more than 3,000 feet high* – einen *munro* erklimmen	
scran [skran]	*food* – Essen, Nahrung	
tae [te]	*to* – zu	
tattie [ˈtate]	*potato* – Kartoffel	
th'morra [ˈmɔrə]	*tomorrow* – morgen	
tidy [ˈtəɪdɪ]	*tasty* – lecker	
wee [wiː]	*small, little* – klein	
yer [jɛr]	*you* – du, ihr	

page	exercise			
22	1a	**gruelling** [ˈgruːəlɪŋ]	*The expedition up the mountain was gruelling.*	zermürbend; schwierig
		to dread [dred]	*He dreaded the test despite having studied for it.*	fürchten; sich scheuen
		excursion [ɪkˈskɜːʃn]	*During the excursion we all filled in our activity logs.*	Ausflug
		to collate [kəˈleɪt]	*Compare and collate your ideas with a partner.* ❗ *Lat. 'conferre (-confero, contuli, collatum)'*	zusammentragen; sammeln
		to allocate [ˈæləkeɪt]	*We allocated work to different people on the team.*	zuteilen
	2	**vegetation** [ˌvedʒəˈteɪʃn]	*I think the observations about vegetation and wildlife are important.*	Vegetation; Pflanzenwelt

page	exercise	Workshop 1		
		to **misplace** [ˌmɪsˈpleɪs]	*Bex misplaced her sunglasses and it took us ages to find them.*	verlegen
		to **scramble** [ˈskræmbl]	*Bex misplaced her sunglasses and everyone was scrambling around for ages looking for them.*	herumkriechen
		to **insist** [ɪnˈsɪst]	**!** *Lat. 'insistere (-sistō, -stiti', --)'; Fr. 'inisister'; Sp. 'insistir'*	bestehen auf
		landform [ˈlændfɔːm]	*Many landforms were created at the end of the ice age.*	Landform; Landschaft
		granite [ˈgrænɪt]	*There are granite landforms throughout the area.*	Granit
		tor [tɔːr]	*The landscape is full of granite tors.*	schroffer Fels
		glacier [ˈglæsiər]	*Many landforms come from ice age glaciers.* **!** *Fr. 'glacier' (m.); glaciar' (m.)*	Gletscher
		pinewood [ˈpaɪnwʊd]	*The chairs are made from a rare kind of pinewood found only in Scotland and Norway.*	Kiefernholz
		shrub [ʃrʌb]	*We planted a row of shrubs in front of the house.*	Busch
		juniper [ˈdʒuːnɪpə]	*Juniper are common plants in this area.*	Wacholder
		shrubby [ˈʃrʌbi]	*The area was full of shrubby plants.*	buschig
		grouse [graʊs]	*There were several grouse which Bex insisted were in fact turkeys.*	Moorhuhn
		to **comply with** [kəmˈplaɪ wɪð]	*You must agree to comply with the school's code of conduct.*	erfüllen
23	3	**logbook** [ˈlɒgbʊk]	*Be sure to write the results down in your logbook each day.*	Logbuch; Fahrtenbuch
	4a	**colloquial** [kəˈləʊkwiəl]	*Colloquial expressions are fine as long as they are not bad language.*	umgangssprachlich
		offensive [əˈfensɪv]	*Humour is fine of course, but make sure what you say is not offensive.*	beleidigend
	4b	to **assure** [əˈʃʊə]	*He assured us that there wouldn't be any need for using a map or a compass because he had studied and memorized the route.*	versichern
		to **memorize** [ˈmeməraɪz]	*He said he didn't need the map because he had memorized the route.*	auswendig lernen; sich merken
	5a	**content** [ˈkɒntent]	*When you talk about an event, make sure you organize the content in chronological order.*	Inhalt
	5b	**constructive** [kənˈstrʌktɪv]	*Make sure your feedback is balanced, constructive and includes concrete examples and suggestions.*	konstruktiv
24	S1	to **appeal** [əˈpiːl]	*How does the songwriter appeal to the reader's emotions?*	appellieren; gefallen; *hier:* ansprechen

page	exercise	**Workshop 1**		
		emotive [ɪˈməʊtɪv]	*Use strong and emotive language but never become aggressive or sarcastic.* ■ *Sp. 'emotivo'*	emotional; gefühlvoll
		rhetorical [rɪˈtɒrɪkl]	*He asks rhetorical questions to make his point.*	rhetorisch
	S3a	to **spiral** [ˈspaɪrəl]	*The forest path was thick with autumn leaves that crackled and spiralled away under her boots.*	sich drehen
		to **grease** [griːs]	*Line and grease the cake tin and pre-heat the oven to 160 degrees.*	(ein)fetten
		to **resemble** [rɪˈzembl]	*He resembled his father more than his mother.*	ähneln
		blade [bleɪd]	*His cheek bones resembled the blades of a knife.*	Schneide
		yolk [jəʊk]	*Separate the egg yolk from the white before mixing the dry ingredients.*	Eigelb
		silent [ˈsaɪlənt]	*Her lips moved in a silent prayer.* ■ *Lat. 'silentium, -i' (n.) = silence*	stumm; still
		thrilling [ˈθrɪlɪŋ]	*The band was musically thrilling and everyone danced.*	aufregend; spannend
		renovation [ˌrenəˈveɪʃn]	*During the renovation of our house we lived in an apartment we rented.*	Renovierung
		to **relocate** [ˌriːləʊˈkeɪt]	*During the renovations, the science lab will be relocated to Block F.*	verlegen; verlagern
		almond [ˈɑːmənd]	*One third of the flour can be replaced with ground almonds if preferred.*	Mandel
25	S1	**fortified** [ˈfɔːtɪfaɪd]	*Edinburgh Castle is one of the oldest fortified places in Europe.*	befestigt
		volcanic [vɒlˈkænɪk]	*The ground here is made of volcanic rock.*	vulkanisch
		residence [ˈrezɪdəns]	*This castle has a long, rich history as a royal residence.*	Residenz; Wohnsitz
		garrison [ˈgærɪsn]	*If you like history, it is worth visiting the old military garrison.*	Garnison; Standort
		fortress [ˈfɔːtrəs]	*This castle is a fortress and a prison.*	Festung
		to **suspect** [səˈspekt]	*Between the 15th and 18th centuries, women who were suspected to be witches were burnt.*	vermuten
		destiny [ˈdestəni]	*We want the power to determine the destiny of our oppressed communities.* ■ *Fr. 'destin' (m.); Sp. 'destino' (m.)*	Schicksal
	S2	**awe** [ɔː]	*They were in awe when they realized what had been achieved.*	Ehrfurcht
		spacious [ˈspeɪʃəs]	*Would you need a spacious family room with facilities for children?*	geräumig
		lone [ləʊn]	*If you are a lone traveller you only need one bed.*	allein

page	exercise	**Workshop 1**		
		toiletry [ˈtɔɪlətri]	*Our hotel offers free toiletries.*	Toilettenartikel
		complimentary [ˌkɒmplɪˈmentri]	*The hotel offers travellers complementary toiletries.*	kostenlos
		to chill (out) [tʃɪl aʊt]	*If you want to chill out after a busy day you can take a dip in our swimming pool.*	relaxen; chillen
		to squeeze [skwiːz]	*After work I squeeze in a workout.*	quetschen
		to equip [ɪˈkwɪp]	*We were equipped with everything we needed for the trip.*	ausrüsten
		leisurely [ˈleʒəli]	*I like to go for a leisurely walk after dinner.*	gemütlich
		exquisite [ɪkˈskwɪzɪt]	*Our chefs offer you exquisite Scottish dishes or prepare meals for your dietary requirements.*	ausgesucht; exquisit
		voucher [ˈvaʊtʃə]	*The hotel offers vouchers for city events.*	Gutschein
	S3	**catchy** [ˈkætʃi]	*You will need a good, catchy title and a short opening paragraph clearly indicating the purpose of your text.*	packend
26	2	**lavish** [ˈlævɪʃ]	*They have a video of their lavish wedding reception.*	großzügig
		wedding [ˈwedɪŋ]	*I was invited to their wedding.*	Hochzeit
		surroundings [səˈraʊndɪŋz]	*I feel that we have to be cautious about our surroundings because it's a dangerous world.*	Umwelt; Umgebung
		ballroom [ˈbɔːlruːm]	*The best part was filmed in a huge ballroom.*	Ballsaal
		fiddle [ˈfɪdl]	*He plays the fiddle and other string instruments.*	Geige; Fiedel
	3	**rural** [ˈrʊərəl]	❗ *Fr. 'rural'; Sp. 'rural'; Lat. 'ruricola, -ae' (f.) = farmer*	ländlich
		celebratory [ˌseləˈbreɪtəri]	*Cakes are common on celebratory occasions such as birthday parties.*	feierlich
		impromptu [ɪmˈprɒmptjuː]	*Impromptu gatherings took place in homes, where neighbours got together to share songs, music, poetry and storytelling.*	spontan
		waltz [wɔːls]	*The dancing varies from high energy dances to slower waltzes.*	Walzer
		assortment [əˈsɔːtmənt]	*The cèilidh band usually consists of two to six players who play an assortment of different instruments.*	Mischung
27	4a	**tacky** [ˈtæki]	*I can't wear those tacky pants!*	kitschig; hässlich
	5	**to retain** [rɪˈteɪn]	*Over the years, Scottish music has retained many traditional aspects.*	behalten
		distinction [dɪˈstɪŋkʃn]	*There is a great distinction between these types of music.* ❗ *Sp. 'distinción' (f.)*	Unterschied

page	exercise	**Workshop 1**		
		to **differ** [ˈdɪfə]	*List what the teenagers have in common and where they differ.*	sich unterscheiden
		somewhat [ˈsʌmwɒt]	*Scottish folk music seems to differ somewhat from Irish music.*	irgendwie
		to **detect** [dɪˈtekt]	*I can detect the influence of Norwegian culture in your music.*	entdecken
28	1	**prolific** [prəˈlɪfɪk]	*I discovered that not only was Robert Burns a famous poet, but that he was also a prolific songwriter.*	produktiv; erfolgreich
		ballad [ˈbæləd]	*There are many ballads about battles between the Scots and the English.*	Ballade
		to **occur** [əˈkɜːr]	*She was at home when the accident occurred.*	passieren
	2a	**isolated** [ˈaɪsəleɪtɪd]	*Today's youngest generation are connected but isolated.*	isoliert
29	1a	**outfit** [ˈaʊtfɪt]	*The six-piece Glasgow outfit practised their arrangements to prepare for the tour.*	Verein; *hier:* Band
		to **complement** [ˈkɒmplɪment]	❗ *Lat. 'complēre (-eō, -ēvī, -ētum)'; Fr. 'completer'*	ergänzen
		upon [əˈpɒn]	*Decisions must be made democratically and not imposed upon people.*	auf; an
		to **burst** [bɜːst]**, burst, burst** [bɜːst, bɜːst]	*He blew air onto the balloon until it burst.*	platzen
		underwhelming [ˌʌndəˈwelmɪŋ]	*The music was underwhelming and everyone looked bored.*	enttäuschend
		anticipation [ænˌtɪsɪˈpeɪʃn]	*There was definitely an eager sense of anticipation before the band started to play.*	Vorfreude
		intimate [ˈɪntɪmət]	*I love to cook and talk with my grandma in the intimate surroundings of her kitchen.*	vertraut
		absolute [ˌæbsəˈluːt]	*It was an absolute surprise when the band played my favourite song.*	absolut; völlig
		joy [dʒɔɪ]	❗ *Fr. 'joie' (f.)*	Freude
		to **bathe** [beɪð]	*The stage was bathed in colour while the band played the song.*	baden; tauchen
		metronomic [ˌmetrəˈnɒmɪk]	*The new material possesses a metronomic quality, but suddenly catches you by surprise.*	metronomisch
		pace [peɪs]	*My grandma lives her life at a slower pace these days.*	Geschwindigkeit; Tempo
		subtle [ˈsʌtl]	*Their most popular song always prompts a very respectful and subtle contribution from the crowd.*	dezent; subtil
		contribution [ˌkɒntrɪˈbjuːʃn]	*Young people do share a concern for the future and their contribution to it.* ❗ *Lat. 'contributo, -i' (n.)*	Beitrag

page	exercise	**Workshop 1**		
		forthcoming [ˌfɔːˈθkʌmɪŋ]	*I'm looking forward to the band's forthcoming album.*	bevorstehend
		liquor [ˈlɪkə]	*She drinks wine but not liquor.*	Spirituosen
		carousel [ˌkærəˈsel]	*On weekends my grandparents would take me to ride the carousel.*	Karussell
	1b	**venue** [ˈvenjuː]	*The Fringe is open-access, meaning that anyone with an act who can find a venue is welcome.*	Veranstaltungsort
	1c	**excitement** [ɪkˈsaɪtmənt]	*There is a lot of excitement about the project in school.*	Aufregung; Spannung
		rhythm [ˈrɪðəm]	*The rhythm of the music reflects its mood.*	Rhythmus
30	1a	**electorate** [ɪˈlektərət]	*The electorate voted for change.*	Wählerschaft
		to **devolve** [dɪˈvɒlv]	*The political powers were devolved.*	dezentralisieren
		administration [ədˌmɪnɪˈstreɪʃn]	❗ *Lat. 'administrātiō, -ōnis' (f.); Fr. 'administration' (f.); Sp. 'administración' (f.)*	Verwaltung
	2	to **propose** [prəˈpəʊz]	*Who proposed the second Scottish independence referendum?*	vorschlagen
		mandate [ˈmændeɪt]	*Nicola Sturgeon said that there was a mandate for independence.*	Mandat; Auftrag
		undeniable [ˌʌndɪˈnaɪəbl]	*Just as the mandate is undeniable, the reason for a referendum is just as important.*	unbestreitbar
		commitment [kəˈmɪtmənt]	*Each one of us was elected on a clear commitment to an independence referendum.*	Verpflichtung
		to **impose** [ɪmˈpəʊz]	*The rules are self-imposed, so no-one forced them on me.*	verhängen; durchsetzen
31	3a	**revenue** [ˈrevənjuː]	*The more advertising, the more revenue for the company.*	Einnahmen
		submarine [ˌsʌbməˈriːn]	*At the moment the UK nuclear weapons are kept on submarines based in Scotland.*	U-Boot
		currency [ˈkʌrənsi]	*What currency do we use to pay here?*	Währung
		to **shrink** [ʃrɪŋk], **shrank, shrunk** [ʃræŋk, ʃrʌŋk]	*Much of the industry here is shrinking.*	schrumpfen
	CC	**conservative** [kənˈsɜːvətɪv]	*The party's policies are conservative.* ❗ *Lat. 'conservare (-o, -avi, atum')* = *to keep, to save*	konservativ
		welfare [ˈwelfeər]	*She cut social welfare programmes and poor people suffered.*	Wohlfahrt
		to **privatize** [ˈpraɪvətaɪz]	*She reduced the power of trade unions and privatized many state-run industries.*	privatisieren
	4	**tender** [ˈtendə]	*She became a member at the tender age of 16.* ❗ *Fr. 'tendre'; Lat. 'tener, -era, -erum'*	zart

page	exercise	Workshop 1		
		helm [helm]	*With a skilled coach at the helm, our team is sure to win.*	Steuer; Ruder
		juggernaut [ˈdʒʌɡənɔːt]	*With the new leadership, the party became an electoral juggernaut.*	Lastzug; *hier:* unbändige Kraft
32	1b	**straightforward** [ˌstreɪtˈfɔːwəd]	*If he asks me a question, I'll give him a straightforward answer.*	direkt; gradlinig
		ballot [ˈbælət]	*On the ballot paper it just said: 'Should Scotland be an independent country?'*	Abstimmung
		speculation [ˌspekjuˈleɪʃn]	*What would happen if Scotland became independent was a matter of speculation.*	Spekulation
		booth [buːð]	*A lot of effort was put into encouraging voters to go to the booths and cast their vote.*	Kabine; Stand
		eligible [ˈelɪdʒəbl]	*Sixty percent of those eligible to vote did so, which was a record.*	berechtigt
		pension [ˈpenʃn]	*My grandma said she was worried she would lose her pension.*	Rente
		turnout [ˈtɜːnaʊt]	*Comment on the high turnout for the referendum.*	Beteiligung
		scaremongering [ˈskeəmʌŋɡərɪŋ]	*There was a lot of scaremongering going on during the campaign.*	Panikmache
	2a	**to mobilize** [ˈməʊbəlaɪz]	*The 2014 Independence vote could be viewed as a turning point that mobilized young people.*	mobilisieren
		prior to [ˈpraɪər tə]	*Prior to the election, I made myself familiar with the candidates.*	vor
		lightly [ˈlaɪtli]	*Prior to the vote these youngsters had proved that they didn't take this opportunity lightly.*	leicht
		enthusiasm [ɪnˈθjuːziæzəm]	*This enthusiasm hasn't worn off after the referendum.*	Enthusiasmus
		cohort [ˈkəʊhɔːt]	*The referendum resulted in a larger cohort of young people who are now in Scottish politics.*	Jahrgang
		forefront [ˈfɔːfrʌnt]	*She is at the forefront of politics today.*	Spitze
		apathetic [ˌæpəˈθetɪk]	*I find it annoying when people say that we are lazy and apathetic – it's completely untrue.*	apathisch; teilnahmslos
		sceptical [ˈskeptɪkl]	*I was initially sceptical about independence for Scotland.* ❗ *Fr. 'sceptique'; Sp. 'escéptico'*	skeptisch
		assumption [əˈsʌmpʃn]	*The debates made me question my assumptions.*	Annahme
		involvement [ɪnˈvɒlvmənt]	*My involvement with the club began while I was still in school.*	Beteiligung

page	exercise	**Workshop 1**		
		ideology [ˌaɪdiˈɒlədʒi]	I met with people who had a different ideology and questioned my beliefs.	Glaube; Ideologie
		to spur [spɜːr]	Engaging with folks who had a different ideology spurred me to dig deep.	anspornen
		ardent [ˈɑːdnt]	One of my best friends is an ardent supporter of the independence movement.	leidenschaftlich
		to crush [krʌʃ]	I was crushed by the result of the election.	zerschlagen; erdrücken
		disappointment [ˌdɪsəˈpɔɪntmənt]	I joined the movement because I wanted to turn my disappointment about failed policy into positive action.	Enttäuschung
33	2b	**outcome** [ˈaʊtkʌm]	She was upset by the outcome of the referendum.	Ergebnis
34	1	**protagonist** [prəˈtægənɪst]	The protagonist in the book is able to solve the crime.	Protagonist(in); Hauptfigur
		profiling [ˈprəʊfaɪlɪŋ]	She is a data analyst who helps the police with profiling.	Profilierung; Profilerstellung
		expertise [ˌekspɜːˈtiːz]	Her expertise as a music journalist gives a glance into Black culture.	Expertise; Erfahrung
		disposal [dɪˈspəʊzl]	The protagonist places her profiling expertise at the disposal of the police.	Verfügung
		romance [rəʊˈmæns]	Romance has changed a lot since the start of online dating.	Romantik
		watershed [ˈwɔːtəʃed]	The mountains form a watershed.	Wasserscheide
		sprawling [ˈsprɔːlɪŋ]	The sprawling district of Sutherland is in the Highlands.	ausgedehnt
		county [ˈkaʊnti]	How many counties are there in the Highlands?	Grafschaft
		to lull [lʌl]	I'd been lulled by the familiarity of rolling fields, so similar to the land of my youth.	beruhigen; einlullen
		fertile [ˈfɜːtaɪl]	The land is fertile and a great place for farmers. ❗ Lat. 'fertilis, -e'; Fr. 'fertile'	fruchtbar
	3a	**to incorporate** [ɪnˈkɔːpəreɪt]	Read the extract again and identify how the data is incorporated into her descriptions.	einbauen; integrieren
35	1	**inlet** [ˈɪnlet]	We drove along the narrow inlet with water on both sides.	Bucht
		lined [laɪnd]	The lake was lined with trees where birds nested.	gesäumt
		conifer [ˈkɑːnɪfə]	The dark water lined with heavy conifer forests looked scary.	Nadelbaum
		sinister [ˈsɪnɪstə]	❗ Fr. 'sinistre'; Lat. sinister, sinistra, sinistrum	unheimlich

page   exercise

Workshop 1			
sunlit [ˈsʌnlɪt]	The sunlit route into the wilderness was beautiful.	sonnenbeschienen
vista [ˈvɪstə]	We hiked up to a beautiful open vista.	Aussicht
rounded [ˈraʊndɪd]	The landscape is full of rounded hills.	rund
rocky [ˈrɒki]	Watch your step: the path is rocky.	steinig
outcropping [ˈaʊtkrɒpɪŋ]	We hiked past rounded hills, their rocky outcroppings grey and random.	Felsvorsprung
to scatter [ˈskætə]	Scattered in the landscape were the ruined walls of houses.	verstreuen
gable [ˈɡeɪbl]	There were ruined houses, often just a pair of gable ends left standing.	Giebel
depopulation [ˌdiːˌpɒpjuˈleɪʃn]	There was a brutal depopulation when crofters were driven off their land.	Entvölkerung
landowner [ˈlændəʊnə]	Rich landowners were eager to make money by using their land themselves.	Landbesitzer(in)
to rear [rɪə]	Landowners were eager to make the easy money that came with rearing this special breed of sheep.	aufziehen
fragment [ˈfræɡmənt]	He picked up the broken fragments of the glass.	Scherbe
diaspora [daɪˈæspərə]	This had been the starting point for the Highland diaspora.	Diaspora
steely [ˈstiːli]	The teacher's voice was steely when she was angry.	stahlhart; stählern
ribbon [ˈrɪbən]	She tied a ribbon in her hair.	Band
to loom [ˈluːm]	For adolescents, there's the pressure of college or university looming.	sich abzeichnen; drohen
to intimidate [ɪnˈtɪmɪdeɪt]	The castle had an intimidating tower. ▋ Fr. 'intimider'; Sp. 'intimidar'	einschüchtern
spire [ˈspaɪə]	A looming Gothic tower with an intimidating spire could be seen from everywhere.	Kirchturm; Turmspitze
to dominate [ˈdɒmɪneɪt]	His presidency was dominated by the American Civil War.	dominieren; beherrschen
porter [ˈpɔːtə]	She asked the porter to carry her suitcase.	Portier; Pförtner(in)
spectacle [ˈspektəkl]	She turned on to the Dean Bridge, enjoying the spectacle of walking above tree-top level.	Spektakel; Sensation
tenement [ˈtenəmənt]	The family lives in a tenement in the centre of town.	Mietshaus
to glow [ɡləʊ]	The light from the house glowed through the fog.	glühen; scheinen
insubstantial [ˌɪnsəbˈstænʃl]	The house looked insubstantial, like the wind could blow it down.	substanzlos; unerheblich

page	exercise	**Workshop 1**		
		mist [mɪst]	*The mist lifted off the loch.* *= fog*	Nebel
	4	**to unfold** [ʌnˈfəʊld]	*The novel engages with the events as they unfold*	entfalten
		empathy [ˈempəθi]	*The writer shows great empathy in her topics.*	Empathie
		hue and cry [hjuː ənd kraɪ]	*Cuts made by the government have raised a hue and cry among the public.*	Geschrei
		auctioneer [ˌɔːkʃəˈnɪə]	*'Yours for 100 Euros,' said the auctioneer.*	Auktionator(in)
		panoramic [ˌpænəˈræmɪk]	*The novel presents a panoramic view of Scottish society.*	panoramisch; panoramaartig
		insightful [ɪnˈsaɪtfl]	*The presentation Debbie gave was very insightful.*	aufschlussreich
		intertwined [ˌɪntəˈtwaɪnd]	*The novel follows several plot lines that become intertwined.*	verflochten
36	S1	**confectionary** [kənˈfekʃənəri]	*The average Scottish diet is high in confectionery, meat and snacks.*	Süßwaren
		fatty [ˈfæti]	*Fatty food is bad for your health.*	fett
		excessive [ɪkˈsesɪv]	*My mum had a conversation with me about my excessive phone use.* **!** *Fr. 'excessif'; Sp. 'excesivo'*	übermäßig
		sugary [ˈʃʊgəri]	*Many people drink excessive amounts of sugary drinks.*	zuckerhaltig
		to satisfy [ˈsætɪsfaɪ]	*Animals suffer a horrible death to satisfy an eating preference.*	befriedigen
	S2a	**adverse** [ˈædvɜːs]	*Some dietary habits have an adverse effect on the nation's health.* *= negative*	negativ; nachteilig
		consumption [kənˈsʌmpʃn]	**!** *Lat. 'consumere (-sumo, -sumpsi, -sumptum)' = to consume*	Verbrauch
		to graze [ˈgreɪz]	*A lot of land is needed for animal grazing and animal feed.*	grasen
		catastrophic [ˌkætəˈstrɒfɪk]	*The world's deforestation has catastrophic consequences.*	katastrophal
		to slash [slæʃ]	*Forests have been slashed and burnt to create fields.*	zerschneiden; reduzieren
		pasture [ˈpɑːstʃə]	*Forests have been slashed and burnt to create pasture for cattle.*	Weide
		filthy [ˈfɪlθi]	*The house was completely filthy.* *≠ clean*	dreckig
		overcrowded [ˌəʊvəˈkraʊdɪd]	*Most meat comes from farming methods where animals live in filthy, overcrowded spaces.*	überfüllt
		compassionate [kəmˈpæʃənət]	*If most compassionate people saw how animals are treated they wouldn't eat meat.*	mitfühlend

page	exercise	Workshop 1		
		beak [biːk]	*If people saw chickens with their beaks removed, they would never eat meat again.*	Schnabel
		nutrient [ˈnjuːtriənt]	**!** *Lat. 'nutrire (-io, -ivi, -itum)' = to feed*	Nährstoff
		wellbeing [ˈwel biːɪŋ]	*The wellbeing of the community is a top priority.*	Wohlbefinden
		alongside [əˌlɒŋˈsaɪd]	*The organizations are working alongside charities to avoid that people go hungry.*	neben; an der Seite von
		to surge [sɜːdʒ]	*The number of Scots adopting a vegan diet has surged in recent years.*	ansteigen; wogen
		widespread [ˈwaɪdspred]	*Veganism is becoming more and more widespread.*	weitverbreitet
		calculation [ˌkælkjuˈleɪʃn]	*Calculations show that a diet based on healthy eating recommendations has a lower footprint than the current average.*	Berechnung; Kalkulation
		wholegrain [ˈhəʊlgreɪn]	*It's best to eat mainly fruit, vegetables and wholegrain foods.*	Vollkorn...
		moderate [ˈmɒdərət]	*Experts recommend that teenagers get 60 minutes or more of moderate to vigorous physical activity each day.*	maßvoll; moderat
		eater [ˈiːtə]	*Meat eaters may argue that meat is the best source of protein.*	Esser(in)
		nutrition [njuˈtrɪʃn]	*A vegan diet gives you the complete nutrition you need.*	Ernährung
		leafy [ˈliːfi]	*Non-meat sources of iron are for example leafy greens and beans.*	blattreich
37	S1	**counterargument** [ˈkaʊntərɑːgjumənt]	*Use paragraphs for arguments and counterarguments.*	Gegenargument
		vigorous [ˈvɪgərəs]	*If you play team sports, you get vigorous activity on practice days.*	kraftvoll; energisch
		mild [maɪld]	*It can help some people who have mild depression.*	mild
		self-esteem [ˌself ɪˈstiːm]	*The programme can help some people who have mild depression and low self-esteem.*	Selbstbewusstsein
		accomplishment [əˈkʌmplɪʃmənt]	*Exercise can give people a sense of accomplishment.*	Erfüllung; Vollendung
		obesity [əʊˈbiːsəti]	**!** *Fr. 'obesité' (f.); Sp. 'obesidad' (f.)*	Fettleibigkeit
		diabetes [ˌdaɪəˈbiːtiːz]	*Exercise helps people lose weight and lower the risk of some diseases, including obesity and diabetes.*	Diabetes
		osteoporosis [ˌɒstiəʊpəˈrəʊsɪs]	*Osteoporosis can be a problem as people get older.*	Osteoporose

page	exercise			
		Workshop 1		
		bearing ['beərɪŋ]	Weight-bearing exercise – like jumping or running can help keep bones strong.	tragend
		brisk [brɪsk]	Brisk walking can be as healthy as jogging.	zügig
		aerobic [eəˈrəʊbɪk]	The three parts of a balanced exercise routine are: aerobic exercise, strength training and flexibility training.	aerobisch
		flexibility [ˌfleksəˈbɪləti]	Dance or martial arts require great flexibility.	Flexibilität; Beweglichkeit
		cell [sel]	Blood cells bring oxygen to all parts of your body.	Zelle
		to row [ˈrəʊ]	Different exercises strengthen different muscles, for example: for arms, rowing is good.	rudern
		pilates [pɪˈlɑːtiːz]	You can do pilates to increase strength.	Pilates
		plank [plæŋk]	We had to do planks in sport and now my arms hurt!	Planke; *hier:* Liegestütze
		crunch [krʌntʃ]	For increasing core strength, try rowing, yoga or pilates, planks and crunches.	Knirschen; *hier:* Sit-up
		martial [ˈmɑːʃl]	He declared martial law and gathered his troops.	martialisch; kriegerisch
		karate [kəˈrɑːti]	Dance or martial arts like karate require great flexibility.	Karate
	T	**aggressive** [əˈgresɪv]	❗ Fr. 'agressif'; Sp. 'agresivo'	aggressiv
		sarcastic [sɑːˈkæstɪk]	Use strong and emotive language but never become aggressive or sarcastic.	sarkastisch
		to anticipate [ænˈtɪsɪpeɪt]	Counterarguments in an essay can anticipate opposition.	erwarten; vorhersehen
		opposition [ˌɒpəˈzɪʃn]	In the presidential campaign, she made her opposition to Brexit very clear.	Opposition
		contrary to [ˈkɒntrəri tuː]	Contrary to expectations, it rained today.	gegen
38	1	**to brief** [ˈbriːf]	After having arrived we were briefed on the safety rules.	instruieren; informieren
		to navigate [ˈnævɪgeɪt]	We let Deepak navigate as he had studied the map.	navigieren
	2a	**bald eagle** [bɔːld ˈiːgəl]	The bald eagle is the national animal of the US.	Weißkopfseeadler
		yew [juː]	Yew trees can grow to be very old.	Eibe
		to dot [dɒt]	There are almost 800 islands dotted around the coast of Scotland.	sprenkeln
		runway [ˈrʌnweɪ]	We flew to Barra and landed on one of the world's last beach runways.	Landebahn

page	exercise	Workshop 1		
		brigade [brɪˈɡeɪd]	*It was also the first city in the world to have its own fire brigade.*	Brigade; Wehr
		raincoat [ˈreɪnkəʊt]	*It's going to rain later, so don't forget your raincoat.*	Regenmantel
		sighting [ˈsaɪtɪŋ]	*The little town is known for UFO sightings.*	Sichtung
39	3	**uninhabited** [ˌʌnɪnˈhæbɪtɪd]	*There are uninhabited islands off the coast of Ireland.*	unbewohnt
		hexagonal [hekˈsæɡənəl]	*A huge sea cave formed entirely of hexagonally jointed rock columns.*	hexagonal; sechseckig
		acoustics [əˈkuːstɪks]	*Fingal's Cave is known for its acoustics, but the origin of its name is unknown.*	Akustik
		numerous [ˈnjuːmərəs]	*There are numerous myths and legends surrounding the USA.* ⓘ *Lat. 'numerosus, -a, -um'*	zahlreich
42	2a	**to unzip** [ˌʌnˈzɪp]	*I unzipped the front of the tent and looked out.*	Reißverschluss aufmachen
		to poke [pəʊk]	*I opened the tent and poked my head out.*	stoßen
43	3a	**explosion** [ɪkˈspləʊʒn]	*Every year, Edinburgh hosts an explosion of creative energy like nowhere else.*	Explosion
		obscure [əbˈskjʊər]	*I love all kinds of music, from big names to the most obscure artists.*	unklar; rätselhaft
		cabaret [ˈkæbəreɪ]	*The Fringe includes theatre, comedy, dance, cabaret, circus skills, music, spoken word and more.*	Kabarett
		circus [ˈsɜːkəs]	*As a child I loved to go to the circus.* ⓘ *Lat. 'circus, -us' (m.)*	Zirkus
		to flock [flɒk]	*Thousands of people were flocking to the city during the festival.*	strömen
	4	**mermaid** [ˈmɜːmeɪd]	*The sailor said he had seen a mermaid.*	Nixe
		to sunbathe [ˈsʌnbeɪð]	*One story is about a man who found a Selkie sunbathing on the beach.*	sonnenbaden
		spooky [ˈspuːki]	*Don't read spooky stories before bed or you'll have bad dreams!*	gruselig

page	exercise	Workshop 2		
53		**triple** [ˈtrɪpl]	*Muhammad Ali was a triple world champion.*	dreifach
		heavyweight [ˈheviweɪt]	*In 1964 he won the first of his three world heavyweight titles.*	Schwergewicht
		segregation [ˌseɡrɪˈɡeɪʃn]	ⓘ *Lat. 'segregare (-o, - avi, -atum)' = to separate*	Trennung; Segregation
		to scrap [skræp]	*It's time to scrap unjust laws.*	verschrotten; abschaffen

page	exercise	**Workshop 2**		
		demonstrator [ˈdemənstreɪtə]	The demonstrators marched through downtown Selma.	Demonstrant(in)
		undisturbed [ˌʌndɪˈstɜːbd]	The demonstrators marched undisturbed through downtown Selma.	ungestört
		trooper [ˈtruːpə]	They were attacked by the state troopers who knocked people to the ground.	Soldat(in)
		to wave [weɪv]	Lots of white spectators were waving confederate flags.	winken; schwenken
		outrage [ˈaʊtreɪdʒ]	There was outrage about the police behaviour.	Empörung
		sympathizer [ˈsɪmpəθaɪzə]	Sympathizers protested his death in cities across the country.	Sympathisant(in)
		to stage [steɪdʒ]	Sympathizers staged sit-ins and demonstrations.	veranstalten; inszenieren
		blockade [blɒˈkeɪd]	They staged sit-ins, traffic blockades and demonstrations.	Blockade
		marcher [ˈmɑːtʃə]	The marchers were met with great sympathy.	Marschierer(in)
		boxer [ˈbɒksə]	He was one of the greatest boxers in the history of the sport.	Boxer(in)
		division [dɪˈvɪʒn]	❗ Lat. 'divisio, -ionis' (f.); Fr. 'division' (f.); Sp. 'división' (f.)	Abteilung; Bereich
		to overturn [ˌəʊvəˈtɜːn]	In 1971 the Supreme Court overturned his conviction and Ali could box again.	(um)stürzen; umwerfen
		thriller [ˈθrɪlə]	One of Ali's greatest boxing matches was called 'The Thriller in Manila.'	Thriller; Krimi
		rumble [ˈrʌmbl]	There was a loud rumble when the building fell.	Grollen; Schlägerei
		jungle [ˈdʒʌŋgl]	I would love to visit a jungle and see the animals that live there.	Dschungel
		butterfly [ˈbʌtəflaɪ]	Ali told reporters: 'Float like a butterfly and sting like a bee – his hands can't hit what his eyes can't see'.	Schmetterling
54	1a	**plantation** [plɑːnˈteɪʃn]	Slave labour was used in the tobacco plantations of the Chesapeake.	Plantage
	1c	**peculiar** [pɪˈkjuːliə]	❗ Lat. 'peculiaris, -e'; Sp. 'peculiar'	seltsam; eigen
		artisan [ˌɑːtɪˈzæn]	The artisans made important objects like tools and clothing.	Kunsthandwerker(in)
		outcry [ˈaʊtkraɪ]	Outcries against slavery on moral grounds began as early as 1724.	Aufschrei; Protest
		ordinance [ˈɔːdɪnəns]	The regulations are laid down in the ordinance.	Verfügung
		to exclude [ɪkˈskluːd]	The Northwest Ordinance excluded slavery from the western territories. ❗ Lat. excludere (- do, -si, -usum)'	ausschließen

page	exercise			
		Workshop 2		
		cotton gin [ˈkɒtn dʒɪn]	*The cotton gin was a machine that rapidly cleaned cotton.*	Baumwollentkörnungs-maschine
		autobiography [ˌɔːtəbaɪˈɒɡrəfi]	*Books like* Uncle Tom's Cabin *and the autobiography of escaped slave Frederick Douglass began national debates about slavery.*	Autobiografie
		mission [ˈmɪʃn]	**!** *Lat. 'missio, -onis' (f.)*	Mission; Aufgabe
		propaganda [ˌprɒpəˈɡændə]	*People in the north were told not to believe southern propaganda.*	Propaganda
		paternal [pəˈtɜːnl]	*In a situation like that our dad would offer some paternal advice to help us.*	väterlich
		to civilize [ˈsɪvəlaɪz]	*Southern propaganda said that slavery was a good thing and that it was civilizing slaves.*	zivilisieren
		to champion [ˈtʃæmpiən]	*The USA championed itself on its respect for individuals and individual freedoms.*	sich einsetzen für; verfechten
		compromise [ˈkɒmprəmaɪz]	*Political compromises in Congress helped prevent civil war for several decades.*	Kompromiss
		congress [ˈkɒŋɡres]	*Congress has held numerous hearings about the increasing role social media plays in people's lives.*	Kongress
		unavoidable [ˌʌnəˈvɔɪdəbl]	*The conflict over slavery became unavoidable.*	unvermeidlich
		to intrigue [ɪnˈtriːɡ]	*The Civil War ended slavery, divided families and communities, and continues to intrigue Americans today.*	faszinieren; neugierig machen
	2a	**to enslave** [ɪnˈsleɪv]	*Enslaved Africans were brought to the British colonies against their will.*	versklaven
		captive [ˈkæptɪv]	*The captives who landed in Virginia are believed to be the first slaves.*	Gefangene(r)
		to constitute [ˈkɒnstɪtjuːt]	*In the tobacco-producing areas of those states, slaves constituted more than 50% of the population by 1776.*	ausmachen
		abolition [ˌæbəˈlɪʃn]	**!** *Lat. 'abolerere (-o, -olevi, -olitum)' = to abolish* *Fr. 'abolir'; Sp. 'abolir'*	Abschaffung
		to secede [sɪˈsiːd]	*Southern states said they wanted to secede to protect states' rights.*	sich abspalten
		entity [ˈentəti]	*Lincoln was worried the British would support the South and recognize it as a separate entity.*	Einheit
55	3	**fluted** [ˈfluːtɪd]	*The monument is surrounded by 36 fluted Doric columns.*	geriffelt
		inscription [ɪnˈskrɪpʃn]	*There are carved inscriptions on the Lincoln Memorial.*	Inschrift
		inaugural [ɪˈnɔːɡjərəl]	*Lincoln's inaugural address is famous.*	Einführung; Antritts...

page	exercise	Workshop 2		
		solitary [ˈsɒlətri]	*In the central hall is the solitary figure of Lincoln sitting and thinking.* ◼ *Lat. 'solitarius, -a, -um'*	einsam
		sculptor [ˈskʌlptə]	*The statue was created under the supervision of the sculptor Daniel Chester French.*	Bildhauer(in)
		to dwarf [dwɔːf]	*The statue of Lincoln was made large so that it would not be dwarfed by the large building.*	klein scheinen lassen
		commission [kəˈmɪʃn]	*A commission to plan a monument was created after Lincoln's death.*	Kommission
	4a	**paramount** [ˈpærəmaʊnt]	*Lincoln's paramount objective was to save the Union, not to save or destroy slavery.*	vorrangig; entscheidend
		impulse [ˈɪmpʌls]		Impuls, Antrieb
56	1	**suppression** [səˈpreʃn]	*Several states are now actively involved in voter suppression.* ◼ *Sp. 'suprésion' (f.)*	Unterdrückung
		registration [ˌredʒɪˈstreɪʃn]	*We will hold a voter registration drive before the election.*	Registrierung
		identification [aɪˌdentɪfɪˈkeɪʃn]	*Several states have created stricter voter identification requirements.*	Identifizierung
		mentality [menˈtæləti]	*The mentality of many people in the southern states hasn't changed much.*	Geisteshaltung
		removal [rɪˈmuːvl]	*There was a protest against the removal of the statue in South Carolina.*	Beseitigung; Entfernung
		to glorify [ˈglɔːrɪfaɪ]	*These monuments tended to glorify leaders of the Confederacy, like General Robert E. Lee.*	verherrlichen
		instrumental [ˌɪnstrəˈmentl]	*White women were instrumental in raising funds to build these Confederate monuments.*	behilflich; instrumentell
		influential [ˌɪnfluˈenʃl]	*Why do you think Black music has been so influential?*	einflussreich
		gigantic [dʒaɪˈgæntɪk]	*The Mount Rushmore of the Confederacy was a gigantic stone carving of Davis, Lee and Jackson in Stone Mountain, Georgia. = huge*	riesig
		to taper off [ˈteɪpər ɒf]	*The construction of Confederate monuments eventually tapered off. ≠ to increase*	abnehmen
		backlash [ˈbæklæʃ]	*The backlash to the Civil Rights Movement led to the spread of Confederate symbols.*	Gegenreaktion
		atop [əˈtɒp]	*In 1962, South Carolina placed the Confederate flag atop its capitol building.*	obenauf

page	exercise	**Workshop 2**		
		capitol [ˈkæpɪtl]	*Black Lives Matter protesters were arrested at the capitol.*	Kapitol
		gradually [ˈɡrædʒuəli]	❗ *Lat. 'gradus,- us' (m.) = step*	allmählich
		to **topple** [ˈtɒpl]		stürzen, kippen
57	2a	**presidency** [ˈprezɪdənsi]	*His presidency was dominated by the American Civil War.*	Präsidentschaft
		to **assume** [əˈsjuːm]	*In the effort to win the war, Lincoln assumed more power than any president before him.*	annehmen; vermuten
		to **suspend** [səˈspend]	❗ *Fr. 'suspendre'; Sp. 'suspender'*	unterbrechen; aussetzen
		conciliatory [kənˈsɪliətəri]	*In his second inaugural address, he was conciliatory towards the southern states.*	versöhnlich
		to **educate** [ˈedʒukeɪt]	*His parents were poor pioneers and Lincoln was largely self-educated.*	erziehen; unterrichten
		legislature [ˈledʒɪsleɪtʃə]	*He sat in the Illinois state legislature before becoming president.*	Gesetzgebung; Legislative
		to **provoke** [prəˈvəʊk]	*Lincoln's victory provoked a crisis for southerners.*	provozieren; auslösen
		to **vow** [vaʊ]	*Lincoln vowed to preserve the Union even if it meant war.*	schwören
		nonetheless [ˌnʌnðəˈles]	*Lincoln always defined the Civil War as a struggle to save the Union, but he nonetheless issued the Emancipation Proclamation.*	trotzdem; nichtsdestoweniger
		emancipation [ɪˌmænsɪˈpeɪʃn]	*After the Civil War and the emancipation of slaves, the blues spread.*	Emanzipation
		symbolic [sɪmˈbɒlɪk]	*The speech was a symbolic gesture that identified the Union's struggle as a war to end slavery.*	symbolisch
		dedication [ˌdedɪˈkeɪʃn]	*the dedication of a building*	*hier:* Einweihung; Einsatz
		cemetery [ˈsemətri]	*Their graves are in a cemetery.*	Friedhof
		decisive [dɪˈsaɪsɪv]	*Education, economic prosperity and popular media are all decisive factors in shaping youth culture.*	entscheidend
		assassin [əˈsæsɪn]	*President Lincoln's assassin, John Wilkes Booth, was a strong supporter of the Confederacy.*	Attentäter(in)
		abolitionist [ˌæbəˈlɪʃənɪst]	*Harriet Tubman was an African American abolitionist and political activist.*	Abolitionist(in); Sklavereigegner(in)
		spy [spaɪ]	*He helped the Union Army during the Civil War by working as a spy.*	Spion(in)
	3a	**reformer** [rɪˈfɔːmə]	*Frederick Douglass was an escaped slave and social reformer.*	Reformator(in)
58	1a	**reconstruction** [ˌriːkənˈstrʌkʃn]	*The reconstruction after the war took a long time.*	Wiederaufbau

page	exercise	**Workshop 2**		
		versus [ˈvɜːsəs]	Most historians date the start of the Civil Rights Movement to Brown versus the Board of Education.	gegen
		to stoke [stəʊk]	She stoked the fire.	schüren
		fervour [ˈfɜːrvə]	The discussion was held with great fervour. ❗ AE = fervor	Eifer; Leidenschaft
		deliberate [dɪˈlɪbərət]	❗ Lat. 'deliberare (-o, -avi, - atum)' = to consider	absichtlich
		to thrust [θrʌst]	When his father died he was thrust into responsibility for his family.	stoßen
		limelight [ˈlaɪmlaɪt]	King was thrust into the limelight following Rosa Park's act of resistance.	Rampenlicht
		preacher [ˈpriːtʃə]	Martin Luther King was a young preacher thrust into the limelight during the bus boycott.	Prediger(in)
		charismatic [ˌkærɪzˈmætɪk]	He would become one of the movement's most charismatic leaders.	charismatisch
		to converge [kənˈvɜːdʒ]	Hundreds of thousands of people converged on the nation's capital for protests.	zusammenlaufen
		to rally [ˈræli]	More than 200,000 people converged on the nation's capital to rally for civil rights.	sich versammeln
		to attain [əˈteɪn]	The Civil Rights Movement attained more attention.	erzielen; erreichen
		visibility [ˌvɪzəˈbɪləti]	As the Civil Rights Movement attained greater visibility it was often met with increased violence.	Sichtbarkeit
		brutality [bruːˈtæləti]	They saw brutality against civil rights protesters as part of a long tradition of police violence.	Brutalität
		midst [mɪdst]	In the midst of so many conflicts, the Civil Rights Movement grew.	Mitte
		sacrifice [ˈsækrɪfaɪs]	In the midst of so much sacrifice the work of civil rights activism became more important.	Opfer
		heartbreak [ˈhɑːtbreɪk]	They had seen a lot of violence and heartbreak.	Kummer
		to desegregate [diːˈsegrɪgeɪt]	The Civil Rights Act of 1964 was designed to desegregate businesses and government employment.	die Rassentrennung aufheben
		monumental [ˌmɒnjuˈmentl]	The passage of the Voting Rights Act was a monumental victory for African-Americans. = huge	riesig
		to assassinate [əˈsæsɪneɪt]	The president was assassinated while sitting in a theatre.	ermorden

page	exercise	Workshop 2		
		resolve [rɪˈzɒlv]	Those who care about equality must fight on and not lose their resolve.	Entschlossenheit
	3	riot [ˈraɪət]	During the Civil Rights Movement, riots also swept major cities.	Aufruhr; Unruhen
		assassination [əˌsæsɪˈneɪʃn]	King was a social activist and Baptist minister from the mid-1950s until his assassination in 1968.	Ermordung; Attentat
		injustice [ɪnˈdʒʌstɪs]	❗ Fr. 'injustice' (f.)	Ungerechtigkeit; Unrecht
		fellow minister [ˌfeləʊ ˈmɪnɪstə]	A lot of civil rights activists were fellow ministers of Martin Luther King.	Amtsbruder, Amtsschwester
		Christian [ˈkrɪstʃən]	Martin Luther King's actions were influenced by his Christian beliefs.	christlich, Christ(in)
		to culminate [ˈkʌlmɪneɪt]	The March on Washington culminated in King's most famous address.	gipfeln; kulminieren
		rhetoric [ˈretərɪk]	King's famous address during the March on Washington is considered a masterpiece of rhetoric.	Rhetorik
		creed [kriːd]	This nation will rise up and live out the true meaning of its creed.	Glaube; Credo
		evident [ˈevɪdənt]	❗ Lat. 'evidentia, -ae' (f.) = visibility	offensichtlich; offenkundig
		to cement [sɪˈment]	The 'I Have a Dream' speech and march cemented King's reputation at home and abroad.	festigen; zementieren
		reputation [ˌrepjuˈteɪʃn]	King was respected and had a good reputation in the US and abroad.	Ansehen; Reputation
		fatal [ˈfeɪtl]	He was fatally shot in Memphis.	tödlich
		balcony [ˈbælkəni]	King was fatally shot while standing on the balcony of a motel in Memphis.	Balkon
		sanitation [ˌsænɪˈteɪʃn]	King had travelled to Mamphis to support a sanitation workers' strike.	Sanitär...
		to recant [rɪˈkænt]	She was forced to recant her beliefs to avoid punishment.	zurückziehen
		confession [kənˈfeʃn]	He later recanted his confession.	Geständnis
		advocate [ˈædvəkət]	❗ Lat. 'advocatus, -i' (m.) Fr. 'avocat' (m.)	Anwalt, Anwältin
59	CC	to clash [klæʃ]	When Rosa Parks refused to give up her bus seat, it wasn't the first time she'd clashed with driver James Blake.	zusammenstoßen
		chilly [ˈtʃɪli]	The weather will be chilly, so take a jacket.	kühl
		fare [feə]	She paid her bus fare and got on the bus.	Fahrgeld
		to disembark [ˌdɪsɪmˈbɑːk]	She refused to disembark and re-enter through the back door. = to get off	aussteigen
		sleeve [sliːv]	He pulled her sleeve to get her attention.	Ärmel

page	exercise	Workshop 2		
		enraged [ɪnˈreɪdʒd]	*She stood her ground until Blake pulled her coat sleeve, enraged, to demand her cooperation.*	wütend
	4	**to boycott** [ˈbɔɪkɒt]	*In response to discrimination, they boycotted the buses.*	boykottieren
		unconstitutional [ˌʌnˌkɒnstɪˈtjuːʃənl]	*The Supreme Court ruled that Segregation was unconstitutional.*	verfassungswidrig
60	1a	**oppressor** [əˈpresə]	*If you say you are neutral in situations of injustice, you are in fact on the side of the oppressor.*	Unterdrücker(in)
		neutrality [njuːˈtræləti]	ⓘ *Fr. 'neutralité' (f.); Sp. 'neutralidad' (f.)*	Neutralität
		archbishop [ˌɑːtʃˈbɪʃəp]	*Archbishop Desmond Tutu died in 2021.*	Erzbischof
		unjust [ˌʌnˈdʒʌst]	*One has a moral responsibility to disobey unjust laws.*	ungerecht
		nonviolence [ˌnɒnˈvaɪələns]	*Concerning nonviolence, it is criminal to teach a man not to defend himself when he is the constant victim of brutal attacks.*	Gewaltlosigkeit
	2b	**nationalism** [ˈnæʃnəlɪzəm]	*Malcolm X was an African American leader in the Civil Rights Movement, minister and supporter of Black nationalism.*	Nationalismus
		fellow [ˈfeləʊ]	*He urged his fellow Black Americans to protect themselves against attacks.*	Gefährte; Gefährtin
		aggression [əˈgreʃn]	*We want an immediate end to all wars of aggression.*	Aggression; Angriff
		stance [stæns]	*You must decide whether to agree, disagree or take a neutral stance toward it.*	Haltung
		nonviolent [ˌnɒnˈvaɪələnt]	*MLK believed in nonviolent protest, while Malcolm X thought violence could be justified.*	gewaltlos
		charisma [kəˈrɪzmə]	ⓘ *Lat. 'charisma, -atis' (n.) = gift*	Ausstrahlung; Charisma
		oratory [ˈɒrətri]	*His charisma and oratory skills helped him to become an important figure.*	Redekunst; Rhetorik
		prominence [ˈprɒmɪnəns]	*He achieved prominence because of his public speaking skills.*	Bedeutung
		to merge [mɜːdʒ]	*The Nation of Islam offered a belief system that merged Islam with Black nationalism.*	verschmelzen
		to popularize [ˈpɒpjələraɪz]	*Malcolm X's book popularized his ideas and inspired the Black Power movement.*	populär machen
		larceny [ˈlɑːsəni]	*Larceny is a legal term for theft of someone's property.* *= theft*	Diebstahl

page	exercise	Workshop 2		
		jail [dʒeɪl]	They weren't being violent, but they were beaten and many were even locked up in jail. = prison	Gefängnis
		devil ['devl]	The Black nationalist group identified white people as the devil.	Teufel
		rejection [rɪ'dʒekʃn]	You must be clear about your rejection of social injustice.	Zurückweisung; Ablehnung
		sermon ['sɜːmən]	His oratory skills and sermons in favour of self-defense gained the organization new admirers.	Predigt
		admirer [əd'maɪərə]	Malcolm X's admirers included celebrities like Muhammad Ali.	Bewunderer; Bewunderin
		disenchanted [ˌdɪsɪn'tʃɑːntɪd]	He was disenchanted with society and went to live in the forest.	enttäuscht
		corruption [kə'rʌpʃn]	Lat. 'corruptio, -ionis' (f.) Fr. 'corruption' (f.); Sp. 'corrupción' (f.)	Korruption
		spiritual ['spɪrɪtʃuəl]	A few months later he travelled to Mecca, where he underwent a spiritual transformation.	spirituell; geistig
		transformation [ˌtrænsfə'meɪʃn]	Generation Z's wider political engagement is going through a period of transformation.	Veränderung
		brotherhood ['brʌðəhʊd]	His spiritual transformation helped him feel true brotherhood with his peers.	Brüderschaft
		anger ['æŋgə]	He saw that anger could be in the way of the truth.	Wut
		to blind [blaɪnd]	He saw that anger could blind people from seeing the truth.	blind
		to foreshadow [fɔː'ʃædəʊ]	Malcolm X foreshadowed his own death in his book.	andeuten
		to bury ['beri]	Malcolm X is buried in Ferncliff Cemetery, New York.	begraben
		to oppose [ə'pəʊz]	You must openly oppose things that you consider wrong. Lat. 'opponere (-o, -posui, -positum)' Fr. 's'opposer'	ablehnen; sich widersetzen
		refusal [rɪ'fjuːzl]	The refusal to accept my apology was terrible.	Weigerung
61	CC	**deputy** ['depjuti]	After he was assassinated, his deputy took over the leadership.	Stellvertreter(in)
		to convert [kən'vɜːt]	He converted to Islam as an adult.	konvertieren; übertreten
	3a	**rally** ['ræli]	The rally was attended by a lot of supporters.	Kundgebung, Demonstration
		telegram ['telɪgræm]	The telegram is an early form of long-distance messaging.	Telegramm

page	exercise	Workshop 2		
		affection [əˈfekʃn]	*Martin Luther King had a deep affection for Malcolm X.*	Zuneigung, Liebe
62	2a	**divisive** [dɪˈvaɪsɪv]	*The Black Panther Party was one of the most divisive organizations to emerge during the Civil Rights Movement in the USA.*	spaltend; trennend
		militant [ˈmɪlɪtənt]	*It became possibly the era's most influential militant black power organization.*	militant
		to liberate [ˈlɪbəreɪt]	*The Black Panthers believed that nonviolent protests could not truly liberate black Americans.*	befreien
		liberation [ˌlɪbəˈreɪʃn]	*They linked the African American liberation movement with liberation movements in Africa and Southeast Asia.*	Befreiung
		fundamental [ˌfʌndəˈmentəl]	*There were fundamental changes in the American society.* **!** *Lat. 'fundamentum, -i' (n.) = base*	grundsätzlich
		disenfranchised [ˌdɪsɪnˈfræntʃaɪzd]	*The Black Panther Party was popular with many poor, disenfranchised African Americans.*	entrechtet
		overt [əʊˈvɜːt]	*I don't feel that the often overt call for violence was right.*	offen
		to further [ˈfɜːrðə]	*I don't feel that the often overt call for violence furthered their cause.*	voranbringen; fördern
		distribution [ˌdɪstrɪˈbjuːʃn]	*They sponsored schools, clothing distribution, local transportation and health clinics.*	Verteilung
		reform [rɪˈfɔːm]	*The organization campaigns for prison reform.*	Reform
		noteworthy [ˈnəʊtwɜːði]	*This is a noteworthy school because of its diversity.*	bemerkenswert
		membership [ˈmembəʃɪp]	*Women made up about half of the Black Panther membership and often held leadership roles.*	Mitgliedschaft
		inspirational [ˌɪnspəˈreɪʃənl]	*Lynn French in Chicago and Audre Dunham in Boston were inspirational local leaders.*	begeisternd
		chairman, chairwoman, chairperson [ˈtʃeəmən, ˈtʃeəˌwʊmən, ˈtʃeəˌpɜːsən]	*She became the first chairwoman of the organization.*	Vorsitzende(r)
		inequality [ˌɪnɪˈkwɒləti]	*The organization's members struggled to overcome gender inequality.*	Ungleichheit
		to outweigh [ˌaʊtˈweɪ]	*I feel that the positive aspects of the Black Panther Party did outweigh the negative aspects.*	aufheben; überwiegen
63	2b	**publicly** [ˈpʌblɪkli]	*If you believe in something, it's important to support it publicly.*	öffentlich

page	exercise	Workshop 2		
	3	**to oppress** [əˈpres]	*We want completely free health care for all Black and oppressed people.*	unterdrücken
		robbery [ˈrɒbəri]	*We want an end to the robbery by those exploiting our heritage.* ❗ *Sp. 'robo' (m.)*	Raubüberfall
		capitalist [ˈkæpɪtəlɪst]	*We want an end to the robbery by the capitalist of our Black communities.*	Kapitalist(in)
		decent [ˈdiːsnt]	*We want decent housing, fit for the shelter of human beings.* ❗ *Fr. 'decent, decente'*	anständig
		to expose [ɪkˈspəʊz]	*We want education for our people that exposes the racism in society.*	entlarven; aufdecken
		decadent [ˈdekədənt]	*We want education for our people that exposes the true nature of this decadent American society.*	dekadent; maßlos
		jury [ˈdʒʊəri]	*We want trials by a jury of peers for all persons charged with so-called crimes under the laws of this country.*	Jury
		establishment [ɪˈstæblɪʃmənt]	*Speculate about the reaction to this document from the American government and establishment.*	Einrichtung; *hier:* Gesellschaft
		revolutionary [ˌrevəˈluːʃənəri]	*How revolutionary is the American Declaration of Independence?*	revolutionär
64	S1	**literary** [ˈlɪtərəri]	*When identifying literary devices, try to relate them to a character, a main theme or the setting.*	literarisch
		alliteration [əˌlɪtəˈreɪʃn]	*Alliteration is a literary technique used in poetry.*	Alliteration
	T	**imagery** [ˈɪmɪdʒəri]	*Writers can use imagery to create their stories, characters and themes.* ❗ *Lat. 'imago, -ginis' (f.)*	Bilder; Bildsprache
		to relate to [rɪˈleɪt]	*Teens need to work out who they are and how they relate to the world they live in.*	sich beziehen auf
	S2	**mockingbird** [ˈmɒkɪŋbɜːd]	*Read these extracts from* To Kill a Mockingbird.	(Spott)drossel
	S3	**allusion** [əˈluːʒn]	*The text is full of allusions to the Bible.*	Anspielung
		climax [ˈklaɪmæks]	*The climax of the story is the most exciting part.*	Höhepunkt
		irony [ˈaɪrəni]	*The irony was that once he could finally join the team he found that he didn't find playing very much fun.* ❗ *Fr. 'ironie' (f.); Sp. 'ironía' (f.)*	Ironie
		metaphor [ˈmetəfə]	*The writer uses metaphor to describe the scene.*	Metapher
		parallelism [ˈpærəlelɪzəm]	*Consider the parallelism between the two topics.*	Parallelität
		personification [pəˌsɒnɪfɪˈkeɪʃn]	*As a literary device, personification gives objects human characteristics.*	Personifizierung

page   exercise

Workshop 2		
to **instil** [ɪnˈstɪl]	*What does Atticus want to instil in the children with the mockingbird example?*	einträufeln
rifle [ˈraɪfl]	*Atticus teaches his son of the moral responsibility of using a rifle.*	Gewehr
blue jay [bluː dʒeɪ]	*Blue jays are birds.*	Blauhäher
sin [sɪn]	*It's a sin to kill a mockingbird.*	Sünde
corn crib [ˈkɔːn krɪb]	*The corn is stored and dried in the corn crib.*	Maisscheune
to **scold** [skəʊld]	*She scolds Scout for her bad behaviour.*	ausschimpfen
to **mock** [mɒk]	*She scolds Scout for mocking a boy from her school.*	verspotten
to **disgrace** [dɪsˈgreɪs]	*It is terrible to disgrace people for being poor!*	blamieren
to **revert** [rɪˈvɜːt]	*She reverts back to her native language when she's tired.* ▪ *Fr. 'revenir'*	zurückkehren
negro [ˈniːgrəʊ]	*They talk about a negro language to refer to a dialect.* ▪ *'Negro' is a term historically used for persons considered to be of Black African heritage. The word 'negro' means the colour black in both Spanish and in Portuguese.*	Neger(in)
outraged [ˈaʊtreɪdʒd]	*We are outraged by acts of injustice.*	entsetzt

Analysing literary texts

act [ækt]	Akt
alliteration [ˌəlɪtəˈreɪʃən]	Alliteration
allusion [əˈluːʒən]	Anspielung
to **annotate** [ˈænəteɪt]	annotieren; kommentieren
author [ˈɔːθə]	Autor(in)
catastrophe [kəˈtæstrəfi]	Bezeichnung für das Ende eines Dramas
climax [ˈklaɪmæks]	Bezeichnung für den Höhepunkt eines Dramas
comic relief [ˌkɒmɪk rɪˈliːf]	Stilmittel der befreienden Komik
comparison [kəmˈpærəsən]	Vergleich
dialect [ˈdaɪəlekt]	Redeweise, Mundart, regionale Variante der Sprache
dialogue [ˈdaɪəlɒg]	Dialog, Gespräch unter zwei oder mehreren Personen
dramatic irony [drəˌmætɪk ˈaɪrəni]	Stilmittel der Ironie, die daraus entsteht, dass das (Theater-)Publikum mehr weiß als auf der Bühne handelnde Charaktere
exposition [ˌekspəˈzɪʃən]	Bezeichnung für den Beginn eines Dramas
falling action [ˈfɔːlɪŋ ˈækʃən]	fallende Handlung; Bezeichnung für den Teil zwischen Höhepunkt und Ende eines Dramas
figurative meaning [ˌfɪgjərətɪv ˈmiːnɪŋ]	übertragener Sinn eines Wortes (im Gegensatz zu wörtlich)
flat character [ˈflæt ˈkærəktə]	ein sich nicht verändernder Charakter (häufig klischeehaft)
formal aspects [ˌfɔːməl ˈæspekts]	formale Aspekte eines Textes wie Strophenaufbau und Reimschema beim Gedicht

page	exercise	**Workshop 2**		

		free verse [friː ˈvɜːs]	freier Vers (ohne Reimschema etc.)	
		hyperbole [haɪˈpɜːbəli]	Übertreibung	
		imagery [ˈɪmɪdʒəri]	sprachliches Bild (Metapher, Vergleich, Personifizierung)	
		irony [ˈaɪrəni]	Stilmittel, durch das das Gegenteil des Gesagten ausgedrückt werden soll	
		literal meaning [ˌlɪtərəl ˈmiːnɪŋ]	wörtlicher Sinn eines Wortes (im Gegenteil zu übertragen)	
		literary devices [ˌlɪtərəri dɪˈvaɪsɪz]	erzählerische Mittel (z. B. Alliteration, Erzählstimme, Ironie, Metapher, übergeordnetes Motiv, Schauplatz der Handlung)	
		metaphor [ˈmetəfə]	bildhafte Sprache, Übertragung	
		monologue [ˈmɒnəlɒg]	Worte eines Charakters, die sich nicht an andere Charaktere richten; Selbstgespräch	
		motif [məʊˈtiːf]	Motiv, Thema	
		narrative voice [ˌnærətɪv ˈvɔɪs]	Erzählstimme	
		narrator [nəˈreɪtə]	Erzähler(in)	
		parallelism [ˈpærəlelɪzəm]	Parallelismus	
		personification [pəˌsɒnɪfɪˈkeɪʃən]	Personifizierung	
		playwright [ˈpleɪraɪt]	Autor(in) eines Dramas	
		plot [plɒt]	Handlung	
		point of view [ˌpɔɪnt ə ˈvjuː]	Erzählperspektive (z. B. Ich-Erzähler(in), allwissende(r) Erzähler(in))	
		property (prop) [ˈprɒpəti]	Requisite	
		protagonist [prəʊˈtægənɪst]	Hauptfigur	
		register [ˈredʒɪstə]	Sprachebene (typische Rede- oder Schreibweise in einer bestimmten Situation, z. B. Bewerbungsschreiben, Gespräch unter Freundinnen)	
		repetition [ˌrepəˈtɪʃən]	Wiederholung	
		rhetorical question [rɪˌtɒrɪkəl ˈkwestʃən]	rhetorische Frage	
		rhyme scheme [ˈraɪm skiːm]	Reimschema	
		rising action [ˈraɪzɪŋ ˈækʃən]	Ansteigen der Handlung; Bezeichnung für den Teil zwischen Beginn und Höhepunkt eines Dramas	
		round character [raʊnd ˈkærəktə]	komplexer, sich entwickelnder Charakter	
		scene [siːn]	Szene	
		setting [ˈsetɪŋ]	Schauplatz der Handlung (Zeit und Ort)	
		sociolect [ˈsəʊʃɪəlɛkt]	soziale Variante der Sprache (im Gegensatz zum Dialekt)	
		soliloquy [səˈlɪləkwi]	Monolog im Drama	
		stage directions [ˈsteɪdʒ dəˈrekʃənz]	Regieanweisung	
		stanza [ˈstænzə]	Strophe	
		stylistic devices [staɪˌlɪstɪk dɪˈvaɪsɪz]	stilistische Mittel, Stilmittel (z. B. Alliteration, Ironie, Personifizierung)	
		symbol [ˈsɪmbəl]	Symbol, Sinnbild	
		theme [θiːm]	Thema, Motiv	
		tone [təʊn]	Erzählhaltung, Einstellung des Erzählers / der Erzählerin zum Erzählten (z. B. distanziert, ironisch, neutral, zustimmend)	

| 65 | S1 | **to prevail** [prɪˈveɪl] | *Read two extracts illustrating the prevailing racism in town.* | überwiegen |
| | | **to precede** [prɪˈsiːd] | *Read two extracts illustrating the prevailing racism in town preceding the Tom Robinson trial.* | vorangehen |

page	exercise	Workshop 2		
		nigger ['nɪɡər]	Don't call anybody 'nigger'. ❗You should not use the word 'nigger' at all, because it is very racist and offensive.	Nigger
		derogative [diˈrɒɡətɪv]	I was shocked when he made derogative comments about religion.	abwertend; abfällig
		firm [fɜːm]	The teacher gave the loud students a firm warning.	fest
		reference [ˈrefrəns]	This sentence is a reference to a well-known literary work.	Referenz
		conscience [ˈkɒnʃəns]	❗Lat. 'conscientia, -ae' (f.); Fr. 'conscience' (f.); Sp. 'la consciencia' (f.)	Gewissen
		entitled [ɪnˈtaɪtld]	You are entitled to your opinion.	berechtigt
		to abide by [əˈbaɪd baɪ]	The one thing that doesn't abide by majority rule is a person's conscience.	befolgen
	T	**narrative** [ˈnærətɪv]	Think about the story's narrative and the character's voice.	Geschichte; Erzählung
	S2	**to arise** [əˈraɪz], **arose, arisen** [əˈrəʊz, əˈrɪzn]	Conflicts arise when people do not discuss their differences.	entstehen
66	2a	**sensation** [senˈseɪʃn]	They were an artistic sensation in America.	Sensation
		motion [ˈməʊʃn]	Once he turned the corner, the events were set in motion.	Bewegung
		corporation [ˌkɔːpəˈreɪʃn]	Motown was a significant black-owned corporation employing multi-racial staff within its teams. = company	Unternehmen
		unmistakeable [ˌʌnmɪˈsteɪkəbl]	The 'Motown Sound' is unmistakeable.	unverwechselbar
		glorious [ˈɡlɔːriəs]	The 'Motown Sound' is famous for its glorious melodies.	herrlich; glorreich
		melody [ˈmelədi]	❗Fr. 'mélodie' (f.); Sp. 'melodía' (f.)	Melodie
		hook [hʊk]	The song had several hooks you can't get out of your head.	Aufhänger; Haken; hier: Hookline
		storey [ˈstɔːri]	We live in the second storey of the house. = floor	Etage
		royalty [ˈrɔɪəlti]	He received a royalty cheque for his hit single.	Tantieme; Lizenzgebühr
		reportedly [rɪˈpɔːtɪdli]	He reportedly told him to stop.	angeblich
		mainstream [ˈmeɪnstriːm]	Language evolves and new terms enter the mainstream.	Mainstream; Hauptrichtung
		exclusionary [ɪkˈskluːʒənri]	The mainstream was an exclusionary zone for many black musicians.	ausgrenzend
		to unify [ˈjuːnɪfaɪ]	We need unifying forces in society right now.	vereinigen
		to shift [ʃɪft]	The company shifted it's offices to LA.	verlagern

page	exercise	Workshop 2		
67	3a	**foundation** [faʊnˈdeɪʃn]	Combined with the African rhythms, these musical styles were the foundation of the blues.	Fundament
		rhythmical [ˈrɪðmɪkl]	Work songs were sung rhythmically in time with the task being done.	rhythmisch
		harmonica [hɑːˈmɒnɪkə]	The guitar and harmonica were used as they were easy to carry around.	Mundharmonika
		delta [ˈdeltə]	There are a lot of birds living in the delta.	Flussmündung
		to adapt [əˈdæpt]	Traditional songs were handed down and old lyrics were often adapted and turned into new ones.	anpassen
		to accompany [əˈkʌmpəni]	The guitar and harmonica were used to accompany vocals in the Delta Blues as they were easy to carry around.	begleiten
		to characterize [ˈkærəktəraɪz]	Blues music is characterized by sad melodies.	kennzeichnen; charakterisieren
		collectively [kəˈlektɪvli]	Different styles of blues emerged, known collectively as city blues or urban blues.	insgesamt
		simplicity [sɪmˈplɪsəti]	❶ Lat. ‘simplicitas, -atis’ (f.); Fr. ‘simplicité’ (f.)	Einfachheit
	4a	**bass** [beɪs]	The band has guitar, bass, keyboard and drums.	Bass
		danceable [dɑːnsəbl]	There was more emphasis on bass and drums to make the music more danceable.	tanzbar
		upbeat [ˈʌpbiːt]	Contrast the upbeat music with the lyrics of the song.	optimistisch
		repertoire [ˈrepətwɑː]	Many artists also included soul music in their repertoire.	Repertoire; Programm
		slangy [ˈslæŋi]	Youth like the band because of its vocal style and slangy lyrics.	salopp
		hardship [ˈhɑːdʃɪp]	A lot of soul songs deal with everyday hardship.	Not, Elend
68	1	**appropriation** [əˌprəʊpriˈeɪʃn]	When traditional Maori tattoos are worn by non-Maori people, it can be viewed as cultural appropriation.	Aneignung
		appreciation [əˌpriːʃiˈeɪʃn]	Show your appreciation if you like something.	Anerkennung
		cornrow [ˈkɔːnrəʊ]	It takes hours to put your hair in cornrows.	Cornrow; dünner Zopf
		hairstyle [ˈheəstaɪl]	I’m not sure that hairstyle would suit me.	Frisur
	CC	**unacknowledged** [ˌʌnəkˈnɒlɪdʒd]	Cultural appropriation is the unacknowledged taking over of customs, practices or ideas.	uneingestanden

page	exercise	Workshop 2		
		adoption [əˈdɒpʃn]	*The adoption of customs, practices or ideas takes place all the time.*	Adoption; Übernahme
	2a	**vernacular** [vəˈnækjələ]	❗ *Lat. 'vernaculus, - a, -um' = native*	(Landes-)Sprache; Mundart
		valid [ˈvælɪd]	*It has its own grammatical structures and vocabulary, which makes it just as valid as British English.*	valid; korrekt
		variant [ˈveəriənt]	*I love this variant of apple.*	Variante
		systemic [sɪˈstiːmɪk]	*Black people are still the targets of systemic racism around the world.*	systembedingt
		to blend [ˈblend]	*Black slang is blended with other forms of English.*	mischen
		exploitation [ˌeksplɔɪˈteɪʃn]	*The blending of black slang into mainstream language is seen as exploitation.*	Ausbeutung; Nutzung
		risky [ˈrɪski]	*It's risky for black people to use their own dialect, but non-black people can pick and choose terms and use them to sound 'cool'.*	riskant
		improper [ɪmˈprɒpə]	*Before black slang is adopted by the non-black masses, it's considered improper by white people.*	unangemessen
		to perceive [pəˈsiːv]	*= to see ≠ to ignore* ❗ *Lat. 'percipere (-cipio, -cepi, -ceptum)'*	wahrnehmen
	3	**to simplify** [ˈsɪmplɪfaɪ]	*We need technologies that simplify life.*	vereinfachen
		habitual [həˈbɪtʃuəl]	*His habitual response to questions was a laugh.*	gewöhnlich; ständig
	4a	**to marginalize** [ˈmɑːdʒɪnəlaɪz]	*Words from marginalized communities often enter the mainstream.*	ausgrenzen; marginalisieren
		to elevate [ˈelɪveɪt]	❗ *Lat. 'elevare (-o, -avi, -atum)'; Sp. 'elevar'*	anheben; nach vorne bringen
		undesirable [ˌʌndɪˈzaɪərəbl]	*Negative effects are undesirable.*	unerwünscht
69	1b	**to bore** [bɔː]	*Keep your speech a bit on the shorter side as then you won't bore your audience.*	langweilen
	2a	**commentator** [ˈkɑːmənteɪtə]	*Which of the points from the tips do the commentators also make?*	Kommentator(in)
		upstart [ˈʌpstɑːt]	*Obama was a political upstart.*	Aufsteiger(in)
		presence [ˈprezns]	*Where did Elvis' stage presence come from?*	Präsenz; Anwesenheit
		to fold [fəʊld]	*Obama was able to fold his life story into the larger American story.*	falten; zusammenlegen
		improbable [ɪmˈprɒbəbl]	*My parents shared not only an improbable love; they shared an abiding faith in this nation.*	unwahrscheinlich

page   exercise

Workshop 2		
debt [det]	*We have climate change and a spiralling debt to worry about.* ❶ *Lat. 'debitum, -i' (n.)*	Schulden
partisan [ˈpɑːtɪzæn]	*All media is partisan in some way.*	parteiisch
antidote [ˈæntɪdəʊt]	*The clinic has the antidote for anyone bitten by the poisonous snake.*	Antidot; Gegenmittel
individualism [ˌɪndɪˈvɪdʒʊəlɪzəm]	*Alongside our famous individualism, there's another ingredient in the American story: a belief that we're all connected as one people.*	Individualismus
saga [ˈsɑːgə]	*Alongside our famous individualism, there's another ingredient in the American saga: a belief that we're all connected as one people.* = story	Geschichte; Sage
prescription [prɪˈskrɪpʃn]	*The doctor writes out prescriptions.*	Rezept
to **presage** [ˈpresɪdʒ]	*She presaged her career in her first book.*	vorhersagen
spin master [spɪn ˈmɑːstə]	*The spin masters are trying to influence us.*	Imageberater(in); Spindoktor
peddler [ˈpedlə]	*Watch out for peddlers of fake news.*	Hausierer(in)
to **embrace** [ɪmˈbreɪs]	*They embraced when they finally saw each other again.* ❶ *Fr. 'embracer'*	umarmen; akzeptieren
liberal [ˈlɪbərəl]	*There is not a liberal America and a conservative America, there's one America.*	liberal
antithesis [ænˈtɪθəsɪs]	*His speeches are based on thesis and antithesis.*	Antithese; Gegensatz
pundit [ˈpʌndɪt]	*The political pundits like to divide our country into red and blue states.*	Experte; Expertin
to **dice** [daɪs]	*She was dicing vegetables.*	würfeln; in Würfel schneiden
to **pledge** [pledʒ]	*The government pledged huge changes.*	geloben
allegiance [əˈliːdʒəns]	*We are pledging allegiance to the stars and stripes, all of us defending the United States of America.*	Treue
solemn [ˈsɒləm]	*He is more solemn and reserved when he gives speeches today.* ❶ *Lat. 'solemnis, -e'*	feierlich; getragen
reflective [rɪˈflektɪv]	*He is more solemn and reserved when he gives speeches today, and I think it's more reflective of his office.*	nachdenklich; reflektierend; *hier:* widerspiegelnd
cynicism [ˈsɪnɪsɪzəm]	*Do we participate in a politics of cynicism, or in a politics of hope?*	Zynismus
naval officer [ˈneɪvl ˈɒfɪsə]	*He was a young naval officer, aboard a ship in the Mekong Delta.*	Marineoffizier(in)
lieutenant [lefˈtenənt]	*He was a young naval lieutenant, aboard a ship in the Mekong Delta.*	Leutnant

page	exercise	Workshop 2		
		to **patrol** [pə'trəʊl]	His job was to patrol the border. ❗ Fr. 'patrouiller'	patrouillieren
		millworker [mɪlwɜ:rkə]	The story is about a millworker's son who dares to defy the odds.	Fabrikarbeiter(in)
		audacity [ɔ:'dæsəti]	He had the audacity to stand on his desk while reading the poem.	Mut; Kühnheit
		to **electrify** [ɪ'lektrɪfaɪ]	His appearance at that convention was electrifying, and without it he wouldn't have become president.	elektrisieren
		sincerity [sɪn'serəti]	Your sincerity means a lot to me.	Ernsthaftigkeit
		to **reclaim** [rɪ'kleɪm]	I believe this country will reclaim its promise and a brighter day will come.	zurückgewinnen; zurückfordern
		to **bless** [bles]	People often say, 'God bless you' when someone sneezes.	segnen
70		**verdict** ['vɜ:dɪkt]	The Black Lives Matter movement was started after the not guilty verdict against George Zimmerman.	Urteil
		ally ['ælaɪ]	Black people and their allies stood up to change the course of history.	Verbündete(r)
		to **kneel** [ni:l], **knelt, knelt** [nelt]	A police officer knelt on George Floyd's neck during his arrest in Minneapolis.	knien
		continually [kən'tɪnjuəli]	He pointed out that the media continually focussed on the wrong issues.	ständig
		neglect [nɪ'glekt]	Nobody talks about the violence that our communities are experiencing because of government neglect.	Vernachlässigung
		vice versa ['vaɪs 'vɜ:sə]	It's unclear whether fashion influenced music or vice versa in the 1920s.	vice versa; umgekehrt
		to **lobby** ['lɒbi]	Many groups lobby politicians to support their causes.	sich einsetzen
71	3	**exclusive** [ɪk'sklu:sɪv]	He gave an exclusive interview after the game.	exklusiv
		affiliated [ə'fɪlieɪtɪd]	He hadn't informed the club or anyone affiliated with the team of his intentions.	verbunden; angegliedert
		approval [ə'pru:vl]	I work hard, but I am not looking for approval.	Zustimmung; Bestätigung
		biracial [ˌbaɪ'reɪʃl]	Kaepernick, who is biracial, was adopted and raised by white parents and siblings.	multi-ethnisch
	5	to **initiate** [ɪ'nɪʃieɪt]	What means are there to initiate discussion between groups? ❗ Lat. 'initialis, -e' = at first	anstoßen; initiieren
72	1a	to **filter** ['fɪltə]	All the stories are filtered so they only send you what they think is important.	filtern
	2a	to **tear** [teə], **tore, torn** [tɔ:, tɔ:n]	Culture wars are tearing us apart.	reißen

page	exercise			
		Workshop 2		
	2b	**to reign** [reɪn]	❗ *Lat. 'regnare (-o, -avi, -atum)'; Fr. 'régner'; Sp. 'reinar'*	regieren; herrschen
		anonymity [ˌænəˈnɪməti]	*The anonymity social media sites created allowed for the advent of internet trolls, keyboard warriors, haters and more.*	Anonymität
		troll [trɒl]	*Internet trolls just try to make people angry and start trouble.*	Troll (Computer)
		hater [ˈheɪtə]	*The anonymity of social media sites creates an opportunity for haters.*	Hasser(in)
		salacious [səˈleɪʃəs]	*The more salacious the story, the more people will view it.*	anzüglich
		to rile up [raɪl ʌp]	*We humans like things that rile us up and make us mad.*	reizen; ärgern
		perpetual [pəˈpetʃuəl]	*People will say anything on social media and this creates perpetual cycles of outrage.*	ständig
	2c	**hurtful** [ˈhɜːtfl]	*Senator Moreno said that you could say hurtful things with little to no consequences.*	verletzend
73	2b	**to crack down on** [kræk daʊn ɒn]	*Social media companies must take steps to crack down on trolls and misinformation campaigns.*	hart vorgehen gegen
		bot [bɒt]	*Social media companies should try harder to keep bots off of their platforms.*	Bot
		insurrection [ˌɪnsəˈrekʃn]	*Too many politicians tolerated the insurrection.*	Aufstand; Revolte
		to perpetuate [pəˈpetʃueɪt]	*Platforms restricted users who were either perpetuating false information or encouraging violence.* ❗ *Lat. 'perpetuare (-o, -avi, -atum)' Sp. 'perpetuar'*	aufrechterhalten
		afterward [ˈɑːftəwəd]	*Afterward, tech companies started to do some serious soul-searching about the role their platforms played in the insurrection.*	danach
		to condone [kənˈdəʊn]	*We do not condone violence under any circumstances.*	dulden; billigen
		to deter [dɪˈtɜː]	*We do our best to deter drug use.*	abhalten; abschrecken
		reasonable [ˈriːznəbl]	*We have to talk about this problem in a reasonable and balanced way.*	vernünftig
	2c	**addicted** [æˈdɪktɪd]	*My mum thinks the only thing that's changed since she was young is how addicted our generation is to their smartphones.*	abhängig; süchtig
		to diminish [dɪˈmɪnɪʃ]	*He thought social media platforms wanted to ignore, deny or diminish their part in creating the problems.*	abschwächen; verringern

page	exercise	**Workshop 2**		
		linkage [ˈlɪŋkɪdʒ]	Social media platforms wanted to ignore the linkage between social media use and teen depression.	Verbindung
	3a	**vulnerable** [ˈvʌlnərəbl]	She wanted to save vulnerable animals. **!** Lat. 'vulnerare (-o, - avi, -atum)' = to hurt	verletzlich; gefährdet
		to manipulate [məˈnɪpjuleɪt]	**!** Fr. 'manipuler'; Sp. 'manipular'	manipulieren
	3c	**inaccuracy** [ɪnˈækjərəsi]	What can be done to deal with the inaccuracy of news stories?	Ungenauigkeit
74	2a	**fame** [feɪm]	She didn't seek out fame when she moved to Hollywood.	Ruhm; Berühmtheit
		trailblazer [ˈtreɪlbleɪzə]	There have been many black Americans in sport who have been trailblazers.	Vorreiter(in); Bahnbrecher(in)
75	3	**championship** [ˈtʃæmpiənʃɪp]	He was part of the championship winning team in 1955.	Meisterschaft
		railroad [ˈreɪlrəʊd]	Harriet Tubman was a major figure in the 'Underground Railroad' helping runaway slaves escape to the North.	Eisenbahn
		influential [ˌɪnfluˈenʃl]		einflussreich
		to embark [ɪmˈbɑːk]	Ruby Bridges embarked on a historic walk to school as the first African-American student to go to an all-white school.	beginnen
	T	**counter-** [kaʊntə, kaʊntər]	Counter-arguments should be factual and supported effectively.	Gegen…
76	S2	**figure of speech** [ˌfɪgə əv ˈspiːtʃ]	It's a figure of speech that compares two unlike things. = rhetorical figure	rhetorisches Stilmittel; rhetorische Figur
	S3	**glory** [ˈglɔːri]	He dreamed of future glory as a songwriter legend.	Ehre; Ruhm
		destined [ˈdestɪnd]	**!** Lat. 'destinatus, -a, -um'	bestimmt; vorgesehen
		blessing [ˈblesɪŋ]	It's a blessing no one was badly hurt in the fight.	Segen; Geschenk
		juxtaposition [ˌdʒʌkstəpəˈzɪʃən]	**!** Lat. 'iuxta' = next to, 'ponere (pono, posui, positum)' = to put	Nebeneinander; Gegenüberstellung; hier als Verb gebraucht (eigtl.: to juxtapose)
		ain't [eɪnt]	= am not, are not, is not, has not, have not	ugs.: ist nicht
		to revisit [ˌriːˈvɪsɪt]	A dead person's spirit is believed by some people to revisit their family as a ghost.	wieder besuchen
		truant [ˈtruːənt]	She will run into problems when she keeps playing truant – she cannot stay away from school forever!	Schulschwänzer(in)
		to woman up [ˈwʊmən ʌp]	You need to woman up and talk to your boss.	in Anlehnung an ‚to man up': ihre Frau stehen

page	exercise	Workshop 2		
		to **man up** [mæn ʌp]	*You need to man up and tell her to leave.*	seinen Mann stehen
		to **pan** [pæn]	*The camera pans to the right to catch the whole scene on film.*	(eine Kamera) schwenken
		finish [ˈfɪnɪʃ]	*They reached the finish line just seconds apart.*	Ende; Ziel
		lethal [ˈliːθəl]	*Just one bite of this snake is lethal.*	tödlich
		regal [ˈriːgəl]	*They dined in regal style, with golden cutlery and large candlesticks.*	königlich; majestätisch
		cut [kʌt]	*The cut was really deep and he had to go to hospital.*	Schnitt
		to **bleed** [bliːd]**, bled, bled** [bled]	*There's a deep cut on my hand that I'm bleeding from.*	bluten
		epiphany [ɪˈpɪfəni]	*The conversation led to an epiphany on both sides and the former enemies finally agreed to live together peacefully and look to the future.*	Erleuchtung; Offenbarung; Eingebung
		to **right** [raɪt]	*She has set her mind to righting the mistakes of the past.*	wiedergutmachen; richtigstellen
		wrong [rɒŋ]	*The movement intends to right the wrongs of history.*	Unrecht
77	S1	**solidarity** [ˌsɒləˈdærəti]	*I have come to speak to you today to express my solidarity with the people of New York City.*	Solidarität; Verbundenheit
		to **contrast** [kɒnˈtrɑːst]	*Contrast the two portraits and talk about similarities and differences.*	vergleichen
		to **depict** [dɪˈpɪkt]	*The documentary depicts the political situation in the Black community today.*	schildern; beschreiben
	S4	to **utilize** [ˈjuːtəlaɪz]	= *to use* 🔢 *Fr. 'utiliser'; Sp. 'utilizar'*	verwenden; nutzen
78	1a	to **commemorate** [kəˈmeməreɪt]	*The public holiday commemorates the end of slavery in the US.*	erinnern an
		unanimously [juˈnænɪməsli]	*The legislation was unanimously approved by the Senate.*	einstimmig
		signature [ˈsɪgnətʃə]	*With the signature of President Biden, it has become law.* 🔢 *Lat. 'signare (-o, -avi, -atum)'* = *to sign*	Unterschrift
		to **dismantle** [dɪsˈmæntl]	*It is time to dismantle racist systems in our country!*	abbauen
		to **rage** [reɪdʒ]	*There is a cultural debate raging over the history of slavery and how it should be taught.*	toben; rasen
	2	to **nominate** [ˈnɒmɪneɪt]	*Black Lives Matter has been nominated for the Nobel Peace Prize.*	nominieren; aufstellen

page	exercise	**Workshop 2**		
		nomination [ˌnɒmɪˈneɪʃn]	*There are several interviews with Petter Eide, a member of the Norwegian parliament, who made the nomination.*	Nominierung; Aufstellung
		racial [ˈreɪʃl]	*There was a racial system discriminating against black people.*	rassisch
		realist [ˈriːəlɪst]	*He is a realist and understands that change takes time.*	Realist(in)
79	3b	**righteous** [ˈraɪtʃəs]	*If anything were to happen to me, I would want it to be for a righteous cause.*	gerecht
		specifically [spəˈsɪfɪkli]	*All lives matter regardless of skin colour, but specifically black lives because of the injustices they face.*	speziell
		to slay [sleɪ]**, slew, slain** [sluː, sleɪn]	*Innocent people were slain in the streets.* = *to murder*	töten; schlachten
		broad daylight [brɔːd ˈdeɪlaɪt]	*We are tired of seeing another innocent person being slain in broad daylight.*	helllichter Tag
		to desensitize [diːˈsensətaɪz]	*I believe that teenagers have been desensitized to violence.*	desensibilisieren
	4a	**nominee** [ˌnɒmɪˈniː]	*Other nominees in the same category included former presidents Bill Clinton and Jimmy Carter.*	Kandidat(in)
		to sanction [ˈsæŋkʃn]	*In 2012, Obama became the first US president to officially sanction same-sex marriage.*	genehmigen
82	1a	**to dispel** [dɪˈspel]	*In the podcast we aim to dispel myths about our country.*	vertreiben
		contentious [kənˈtenʃəs]	*We aim to dispel some of the most contentious myths that surround him.*	umstritten
		enigmatic [ˌenɪɡˈmætɪk]	*We aim to dispel the myths that surround this enigmatic character.*	geheimnisvoll; rätselhaft
		rag [ræɡ]	*Is it true that the story of Abraham Lincoln is one of rags to riches?*	Lumpen
		barely [ˈbeəli]	*His father barely made enough money to feed his family.*	kaum
		affectionate [əˈfekʃənət]	*He was affectionately known as Abe.* ❗ *Fr. 'afectueux'; Sp. 'afectuoso'*	liebevoll
		avail [əˈveɪl]	*Often President Lincoln tried to compromise with the Confederate States, but to no avail.*	Nutzen
		copper beech [ˈkɒpə biːtʃ]	*He played with his son under the copper beech tree.*	Rotbuche
	1b	**mysterious** [mɪˈstɪəriəs]	*The circumstances of his death are mysterious.*	geheimnisvoll; rätselhaft
	2a	**to impact** [ˈɪmpækt]	*How has Black music impacted social movements?*	beeinflussen

page	exercise	Workshop 2		
		radar [ˈreɪdɑː]	*What fact about the American music industry often flies under the radar?*	Radar
		intersection [ˈɪntəsekʃn]	*The show is about the intersections of music and culture.*	Schnittpunkt; Kreuzung
		glance [glɑːns]	*Her expertise gives a glance into how Black culture affected the music industry.*	Blick
		fingerprint [ˈfɪŋgəprɪnt]	*The fingerprints of Black creators are all over what makes American music so unique.*	Fingerabdruck
		fabric [ˈfæbrɪk]	*We'll make shirts from this fabric.*	Stoff
		bedrock [ˈbedrɒk]	*Theft of Black creativity is something that is in the bedrock of American society.*	Fundament
		bravado [brəˈvɑːdəʊ]	*Elvis had a lot of bravado in his stage presence.*	Draufgängertum
		titan [ˈtaɪtn]	*He is a titan in the music industry right now.*	Titan; Riese
		to permeate [ˈpɜːmieɪt]	**!** *Lat. 'permeate, -o, -avi, -atum'*	durchdringen
		soundtrack [ˈsaʊndtræk]	*There would be no soundtrack to the Black Lives Matter protest without Black music.*	Tonspur
		limitless [ˈlɪmɪtləs]	*The future of Black music is going where Black people are going, and that's limitless.*	grenzenlos
		applicable [əˈplɪkəbl]	*The same factors that prompt teens to experiment with new language are applicable to people at many stages of life.*	zutreffend; anwendbar
83	3	**citizenship** [ˈsɪtɪzənʃɪp]	*Differences of race, nationality or religion should not be used to deny any human being citizenship rights or privileges.*	Staatsbürgerschaft
		coward [ˈkaʊəd]	*Some people are cowards and some are brave.*	Feigling
	4a	**stark** [stɑːk]	*Figures show a stark difference in the numbers of arrests during the two protests.*	krass; deutlich
		to certify [ˈsɜːtɪfaɪ]	*After the insurrection, Congress certified Joe Biden as the next president of the USA.*	bestätigen
	5	**socio-economic** [ˌsəʊsiəʊˌiːkəˈnɒmɪk]	*Socio-economic characteristics are important to consider when analysing data.*	sozioökonomisch
		to distinguish [dɪˈstɪŋgwɪʃ]	*What distinguishes these activists from the others?* **!** *Lat. 'distinguere (distinguo, distinxi, distinctum)'*	unterscheiden

page	exercise	**Workshop 3**		
93		**lecturer** [ˈlektʃərə]	Our guest is a psychologist and guest university lecturer. ❗ Lat. 'lector, -oris' (m.)	Dozent(in)
		to vouch [vaʊtʃ]	Yes, I can vouch for that.	bürgen; sich verbürgen
		conscious [ˈkɒnʃəs]	Dr Spellman shows that teenagers today are health conscious.	bewusst
		reduction [rɪˈdʌkʃn]	There has been a great reduction in green spaces in our city. ❗ Lat. 'reductio, -onis' (f.); Fr. 'réduction' (f.); Sp. 'reducción (f.)	Verringerung; Reduzierung
		to deem [diːm]	Some fashion trends are deemed by teens to be not cool.	meinen
		slick [slɪk]	Slick marketing is good for selling products.	clever; glatt
94	2b	**to pertain to** [pəˈteɪn]	Youth culture can pertain to interests, styles, behaviours, music, beliefs, vocabulary, clothes, sports and dating.	zu etwas gehören
		subculture [ˈsʌbkʌltʃə]	The concept behind youth culture is that adolescents have their own subculture.	Subkultur
		indicator [ˈɪndɪkeɪtə]	Personal appearance is one of the most visible indicators of teen culture.	Indikator; Anzeige
		mindset [ˈmaɪndset]	Twenty-first century youth seem to have a 'less is more' mindset.	Mentalität
		turbulent [ˈtɜːbjələnt]	The 1960s were a turbulent time in recent history.	turbulent; unruhig
		tyranny [ˈtɪrəni]	All people want to be free from tyranny. ❗ Lat. 'tyrannis, -idis' (f.)	Tyrannei
		fringed [frɪndʒd]	Short skirts and fringed jackets were popular fashions.	fransig
		bond [bɒnd]	Teens today form bonds with gamers that they get to know in the virtual world.	*hier:* Verbindung
	2c	**to contradict** [ˌkɒntrəˈdɪkt]	Find arguments that support or contradict Erikson's point. ≠ to support	widersprechen
95		**adolescence** [ˌædəˈlesns]	As kids move into adolescence, their entertainment preferences often change.	Jugend(alter)
	2b	**to minimize** [ˈmɪnɪmaɪz]	Many teens minimize their environmental impact.	minimieren; verkleinern
		inclusiveness [ɪnˈkluːsɪvnəs]	Youth in the 21st century tend to favour inclusiveness more than previous generations.	Inklusivität
		to assert [əˈsɜːt]	Youth assert their independence through rebellious action.	durchsetzen; behaupten
		conformity [kənˈfɔːməti]	They want to challenge conformity.	Konformität; Anpassung

page	exercise	Workshop 3		
		perception [pəˈsepʃn]	*Youth sometimes change their perceptions under peer pressure.*	Wahrnehmung
		kindness [ˈkaɪndnəs]	*It is important to show kindness to others.*	Freundlichkeit; Güte
		aloofness [əˈluːfnəs]	*Depending on peer group members, youth may show greater kindness or more aloofness.*	Zurückhaltung
		to **theorize** [ˈθɪəraɪz]	*Psychologists theorize that the primary goal in adolescence is to answer the question, 'Who am I'.*	theoretisieren
		developmental [dɪˌveləpˈmentl]	*Adolescence is an important developmental stage.*	entwicklungsbedingt
	4	**telenovela** [ˌtɑlenəˈvelə]	*When I'm not dancing, I enjoy watching telenovelas, which are soap operas.*	Seifenoper
		episode [ˈepɪsəʊd]	*I enjoy watching telenovelas and then chat with friends about the latest episodes.*	Episode
96	1a	**component** [kəmˈpəʊnənt]	*One very important component of youth culture is language.*	Bestandteil
	2	**secretive** [ˈsiːkrətɪv]	*What are you up to? You're being so secretive.* ⚠ *Lat. 'secreto, -a, -um'*	geheimnisvoll
	3a	to **overstate** [ˌəʊvəˈsteɪt]	*The influence teenagers have on language change has been grossly overstated*	überbewerten
		shorthand [ˈʃɔːthænd]	*Text messages by teenagers are often written in shorthand.*	Kurzform
		infancy [ˈɪnfənsi]	*Language development usually starts during the first year of infancy.*	Kindheit
		sound wave [ˈsaʊnd weɪv]	*The researcher studied sound waves to find out how words are pronounced.*	Schallwelle
		subgroup [ˈsʌbɡruːp]	*They found out that all subgroups experience language change.*	Untergruppe
		to **stand out** [ˈstænd aʊt], **stood, stood** [stʊd]	*The teenagers did not stand out as the most distinct group.*	hervorstechen
		crucial [ˈkruːʃəl]	*A crucial point when language changes is when children enter school.*	wesentlich; zentral
		to **meet a demand** [miːt ə dɪˈmɑːnd], **met, met** [met]	*Teenagers change the way they speak to meet the demand of their jobs.*	einen Anspruch befriedigen
		monograph [ˈmɒnəɡrɑːf]	*She published her results in her monograph, which was published last year.*	Monografie
		to **skyrocket** [ˈskaɪrɒkɪt]	*Some songs skyrocket and become very famous while others do not.*	in die Höhe schießen

page	exercise	Workshop 3		
		to **doom** [duːm]	Some ideas are doomed to fail because they are too silly.	verdammen
		acceptable [əkˈseptəbl]	Even grammar geeks are warming up to 'they' as an acceptable gender-neutral pronoun.	akzeptabel; zulässig
		tendency [ˈtendənsi]	There is a tendency for older adults to criticize younger generations.	Tendenz
		to **stake** [steɪk]	Teens are establishing identity and staking a space in a social group.	abstecken
97	3a	**worthy** [ˈwɜːði]	In my opinion our generation is worthy of being listened to, yet it doesn't seem to happen frequently enough.	würdig; wert
		to **discredit** [dɪsˈkredɪt]	As soon as we give our thoughts on an important issue, we're discredited for being too young.	diskreditieren
		immature [ˌɪməˈtjʊə]	❗ Lat. 'immaturus, -a, -um'; Fr. 'immature'; Sp. 'immaduro'	unreif
		to **get to grips** [get tə grɪps]**, got, got** [gɒt]	I need to get to grips with my homework to do well in school.	in den Griff bekommen
		to **mold** [məʊld]	Every decision that you're making right now might mold your future. ❗ BE = to mould	formen
		fingertip [ˈfɪŋgətɪp]	Being a teenager in this decade is awesome with all the different things that we have at our fingertips.	Fingerspitze
		avenue [ˈævənjuː]	There are many avenues for your voice to be heard.	Allee; Weg
		bitter [ˈbɪtə]	These days life is bitter because of all the pressure that is put on us.	bitter
		pensive [ˈpensɪv]	She looked pensive while reading the book.	nachdenklich
		obtainable [əbˈteɪnəbl]	Teenagers want a certain lifestyle that isn't obtainable for everyone.	erreichbar
		interconnectedness [ˌɪntəkəˈnektɪdnəs]	Some things in life, like family and tradition, are great because of all the interconnectedness.	Vernetzung
		cautious [ˈkɔːʃəs]	We have to be twice as cautious about where we are because it's a dangerous world.	vorsichtig
	3b	**outlook** [ˈaʊtlʊk]	Many teenagers have a positive outlook.	Einstellung
	5a	**similarity** [ˌsɪməˈlærəti]	❗ Lat. 'similtudo, -dinis' (f.); Fr. 'similitude'; Sp. 'similitud' (f.)	Ähnlichkeit
98	2	**hand-eye coordination** [hænd aɪ kəʊˌɔːdɪˈneɪʃn]	Some video games can improve your hand-eye-coordination.	Hand-Auge-Koordination
		to **change one's tune** [tʃeɪndʒ wʌnz tjuːn]	When she realized she was talking to the president, she quickly changed her tune.	eine andere Tonlage anschlagen, seine Meinung wechseln

page	exercise	**Workshop 3**		
	3	**sociable** [ˈsəʊʃəbl]	She's very sociable and gets along with a lot of people.	gesellig, kontaktfreudig
		to **push sth.** [pʊʃ]	Don't push your luck!	mit etw. übertreiben
99	4	**underway** [ˌʌndəˈweɪ]	A new culture of video gaming is underway.	im Gange, in Bearbeitung
		to **take the torch** [ˌteɪk ðə ˈtɔːtʃ], **took, taken** [tʊk, ˈteɪkən]	Generation Z has taken over the torch from previous generations.	den Staffelstab übernehmen
		cohort [ˈkəʊhɔːt]	Generation Z is made up of those belonging to the birth cohorts between 1997 and 2012.	Kohorte, Jahrgang
		tech-savvy [ˈtek sævi]	A lot of today's teenagers are very tech-savvy.	technikerfahren, computererfahren
		to **bloom** [bluːm]	These plants bloom in early summer.	blühen
		profitable [ˈprɒfɪtəbl]	The gaming industry has become very profitable in recent years.	profitabel
		processor [ˈprəʊsesə]	A lot of the newer computer games demand powerful processors.	Prozessor
		like-minded [ˌlaɪk ˈmaɪndɪd]	Gen Z teenagers want to connect online with like-minded people.	gleichgesinnt
		AI, artificial intelligence [ˌeɪ ˈaɪ], [ˌɑːtɪˈfɪʃl ɪnˈtelɪdʒəns]	Driverless cars use artificial intelligence to know where they're going.	KI, künstliche Intelligenz
		VR, virtual reality [ˌviː ˈɑː], [ˈvɜːtʃuəl riˈæləti]	Virtual reality uses computer models to create a simulated world.	VR, virtuelle Realität
		aforementioned [əˈfɔːmenʃənd]	The contract covers all aforementioned aspects.	zuvor genannt
100	2a	**elite** [ɪˈliːt]	Tattoos started to become fashionable among the elite.	Elite, Oberschicht
		to **go out of fashion** [gəʊ aʊt əv ˈfæʃn], **went, gone** [went, gɒn]	Tattoos went out of fashion.	aus der Mode kommen
		reminder [rɪˈmaɪndə]	Some styles will never go out of fashion.	Mahnung, Erinnerung
101	3a	**fanciful** [ˈfænsɪfl]	They have fanciful ideas about how to get rich.	fantastisch
		notion [ˈnəʊʃn]	Youth have funny notions about older generations. = idea	Idee; Vorstellung
		enthusiast [ɪnˈθjuːziæst]	I asked Will Spratley, 15-year-old music and drama enthusiast, whose style he admired.	Liebhaber(in)
		to **flick** [flɪk]	He pulled out the magazine and flicked to an article about gorillas.	(um)blättern
		to **scorn** [skɔːn]	They scorn our rules, but control their own society with strict laws.	verachten
		exacting [ɪgˈzæktɪŋ]	The teacher was so exacting, she took points off because my handwriting was messy.	anspruchsvoll

page	exercise	Workshop 3		
		etiquette ['etɪkət]	They scorn our rules but police their own society with exacting systems of etiquette.	Etikette
		nub [nʌb]	At the nub of teenage rebellion is their wish to be different.	Kernpunkt
		compulsion [kəmˈpʌlʃn]	A highlight of teenage rebellion is their compulsion to be different.	Zwang
		to flaunt [flɔːnt]	Teenagers want to flaunt their youth and difference from their parents.	zur Schau stellen
		absence [ˈæbsəns]	The first surprise was the almost complete absence of trends. ❗ Lat. 'absentia, -ae' (f.)	Abwesenheit; Mangel
		motif [məʊˈtiːf]	She wore a T-shirt with a motif of a peace sign.	Motiv
		mesh [meʃ]	The clothing was made of mesh, so she wore a t-shirt under it.	Netz
		denim [ˈdenɪm]	Denim clothing is very good to wear when you have to do farm work.	Jeansstoff
		to wrinkle [ˈrɪŋkl]	She wrinkles her nose when I ask her how she would define her own style.	rümpfen; runzeln
		knickers [ˈnɪkəz]	She wore black knickers under her trousers.	Schlüpfer
		heartfelt [ˈhɑːtfelt]	He gave me such a heartfelt look, I had to forgive him.	aufrichtig; herzlich
		literally [ˈlɪtərəli]	When it's cold, she sometimes literally makes me wear a jacket.	buchstäblich
102	1c	tracksuit [ˈtræksuːt]	Teenagers wore bright-coloured tracksuits.	Trainingsanzug
		flared [fleəd]	Teenagers wore flared trousers in the 1970s.	ausgestellt
104	S1a	to purchase [ˈpɜːtʃəs]	Nowadays, a lot of clothes are purchased online.	kaufen, beschaffen
		shiny [ˈʃaɪni]	Wow, you look stunning in that shiny dress!	glänzend, funkelnd
		eternal [ɪˈtɜːnl]	Christians believe in eternal life in heaven.	ewig
		guilt-free [gɪlt friː]	You can buy our product guilt-free – it's completely sustainable.	schuldfrei
		gem [dʒem]	This album is the gem of his record collection.	Edelstein, Prachtstück
		discarded [dɪˈskɑːdɪt]	A lot of clothes are too easily discarded and never used again.	ausrangiert
		dent [dent]	There were a few dents in the back of the car after Simon had crashed it.	Beule, Delle
		bank balance [ˈbæŋk bæləns]	My bank balance is always low at the end of the month.	Kontostand
		synthetic [sɪnˈθetɪk]	This jumper is made of synthetic material.	synthetisch, künstlich

page	exercise	**Workshop 3**		
		biodiversity [ˌbaɪəʊdaɪˈvɜːsəti]	*If the pollution of air, land and water continues, the biodiversity will even be more reduced than it already has been.*	Artenvielfalt
105	S1	**to mutter** [ˈmʌtə]	*He muttered something about it all being lies.*	murmeln
		damned [dæmd]	*He muttered something about lies, damned lies, and statistics.*	verdammt
		fool [fuːl]	*Nobody likes to be taken for a fool.*	Idiot(in)
		to reject [rɪˈdʒekt]	❗ *Fr. 'rejecter'*	ablehnen
		to exert [ɪgˈzɜːt]	*We have to exert a bit of brain power to figure out what is true.*	aufbieten
		wisdom [ˈwɪzdəm]	*The three Cs of data wisdom are, be calm, check claims and be careful.*	Weisheit
		baggage [ˈbægɪdʒ]	*A lot of kids these days carry emotional baggage.*	Gepäck; Ballast
		joyful [ˈdʒɔɪfl]	*The song makes everyone who hears it joyful.*	fröhlich
		deficit [ˈdefɪsɪt]	*Staggering deficits and shocking rates of crime have inspired people to collect money to help others.*	Mangel
		instinctive [ɪnˈstɪŋktɪv]	*My instinctive reaction was anger, not sadness.* ❗ *Lat. 'instinctus, -us' (m.)*	instinktiv
		denial [dɪˈnaɪəl]	❗ *Fr. 'deni' (f.)*	Verweigerung
		vindication [ˌvɪndɪˈkeɪʃn]	*They felt that the accident was vindication of their campaign for safer streets.*	Rechtfertigung
		overweight [ˌəʊvəˈweɪt]	*Many people in the US and UK are overweight.*	übergewichtig
		fancy [ˈfænsi]	*You don't need a lot of fancy skills, just a search engine and a curious mind.*	ausgefallen
		preconception [ˌpriːkənˈsepʃn]	*News sources can change your preconceptions.*	Vorurteil
		telescope [ˈtelɪskəʊp]	*A telescope is an instrument for watching the stars.*	Teleskop
		astronomer [əˈstrɑːnəmə]	*We should think about statistics as a tool to understand the world, like a telescope for an astronomer.*	Astronom(in)
		curiosity [ˌkjʊəriˈɒsəti]	*A good journalist will feed your curiosity.*	Neugier
		unthinkingly [ʌnˈθɪŋkɪŋli]	*We shouldn't just accept the things we read unthinkingly.*	ohne nachzudenken
		to dismiss [dɪsˈmɪs]	*We don't need to accept statistical claims at face value, but we shouldn't dismiss them out of hand either.*	ablehnen; entlassen
	S1b	**untrustworthy** [ʌnˈtrʌstwɜːði]	*People begin to think that the news media is untrustworthy.*	unglaubwürdig

page	exercise	Workshop 3		
	S2b	**comprehensive** [ˌkɒmprɪˈhensɪv]	*Combine the lists to make a more comprehensive one.*	umfassend
	S2c	**breakdown** [ˈbreɪkdaʊn]	*The data doesn't give information about the breakdown of ages.*	hier: Aufgliederung
		prospective [prəˈspektɪv]	*How many prospective students will be able to take this class?*	zukünftig
		to enroll [ɪnˈrəʊl]	*Most students enroll after finishing secondary school.*	(sich) anmelden
		mature [məˈtʃʊə]	*Many mature students only study part-time.*	reif; erwachsen
		privileged [ˈprɪvəlɪdʒd]	*There is no data about the proportion of the students who are middle-class, privileged or less well-off.*	privilegiert
		ethnicity [eθˈnɪsəti]	*Black students or students of other ethnicities make up about one third of the students.*	Ethnizität
	S3	**assessment** [əˈsesmənt]	*Write an assessment of your experience with the programme.*	Einschätzung; Bewertung
106	1	**digitalization** [ˌdɪdʒɪtəlaɪˈzeɪʃn]	*Brendan decides to write some advice and information about digitalization and digital detox.*	Digitalisierung
		instantly [ˈɪnstəntli]	*In today's world we expect to be able to know everything instantly. = at once*	sofort
	2a	**literacy** [ˈlɪtərəsi]	*Outline the three key areas of data literacy.*	Lesekompetenz; Gebildetsein
		extensive [ɪkˈstensɪv]	*These are extensive political, economic and social problems.*	umfangreich
		probability [ˌprɒbəˈbɪləti]	**❗** *Lat. 'probabilitas, -atis' (f.); Fr. 'probabilité' (f.); Sp. 'probabilidad' (f.)*	Wahrscheinlichkeit
		archetypal [ˌɑːkiˈtaɪpl]	*If you listen to them talk, they sound like your archetypal digital natives.*	archetypisch
		reliability [rɪˌlaɪəˈbɪləti]	*You have to think about the reliability of the information you read online.*	Zuverlässigkeit
		target [ˈtɑːgɪt]	*Black people are often the targets of violence.*	Ziel
		retailer [ˈriːteɪlər]	*Young people buy things online and trust online retailers with their data.*	Händler(in)
		to correspond [ˌkɒrəˈspɒnd]	*Digital inequalities correspond with other key elements of economic, social and cultural inequality.*	übereinstimmen
		to acquire [əˈkwaɪə]	*Education helps us acquire skills and the ability to think critically.*	erwerben; akquirieren
107	2b	**overuse** [ˌəʊvəˈjuːs]	*The overuse of social media is dangerous and harmful to the user.*	Überbeanspruchung
		on par [ɒn pɑː]	*Economic, social and cultural inequalities in society are on par with digital inequality.*	gleichgestellt

page	exercise	Workshop 3		
	3a	**indisputable** [ˌɪndɪˈspjuːtəbl]	*What seems like an indisputable fact can be more complex than you think.*	unbestritten
	3b	**tentative** [ˈtentətɪv]	*Skim the article and find other examples of tentative language.*	zaghaft; vorsichtig
	4a	**competency** [ˈkɒmpɪtənsi]	*He started making notes about what each competency entails.* ⓘ *Lat. 'competens' = suitable*	Kompetenz
		collaborative [kəˈlæbərətɪv]	*The second step is what I call collaborative creativity.*	gemeinschaftlich
108	1	**to peel** [piːl]	*Oranges have to be peeled.*	schälen
		detox [ˈdiːtɒks]	*I am still using my phone or laptop, but I am on a kind of digital detox.*	Entgiftung; Entzug
	2a	**to compel** [kəmˈpel]	*I felt compelled to check social media as soon as I woke up.*	zwingen
		grunt [grʌnt]	*She tried to talk to me, but all she had from me was the occasional grunt.*	Grunzen
		to distract [dɪˈstrækt]	*I try hard not to get distracted when I am studying.*	ablenken
		temptation [tempˈteɪʃn]	*Chocolate is a big temptation for me.*	Versuchung
		acronym [ˈækrənɪm]	*He uses so many acronyms I'm not sure what he's talking about.*	Akronym
		symptom [ˈsɪmptəm]	*I showed all the symptoms of FOMO – that is 'fear of missing out'.*	Symptom; Anzeichen
		craze [kreɪz]	*I was always trying to catch up with the latest social media craze.*	Wahn
		notification [ˌnəʊtɪfɪˈkeɪʃn]	*I try to resist the urge to check constantly what others post, so I turned off my push notifications.*	Benachrichtigung
		span [spæn]	*I learned that I have a short attention span.*	Spanne
		to disconnect [ˌdɪskəˈnekt]	*I am doing digital detox, but I am not completely disconnected.*	trennen; abschalten
	3b	**whopping** [ˈwɒpɪŋ]	*A whopping 78% of the teen respondents said that they checked their digital devices hourly.*	*hier:* überwältigend
		depressive [dɪˈpresɪv]	*Heavy technology use was linked to sleeping problems and depressive symptoms.*	depressiv
		likelihood [ˈlaɪklihʊd]	*The likelihood of anxiety increased with social media use.*	Wahrscheinlichkeit
		insomnia [ɪnˈsɒmniə]	ⓘ *Lat. 'insomnia, -ae' (f.)*	Schlaflosigkeit
		duration [djuˈreɪʃn]	*Reading on your phone before going to sleep will lead to shorter sleep duration.*	Dauer
109	2	**precarious** [prɪˈkeəriəs]	*She fell to her death after trying to take a photo in a precarious location.*	gefährlich

page	exercise	Workshop 3		
		to pose [pəʊz]	She climbed past safety barriers and warning signs to pose on a rock for a photo when she tripped over the edge.	posieren; darstellen
		aftermath [ˈɑːtəmæθ]	In the aftermath of the accident, authorities reminded the public to pay attention to safety signs.	Nachwirkungen
	T	**argumentative** [ˌɑːgjuˈmentətɪv]	Write an argumentative essay about the advantages and disadvantages of digital technology.	argumentativ
110	1a	**globalization** [ˌgləʊbəlaɪˈzeɪʃn]	People are divided about whether globalization is a good or bad thing.	Globalisierung
	2	**relevance** [ˈreləvəns]	List the issues the article highlights and evaluate their relevance to your life.	Bedeutung
		fluid [ˈfluːɪd]	Gender is a rather fluid concept. ❗ Lat. 'fluere (fluo, fluxi, fluxum)' = to flow	fließend
		to indulge [ɪnˈdʌldʒ]	The child is so indulged, it behaves badly.	verwöhnen
		proliferation [prəˌlɪfəˈreɪʃn]	They have grown up with social media, a constant proliferation of information on a fully mobile internet.	Verbreitung
		connectivity [kəˌnekˈtɪvəti]	Connectivity is disconnecting people from real friendships and the opportunity to enjoy the world together.	Vernetzung
		feminism [ˈfemənɪzəm]	Young voters' focus has shifted away from party politics to single-topic issues such as feminism or climate change.	Feminismus
		civic [ˈsɪvɪk]	❗ Lat. 'civis, -is' (m./f.) = citizen	bürgerlich
	T	**connotation** [ˌkɒnəˈteɪʃn]	Interpret the use of adjectives with positive and negative connotations.	Konnotation; Beiklang
		hence [hens]		daher
111	2	**isolation** [ˌaɪsəˈleɪʃn]	The feelings of social isolation reported by many teenagers can be hard for older people to understand.	Isolation
		contradiction [ˌkɒntrəˈdɪkʃn]	The contradictions of connectivity are the real challenge for Generation Z and for society at large.	Widerspruch
		predecessor [ˈpriːdəsesə]	Young politicians appear more eager for change than their predecessors.	Vorgänger(in)
		to reframe [ˌriːˈfreɪm]	Youth are more politically engaged and eager to reframe perspectives on sexual orientation and gender.	umstrukturieren
		orientation [ˌɔːriənˈteɪʃn]	Perspectives on sexual orientation and gender are being reframed.	Orientierung; Ausrichtung

page	exercise	**Workshop 3**		
		adulthood [ˈædʌlthʊd]	*As they emerge into adulthood, we will see what world they make.*	Erwachsenenalter
	3b	façade [fəˈsɑːd]	*I wanted to break the façade and share my real feelings with my friends.*	Fassade
		to delve into [ˈdelv ɪntə]	*Let's delve into the details of the project.*	sich vertiefen
		introverted [ˈɪntrəvɜːtɪd]	*I've learned that I'm a lot more introverted than I thought I was.* ❗ *Lat. 'intro' = inside, 'vertere, -o, -i, -um' = to turn*	in sich gekehrt
		comfort [ˈkʌmfət]	*I find comfort in the realization that there's always hope in the future.*	Geborgenheit
		ukulele [ˌjuːkəˈleɪli]	*I gave up on trying to learn the ukulele, but now I'm playing chords.*	Ukulele
		chord [kɔːd]	*A while ago I gave up on trying to learn the guitar, but now I'm playing chords.*	Akkord
		empathetic [ˌempəˈθetɪk]	*Adults can be supportive by just trying to be empathetic.*	einfühlsam
		to adjust [əˈdʒʌst]	*Adjusting to a new way of learning is difficult and takes time.*	(sich) anpassen
		outreach [ˈaʊtriːtʃ]	*He has tried to create a culture of caring, compassion and outreach.*	Reichweite
		on behalf of [ɒn bɪˈhɑːf əv]	*We encourage each member of the community to reach out on behalf of their family.*	im Auftrag; im Namen von
	5	to accomplish [əˈkʌmplɪʃ]	*What did they accomplish and what are they proud of?*	erreichen; schaffen
112	1	urgent [ˈɜːdʒənt]	*For some young people, climate change is urgent.* ❗ *Lat. 'urgens, urgentis'; Fr. 'urgent'; Sp. 'urgente'*	dringend
		reconciliation [ˌrekənsɪliˈeɪʃn]	*From truth and reconciliation to inclusion and diversity, young people are aware of today's issues.*	Versöhnung
		inclusion [ɪnˈkluːʒn]	*Young people are bringing awareness to issues such as inclusion.*	Inklusion
		societal [səˈsaɪətl]	*There are many societal crises for younger generations to deal with.*	gesellschaftlich
		affordable [əˈfɔːdəbl]	*There is hardly any affordable housing so young adults continue living with their parents.*	erschwinglich
		parental [pəˈrentl]	*Unemployment leaves many young people under the parental roof.*	elterlich
		ubiquity [juːˈbɪkwəti]	*The ubiquity of the internet and social media has put new pressures on youth.* ❗ *Lat. 'ubique' = everywhere*	Allgegenwart

page	exercise	**Workshop 3**		
		to **shame** [ˈʃeɪm]	*Body shaming happens too often on social media.*	(be)schämen
		to **encroach** [ɪnˈkrəʊtʃ]	*The ubiquity of the internet and social media is encroaching on teens wellbeing.*	eingreifen; vordringen
		relentless [rɪˈlentləs]	*He had a relentless focus on his academic work.*	unerbittlich
		enviable [ˈenviəbl]	*Youth is thought to be the most enviable time of life.*	beneidenswert
		psychotherapist [ˌsaɪkəʊˈθerəpɪst]	*The child and adolescent psychotherapist will discuss how childhood has changed.*	Psychotherapeut(in)
		to **hinge on** [ˈhɪndʒ ɒn]	*There is a lot of pressure since so much hinges on this exam.*	abhängen von
		distress [dɪˈstres]	*Teachers are concerned about the mental distress they are seeing in students.*	Not; Leid
		non-binary [ˌnɒn ˈbaɪnəri]	*Non-binary people do not feel that they have solely a male or female gender.*	nicht binär
		apparent [əˈpærənt]	*These days, it's increasingly apparent that gender is a fluid concept.*	offensichtlich; erkennbar
		polysexual [pɒlɪˈsekʃʊəl]	*Polysexual people are sexually attracted to more than one gender.*	polysexuell
		to **strive** [straɪv], **strove, striven** [strəʊv, ˈstrɪvən]	*I pride myself on striving to use inclusive language.*	sich bemühen
		to **bite** [baɪt], **bit, bitten** [bɪt, ˈbɪtn]	*I work hard on biting my tongue when I want to say something critical.*	beißen
113	2b	**thought-provoking** [ˈθɔːt prəvəʊkɪŋ]	*Explain why you find the article so thought-provoking.*	nachdenkenswert
		furious [ˈfjʊəriəs]	*She looked furious after their conversation.*	wütend
		laughing stock [ˈlɑːfɪŋ stɒk]	*I'll be a laughing stock, nobody wil take me seriously.*	Lachnummer
		humiliating [hjuːˈmɪlieɪtɪŋ]	*I'll be a laughing stock, it's so humiliating.*	demütigend
	4a	**clueless** [ˈkluːləs]	*Her generation might be digital natives but when it comes to online security they seem to be clueless.*	ahnungslos
		to **shrug** [ʃrʌg]	*When I ask him a question, he just shrugs.*	mit den Schultern zucken
		immune [ɪˈmjuːn]	⚠ *Lat. 'immunis, -e' = free (from), unaffected*	immun
114	2	**exhaustive** [ɪgˈzɔːstɪv]	*The press exhaustively tracks the apps young people use.*	gründlich; vollständig
		gerontocratic [dʒəˌrɒntəˈkrætɪk]	*Most ancient cultures were gerontocratic, meaning they were ruled by the old.*	gerontokratisch

page   exercise

Workshop 3		
teenocratic [ˈtiːnəˈkrætɪk]	*Modern culture is fully teenocratic, governed by the tastes of young people.*	teenokratisch
confluence [ˈkɒnfluəns]	❗ *Lat. 'confluere, -fluo, - fluxi, --' = to flow into one another; to join*	Zusammenströmen
watchful [ˈwɒtʃfl]	*High schools gave young people a place to build a separate culture outside the watchful eye of family.*	wachsam
to **localize** [ˈləʊkəlaɪz]	*As the US economy shifted from a more localized agrarian society to a mass-production machine, families relocated closer to cities.*	lokalisieren
countermovement [kaʊntəmuːvmənt]	*This triggered a countermovement to prevent kids from being forced to work.*	Gegenbewegung
to **toil** [tɔɪl]	*Kids of a young age were forced to toil in factories.*	schuften
mill [mɪl]	*This triggered a countermovement to prevent kids from being forced to toil in mills.*	Fabrik; Mühle
in earnest [ɪn ˈɜːnɪst]	*A serious commercial interest in teenagers didn't begin in earnest until after World War II.*	ernsthaft
to **entice** [ɪnˈtaɪs]	*Teenagers entice marketers because they have money to spend.*	locken; ködern
marketer [ˈmɑːkɪtə]	*Marketers try to entice teens with their products.*	Vermarkter(in)
expansion [ɪkˈspænʃn]	❗ *Fr. 'expansion' (f.); Sp. 'expansión' (f.)*	Ausdehnung; Expansion
unionized [ˈjuːnɪənaɪzd]	*With full employment came rising wages for unionized adults and older teenage workers.*	gewerkschaftlich organisiert
enrichment [ɪnˈrɪtʃmənt]	*Since the 1970s, the richest 20% of US households have more than doubled their spending on childhood 'enrichment'.*	Bereicherung
consideration [kən,sɪdəˈreɪʃn]	*Today's singles would find it a strange consideration to have to meet their date's parents before going out.*	Überlegung; Beachtung
awkward [ˈɔːkwəd]	*After my parents' fight we sat down to an awkward family dinner.*	umständlich; peinlich
to **emancipate** [ɪˈmænsɪpeɪt]	*It is hard to emancipate oneself from peer pressure.*	(sich) emanzipieren; befreien
stilted [ˈstɪltɪd]	*I like lively conversations and not stilted small talk.*	gekünstelt
parlour [ˈpɑːlə]	*In the past, rich people had a parlour to receive guests.* ❗ *AE = parlor*	Salon

page	exercise	**Workshop 3**		
		permissible [pəˈmɪsəbl]	❗ *Lat. 'permittere, -mitto, -misi, - missum'*	erlaubt
		normalization [ˌnɔːməlaɪˈzeɪʃn]	*When injustice is everywhere there is the risk of the normalization of it.*	Normalisierung
		to upend [ʌpˈend]	*The fear that young men and fast cars were upending romantic norms was widespread.*	umdrehen
		illegitimate [ˌɪləˈdʒɪtəmət]	*When you're young, every rule is illegitimate until proven otherwise.*	unrechtmäßig
		precisely [prɪˈsaɪsli]	*It is precisely because they have so little to lose that young people will challenge culture.*	genau
		inexhaustible [ˌɪnɪgˈzɔːstəbl]	*Young people will continue to be the inexhaustible motor of culture.*	unerschöpflich
115	4b	**compulsory** [kəmˈpʌlsəri]	*This course is compulsory – you have to take it.*	verpflichtend, obligatorisch
116	S1b	**discipline** [ˈdɪsəplɪn]	*It is important to learn skills in all academic disciplines.*	Disziplin; Fachrichtung
		robust [rəʊˈbʌst]	*Your analysis can show that evidence is not robust.*	solide; robust
		to synthesize [ˈsɪnθəsaɪz]	*Writing the paper will require synthesizing, analysing and evaluating what you have learned.*	synthetisieren
		postgraduate [ˌpəʊstˈgrædʒuət]	*Critical thinking is required for pre-university, undergraduate and postgraduate levels of study.*	Graduierten...
		purposeful [ˈpɜːpəsfl]	*Purposeful reading can help with critical thinking because it encourages you to read actively.*	zielgerichtet
		validity [vəˈlɪdəti]	❗ *Fr. 'validité' (f.); Sp. 'validez' (f.)*	Gültigkeit
	S2a	**confirmation** [ˌkɒnfəˈmeɪʃn]	*We need confirmation for our ideas.*	Bestätigung
		prejudice [ˈpredʒədɪs]	❗ *Lat. praeiudicare (-o, -avi, -atus)' = to decide in advance*	Vorurteil
		nuanced [ˈnjuːɑːnst]	*What seems like a fact can be more nuanced than you think.*	differenziert
		intellectual [ˌɪntəˈlektʃuəl]	*Having intellectual empathy can have very successful results when you are thinking something out.*	geistig; intellektuell
		ulterior [ʌlˈtɪəriə]	*Critical thinking depends on being aware of ulterior motives.*	versteckt
		motive [ˈməʊtɪv]	*Critical thinking depends on being aware of ulterior motives.*	Beweggrund; Motiv
		vested interest [ˌvestɪd ˈɪntrəst]	*Does the person or organization making the claim have a vested interest?*	persönliches Interesse
		to sway [sweɪ]	*Ads you see on social media can sway your vote in a government election.*	beeinflussen; schwanken

page	exercise	**Workshop 3**		
117	T	**to alter** [ˈɔːltə]	Photos can be altered or taken from an unrelated site. = to change	verändern
		reverse [rɪˈvɜːs]	Use a tool like a reverse image search to show you if the same image has already been used.	umgekehrt
		elsewhere [ˌelsˈweə]	A reverse image search can show you if the same image is used elsewhere.	woanders
	S1	**to cure** [kjʊər]	She made a fortune by claiming she had cured herself.	heilen
		cancer [ˈkænsər]	She made a fortune by claiming she had cured herself of cancer.	Krebs
		slim [slɪm]	All the people in adverts are slim.	schlank
		gorgeous [ˈgɔːdʒəs]	You look amazing and your hair is gorgeous!	wunderschön
		to sculpt [skʌlpt]	He sculpts his body by going to the gym.	formen
		insane [ɪnˈseɪn]	I have so much school work, it's insane. ❗ Sp. 'insano'	verrückt
		to heal [hiːl]	Because they believed they could heal their illness naturally, they stopped taking medicine. = to cure	heilen
	S3	**to verify** [ˈverɪfaɪ]	Describe how the argument can or cannot be verified and share your analysis in class.	überprüfen; belegen
118	3	**to reshuffle** [riːˈʃʌfl]	Reshuffle the cards, please.	neu mischen
119	4a	**toll** [təʊl]	Exams, peer pressure and personal stresses can really put a toll on your life.	Tribut; Zoll
		positivity [ˌpɒzəˈtɪvəti]	A lot of people think positivity just means happiness, but it doesn't.	positive Einstellung
		admirable [ˈædmərəbl]	Being proud of who you are and what you believe in is admirable. ❗ Lat. 'admirari, admiror' = to admire	bewundernswert
		relevancy [ˈreləvənsi]	There is no relevancy in comparing your work to others.	Relevanz; Bedeutung
	5	**to hurl** [hɜːl]	She has hurled herself into her schoolwork, hoping to get great marks.	schleudern; werfen
		headfirst [ˌhedˈfɜːst]	Japan has hurled itself headfirst into the 21st century.	kopfüber
		to recreate [ˌriːkriˈeɪt]	Japan has recreated itself as a powerful economy.	wiederherstellen
		powerhouse [ˈpaʊəhaʊs]	Japan has recreated itself as an economic powerhouse.	Kraftzentrum
		to baffle [ˈbæfl]	Some teens have the baffling desire to go to school in ripped clothing.	verblüffen

page	exercise	Workshop 3		
		delicate ['delɪkət]	The flower is beautiful and delicate. ❗ Fr. 'delicat'; Sp. 'delicado'	zart
		jowl [dʒaʊl]	His jowls were trembling in fear.	Wange
		heel [hi:l]	Her shoes were too small and hurt her heels.	Absatz; Ferse
		bewildered [bɪˈwɪldəd]	Older people are often bewildered by youth.	verwirrt
		productive [prəˈdʌktɪv]	Most rebellious youth will become productive citizens some day.	produktiv
		meantime [ˈmi:ntaɪm]	In the meantime, there's no telling who's going to show up to enjoy the show.	Zwischenzeit
		to lace [leɪs]	She laced up her shoes.	schnüren
		dropout [ˈdrɒpaʊt]	Those kids aren't dropouts, they only have a half day of school today!	Aussteiger(in); Abbrecher(in)
		dedicated [ˈdedɪkeɪtɪd]	They're just as dedicated to their success as their parents are.	engagiert
		tissue [ˈtɪʃu:]	He sneezed, so I gave him a tissue.	Papiertaschentuch
		assertion [əˈsɜ:ʃn]	Evaluate the assertion that parents put too much pressure on kids.	Behauptung
122	2	immense [ɪˈmens]	While there are immense advantages to social media use, there are also problems with it. = huge ≠ small	riesig
		to bombard [bɒmˈbɑ:d]	Teens are bombarded by news, social media posts and adverts.	bombardieren
		flow [fləʊ]	Being bombarded by the never-ending flow of news, social media posts and adverts makes it hard to stay focused.	Fluss; Strom
	3	phase [feɪz]	Much happens in this phase of adolescent development.	Phase; Abschnitt
		gist [dʒɪst]	I think you get my gist.	Hauptpunkt
		exploratory [ɪkˈsplɒrətri]	After the exploratory stage, you'll need to decide on a topic.	exploratisch; forschend
		diffused [dɪˈfju:zd]	This is a highly diffused fashion style.	verbreitet; diffus
		painful [ˈpeɪnfl]	It's painful to lose a friend.	schmerzhaft
		separation [ˌsepəˈreɪʃn]	The separation from one another was hard for the family. ❗ Lat. 'separatio, -ionis' (f.)	Trennung
		individuation [ɪndɪvɪdʒʊˈeɪʃən]	Individuation helps develop a healthy identity.	Individualisierung
		identical [aɪˈdentɪkl]	The teens dress so alike they're almost identical.	identisch
		to lessen [ˈlesn]	Playing sport lessens his anxiety.	mindern; nachlassen
		to elaborate [ɪˈlæbərət]	Allow me to elaborate on this last point I made.	weiter ausführen

page	exercise	**Workshop 3**		
		to occupy [ˈɒkjupaɪ]	*Friendships occupy a lot of teens' attention.* ❗ *Lat. 'occupare (-o, -avi, -atum)'; Fr. 'occuper'; Sp. 'ocupar'*	einnehmen; besetzen
		socialization [ˌsəʊʃəlaɪˈzeɪʃn]	*During the socialization process teenagers often rebel.*	Sozialisierung
		ethic [ˈeθɪk]	*What values and ethics do they identify with?*	Ethik
		behavioural [bɪˈheɪvjərəl]	*Talking things through helps teenagers with behavioural problems.*	Verhaltens…
		resolution [ˌrezəˈluːʃn]	*It is good to learn skills in conflict resolution.*	hier: Auflösung
		interpretation [ɪnˌtɜːprəˈteɪʃn]	*How is the way she views the poem different from his interpretation?*	Interpretation
123	4a	**prestigious** [preˈstɪdʒəs]	*He received a prestigious scholarship.*	angesehen
		dot [dɒt]	*There was a dot-based code system, but it was complicated and slow.*	Punkt

page	exercise	**Workshop 4**		
134		**proposition** [ˌprɒpəˈzɪʃn]	*Choose one of the topic areas and respond to one of the propositions given for that topic area.*	Vorschlag
		to choke [tʃəʊk]	*Air pollution is choking our cities and causing a global health crisis.*	ersticken
		culprit [ˈkʌlprɪt]	*In the UK the main culprit in fossil fuel pollution is diesel-using vehicles.*	Schuldige
		addictive [əˈdɪktɪv]	*Tech companies use design techniques to encourage impulsive or addictive behaviour.*	süchtig machend
135		**unchaperoned** [ʌnˈʃæpərəʊnd]	*Teens today navigate new relationships unchaperoned by adults.*	ohne Begleitung
		protection [prəˈtekʃn]	*There are not enough protections for children online.* ❗ *Lat. 'protegere (-tego, -texi, -tectum)'*	Schutz
		to pollinate [ˈpɒləneɪt]	*Insects and small birds pollinate plants.*	befruchten; bestäuben
		soy [ˈsɔɪ]	*Soy beans are an excellent source of protein.*	Soja
		reliant [rɪˈlaɪənt]	*The agricultural industry has become reliant on soy for animal feed.*	angewiesen
		to accelerate [əkˈseləreɪt]	*The drive to produce greater amounts of cheap meat and dairy is accelerating climate change and destroying forests.*	beschleunigen
		to compound [kəmˈpaʊnd]	*Technology is compounding problems of division in society.*	verschlimmern

page   exercise

Workshop 4		
exclusion [ɪkˈskluːʒn]	The exclusion of children with disabilities is not allowed. ≠ inclusion	Ausschluss
to **reproduce** [ˌriːprəˈdjuːs]	Social media reproduces divides in society. ❗ Fr. 'reproduir'; Sp. 'reproducir'	vervielfältigen
to **amplify** [ˈæmplɪfaɪ]	These news stories amplify divides that exist between socioeconomic groups.	verstärken
classification [ˌklæsɪfɪˈkeɪʃn]	Our society is divided by socio-economic classifications.	Einstufung
dependent on [dɪˈpendənt ɒn]	Babies are dependent on their parents for survival. ≠ independent of	abhängig von
seafloor [siːflɔː]	It would be amazing to be able to see the seafloor and the life there.	Meeresgrund
animation [ˌænɪˈmeɪʃn]	Sounds, animations, endless content and notifications from social media take our attention.	Animation
to **activate** [ˈæktɪveɪt]	You have to activate the account before you can use it.	aktivieren; auslösen
dopamine [ˈdəʊpəmiːn]	The rewards of social media activate the dopamine reward systems of the brain.	Dopamin
to **harness** [ˈhɑːnɪs]	They are harnessing different techniques to reach the user.	nutzen
loader [ˈləʊdə]	When you pull down on your Instagram, it shows a little loader as it updates.	Ladesymbol
slot machine [ˈslɒt məʃiːn]	Sometimes you can win when you play a slot machine, but not often.	Spielautomat
periodically [ˌpɪəriˈɒdɪkli]	Social media companies periodically send updates in order to get you to check their app.	regelmäßig
sophisticated [səˈfɪstɪkeɪtɪd]	Teens become increasingly sophisticated as they grow older.	anspruchsvoll; gebildet
dwell time [dwel taɪm]	Dwell time is how long you spend looking at a piece of content in your social media feed.	Verweilzeit
to **backtrack** [ˈbæktræk]	If you lose something, try backtracking to see where you left it.	zurückverfolgen
to **monitor** [ˈmɒnɪtər]	I use an alarm to help monitor my use of social media.	kontrollieren
usage [ˈjuːsɪdʒ]	There are applications to help us monitor and cut down on social media usage.	Gebrauch
impulsive [ɪmˈpʌlsɪv]	❗ Fr. 'impulsif'; Sp. 'impulsivo'	impulsiv; spontan
in-depth [ˌɪn ˈdepθ]	Have an in-depth discussion of the topic.	gründlich

page	exercise	Workshop 4		
136	1a	**disastrous** [dɪˈzɑːstrəs]	*We must avoid the disastrous effects of climate change.*	verheerend
		to **halve** [hɑːv]	*We must halve global emissions in the next 10 years.*	halbieren
		prosperity [prɒˈsperəti]	*Our goal is for a world of net zero carbon emissions by 2050, with greater prosperity for all.*	Wohlstand
		to **multiply** [ˈmʌltɪplaɪ]	❗ *Lat. 'multiplicare (-o, -avi, -atum)'*	multiplizieren; vervielfachen
		to **unlock** [ˌʌnˈlɒk]	*We join up organizations to unlock the power of collective action.*	entriegeln
		to **hold accountable** [həʊld əˈkaʊntəbl], **held, held** [held, held]	*We power large networks and hold each organization accountable.*	verantwortlich machen
		decision maker [dɪˈsɪʒn meɪkə]	*We work with leaders and decision makers from business and government.*	Entscheidungsträger(in)
138	1	**biodiversity** [ˌbaɪəʊdaɪˈvɜːsəti]	*Biodiversity is being threatened.*	Artenvielfalt
		to **annihilate** [əˈnaɪəleɪt]	*Biodiversity is being annihilated around the world.*	vernichten
		desertification [dɪˌzɜːtɪfɪˈkeɪʃn]	*Flooding and desertification will make vast areas of land uninhabitable.*	Wüstenbildung
		to **render** [ˈrendə]	*Flooding and desertification will render vast areas of land uninhabitable.* = make	machen
		tract [trækt]	*Flooding and desertification will render vast tracts of land uninhabitable.* = area	Gebiet
		toxic [ˈtɒksɪk]	*Toxic waste is polluting our earth.* ❗ *Fr. 'toxique'; Sp. 'toxico'*	giftig
		unborn [ˌʌnˈbɔːn]	*A population's poor nutrition harms the unborn.*	Ungeborene(r)
		untold [ˌʌnˈtəʊld]	*Humans are causing untold damage to the environment.*	unermesslich
		bystander [ˈbaɪstændə]	*If you see an act of violence, get help, don't just be a bystander.*	Zuschauer(in)
		to **prioritize** [praɪˈɒrətaɪz]	*Now is the moment to begin building a world where love, care and freedom are prioritized.*	priorisieren
		cascading [kæˈskeɪdɪŋ]	*We must be clear about the extreme cascading risks we now face.*	kaskadierend
		humanity [hjuːˈmænəti]	*We must be clear about the extreme cascading risks humanity now faces.*	Menschheit
	2a	**explanatory** [ɪkˈsplænətri]	*Read the explanatory text and answer the questions.*	erklärend; erläuternd
		uncontracted [ʌnkənˈtræktɪd]	*Use uncontracted forms of a verb to make your writing more formal.* ≠ contracted	nicht zusammengezogen

page	exercise	**Workshop 4**		
139	3b	**hyperbole** [haɪˈpɜːbəli]	*Hyperbole is exaggerated language that is used to have an effect on the listener.*	Übertreibung
140	1a	**exhibitor** [ɪgˈzɪbɪtə]	*Read the abstract introducing an exhibitor at an exhibition.*	Aussteller(in)
		trustworthy [ˈtrʌstwɜːði]	*Evaluate whether these sources are trustworthy or not.*	vertrauenswürdig
		scenario [səˈnɑːriəʊ]	*Usually in bleak future scenarios, it's the robots that are causing all the problems.*	Szenario
		robotic [rəʊˈbɒtɪk]	*It's a robotic bee that can pollinate plants.*	Roboter...
		to buzz [bʌz]	*It's a robotic bee that can buzz between flowers and pollinate plants.*	schwirren
		fungus [ˈfʌŋgəs]	**!** *Lat. 'fungus, -i' (m.)*	Pilz
		virus [ˈvaɪrəs]	*Wear a mask so that you don't catch the virus.*	Virus
		parasite [ˈpærəsaɪt]	*Parasites might be to blame for bee deaths.*	Parasit
		pollination [ˌpɒləˈneɪʃn]	*Most plants growing in the wild require pollination.*	Bestäubung
		fatigue [fəˈtiːg]	*We walked for so long, I thought I would die of fatigue.* = tiredness	Müdigkeit
		dire [ˈdaɪər]	*The effects of such a situation may be direr than we all think.*	entsetzlich; furchtbar
		pollinator [ˈpɒləneɪtə]	*Bees are the planet's main pollinators.*	Bestäuber
		recognition [ˌrekəgˈnɪʃn]	*The autonomous device's recognition of flowers is amazing.*	Erkennung
		to locate [ləʊˈkeɪt]	*This autonomous device locates problems with the system and repairs them.* **!** *Lat. 'locus, -i' (m.) = place*	finden; orten
		pollen [ˈpɒlən]	*Bees help collect and transport pollen.*	Pollen
	2a	**groundbreaker** [ˈgraʊndbreɪkə]	*These young people have been groundbreakers in developing new technologies.*	Wegbereiter(in)
	4	**cluster** [ˈklʌstə]	*A cluster of students stood around the teacher.*	Gruppe; Ansammlung
141	3a	**coherent** [kəʊˈhɪərənt]	*Tie your ideas together to create a coherent argument.*	schlüssig
		mash [mæʃ]	*We mix the ingredients together to make a mash.*	Brei
		representation [ˌreprɪzenˈteɪʃn]	*You need a visual representation of how you can organize your ideas.*	*hier:* Darstellung
		to fasten [ˈfɑːsn]	*He fastened the list of new words to the wall.*	festmachen

page	exercise	**Workshop 4**		
		to **delete** [dɪˈliːt]	*Delete useless information from your presentation.*	löschen
		duplication [ˌdjuːplɪˈkeɪʃn]	*Find all of the duplications on the guest list and delete them.*	Doppelung
		to **crystallize** [ˈkrɪstəlaɪz]	*As your plan crystallizes, organize your ideas in writing.*	sich herausbilden
142		**sturdy** [ˈstɜːdi]	*Don't climb the tree if the branches aren't sturdy!*	kräftig
	3b	**edible** [ˈedəbl]	*Edible cutlery is a clever way of getting rid of plastic forks, spoons and knives.*	essbar
		to **convert** [kənˈvɜːt]	*The article is about the converting of fog into drinking water.* ❗ *Fr. 'convertir'; Sp. 'convertir'*	umwandeln
	4	**fishbone** [fɪʃbəʊn]	*The fishbone diagram provides another way of organizing information.*	Gräte
		doodle [ˈduːdl]	*Creative doodles can help you organize ideas.*	Gekritzel
		causal [ˈkɔːzl]	*There is a causal relationship between poverty and crime.*	ursächlich
		loop [luːp]	*Causal loop diagrams show causal relationships between things.*	Schleife
143	1a	**bluff** [blʌf]	*He said he would stop if we gave him sweets, but it was a bluff.*	Täuschung
	1b	**plausible** [ˈplɔːzəbl]	*Each person in a team must define the same English word so there are several plausible definitions.*	einleuchtend
	T	**provenance** [ˈprɒvənəns]	*What is the provenance of these words?* = origin	Herkunft
144	2a	**economist** [ɪˈkɒnəmɪst]	❗ *Fr. 'economiste' (m./f.);* *Sp. 'economista' (m./f.)*	Wirtschaftswissenschaftler(in)
		desirable [dɪˈzaɪərəbl]	*My own view is that Net Zero is achievable and desirable, but there will be many problems.*	wünschenswert
		trillion [ˈtrɪljən]	*We will need to spend about $275 trillion on renewable energies.*	Billion
		catastrophe [kəˈtæstrəfi]	*It would be a catastrophe if schools closed again.* = disaster	Katastrophe
146	2	**everlasting** [ˌevəˈlɑːstɪŋ]	*The social media we use has an everlasting effect on us – whether we notice it or not.*	andauernd
		trait [treɪt]	*We have to define the traits that help us survive in the future.*	Charakterzug
		utopia [juːˈtəʊpiə]	*I would love to create a future that is a utopia for everyone.*	Utopie

page	exercise	**Workshop 4**		
		stressor [ˈstresə]	*If we aren't careful, these stressors could easily turn into full-blown mental health problems.*	Stressfaktor
		insecurity [ˌɪnsɪˈkjʊərəti]	*Insecurity is basically one's lack of confidence in themselves.*	Unsicherheit
		reel [riːl]	*A highlight reel is a collection of your best and brightest moments.*	Reel; Rolle
		transaction [trænˈzækʃn]	*When you post a photo and you get a like or a comment in return, it becomes a recorded transaction.*	Transaktion; Geschäft
		to **quantify** [ˈkwɒntɪfaɪ]	*Our self-worth depends on what others think of us, and then we quantify it for everyone to see.*	messen; quantifizieren
		irrational [ɪˈræʃənl]	*Some expectations are totally irrational.*	irrational
		withdrawal [wɪðˈdrɔːəl]	*Using social media and phones can cause social anxiety and irrational withdrawal symptoms.*	Entzug
		tirelessly [ˈtaɪələsli]	*People like Greta Thunberg work tirelessly for their movements.*	unermüdlich
		to **collaborate** [kəˈlæbəreɪt]	*So why not use your time on social media to collaborate with some of these individuals.* ❗ Lat. 'collaboratio, -onis' (f.) = outcome, gain	zusammenarbeiten
	T	to **gesticulate** [dʒeˈstɪkjuleɪt]	*Your body language was good, but maybe you could gesticulate a bit less.*	gestikulieren
	3	**appreciable** [əˈpriːʃəbl]	*It might make an appreciable difference if you call to check in on her.*	spürbar; erheblich

Dictionary: English – German

A

abbey [ˈæbi] Kloster **WS 1**, 17

abbreviated [əˈbriːvieɪtɪd] abgekürzt OT 5

abbreviation [əˌbriːviˈeɪʃn] Abkürzung OT 2

to abide by [əˈbaɪd baɪ] befolgen **WS 2**, 65

ability [əˈbɪləti] Fähigkeit; Möglichkeit OT 4

to able: be able [bi ˈeɪbl] fähig sein; können OT 2

aboard [əˈbɔːd] an Bord OT 4

to abolish [əˈbɒlɪʃ] abschaffen **WW**, 10

abolition [ˌæbəˈlɪʃn] Abschaffung **WS 2**, 54

abolitionist [ˌæbəˈlɪʃənɪst] Abolitionist(in); Sklavereigegner(in) **WS 2**, 57

about [əˈbaʊt] über; wegen; ungefähr OT 1

above [əˈbʌv] oben; oberhalb OT 2

abroad [əˈbrɔːd] im Ausland OT 2

to abseil [ˈæbseɪl] (sich) abseilen OT 2

absence [ˈæbsəns] Abwesenheit; Mangel **WS 3**, 101

absolute [ˌæbsəˈluːt] absolut; völlig **WS 1**, 29

  absolutely [ˈæbsəluːtli] absolut; wirklich OT 2

abstract [ˈæbstrækt] Zusammenfassung; Auszug OT 4

academic [ˌækəˈdemɪk] akademisch OT 4

to accelerate [əkˈseləreɪt] beschleunigen **WS 4**, 135

accent [ˈæksənt] Akzent; Akzentzeichen; Betonung OT 2

to accept [əkˈsept] annehmen OT 2

acceptable [əkˈseptəbl] akzeptabel; zulässig **WS 3**, 96

acceptance [əkˈseptəns] Akzeptanz OT 5

access [ˈækses] Zugang OT 2

to access [ˈækses] zugreifen auf OT 4

accessible [əkˈsesəbl] zugänglich; barrierefrei OT 2

accessory [əkˈsesəri] Zubehör OT 3

accident [ˈæksɪdənt] Unfall; Missgeschick; Zufall OT 1

  by accident [baɪ ˈæksɪdənt] versehentlich OT 2

  Accident and Emergency [ˈæksɪdənt ənd iˌmɜːdʒənsi] Notaufnahme OT 1

accidentally [ˌæksɪˈdentəli] zufällig; versehentlich OT 3

to accommodate [əˈkɒmədeɪt] unterbringen **WS 1**, 15

accommodation [əˌkɒməˈdeɪʃn] Unterkunft OT 4

to accompany [əˈkʌmpəni] begleiten **WS 2**, 67

accompanied [əˈkʌmpəniːd] in Begleitung OT 3

to accomplish [əˈkʌmplɪʃ] erreichen; schaffen **WS 3**, 111

accomplishment [əˈkʌmplɪʃmənt] Erfüllung; Vollendung **WS 1**, 37

according to [əˈkɔːdɪŋ tə] nach; gemäß OT 4

accordion [əˈkɔːdiən] Akkordeon OT 2

account [əˈkaʊnt] Konto OT 3

to account for [əˈkaʊnt fər] ausmachen OT 5

to hold accountable [həʊld əˈkaʊntəbl] zur Rechenschaft ziehen OT 5

accurate [ˈækjərət] genau; präzise OT 4

to accuse [əˈkjuːz] beschuldigen; anklagen OT 5

ache [eɪk] Schmerz OT 3

achievable [əˈtʃiːvəbl] erreichbar **WS 1**, 12

to achieve [əˈtʃiːv] erreichen; schaffen OT 4

achievement [əˈtʃiːvmənt] Errungenschaft OT 4

aching [ˈeɪkɪŋ] schmerzend; schmerzhaft **WS 1**, 12

acidic [əˈsɪdɪk] sauer OT 5

to acknowledge [əkˈnɒlɪdʒ] bestätigen; anerkennen OT 5

acoustic [əˈkuːstɪk] akustisch OT 2

acoustics [əˈkuːstɪks] Akustik **WS 1**, 39

acquaintance [əˈkweɪntəns] Bekannte(r); Bekanntschaft OT 3

to acquire [əˈkwaɪə] erwerben; akquirieren **WS 3**, 106

acre [ˈeɪkə] Morgen (Fläche) OT 4

acronym [ˈækrənɪm] Akronym **WS 3**, 108

across [əˈkrɒs] auf der anderen Seite; hinüber; über OT 1

act [ækt] Gesetz; Verordnung OT 5

to act [ækt] sich verhalten; handeln; Theater spielen OT 1

  to act out [ækt aʊt] ausspielen OT 2

action [ˈækʃn] Aktion OT 2

  in action [ɪn ˈækʃn] im Einsatz OT 2

to activate [ˈæktɪveɪt] aktivieren; auslösen **WS 4**, 135

actively [ˈæktɪvli] aktiv OT 4

activism [ˈæktɪvɪzəm] Aktivismus OT 5

activist [ˈæktɪvɪst] Aktivist(in) OT 5

activity [ækˈtɪvəti] Aktivität; Beschäftigung OT 1

actor [ˈæktə] Schauspieler(in) OT 1

actual [ˈæktʃuəl] richtig; wirklich OT 4

  actually [ˈæktʃuəli] eigentlich; um genau zu sein OT 3

ad [æd] Werbung OT 2

AD (Anno Domini) [ˌeɪ ˈdiː] n. Chr.; unserer Zeitrechnung OT 2

to adapt [əˈdæpt] sich anpassen **WS 2**, 67

adaptation [ˌædæpˈteɪʃn] Adaptierung OT 4

to add [æd] hinzufügen; addieren; zusammenzählen OT 1

addicted [əˈdɪktɪd] abhängig; süchtig **WS 2**, 73

addiction [əˈdɪkʃn] Sucht; Süchtigkeit OT 5

addictive [əˈdɪktɪv] süchtig machend **WS 4**, 134

addition [əˈdɪʃn] Zusatz; Ergänzung OT 4

additional [əˈdɪʃənl] zusätzlich; ergänzend OT 5

address [əˈdres] Adresse; Anschrift; Ansprache OT 1

to address [əˈdres] ansprechen OT 5

adjective [ˈædʒɪktɪv] Adjektiv OT 2

to adjust [əˈdʒʌst] (sich) anpassen **WS 3**, 111

administration [ədˌmɪnɪˈstreɪʃn] Verwaltung **WS 1**, 30

admirable [ˈædmərəbl] bewundernswert **WS 3**, 119

to admire [ədˈmaɪə] bewundern OT 4

admirer [ədˈmaɪərə] Bewunderer; Bewunderin **WS 2**, 60

admission [ədˈmɪʃn] Eintritt OT 2

to admit [ədˈmɪt] zugeben OT 5

adolescence [ˌædəˈlesns] Jugend(alter) **WS 3**, 94

adolescent [ˌædəˈlesnt] Jugendliche; Jugend... OT 5

to adopt [əˈdɒpt] annehmen OT 5

adoption [əˈdɒpʃn] Adoption; Übernahme **WS 2**, 68

to adore [əˈdɔː] anbeten; bewundern OT 4

adult ['ædʌlt] Erwachsene(r) OT 1

adulthood ['ædʌlthʊd] Erwachsenenalter **WS 3**, 111

advance [əd'vɑːns] Fortschritt OT 4

advantage [əd'vɑːntɪdʒ] Vorteil OT 3

advent ['ædvent] Beginn; Einführung OT 5

adventure [əd'ventʃə] Abenteuer OT 1

adventurous [əd'ventʃərəs] abenteuerlustig OT 2

adverse ['ædvɜːs] negativ; nachteilig **WS 1**, 36

adversity [əd'vɜːsəti] Widrigkeit **WS 1**, 16

advert ['ædvɜːt] Werbung OT 2

to **advertise** ['ædvətaɪz] Werbung machen für OT 2

advertisement [əd'vɜːtɪsmənt] Werbung; Reklame; Anzeige OT 1

advertising ['ædvətaɪzɪŋ] Werbung OT 2

advice [əd'vaɪs] Rat OT 2

to **advise** [əd'vaɪz] raten OT 4

advisor [əd'vaɪzə] Berater(in) OT 5

advocate ['ædvəkət] Anwalt, Anwältin **WS 2**, 58

advocate (for) ['ædvəkət fə] Fürsprecher(in) OT 5

aerobic [eə'rəʊbɪk] aerobisch **WS 1**, 37

aeroplane ['eərəpleɪn] Flugzeug OT 4

aerospace ['eərəʊspeɪs] Luftfahrt OT 4

affair [ə'feə] Angelegenheit; Affäre OT 4

to **affect** [ə'fekt] sich auswirken auf OT 3

affection [ə'fekʃn] Zuneigung **WS 1**, 13

affectionate [ə'fekʃənət] liebevoll **WS 2**, 82

affiliated [ə'fɪlieɪtɪd] verbunden; angegliedert **WS 2**, 71

affirmative [ə'fɜːmətɪv] zustimmend OT 3

to **afford** [ə'fɔːd] sich leisten OT 2

affordable [ə'fɔːdəbl] erschwinglich **WS 3**, 112

afield [ə'fiːld] draußen **WS 1**, 15

aforementioned [ə'fɔːmenʃənd] zuvor genannt **WS 3**, 99

afraid [ə'freɪd] ängstlich OT 2

African ['æfrɪkən] afrikanisch OT 2

after ['ɑːftə] nach; hinter; hinterher OT 1

afterlife ['ɑːftəlaɪf] Leben nach dem Tod OT 5

aftermath ['ɑːftəmæθ] Nachwirkungen **WS 3**, 109

afternoon [ˌɑːftə'nuːn] Nachmittag OT 1

afterward ['ɑːftəwəd] danach **WS 2**, 73

afterwards ['ɑːftəwədz] danach OT 4

again [ə'gen] wieder; gleich wieder OT 1

against [ə'genst] gegen; gegenüber; an OT 1

age [eɪdʒ] Alter; Zeitalter; Zeit OT 1

aged ['eɪdʒd] im Alter von OT 3

agency ['eɪdʒənsi] Agentur; Organisation OT 4

agenda [ə'dʒendə] Tagesordnung OT 3

agent ['eɪdʒənt] Mittel OT 5

aggravated assault [ˌægrəveɪtɪd ə'sɔːlt] schwere Körperverletzung OT 5

aggression [ə'greʃn] Aggression; Angriff **WS 2**, 60

aggressive [ə'gresɪv] aggressiv **WS 1**, 37

aghast [ə'gɑːst] entsetzt OT 3

agile ['ædʒaɪl] beweglich OT 3

ago [ə'gəʊ] vor OT 1

agonizingly ['ægənaɪzɪŋli] quälend; sehr OT 3

agrarian [ə'greəriən] landwirtschaftlich OT 5

to **agree** [ə'griː] sich einig sein; zustimmen OT 1

agreement [ə'griːmənt] Vereinbarung OT 3

agricultural [ˌægrɪ'kʌltʃərəl] landwirtschaftlich OT 4

agriculture ['ægrɪkʌltʃə] Landwirtschaft OT 2

ahead [ə'hed] weiter vorn OT 2

AI, artificial intelligence [ˌeɪ 'aɪ, ˌɑːtɪ'fɪʃl ɪn'telɪdʒəns] KI; künstliche Intelligenz **WS 3**, 99

aid [eɪd] Hilfe; Unterstützung OT 5

first aid [ˌfɜːst 'eɪd] Erste Hilfe OT 2

aim [eɪm] Ziel OT 4

to **aim** [eɪm] zielen; beabsichtigen OT 4

ain't [eɪnt] *hier:* ist nicht **WS 2**, 76

air [eə] Luft OT 2

airline ['eəlaɪn] Fluggesellschaft OT 5

airplane ['eəpleɪn] Flugzeug OT 2

airport ['eəpɔːt] Flughafen OT 1

alarm [ə'lɑːm] Wecker; Alarm OT 2

alarmed [ə'lɑːmd] beunruhigt OT 3

alarming [ə'lɑːmɪŋ] erschreckend OT 4

Alaskan [ə'læskən] alaskisch OT 2

album ['ælbəm] Album OT 3

alcohol ['ælkəhɒl] Alkohol OT 3

alcoholic [ˌælkə'hɒlɪk] alkoholisch OT 3

to **alert** [ə'lɜːt] alarmieren OT 2

algorithm ['ælgərɪðəm] Algorithmus OT 5

alien ['eɪliən] Außerirdische(r); Alien OT 2

alike [ə'laɪk] ebenso OT 4

alive [ə'laɪv] lebendig OT 2

all [ɔːl] alles; alle OT 1

allegiance [ə'liːdʒəns] Treue **WS 2**, 69

to **alleviate** [ə'liːvieɪt] lindern; erleichtern OT 5

alliteration [əˌlɪtə'reɪʃn] Alliteration **WS 2**, 64

to **allocate** ['æləkeɪt] zuordnen OT 4

to **allow** [ə'laʊ] erlauben OT 3

allowed [ə'laʊd] erlaubt OT 2

allusion [ə'luːʒn] Anspielung **WS 2**, 64

ally ['ælaɪ] Verbündete(r) **WS 2**, 70

almond ['ɑːmənd] Mandel **WS 1**, 24

almost ['ɔːlməʊst] fast OT 2

alone [ə'ləʊn] allein OT 2

to **leave alone** [liːv ə'ləʊn] in Ruhe lassen OT 2

along [ə'lɒŋ] entlang; dahin; mit... OT 2

alongside [əˌlɒŋ'saɪd] neben; an der Seite von **WS 1**, 36

aloofness [ə'luːfnəs] Zurückhaltung **WS 3**, 95

aloud [ə'laʊd] laut; mit lauter Stimme OT 2

alpaca [æl'pækə] Alpaka OT 2

alphabet ['ælfəbet] Alphabet OT 1

alphabetical [ˌælfə'betɪkl] alphabetisch OT 2

already [ɔːl'redi] schon OT 2

alright [ɔːl'raɪt] in Ordnung OT 5

also ['ɔːlsəʊ] auch; außerdem OT 1

to **alter** ['ɔːltə] verändern **WS 3**, 117

alternative [ɔːl'tɜːnətɪv] alternativ OT 5

alternatively [ɔːl'tɜːnətɪvli] alternativ OT 4

although [ɔːl'ðəʊ] obwohl OT 2

always ['ɔːlweɪz] immer; immer noch OT 1

amazed [ə'meɪzd] erstaunt; überrascht OT 3

amazing [ə'meɪzɪŋ] fantastisch OT 1

ambition [æm'bɪʃn] Ehrgeiz; Ambition OT 5

ambitious [æm'bɪʃəs] ehrgeizig OT 3

ambulance ['æmbjələns] Krankenwagen OT 1

amends [ə'mendz] Wiedergutmachung; Schadenersatz OT 5

amendment [ə'mendmənt] Ergänzung OT 4

amenity [ə'miːnəti] Einrichtung OT 4

American [ə'merɪkən] amerikanisch OT 1

among [ə'mʌŋ] unter; zwischen OT 3

amount [ə'maʊnt] Betrag OT 2

ample ['æmpl] ausreichend **WS 1**, 15

to **amplify** ['æmplɪfaɪ] verstärken **WS 4**, 135

amused [ə'mjuːzd] amüsiert OT 3

to **analyse** ['ænəlaɪz] analysieren OT 3

analysis [ə'næləsɪs] Analyse; Untersuchung OT 5

analyst ['ænəlɪst] Analytiker(in); Analyst(in) OT 5

ancestor ['ænsestə] Vorfahr(in) OT 3

ancestral [æn'sestrəl] zur Familie gehörend; den Vorfahren gehörend OT 4

ancestry ['ænsestri] Abstammung OT 3

to **anchor** ['æŋkə] ankern OT 4

ancient ['eɪnʃənt] antik OT 2

and [ənd] und OT 1

anecdote ['ænɪkdəʊt] Anekdote OT 4

anger ['æŋgə] Wut **WS 2**, 60

Anglican ['æŋglɪkən] anglikanisch OT 3

Anglo-Saxon [ˌæŋgləʊ'sæksn] angelsächsisch OT 3

angry ['æŋgri] wütend; verärgert OT 1

animal ['ænɪml] Tier OT 1

animated ['ænɪmeɪtɪd] animiert OT 4

animation [ˌænɪ'meɪʃn] Animation **WS 4**, 135

ankle ['æŋkl] Knöchel; Fußknöchel OT 1

to **annihilate** [ə'naɪəleɪt] vernichten **WS 4**, 138

to **annotate** ['ænəteɪt] annotieren; kommentieren **WS 2**, 65

to **announce** [ə'naʊns] ansagen; bekannt geben OT 2

announcement [ə'naʊnsmənt] Bekanntgabe; Ansage OT 2

announcer [ə'naʊnsə] Ansager(in) OT 2

to **annoy** [ə'nɔɪ] ärgern; aufregen OT 5

annoyed [ə'nɔɪd] verärgert OT 3

annoying [ə'nɔɪɪŋ] ärgerlich OT 2

annual ['ænjuəl] jährlich OT 5

anonymity [ˌænə'nɪməti] Anonymität **WS 2**, 72

another [ə'nʌðə] noch ein(e); ein(e) andere(r, -s); ein(e) weitere(r, -s) OT 1

answer ['ɑːnsə] Antwort; Lösung OT 1

to **answer** ['ɑːnsə] antworten; beantworten OT 1

antelope ['æntɪləʊp] Antilope OT 4

anthem ['ænθəm] Nationalhymne; Hymne OT 5

anthropology [ˌænθrə'pɒlədʒi] Anthropologie OT 4

to **anticipate** [æn'tɪsɪpeɪt] erwarten; vorhersehen **WS 1**, 37

anticipation [ænˌtɪsɪ'peɪʃn] Vorfreude **WS 1**, 29

antidote ['æntidəʊt] Antidot; Gegenmittel **WS 2**, 69

antithesis [æn'tɪθəsɪs] Antithese; Gegensatz **WS 2**, 69

anxiety [æŋ'zaɪəti] Sorge; Ängstlichkeit OT 5

anxious ['æŋkʃəs] besorgt; ängstlich OT 5

anxiously ['æŋkʃəsli] besorgt OT 3

any ['eni] irgendein(e); jede(r, -s) (beliebige) OT 1

anybody ['enibɒdi] irgend jemand; jede(r, -s) OT 1

any more [ˌeni 'mɔː] nicht mehr OT 3

anymore [ˌeni'mɔː] nicht mehr OT 4

anyone ['eniwʌn] (irgend)jemand OT 2

anything ['eniθɪŋ] irgend etwas; alles OT 1

anytime ['enitaɪm] jederzeit OT 3

anyway ['eniweɪ] trotzdem; sowieso; jedenfalls OT 1

anywhere ['eniweə] irgendwo OT 2

apart [ə'pɑːt] auseinander OT 5

apart from [ə'pɑːt] abgesehen von OT 3

apartment [ə'pɑːtmənt] Wohnung OT 1

apathetic [ˌæpə'θetɪk] apathisch; teilnahmslos **WS 1**, 32

to **apologize** [ə'pɒlədʒaɪz] sich entschuldigen OT 2

apology [ə'pɒlədʒi] Entschuldigung OT 3

app [æp] App OT 3

apparent [ə'pærənt] offensichtlich; erkennbar **WS 3**, 112

apparently [ə'pærəntli] anscheinend OT 3

appeal [ə'piːl] Aufruf OT 2

to **appeal** [ə'piːl] appellieren; gefallen; *hier:* ansprechen **WS 1**, 24

to **appear** [ə'pɪə] erscheinen; scheinen; auftauchen OT 3

appearance [ə'pɪərəns] Aussehen OT 2

appetizing ['æpɪtaɪzɪŋ] appetitlich OT 3

to **applaud** [ə'plɔːd] applaudieren OT 2

applause [ə'plɔːz] Applaus OT 2

round of applause [ˌraʊnd əv ə'plɔːz] ein Applaus OT 2

apple ['æpl] Apfel OT 1

appliance [ə'plaɪəns] Gerät OT 3

applicable [ə'plɪkəbl] zutreffend; anwendbar **WS 2**, 82

applicant ['æplɪkənt] Bewerber(in); Anmelder(in) OT 5

application [ˌæplɪ'keɪʃn] Anwendung OT 4

to **apply** [ə'plaɪ] sich bewerben OT 3

to **appoint** [ə'pɔɪnt] ernennen OT 4

appointment [ə'pɔɪntmənt] Termin OT 3

appreciable [ə'priːʃəbl] spürbar; erheblich **WS 4**, 146

to **appreciate** [ə'priːʃieɪt] anerkennen; schätzen OT 4

appreciation [əˌpriːʃi'eɪʃn] Anerkennung **WS 2**, 68

apprentice [ə'prentɪs] Auszubildende(r); Lehrling OT 5

apprenticeship [ə'prentɪʃɪp] Lehrstelle; Ausbildung OT 5

approach [ə'prəʊtʃ] Vorgehen; Ansatz OT 5

to **approach** [ə'prəʊtʃ] näher kommen; sich nähern OT 3

approachable [ə'prəʊtʃəbl] aufgeschlossen OT 4

appropriate [ə'prəʊpriət] angemessen OT 4

appropriation [əˌprəʊpri'eɪʃn] Aneignung **WS 2**, 68

approval [ə'pruːvl] Zustimmung; Bestätigung **WS 2**, 71

to **approve** [ə'pruːv] zustimmen; genehmigen OT 4

approximately [ə'prɒksɪmətli] ungefähr; etwa OT 5

April ['eɪprəl] April OT 1

aquarium [ə'kweəriəm] Aquarium OT 2

aqueduct ['ækwɪdʌkt] Aquädukt OT 3

arch [ɑːtʃ] Bogen OT 3

archaeological [ˌɑːkiə'lɒdʒɪkl] archäologisch OT 2

archaeologist [ˌɑːki'ɒlədʒɪst] Archäologe(-in) OT 2

archbishop [ˌɑːtʃ'bɪʃəp] Erzbischof **WS 2**, 60

archer ['ɑːtʃə] Bogenschütze(-in) OT 3

archetypal [ˌɑːki'taɪpl] archetypisch **WS 3**, 106

architect ['ɑːkɪtekt] Architekt(in) OT 4

architecture ['ɑːkɪtektʃə] Architektur OT 4

archive ['ɑːkaɪv] Archiv OT 5

arctic ['ɑːktɪk] arktisch; Arktis OT 4

ardent ['ɑːdnt] leidenschaftlich **WS 1**, 32

area [ˈeəriə] Gebiet; Gegend; Bereich OT 1

arena [əˈriːnə] Arena; Bühne OT 1

to **argue** [ˈɑːgjuː] sich streiten OT 3

argument [ˈɑːgjumənt] Streit; Auseinandersetzung; Argument OT 1

argumentative [ˌɑːgjuˈmentətɪv] argumentativ **WS 3**, 109

arid [ˈærɪd] dürr; trocken OT 5

to **arise** [əˈraɪz] entstehen **WS 2**, 65

arm [ɑːm] Arm; Ärmel; Armlehne OT 1

armchair [ˈɑːmtʃeə] Sessel OT 1

armed [ɑːmd] bewaffnet OT 5

armed forces [ˌɑːmd ˈfɔːsɪz] Streitkräfte OT 4

army [ˈɑːmi] Armee OT 2

around [əˈraʊnd] um; um...herum; in... herum OT 1

to **arrange** [əˈreɪndʒ] planen; vereinbaren OT 2

arrangement [əˈreɪndʒmənt] Vereinbarung OT 5

to **arrest** [əˈrest] gefangen nehmen; verhaften OT 4

arrival [əˈraɪvl] Ankunft OT 2

to **arrive** [əˈraɪv] ankommen; kommen OT 1

arrow [ˈærəʊ] Pfeil OT 3

art [ɑːt] Kunst OT 1

artefact [ˈɑːtɪfækt] Artefakt OT 2

article [ˈɑːtɪkl] Artikel OT 1

definite article [ˈdefɪnət ˌɑːtɪkl] bestimmter Artikel OT 1

artificial [ˌɑːtɪˈfɪʃl] künstlich OT 4

artificial intelligence [ˌɑːtɪfɪʃl ɪnˈtelɪdʒəns] künstliche Intelligenz OT 5

artisan [ˌɑːtɪˈzæn] Kunsthandwerker(in) **WS 2**, 54

artist [ˈɑːtɪst] Künstler(in); Unterhaltungskünstler(in) OT 1

artistic [ɑːˈtɪstɪk] künstlerisch **WS 1**, 18

arty [ˈɑːti] gewollt künstlerisch OT 5

as [æz] als; wie OT 1

asexual [ˌeɪˈsekʃuəl] asexuell OT 5

ash [æʃ] Asche OT 2

ashamed [əˈʃeɪmd] beschämt OT 3

aside [əˈsaɪd] beiseite OT 5

to **ask** [ɑːsk] fragen; bitten; einladen OT 1

asleep [əˈsliːp] schlafend OT 2

aspect [ˈæspekt] Aspekt OT 4

assassin [əˈsæsɪn] Attentäter(in) **WS 2**, 57

to **assassinate** [əˈsæsɪneɪt] ermorden **WS 2**, 58

assassination [əˌsæsɪˈneɪʃn] Ermordung; Attentat **WS 2**, 58

assault [əˈsɔːlt] Angriff; Überfall OT 5

assembly [əˈsembli] Versammlung; morgendliche Schulversammlung; Montage OT 1

assembly hall [əˈsembli hɔːl] Aula; Montagehalle OT 1

to **assert** [əˈsɜːt] durchsetzen; behaupten **WS 3**, 95

assertion [əˈsɜːʃn] Behauptung **WS 3**, 119

to **assess** [əˈses] beurteilen OT 4

assessment [əˈsesmənt] Einschätzung; Bewertung **WS 3**, 105

assessor [əˈsesə] Gutacher(in); Bewerter(in) **WS 1**, 16

assignment [əˈsaɪnmənt] Aufgabe OT 4

assimilation [əˌsɪməˈleɪʃn] Assimilation; Anpassung OT 4

to **assist** [əˈsɪst] unterstützen OT 4

assistance [əˈsɪstəns] Unterstützung OT 5

assistant [əˈsɪstənt] Assistent(in); Verkäufer(in) OT 4

to **associate (with)** [əˈsəʊsieɪt] assoziieren; in Verbindung bringen OT 5

assortment [əˈsɔːtmənt] Mischung **WS 1**, 26

to **assume** [əˈsjuːm] annehmen; vermuten **WS 2**, 57

assumption [əˈsʌmpʃn] Annahme **WS 1**, 32

to **assure** [əˈʃʊə] versichern **WS 1**, 23

astonishingly [əˈstɒnɪʃɪŋli] erstaunlicherweise OT 3

astronaut [ˈæstrənɔːt] Astronaut(in) OT 3

astronomer [əˈstrɑːnəmə] Astronom(in) **WS 3**, 105

at [ət] an; in; bei OT 1

athlete [ˈæθliːt] Sportler(in) OT 2

athletics [æθˈletɪks] Leichtathletik; Sport OT 1

atmosphere [ˈætməsfɪə] Atmosphäre OT 3

atop [əˈtɒp] obenauf **WS 2**, 56

attack [əˈtæk] Angriff OT 2

to **attack** [əˈtæk] angreifen OT 4

attacking [əˈtækɪŋ] angreifend OT 3

to **attain** [əˈteɪn] erzielen; erreichen **WS 2**, 58

attainment [əˈteɪnmənt] Leistungen OT 5

attempt [əˈtempt] Versuch OT 2

to **attempt** [əˈtempt] versuchen **WS 1**, 12

to **attend** [əˈtend] besuchen OT 2

attendant [əˈtendənt] Aufseher(in); Diener(in) OT 2

attention [əˈtenʃn] Aufmerksamkeit OT 2

to **pay attention** [ˌpeɪ əˈtenʃn] aufpassen OT 2

attention deficit hyperactivity disorder (ADHD) [əˌtenʃn ˈdefɪsɪt haɪpərækˈtɪvəti dɪsɔːdə] Aufmerksamkeitsdefizit-Hyperaktivitätsstörung OT 5

attic [ˈætɪk] Dachboden OT 2

attitude [ˈætɪtjuːd] Ansicht; Einstellung OT 4

to **attract** [əˈtrækt] anziehen OT 4

attraction [əˈtrækʃn] Sehenswürdigkeit OT 2

attractive [əˈtræktɪv] reizvoll OT 5

auctioneer [ˌɔːkʃəˈnɪə] Auktionator(in) **WS 1**, 35

audacity [ɔːˈdæsəti] Mut; Kühnheit **WS 2**, 69

audience [ˈɔːdiəns] Publikum; Zuschauer(innen) OT 1

audio [ˈɔːdiəʊ] Audio... OT 2

audition [ɔːˈdɪʃn] Vorsprechen OT 3

to **audition** [ɔːˈdɪʃn] vorsingen; vorsprechen OT 3

August [ˈɔːgəst] August OT 1

aunt [ɑːnt] Tante OT 1

auntie [ˈɑːnti] Tantchen OT 2

authentic [ɔːˈθentɪk] authentisch; echt OT 4

author [ˈɔːθə] Autor(in) OT 2

authority [ɔːˈθɒrəti] Autorität; Behörde OT 3

autism [ˈɔːtɪzəm] Autismus OT 5

autobiography [ˌɔːtəbaɪˈɒgrəfi] Autobiografie **WS 2**, 54

automobile [ˈɔːtəməbiːl] Automobil OT 4

autonomous [ɔːˈtɒnəməs] unabhängig; autonom OT 4

autumn [ˈɔːtəm] Herbst OT 2

avail [əˈveɪl] Nutzen **WS 2**, 82

availability [əˌveɪləˈbɪləti] Verfügbarkeit OT 4

available [əˈveɪləbl] verfügbar; erhältlich OT 4

avatar [ˈævətɑː] Avatar OT 3

avenue [ˈævənjuː] Allee; Weg **WS 3**, 97

average [ˈævərɪdʒ] durchschnittlich OT 3

  on average [ɒn ˈævərɪdʒ] im Durchschnitt OT 5

avocado [ˌævəˈkɑːdəʊ] Avocado OT 5

to **avoid** [əˈvɔɪd] vermeiden OT 4

awake [əˈweik] wach OT 2

award [əˈwɔːd] Auszeichnung OT 2

to **award** [əˈwɔːd] vergeben; verleihen OT 4

aware [əˈweər] bewusst OT 5

  to **be aware** [bi əˈweə] sich bewusst sein; vorsichtig sein OT 4

awareness [əˈweənəs] Bewusstsein OT 4

away [əˈwei] weg OT 2

awe [ɔː] Ehrfurcht **WS 1**, 25

awesome [ˈɔːsəm] toll OT 2

awful [ˈɔːfl] fürchterlich; schrecklich OT 1

awkward [ˈɔːkwəd] umständlich; peinlich **WS 3**, 114

aye [ai] ja OT 2

B

baby [ˈbeibi] Säugling; Baby OT 1

  to **have a baby** [ˌhəv ə ˈbeibi] ein Baby bekommen OT 2

back [bæk] zurück OT 1

back [bæk] Rücken; hinterer Teil; hinterer Teil OT 1

backbone [ˈbækbəʊn] Rückgrat OT 2

to **backfire** [ˌbækˈfaiə] fehlschlagen; daneben gehen OT 4

background [ˈbækgraʊnd] Hintergrund... OT 3

backing [ˈbækiŋ] Unterstützung OT 4

backlash [ˈbæklæʃ] Gegenreaktion **WS 2**, 56

backpack [ˈbækpæk] Rucksack OT 2

to **backpack** [ˈbækpæk] mit dem Rucksack reisen OT 3

backstage [ˌbækˈsteidʒ] hinter der Bühne OT 3

to **backtrack** [ˈbæktræk] zurückverfolgen **WS 4**, 135

backwards [ˈbækwədz] nach hinten; rückwärts OT 3

backyard [ˌbækˈjɑːd] Garten hinter dem Haus; Hinterhof OT 5

bacon [ˈbeikən] Speck OT 1

bad [bæd] schlecht; ungünstig OT 1

badge [bædʒ] Abzeichen; Plakette OT 5

badminton [ˈbædmintən] Badminton; Federball OT 1

to **baffle** [ˈbæfl] verblüffen **WS 3**, 119

bag [bæg] Tasche; Beutel OT 1

baggage [ˈbægɪdʒ] Gepäck **WS 3**, 105

bagger [bægə] Packer(in) OT 4

bagless [ˈbægles] ohne Beutel OT 4

bagpipe [ˈbægpaip] Dudelsack **WS 1**, 12

to **bake** [beik] backen; ausdörren; brennen OT 1

baked beans [beikt ˈbiːns] weiße Bohnen in Tomatensoße OT 1

baker [ˈbeikə] Bäcker(in) OT 4

balance [ˈbæləns] Balance OT 3

to **balance** [ˈbæləns] ausgleichen OT 5

balcony [ˈbælkəni] Balkon **WS 2**, 58

bald [bɔːld] kahl OT 3

ball [bɔːl] Ball; Kugel; Knäuel OT 1

ballad [ˈbæləd] Ballade **WS 1**, 28

ballet [ˈbælei] Ballett OT 4

ballot [ˈbælət] Abstimmung **WS 1**, 32

ballroom [ˈbɔːlruːm] Ballsaal **WS 1**, 26

ban [bæn] Verbot; Sperre OT 5

to **ban** [bæn] verbieten OT 3

banana [bəˈnɑːnə] Banane OT 1

band [bænd] Band; Musikkapelle OT 1

bandage [ˈbændɪdʒ] Verband OT 2

bank [bæŋk] Ufer; Bank OT 3

bank balance [ˈbæŋk bæləns] Kontostand **WS 3**, 104

banking [ˈbæŋkiŋ] Banking; Bankwesen OT 5

banner [ˈbænə] Transparent OT 4

bar [bɑː] Bar; Riegel; Kneipe OT 1

barbecue [ˈbɑːbikjuː] Grillen OT 2

bard [bɑːd] Barde **WS 1**, 17

bare [beə] nackt; kahl **WS 1**, 13

barely [ˈbeəli] kaum **WS 2**, 82

barge [bɑːdʒ] Frachtkahn OT 3

to **bark** [bɑːk] bellen OT 2

barn [bɑːn] Scheune OT 2

barrier [ˈbæriə] Barriere OT 3

barrow [ˈbærəʊ] Karre OT 4

base [beis] Fuß; Basis OT 5

baseball [ˈbeisbɔːl] Baseball OT 1

based on [ˈbeist ɒn] basierend auf; bezogen auf OT 4

basic [ˈbeisik] Grund-; grundsätzlich; einfach OT 4

basically [ˈbeisikli] im Grunde OT 3

basics [ˈbeisiks] Grundlagen OT 2

basin [ˈbeisn] Becken OT 3

basis [ˈbeisis] Grundlage; Basis OT 4

basket [ˈbɑːskit] Korb OT 4

basketball [ˈbɑːskitbɔːl] Basketball OT 3

bass [beis] Bass **WS 2**, 67

  double bass [ˌdʌbl ˈbeis] Kontrabass OT 2

bat [bæt] Fledermaus; Schläger (Sport) OT 1

bath [bɑːθ] Badewanne; Bad OT 1

to **bathe** [beið] baden **WS 1**, 29

bathhouse [ˈbɑːθhaʊs] Badehaus OT 2

bathroom [ˈbɑːθruːm] Badezimmer; Toilette OT 1

to **batter** [ˈbætə] schlagen; zertrümmern OT 4

battery [ˈbætri] Batterie OT 2

battle [ˈbætl] Schlacht OT 4

battleship [ˈbætlʃip] Schlachtschiff OT 3

bay [bei] Bucht OT 2

BCE (before the Common Era) [ˌbiː siː ˈiː] v. Chr.; vor unserer Zeitrechnung OT 2

to **be** [biː] sein OT 1

  to **be into** [bi ˈintə] auf etwas stehen OT 2

  to **be fed up** [fed ˈʌp] satthaben OT 1

beach [biːtʃ] Strand OT 1

beak [biːk] Schnabel **WS 1**, 36

beam [biːm] Balken OT 3

to **beam** [biːm] strahlen; glänzen **WS 1**, 13

bean [biːn] Bohne OT 1

bear [beə] Bär OT 1

to **bear** [beər] ertragen OT 5

beard [biəd] Bart OT 1

bearing [ˈbeəriŋ] tragend **WS 1**, 37

beast [biːst] Tier OT 2

beat [biːt] Schlag; Takt OT 4

to **beat** [biːt] schlagen; übertreffen OT 4

beautiful [ˈbjuːtifl] schön; wunderschön; herrlich OT 1

beauty [ˈbjuːti] Schönheit OT 3

beaver [ˈbiːvə] Biber OT 4

because [biˈkɒz] weil OT 1

to **become** [biˈkʌm] werden OT 2

bed [bed] Bett; Beet; Boden OT 1

bedrock [ˈbedrɒk] Fundament **WS 2**, 82

bedroom [ˈbedruːm] Schlafzimmer OT 1

bedtime [ˈbedtaim] Schlafenszeit OT 2

bee [biː] Biene OT 1

beef [biːf] Rindfleisch OT 2

beer [biə] Bier OT 1

before [biˈfɔː] vor OT 1

to **beg** [beg] betteln OT 5

to **begin** [biˈgin] anfangen OT 2

beginning [biˈginiŋ] Beginn; Anfang OT 1

behalf: on behalf of [ɒn biˈhɑːf əv] im Auftrag; im Namen von **WS 3**, 111

to **behave** [biˈheiv] sich benehmen OT 2

behaviour [bɪˈheɪvjə] Benehmen; Verhalten OT 2

behavioural [bɪˈheɪvjərəl] Verhaltens... WS 3, 122

to behead [bɪˈhed] köpfen OT 3

behind [bɪˈhaɪnd] hinter; hinterher OT 1

to behold [bɪˈhəʊld] anschauen OT 3

being [ˈbiːɪŋ] Wesen OT 4

belief [bɪˈliːf] Glaube OT 3

to believe [bɪˈliːv] glauben OT 2

bell [bel] Glocke; Klingel OT 1

to belong [bɪˈlɒŋ] gehören OT 2

belongings [bɪˈlɒŋɪŋz] persönliche Gegenstände OT 4

below [bɪˈləʊ] unter OT 2

bench [bentʃ] Bank OT 3

beneath [bɪˈniːθ] unten; unter OT 3

beneficial [ˌbenɪˈfɪʃl] vorteilhaft OT 2

benefit [ˈbenɪfɪt] Vorteil OT 4

to benefit [ˈbenɪfɪt] profitieren OT 4

berry [ˈberi] Beere OT 4

beside [bɪˈsaɪd] neben OT 2

besides [bɪˈsaɪdz] außerdem OT 5

best [best] beste(r, -s) OT 1

to bet [bet] wetten OT 1

better [ˈbetə] besser OT 1

between [bɪˈtwiːn] zwischen; unter OT 1

to beware [bɪˈweə] vorsichtig sein OT 2

bewildered [bɪˈwɪldəd] verwirrt WS 3, 119

beyond [bɪˈjɒnd] dahinter OT 3

bias [ˈbaɪəs] Voreingenommenheit OT 5

biased [ˈbaɪəst] parteiisch; voreingenommen OT 5

bicultural [ˌbaɪˈkʌltʃərəl] bikulturell OT 4

bicycle [ˈbaɪsɪkl] Fahrrad OT 3

to bid for [bɪd] sich bewerben um; ein Angebot machen OT 5

big [bɪg] groß; älter; größer OT 1

bike [baɪk] Fahrrad; Motorrad OT 1

bilingual [ˌbaɪˈlɪŋgwəl] zweisprachig OT 3

bilingualism [ˌbaɪˈlɪŋgwəlɪzəm] Zweisprachigkeit OT 4

bill [bɪl] Gesetz; Rechnung OT 4

billion [ˈbɪljən] Milliarde OT 4

bin [bɪn] Tonne OT 4

binoculars [bɪˈnɒkjələz] Fernglas OT 2

biodiverse [ˌbaɪəʊdaɪˈvɜːs] artenreich WS 1, 12

biodiversity [ˌbaɪəʊdaɪˈvɜːsəti] Artenvielfalt WS 3, 104

biofuel [ˈbaɪəʊfjuːəl] Biokraftstoff OT 3

biography [baɪˈɒgrəfi] Biografie OT 4

biological [ˌbaɪəˈlɒdʒɪkl] biologisch OT 5

biology [baɪˈɒlədʒi] Biologie OT 1

bipolar [ˌbaɪˈpəʊlə] bipolar OT 5

biracial [ˌbaɪˈreɪʃl] multi-ethnisch WS 2, 71

bird [bɜːd] Vogel OT 1

birth [bɜːθ] Geburt OT 2

date of birth [ˌdeɪt əv ˈbɜːθ] Geburtsdatum OT 2

birthday [ˈbɜːθdeɪ] Geburtstag OT 1

birthplace [ˈbɜːθpleɪs] Geburtsort OT 4

biscuit [ˈbɪskɪt] Keks; Plätzchen; Cracker OT 1

bisexual [ˌbaɪˈsekʃuəl] bisexuell OT 5

bison [ˈbaɪsn] Bison OT 4

bit [bɪt] Stück OT 2

a bit [bɪt] Stück; ein bisschen; Bit OT 1

bite [baɪt] Biss OT 2

to bite [baɪt] beißen WS 3, 112

bitter [ˈbɪtər] bitter WS 3, 97

bitterly [ˈbɪtəli] bitterlich OT 5

black [blæk] schwarz OT 1

blackberry [ˈblækbəri] Brombeere OT 1

blackbird [ˈblækbɜːd] Amsel OT 1

blackboard [ˈblækbɔːd] Tafel OT 1

bladder [ˈblædə] Blase OT 4

blade [bleɪd] Schneide WS 1, 24

blame [bleɪm] Schuld; Vorwurf OT 4

blank [blæŋk] leer OT 4

blanket [ˈblæŋkɪt] Decke OT 2

blast [blɑːst] Tuten OT 3

to blast [blɑːst] bombadieren OT 5

blazer [ˈbleɪzər] Blazer; leichte Sportjacke OT 5

bleak [bliːk] düster OT 4

to bleed [bliːd] bluten WS 2, 76

blended [ˈblendɪd] gemischt OT 5

to blend [ˈblend] mischen WS 2, 68

to bless [bles] segnen WS 2, 69

blessing [ˈblesɪŋ] Segen; Geschenk WS 2, 76

to blind [blaɪnd] blind machen WS 2, 60

block [blɒk] Block OT 4

to block [blɒk] blockieren OT 5

blockade [blɒˈkeɪd] Blockade WS 2, 53

blockbuster [ˈblɒkbʌstə] Blockbuster; Hit WS 1, 17

blocker [blɒkər] Blocker OT 5

blog [blɒg] Blog OT 1

blogger [ˈblɒgə] Blogger(in) OT 3

blogpost [ˈblɒgpəʊst] Blogeintrag OT 4

blonde [blɒnd] blond OT 1

blood [blʌd] Blut OT 2

bloodshed [ˈblʌdʃed] Blutvergießen OT 5

bloody [ˈblʌdi] blutig WS 1, 13

to bloom [bluːm] blühen WS 3, 99

to blow [bləʊ] blasen; pfeifen; wehen OT 2

blubber [ˈblʌbə] Walspeck OT 2

blue [bluː] blau OT 1

blue jay [bluː dʒeɪ] Blauhäher WS 2, 64

blues [bluːz] Blues WW, 10

bluff [blʌf] Täuschung WS 4, 143

to blurt [blɜːt] herausplatzen WS 1, 20

BMXing [ˌbiː em ˈeksɪŋ] BMX-Rad fahren OT 5

to board [bɔːd] an Bord gehen OT 4

boarding pass [ˈbɔːdɪŋ pɑːs] Bordkarte OT 2

to boast [bəʊst] sich rühmen WS 1, 17

boat [bəʊt] Boot; Schiff; Fähre OT 1

boater [ˈbəʊtə] Bootsfahrer(in) OT 3

boating [ˈbəʊtɪŋ] Bootfahren OT 3

body [ˈbɒdi] Körper; Rumpf; Leiche OT 1

bog [bɒg] Sumpf; Moor WS 1, 16

boggy [ˈbɒgi] matschig WS 1, 16

to boil [bɔɪl] kochen; zum Kochen bringen OT 1

boiling [ˈbɔɪlɪŋ] kochend heiß OT 1

bold [bəʊld] mutig; fettgedruckt; gewagt OT 1

to bombard [bɒmˈbɑːd] bombardieren WS 3, 122

bond [bɒnd] Verbindung WS 3, 94

bone [bəʊn] Knochen; Gräte OT 1

book [bʊk] Buch; Heft; Heftchen OT 1

to book [bʊk] buchen OT 4

bookcase [ˈbʊkkeɪs] Bücherregal; Bücherschrank OT 1

booking [ˈbʊkɪŋ] Buchung OT 2

booklet [ˈbʊklət] Broschüre OT 2

to bookmark [ˈbʊkmɑːk] markieren OT 4

boot [buːt] Stiefel; Kofferraum; Kralle OT 1

booth [buːð] Kabine; Stand WS 1, 32

border [ˈbɔːdə] Grenze OT 3

to border [ˈbɔːdə] angrenzen; begrenzen OT 4

to bore [bɔː] langweilen WS 2, 69

bored [bɔːd] gelangweilt OT 1

boring [ˈbɔːrɪŋ] langweilig OT 1

to be born [bi bɔːn] geboren sein OT 2

to borrow [ˈbɒrəʊ] (aus)leihen OT 2

boss [bɒs] Chef(in) OT 2

bossy [ˈbɒsi] herrisch OT 3

bot [bɒt] Bot WS 2, 73

botanical [bəˈtænɪkl] botanisch OT 4

botany [ˈbɒtəni] Pflanzenkunde WS 1, 21

both [bəʊθ] beide OT 1

to bother [ˈbɒðə] stören OT 4

bothy [ˈbɒθi] Schutzhütte **WS 1**, 15

bottle [ˈbɒtl] Flasche OT 1

bottom [ˈbɒtəm] Boden; unterster Teil; Sohle OT 1

bound: to be bound [bi: baʊnd] etwas zwangsläufig tun **WS 1**, 12

boundary [ˈbaʊndri] Grenze OT 4

bow [baʊ] Bogen OT 2

bowl [bəʊl] Schüssel; Schale; Futternapf OT 1

box [bɒks] Kiste; Kasten; Schachtel OT 1

boxer [ˈbɒksə] Boxer(in) **WS 2**, 53

boy [bɔɪ] Junge OT 1

boyband [ˈbɔɪbænd] Boygroup OT 2

to boycott [ˈbɔɪkɒt] boykottieren **WS 2**, 59

bracket [ˈbrækɪt] Klammer; Gruppe; Klasse OT 2

brain [breɪn] Gehirn OT 2

to brainstorm [ˈbreɪnstɔ:m] brainstormen OT 2

branch [brɑ:ntʃ] Ast OT 2

brand [brænd] Marke OT 5

bravado [brəˈvɑ:dəʊ] Draufgängertum **WS 2**, 82

brave [breɪv] tapfer; mutig; tapfer OT 1

bravery [ˈbreɪvəri] Mut OT 2

bread [bred] Brot OT 1

bread roll [ˌbredˈrəʊl] Brötchen OT 1

breadwinner [ˈbredwɪnə] Ernährer(in); Brotverdiener(in) OT 5

break [breɪk] Pause; Urlaub; Werbepause OT 1

to break [breɪk] brechen; zerbrechen; kaputtgehen OT 1

to break down [breɪk daʊn] in Schritte unterteilen; aufschlüsseln OT 5

breakdown [ˈbreɪkdaʊn] Aufgliederung **WS 3**, 105

breakfast [ˈbrekfəst] Frühstück OT 1

breakout area [ˈbreɪkaʊt ˈeəriə] Gruppenfläche; Breakout-Bereich OT 5

breakthrough [ˈbreɪkθru:] Durchbruch OT 4

breath [breθ] Atem(zug) OT 2

to take a deep breath [ˌteɪk ə ˈdi:p breθ] tief einatmen OT 2

to breathe [bri:ð] atmen OT 2

breathless [ˈbreθləs] atemlos OT 3

breathtaking [ˈbreθteɪkɪŋ] atemberaubend OT 2

breeches [ˈbrɪtʃɪz] Kniehose OT 3

to breed [bri:d] brüten; züchten OT 5

breeze [bri:z] Brise OT 3

bridge [brɪdʒ] Brücke OT 1

brief [bri:f] kurz OT 5

briefly [ˈbri:fli] kurz OT 3

to brief [bri:f] instruieren; informieren **WS 1**, 38

brigade [brɪˈgeɪd] Brigade; Wehr **WS 1**, 38

bright [braɪt] leuchtend; glänzend; strahlend OT 1

brilliant [ˈbrɪliənt] genial; großartig OT 1

to bring [brɪŋ] bringen; einbringen OT 1

brisk [brɪsk] zügig **WS 1**, 37

British [ˈbrɪtɪʃ] britisch OT 1

Briton [ˈbrɪtn] Brite OT 2

broadcast [ˈbrɔ:dkɑ:st] Sendung OT 3

broccoli [ˈbrɒkəli] Brokkoli OT 1

brochure [ˈbrəʊʃə] Broschüre; Prospekt OT 1

broken [ˈbrəʊkən] gebrochen OT 1

broom [bru:m] Besen OT 4

brother [ˈbrʌðə] Bruder OT 1

brotherhood [ˈbrʌðəhʊd] Brüderschaft **WS 2**, 60

brown [braʊn] braun OT 1

brush [brʌʃ] Bürste; Pinsel OT 2

to brush [brʌʃ] putzen; bürsten OT 4

brutality [bru:ˈtæləti] Brutalität **WS 2**, 58

bubble [ˈbʌbl] Blase OT 2

bucket [ˈbʌkɪt] Eimer OT 3

buddy [ˈbʌdi] Kumpel OT 2

to budget [ˈbʌdʒɪt] einplanen OT 3

budgie [ˈbʌdʒi] Wellensittich OT 1

buffalo [ˈbʌfələʊ] Büffel OT 4

buffet [ˈbʊfeɪ] Buffet OT 4

to build [bɪld] bauen; aufbauen OT 1

builder [ˈbɪldə] Baumeister(in); Bauherr(in) OT 5

building [ˈbɪldɪŋ] Gebäude; Bau; Bauen OT 1

to bulk up [bʌlk ʌp] Masse zusetzen; hier: Muskeln aufbauen OT 5

bullet [ˈbʊlɪt] Kugel OT 2

to bully [ˈbʊli] mobben OT 3

to bump into [bʌmp ˈɪntə] anstoßen OT 2

bumpy [ˈbʌmpi] holprig; uneben OT 4

bundle [ˈbʌndl] Bündel OT 2

to buoy [bɔɪ] Auftrieb geben OT 3

burden [ˈbɜ:dn] Last OT 3

burger [ˈbɜ:gə] Hamburger OT 1

to burn [bɜ:n] brennen OT 2

to burst [bɜ:st] platzen **WS 1**, 29

to bury [ˈberi] begraben **WS 2**, 60

bus [bʌs] Bus OT 1

bush [bʊʃ] Busch; Gebüsch; Buschland OT 5

bushfire [ˈbʊʃfaɪər] Buschfeuer OT 5

bushland [ˈbʊʃlænd] Buschland OT 5

business [ˈbɪznəs] Geschäft(e) OT 3

businessman, -woman [ˈbɪznəsmæn, -wʊmən] Geschäftsmann, -frau OT 4

busker [ˈbʌskər] Straßenmusiker(in) OT 5

busload [ˈbʌsləʊd] Busladung OT 5

busted [ˈbʌstɪd] kaputt OT 4

busy [ˈbɪzi] beschäftigt; beschäftigt; arbeitsreich OT 1

butter [ˈbʌtə] Butter OT 1

butterfly [ˈbʌtəflaɪ] Schmetterling **WS 2**, 53

butternut squash [ˈbʌtənʌt skwɒʃ] Butternut-Kürbis OT 3

button [ˈbʌtn] Knopf; Taste; Schaltfläche OT 1

to buy [baɪ] kaufen; glauben; abkaufen OT 1

buyer [ˈbaɪə] Käufer(in) OT 5

to buzz [bʌz] schwirren **WS 4**, 140

buzzard [ˈbʌzəd] Bussard OT 2

by [baɪ] bei; von OT 1

bye [baɪ] Tschüss! OT 1

bystander [ˈbaɪstændə] Zuschauer(in) **WS 4**, 138

C

cab [kæb] Taxi; Fahrerkabine; Führerhaus OT 1

cabaret [ˈkæbəreɪ] Kabarett **WS 1**, 43

cabbage [ˈkæbɪdʒ] Kohl OT 1

cabin [ˈkæbɪn] Kabine OT 2

cabinet [ˈkæbɪnət] Schrank; Kabinett OT 5

cabinet minister [ˈkæbɪnət ˈmɪnɪstə] Kabinettsminister(in) OT 4

cable [ˈkeɪbl] Kabel OT 3

cactus [ˈkæktəs] Kaktus OT 4

caddie [ˈkædi] Caddie OT 4

café [ˈkæfeɪ] Café; Kaffeehaus OT 1

cafeteria [ˌkæfəˈtɪəriə] Cafeteria OT 2

caffeine [ˈkæfi:n] Koffein OT 5

cage [keɪdʒ] Käfig OT 5

cake [keɪk] Kuchen; Torte OT 1

calcified [ˈkælsɪfaɪd] verkalkt **WS 1**, 12

calculation [ˌkælkjuˈleɪʃn] Berechnung; Kalkulation **WS 1**, 36

calendar [ˈkælɪndə] Kalender OT 1

call [kɔ:l] Anruf OT 2

to take a call [teɪk ə kɔ:l] einen Anruf entgegennehmen OT 2 to **call** [kɔːl] anrufen; nennen; rufen OT 1

called [kɔːld] namens; mit dem Namen; genannt OT 1

caller [ˈkɔːlə] Anrufer(in) OT 2

calm [kɑːm] ruhig OT 2

to **keep calm** [kiːp kɑːm] Ruhe bewahren OT 2

to **calm down** [kɑːm daʊn] beruhigen OT 2

calmly [ˈkɑːmli] ruhig OT 3

calorie [ˈkæləri] Kalorie OT 5

camel [ˈkæml] Kamel OT 5

camera [ˈkæmərə] Fotoapparat; Kamera OT 1

cameraman [ˈkæmrəmæn] Kameramann OT 5

camp [kæmp] Camp; Lager; Feldlager OT 1

to **camp** [kæmp] zelten; campen; kampieren OT 1

to **camp out** [kæmp aʊt] zelten OT 5

campaign [kæmˈpeɪn] Kampagne; Aktion OT 3

to **campaign (for)** [kæmˈpeɪn] kämpfen (um); sich einsetzen (für) OT 5

camper [ˈkæmpə] Camper(in) OT 2

campfire [ˈkæmpfaɪə] Lagerfeuer OT 2

to **build a campfire** [ˌbɪld ə ˈkæmpfaɪə] ein Lagerfeuer machen OT 2

campground [ˈkæmpgraʊnd] Zeltplatz OT 2

campsite [ˈkæmpsaɪt] Zeltplatz; Campingplatz OT 2

campus [ˈkæmpəs] Campus OT 2

can [kæn] Dose OT 2

can [kæn] können; dürfen OT 1

canal [kəˈnæl] Kanal OT 3

canary [kəˈneəri] Kanarienvogel OT 2

cancer [ˈkænsər] Krebs **WS 3**, 117

candidate [ˈkændɪdət] Kandidat(in) OT 4

candle [ˈkændl] Kerze OT 2

candlelight [ˈkændllaɪt] Kerzenlicht OT 4

canned [kænd] Dosen... OT 2

canoe [kəˈnuː] Kanu OT 2

canoeing [kəˈnuːɪŋ] Kanufahren OT 2

canteen [kænˈtiːn] Kantine; Feldflasche OT 1

canvas [ˈkænvəs] Leinen OT 3

canyon [ˈkænjən] Schlucht; Canyon OT 3

cap [kæp] Mütze; Deckel; Schirmmütze OT 1

capable [ˈkeɪpəbl] fähig OT 4

capacity [kəˈpæsəti] Fähigkeit OT 5

capital [ˈkæpɪtl] Hauptstadt OT 1

capitalist [ˈkæpɪtəlɪst] Kapitalist(in) **WS 2**, 63

capitol [ˈkæpɪtl] Kapitol **WS 2**, 56

caption [ˈkæpʃn] Bildunterschrift; Bildtext; Untertitel OT 2

captive [ˈkæptɪv] Gefangene(r) **WS 2**, 54

captivity [kæpˈtɪvəti] Gefangenschaft **WS 1**, 18

to **capture** [ˈkæptʃə] einfangen; festnehmen OT 4

car [kɑː] Auto; Wagen; Waggon OT 1

caravan [ˈkærəvæn] Wohnwagen; Karawane OT 1

carbohydrate [ˌkɑːbəʊˈhaɪdreɪt] Kohlenhydrat OT 5

carbon [ˈkɑːbən] Kohlenstoff OT 4

carbon dioxide [ˌkɑːbəndaɪˈɒksaɪd] Kohlendioxid OT 3

carbon emission [ˌkɑːbəniˈmɪʃn] CO_2-Ausstoß OT 3

carbon footprint [ˌkɑːbənˈfʊtprɪnt] CO_2-Bilanz; ökologischer Fußabdruck OT 3

card [kɑːd] Karte; Karton; Pappe OT 1

care [keə] Betreuung; Sorge OT 2

to **care** [keə] besorgt sein OT 2

I don't care! [aɪ dəʊnt keə] Das ist mir egal! OT 2

career [kəˈrɪə] Karriere OT 3

careful [ˈkeəfl] vorsichtig; sorgfältig OT 1

careless [ˈkeələs] sorglos OT 2

carer [ˈkeərər] Betreuer(in) OT 5

caretaker [ˈkeəteɪkə] Hausmeister(in) OT 1

cargo [ˈkɑːgəʊ] Ladung OT 3

caribou [ˈkærɪbuː] Karibu OT 4

carnival [ˈkɑːnɪvl] Karneval OT 4

carousel [ˌkærəˈsel] Karussell **WS 1**, 29

car park [ˈkɑː pɑːk] Parkplatz OT 2

carpenter [ˈkɑːpəntə] Zimmermann; Tischler(in) OT 3

carriage [ˈkærɪdʒ] Wagen; Beförderung; Transport OT 2

carrier [ˈkæriə] Trage... OT 5

carrot [ˈkærət] Karotte; Möhre OT 1

to **carry** [ˈkæri] tragen; befördern; bei sich haben OT 1

to **carry out** [ˈkæri aʊt] ausführen **WS 1**, 19

cartoonist [kɑːˈtuːnɪst] Karikaturist(in) OT 4

to **carve** [kɑːv] schnitzen OT 2

carver [kɑːvə] Schnitzer(in) OT 4

carving [ˈkɑːvɪŋ] Schnitzerei OT 4

cascading [kæˈskeɪdɪŋ] kaskadierend **WS 4**, 138

case [keɪs] Koffer; Aktentasche; Etui; Tasche; Fall OT 1

cash [kæʃ] Kleingeld; Bargeld; Geld OT 1

cashier [kæˈʃɪə] Kassierer(in) OT 4

cast [kɑːst] Besetzung OT 3

castle [ˈkɑːsl] Burg; Schloss; Turm OT 1

casual [ˈkæʒuəl] locker; lässig OT 5

cat [kæt] Katze OT 1

catastrophe [kəˈtæstrəfi] Katastrophe **WS 4**, 144

catastrophic [ˌkætəˈstrɒfɪk] katastrophal **WS 1**, 36

to **catch** [kætʃ] fangen; nehmen; kriegen OT 1

catchy [ˈkætʃi] packend **WS 1**, 25

category [ˈkætəgəri] Kategorie OT 3

catering [ˈkeɪtərɪŋ] Versorgung; Catering OT 3

catfish [ˈkætfɪʃ] Wels **WS 1**, 12

cathedral [kəˈθiːdrəl] Kathedrale; Dom OT 1

Catholic [ˈkæθəlɪk] Katholik(in) OT 3

catshark [kætʃɑːk] Katzenhai **WS 1**, 12

cattle [ˈkætl] Rinder OT 4

causal [ˈkɔːzl] ursächlich **WS 4**, 142

to **cause** [kɔːz] verursachen OT 2

to **cause an accident** [ˌkɔːz ən ˈæksɪdənt] einen Unfall verursachen OT 2

caution [ˈkɔːʃn] Verwarnung; Warnung OT 5

cautious [ˈkɔːʃəs] vorsichtig **WS 3**, 97

cavalry [ˈkævlri] Kavallerie OT 3

cave [keɪv] Höhle OT 3

CE (Common Era) [ˌsiː ˈiː] n. Chr.; unserer Zeitrechnung OT 2

ceiling [ˈsiːlɪŋ] Decke OT 2

to **celebrate** [ˈselɪbreɪt] feiern OT 3

celebration [ˌselɪˈbreɪʃn] Feier OT 2

celebratory [ˌseləˈbreɪtəri] feierlich **WS 1**, 26

celebrity [səˈlebrəti] Prominente(r) OT 5

cell [sel] Zelle **WS 1**, 37

cello [ˈtʃeləʊ] Cello OT 1

cell phone [ˈsel fəʊn] Handy OT 4

Celtic [ˈkeltɪk] Keltisch OT 2

to **cement** [sɪˈment] festigen; zementieren **WS 2**, 58

cemetery [ˈsemətri] Friedhof **WS 2**, 57

center [ˈsentə] Mitte; Zentrum OT 2

centimetre [ˈsentɪmiːtə] Zentimeter OT 2

central [ˈsentrəl] Zentral- OT 1
  central heating [ˌsentrəl ˈhiːtɪŋ]
    Zentralheizung OT 2
centre [ˈsentə] Mitte; Stadtmitte;
  Zentrum OT 1
century [ˈsentʃəri] Jahrhundert OT 2
cereal [ˈsɪəriəl] Cerealien;
  Frühstücksflocken OT 1
cerebral palsy [səˈriːbrəl ˈpɔːlzi]
  zerebrale Kinderlähmung OT 5
ceremonial [ˌserɪˈməʊniəl] zeremoniell;
  feierlich OT 3
ceremony [ˈserəməni] Feier OT 2
certain [ˈsɜːtn] sicher OT 3
certainly [ˈsɜːtnli] sicher; sicherlich;
  bestimmt OT 2
certainty [ˈsɜːtnti] Gewissheit OT 4
certificate [səˈtɪfɪkət] Zeugnis;
  Zertifikat OT 2
certified [ˈsɜːtɪfaɪd] beglaubigt;
  anerkannt OT 5
to certify [ˈsɜːtɪfaɪ] bestätigen WS 2, 83
chain [tʃeɪn] Kette OT 3
chair [tʃeə] Stuhl; Vorsitz;
  Vorsitzende(r) OT 1
chairlift [ˈtʃeəlɪft] Sessellift OT 5
chairman [ˈtʃeəmən] Vorsitzender
  WS 2, 62
chairperson [ˈtʃeəˌpɜːsən] Vorsitzende(r)
  WS 2, 62
chairwoman [ˈtʃeəˌwʊmən] Vorsitzende
  WS 2, 62
challenge [ˈtʃælɪndʒ] Herausforderung
  OT 3
to challenge [ˈtʃælɪndʒ] herausfordern
  OT 4
challenging [ˈtʃælɪndʒɪŋ] schwierig
  OT 2
chamber [ˈtʃeɪmbə] Kammer OT 2
chamber pot [ˈtʃeɪmbə pɒt] Nachttopf
  OT 3
to champion [ˈtʃæmpiən] sich einsetzen
  für; verfechten WS 2, 54
champion [ˈtʃæmpiən] Champion OT 4
championship [ˈtʃæmpiənʃɪp]
  Meisterschaft WS 2, 75
chance [tʃɑːns] Zufall; Möglichkeit OT 2
chandelier [ˌʃændəˈlɪə] Kronleuchter
  OT 2
change [tʃeɪndʒ] Wechselgeld OT 1
to change [tʃeɪndʒ] ändern; sich
  umziehen; wechseln OT 1
channel [ˈtʃænl] Kanal OT 3
chaos [ˈkeɪɒs] Chaos OT 4
chapter [ˈtʃæptə] Kapitel OT 1

character [ˈkærəktə] Charakter OT 2
characteristic [ˌkærəktəˈrɪstɪk]
  charakteristisches Merkmal OT 2
to characterize [ˈkærəktəraɪz]
  kennzeichnen; charakterisieren
  WS 2, 67
charge: in charge [ˈɪn tʃɑːdʒ] zuständig;
  verantwortlich OT 1
to charge [tʃɑːdʒ] aufladen OT 2
  to charge (with) [tʃɑːdʒ] anklagen
    (wegen) OT 5
charisma [kəˈrɪzmə] Ausstrahlung;
  Charisma WS 2, 60
charismatic [ˌkærɪzˈmætɪk]
  charismatisch WS 2, 58
charitable [ˈtʃærətəbl] Wohltätigkeits...
  WS 1, 14
charity [ˈtʃærəti]
  Wohlfahrtsorganisation OT 2
to charm [tʃɑːm] einnehmen;
  bezaubern WS 1, 17
charming [ˈtʃɑːmɪŋ] charmant OT 3
chart [tʃɑːt] Diagramm; Chart OT 4
to chase [tʃeɪs] jagen OT 2
to chat [tʃæt] plaudern OT 3
to chatter [ˈtʃætə] plaudern OT 2
chatty [ˈtʃæti] gesprächig OT 5
cheap [tʃiːp] billig OT 2
to cheat [tʃiːt] schummeln; mogeln
  OT 4
to check [tʃek] überprüfen;
  kontrollieren; checken OT 1
checklist [ˈtʃeklɪst] Checkliste OT 2
check-out [ˈtʃekaʊt] Kasse OT 4
cheek [tʃiːk] Backe OT 4
cheeky [ˈtʃiːki] frech OT 3
cheerful [ˈtʃɪəfl] fröhlich OT 2
cheerleader [ˈtʃɪəliːdə] Cheerleader(in)
  OT 3
to cheer up [tʃɪə ʌp] fröhlich sein;
  aufmuntern OT 3
cheese [tʃiːz] Käse OT 1
cheetah [ˈtʃiːtə] Gepard OT 3
chef [ʃef] Küchenchef(in); Koch/Köchin
  OT 1
chemical [ˈkemɪkl] Chemikalie OT 3
chemistry [ˈkemɪstri] Chemie OT 5
cheque [tʃek] Scheck OT 4
cherry [ˈtʃeri] Kirsche OT 4
chess [tʃes] Schach OT 1
chest [tʃest] Truhe; Brust OT 1
chest of drawers [ˌtʃest əv ˈdrɔːz]
  Kommode OT 1
chicken [ˈtʃɪkɪn] Huhn; Hähnchen;
  Hühnchen OT 1

Chief Executive Officer (CEO) [ˌtʃiːf
  ɪɡˌzekjətɪv ˈɒfɪsə] Geschäftsführer(in)
  OT 5
child [tʃaɪld] Kind OT 1
childhood [ˈtʃaɪldhʊd] Kindheit OT 3
childish [ˈtʃaɪldɪʃ] kindisch OT 3
chili [ˈtʃɪli] Chili OT 2
to chill (out) [tʃɪl aʊt] relaxen; chillen
  WS 1, 25
chilly [ˈtʃɪli] kühl WS 2, 59
chimney [ˈtʃɪmni] Schornstein OT 3
Chinese [ˌtʃaɪˈniːz] chinesisch OT 1
chip [tʃɪp] Chip; Fritte; angeschlagene
  Stelle OT 1
choc-chip [ˈtʃɒk tʃɪp]
  Schockoladensplitter OT 1
chocoholic [ˌtʃɒkəˈhɒlɪk]
  Schokoladensüchtige(r) OT 3
chocolate [ˈtʃɒklət] Schokolade;
  Praline; heiße Schokolade OT 1
choice [tʃɔɪs] Wahl; Auswahl OT 1
choir [ˈkwaɪə] Chor OT 1
to choke [tʃəʊk] ersticken WS 4, 134
cholera [ˈkɒlərə] Cholera OT 4
to choose [tʃuːz] auswählen;
  aussuchen OT 1
to chop [tʃɒp] schneiden OT 3
chopped [tʃɒpt] gehackt OT 2
chord [kɔːd] Akkord WS 3, 111
chore [tʃɔː] Hausarbeit OT 4
chowder [ˈtʃaʊdə] dickflüssige
  Fischsuppe OT 3
Christian [ˈkrɪstʃən] christlich;
  Christ(in) WS 2, 58
chromosome [ˈkrəʊməsəʊm]
  Chromosom OT 5
chronological [ˌkrɒnəˈlɒdʒɪkl]
  chronologisch OT 4
church [tʃɜːtʃ] Kirche OT 1
cinema [ˈsɪnəmə] Kino OT 1
circle [ˈsɜːkl] Kreis OT 2
to circulate [ˈsɜːkjəleɪt] kursieren;
  zirkulieren OT 4
circumstance [ˈsɜːkəmstəns] Umstand;
  Lage OT 5
circus [ˈsɜːkəs] Zirkus WS 1, 43
to cite [saɪt] anführen OT 2
citizen [ˈsɪtɪzn] Einwohner(in) OT 2
citizenship [ˈsɪtɪzənʃɪp]
  Staatsbürgerschaft WS 2, 83
city [ˈsɪti] Stadt; Großstadt OT 1
city hall [ˌsɪti ˈhɔːl] Rathaus OT 5
civic [ˈsɪvɪk] bürgerlich WS 3, 110
civil [ˈsɪvl] Bürger...; bürgerlich
  WW, 10

civilization [ˌsɪvəlaɪˈzeɪʃn] Zivilisation **WS 1**, 15

to civilize [ˈsɪvəlaɪz] zivilisieren **WS 2**, 54

civilized [ˈsɪvəlaɪz] zivilisiert; kultiviert OT 5

claim [kleɪm] Behauptung OT 5

to claim [kleɪm] behaupten OT 3

clam [klæm] Venusmuschel OT 3

clan [klæn] Stamm OT 5

to clap [klæp] klatschen OT 1

clarification [ˌklærəfɪˈkeɪʃn] Abklärung OT 4

to clarify [ˈklærəfaɪ] etw. klären OT 4

clarinet [ˌklærəˈnet] Klarinette OT 2

to clash [klæʃ] zusammenstoßen **WS 2**, 59

class [klɑːs] Stunde; Klasse; Kurs OT 1

classic [ˈklæsɪk] klassisch OT 2

classical [ˈklæsɪkl] klassisch OT 2

classification [ˌklæsɪfɪˈkeɪʃn] Einstufung **WS 4**, 135

to classify [ˈklæsɪfaɪ] etw. einstufen OT 4

classmate [ˈklɑːsmeɪt] Klassenkamerad(in) OT 3

classroom [ˈklɑːsruːm] Klassenzimmer OT 1

to clean [kliːn] putzen; reinigen OT 1

cleaner [ˈkliːnə] Reinigungsmittel OT 3

clear [klɪə] klar OT 2

clearing [ˈklɪərɪŋ] Lichtung **WS 1**, 16

clearly [ˈklɪəli] deutlich OT 3

clever [ˈklevə] intelligent OT 2

to click [klɪk] klicken OT 3

client [ˈklaɪənt] Mandant(in); Kunde/ Kundin OT 5

cliff [klɪf] Klippe; Felsen OT 5

climate [ˈklaɪmət] Klima OT 2

climax [ˈklaɪmæks] Höhepunkt **WS 2**, 64

to climb [klaɪm] klettern; steigen OT 1

climber [ˈklaɪmə] Kletterer(in) OT 2

climbing [ˈklaɪmɪŋ] Klettern; Bergsteigen OT 1

clinic [ˈklɪnɪk] Klinik OT 5

clip [klɪp] Ausschnitt OT 2

to clip to [klɪp tə] klemmen an OT 5

cloak [kləʊk] Umhang; Deckmantel OT 2

cloakroom [ˈkləʊkruːm] Garderobe OT 4

clock [klɒk] Uhr; Tacho; Taxameter OT 1

to clog [klɒg] verstopfen OT 4

to close [kləʊz] schließen; zumachen; zugehen OT 1

close [kləʊs] nah OT 1

closely [ˈkləʊsli] eng; nah OT 3

closed [kləʊzd] geschlossen OT 1

cloth [klɒθ] Stoff OT 2

clothes [kləʊðz] Kleidung; Kleider OT 1

clothing [ˈkləʊðɪŋ] Kleidung OT 4

cloud [klaʊd] Wolke; Schatten OT 1

cloudy [ˈklaʊdi] wolkig; bewölkt; trüb OT 1

club [klʌb] Klub; Verein; Stock OT 1

clue [kluː] Hinweis; Anhaltspunkt OT 1

clueless [ˈkluːləs] ahnungslos **WS 3**, 113

clumsy [ˈklʌmzi] ungeschickt OT 2

cluster [ˈklʌstə] Gruppe; Ansammlung **WS 4**, 140

coach [kəʊtʃ] Reisebus; Trainer(in) OT 1

coal [kəʊl] Kohle OT 2

coast [kəʊst] Küste OT 1

coastal [ˈkəʊstl] Küsten…; an der Küste OT 4

coastguard [ˈkəʊstgɑːd] Küstenwache OT 2

coastline [ˈkəʊstlaɪn] Küstenlinie; Küste OT 5

coat [kəʊt] Mantel OT 2

cocoa [ˈkəʊkəʊ] Kakao OT 4

code [kəʊd] Code; Vorwahl OT 2

to code [kəʊd] kodieren; programmieren OT 5

co-ed, co-educational [ˌkəʊˈed] gemischtgeschlechtlich OT 2

coffee [ˈkɒfi] Kaffee OT 1

coffin [ˈkɒfɪn] Sarg OT 4

coherent [kəʊˈhɪərənt] schlüssig **WS 4**, 141

cohort [ˈkəʊhɔːt] Jahrgang; Kohorte **WS 1**, 32

coin [kɔɪn] Münze OT 1

cold [kəʊld] kalt; unfreundlich; kühl OT 1

cold-blooded [ˌkəʊld ˈblʌdɪd] kaltblütig **WS 1**, 18

to collaborate [kəˈlæbəreɪt] zusammenarbeiten **WS 4**, 146

collaboration [kəˌlæbəˈreɪʃn] Zusammenarbeit; Kollaboration OT 4

collaborative [kəˈlæbərətɪv] gemeinschaftlich **WS 3**, 107

collar [ˈkɒlə] Halsband OT 2

to collate [kəˈleɪt] zusammentragen; sammeln **WS 1**, 22

colleague [ˈkɒliːg] Kollege, Kollegin; Mitarbeiter(in) OT 4

to collect [kəˈlekt] sammeln; einsammeln OT 1

collection [kəˈlekʃn] Sammlung OT 2

collectively [kəˈlektɪvli] insgesamt **WS 2**, 67

college [ˈkɒlɪdʒ] Hochschule; Universität OT 2

colloquial [kəˈləʊkwiəl] umgangssprachlich **WS 1**, 23

colonial [kəˈləʊniəl] kolonial OT 3

colonialism [kəˈləʊniəlɪzəm] Kolonialismus OT 5

colonist [ˈkɒlənɪst] Kolonist(in) OT 4

colonization [ˌkɒlənaɪˈzeɪʃn] Kolonialisierung OT 5

to colonize [ˈkɒlənaɪz] kolonisieren OT 3

colony [ˈkɒləni] Kolonie OT 3

colour [ˈkʌlə] Farbe; Gesichtsfarbe; Hautfarbe OT 1

to colour [ˈkʌlə] ausmalen OT 1

coloured [ˈkʌləd] farbig; bunt; farbig OT 1

colourful [ˈkʌləfl] farbenfroh OT 3

column [ˈkɒləm] Säule; Spalte OT 1

comb [kəʊm] Kamm OT 2

combination [ˌkɒmbɪˈneɪʃn] Kombination OT 4

to combine [kəmˈbaɪn] kombinieren; mischen OT 4

combustion: internal combustion [ɪnˈtɜːnl kəmˈbʌstʃən] Verbrennungs- OT 4

to come [kʌm] kommen; bevorstehen OT 1

to come first / second / third [kʌm ˈfɜːst / ˈsekənd / ˈθɜːd] den ersten / zweiten / dritten Platz belegen OT 2

to come from [kʌm frəm] kommen aus OT 5

to come to know [kʌm tə nəʊ] erfahren; kennenlernen OT 5

comedy [ˈkɒmədi] Komödie OT 4

comfort [ˈkʌmfət] Geborgenheit **WS 3**, 111

comfortable [ˈkʌmftəbl] bequem; komfortabel OT 1

comic [ˈkɒmɪk] Comicheft; Komiker(in) OT 1

comma [ˈkɒmə] Komma OT 3

commander [kəˈmɑːndə] Kommandant(in) OT 2

Commander-in-Chief [kəˌmɑːndər ɪn ˈtʃiːf] Oberbefehlshaber(in) OT 4

commanding [kəˈmɑːndɪŋ] befehlshabend OT 2

to commemorate [kəˈmeməreɪt] erinnern an **WS 2**, 78

comment [ˈkɒment] Bemerkung OT 3

to comment [ˈkɒment] bemerken; kommentieren OT 3

commentator [ˈkɒmənteɪtə] Kommentator(in) **WS 2**, 69

commerce [ˈkɒmɜːs] Handel; Kommerz OT 5

commercial [kəˈmɜːʃl] kommerziell OT 4

commission [kəˈmɪʃn] Kommission **WS 2**, 55

to **commit** [kəˈmɪt] begehen OT 3

commitment [kəˈmɪtmənt] Verpflichtung **WS 1**, 30

committee [kəˈmɪti] Kommission; Komitee OT 4

common [ˈkɒmən] Gemeindeland OT 2

  Common Era [ˌkɒmən ˈɪərə] unsere Zeitrechnung OT 2

commonly [ˈkɒmənli] gewöhnlich; häufig OT 5

to **communicate** [kəˈmjuːnɪkeɪt] kommunizieren; etw. vermitteln OT 4

communication [kəˌmjuːnɪˈkeɪʃn] Kommunikation OT 1

community [kəˈmjuːnəti] Gemeinschaft OT 2

to **commute** [kəˈmjuːt] pendeln OT 5

commuter [kəˈmjuːtə] Pendler(in) OT 2

commuter rail [kəˌmjuːtə ˈreɪl] Pendlerbahn OT 2

company [ˈkʌmpəni] Unternehmen OT 1

comparable to [ˈkɒmpərəbl tə] vergleichbar mit OT 5

comparative [kəmˈpærətɪv] Komparativ OT 2

to **compare** [kəmˈpeə] vergleichen; vergleichen OT 1

comparison [kəmˈpærɪsn] Vergleich OT 5

compass [ˈkʌmpəs] Kompass OT 2

compassion [kəmˈpæʃn] Mitgefühl; Anteilnahme **WS 1**, 14

compassionate [kəmˈpæʃənət] mitfühlend **WS 1**, 36

compatible [kəmˈpætəbl] kompatibel OT 5

to **compel** [kəmˈpel] zwingen **WS 3**, 108

compensation [ˌkɒmpenˈseɪʃn] Entschädigung OT 5

to **compete** [kəmˈpiːt] konkurrieren OT 2

competency [ˈkɒmpɪtənsi] Kompetenz **WS 3**, 107

competent [ˈkɒmpɪtənt] fähig; kompetent OT 4

competition [ˌkɒmpəˈtɪʃn] Konkurrenz; Wettbewerb; Preisausschreiben OT 1

competitive [kəmˈpetətɪv] konkurrenzorientiert OT 3

  competitively [kəmˈpetətɪvli] konkurrierend; wetteifernd OT 4

competitor [kəmˈpetɪtə] Konkurrent(in); Wettbewerber(in) OT 4

to **complain** [kəmˈpleɪn] sich beklagen; sich beschweren OT 3

complaint [kəmˈpleɪnt] Beschwerde OT 2

to **complement** [ˈkɒmplɪment] ergänzen **WS 1**, 29

to **complete** [kəmˈpliːt] vervollständigen OT 1

completely [kəmˈpliːtli] ganz; komplett OT 4

completion [kəmˈpliːʃn] Vervollständigung; Erfüllung OT 4

complex [ˈkɒmpleks] Anlage; Komplex OT 4

complicated [ˈkɒmplɪkeɪtɪd] kompliziert OT 3

compliment [ˈkɒmplɪmənt] Kompliment OT 3

to **compliment** [ˈkɒmplɪmənt] loben OT 3

complimentary [ˌkɒmplɪˈmentri] kostenlos **WS 1**, 25

to **comply (with)** [kəmˈplaɪ wɪð] erfüllen **WS 1**, 22

component [kəmˈpəʊnənt] Bestandteil **WS 3**, 96

to **compose** [kəmˈpəʊz] komponieren OT 3

composer [kəmˈpəʊzə] Komponist(in) OT 2

compost [ˈkɒmpɒst] Kompost OT 3

composting [ˈkɒmpɒstɪŋ] Kompostierungs- OT 4

  composting toilet [ˈkɒmpɒstɪŋ ˈtɔɪlət] kompostierende Toilette OT 3

to **compound** [kəmˈpaʊnd] verschlimmern **WS 4**, 135

comprehensive [ˌkɒmprɪˈhensɪv] umfassend **WS 3**, 105

compromise [ˈkɒmprəmaɪz] Kompromiss **WS 2**, 54

compulsory [kəmˈpʌlsəri] verpflichtend; obligatorisch **WS 3**, 115

compulsion [kəmˈpʌlʃn] Zwang **WS 3**, 101

computer [kəmˈpjuːtər] Computer OT 5

  computer lab [kəmˈpjuːtə ˌlæb] Computerraum OT 2

computing [kəmˈpjuːtɪŋ] Computing OT 5

con [kɒn] Nachteil OT 2

to **conceal** [kənˈsiːl] verbergen OT 5

to **concentrate** [ˈkɒnsntreɪt] konzentrieren OT 3

concept [ˈkɒnsept] Konzept; Begriff OT 4

concern [kənˈsɜːn] Sorge; Bedenken OT 5

concerned [kənˈsɜːnd] besorgt OT 3

concerning [kənˈsɜːnɪŋ] betreffend; bezüglich OT 5

concert [ˈkɒnsət] Konzert OT 1

conciliatory [kənˈsɪliətəri] versöhnlich **WS 2**, 57

to **conclude** [kənˈkluːd] schließen (aus etwas); beenden OT 3

conclusion [kənˈkluːʒn] Schluss OT 3

concrete [ˈkɒŋkriːt] Beton OT 2

condition [kənˈdɪʃn] Zustand OT 2

to **condone** [kənˈdəʊn] dulden; billigen **WS 2**, 73

condor [ˈkɒndɔː] Condor OT 3

to **conduct** [kənˈdʌkt] durchführen OT 3

confectionary [kənˈfekʃənəri] Süßwaren **WS 1**, 36

conference [ˈkɒnfərəns] Konferenz OT 3

confession [kənˈfeʃn] Geständnis **WS 2**, 58

confidence [ˈkɒnfɪdəns] Selbstvertrauen OT 5

confident [ˈkɒnfɪdənt] selbstsicher OT 3

to **confirm** [kənˈfɜːm] bestätigen OT 4

confirmation [ˌkɒnfəˈmeɪʃn] Bestätigung **WS 3**, 116

conflict [ˈkɒnflɪkt] Konflikt OT 4

confluence [ˈkɒnfluəns] Zusammenströmen **WS 3**, 114

to **conform (to)** [kənˈfɔːm] (sich) anpassen an; übereinstimmen (mit) OT 5

conformity [kənˈfɔːməti] Konformität; Anpassung **WS 3**, 95

to **confront** [kənˈfrʌnt] konfrontieren; entgegentreten **WS 1**, 20

confused [kənˈfjuːzd] verwirrt OT 2

confusing [kənˈfjuːzɪŋ] verwirrend OT 2

congestion [kənˈdʒestʃən] Stau; Stauung OT 4

to **congratulate** [kənˈgrætʃuleɪt] gratulieren OT 2

congratulations [kənˌgrætʃuˈleɪʃnz] Glückwünsche OT 2

Congress [ˈkɒŋgres] Kongress OT 4

congressman, -woman [ˈkɒŋgrəsmən, -wʊmən] Abgeordnete(r) OT 4

conifer [ˈkɑːnɪfə] Nadelbaum **WS 1**, 35

conjunction [kənˈdʒʌŋkʃn] Konjunktion OT 2

to **connect** [kə'nekt] verbinden OT 2

connection [kə'nekʃn] Verbindung OT 2

connectivity [kə,nek'tɪvəti] Vernetzung **WS 3**, 110

connotation [,kɒnə'teɪʃn] Konnotation; Beiklang **WS 3**, 110

to **conquer** ['kɒŋkə] erobern OT 2

conscience ['kɒnʃəns] Gewissen **WS 2**, 65

conscious ['kɒnʃəs] bewusst **WS 3**, 93

consequence ['kɒnsɪkwəns] Folge; Konsequenz OT 4

conservation [,kɒnsə'veɪʃn] Schutz OT 2

conservative [kən'sɜ:vətɪv] konservativ **WS 1**, 31

to **consider** [kən'sɪdə] nachdenken über OT 3

consideration [kən,sɪdə'reɪʃn] Überlegung; Beachtung **WS 3**, 114

to **consist** [kən'sɪst] bestehen OT 3

consistent [kən'sɪstənt] konsequent OT 5

console: game console ['geɪm kɒnsəʊl] Spielekonsole OT 4

consonant ['kɒnsənənt] Konsonant; Mitlaut OT 1

constant ['kɒnstənt] ständig OT 5

constantly ['kɒnstəntli] ständig; konstant OT 4

constituency [kən'stɪtʃuənsi] Wahlbezirk; Interessengemeinschaft OT 4

constituent [kən'stɪtʃuənt] Wähler OT 4

to **constitute** ['kɒnstɪtju:t] ausmachen **WS 2**, 54

constitution [,kɒnstɪ'tju:ʃn] Verfassung OT 4

constitutional [,kɒnstɪ'tju:ʃənl] konstitutionell; Verfassungs... OT 4

to **construct** [kən'strʌkt] bauen; errichten OT 4

construction [kən'strʌkʃn] Bau OT 4

constructive [kən'strʌktɪv] konstruktiv **WS 1**, 23

consultant [kən'sʌltənt] Berater(in) OT 5

to **consume** [kən'sju:m] konsumieren; verbrauchen OT 4

consumer [kən'sju:mər] Verbraucher(in) OT 5

consumption [kən'sʌmpʃn] Verbrauch **WS 1**, 36

contact ['kɒntækt] Kontakt; Kontaktperson OT 1

to **contact** ['kɒntækt] kontaktieren OT 2

to **contain** [kən'teɪn] etw. enthalten OT 4

container [kən'teɪnə] Behälter; Container OT 4

to **contaminate** [kən'tæmɪneɪt] verunreinigen; kontaminieren OT 5

contemporary [kən'temprəri] zeitgenössisch OT 4

content ['kɒntent] Inhalt **WS 1**, 23

contents [kən'tents] Inhalt OT 2

contentious [kən'tenʃəs] umstritten **WS 2**, 82

contestant [kən'testənt] Wettkämpfer(in) OT 4

context ['kɒntekst] Kontext; Zusammenhang OT 4

continent ['kɒntɪnənt] Kontinent OT 5

continually [kən'tɪnjuəli] ständig **WS 2**, 70

to **continue** [kən'tɪnju:] weitermachen OT 2

continuous [kən'tɪnjuəs] laufend; kontinuierlich OT 4

contract ['kɒntrækt] Vertrag OT 4

contractor [kən'træktə] Auftragnehmer(in) OT 5

to **contradict** [,kɒntrə'dɪkt] widersprechen **WS 3**, 94

contradiction [,kɒntrə'dɪkʃn] Widerspruch **WS 3**, 111

contrary to ['kɒntrəri tu:] gegen **WS 1**, 37

contrast ['kɒntrɑ:st] Gegenteil; Kontrast OT 3

to **contrast** [kən'trɑ:st] vergleichen **WS 2**, 77

to **contribute (to)** [kən'trɪbju:t] mitarbeiten (an); beitragen (zu) OT 5

contribution [,kɒntrɪ'bju:ʃn] Beitrag **WS 1**, 29

control [kən'trəʊl] Kontrolle OT 2

to **control** [kən'trəʊl] kontrollieren OT 4

controversial [,kɒntrə'vɜ:ʃl] umstritten OT 3

controversy ['kɒntrəvɜ:si] Kontroverse OT 4

convenience [kən'vi:niəns] Bequemlichkeit; zweckmäßiges Gerät OT 4

convenient [kən'vi:niənt] günstig; praktisch OT 4

convention [kən'venʃn] Konvention **WS 1**, 21

to **converge** [kən'vɜ:dʒ] zusammenlaufen **WS 2**, 58

conversation [,kɒnvə'seɪʃn] Gespräch; Unterhaltung OT 1

conversational [,kɒnvə'seɪʃənl] Gesprächs... OT 5

to **convert** [kən'vɜ:t] konvertieren; übertreten; umwandeln **WS 2**, 61

to **convey** [kən'veɪ] vermitteln OT 5

convict ['kɒnvɪkt] Verurteilte(r) OT 5

to **convict** [kən'vɪkt] verurteilen OT 5

conviction [kən'vɪkʃn] Verurteilung OT 5

to **convince** [kən'vɪns] überzeugen OT 5

to **cook** [kʊk] kochen OT 1

cooker ['kʊkə] Herd OT 3

cookery ['kʊkəri] Kochen OT 2

cookie ['kʊki] Keks OT 3

cooking ['kʊkɪŋ] Kochen; Küche OT 1

cool [ku:l] kühl; cool; gelassen OT 1

to **cool** [ku:l] abkühlen OT 5

cooling system ['ku:lɪŋ sɪstəm] Kühlsystem OT 3

cooperation [kəʊ,ɒpə'reɪʃn] Zusammenarbeit OT 5

to **cope** [kəʊp] zurechtkommen OT 5

copper beech ['kɒpə bi:tʃ] Rotbuche **WS 2**, 82

copy ['kɒpi] Kopie OT 1

to **copy** ['kɒpi] kopieren; nachahmen OT 1

coral ['kɒrəl] Korallen... **WS 1**, 12

core [kɔ:] Kern; Haupt... OT 4

corn [kɔ:n] Mais OT 3

corn crib ['kɔ:n krɪb] Maisscheune **WS 2**, 64

corner ['kɔ:nə] Ecke; Kurve; Winkel OT 1

cornrow ['kɔ:nrəʊ] Cornrow; dünner Zopf **WS 2**, 68

coronation [,kɒrə'neɪʃn] Krönung OT 3

corporation [,kɔ:pə'reɪʃn] Unternehmen **WS 2**, 66

correct [kə'rekt] richtig; korrekt; einwandfrei OT 1

to **correct** [kə'rekt] verbessern; korrigieren OT 1

correction [kə'rekʃn] Korrektur OT 4

to **correspond** [,kɒrə'spɒnd] übereinstimmen **WS 3**, 106

correspondent [,kɒrə'spɒndənt] Korrespondent(in); Reporter(in) OT 4

corridor ['kɒrɪdɔ:] Korridor OT 2

corruption [kə'rʌpʃn] Korruption **WS 2**, 60

corset ['kɔ:sɪt] Korsett OT 3

cosmopolitan city [,kɒzməpɒlɪtən 'sɪti] Weltstadt OT 4

cost [kɒst] Kosten; Preis OT 1

to **cost** [kɒst] kosten OT 1

costume ['kɒstju:m] Kostüm OT 2

cottage [ˈkɒtɪdʒ] Häuschen OT 3
cotton [ˈkɒtn] Baumwolle OT 4
cotton gin [ˈkɒtn dʒɪn]
Baumwollentkörnungsmaschine
WS 2, 54
cougar [ˈkuːgə] Puma OT 2
could [kʊd] konnte; könnte(n) OT 1
council [ˈkaʊnsl] Rat OT 3
counselling [ˈkaʊnsəlɪŋ] Beratung OT 5
counselor [ˈkaʊnsələ]
Jugendbetreuer(in) OT 2
to **count** [kaʊnt] zählen OT 2
countable [ˈkaʊntəbl] zählbar OT 1
counter- [kaʊntə, kaʊntər] Gegen…
WS 2, 75
counterargument [ˈkaʊntərɑːgjumənt]
Gegenargument **WS 1**, 37
countermovement [kaʊntəmuːvmənt]
Gegenbewegung **WS 3**, 114
counterpart [ˈkaʊntəpɑːt] Kollege;
Kollegin OT 5
country [ˈkʌntri] Land; Landschaft OT 1
countryside [ˈkʌntrisaɪd] Land(schaft)
OT 1
county [ˈkaʊnti] Grafschaft **WS 1**, 34
couple [ˈkʌpl] Paar OT 2
coupon [ˈkuːpɒn] Gutschein OT 2
courage [ˈkʌrɪdʒ] Mut **WS 1**, 14
courier [ˈkʊriə] Kurier(in) OT 2
course [kɔːs] Kurs OT 3
of course [əv ˈkɔːs] natürlich OT 1
coursework [ˈkɔːswɜːk] Facharbeit OT 4
court [kɔːt] Gericht OT 4
cousin [ˈkʌzn] Cousin(e) OT 1
to **cover** [ˈkʌvə] abdecken OT 2
covered [ˈkʌvəd] bedeckt OT 2
cow [kaʊ] Kuh OT 1
coward [ˈkaʊəd] Feigling **WS 2**, 83
coyote [kaɪˈəʊti] Kojote; hier:
Schlepper(in) OT 5
to **crack down on** [kræk daʊn ɒn] hart
vorgehen gegen **WS 2**, 73
cracker [ˈkrækə] Cracker OT 3
cradle [ˈkreɪdl] Wiege OT 3
craft [krɑːft] Handwerk;
Kunsthandwerk OT 4
cramp [kræmp] Krampf OT 2
cramped [kræmpt] beengt OT 3
cranberry [ˈkrænbəri] Preiselbeere OT 3
to **crash** [kræʃ] abstürzen OT 3
crash diet [ˈkræʃ ˈdaɪət] Crash-Diät OT 5
crate [kreɪt] Kiste OT 4
to **crawl** [krɔːl] krabbeln; kriechen OT 5
craze [kreɪz] Wahn **WS 3**, 108
crazy [ˈkreɪzi] verrückt OT 2

cream [kriːm] Sahne; Rahm OT 1
to **create** [kriˈeɪt] schaffen; kreieren
OT 2
creation [kriˈeɪʃn] Schöpfung OT 5
creative [kriˈeɪtɪv] kreativ OT 2
creativity [ˌkriːeɪˈtɪvəti] Kreativität OT 3
creator [kriˈeɪtər] Schöpfer(in);
Erschaffer(in) OT 5
creature [ˈkriːtʃər] Geschöpf;
Lebewesen OT 5
credit [ˈkredɪt] Credit; Notenpunkt OT 5
credit card [ˈkredɪt kɑːd] Kreditkarte
OT 1
creed [kriːd] Glaube; Credo **WS 2**, 58
creepy [ˈkriːpi] gruselig OT 5
creepy-crawly [ˌkriːpiˈkrɔːli]
Krabbeltier OT 2
crew [kruː] Mannschaft; Personal OT 2
cricket [ˈkrɪkɪt] Kricket; Grille OT 1
crime [kraɪm] Verbrechen OT 4
criminal [ˈkrɪmɪnl] Kriminelle(r) OT 3
criminal record [ˌkrɪmɪnl ˈrekɔːd]
Vorstrafregister OT 5
crisis [ˈkraɪsɪs] Krise OT 4
crisp [krɪsp] Kartoffelchip OT 1
criterion [kraɪˈtɪəriən] Kriterium OT 5
critic [ˈkrɪtɪk] Kritiker(in) OT 5
critical [ˈkrɪtɪkl] kritisch OT 4
criticism [ˈkrɪtɪsɪzəm] Kritik OT 3
to **criticize** [ˈkrɪtɪsaɪz] kritisieren OT 3
croft [krɒft] kleiner Hof **WS 1**, 19
crop [krɒp] Getreide; Feldfrüchte OT 3
cross [krɒs] verärgert OT 2
to **cross** [krɒs] überqueren; sich
kreuzen OT 1
cross country [ˌkrɒs ˈkʌntri]
Querfeldein- OT 2
cross-country skiing [ˌkrɒs ˌkʌntri
ˈskiːɪŋ] Langlaufen; Skilanglauf OT 5
crossly [ˈkrɒsli] mürrisch OT 3
crow [krəʊ] Krähe OT 3
crowd [kraʊd] Menge;
Menschenmenge; Zuschauer OT 1
crowded [ˈkraʊdɪd] überfüllt OT 2
crown [kraʊn] Krone OT 1
to **crown** [kraʊn] krönen; überkronen
OT 1
crucial [ˈkruːʃəl] wesentlich; zentral
WS 3, 96
cruel [ˈkruːəl] grausam OT 3
to **cruise** [kruːz] mit dem Boot fahren;
eine Kreuzfahrt machen OT 3
cruise ship [ˈkruːz ʃɪp] Kreuzfahrtschiff
OT 2

crunch [krʌntʃ] Knirschen; hier: Sit-up
WS 1, 37
crush: to have a crush (on) [həv ə ˈkrʌʃ]
in jmdn. verknallt sein OT 4
to **crush** [krʌʃ] zerschlagen; erdrücken
WS 1, 32
crutch [krʌtʃ] Krücke OT 2
to **cry** [kraɪ] weinen; schreien; rufen OT 1
to **crystallize** [ˈkrɪstəlaɪz] sich
herausbilden **WS 4**, 141
cub [kʌb] Junge(s) OT 2
cucumber [ˈkjuːkʌmbə] Gurke;
Salatgurke OT 1
cuddly [ˈkʌdli] knuddelig OT 3
cue [kjuː] Hinweis; Stichwort OT 5
cuisine [kwɪˈziːn] Küche OT 3
cull [kʌl] Schlachten; Keulen OT 5
to **cull** [kʌl] keulen; selektiv schlachten
OT 5
to **culminate** [ˈkʌlmɪneɪt] gipfeln;
kulminieren **WS 2**, 58
culprit [ˈkʌlprɪt] Schuldige **WS 4**, 134
cultural [ˈkʌltʃərəl] kulturell OT 4
culture [ˈkʌltʃə] Kultur OT 1
Cumbrian [ˈkʌmbriən] von/aus
Cumbria OT 2
cup [kʌp] Tasse; Pokal; Kelch OT 1
cup [kʌp] Meisterschaft OT 5
cupboard [ˈkʌbəd] Schrank OT 1
curb [kɜːb] Bordstein OT 5
to **cure** [kjʊər] heilen **WS 3**, 117
curfew [ˈkɜːfjuː] Ausgangssperre OT 3
curiosity [ˌkjʊəriˈɒsəti] Neugier
WS 3, 105
curious [ˈkjʊəriəs] neugierig; gespannt
OT 4
curlew [ˈkɜːljuː] Brachvogel OT 2
curling [ˈkɜːlɪŋ] Curling OT 4
curly [ˈkɜːli] gelockt OT 3
currency [ˈkʌrənsi] Währung **WS 1**, 31
current [ˈkʌrənt] aktuell OT 2
currently [ˈkʌrəntli] derzeit; gerade
OT 4
curriculum [kəˈrɪkjələm] Curriculum;
Lehrplan OT 4
curry [ˈkʌri] Currygericht OT 1
curtain [ˈkɜːtn] Vorhang OT 2
cushion [ˈkʊʃn] Kissen; Polster; Bande
OT 1
custard [ˈkʌstəd] Vanillesoße OT 1
custodial sentence [kʌˈstəʊdiəl ˈsentəns]
Freiheitsstrafe OT 5
custody [ˈkʌstədi] Verwahrung; Schutz;
Sorgerecht OT 5
customer [ˈkʌstəmə] Kunde(-in) OT 2

customs [ˈkʌstəmz] Zoll OT 2

cut [kʌt] Schnitt **WS 2**, 76

to cut [kʌt] schneiden OT 2

cute [kjuːt] niedlich OT 3

cutlery [ˈkʌtləri] Besteck OT 3

CV (curriculum vitae) [ˌsiː ˈviː]
   Lebenslauf OT 4

cyberbullying [ˈsaɪbəbʊliŋ]
   Cyber-Mobbing OT 5

cyberthreat [ˈsaɪbəθret]
   Cyber-Bedrohung OT 5

cycle [ˈsaɪkl] Periode; Zyklus OT 4

to cycle [ˈsaɪkl] radfahren; einen
   Kreislauf durchlaufen OT 1

cyclist [ˈsaɪklɪst] Radfahrer(in) OT 3

cyclone [ˈsaɪkləʊn] Zyklon OT 5

cynicism [ˈsɪnɪsɪzəm] Zynismus
   WS 2, 69

D

dad [dæd] Papa; Vati OT 1

daily [ˈdeɪli] täglich OT 2

dairy [ˈdeəri] Milchprodukte OT 4

damage [ˈdæmɪdʒ] Beschädigung OT 3

to damage [ˈdæmɪdʒ] beschädigen OT 3

damaged [ˈdæmɪdʒd] beschädigt OT 2

damned [dæmd] verdammt **WS 3**, 105

dance [dɑːns] Tanz OT 5

danceable [dɑːnsəbl] tanzbar **WS 2**, 67

dancing [ˈdɑːnsɪŋ] Tanzen OT 1

danger [ˈdeɪndʒə] Gefahr OT 2

dangerous [ˈdeɪndʒərəs] gefährlich OT 1

to dare [deə] wagen OT 2

dark [dɑːk] dunkel; finster;
   geheimnisvoll OT 1

dark-haired [ˌdɑːk ˈheəd] dunkelhaarig
   OT 3

darkness [ˈdɑːknəs] Dunkelheit OT 5

data [ˈdeɪtə] Daten OT 5

date [deɪt] Verabredung OT 3

to date back [deɪt bæk] stammen aus
   OT 4

daughter [ˈdɔːtə] Tochter OT 1

dawn [dɔːn] Morgendämmerung OT 3

day [deɪ] Tag; Zeit OT 1

   one day [ˈwʌn deɪ] eines Tages;
      später einmal OT 2

   day out [deɪ ˈaʊt] Tagesausflug OT 2

daylight [ˈdeɪlaɪt] Tageslicht **WS 2**, 79

   broad daylight [brɔːd ˈdeɪlaɪt]
      helllichter Tag **WS 2**, 79

dead [ded] tot; taub; gefühllos OT 1

deadly [ˈdedli] tödlich OT 5

deaf [def] taub OT 3

deal [diːl] Geschäft; hier: Angelegenheit
   OT 5

to deal with [diːl wɪð] umgehen OT 2

death [deθ] Tod OT 2

   date of death [ˌdeɪt əv ˈdeθ]
      Todesdatum OT 2

debate [dɪˈbeɪt] Debatte OT 4

debt [det] Schulden **WS 2**, 69

to debunk [diːˈbʌŋk] widerlegen;
   entlarven **WS 1**, 12

debut [ˈdeɪbjuː] Debüt; Auftreten OT 4

decade [ˈdekeɪd] Dekade; Jahrzehnt
   OT 4

decadent [ˈdekədənt] dekadent;
   maßlos **WS 2**, 63

December [dɪˈsembə] Dezember OT 1

decent [ˈdiːsnt] anständig **WS 2**, 63

to decide [dɪˈsaɪd] entscheiden;
   beschließen OT 1

decision [dɪˈsɪʒn] Entscheidung;
   Entschluss OT 1

   decision maker [dɪˈsɪʒn meɪkə]
      Entscheidungsträger(in) **WS 4**, 136

decisive [dɪˈsaɪsɪv] entscheidend
   WS 2, 57

deck [dek] Deck OT 3

to declare [dɪˈkleə] ausrufen;
   verkünden OT 4

decline [dɪˈklaɪn] Rückgang OT 5

to decline [dɪˈklaɪn] verfallen OT 5

to decorate [ˈdekəreɪt] dekorieren;
   schmücken OT 2

decoration [ˌdekəˈreɪʃn] Dekoration OT 3

to decrease [dɪˈkriːs] fallen;
   zurückgehen OT 5

dedicated [ˈdedɪkeɪtɪd] engagiert
   WS 3, 119

dedication [ˌdedɪˈkeɪʃn] hier:
   Einweihung; Einsatz **WS 2**, 57

deed [diːd] Urkunde OT 5

to deem [diːm] meinen **WS 3**, 93

deep [diːp] tief; schwer; dunkel OT 1

deer [dɪə] Hirsch OT 1

deerskin [ˈdɪəskin] Hirschleder OT 3

de facto [ˌdeɪ ˈfæktəʊ] de facto OT 5

default [dɪˈfɔːlt] Standard OT 3

to defeat [dɪˈfiːt] besiegen **WW**, 10

defence [dɪˈfens] Verteidigung OT 5

to defend [dɪˈfend] verteidigen OT 5

deficit [ˈdefɪsɪt] Mangel **WS 3**, 105

to define [dɪˈfaɪn] definieren;
   bestimmen OT 4

defining [dɪˈfaɪnɪŋ] bestimmend OT 2

definite [ˈdefɪnət] eindeutig; fest OT 1

definitely [ˈdefɪnətli] bestimmt;
   definitiv OT 2

definition [ˌdefɪˈnɪʃn] Definition;
   Schärfe; Bildschärfe OT 1

deforestation [ˌdiːˌfɒrɪˈsteɪʃn]
   Abholzung OT 5

to defy [dɪˈfaɪ] trotzen; sich widersetzen
   WS 1, 21

degree [dɪˈɡriː] Grad OT 5

dehydrated [ˌdiːhaɪˈdreɪtɪd] dehydriert
   OT 2

delay [dɪˈleɪ] Verzögerung; Verspätung
   OT 4

delegate [ˈdelɪɡət] Abgeordnete(r) OT 4

to delete [dɪˈliːt] löschen **WS 4**, 141

deli [ˈdeli] Feinkostladen OT 5

deliberate [dɪˈlɪbərət] absichtlich
   WS 2, 58

delicate [ˈdelɪkət] zart **WS 3**, 119

delicious [dɪˈlɪʃəs] lecker; köstlich
   OT 1

to deliver [dɪˈlɪvə] liefern OT 3

delivery [dɪˈlɪvəri] Zustellung;
   Zustellung OT 5

delta [ˈdeltə] Flußmündung **WS 2**, 67

to delve into [ˈdelv ɪntə] sich vertiefen
   WS 3, 111

demand [dɪˈmɑːnd] Nachfrage;
   Verlangen OT 5

demanding [dɪˈmɑːndɪŋ] anspruchsvoll
   OT 4

demise [dɪˈmaɪz] Niedergang **WS 1**, 12

democracy [dɪˈmɒkrəsi] Demokratie
   OT 3

to demolish [dɪˈmɒlɪʃ] abreißen OT 5

to demonstrate [ˈdemənstreɪt] zeigen;
   vorführen OT 5

demonstration [ˌdemənˈstreɪʃn]
   Demonstration OT 5

demonstrative [dɪˈmɒnstrətɪv]
   Demonstrativbegleiter OT 1

demonstrator [ˈdemənstreɪtə]
   Demonstrant(in) **WS 2**, 53

denial [dɪˈnaɪəl] Verweigerung
   WS 3, 105

denim [ˈdenɪm] Jeansstoff **WS 3**, 101

dent [dent] Beule; Delle **WS 3**, 104

deny [dɪˈnaɪ] leugnen OT 4

department [dɪˈpɑːtmənt] Abteilung
   OT 4

department store [dɪˈpɑːtmənt stɔː]
   Kaufhaus OT 4

departure [dɪˈpɑːtʃə] Abfahrt; Abflug
   OT 2

to depend [dɪˈpend] abhängen OT 2

dependent on [dɪˈpendənt ɒn] abhängig von **WS 4**, 135

to **depict** [dɪˈpɪkt] schildern; beschreiben **WS 2**, 77

depopulation [ˌdiːˌpɒpjuˈleɪʃn] Entvölkerung **WS 1**, 35

depression [dɪˈpreʃn] Depression OT 5

depressive [dɪˈpresɪv] depressiv **WS 3**, 108

deputy [ˈdepjuti] Stellvertreter(in) **WS 2**, 61

derogative [diˈrɒgətɪv] abwertend; abfällig **WS 2**, 65

to **descend (from)** [dɪˈsend] abstammen (von) OT 5

to **be descended** [bi dɪˈsendɪd] abstammen von OT 3

descendant [dɪˈsendənt] Nachkomme OT 3

descent [dɪˈsent] Abstammung OT 5

to **describe** [dɪˈskraɪb] beschreiben OT 1

description [dɪˈskrɪpʃn] Beschreibung; Schilderung OT 1

descriptive [dɪˈskrɪptɪv] beschreibend OT 4

to **desegregate** [diːˈsegrɪgeɪt] die Rassentrennung aufheben **WS 2**, 58

to **desensitize** [diːˈsensətaɪz] desensibilisieren **WS 2**, 79

desert [ˈdezət] Wüste OT 3

desertification [dɪˌzɜːtɪfɪˈkeɪʃn] Wüstenbildung **WS 4**, 138

to **deserve** [dɪˈzɜːv] verdienen OT 2

design [dɪˈzaɪn] Entwurf; Design; Gestaltung OT 1

to **design** [dɪˈzaɪn] planen OT 4

designated [ˈdezɪgneɪtɪd] bestimmt OT 3

designer [dɪˈzaɪnə] Designer(in) OT 3

desirable [dɪˈzaɪərəbl] wünschenswert **WS 4**, 144

desire [dɪˈzaɪə] Wunsch OT 5

desk [desk] Schreibtisch; Empfang; Redaktion OT 1

desperate [ˈdespərət] verzweifelt OT 3

desperately [ˈdespərətli] verzweifelt OT 3

despite [dɪˈspaɪt] obwohl; trotz OT 4

dessert [dɪˈzɜːt] Nachtisch; Dessert OT 1

destination [ˌdestɪˈneɪʃn] Reiseziel OT 4

destined [ˈdestɪnd] bestimmt; vorgesehen **WS 2**, 76

destiny [ˈdestəni] Schicksal **WS 1**, 25

to **destroy** [dɪˈstrɔɪ] zerstören OT 2

destruction [dɪˈstrʌkʃn] Zerstörung OT 4

detail [ˈdiːteɪl] Detail OT 2

detailed [ˈdiːteɪld] detailliert; ausführlich OT 4

to **detect** [dɪˈtekt] entdecken **WS 1**, 27

to **deter** [dɪˈtɜː] abhalten; abschrecken **WS 2**, 73

determination [dɪˌtɜːmɪˈneɪʃn] Entschlossenheit OT 4

to **determine** [dɪˈtɜːmɪn] ausmachen; bestimmen OT 4

determined [dɪˈtɜːmɪnd] entschlossen OT 5

determiner [dɪˈtɜːmɪnə] Bestimmungswort OT 1

detox [ˈdiːtɒks] Entgiftung; Entzug **WS 3**, 108

devastating [ˈdevəsteɪtɪŋ] verheerend OT 5

to **develop** [dɪˈveləp] entwickeln OT 2

developer [dɪˈveləpə] Entwickler(in) OT 5

development [dɪˈveləpmənt] Entwicklung OT 4

developmental [dɪˌveləpˈmentl] entwicklungsbedingt **WS 3**, 95

device [dɪˈvaɪs] Gerät OT 3

devil [ˈdevl] Teufel **WS 2**, 60

to **devolve** [dɪˈvɒlv] dezentralisieren **WS 1**, 30

devoted [dɪˈvəʊtɪd] verbunden OT 4

diabetes [ˌdaɪəˈbiːtiːz] Diabetes **WS 1**, 37

diagram [ˈdaɪəgræm] Schaubild; Diagramm; grafische Darstellung OT 1

to **dial** [ˈdaɪəl] wählen OT 2

dialect [ˈdaɪəlekt] Dialekt OT 4

dialogue [ˈdaɪəlɒg] Dialog OT 1

dial phone [ˈdaɪəl fəʊn] Telefon mit Wählscheibe OT 5

diaper [ˈdaɪəpə] Windel OT 3

diary [ˈdaɪəri] Terminkalender; Tagebuch OT 1

diaspora [daɪˈæspərə] Diaspora **WS 1**, 35

to **dice** [daɪs] würfeln; in Würfel schneiden **WS 2**, 69

to **dictate** [dɪkˈteɪt] bestimmen OT 5

dictionary [ˈdɪkʃənri] Wörterbuch OT 2

didgeridoo [ˌdɪdʒəriˈduː] Didgeridoo OT 5

to **die** [daɪ] sterben; eingehen; verenden OT 1

diesel [ˈdiːzl] Diesel OT 3

diet [ˈdaɪət] Diät OT 3

dietary [ˈdaɪətəri] diätetisch OT 5

dietician [ˌdaɪəˈtɪʃn] Ernährungswissenschaftler(in) OT 5

dieting [ˈdaɪətɪŋ] Schlankheitskuren; Diäten OT 5

to **differ** [ˈdɪfə] sich unterscheiden **WS 1**, 27

difference [ˈdɪfrəns] Unterschied OT 1

different [ˈdɪfrənt] unterschiedlich; anders; verschieden OT 1

difficult [ˈdɪfɪkəlt] schwer; schwierig OT 1

difficulty [ˈdɪfɪkəlti] Schwierigkeit OT 2

diffused [dɪˈfjuːzd] verbreitet; diffus **WS 3**, 122

to **dig** [dɪg] graben OT 5

digit [ˈdɪdʒɪt] Ziffer OT 2

digital [ˈdɪdʒɪtl] digital; Digital... OT 1

digitalization [ˌdɪdʒɪtəlaɪˈzeɪʃn] Digitalisierung **WS 3**, 106

dilemma [dɪˈlemə] Dilemma OT 5

dimension [daɪˈmenʃn] Abmessung OT 2

to **diminish** [dɪˈmɪnɪʃ] abschwächen; verringern **WS 2**, 73

dingo [ˈdɪŋgəʊ] Dingo OT 5

dining room [ˈdaɪnɪŋ ruːm] Esszimmer OT 1

dinner [ˈdɪnə] Abendessen OT 1

dinosaur [ˈdaɪnəsɔː] Dinosaurier OT 1

to **dip** [dɪp] tauchen OT 4

diploma [dɪˈpləʊmə] Diplom; Urkunde OT 4

dire [ˈdaɪə] entsetzlich; furchtbar **WS 4**, 140

to **direct** [dəˈrekt] Regie führen OT 3

direction [dəˈrekʃn] Anweisung OT 2

directions [dəˈrekʃnz] Wegbeschreibungen OT 2

directly [dəˈrektli] direkt OT 3

director [dəˈrektə] Leiter(in) OT 2

dirt [dɜːt] Dreck; Schmutz OT 4

dirty [ˈdɜːti] schmutzig; dreckig; unfair OT 1

disability [ˌdɪsəˈbɪləti] Behinderung OT 2

disabled [dɪsˈeɪbld] Behinderte(r) OT 4

disadvantage [ˌdɪsədˈvɑːntɪdʒ] Nachteil OT 4

disadvantaged [ˌdɪsədˈvɑːntɪdʒd] benachteiligt OT 5

to **disagree** [ˌdɪsəˈgriː] anderer Meinung sein; nicht übereinstimmen; sich widersprechen OT 1

disagreement [ˌdɪsəˈgriːmənt] Uneinigkeit OT 3

to **disappear** [ˌdɪsəˈpɪə] verschwinden OT 3

disappointed [ˌdɪsəˈpɔɪntɪd] enttäuscht OT 2

disappointing [ˌdɪsəˈpɔɪntɪŋ] enttäuschend OT 4

disappointment [ˌdɪsəˈpɔɪntmənt] Enttäuschung WS 1, 32

disaster [dɪˈzɑːstə] Katastrophe OT 2

disastrous [dɪˈzɑːstrəs] verheerend WS 4, 136

to discard [dɪˈskɑːd] ausrangieren; wegwerfen WS 3, 104

discipline [ˈdɪsəplɪn] Disziplin; Fachrichtung WS 3, 116

to disconnect [ˌdɪskəˈnekt] trennen; abschalten WS 3, 108

discount [ˈdɪskaʊnt] Rabatt; Nachlass OT 4

to discover [dɪˈskʌvə] entdecken OT 2

discovery [dɪˈskʌvəri] Entdeckung OT 4

to discredit [dɪsˈkredɪt] diskreditieren WS 3, 97

to discriminate [dɪˈskrɪmɪneɪt] unterschiedlich behandeln; diskriminieren OT 5

discrimination [dɪˌskrɪmɪˈneɪʃn] Diskriminierung; Ausgrenzung OT 5

to discuss [dɪˈskʌs] besprechen; diskutieren; erörtern OT 1

discussion [dɪˈskʌʃn] Besprechung; Diskussion; Erörterung OT 1

disease [dɪˈziːz] Krankheit OT 2

to disembark [ˌdɪsɪmˈbɑːk] aussteigen WS 2, 59

disenchanted [ˌdɪsɪnˈtʃɑːntɪd] enttäuscht WS 2, 60

disenfranchised [ˌdɪsɪnˈfræntʃaɪzd] entrechtet WS 2, 62

to disgrace [dɪsˈɡreɪs] blamieren WS 2, 64

disgusted [dɪsˈɡʌstɪd] empört; angewidert OT 5

disgusting [dɪsˈɡʌstɪŋ] ekelhaft OT 2

dish [dɪʃ] Gericht; Schale OT 2

dishes [ˈdɪʃɪz] Geschirr OT 2

to do the dishes [ˌduː ðə ˈdɪʃɪz] den Abwasch machen OT 2

disinfectant [ˌdɪsɪnˈfektənt] Desinfektionsmittel OT 3

to dislike [dɪsˈlaɪk] nicht mögen OT 2

to dismantle [dɪsˈmæntl] abbauen WS 2, 78

to dismiss [dɪsˈmɪs] ablehnen; entlassen WS 3, 105

to disobey [ˌdɪsəˈbeɪ] nicht gehorchen OT 3

disorder [dɪsˈɔːdə] Störung OT 5

disorganized [dɪsˈɔːɡənaɪzd] chaotisch OT 2

to dispel [dɪˈspel] vertreiben WS 2, 82

dispenser [dɪˈspensə] Spender OT 5

display [dɪˈspleɪ] Ausstellung OT 2

disposable [dɪˈspəʊzəbl] verfügbar WS 1, 12

disposal [dɪˈspəʊzl] Verfügung WS 1, 34

to dispute [dɪˈspjuːt] bestreiten; anfechten WS 1, 20

disrespectful [ˌdɪsrɪˈspektfl] respektlos OT 3

disruption [dɪsˈrʌpʃn] Störung; Unterbrechung OT 4

dissatisfaction [ˌdɪsˌsætɪsˈfækʃn] Unzufriedenheit OT 5

distance [ˈdɪstəns] Entfernung OT 2

to distance oneself [ˈdɪstəns] (sich) distanzieren OT 4

distant [ˈdɪstənt] weit entfernt OT 4

distinct [dɪˈstɪŋkt] eindeutig; eigenständig OT 5

distinction [dɪˈstɪŋkʃn] Unterschied WS 1, 27

distinctive [dɪˈstɪŋktɪv] unverwechselbar; ausgeprägt OT 5

to distinguish [dɪˈstɪŋɡwɪʃ] unterscheiden WS 2, 83

to distract [dɪˈstrækt] ablenken WS 3, 108

distress [dɪˈstres] Not; Leid WS 3, 112

to distribute [dɪˈstrɪbjuːt] verteilen OT 4

distribution [ˌdɪstrɪˈbjuːʃn] Verteilung WS 2, 62

district [ˈdɪstrɪkt] Bezirk OT 5

to disturb [dɪˈstɜːb] stören OT 3

to dive [daɪv] tauchen; hineinspringen OT 3

diver [ˈdaɪvər] Taucher(in) OT 3

diverse [daɪˈvɜːs] vielfältig; verschieden OT 4

diversity [daɪˈvɜːsəti] Vielfältigkeit OT 4

to divide [dɪˈvaɪd] (sich) teilen OT 2

diving [ˈdaɪvɪŋ] Tauchen; Kunstspringen OT 1

division [dɪˈvɪʒn] Abteilung; Bereich WS 2, 53

divisive [dɪˈvaɪsɪv] spaltend; trennend WS 2, 62

divorce [dɪˈvɔːs] Scheidung OT 3

divorced: get divorced [ɡet dɪˈvɔːst] sich scheiden lassen OT 3

dizzy [ˈdɪzi] schwindlig OT 3

to do [duː] tun; machen; vorankommen OT 1

doctor [ˈdɒktə] Arzt/Ärztin; Doktor(in) OT 1

document [ˈdɒkjumənt] Dokument OT 4

documentary [ˌdɒkjuˈmentri] Dokumentation OT 2

dog [dɒɡ] Hund OT 1

doll [dɒl] Puppe OT 2

dollar [ˈdɒlə] Dollar OT 1

dolphin [ˈdɒlfɪn] Delfin OT 1

dome [dəʊm] Kuppel OT 4

dominant [ˈdɒmɪnənt] wichtig; überwiegend OT 4

to dominate [ˈdɒmɪneɪt] dominieren; beherrschen WS 1, 35

to donate [dəʊˈneɪt] spenden OT 2

donation [dəʊˈneɪʃn] Spende OT 2

donkey [ˈdɒŋki] Esel OT 4

doodle [ˈduːdl] Gekritzel WS 4, 142

to doom [duːm] verdammen WS 3, 96

door [dɔː] Tür OT 1

doorbell [ˈdɔːbel] Klingel OT 2

doorstep [ˈdɔːstep] Türschwelle OT 5

dopamine [ˈdəʊpəmiːn] Dopamin WS 4, 135

dot [dɒt] Punkt WS 3, 123

to dot [dɒt] sprenkeln WS 1, 38

double [ˈdʌbl] doppelt; Doppel... OT 1

to double [ˈdʌbl] sich verdoppeln OT 5

doublet [ˈdʌblət] Wams OT 3

doubt [daʊt] Zweifel OT 5

doughnut [ˈdəʊnʌt] Krapfen OT 2

down [daʊn] (nach) unten OT 1

downhill [ˌdaʊnˈhɪl] bergab OT 5

to download [ˈdaʊnləʊd] herunterladen OT 3

downside [ˈdaʊnsaɪd] Nachteil OT 3

to downsize [ˈdaʊnsaɪz] reduzieren; sich einschränken OT 3

downstairs [ˈdaʊnsteəz] im unteren Stockwerk; Parterre OT 1

Down syndrome [ˈdaʊn sɪndrəʊm] Downsyndrom OT 5

downtown [ˌdaʊnˈtaʊn] Innenstadt OT 4

to doze [dəʊz] ein Nickerchen machen OT 2

dozen [ˈdʌzn] Dutzend OT 4

draft [drɑːft] Entwurf OT 2

to draft [drɑːft] entwerfen OT 5

to drag [dræɡ] schleppen WS 1, 20

to drain [dreɪn] abgießen OT 2

drained [dreɪnd] abgetropft OT 2

drama [ˈdrɑːmə] Drama; Dramatik OT 1

dramatic [drəˈmætɪk] dramatisch OT 4

drastic [ˈdræstɪk] drastisch; extrem OT 5

to **draw** [drɔ:] ziehen; zeichnen; aufziehen OT 1

drawer [drɔ:] Schublade OT 1

drawing ['drɔ:ɪŋ] Zeichnung OT 4

to **dread** [dred] fürchten; sich scheuen **WS 1**, 22

dreadful ['dredfl] schrecklich OT 2

dream [dri:m] Traum OT 2

dreamtime ['dri:mtaɪm] Traumzeit OT 5

dress [dres] Kleid OT 5

to **dress** [dres] anziehen; sich anziehen OT 3

dried [draɪd] getrocknet OT 3

drink [drɪŋk] Getränk; Drink; Gläschen OT 1

to **drink** [drɪŋk] trinken OT 1

to **drip** [drɪp] tropfen OT 3

drive [draɪv] Fahrt OT 5

to **drive** [draɪv] fahren; bringen; antreiben OT 1

to **drive** [draɪv] treiben OT 5

driver ['draɪvə] Fahrer(in) OT 2

driveway ['draɪvweɪ] Zufahrt; Auffahrt OT 4

drone [drəʊn] Drone OT 4

to **drop** [drɒp] fallen (lassen); fallen; sich fallen lassen OT 1

drop kick ['drɒp kɪk] Dropkick OT 5

dropout ['drɒpaʊt] Aussteiger(in); Abbrecher(in) **WS 3**, 119

drought [draʊt] Dürre OT 5

to **drown** [draʊn] ertrinken OT 3

drug [drʌg] Droge OT 3

drummer ['drʌmə] Schlagzeuger(in) OT 2

drums [drʌmz] Schlagzeug OT 1

dry [draɪ] trocken OT 2

dual ['dju:əl] zweifach; dual OT 4

duality [dju:'æləti] Dualität OT 4

duck [dʌk] Ente OT 2

due to [dju: tə] wegen OT 5

dull [dʌl] öde; langweilig **WS 1**, 16

dumb [dʌm] blöd; dumm OT 5

to **dump** [dʌmp] abkippen OT 2

dumpster ['dʌmpstə] Müllcontainer OT 4

dunk [dʌŋk] Treffer OT 3

duplication [ˌdju:plɪ'keɪʃn] Doppelung **WS 4**, 141

duration [dju'reɪʃn] Dauer **WS 3**, 108

during ['djʊərɪŋ] während OT 2

dust [dʌst] Staub OT 2

to **dust** [dʌst] abstauben **WS 1**, 20

dusty ['dʌsti] verstaubt OT 4

duty free [ˌdju:ti 'fri:] zollfrei OT 2

duvet ['du:veɪ] Bettdecke OT 2

to **dwarf** [dwɔ:f] klein scheinen lassen **WS 2**, 55

dwell time [dwel taɪm] Verweilzeit **WS 4**, 135

dwelling ['dwelɪŋ] Behausung OT 4

to **dye** [daɪ] färben OT 3

dynamic [daɪ'næmɪk] Dynamik OT 5

dyscalculia [ˌdɪskæl'kju:liə] Dyskalkulie OT 5

dyslexia [dɪs'leksiə] Legasthenie OT 5

dyslexic [dɪs'leksɪk] legasthenisch OT 5

dyspraxia [dɪs'præksiə] Dyspraxie OT 5

dystopian [dɪs'təʊpiən] dystopisch OT 5

E

each [i:tʃ] jede(r, -s); je OT 1

each other [ˌi:tʃ 'ʌðə] (sich) gegenseitig OT 3

eager ['i:gə] eifrig OT 2

eagle ['i:gl] Adler OT 2

bald eagle [bɔ:ld 'i:gəl] Weißkopfseeadler **WS 1**, 38

ear [ɪə] Ohr; Ähre OT 1

early ['ɜ:li] früh; zeitig; vorzeitig OT 1

to **earn** [ɜ:n] verdienen OT 3

earnest: in earnest [ɪn 'ɜ:nɪst] ernsthaft **WS 3**, 114

earring ['ɪərɪŋ] Ohrring OT 3

Earth [ɜ:θ] Erde OT 1

earthquake ['ɜ:θkweɪk] Erdbeben OT 2

east [i:st] Ost- OT 2

eastern ['i:stən] östlich OT 2

easy ['i:zi] einfach; leicht; sorgenfrei OT 1

to **eat** [i:t] essen; fressen OT 1

eater ['i:tə] Esser(in) **WS 1**, 36

to **echo** ['ekəʊ] nachhallen; nachklingen OT 5

eco-friendly [ˌi:kəʊ 'frendli] umweltfreundlich OT 3

ecological [ˌi:kə'lɒdʒɪkl] ökologisch OT 5

economic [ˌi:kə'nɒmɪk] wirtschaftlich OT 5

economist [ɪ'kɒnəmɪst] Wirtschaftswissenschaftler(in) **WS 4**, 144

economy [ɪ'kɒnəmi] Ökonomie; Wirtschaft OT 5

ecosystem ['i:kəʊsɪstəm] Ökosystem **WS 1**, 12

ecotourism ['i:kəʊtʊərɪzəm] Ökotourismus OT 3

edge [edʒ] Rand OT 3

edible ['edəbl] essbar **WS 4**, 142

edit ['edɪt] Überarbeitung; Schnitt OT 4

to **edit** ['edɪt] bearbeiten OT 4

editor ['edɪtə] Redakteur(in); Herausgeber(in) OT 2

to **educate** ['edʒukeɪt] erziehen; unterrichten **WS 2**, 57

education [ˌedjʊ'keɪʃən] Ausbildung OT 3

educational [ˌedʒu'keɪʃənl] Bildungs- OT 4

eel [i:l] Aal **WS 1**, 12

effect [ɪ'fekt] Wirkung OT 3

special effects [ˌspeʃlɪ'fekts] Spezialeffekte OT 2

effective [ɪ'fektɪv] wirksam OT 3

efficient [ɪ'fɪʃnt] effizient; wirksam OT 5

efficiently [ɪ'fɪʃntli] effizient OT 3

effort ['efət] Anstrengung; Mühe OT 3

egg [eg] Ei OT 1

eight [eɪt] acht OT 1

eighteen [ˌeɪ'ti:n] achtzehn OT 1

eighty ['eɪti] achtzig OT 1

either ['aɪðə] auch nicht OT 2

to **elaborate** [ɪ'læbərət] weiter ausführen **WS 3**, 122

elbow ['elbəʊ] Ellbogen OT 1

elder ['eldə] Älteste(r) OT 4

elderly ['eldəli] älter OT 4

to **elect** [ɪ'lekt] wählen; auswählen OT 4

election [ɪ'lekʃn] Wahl OT 3

elective [ɪ'lektɪv] Auswahlfach OT 4

elector [ɪ'lektə] Wahlmann OT 4

electoral [ɪ'lektərəl] Wahl- OT 4

electorate [ɪ'lektərət] Wählerschaft **WS 1**, 30

electric [ɪ'lektrɪk] elektrisch; spannungsgeladen OT 1

electrical [ɪ'lektrɪkl] elektrisch; elektronisch OT 5

electrician [ɪˌlek'trɪʃn] Elektriker(in) OT 5

electricity [ɪˌlek'trɪsəti] Strom OT 2

to **electrify** [ɪ'lektrɪfaɪ] elektrisieren **WS 2**, 69

electronic [ɪˌlek'trɒnɪk] elektronisch OT 2

element ['elɪmənt] Element OT 4

elementary school [ˌelɪ'mentri sku:l] Grundschule OT 2

elephant ['elɪfənt] Elefant OT 1

to **elevate** ['elɪveɪt] anheben; nach vorne bringen **WS 2**, 68

eleven [ɪ'levn] elf OT 1

eligible [ˈelɪdʒəbl] berechtigt **WS 1**, 32

to **eliminate** [ɪˈlɪmɪneɪt] beseitigen OT 3

elite [ɪˈliːt] Elite; Oberschicht **WS 3**, 100

else [els] sonst noch; andere(r, -s) OT 1

elsewhere [ˌelsˈweə] woanders **WS 3**, 117

emaciated [ɪˈmeɪsieɪtɪd] ausgemergelt OT 3

email [ˈiːmeɪl] Email OT 3

to **email** [ˈiːmeɪl] emailen OT 3

to **emancipate** [ɪˈmænsɪpeɪt] (sich) emanzipieren; befreien **WS 3**, 114

emancipation [ɪˌmænsɪˈpeɪʃn] Emanzipation **WS 2**, 57

to **embark** [ɪmˈbɑːk] beginnen **WS 2**, 75

embarrassing [ɪmˈbærəsɪŋ] peinlich OT 2

to **embed** [ɪmˈbed] einbetten; verankern **WS 1**, 12

ember [ˈembər] glühende Kohle OT 5

to **embrace** [ɪmˈbreɪs] umarmen; akzeptieren **WS 2**, 69

to **emerge** [iˈmɜːdʒ] ans Licht kommen OT 3

emergency [iˈmɜːdʒənsi] Notfall; Not... OT 1

to **emigrate** [ˈemɪgreɪt] auswandern OT 4

emission [ɪˈmɪʃn] Ausstoß; Emission OT 4

emoji [ɪˈməʊdʒi] Emoji OT 2

emotion [ɪˈməʊʃn] Emotion; Gefühl OT 5

emotional [ɪˈməʊʃənl] emotional OT 4

emotive [ɪˈməʊtɪv] emotional; gefühlvoll **WS 1**, 24

empathetic [ˌempəˈθetɪk] einfühlsam **WS 3**, 111

empathy [ˈempəθi] Empathie **WS 1**, 35

emperor [ˈempərə] Kaiser OT 2

emphasis (on) [ˈemfəsɪs] Betonung (auf) OT 5

to **emphasize** [ˈemfəsaɪz] betonen OT 4

emphatic [ɪmˈfætɪk] emphatisch OT 5

empire [ˈempaɪə] Reich OT 2

to **employ** [ɪmˈplɔɪ] beschäftigen OT 4

employee [ɪmˈplɔɪiː] Angestellte(r) OT 5

employer [ɪmˈplɔɪə] Arbeitgeber(in) OT 3

employment [ɪmˈplɔɪmənt] Beschäftigung; Arbeit OT 4

to **empower** [ɪmˈpaʊə] stärken; ermächtigen OT 5

empty [ˈempti] leer OT 1

to **empty out** [ˌemptiˈaʊt] ausleeren; herausfließen OT 3

to **enable** [ɪˈneɪbl] ermöglichen OT 4

to **encounter** [ɪnˈkaʊntə] begegnen OT 3

to **encourage** [ɪnˈkʌrɪdʒ] ermutigen OT 4

to **encroach** [ɪnˈkrəʊtʃ] eingreifen; vordringen **WS 3**, 112

encyclopedia [ɪnˌsaɪkləˈpiːdiə] Enzyklopädie; Lexikon OT 4

end [end] Ende OT 1

to **end** [end] enden; beenden OT 1

to **endanger** [ɪnˈdeɪndʒər] gefährden OT 5

endangered [ɪnˈdeɪndʒəd] gefährdet OT 2

endeavour [ɪnˈdəvə] Bemühen; Anstrengung **WS 1**, 13

ending [ˈendɪŋ] Ende; Schluss; Endung OT 1

endless [ˈendləs] endlos; unendlich OT 4

end zone [ˈend zəʊn] Endzone OT 3

enemy [ˈenəmi] Feind(in) OT 3

energetic [ˌenəˈdʒetɪk] aktiv OT 2

energy [ˈenədʒi] Energie OT 2

to **enforce** [ɪnˈfɔːs] durchsetzen OT 4

enforcement [ɪnˈfɔːsmənt] Vollstreckung OT 5

to **engage** [ɪnˈgeɪdʒ] fesseln; engagieren OT 5

to **engage with** [ɪnˈgeɪdʒ wɪð] sich befassen mit OT 4

engagement [ɪnˈgeɪdʒmənt] Engagement; Einsatz OT 4

engine [ˈendʒɪn] Motor; Lokomotive OT 2

engineer [ˌendʒɪˈnɪə] Ingenieur(in); Lokführer(in) OT 2

engineering [ˌendʒɪˈnɪərɪŋ] Ingenieurwesen OT 2

English [ˈɪŋglɪʃ] englisch OT 1

to **engrave** [ɪnˈgreɪv] gravieren; eingravieren OT 4

to **enhance** [ɪnˈhɑːns] verbessern OT 4

enigmatic [ˌenɪgˈmætɪk] geheimnisvoll; rätselhaft **WS 2**, 82

to **enjoy** [ɪnˈdʒɔɪ] genießen; sich schmecken lassen OT 1

enjoyable [ɪnˈdʒɔɪəbl] angenehm OT 2

enormous [ɪˈnɔːməs] riesig; gewaltig; ungeheuer OT 1

enough [ɪˈnʌf] genug; genügend OT 1

enraged [ɪnˈreɪdʒd] wütend **WS 2**, 59

to **enrich** [ɪnˈrɪtʃ] verbessern; bereichern OT 4

enrichment [ɪnˈrɪtʃmənt] Bereicherung **WS 3**, 114

to **enroll** [ɪnˈrəʊl] (sich) anmelden **WS 3**, 105

to **enslave** [ɪnˈsleɪv] versklaven **WS 2**, 54

to **ensure** [ɪnˈʃʊə] sicherstellen OT 4

to **entail** [ɪnˈteɪl] beinhalten OT 4

to **enter** [ˈentə] eintreten; eintragen OT 2

enterprise [ˈentəpraɪz] Unternehmen OT 5

to **entertain** [ˌentəˈteɪn] unterhalten OT 4

entertainment [ˌentəˈteɪnmənt] Unterhaltung OT 2

enthusiasm [ɪnˈθjuːziæzəm] Enthusiasmus **WS 1**, 32

enthusiast [ɪnˈθjuːziæst] Liebhaber(in) **WS 3**, 101

enthusiastic [ɪnˌθjuːziˈæstɪk] begeistert OT 3

to **entice** [ɪnˈtaɪs] locken; ködern **WS 3**, 114

entire [ɪnˈtaɪə] ganze(r, -s) OT 3

entitled [ɪnˈtaɪtld] berechtigt **WS 2**, 65

entity [ˈentəti] Einheit **WS 2**, 54

entrance [ˈentrəns] Eingang; Eintreten; Aufnahme OT 1

entrance hall [ˈentrəns ˌhɔːl] Eingangsbereich; Eingangshalle OT 1

entrepreneur [ˌɒntrəprəˈnɜː] Unternehmer(in) OT 5

entrepreneurship [ˌɒntrəprəˈnɜːʃɪp] Unternehmertum OT 4

entry [ˈentri] Eintrag; Einsendung OT 2

to **entwine** [ɪnˈtwaɪn] verflechten **WS 1**, 17

envelope [ˈenvələʊp] Briefumschlag OT 2

enviable [ˈenviəbl] beneidenswert **WS 3**, 112

environment [ɪnˈvaɪrənmənt] Umfeld; Umwelt OT 2

environmental [ɪnˌvaɪrənˈmentl] Umwelt-; ökologisch OT 4

environmentally [ɪnˌvaɪrənˈmentəli] umwelt... OT 3

environmentalist [ɪnˌvaɪrənˈmentəlɪst] Umweltschützer(in) OT 3

to **envy** [ˈenvi] beneiden OT 5

epidemic [ˌepɪˈdemɪk] epidemisch OT 5

epiphany [ɪˈpɪfəni] Erleuchtung; Offenbarung; Eingebung **WS 2**, 76

episode [ˈepɪsəʊd] Episode **WS 3**, 95

equal [ˈiːkwəl] gleich; gleichberechtigt OT 4

equality [ɪˈkwɒləti] Gleichberechtigung OT 5

equator [ɪˈkweɪtər] Äquator OT 5

to **equip** [ɪˈkwɪp] ausrüsten **WS 1**, 25

equipment [ɪˈkwɪpmənt] Ausrüstung OT 2

equivalent (to) [ɪˈkwɪvələnt] entsprechend OT 5

to **erase** [ɪˈreɪz] auslöschen **WS 1**, 12

to **erect** [ɪˈrekt] errichten OT 4

errand [ˈerənd] Besorgung OT 4

erratic [ɪˈrætɪk] erratisch; sprunghaft OT 5

to **erupt** [ɪˈrʌpt] ausbrechen OT 2

escalator [ˈeskəleɪtə] Rolltreppe OT 1

to **escape** [ɪˈskeɪp] entkommen OT 2

e-scooter [ˈiːskuːtə] E-Roller OT 5

to **escort** [ˈeskɔːt] begleiten OT 4

especially [ɪˈspeʃəli] besonders OT 2

essay [ˈeseɪ] Aufsatz OT 3

essence [ˈesns] Wesen; Wesentliche **WS 1**, 13

in **essence** [ɪn ˈesns] im Wesentlichen OT 4

essential [ɪˈsenʃl] wichtig; wesentlich OT 4

to **establish** [ɪˈstæblɪʃ] gründen OT 5

establishment [ɪˈstæblɪʃmənt] Einrichtung; Gesellschaft **WS 2**, 63

estate [ɪˈsteɪt] Anwesen **WS 1**, 15

to **estimate** [ˈestɪmeɪt] schätzen OT 4

ETA (estimated time of arrival) [ˌiː tiː ˈeɪ] geschätzte Ankunftszeit OT 2

etc. [ˌet ˈsetərə] usw.; und so weiter OT 3

eternal [ɪˈtɜːnl] ewig **WS 3**, 104

ethic [ˈeθɪk] Ethik **WS 3**, 122

ethical [ˈeθɪkl] ethisch; moralisch vertretbar OT 3

ethnic [ˈeθnɪk] ethnisch OT 5

ethnicity [eθˈnɪsəti] Ethnizität **WS 3**, 105

etiquette [ˈetɪkət] Etikette **WS 3**, 101

eureka moment [juˈriːkə ˈməʊmənt] Heureka-Erlebnis OT 4

European [ˌjʊərəˈpiːən] Europäer(in) OT 3

to **evacuate** [ɪˈvækjueɪt] verlassen; evakuieren OT 4

evacuation [ɪˌvækjuˈeɪʃn] Evakuierung OT 4

to **evaluate** [ɪˈvæljueɪt] bewerten OT 4

evaluation [ɪˌvæljuˈeɪʃn] Bewertung OT 5

even [ˈiːvn] sogar; selbst OT 1

evening [ˈiːvnɪŋ] Abend OT 1

event [ɪˈvent] Ereignis; Veranstaltung; Disziplin OT 1

eventually [ɪˈventʃuəli] schließlich OT 3

ever [ˈevə] je; jemals OT 1

everlasting [ˌevəˈlɑːstɪŋ] andauernd **WS 4**, 146

every [ˈevri] jede(r, -s) OT 1

everybody [ˈevribɒdi] jeder; alle; jedermann OT 1

everyday [ˈevrideɪ] alltäglich OT 3

everyone [ˈevriwʌn] jeder; alle; jedermann OT 1

everything [ˈevriθɪŋ] alles OT 1

everywhere [ˈevriweə] überall; überallhin OT 1

evidence [ˈevɪdəns] Nachweis; Beweis OT 4

evident [ˈevɪdənt] offensichtlich; offenkundig **WS 2**, 58

evil [ˈiːvl] Übel; Böse OT 5

evolution [ˌiːvəˈluːʃn] Evolution; Entwicklung OT 5

to **evolve** [ɪˈvɒlv] sich entwickeln OT 4

ewe [juː] Mutterschaf OT 2

exact [ɪgˈzækt] genau OT 2

exacting [ɪgˈzæktɪŋ] anspruchsvoll **WS 3**, 101

exaggerated [ɪgˈzædʒəreɪtɪd] übertrieben OT 5

exaggeration [ɪgˌzædʒəˈreɪʃn] Übertreibung OT 4

exam [ɪgˈzæm] Prüfung; Examen OT 1

to **examine** [ɪgˈzæmɪn] untersuchen OT 4

example [ɪgˈzɑːmpl] Beispiel OT 1

to **excavate** [ˈekskəveɪt] ausgraben OT 2

excavation [ˌekskəˈveɪʃn] Ausgrabung OT 2

to **excel** [ɪkˈsel] sich selbst übertreffen; sich hervortun OT 4

excellent [ˈeksələnt] ausgezeichnet OT 2

except [ɪkˈsept] außer OT 2

exception [ɪkˈsepʃn] Ausnahme OT 5

excerpt [ekˈsɜːpt] Ausschnitt; Auszug OT 4

excessive [ɪkˈsesɪv] übermäßig **WS 1**, 36

exchange [ɪksˈtʃeɪndʒ] Austausch; Wechseln; Wechsel OT 1

to **exchange** [ɪksˈtʃeɪndʒ] austauschen; wechseln OT 5

excited [ɪkˈsaɪtɪd] begeistert; aufgeregt OT 1

excitement [ɪkˈsaɪtmənt] Aufregung; Spannung **WS 1**, 29

exciting [ɪkˈsaɪtɪŋ] aufregend; spannend OT 1

to **exclaim** [ɪkˈskleɪm] rufen OT 3

to **exclude** [ɪkˈskluːd] ausschließen **WS 2**, 54

exclusion [ɪkˈskluːʒn] Ausschluss **WS 4**, 135

exclusionary [ɪkˈskluːʒənri] ausgrenzend **WS 2**, 66

exclusive [ɪkˈskluːsɪv] exklusiv **WS 2**, 71

excursion [ɪkˈskɜːʃn] Ausflug **WS 1**, 22

excuse [ɪkˈskjuːs] Entschuldigung OT 5

to **excuse** [ɪkˈskjuːz] entschuldigen OT 1

to **execute** [ˈeksɪkjuːt] hinrichten OT 3

executive [ɪgˈzekjətɪv] Exekutive; ausführend OT 4

exercise [ˈeksəsaɪz] körperliche Bewegung; Übung; Manöver OT 1

exercise book [ˈeksəsaɪz bʊk] Übungsheft; Schulheft; Heft OT 1

to **exert** [ɪgˈzɜːt] aufbieten **WS 3**, 105

exhausted [ɪgˈzɔːstɪd] erschöpft OT 2

exhaustive [ɪgˈzɔːstɪv] gründlich; vollständig **WS 3**, 114

to **exhibit** [ɪgˈzɪbɪt] ausstellen OT 2

exhibition [ˌeksɪˈbɪʃn] Ausstellung; Messe OT 1

exhibitor [ɪgˈzɪbɪtə] Aussteller(in) **WS 4**, 140

to **exist** [ɪgˈzɪst] existieren OT 3

existence [ɪgˈzɪstəns] Existenz OT 4

exit [ˈeksɪt] Ausgang; Abfahrt OT 2

exotic [ɪgˈzɒtɪk] exotisch **WS 1**, 12

to **expand** [ɪkˈspænd] wachsen; ausbauen OT 5

expansion [ɪkˈspænʃn] Ausdehnung; Expansion **WS 3**, 114

to **expect** [ɪkˈspekt] erwarten OT 2

expectation [ˌekspekˈteɪʃn] Erwartung OT 4

expedition [ˌekspəˈdɪʃn] Expedition OT 2

expense [ɪkˈspens] Kosten; Ausgabe OT 4

expensive [ɪkˈspensɪv] teuer OT 1

experience [ɪkˈspɪəriəns] Erfahrung OT 2

to **experience** [ɪkˈspɪəriəns] erfahren; erleben OT 5

experienced [ɪkˈspɪəriənst] erfahren OT 3

experiential [ɪkˌspɪəriˈenʃl] erfahrungsmäßig; auf Erfahrung beruhend OT 4

experiment [ɪkˈsperɪmənt] Experiment; Test; Versuch OT 2

to **experiment** [ɪkˈsperɪmənt]
experimentieren OT 4

expert [ˈekspɜːt] Experte(in) OT 3

expertise [ˌekspɜːˈtiːz] Expertise;
Erfahrung **WS 1**, 34

to **explain** [ɪkˈspleɪn] erklären OT 1

explanation [ˌekspləˈneɪʃn] Erklärung;
Erläuterung OT 1

explanatory [ɪkˈsplænətri] erklärend;
erläuternd **WS 4**, 138

to **explode** [ɪkˈspləʊd] explodieren OT 5

to **exploit** [ɪkˈsplɔɪt] ausbeuten OT 3

exploitation [ˌeksplɔɪˈteɪʃn]
Ausbeutung; Nutzung **WS 2**, 68

exploration [ˌekspləˈreɪʃn] Exploration;
Erforschung OT 5

exploratory [ɪkˈsplɒrətri] exploratisch;
forschend **WS 3**, 122

to **explore** [ɪkˈsplɔː] erforschen;
erkunden; untersuchen OT 1

explorer [ɪkˈsplɔːrə] Forscher(in) OT 3

explosion [ɪkˈspləʊʒn] Explosion
WS 1, 43

exporter [ekˈspɔːtər] Exporteur(in) OT 5

to **expose** [ɪkˈspəʊz] entlarven;
aufdecken **WS 2**, 63

exposure [ɪkˈspəʊʒə] Sichtbarkeit OT 4

to **express** [ɪkˈspres] äußern; etw.
ausdrücken OT 4

expression [ɪkˈspreʃn] Ausdruck;
Äußerung; Gesichtsausdruck OT 1

exquisite [ɪkˈskwɪzɪt] ausgesucht;
exquisit **WS 1**, 25

extended [ɪkˈstendɪd] erweitert OT 5

extensive [ɪkˈstensɪv] umfangreich
WS 3, 106

extent [ɪkˈstent] Ausmaß OT 3

extinct [ɪkˈstɪŋkt] ausgestorben OT 2

extinction [ɪkˈstɪŋkʃn] Aussterben OT 4

extra [ˈekstrə] Extra...; besonders OT 1

extract [ɪkˈstrækt] Auszug OT 3

extreme [ɪkˈstriːm] Extrem OT 4

extreme [ɪkˈstriːm] extrem OT 4

extremely [ɪkˈstriːmli] extrem OT 3

eye [aɪ] Auge; Blick; Öhr OT 1

eyebrow [ˈaɪbraʊ] Augenbraue OT 5

eyelid [ˈaɪlɪd] Augenlid OT 2

eyepiece [ˈaɪpiːs] Okular OT 2

F

fabric [ˈfæbrɪk] Stoff **WS 2**, 82

fabulous [ˈfæbjələs] fabelhaft OT 2

façade [fəˈsɑːd] Fassade **WS 3**, 111

face [feɪs] Gesicht; Seite; Zifferblatt OT 1

to **make a face** [ˌmeɪk ə ˈfeɪs] eine
Grimasse schneiden OT 2

to **face** [feɪs] begegnen OT 4

facial [ˈfeɪʃl] Gesichts- OT 4

facility [fəˈsɪləti] Anlage OT 3

fact [fækt] Tatsache; Fakt OT 1

factor [ˈfæktə] Faktor OT 3

factory [ˈfæktri] Fabrik OT 2

factual [ˈfæktʃuəl] sachlich OT 4

to **fail** [feɪl] scheitern OT 4

failure [ˈfeɪljə] Misserfolg OT 4

faint [feɪnt] schwindlig OT 2

to **faint** [feɪnt] ohnmächtig werden
OT 2

fair [feə] Jahrmarkt OT 2

fair [feə] gerecht; schön; blond OT 1

fairground [ˈfeəgraʊnd] Jahrmarkt OT 2

fairy tale [ˈfeəri teɪl] Märchen OT 1

faith [feɪθ] Vertrauen; Glaube OT 3

fake [feɪk] falsch; fake **WS 1**, 18

fall [fɔːl] Herbst; Wasserfall OT 1

to **fall** [fɔːl] fallen; stürzen; hinfallen OT 1

to **fall over** [fɔːl ˈəʊvə] hinfallen;
umfallen OT 2

to **fall in love** [fɔːl ɪn lʌv] sich
verlieben OT 5

false [fɔːls] falsch; erfunden; gefälscht
OT 1

fame [feɪm] Ruhm; Berühmtheit
WS 2, 74

familiar [fəˈmɪliə] vertraut; bekannt
OT 2

familiarity [fəˌmɪliˈærəti] Vertrautheit
OT 4

family [ˈfæməli] Familie OT 1

famine [ˈfæmɪn] Hungersnot OT 2

famous [ˈfeɪməs] berühmt; bekannt OT 1

fan [fæn] Fan; Ventilator; Fächer OT 1

fanatic [fəˈnætɪk] Fanatiker(in) OT 5

fanciful [ˈfænsɪfl] fantastisch **WS 3**, 101

fancy [ˈfænsi] ausgefallen **WS 3**, 105

fantastic [fænˈtæstɪk] fantastisch; toll;
riesig OT 1

fantasy [ˈfæntəsi] Fantasy; Fantasie OT 2

FAQ [ˌefeɪˈkjuː] FAQ; häufig gestellte
Fragen OT 3

far [fɑː] weit OT 1

faraway [ˈfɑːrəweɪ] fern OT 5

fare [feə] Fahrgeld **WS 2**, 59

farewell [ˌfeəˈwel] Lebe wohl! OT 2

farm [fɑːm] Bauernhof OT 1

farmer [ˈfɑːmə] Bauer/Bäuerin;
Hühnerzüchter OT 2

farmhouse [ˈfɑːmhaʊs] Bauernhaus
OT 2

farming [ˈfɑːmɪŋ] Landwirtschaft OT 2

farmland [ˈfɑːmlænd] Ackerland OT 4

farmyard [ˈfɑːmjɑːd] Hof OT 2

far-off [ˈfɑː ɒf] fern OT 2

to **fascinate** [ˈfæsɪneɪt] faszinieren OT 4

fascinating [ˈfæsɪneɪtɪŋ] faszinierend
OT 2

fascination [ˌfæsɪˈneɪʃn] Faszination
OT 3

fashion [ˈfæʃn] Trend; Mode; Art(und
Weise) OT 1

to **go out of fashion** [gəʊ aʊt əv ˈfæʃn]
aus der Mode kommen **WS 3**, 100

fashionable [ˈfæʃnəbl] modisch OT 2

fast [fɑːst] schnell; fest OT 1

to **fasten** [ˈfɑːsn] festmachen **WS 4**, 141

fat [fæt] Fett OT 2

fatal [ˈfeɪtl] tödlich **WS 2**, 58

father [ˈfɑːðə] Vater OT 1

fatigue [fəˈtiːg] Müdigkeit **WS 4**, 140

fatty [ˈfæti] fett **WS 1**, 36

fault [fɔːlt] Schuld; Fehler OT 2

to **fault** [fɔːlt] bemängeln OT 2

favour: in favour [ɪn ˈfeɪvə] für;
zugunsten OT 4

favoured [ˈfeɪvəd] favorisiert;
bevorzugt OT 4

favourite [ˈfeɪvərɪt] Lieblings... OT 1

fear [fɪə] Angst; Furcht OT 3

to **fear** [fɪər] befürchten OT 5

fearless [ˈfɪələs] furchtlos **WS 1**, 13

feast [fiːst] Fest OT 3

feat [fiːt] Meisterleistung OT 2

feather [ˈfeðə] Feder OT 2

feature [ˈfiːtʃə] Merkmal, Beitrag OT 2

to **feature** [ˈfiːtʃə] haben; präsentieren
OT 2

February [ˈfebruəri] Februar OT 1

federal [ˈfedərəl] Bundes... OT 4

fee [fiː] Gebühr OT 3

to **feed** [fiːd] füttern OT 2

feedback [ˈfiːdbæk] Feedback OT 2

feeding [ˈfiːdɪŋ] Füttern OT 2

to **feel** [fiːl] (sich) fühlen; empfinden;
spüren; fühlen; anfassen OT 1

feeling [ˈfiːlɪŋ] Gefühl OT 2

fell [fel] (in Nordengland) Berg OT 2

fellow [ˈfeləʊ] Gefährte; Gefährtin
WS 2, 60

fellow minister [ˌfeləʊ ˈmɪnɪstə]
Amtsbruder; Amtsschwester **WS 2**, 58

female [ˈfiːmeɪl] weiblich OT 2

feminism [ˈfemənɪzəm] Feminismus
WS 3, 110

fence [fens] Zaun OT 1

feral [ˈferəl] wild OT 5

fertile [ˈfɜːtaɪl] fruchtbar **WS 1**, 34

fertilizer [ˈfɜːtəlaɪzə] Dünger OT 3

fervour [ˈfɜːrvə] Eifer; Leidenschaft **WS 2**, 58

festival [ˈfestɪvl] Festival; Fest OT 1

festival-goer [ˈfestɪvl ˈɡəʊə] Festivalbesucher(in) OT 4

few [fjuː] wenige OT 1

fictional [ˈfɪkʃənl] erfunden OT 2

fiddle [ˈfɪdl] Geige; Fiedel **WS 1**, 26

field [fiːld] Feld; Acker; Platz OT 1

field trip [ˈfiːld trɪp] Schulausflug OT 2

fiercely [ˈfɪəsli] heftig; verbissen **WS 1**, 15

fifteen [ˌfɪfˈtiːn] fünfzehn OT 1

fifty [ˈfɪfti] fünfzig OT 1

fight [faɪt] Kampf; Schlägerei; Streit OT 1

to **fight** [faɪt] kämpfen OT 1

fighter [ˈfaɪtə] Kämpfer(in) OT 2

figure [ˈfɪɡə] Zahl; Figur OT 3

figure of speech [ˌfɪɡə əv ˈspiːtʃ] rhetorisches Stilmittel; rhetorische Figur **WS 2**, 76

file [faɪl] Datei OT 2

file card [ˈfaɪl ˌkɑːd] Karteikarte OT 2

to **fill** [fɪl] füllen; füllen; ausfüllen OT 1

film [fɪlm] Film; Ausschnitte; Kino OT 1

to **film** [fɪlm] drehen; filmen OT 5

filmmaker [ˈfɪlm meɪkə] Filmemacher(in) OT 4

filter [ˈfɪltə] Filter OT 4

to **filter** [ˈfɪltə] filtern **WS 2**, 72

filthy [ˈfɪlθi] dreckig **WS 1**, 36

final [ˈfaɪnl] endgültig; letzte(r, -s) OT 2

finalist [ˈfaɪnəlɪst] Finalist(in) OT 5

to **finalize** [ˈfaɪnəlaɪz] fertigstellen; abschließen OT 4

finally [ˈfaɪnəli] schließlich; endlich; zum Schluss OT 1

to **finance** [ˈfaɪnæns] finanzieren OT 4

financial [faɪˈnænʃl] finanziell OT 4

to **find** [faɪnd] finden; feststellen OT 1

to **find out** [faɪnd aʊt] herausfinden OT 2

finding [ˈfaɪndɪŋ] Ergebnis; Erkenntnis OT 4

fine [faɪn] gut; prima OT 1

finger [ˈfɪŋɡə] Finger OT 1

fingernail [ˈfɪŋɡəneɪl] Fingernagel OT 2

fingerprint [ˈfɪŋɡəprɪnt] Fingerabdruck **WS 2**, 82

fingertip [ˈfɪŋɡətɪp] Fingerspitze **WS 3**, 97

finish [ˈfɪnɪʃ] Ende; Ziel **WS 2**, 76

to **finish** [ˈfɪnɪʃ] abschließen; aufhören OT 1

fire [faɪə] Feuer OT 2

to **fire** [faɪə] schießen; feuern; entlassen OT 4

fire-builder [ˈfaɪə bɪldə] Feuermacher(in) OT 2

fire escape [ˈfaɪər ɪskeɪp] Fluchtweg OT 5

fire extinguisher [ˈfaɪər ɪkstɪŋɡwɪʃə] Feuerlöscher OT 5

firefighter [ˈfaɪəfaɪtə] Feuerwehrmann; Feuerwehrfrau OT 2

firefighting [ˈfaɪəfaɪtɪŋ] Brandbekämpfung OT 2

fireplace [ˈfaɪəpleɪs] Kamin OT 1

firewood [ˈfaɪəwʊd] Brennholz OT 4

fireworks [ˈfaɪəwɜːks] Feuerwerk OT 3

firm [fɜːm] fest **WS 2**, 65

firmly [ˈfɜːmli] fest OT 4

first [fɜːst] erste(r, -s); erster Gang; Eins OT 1

at first [ət ˈfɜːst] zuerst; anfangs OT 2

for the first time [fɔː ðə ˈfɜːst taɪm] zum ersten Mal OT 2

firstly [ˈfɜːstli] zuerst OT 3

fish [fɪʃ] Fisch OT 1

fishbone [ˈfɪʃbəʊn] Gräte **WS 4**, 142

fisherman [ˈfɪʃəmən] Fischer OT 2

fish finger [ˈfɪʃ ˌfɪŋɡə] Fischstäbchen OT 1

fishing [ˈfɪʃɪŋ] Fischerei OT 3

fit [fɪt] in Form; geeignet OT 2

to **keep fit** [kiːp ˈfɪt] sich fit halten OT 2

fitness [ˈfɪtnəs] Fitness OT 5

fitting [ˈfɪtɪŋ] passend **WS 1**, 17

five [faɪv] fünf OT 1

to **fix** [fɪks] korrigieren OT 2

fizzy [ˈfɪzi] kohlensäurehaltig OT 2

flag [flæɡ] Fahne OT 5

flagship [ˈflæɡʃɪp] Flaggschiff OT 3

flamingo [fləˈmɪŋɡəʊ] Flamingo OT 2

flared [fleəd] ausgestellt **WS 3**, 102

flash [flæʃ] Blitz OT 4

flashlight [ˈflæʃlaɪt] Taschenlampe OT 2

flat [flæt] Wohnung; Apartment; Reifenpanne OT 1

to **flaunt** [flɔːnt] zur Schau stellen **WS 3**, 101

flea [fliː] Floh OT 5

fleet [fliːt] Flotte OT 3

flexibility [ˌfleksəˈbɪləti] Flexibilität; Beweglichkeit **WS 1**, 37

flexible [ˈfleksəbl] flexibel OT 5

to **flick** [flɪk] (um)blättern **WS 3**, 101

flight [flaɪt] Flug; Flucht OT 1

to **flip** [flɪp] umdrehen OT 5

to **float** [fləʊt] treiben; schweben OT 3

to **flock** [flɒk] strömen **WS 1**, 43

flood [flʌd] Hochwasser; Flut OT 2

flooding [ˈflʌdɪŋ] Fluten; Flut OT 5

floor [flɔː] Boden; Stock(werk) OT 1

flora [ˈflɔːrə] Flora OT 4

flour [ˈflaʊə] Mehl OT 2

to **flourish** [ˈflʌrɪʃ] (auf)blühen; gedeihen **WS 1**, 12

flow [fləʊ] Fluss; Strom **WS 3**, 122

flower [ˈflaʊə] Blume OT 1

flowing [ˈfləʊɪŋ] fließend OT 5

fluent [ˈfluːənt] fließend OT 3

fluently [ˈfluːəntli] fließend OT 3

fluffy [ˈflʌfi] flauschig OT 2

fluid [ˈfluːɪd] fließend **WS 3**, 110

flute [fluːt] Querflöte OT 1

fluted [ˈfluːtɪd] geriffelt **WS 2**, 55

to **fly** [flaɪ] fliegen; steigen lassen; hissen OT 1

flyer [ˈflaɪə] Flyer OT 4

to **focus** [ˈfəʊkəs] fokusieren OT 2

to **focus on** [ˈfəʊkəs ɒn] sich konzentrieren OT 5

fog [fɒɡ] Nebel **WS 1**, 16

foggy [ˈfɒɡi] nebelig OT 3

foil [fɔɪl] Folie OT 2

to **fold** [fəʊld] falten; zusammenlegen **WS 2**, 69

folk [fəʊk] Volks... OT 2

folklore [ˈfəʊklɔːr] Folklore OT 5

folks [fəʊks] Leute OT 2

to **follow** [ˈfɒləʊ] folgen OT 2

follower [ˈfɒləʊə] Anhänger(in) OT 3

food [fuːd] Nahrungsmittel; Essen OT 1

food bank [ˈfuːd bæŋk] Essensausgabe; Lebensmittelsammelstelle OT 5

food poisoning [ˈfuːd pɔɪzənɪŋ] Lebensmittelvergiftung OT 2

food supplement [ˈfuːd ˌsʌplɪmənt] Nahrungsergänzungsmittel OT 5

fool [fuːl] Idiot(in) **WS 3**, 105

foolishly [ˈfuːlɪʃli] unvernünftig OT 5

foot [fʊt] Fuß; Fußende; Fuß (Längenmaß: 30,48 cm) OT 1

footage [ˈfʊtɪdʒ] Filmmaterial; Filmaufnahmen OT 4

football [ˈfʊtbɔːl] Fußball; Football OT 1

footpath [ˈfʊtpɑːθ] Fußweg; Pfad **WS 1**, 12

footprint [ˈfʊtprɪnt] Fußabdruck OT 2

footstep [ˈfʊtstep] Fußstapfen OT 5

for ['fə] für; dafür; wegen OT 1
to force [fɔːs] zwingen OT 5
force [fɔːs] Wasserfall; Kraft OT 2
forecast ['fɔːkɑːst] Prognose OT 2
forefather ['fɔːfɑːðə] Ahne; Urvater OT 4
forefront ['fɔːfrʌnt] Spitze WS 1, 32
foreground ['fɔːɡraʊnd] Vordergrund OT 4
foreign ['fɒrən] ausländisch; fremd; Außen… OT 1
to foreshadow [fɔːˈʃædəʊ] andeuten WS 2, 60
forest ['fɒrɪst] Wald OT 1
forested ['fɒrɪstɪd] bewaldet OT 4
forever [fərˈevə] für immer OT 2
to forge [fɔːdʒ] schmieden WS 1, 18
to forget [fəˈɡet] vergessen OT 1
to forgive [fəˈɡɪv] vergeben OT 2
forklift [ˌfɔːklɪft] Gabelstapler OT 5
form [fɔːm] Form; Formular; Verfassung OT 1
to form [fɔːm] gründen; bilden OT 4
formal ['fɔːml] förmlich; formell OT 3
format ['fɔːmæt] Format OT 5
formation [fɔːˈmeɪʃn] Formation OT 5
former ['fɔːmə] frühere(r) OT 5
formidable [fəˈmɪdəbl] beachtlich; gewaltig WS 1, 12
formula ['fɔːmjələ] Formel OT 2
fort [fɔːt] Festung OT 2
forthcoming [ˌfɔːθˈkʌmɪŋ] bevorstehend WS 1, 29
fortification [ˌfɔːtɪfɪˈkeɪʃn] Festung WS 1, 18
fortified ['fɔːtɪfaɪd] befestigt WS 1, 25
fortress ['fɔːtrəs] Festung WS 1, 25
fortunate ['fɔːtʃənət] glücklich OT 3
fortune ['fɔːtʃuːn] Glück; Reichtum OT 3
forty ['fɔːti] vierzig OT 1
forum ['fɔːrəm] Forum OT 2
forwards ['fɔːwədz] vorwärts OT 2
fossil ['fɒsl] fossil OT 3
foul [faʊl] Foul OT 3
to foul [faʊl] foulen OT 3
to foul [faʊl] verschmutzen; verseuchen OT 5
to found [faʊnd] gründen OT 4
foundation [faʊnˈdeɪʃn] Grundlage; Fundament OT 4
to founder ['faʊndə] sinken OT 3
fountain ['faʊntən] Springbrunnen; Fontäne; Quelle OT 1
four [fɔː] vier OT 1

fourteen [ˌfɔːˈtiːn] vierzehn OT 1
fox [fɒks] Fuchs OT 1
to frack [fræk] fracken OT 5
fragment ['fræɡmənt] Scherbe WS 1, 35
frame [freɪm] Rahmen OT 3
framework ['freɪmwɜːk] Rahmen OT 4
frankly ['fræŋkli] offen gesagt; ehrlich gesagt OT 4
frantic ['fræntɪk] hektisch; aufgeregt OT 3
freckles ['frekelz] Sommersprossen OT 3
free [friː] frei; kostenlos OT 1
freedom ['friːdəm] Freiheit OT 3
freelance ['friːlɑːns] freiberuflich OT 5
freelancer ['friːlɑːnsə] Freiberufler(in) OT 5
freezer ['friːzə] Gefrierschrank OT 3
freezing ['friːzɪŋ] kalt OT 2
freight [freɪt] Fracht OT 2
French [frentʃ] französisch OT 1
French fries [ˌfrentʃˈfraɪz] Pommes frites OT 2
frequency ['friːkwənsi] Häufigkeit OT 3
frequent ['friːkwənt] häufig OT 5
frequently ['friːkwəntli] häufig OT 3
fresh [freʃ] frisch OT 3
freshman ['freʃmən] Student im ersten Jahr; Studienanfänger(in) OT 4
freshwater ['freʃwɔːtə] Süßwasser WS 1, 13
Friday ['fraɪdeɪ] Freitag OT 1
fridge [frɪdʒ] Kühlschrank OT 1
fried [fraɪd] frittiert OT 2
friend [frend] Freund(in); Bekannte(r); Förderer(-in) OT 1
friendliness ['frendlinəs] Freundlichkeit OT 4
friendly ['frendli] freundlich; freundschaftlich OT 1
frightened ['fraɪtnd] verängstigt OT 1
frightening ['fraɪtnɪŋ] erschreckend OT 1
fringed [frɪndʒd] fransig WS 3, 94
frizzy ['frɪzi] kraus OT 3
from [frəm] von; aus; von…(entfernt) OT 1
front [frʌnt] Vorderseite; Bauch; Front OT 1
to frown [fraʊn] die Stirn runzeln OT 3
frozen ['frəʊzn] gefroren OT 4
fruit [fruːt] Obst; Frucht; Früchte OT 1
frustrated [frʌˈstreɪtɪd] frustriert OT 4
fuel ['fjuːəl] Brennstoff OT 2

full [fʊl] voll; komplett; füllig OT 1
full-time [ˌfʊlˈtaɪm] ganztags OT 5
fun [fʌn] Spaß OT 1
function ['fʌŋkʃn] Funktion OT 4
fund [fʌnd] Geldmittel OT 4
fundamental [ˌfʌndəˈmentəl] grundsätzlich WS 2, 62
fundraiser ['fʌndreɪzə] Wohltätigkeitsveranstaltung OT 2
fundraising ['fʌndreɪzɪŋ] Spendensammlung OT 2
funeral ['fjuːnərəl] Beerdigung OT 4
fungus ['fʌŋɡəs] Pilz WS 4, 140
funny ['fʌni] lustig; merkwürdig OT 1
fur ['fɜː] Fell OT 4
fur-lined ['fɜː laɪnd] mit Fell gefüttert OT 4
furious ['fjʊəriəs] wütend WS 3, 113
furniture ['fɜːnɪtʃə] Möbel OT 1
further ['fɜːðə] weiter OT 4
    furthest ['fɜːðɪst] am weitesten entfernt OT 2
to further ['fɜːrðə] voranbringen; fördern WS 2, 62
future ['fjuːtʃə] Zukunft OT 2
fuzz [fʌz] Fussel OT 4

G
gable ['ɡeɪbl] Giebel WS 1, 35
gadget ['ɡædʒɪt] Gerät; technische Spielerei OT 4
to gain [ɡeɪn] bekommen; erreichen OT 4
gallant ['ɡælənt] furchtlos; höflich WS 1, 13
gallery ['ɡæləri] Galerie; Empore; Gang OT 1
galley ['ɡæli] Kombüse OT 3
gallon ['ɡælən] Gallone OT 3
game [ɡeɪm] Spiel; Wild OT 1
gamer ['ɡeɪmə] Gamer(in); Spieler(in) OT 4
gang [ɡæŋ] Bande; Gang OT 5
gap [ɡæp] Lücke; Pause; Unterbrechung OT 1
garage ['ɡærɑːʒ] Garage; Werkstatt OT 4
garbage ['ɡɑːbɪdʒ] Abfall OT 2
garden ['ɡɑːdn] Garten OT 1
gardener ['ɡɑːdnə] Gärtner(in) OT 4
gardening ['ɡɑːdnɪŋ] Gartenarbeit OT 1
garrison ['ɡærɪsn] Garnison; Standort WS 1, 25
gas [ɡæs] Gas OT 4
gas cooker ['ɡæs kʊkə] Gaskocher OT 3
gate [ɡeɪt] Tor; Pforte; Flugsteig OT 1

gateway ['geɪtweɪ] Zugang; Gateway OT 5

to **gather** ['gæðə] sammeln OT 4

gay [geɪ] schwul; früher: fröhlich OT 5

to **gaze** [geɪz] blicken OT 5

GCSE (General Certificate of Secondary Education) [,dʒi: si: es 'i:] mittlerer Schulabschluss OT 4

gear [gɪər] Ausrüstung **WS 1**, 12

geared: to be geared towards [bi gɪəd tə'wɔːdz] auf etw. ausgerichtet sein OT 5

geek [giːk] Geek; Spezialist(in) OT 5

gel [dʒel] Gel OT 2

gelateria [dʒelə'tɪəriə] italienisches Eiscafé OT 5

gelato ['dʒelɑːtəʊ] italienische Eiscreme OT 5

gem [dʒem] Edelstein; Prachtstück **WS 3**, 104

gender ['dʒendə] Geschlecht; Gender OT 4

gendered ['dʒendəd] geschlechtsspezifisch OT 5

genderless ['dʒendələs] geschlechtslos OT 5

gender-neutral [,dʒendə 'njuːtrəl] geschlechtsneutral OT 5

general ['dʒenrəl] allgemein; generell OT 4

   generally ['dʒenrəli] im Allgemeinen; hauptsächlich OT 4

   general manager ['dʒenrəl 'mænɪdʒər] Geschäftsführer(in) OT 3

generalization [,dʒenrəlaɪ'zeɪʃn] Generalisierung OT 5

to **generate** ['dʒenəreɪt] erzeugen OT 4

generation [,dʒenə'reɪʃn] Generation OT 3

genetic [dʒə'netɪk] genetisch OT 5

genre ['ʒɒnrə] Genre OT 5

gentle ['dʒentl] sanft **WS 1**, 15

gently ['dʒentli] sachte OT 3

genuinely ['dʒenjuɪnli] echt OT 5

geocache [dʒiːəʊkæʃ] Geocache OT 2

geocaching ['dʒiːəʊkæʃɪŋ] Geocaching OT 2

geographical [,dʒiːə'græfɪkl] geografisch OT 4

geography [dʒi'ɒɡrəfi] Erdkunde; Geografie OT 1

geology [dʒi'ɒlədʒi] Geologie OT 2

German ['dʒɜːmən] deutsch OT 1

gerontocratic [dʒə,rɒntə'krætɪk] gerontokratisch **WS 3**, 114

to **gesticulate** [dʒe'stɪkjuleɪt] gestikulieren **WS 4**, 146

gesture ['dʒestər] Geste OT 5

to **get** [get] bekommen; holen; werden OT 1

   to **get** [get] werden OT 2

   to **get in** [get ɪn] einsteigen OT 1

   to **get off** [get ɒf] aussteigen OT 2

   to **get on** [get ɒn] zusteigen OT 2

   to **get out** ['get aʊt] aussteigen OT 1

   Get out! [get aʊt] Raus hier! OT 2

   to **get ready** ['get redi] vorbereiten OT 1

   to **get rid of** [get rɪd əv] los werden OT 3

   to **get there** [get ðeə] ankommen OT 2

   to **get to (a place)** [get tʌ:] ankommen OT 2

   to **get up** ['get ʌp] aufstehen OT 1

ghost [gəʊst] Geist OT 2

ghyll [gɪl] (in Nordengland) enges Tal OT 2

giant ['dʒaɪənt] riesig OT 2

gift [gɪft] Geschenk; Talent OT 1

gifted ['gɪftɪd] begabt OT 5

gig [gɪg] Gig; Auftritt; Mini-Job OT 5

gigantic [dʒaɪ'gæntɪk] riesig **WS 2**, 56

ginger ['dʒɪndʒə] Ingwer; rötlich braun OT 1

giraffe [dʒə'rɑːf] Giraffe OT 1

girl [gɜːl] Mädchen OT 1

Girl Scout [,gɜːl'skaʊt] Pfadfinderin OT 3

gist [dʒɪst] Hauptpunkt **WS 3**, 122

to **give** [gɪv] geben; schenken; aufgeben OT 1

   to **give up** [gɪv ʌp] aufgeben OT 2

glacier ['glæsiər] Gletscher **WS 1**, 22

glad [glæd] froh OT 2

gladiator ['glædieɪtə] Gladiator(in) OT 2

glam [glæm] schick OT 4

glamorous ['glæmərəs] glamourös OT 4

glamping ['glæmpɪŋ] glamouröses Zelten OT 4

glance [glɑːns] Blick **WS 2**, 82

glass [glɑːs] Glas OT 1

glass ceiling [,glɑːs 'siːlɪŋ] gläserne Decke; unsichtbare Barriere OT 5

glen [glen] Tal **WS 1**, 15

glimpse [glɪmps] flüchtiger Blick OT 5

global ['gləʊbl] global; weltweit OT 4

globalization [,gləʊbəlaɪ'zeɪʃn] Globalisierung **WS 3**, 110

globe [gləʊb] Globus; Erdkugel OT 5

gloomy ['gluːmi] trübe; schlechtgelaunt **WS 1**, 16

to **glorify** ['glɔːrɪfaɪ] verherrlichen **WS 2**, 56

glorious ['glɔːriəs] herrlich; glorreich **WS 2**, 66

glory ['glɔːri] Ehre; Ruhm **WS 2**, 76

glove [glʌv] Handschuh OT 1

to **glow** [gləʊ] glühen; scheinen **WS 1**, 35

glue [gluː] Klebstoff; Leim OT 1

to **go** [gəʊ] gehen; fahren; fliegen OT 1

   to **go ahead** [,gəʊ ə'hed] weitermachen OT 2

goal [gəʊl] Tor; Ziel OT 1

goalkeeper ['gəʊlkiːpə] Torwart OT 4

goat [gəʊt] Ziege OT 3

God [gɒd] Gott OT 3

godmother ['gɒdmʌðər] Patentante OT 5

gold [gəʊld] Gold OT 2

golden ['gəʊldən] golden OT 2

gold rush ['gəʊld rʌʃ] Goldrausch OT 5

golf [gɒlf] Golf OT 4

golfer ['gɒlfə] Golfer(in) OT 4

to **gongoozle** [gɒŋ'guːzl] gaffen OT 3

gongoozler [gɒŋ'guːzlə] Gaffer OT 3

good [gʊd] gut; gut(geeignet); nett OT 1

goody ['gʊdi] tolle Kleinigkeit OT 2

goods [gʊdz] Güter OT 3

gorgeous ['gɔːdʒəs] wunderschön **WS 3**, 117

to **govern** ['gʌvn] regieren OT 3

government ['gʌvənmənt] Regierung OT 2

governmental [,gʌvn'mentl] Regierungs- OT 4

governor ['gʌvənə] Gouverneur(in) OT 3

GPS (global positioning system) [,dʒi: pi: 'es] Navigationssystem; Globales Positionsbestimmungssystem OT 2

to **grab** [græb] greifen OT 3

to **grace** [greɪs] zieren; schmücken **WS 1**, 17

grade [greɪd] Klassenstufe OT 2

   sixth grader ['sɪksθ ,greɪdə] Sechstklässler(in) OT 2

grading ['greɪdɪŋ] Noten... OT 5

gradually ['grædʒuəli] allmählich **WS 2**, 56

to **graduate** ['grædʒuət] den Schulabschluss machen OT 4

grain [greɪn] Getreide OT 5

gram [græm] Gramm OT 2

grammar ['græmə] Grammatik OT 1

grandchild [ˈgræntʃaɪld] Enkel(in); Enkelkind OT 1

grandfather [ˈgrænfɑːðə] Großvater OT 1

grandma [ˈgrænmɑː] Oma OT 1

grandmother [ˈgrænmʌðə] Großmutter OT 1

grandpa [ˈgrænpɑː] Opa OT 1

grandparents [ˈgrænpeərənts] Großeltern OT 1

grandson [ˈgrænsʌn] Enkel OT 1

granite [ˈgrænɪt] Granit **WS 1**, 22

grant [grɑːnt] Förderung; Zuschuss OT 4

graph [grɑːf] Diagramm OT 5

graphic [ˈgræfɪk] Grafik OT 3

graphic novel [ˌgræfɪk ˈnɒvl] Bildroman OT 5

to **grasp** [grɑːsp] greifen; festhalten OT 5

grass [grɑːs] Gras; Rasen; Rasenfläche OT 1

grassland [ˈgrɑːslænd] Grasland; Grünland OT 4

grateful [ˈgreɪtfl] dankbar OT 3

gravy [ˈgreɪvi] Bratensoße OT 1

to **graze** [greɪz] grasen **WS 1**, 36

to **grease** [griːs] fetten **WS 1**, 24

great [greɪt] groß; toll; bedeutend; toll OT 1

Greek [griːk] Grieche(-in) OT 2

green [griːn] grün; Grünfläche OT 1

to **greet** [griːt] grüßen OT 2

greeting [ˈgriːtɪŋ] Gruß OT 2

grey [greɪ] grau; trüb OT 1

to **grin** [grɪn] grinsen OT 2

grips: to get to grips [get tə grɪps] in den Griff bekommen **WS 3**, 97

grizzly [ˈgrɪzli] Grizzlybär OT 2

grocery [ˈgrəʊsəri] Lebensmittel OT 4

gross [grəʊs] ätzend OT 3

grouchy [ˈgraʊtʃi] griesgrämig OT 2

ground [graʊnd] Boden; Erde; Platz OT 2

groundbreaker [ˈgraʊndbreɪkə] Wegbereiter(in) **WS 4**, 140

group [gruːp] Gruppe OT 1

to **group** [gruːp] gruppieren OT 4

grouse [graʊs] Moorhuhn **WS 1**, 22

to **grow** [grəʊ] wachsen; anbauen OT 1

grown up [ˈgrəʊn ʌp] erwachsen OT 2

growth [grəʊθ] Wachstum OT 5

gruelling [ˈgruːəlɪŋ] zermürbend; schwierig **WS 1**, 22

grunge [grʌndʒ] Grunge **WW**, 11

grunt [grʌnt] Grunzen **WS 3**, 108

to **guarantee** [ˌgærənˈtiː] garantieren OT 4

guard [gɑːd] Sicherheitsbeamter(in); Wächter(in) OT 5

guardian [ˈgɑːdiən] Betreuer(in) OT 2

guess [ges] Schätzung OT 1

to **guess** [ges] schätzen; raten OT 1

guest [gest] Gast OT 2

guestbook [ˈgestbʊk] Gästebuch OT 2

guidance [ˈgaɪdns] Anleitung OT 4

guidance counsellor [ˈgaɪdnsˈkaʊnsələ] Beratungslehrer(in) OT 3

guide [gaɪd] Führer(in); Leitfaden; Reiseführer OT 1

to **guide** [gaɪd] führen; leiten OT 1

guidebook [ˈgaɪdbʊk] Reiseführer OT 3

guide dog [ˈgaɪd dɒg] Blindenführhund OT 2

guideline [ˈgaɪdlaɪn] Richtlinie; Regel OT 3

guilt-free [ˈgɪlt friː] schuldfrei **WS 3**, 104

guilty [ˈgɪlti] schuldig OT 4

guitar [gɪˈtɑː] Gitarre OT 1

guitarist [gɪˈtɑːrɪst] Gitarrist(in) OT 4

gun [gʌn] Schusswaffe OT 3

gunfire [ˈgʌnfaɪə] Schießerei; Schüsse OT 3

gunman [ˈgʌnmən] Schütze OT 4

gurning [ˈgɜːnɪŋ] Grimassieren OT 2

guy [gaɪ] Kerl; Typ OT 5

guys [gaɪz] Leute OT 2

gym [dʒɪm] Turnen; Turnhalle; Fitnesscenter OT 1

gymnasium [dʒɪmˈneɪziəm] Sporthalle; Turnhalle OT 4

gymnastics [dʒɪmˈnæstɪks] Gymnastik OT 1

H

habit [ˈhæbɪt] Angewohnheit OT 4

habitable [ˈhæbɪtəbl] bewohnbar OT 4

habitat [ˈhæbɪtæt] Habitat OT 5

habitual [həˈbɪtʃuəl] gewöhnlich; ständig **WS 2**, 68

to **hail** [heɪl] grüßen OT 2

hair [heə] Haare; Haar OT 1

haircut [ˈheəkʌt] Haarschnitt OT 2

hairstyle [ˈheəstaɪl] Frisur **WS 2**, 68

half [hɑːf] halbe(r, -s); halb; zur Hälfte OT 1

half past [ˈhɑːf pɑːst] eine halbe Stunde nach OT 1

halfway [ˌhɑːfˈweɪ] halbwegs; halb OT 4

hall [hɔːl] Halle; Flur OT 1

Halloween [ˌhæləʊˈiːn] Halloween OT 2

halo [ˈheɪləʊ] Strahlenkranz **WS 1**, 12

halt [hɔːlt] Haltestelle OT 2

to **halve** [hɑːv] halbieren **WS 4**, 136

ham [hæm] Schinken OT 1

hamster [ˈhæmstə] Hamster OT 1

hand-eye coordination [hænd aɪ kəʊˌɔːdɪˈneɪʃn] Hand-Auge-Koordination **WS 3**, 98

hand [hænd] Hand; Hilfe; Arbeiter(in) OT 1

to **hand in** [hænd ɪn] einreichen OT 2

handbag [ˈhændbæg] Handtasche OT 3

handbook [ˈhændbʊk] Handbuch OT 3

handful [ˈhændfʊl] Handvoll OT 4

handicraft [ˈhændikrɑːft] Handwerk; Handarbeit OT 4

handle [ˈhændl] Griff OT 2

to **handle** [ˈhændl] handhaben OT 4

handout [ˈhændaʊt] Handout; Flugblatt OT 4

handset [ˈhændset] Handapparat OT 2

handsome [ˈhænsəm] gut aussehend; attraktiv; ansehnlich OT 1

handwoven [hændˈwəʊvn] handgewebt **WS 1**, 17

to **handwrite** [ˈhændraɪt] mit der Hand schreiben OT 5

handwriting [ˈhændraɪtɪŋ] Handschrift OT 2

to **hang on** [ˌhæŋˈɒn] warten OT 2

to **hang out** [hæŋ aʊt] herumhängen OT 3

to **happen** [ˈhæpən] geschehen; passieren; geschehen OT 1

to **happen upon** [ˈhæpən əˈpɒn] zufällig entdecken OT 4

happiness [ˈhæpinəs] Glück; Freude OT 5

happy [ˈhæpi] glücklich; herzlich OT 1

harbour [ˈhɑːbə] Hafen OT 4

hard [hɑːd] hart OT 2

hardly [ˈhɑːdli] kaum OT 4

hardship [ˈhɑːdʃɪp] Not; Elend **WS 2**, 67

to **hark** [hɑːk] (zu)hören **WS 1**, 13

harm [hɑːm] Schaden OT 3

harmful [ˈhɑːmfl] schädlich OT 5

harmonica [hɑːˈmɒnɪkə] Mundharmonika **WS 2**, 67

to **harness** [ˈhɑːnɪs] nutzen **WS 4**, 135

harpoon [hɑːˈpuːn] Harpune OT 4

harsh [hɑːʃ] rau OT 3

harvest [ˈhɑːvɪst] Ernte OT 3

to **harvest** [ˈhɑːvɪst] ernten OT 4

hat [hæt] Hut; Mütze OT 1

to **hate** [heɪt] hassen OT 1

hater [ˈheɪtə] Hasser(in) **WS 2**, 72

to **have got** [ˈhæv gɒt] haben OT 1

hazardous [ˈhæzədəs] gefährlich OT 4

head [hed] Kopf; Verstand; Leiter(in) OT 1

headache [ˈhedeɪk] Kopfschmerzen; Problem OT 1

header [ˈhedə] Kopfball OT 3

headfirst [ˌhedˈfɜːst] kopfüber **WS 3**, 119

heading [ˈhedɪŋ] Überschrift OT 3

headline [ˈhedlaɪn] Schlagzeile OT 2

to **headline** [ˈhedlaɪn] hier: der wichtigste Künstler sein OT 3

headset [ˈhedset] Headset; Kopfhörer OT 5

headphones [ˈhedfəʊnz] Kopfhörer OT 2

headshot [ˈhedʃɒt] Portraitfoto OT 5

head teacher [ˌhed ˈtiːtʃə] Schulleiter(in); Rektor(in) OT 1

headword [ˈhedwɜːd] Stichwort OT 2

to **heal** [hiːl] heilen **WS 3**, 117

health [helθ] Gesundheit OT 3

healthcare [ˈhelθkeə] Gesundheitsfürsorge OT 4

healthy [ˈhelθi] gesund OT 2

heap [hiːp] Haufen OT 5

to **hear** [hɪə] hören; erfahren; anhören OT 1

heart [hɑːt] Herz OT 2

heartbreak [ˈhɑːtbreɪk] Kummer **WS 2**, 58

heartfelt [ˈhɑːtfelt] aufrichtig; herzlich **WS 3**, 101

to **heat** [hiːt] heizen OT 2

heater [ˈhiːtə] Ofen OT 2

heathered [ˈheðəd] mit Heide bewachsen **WS 1**, 15

heatwave [ˈhiːtweɪv] Hitzewelle OT 5

heaven [ˈhevn] Himmel **WS 1**, 16

heavy [ˈhevi] schwer; stark OT 1

heavyweight [ˈheviweɪt] Schwergewicht **WS 2**, 53

hectic [ˈhektɪk] hektisch OT 4

hedgehog [ˈhedʒhɒg] Igel OT 1

heel [hiːl] Absatz; Ferse **WS 3**, 119

height [haɪt] Höhe; Größe; Höhepunkt OT 1

hell [hel] Hölle OT 5

hello [həˈləʊ] Hallo OT 1

helm [helm] Steuer; Ruder **WS 1**, 31

helmet [ˈhelmɪt] Helm OT 1

to **help** [help] helfen OT 1

helper [ˈhelpə] Helfer(in) OT 5

helpful [ˈhelpfl] hilfreich; hilfsbereit OT 1

helpline [ˈhelplaɪn] Hotline OT 2

hemisphere [ˈhemɪsfɪər] Hemisphäre OT 5

hemp [hemp] Hanf **WS 1**, 20

hen [hen] Henne; Huhn OT 4

hence [hens] daher **WS 3**, 110

heptathlon [hepˈtæθlən] Siebenkampf OT 2

her [hə] sie; ihr; sie/ihr OT 1

herb [hɜːb] Kraut; Heilkraut OT 3

herd [hɜːd] Herde OT 5

to **herd** [hɜːd] treiben OT 2

herder [ˈhɜːdə] Hirte(-in) OT 3

here [hɪə] hier; hierher; jetzt OT 1

heritage [ˈherɪtɪdʒ] Erbe; Tradition OT 4

hero [ˈhɪərəʊ] Held(in) OT 4

hers [hɜːz] ihre(r, -s) OT 3

hesitantly [ˈhezɪtəntli] zögerlich OT 4

to **hesitate** [ˈhezɪteɪt] zögern OT 3

hesitation [ˌhezɪˈteɪʃn] Zögern OT 3

heterosexual [ˌhetərəˈsekʃuəl] heterosexuell OT 5

hexagonal [hekˈsægənəl] hexagonal; sechseckig **WS 1**, 39

to **hide** [haɪd] sich verstecken OT 3

hi-fi [ˈhaɪ faɪ] Hi-Fi-Anlage OT 3

high [haɪ] Höchststand OT 1

high [haɪ] hoch OT 1

   highly [ˈhaɪli] höchst; äußerst OT 4

high-heeled [ˌhaɪ ˈhiːld] hochhackig OT 3

to **highlight** [ˈhaɪlaɪt] betonen OT 5

highway [ˈhaɪweɪ] Highway; Landstrasse OT 3

to **hike** [haɪk] wandern OT 1

hill [hɪl] Hügel OT 1

hillwalking [ˈhɪlwɔːkɪŋ] Wandern **WS 1**, 12

him [hɪm] ihn; ihm; ihm/ihn OT 1

Hindu [ˈhɪnduː] hinduistisch; Hindu... OT 1

to **hinge on** [ˈhɪndʒ ɒn] abhängen von **WS 3**, 112

to **hint** [hɪnt] andeuten OT 4

hip [hɪp] Hüfte OT 1

to **hire** [ˈhaɪə] mieten OT 3

his [hɪz] seine(r, -s); sein Haus/seine Wohnung OT 1

Hispanic [hɪˈspænɪk] hispanisch OT 3

historian [hɪˈstɔːriən] Historiker(in) OT 2

historic [hɪˈstɒrɪk] historisch OT 2

historical [hɪˈstɒrɪkl] geschichtlich OT 2

history [ˈhɪstri] Geschichte; Geschichtswissenschaft; Vergangenheit OT 1

to **hit** [hɪt] schlagen; treffen; prallen gegen OT 1

hoax [həʊks] Falschmeldung; Schwindel **WS 1**, 20

hob [hɒb] Kochfeld OT 3

hobby [ˈhɒbi] Hobby OT 1

hockey [ˈhɒki] Hockey; Eishockey OT 1

to **hold** [həʊld] halten; tragen OT 1

holder [ˈhəʊldə] Träger(in); Halter(in) **WS 1**, 14

hole [həʊl] Loch; Bau; Höhle OT 1

holiday [ˈhɒlədeɪ] Urlaub OT 1

hologram [ˈhɒləgræm] Hologramm OT 2

home [həʊm] Zuhause; Haus; Wohnung OT 1

homecoming [ˈhəʊmkʌmɪŋ] traditionelles Event in Highschools OT 5

homeland [ˈhəʊmlænd] Heimat OT 5

homeless [ˈhəʊmləs] obdachlos; Obdachlose(r) OT 4

homemade [ˈhəʊmmeɪd] selbst gemacht; selbst zubereitet OT 1

home-schooled [ˌhəʊmˈskuːld] zu Hause unterrichtet OT 4

homesick [ˈhəʊmsɪk] voll Heimweh OT 2

homesickness [ˈhəʊmsɪknəs] Heimweh OT 5

homework [ˈhəʊmwɜːk] Hausaufgaben OT 1

honest [ˈɒnɪst] ehrlich OT 2

honey [ˈhʌni] Honig; Schatz (als Kosename) OT 2

to **honour** [ˈɒnə] ehren OT 4

hoodie [ˈhʊdi] Kapuzenpullover; Kapuzenjacke OT 1

hook [hʊk] Aufhänger; Haken; Hookline **WS 2**, 66

to **hope** [həʊp] hoffen OT 1

hopeful [ˈhəʊpfl] hoffnungsvoll OT 4

   hopefully [ˈhəʊpfəli] hoffentlich OT 3

hopeless [ˈhəʊpləs] hoffnungslos OT 4

horizon [həˈraɪzn] Horizont OT 5

horizontal [ˌhɒrɪˈzɒntl] horizontal OT 5

hormone [ˈhɔːməʊn] Hormon OT 5

horn [hɔːn] Horn; Hupe OT 3

horrendous [həˈrendəs] schrecklich **WS 1**, 16

horrible [ˈhɒrəbl] furchtbar OT 2

horrified [ˈhɒrɪfaɪd] entsetzt OT 5

horror [ˈhɒrə] Schrecken; Horror OT 4

horse [hɔːs] Pferd OT 1

horseback: on horseback [ˈhɔːsbæk]
zu Pferde OT 3

horse riding [ˈhɔːs ˈraɪdɪŋ] Reiten OT 1

hospital [ˈhɒspɪtl] Krankenhaus OT 1

hospitality [ˌhɒspɪˈtæləti]
Gastfreundlichkeit OT 2

host [həʊst] Gastgeber(in) OT 3

to host [həʊst] ausrichten OT 3

hot [hɒt] heiß; scharf OT 1

hotel [həʊˈtel] Hotel OT 1

hound [haʊnd] Spürhund OT 2

hour [ˈaʊə] Stunde; Zeit; Stunden OT 1

house [haʊs] Haus OT 1

household [ˈhaʊshəʊld] häuslich;
Haushalts- OT 4

housekeeper [ˈhaʊskiːpə]
Haushälter(in) OT 3

housewife [ˈhaʊswaɪf] Hausfrau OT 5

housework [ˈhaʊswɜːk] Hausarbeit OT 1

housing [ˈhaʊzɪŋ] Wohn...; Wohnungs...
OT 5

how [haʊ] wie OT 1

however [haʊˈevə] jedoch OT 2

howl [haʊl] Geheul OT 5

to huddle [ˈhʌdl] hocken WS 1, 19

hue and cry [hjuː ənd ˈkraɪ] Geschrei
WS 1, 35

hug [hʌg] Umarmung OT 1

huge [hjuːdʒ] riesig OT 2

hull [hʌl] Rumpf OT 3

to hum [hʌm] summen OT 4

human [ˈhjuːmən] menschlich OT 2

human being [ˌhjuːmənˈbiːɪŋ] Mensch
OT 2

humanity [hjuːˈmænəti] Menschheit
WS 4, 138

humanities [hjuːˈmænətis]
Geisteswissenschaften OT 4

human right [ˌhjuːmən ˈraɪt]
Menschenrecht OT 5

humid [ˈhjuːmɪd] humid; feucht OT 4

humiliating [hjuːˈmɪlieɪtɪŋ] demütigend
WS 3, 113

humour [ˈhjuːmə] Humor OT 4

hundred [ˈhʌndrəd] hundert OT 1

Hungarian [hʌŋˈɡeəriən] ungarisch
OT 2

hunger [ˈhʌŋɡə] Hunger OT 3

hungry [ˈhʌŋɡri] hungrig OT 1

to hunt [hʌnt] jagen OT 2

hunter [ˈhʌntə] Jäger(in) OT 3

hunter-gatherer [ˌhʌntə ˈɡæðərər]
Jäger und Sammler OT 5

hunting [ˈhʌntɪŋ] Jagen OT 2

to hurl [hɜːl] schleudern; werfen
WS 3, 119

hurricane [ˈhʌrɪkən] Hurrikan; Orkan
OT 4

to hurry [ˈhʌri] sich beeilen; antreiben;
hetzen OT 1

to hurry up [ˈhʌri ʌp] sich beeilen
OT 2

hurt [hɜːt] verletzt; gekränkt OT 1

to hurt [hɜːt] schmerzen; wehtun;
schaden OT 1

hurtful [ˈhɜːtfl] verletzend WS 2, 72

husband [ˈhʌzbənd] Ehemann; Mann
OT 2

hydro-electric [ˌhaɪdrəʊˈlektrɪk]
Wasserkraft OT 4

hyper [ˈhaɪpə] über- OT 4

hyperactive [ˌhaɪpərˈæktɪv] hyperaktiv
OT 5

hyperbole [haɪˈpɜːbəli] Übertreibung
WS 4, 139

hypothermia [ˌhaɪpəˈθɜːmiə]
Unterkühlung OT 2

I

ice [aɪs] Eis; Eiscreme OT 1

ice cream [ˌaɪsˈkriːm] Eis; Eiscreme OT 1

iconic [aɪˈkɒnɪk] ikonisch; Kult... OT 3

ICT (information and communications
technology) [ˌaɪ siːˈtiː] Informations-
und Kommunikationstechnologie;
Informatikunterricht OT 1

icy [ˈaɪsi] eisig OT 5

ID card (identification card) [ˌaɪ ˈdiː
kɑːd] Ausweis OT 5

idea [aɪˈdɪə] Idee; Ansicht; Bild OT 1

ideal [aɪˈdiːəl] ideal OT 4

identical [aɪˈdentɪkl] identisch
WS 3, 122

identification [aɪˌdentɪfɪˈkeɪʃn]
Identifizierung WS 2, 56

to identify [aɪˈdentɪfaɪ] identifizieren
OT 4

identity [aɪˈdentəti] Identität OT 3

ideology [ˌaɪdiˈɒlədʒi] Glaube; Ideologie
WS 1, 32

idol [ˈaɪdl] Idol OT 5

if [ɪf] falls; immer, wenn; ob OT 1

igloo [ˈɪɡluː] Iglu OT 4

to ignore [ɪɡˈnɔː] ignorieren OT 4

ill [ɪl] krank OT 2

illegal [ɪˈliːɡl] illegal OT 3

illegitimate [ˌɪləˈdʒɪtəmət]
unrechtmäßig WS 3, 114

illiterate [ɪˈlɪtərət] analphabetisch OT 4

illness [ˈɪlnəs] Krankheit OT 2

to illustrate [ˈɪləstreɪt] verdeutlichen;
illustrieren OT 4

illustration [ˌɪləˈstreɪʃn] Illustration
OT 2

image [ˈɪmɪdʒ] Bild OT 3

imagery [ˈɪmɪdʒəri] Bilder; Bildsprache
WS 2, 64

imaginary [ɪˈmædʒɪnəri] erfunden;
fiktiv OT 4

to imagine [ɪˈmædʒɪn] sich etwas
vorstellen; sich einbilden; glauben
OT 1

immature [ˌɪməˈtjʊə] unreif WS 3, 97

immediate [ɪˈmiːdiət] unmittelbar;
umgehend OT 5

immediately [ɪˈmiːdiətli] sofort OT 4

immense [ɪˈmens] riesig WS 3, 122

to immerse [ɪˈmɜːs] eintauchen WS 1, 17

immigrant [ˈɪmɪɡrənt] Einwanderer(in)
OT 4

to immigrate [ˈɪmɪɡreɪt] einwandern
OT 5

immigration [ˌɪmɪˈɡreɪʃn]
Einwanderung OT 2

immune [ɪˈmjuːn] immun WS 3, 113

impact [ˈɪmpækt] Auswirkung OT 3

to impact [ɪmˈpækt] beeinflussen
WS 2, 82

impaired [ɪmˈpeəd] beeinträchtigt OT 5

to impart [ɪmˈpɑːt] vermitteln OT 4

impatient [ɪmˈpeɪʃnt] ungeduldig OT 5

imperative [ɪmˈperətɪv] Imperativ;
Befehlsform OT 1

to implement [ˈɪmplɪment] umsetzen;
durchführen OT 4

importance [ɪmˈpɔːtns] Wichtigkeit;
Bedeutung OT 3

important [ɪmˈpɔːtnt] wichtig;
einflussreich; bedeutend OT 1

to impose [ɪmˈpəʊz] verhängen;
durchsetzen WS 1, 30

impossible [ɪmˈpɒsəbl] unmöglich OT 2

to impress [ɪmˈpres] beeindrucken OT 4

impression [ɪmˈpreʃn] Eindruck OT 5

impressive [ɪmˈpresɪv] beeindruckend
OT 2

to imprison [ɪmˈprɪzn] einsperren
WS 1, 18

improbable [ɪmˈprɒbəbl]
unwahrscheinlich WS 2, 69

impromptu [ɪmˈprɒmptjuː] spontan
WS 1, 26

improper [ɪmˈprɒpə] unangemessen
WS 2, 68

to **improve** [ɪmˈpruːv] sich verbessern OT 3

improvement [ɪmˈpruːvmənt] Verbesserung OT 3

impulse [ˈɪmpʌls] Impuls; Anstoß **WS 1**, 21

impulsive [ɪmˈpʌlsɪv] impulsiv; spontan **WS 4**, 135

in [ɪn] in OT 1

inaccessible [ˌɪnækˈsesəbl] unzugänglich OT 3

inaccuracy [ɪnˈækjərəsi] Ungenauigkeit **WS 2**, 73

inaccurate [ɪnˈækjərət] ungenau OT 4

inaugural [ɪˈnɔːgjərəl] Einführung; Antritts... **WS 2**, 55

incentive [ɪnˈsentɪv] Anreiz; Antrieb OT 5

inception [ɪnˈsepʃn] Einführung **WS 1**, 14

inch [ɪntʃ] Zoll (2,54 cm) OT 2

incident [ˈɪnsɪdənt] Vorfall; Ereignis OT 5

to **include** [ɪnˈkluːd] einschließen OT 2

including [ɪnˈkluːdɪŋ] einschließlich; inklusive OT 1

inclusion [ɪnˈkluːʒn] Inklusion **WS 3**, 112

inclusive [ɪnˈkluːsɪv] integrativ OT 4

inclusiveness [ɪnˈkluːsɪvnəs] Inklusivität **WS 3**, 95

income [ˈɪnkʌm] Einkommen OT 5

incomplete [ˌɪnkəmˈpliːt] unvollständig OT 5

to **incorporate** [ɪnˈkɔːpəreɪt] einbauen; integrieren **WS 1**, 34

incorrectly [ˌɪnkəˈrektli] falsch; fehlerhaft OT 5

increase [ˈɪnkriːs] Zunahme OT 3

to **increase** [ɪnˈkriːs] erhöhen OT 5

increased [ɪnˈkriːst] erhöht OT 5

increasingly [ɪnˈkriːsɪŋli] zunehmend OT 5

incredible [ɪnˈkredəbl] unglaublich OT 2

incubator [ˈɪŋkjubeɪtər] Inkubator; Unterstützer von Start-ups OT 5

independence [ˌɪndɪˈpendəns] Unabhängigkeit OT 2

independent [ˌɪndɪˈpendənt] unabhängig OT 4

in-depth [ˌɪn ˈdepθ] gründlich **WS 4**, 135

to **indicate** [ˈɪndɪkeɪt] angeben; zeigen OT 4

indicator [ˈɪndɪkeɪtə] Indikator; Anzeige **WS 3**, 94

indigenous [ɪnˈdɪdʒənəs] einheimisch OT 4

indisputable [ˌɪndɪˈspjuːtəbl] unbestritten **WS 3**, 107

individual [ˌɪndɪˈvɪdʒuəl] individuell OT 3

individually [ˌɪndɪˈvɪdʒuəli] einzeln OT 5

individualism [ˌɪndɪˈvɪdʒuəlɪzəm] Individualismus **WS 2**, 69

individuation [ɪndɪvɪdʒuˈeɪʃən] Individualisierung **WS 3**, 122

indoor [ˈɪndɔː] Innen... OT 2

indoors [ˌɪnˈdɔːz] drinnen OT 3

induction [ɪnˈdʌkʃn] Einführung OT 5

to **indulge** [ɪnˈdʌldʒ] verwöhnen **WS 3**, 110

industrial [ɪnˈdʌstriəl] Industrie... OT 2

industry [ˈɪndəstri] Industrie OT 2

inequality [ˌɪnɪˈkwɒləti] Ungleichheit **WS 2**, 62

inexhaustible [ˌɪnɪgˈzɔːstəbl] unerschöpflich **WS 3**, 114

infamous [ˈɪnfəməs] berüchtigt OT 4

infancy [ˈɪnfənsi] Kindheit **WS 3**, 96

infection [ɪnˈfekʃn] Entzündung OT 2

infinitive [ɪnˈfɪnətɪv] Infinitiv OT 1

influence [ˈɪnfluəns] Einfluss OT 5

to **influence** [ˈɪnfluəns] beeinflussen OT 3

influencer [ˈɪnfluənsə] Influencer(in) OT 5

influential [ˌɪnfluˈenʃl] einflussreich **WS 2**, 75

influenza [ˌɪnfluˈenzə] Grippe; Influenza OT 5

infographic [ˌɪnfəʊˈgræfɪk] Infografik OT 3

infomercial [ˌɪnfəʊˈmɜːʃl] Infomercial OT 4

to **inform** [ɪnˈfɔːm] informieren OT 4

informal [ɪnˈfɔːml] informell OT 5

information [ˌɪnfəˈmeɪʃn] Information; Auskunft OT 1

informative [ɪnˈfɔːmətɪv] informativ OT 4

infrastructure [ˈɪnfrəstrʌktʃə] Infrastruktur OT 4

ingredient [ɪnˈgriːdiənt] Zutat OT 2

to **inhabit** [ɪnˈhæbɪt] bewohnen OT 4

to **inherit** [ɪnˈherɪt] erben OT 4

initial [ɪˈnɪʃl] ursprünglich; anfänglich OT 5

initially [ɪˈnɪʃəli] zunächst; anfangs OT 5

to **initiate** [ɪˈnɪʃieɪt] anstoßen; initiieren **WS 2**, 71

initiative [ɪˈnɪʃətɪv] Initiative; Kampagne OT 4

to **injure** [ˈɪndʒə] verletzen OT 2

injury [ˈɪndʒəri] Verletzung OT 2

injustice [ɪnˈdʒʌstɪs] Ungerechtigkeit; Unrecht **WS 2**, 58

inlet [ˈɪnlet] Bucht **WS 1**, 35

inn [ɪn] Gasthaus OT 2

to **innovate** [ˈɪnəveɪt] innovieren; verbessern OT 4

innovation [ˌɪnəˈveɪʃn] Innovation; Neuheit OT 4

innovative [ˈɪnəveɪtɪv] innovativ OT 4

innovator [ˈɪnəveɪtə] Innovator(in) OT 4

insane [ɪnˈseɪn] verrückt **WS 3**, 117

inscription [ɪnˈskrɪpʃn] Inschrift **WS 2**, 55

insect [ˈɪnsekt] Insekt OT 2

insecure [ˌɪnsɪˈkjʊər] unsicher; instabil OT 5

insecurity [ˌɪnsɪˈkjʊərəti] Unsicherheit **WS 4**, 146

inside [ˌɪnˈsaɪd] in; innerhalb; innen OT 1

insightful [ˈɪnsaɪtfəl] aufschlussreich **WS 1**, 35

to **insist** [ɪnˈsɪst] bestehen auf **WS 1**, 22

insomnia [ɪnˈsɒmniə] Schlaflosigkeit **WS 3**, 108

inspiration [ˌɪnspəˈreɪʃn] Inspiration; Eingebung OT 4

inspirational [ˌɪnspəˈreɪʃənl] begeisternd **WS 2**, 62

to **inspire** [ɪnˈspaɪə] inspirieren; anregen OT 4

to **install** [ɪnˈstɔːl] installieren OT 3

installation [ˌɪnstəˈleɪʃn] Installation OT 4

instance: for instance [fə ˈɪnstəns] zum Beispiel OT 4

instantly [ˈɪnstəntli] sofort **WS 3**, 106

instead [ɪnˈsted] stattdessen OT 2

to **instil** [ɪnˈstɪl] einträufeln **WS 2**, 64

instinctive [ɪnˈstɪŋktɪv] instinktiv **WS 3**, 105

institution [ˌɪnstɪˈtjuːʃn] Einrichtung OT 4

instruction [ɪnˈstrʌkʃn] Anweisung; Anleitung; Unterricht OT 1

instructive [ɪnˈstrʌktɪv] instruktiv; lehrreich OT 5

instructor [ɪnˈstrʌktə] Lehrer(in) OT 2

instrument [ˈɪnstrəmənt] Instrument; Gerät; Mittel OT 1

instrumental [ˌɪnstrəˈmentl] behilflich; instrumentell **WS 2**, 56

insubstantial [ˌɪnsəbˈstænʃl] substanzlos; unerheblich **WS 1**, 35

to insult [ˈɪnsʌlt] beleidigen; verletzen OT 5

insurrection [ˌɪnsəˈrekʃn] Aufstand; Revolte **WS 2**, 73

to integrate [ˈɪntɪgreɪt] integrieren OT 4

integration [ˌɪntɪˈgreɪʃn] Integration OT 5

intellectual [ˌɪntəˈlektʃuəl] geistig; intellektuell **WS 3**, 116

intelligence [ɪnˈtelɪdʒəns] Intelligenz OT 4

intelligent [ɪnˈtelɪdʒənt] intelligent OT 2

to intend [ɪnˈtend] beabsichtigen OT 4

intense [ɪnˈtens] stark; ernsthaft OT 5

intention [ɪnˈtenʃn] Absicht OT 5

to interact [ˌɪntərˈækt] interagieren OT 4

interaction [ˌɪntərˈækʃn] Interaktion OT 4

interactive [ˌɪntərˈæktɪv] interaktiv OT 4

interconnectedness [ˌɪntəkəˈnektɪdnəs] Vernetzung **WS 3**, 97

interest [ˈɪntrəst] Interesse; Reiz; Zinsen OT 1

interested [ˈɪntrəstɪd] interessiert OT 1

interesting [ˈɪntrəstɪŋ] interessant OT 1

interior [ɪnˈtɪəriər] Binnenland; das Innere OT 5

intern [ˈɪntɜːn] Praktikant(in); Volontär(in) OT 5

international [ˌɪntəˈnæʃnəl] international OT 1

internet [ˈɪntənet] Internet OT 3

internship [ˈɪntɜːnʃɪp] Praktikum OT 4

interpersonal [ˌɪntəˈpɜːsənl] interpersonell; zwischenmenschlich OT 5

to interpret [ɪnˈtɜːprət] interpretieren OT 4

interpretation [ɪnˌtɜːprəˈteɪʃn] Interpretation **WS 3**, 122

interpreter [ɪnˈtɜːprɪtə] Dolmetscher(in) OT 3

to interrupt [ˌɪntəˈrʌpt] unterbrechen OT 2

intersection [ˈɪntəsekʃn] Schnittpunkt; Kreuzung **WS 2**, 82

intersex [ˈɪntəseks] Intersex OT 5

intertwined [ˌɪntəˈtwaɪnd] verflochten **WS 1**, 35

to intervene [ˌɪntəˈviːn] eingreifen OT 5

intervention [ˌɪntəˈvenʃn] Eingriff; Eingreifen OT 5

interview [ˈɪntəvjuː] Vorstellungsgespräch; Interview OT 1

to interview [ˈɪntəvjuː] ein Vorstellungsgespräch führen; interviewen; befragen OT 1

interviewee [ˌɪntəvjuˈiː] Interviewte(r) OT 3

interviewer [ˈɪntəvjuːə] Interviewer(in) OT 5

intimate [ˈɪntɪmət] vertraut **WS 1**, 29

to intimidate [ɪnˈtɪmɪdeɪt] einschüchtern **WS 1**, 35

into [ˈɪntuː] in OT 1

intolerant [ɪnˈtɒlərənt] intolerant OT 5

intonation [ˌɪntəˈneɪʃn] Intonation OT 5

to intrigue [ɪnˈtriːg] faszinieren; neugierig machen **WS 2**, 54

intriguing [ɪnˈtriːgɪŋ] faszinierend OT 5

to introduce [ˌɪntrəˈdjuːs] vorstellen OT 2

introduction [ˌɪntrəˈdʌkʃn] Vorstellung; Einführung OT 2

introductory [ˌɪntrəˈdʌktəri] Anfangs...; Einführungs... OT 5

introverted [ˈɪntrəvɜːtɪd] in sich gekehrt **WS 3**, 111

to invade [ɪnˈveɪd] einmarschieren OT 3

invader [ɪnˈveɪdə] Angreifer(in) OT 3

invasive [ɪnˈveɪsɪv] invasiv OT 5

to invent [ɪnˈvent] erfinden OT 2

invention [ɪnˈvenʃn] Erfindung OT 2

inventor [ɪnˈventə] Erfinder(in) OT 2

to invert [ɪnˈvɜːt] umkehren; umstellen OT 5

inverted commas [ɪnˌvɜːtɪd ˈkɒməz] Anführungszeichen OT 3

to invest [ɪnˈvest] investieren OT 4

to investigate [ɪnˈvestɪgeɪt] untersuchen OT 3

investment [ɪnˈvestmənt] Investition OT 4

investor [ɪnˈvestə] Investor(in); Geldgeber(in) OT 4

invisible [ɪnˈvɪzəbl] unsichtbar OT 5

invitation [ˌɪnvɪˈteɪʃn] Einladung; Aufforderung OT 1

to invite [ɪnˈvaɪt] einladen OT 2

to involve [ɪnˈvɒlv] einbeziehen; umfassen OT 4

involved [ɪnˈvɒlvd] beteiligt OT 3

involvement [ɪnˈvɒlvmənt] Beteiligung **WS 1**, 32

Irish [ˈaɪrɪʃ] irisch OT 1

iron [ˈaɪən] Eisen OT 3

ironing [ˈaɪənɪŋ] Bügeln OT 5

irony [ˈaɪrəni] Ironie **WS 2**, 64

irrational [ɪˈræʃənl] irrational **WS 4**, 146

irregular [ɪˈregjələ] unregelmäßig; uneben; ungehörig OT 1

irritated [ˈɪrɪteɪtɪd] verärgert OT 2

island [ˈaɪlənd] Insel OT 1

islander [ˈaɪləndə] Insulaner(in) OT 4

isolated [ˈaɪsəleɪtɪd] isoliert **WS 1**, 28

isolation [ˌaɪsəˈleɪʃn] Isolation **WS 3**, 111

issue [ˈɪsjuː] Thema; Ausgabe OT 2

to issue [ˈɪsjuː] erteilen OT 4

it [ɪt] es; ihm; er/ihm/ihn OT 1

Italian [ɪˈtæliən] italienisch OT 2

to itch [ɪtʃ] jucken OT 2

itchy [ˈɪtʃi] juckend OT 2

item [ˈaɪtəm] Gegenstand; Punkt OT 3

its [ɪts] sein; ihr OT 1

itself [ɪtˈself] sich (selbst) OT 3

ivory [ˈaɪvəri] Elfenbein OT 4

J

jacket [ˈdʒækɪt] Jacke; Jackett; Sakko OT 1

jail [dʒeɪl] Gefängnis **WS 2**, 60

jam [dʒæm] Marmelade; Stau OT 1

January [ˈdʒænjuəri] Januar OT 1

Japanese [ˌdʒæpəˈniːz] japanisch OT 1

jar [dʒɑː] Einweckglas OT 2

jazz [dʒæz] Jazz OT 2

jealous [ˈdʒeləs] eifersüchtig OT 2

jerk chicken [ˌdʒɜːk ˈtʃɪkɪn] gegrilltes Huhn OT 4

jewel [ˈdʒuːəl] Edelstein; Schmuckstück OT 3

jewelry [ˈdʒuːəlri] Schmuck OT 2

job [dʒɒb] Stelle; Job OT 1

job hopping [dʒɒb ˈhɒpɪŋ] wiederholter Stellenwechsel OT 5

to join [dʒɔɪn] Mitglied werden in; eintreten in; sich anschließen OT 1

to join up [dʒɔɪn ʌp] verbinden OT 2

joke [dʒəʊk] Witz OT 2

to take a joke [teɪk ə dʒəʊk] Spaß verstehen OT 2

to joke [dʒəʊk] Witze machen OT 2

journal [ˈdʒɜːnl] Journal; Fachzeitschrift OT 3

journalism [ˈdʒɜːnəlɪzəm] Journalismus OT 4

journalist [ˈdʒɜːnəlɪst] Journalist(in) OT 2

journey [ˈdʒɜːni] Reise; Fahrt OT 1

joust [dʒaʊst] Turnier OT 2

jowl [dʒaʊl] Wange **WS 3**, 119

joy [dʒɔɪ] Freude **WS 1**, 29

joyful [ˈdʒɔɪfl] fröhlich **WS 3**, 105

joyride [ˈdʒɔɪraɪd] Spritztour (mit einem gestohlenen Auto) OT 5

judge [dʒʌdʒ] Richter(in) OT 2

to **judge** [dʒʌdʒ] einschätzen OT 2

judging [ˈdʒʌdʒɪŋ] Beurteilen OT 2

judicial [dʒuˈdɪʃl] Justiz- OT 4

judo [ˈdʒuːdəʊ] Judo OT 1

juggernaut [ˈdʒʌgənɔːt] Lastzug; *hier:* unbändige Kraft **WS 1**, 31

juice [dʒuːs] Saft; Sprit OT 1

July [dʒuˈlaɪ] Juli OT 1

to **jump** [dʒʌmp] springen OT 2

jumper [ˈdʒʌmpə] Pullover OT 1

June [dʒuːn] Juni OT 1

jungle [ˈdʒʌŋgl] Dschungel **WS 2**, 53

junior [ˈdʒuːniə] Junior(in) OT 2

juniper [ˈdʒuːnɪpə] Wacholder **WS 1**, 22

junk food [ˈdʒʌŋk fuːd] ungesundes Essen OT 4

jury [ˈdʒʊəri] Jury **WS 2**, 63

just [dʒʌst] genau; nur; gerade OT 1

justice [ˈdʒʌstɪs] Justiz OT 5

to **justify** [ˈdʒʌstɪfaɪ] rechtfertigen OT 4

juxtaposition [ˌdʒʌkstəpəˈzɪʃən] Nebeneinander; Gegenüberstellung; *hier als Verb gebraucht (eigtl.: to juxtapose)* **WS 2**, 76

K

kangaroo [ˌkæŋgəˈruː] Känguru OT 3

karate [kəˈrɑːti] Karate **WS 1**, 37

kayak [ˈkaɪæk] Kajak OT 4

kayaking [ˈkaɪækɪŋ] Kajakfahren OT 2

keen [kiːn] leidenschaftlich OT 2

to **keep** [kiːp] bleiben; behalten OT 2

keeper [ˈkiːpə] Hüter(in) OT 4

ketchup [ˈketʃəp] Ketchup OT 3

kettle [ˈketl] Kessel OT 2

key [kiː] Schlüssel; Taste; Tonart OT 1

to **key** [kiː] tippen OT 2

keyboard [ˈkiːbɔːd] Tastatur; Keyboard OT 1

keyword [ˈkiːwɜːd] Stichwort OT 2

to **kick** [kɪk] treten; einen Tritt versetzen; schießen OT 1

kid [kɪd] Kind; Jugendliche(r); Kleine(r) OT 1

to **kidnap** [ˈkɪdnæp] entführen OT 3

kidnapper [ˈkɪdnæpə] Entführer(in) OT 2

kidney bean [ˈkɪdni biːn] Kidneybohne OT 2

to **kill** [kɪl] töten; umbringen OT 1

kiln [kɪln] Brennofen OT 3

kilo [ˈkiːləʊ] Kilo OT 2

kilometre [ˈkɪləmiːtə] Kilometer OT 1

kilt [kɪlt] Schottenrock; Kilt OT 2

kind [kaɪnd] Art; Sorte OT 1

kind [kaɪnd] freundlich; nett OT 1

kindling [ˈkɪndlɪŋ] Kleinholz OT 2

kindness [ˈkaɪndnəs] Freundlichkeit; Güte **WS 3**, 95

king [kɪŋ] König; Dame OT 1

kinsman [ˈkɪnzmən] Verwandter OT 4

kiss [kɪs] Kuss OT 2

to **kiss** [kɪs] küssen OT 2

kit [kɪt] Ausrüstung; Sportzeug; Bausatz OT 2

kitchen [ˈkɪtʃɪn] Küche OT 1

kiwi [ˈkiːwiː] Kiwi; Neuseeländer(in) OT 1

knee [niː] Knie OT 1

to **kneel** [niːl] knien **WS 2**, 70

knicker [ˈnɪkə] Schlüpfer **WS 3**, 101

knife [naɪf] Messer OT 2

knight [naɪt] Ritter **WS 1**, 20

to **knock** [nɒk] klopfen; stoßen OT 2

to **knock over** [nɒk əʊvə] umstoßen OT 2

to **know** [nəʊ] wissen; kennen; können OT 1

knowledge [ˈnɒlɪdʒ] Wissen OT 4

knowledgeable [ˈnɒlɪdʒəbl] kenntnisreich OT 3

koala [kəʊˈɑːlə] Koala OT 5

kookaburra [ˈkʊkəbʌrə] Kookaburra; Lachender Hans OT 5

Korean [kəˈriːən] koreanisch OT 1

L

lab [læb] Labor OT 4

label [ˈleɪbl] Etikett OT 5

to **label** [ˈleɪbl] beschriften; etikettieren; auszeichnen OT 1

labour [ˈleɪbər] Arbeits... OT 5

to **lace** [leɪs] schnüren **WS 3**, 119

lack [læk] Mangel OT 3

lacrosse [ləˈkrɒs] Lacrosse OT 4

lad [læd] Bursche; Kerl OT 5

ladder [ˈlædə] Leiter OT 3

lady [ˈleɪdi] Dame OT 2

lake [leɪk] See OT 1

lamb [læm] Lamm OT 2

lamp [læmp] Lampe; Laterne OT 1

land [lænd] Land OT 2

to **land** [lænd] landen OT 2

landfill [ˈlændfɪl] Mülldeponie OT 3

landform [ˈlændfɔːm] Landform; Landschaft **WS 1**, 22

landline [ˈlændlaɪn] Festnetz OT 4

landlord [ˈlændlɔːd] Grundbesitzer; Verpächter **WS 1**, 19

landlordism [ˈlændlɔːdɪzəm] Großgrundbesitzertum **WS 1**, 17

landmark [ˈlændmɑːk] Wahrzeichen OT 3

landowner [ˈlændəʊnə] Landbesitzer(in) **WS 1**, 35

landscape [ˈlændskeɪp] Landschaft OT 2

lane [leɪn] Fahrbahn; Gasse OT 4

laneway [leɪnweɪ] Sträßchen OT 5

language [ˈlæŋgwɪdʒ] Sprache OT 1

lantern [ˈlæntən] Laterne OT 2

lanyard [ˈlænjɑːd] Umhängeband; Kordel OT 5

laptop [ˈlæptɒp] Laptop OT 3

larceny [ˈlɑːsəni] Diebstahl **WS 2**, 60

large [lɑːdʒ] groß OT 1

last [lɑːst] letzte(r, -s) OT 1

at **last** [ət ˈlɑːst] endlich OT 2

to **last** [lɑːst] dauern; anhalten OT 2

late [leɪt] spät; zu spät; verstorben OT 1

Latin [ˈlætɪn] Latein OT 2

Latino [læˈtiːnəʊ] lateinamerikanisch OT 2

to **laugh** [lɑːf] lachen OT 1

to **laugh at** [lɑːf ət] auslachen OT 2

laughing stock [ˈlɑːfɪŋ stɒk] Lachnummer **WS 3**, 113

to **launch** [lɔːntʃ] starten; auf den Markt bringen OT 4

laundry [ˈlɔːndri] Wäsche; Wäscherei OT 3

lava [ˈlɑːvə] Lava OT 5

lavish [ˈlævɪʃ] großzügig **WS 1**, 26

law [lɔː] Gesetz OT 3

lawn [lɔːn] Rasen OT 5

lawyer [ˈlɔɪə] Rechtsanwalt, Rechtsanwältin OT 4

lazy [ˈleɪzi] faul OT 2

to **lead** [liːd] führen OT 3

leading [ˈliːdɪŋ] führend OT 2

leader [ˈliːdə] Leiter(in) OT 2

leadership [ˈliːdəʃɪp] Führung OT 2

leaflet [ˈliːflət] Reklamezettel OT 2

leafy [ˈliːfi] blattreich **WS 1**, 36

league [liːg] Liga OT 2

lean [liːn] mager OT 5

to **lean** [liːn] lehnen OT 3

to **leap** [liːp] springen **WS 1**, 13

to **learn** [lɜːn] lernen; erfahren; erkennen OT 1

learner [ˈlɜːnə] Lernende(r); Fahranfänger{in} OT 3

least: at least [ət ˈliːst] mindestens OT 1
leather [ˈleðə] Leder OT 3
leatherback turtle [ˈleðəbæk ˌtɜːtl] Lederrückenschildkröte OT 2
to **leave** [liːv] verlassen; lassen; hinterlassen OT 1
   to **leave behind** [ˌliːv bɪˈhaɪnd] hinterlassen OT 2
leaver [ˈliːvə] Schulabgänger(in) OT 5
leaving [ˈliːvɪŋ] Abschieds... OT 2
lecture [ˈlektʃə] Vorlesung OT 4
lecturer [ˈlektʃərə] Dozent(in) **WS 3**, 93
leftover [ˈleftəʊvə] übriggeblieben OT 4
leg [leg] Bein; Keule; Etappe OT 1
legacy [ˈlegəsi] Vermächtnis; Erbe OT 4
legal [ˈliːgl] rechtlich; legal OT 3
to **legalize** [ˈliːgəlaɪz] legalisieren OT 5
legal pad [ˈliːgl pæd] Schreibblock mit speziellem Papier OT 5
legend [ˈledʒənd] Legende; Sage OT 4
legendary [ˈledʒəndri] legendär **WS 1**, 16
legion [ˈliːdʒən] Legion OT 2
legislation [ˌledʒɪsˈleɪʃn] Gesetzgebung **WS 1**, 17
legislative [ˈledʒɪslətɪv] Legislative; gesetzgebend OT 4
legislature [ˈledʒɪsleɪtʃə] Gesetzgebung; Legislative **WS 2**, 57
leisure [ˈleʒə] Freizeit OT 3
leisurely [ˈleʒəli] gemütlich **WS 1**, 25
lemonade [ˌleməˈneɪd] Zitronenlimonade; Getränk aus frischem Zitronensaft, Zucker und Wasser OT 1
to **lend** [lend] leihen OT 2
length [leŋθ] Länge OT 3
lens [lenz] Objektiv; Linse OT 2
lesbian [ˈlezbiən] Lesbe OT 5
less [les] weniger OT 2
to **lessen** [ˈlesn] mindern; nachlassen **WS 3**, 122
lesson [ˈlesn] Unterricht; Lektion OT 1
to **let** [let] lassen; vermieten OT 1
lethal [ˈliːθəl] tötlich **WS 2**, 76
letter [ˈletə] Brief; Buchstabe OT 1
   letter of reference [ˌletə əv ˈrefrəns] Referenzschreiben; Empfehlungsschreiben OT 5
letterbox [ˈletəbɒks] Briefkasten OT 1
lettuce [ˈletɪs] Kopfsalat OT 2
levee [ˈlevi] Deich OT 4
level [ˈlevl] Niveau; Stufe; Standard OT 1
to **level off** [ˈlevl ɒf] sich ebnen; abflachen OT 5
lexicon [ˈleksɪkən] Wortschatz OT 5

LGBT (lesbian, gay, bisexual, transgender) [el dʒiː biː ˈtiː] LGBT OT 5
liberal [ˈlɪbərəl] liberal **WS 2**, 69
to **liberate** [ˈlɪbəreɪt] befreien **WS 2**, 62
liberation [ˌlɪbəˈreɪʃn] Befreiung **WS 2**, 62
liberty [ˈlɪbəti] Freiheit OT 2
library [ˈlaɪbrəri] Bücherei; Bibliothek; Sammlung OT 1
licence [ˈlaɪsns] Erlaubnis OT 3
lid [lɪd] Deckel OT 2
to **lie** [laɪ] liegen; gelegen sein OT 1
lieutenant [lefˈtenənt] Leutnant **WS 2**, 69
life [laɪf] Leben; Lebensdauer; Schwung OT 1
lifebuoy [ˈlaɪfbɔɪ] Rettungsring OT 3
lifeguard [ˈlaɪfgɑːd] Rettungsschwimmer(in) OT 4
life jacket [ˈlaɪf dʒækɪt] Schwimmweste OT 3
lifeline [ˈlaɪflaɪn] Rettungsleine OT 3
lifelong [ˈlaɪflɒŋ] lebenslang **WS 1**, 21
lifestyle [ˈlaɪfstaɪl] Lebensstil; Lifestyle OT 4
life-threatening [ˈlaɪf θretnɪŋ] lebensbedrohlich OT 2
lifetime [ˈlaɪftaɪm] Lebenszeit; Lebensdauer OT 3
lift [lɪft] Anheben; Lift; Mitfahrgelegenheit OT 3
to **lift** [lɪft] heben OT 3
light [laɪt] Licht; Lampe; Feuer OT 1
light bulb [ˈlaɪtbʌlb] Glühbirne OT 4
to **light** [laɪt] anzünden OT 2
lightheartedly [ˌlaɪt ˈhɑːtɪdli] unbeschwert OT 4
lightly [ˈlaɪtli] leicht **WS 1**, 32
like [laɪk] wie OT 1
   like [laɪk] halt OT 5
to **like** [laɪk] gernhaben; mögen; wollen OT 1
likelihood [ˈlaɪklihʊd] Wahrscheinlichkeit **WS 3**, 108
likely [ˈlaɪkli] wahrscheinlich OT 2
like-minded [ˌlaɪk ˈmaɪndɪd] gleichgesinnt **WS 3**, 99
limelight [ˈlaɪmlaɪt] Rampenlicht **WS 2**, 58
limit [ˈlɪmɪt] Grenze OT 4
to **limit** [ˈlɪmɪt] begrenzen OT 4
limited [ˈlɪmɪtɪd] begrenzt OT 4
limitless [ˈlɪmɪtləs] grenzenlos **WS 2**, 82
line [laɪn] Linie; Reihe; Zeile OT 1

lined [laɪnd] gesäumt **WS 1**, 35
linen [ˈlɪnɪn] Leinen OT 3
linguist [ˈlɪŋgwɪst] Sprachwissenschaftler(in); Linguist(in) OT 5
linguistic [lɪŋˈgwɪstɪk] sprachlich OT 4
linguistics [lɪŋˈgwɪstɪks] Linguistik OT 5
link [lɪŋk] Verbindung OT 2
linkage [ˈlɪŋkɪdʒ] Verbindung **WS 2**, 73
linked [lɪŋkt] verbunden OT 2
lion [ˈlaɪən] Löwe(-in) OT 1
lip [lɪp] Lippe OT 2
liquid [ˈlɪkwɪd] flüssig OT 2
liquor [ˈlɪkə] Spirituosen **WS 1**, 29
list [lɪst] Liste OT 1
to **list** [lɪst] auflisten; listen OT 5
to **listen** [ˈlɪsn] hören; zuhören OT 1
listener [ˈlɪsnə] Hörer(in) OT 3
literacy [ˈlɪtərəsi] Lesekompetenz; Gebildetsein **WS 3**, 106
literally [ˈlɪtərəli] buchstäblich **WS 3**, 101
literary [ˈlɪtərəri] literarisch **WS 2**, 64
litre [ˈliːtə] Liter OT 4
litter bin [ˈlɪtə bɪn] Abfalleimer OT 2
little [ˈlɪtl] klein; kurz; geringfügig OT 1
little-known [ˈlɪtlnəʊn] wenig bekannt OT 2
to **live** [lɪv] leben; wohnen; führen OT 1
lively [ˈlaɪvli] lebhaft OT 2
liver [ˈlɪvər] Leber OT 5
livestock [ˈlaɪvstɒk] Vieh; Viehbestand OT 5
living room [ˈlɪvɪŋ ruːm] Wohnzimmer OT 1
to **load** [ləʊd] (be)laden OT 3
loader [ˈləʊdə] Ladesymbol **WS 4**, 135
loads of [ˈləʊds əv] jede Menge OT 3
loaf [ləʊf] Brotlaib; Brot OT 1
loan [ləʊn] Darlehen; Leihgabe OT 4
to **loath** [ləʊð] hassen; verabscheuen OT 5
to **lobby** [ˈlɒbi] sich einsetzen **WS 2**, 70
local [ˈləʊkl] Einheimische(r) OT 2
local [ˈləʊkl] einheimisch OT 2
   locally [ˈləʊkəli] örtlich; am Ort OT 4
to **localize** [ˈləʊkəlaɪz] lokalisieren **WS 3**, 114
to **locate** [ləʊˈkeɪt] finden; orten **WS 4**, 140
located [ləʊˈkeɪtɪd] gelegen OT 4
location [ləʊˈkeɪʃn] Standort OT 2
loch [lɒk, lɒx] Loch; See **WS 1**, 12
lock [lɒk] Schleuse OT 3
locker [ˈlɒkə] Spind; Schließfach OT 2

lock keeper [ˈlɒk kiːpə]
Schleusenwärter(in) OT 3

lodge [lɒdʒ] Pension OT 2

log [lɒg] Holzscheit OT 3

to **log on** [lɒg ɒn] sich einloggen OT 3

logbook [ˈlɒgbʊk] Logbuch;
Fahrtenbuch **WS 1**, 23

logical [ˈlɒdʒɪkl] logisch; folgerichtig
OT 5

logically [ˈlɒdʒɪkli] logisch OT 4

logline [lɒglaɪn] Logline OT 4

logo [ˈləʊgəʊ] Logo; Firmenzeichen OT 1

lone [ləʊn] allein **WS 1**, 25

lonely [ˈləʊnli] einsam OT 3

long [lɒŋ] lang; weit; lange OT 1

to **long for** [lɒŋ fə] sich sehnen nach
WS 1, 13

long-eared bat [ˌlɒŋɪəd ˈbæt]
(Fledermaus) Braunes Langohr OT 2

loo [luː] Klo OT 2

look [lʊk] Aussehen; Blick OT 2

to **take a look** [ˌteɪk ə ˈlʊk] einen Blick
werfen OT 2

to **look** [lʊk] sehen; aussehen; suchen
OT 1

to **look after** [lʊk ˈɑːftə] auf jdn.
aufpassen; sich um jdn. kümmern
OT 1

to **look forward to** [lʊk ˈfɔːwəd]
sich auf etwas freuen OT 1

to **loom** [ˈluːm] sich abzeichnen;
drohen **WS 1**, 35

loop [luːp] Schleife **WS 4**, 142

lord [lɔːd] Herr OT 2

to **lose** [luːz] verlieren OT 1

loss [lɒs] Verlust OT 4

lot: a lot [lɒt] eine Menge; viel OT 1

lots, a lot [lɒts] viel OT 1

loud [laʊd] laut; grell OT 1

loudspeaker [ˌlaʊdˈspiːkə] Lautsprecher
OT 2

lounge [laʊndʒ] Aufenthaltsraum OT 4

to **love** [lʌv] lieben OT 1

lovely [ˈlʌvli] hübsch; schön;
liebenswert OT 1

low [ləʊ] tief OT 2; arm an **WS 1**, 36

lowland [ˈləʊlənd] Ebene **WS 1**, 17

loyal [ˈlɔɪəl] treu OT 4

loyalty [ˈlɔɪəlti] Loyalität; Treue OT 5

luck [lʌk] Glück; Schicksal OT 1

lucky [ˈlʌki] glücklich OT 4

to **be lucky** [bi ˈlʌki] Glück haben OT 3

luckily [ˈlʌkɪli] glücklicherweise OT 3

luggage [ˈlʌgɪdʒ] Gepäck OT 4

---

to **lull** [lʌl] beruhigen; einlullen
WS 1, 34

lunch [lʌntʃ] Mittagessen OT 1

lunch break [ˈlʌntʃ breɪk] Mittagspause
OT 1

lunchtime [ˈlʌntʃtaɪm] Mittagszeit OT 1

lung [lʌŋ] Lunge OT 3

luxurious [lʌɡˈʒʊəriəs] luxuriös OT 2

lynx [lɪŋks] Luchs OT 2

lyrics [ˈlɪrɪks] Liedtext **WS 1**, 13

M

ma'am [mæm] gnädige Frau OT 2

machine [məˈʃiːn] Maschine OT 2

machinery [məˈʃiːnəri] Maschinen OT 2

mad [mæd] böse (AmE); verrückt (BrE)
OT 2

madam [ˈmædəm] gnädige Frau OT 1

magazine [ˌmægəˈziːn] Zeitschrift;
Illustrierte; Magazin OT 1

magic [ˈmædʒɪk] Zauber OT 1

magical [ˈmædʒɪkl] magisch OT 2

magician [məˈdʒɪʃn] Zauberer/
Zauberin; Zauberkünstler(in) OT 1

magnet [ˈmægnət] Magnet OT 4

magnetic [mægˈnetɪk] magnetisch
OT 2

magnificent [mægˈnɪfɪsnt] großartig;
herrlich OT 5

magnifying glass [ˈmægnɪfaɪɪŋ glɑːs]
Lupe OT 2

magpie [ˈmægpaɪ] Elster OT 1

maiden [ˈmeɪdn] Maid (altmodisch);
unverheiratete Frau **WS 1**, 13

mail [meɪl] Post OT 4

mailbox [ˈmeɪlbɒks] Briefkasten;
Mailbox OT 4

mail carrier [ˈmeɪl kæriə] Postbote;
Postbotin OT 4

main [meɪn] Haupt... OT 1

main course [ˈmeɪn kɔːs] Hauptgang
OT 1

mainland [ˈmeɪnlænd] Festland OT 3

mainstream [ˈmeɪnstriːm] Mainstream;
Hauptrichtung **WS 2**, 66

mainstream school [ˈmeɪnstriːmˈskuːl]
Regelschule OT 5

to **maintain** [meɪnˈteɪn] pflegen;
aufrechterhalten OT 4

maintenance [ˈmeɪntənəns] Wartung
OT 3

majestic [məˈdʒestɪk] majestätisch
OT 4

major [ˈmeɪdʒə] wichtig OT 3

majority [məˈdʒɒrəti] Mehrheit OT 4

---

to **make** [meɪk] kochen; machen;
zubereiten OT 1

makeup [ˈmeɪk ʌp] Schminke OT 5

malaria [məˈleəriə] Malaria OT 5

male [meɪl] männlich OT 2

mall [mɔːl] Einkaufszentrum OT 3

mammal [ˈmæml] Säugetier OT 2

man [mæn] Mann; Mensch; der Mensch
OT 1

to **man up** [mæn ˈʌp] seinen Mann
stehen **WS 2**, 76

to **manage** [ˈmænɪdʒ] leiten; managen;
zurechtkommen OT 1

management [ˈmænɪdʒmənt]
Management ; Geschäftsführung OT 4

manager [ˈmænɪdʒə]
Geschäftsführer(in); Manager(in);
Leiter(in) OT 1

mandate [ˈmændeɪt] Mandat; Auftrag
WS 1, 30

mandatory [ˈmændətəri] verpflichtend
OT 4

manifesto [ˌmænɪˈfestəʊ] Manifest OT 4

to **manipulate** [məˈnɪpjuleɪt]
manipulieren **WS 2**, 73

manner [ˈmænə] Art und Weise OT 3

manual [ˈmænjuəl] Handbuch OT 3

to **manufacture** [ˌmænjuˈfæktʃə]
herstellen OT 4

manure [məˈnjʊə] Dung OT 3

many [ˈmeni] viele OT 1

map [mæp] Karte; Stadtplan OT 1

marathon [ˈmærəθən] Marathon OT 2

March [mɑːtʃ] März OT 1

march [mɑːtʃ] Marsch OT 5

to **march** [mɑːtʃ] marschieren OT 4

marcher [ˈmɑːrtʃə] Marschierer(in)
WS 2, 53

margin [ˈmɑːdʒɪn] Rand OT 5

to **marginalize** [ˈmɑːdʒɪnəlaɪz]
ausgrenzen; marginalisieren **WS 2**, 68

marine [məˈriːn] marin; Meeres... OT 5

to **mark** [mɑːk] korrigieren OT 2

marker [ˈmɑːkə] Markierung;
Textmarker; Textmarker OT 1

market [ˈmɑːkɪt] Markt; Börse OT 1

marketer [ˈmɑːkɪtə] Vermarkter(in)
WS 3, 114

marketing [ˈmɑːkɪtɪŋ] Marketing OT 5

marquee [mɑːˈkiː] Festzelt OT 2

marriage [ˈmærɪdʒ] Ehe OT 3

to **marry** [ˈmæri] heiraten; trauen OT 1

marshmallow [ˌmɑːʃˈmæləʊ]
Marshmallow OT 2

martial [ˈmɑːʃl] martialisch; kriegerisch **WS 1**, 37

mascot [ˈmæskət] Maskottchen OT 2

mash [mæʃ] Brei **WS 4**, 141

mashed potato [ˌmæʃt pəˈteɪtəʊ] Kartoffelbrei OT 1

mask [mɑːsk] Maske OT 3

mass [mæs] Masse OT 5

massacre [ˈmæsəkə] Massaker OT 5

massage [ˈmæsɑːʒ] Massage OT 2

massive [ˈmæsɪv] riesig OT 3

to **master** [ˈmɑːstə] beherrschen OT 4

masterpiece [ˈmɑːstəpiːs] Meisterstück OT 4

match [mætʃ] Spiel, Wettkampf; Streichholz OT 1

mate [meɪt] Kumpel OT 4

material [məˈtɪəriəl] Material OT 4

maths [mæθs] Mathematik OT 1

matter [ˈmætə] Angelegenheit; Problem OT 2

   no matter [nəʊ ˈmætə] was auch immer; egal wie OT 5

   What's the matter? [wɒts ðə ˈmætə] Was ist los? OT 2

to **matter** [ˈmætə] von Bedeutung sein OT 2

mattress [ˈmætrəs] Matratze OT 4

mature [məˈtʃʊə] reif; erwachsen **WS 3**, 105

maximum [ˈmæksɪməm] Maximum OT 2

May [meɪ] Mai OT 1

maybe [ˈmeɪbi] vielleicht; möglicherweise OT 1

mayonnaise [ˌmeɪəˈneɪz] Mayonnaise OT 1

mayor [meə] Bürgermeister(in) OT 3

maze [meɪz] Irrgarten OT 3

MBA (Master of Business Administration) [ˌem biː ˈeɪ] MBA OT 5

me [miː] mich; mir; mich/mir; ich OT 1

meadow [ˈmedəʊ] Wiese OT 2

meal [miːl] Mahlzeit; Essen OT 1

to **mean** [miːn] bedeuten; meinen; etwas ernst meinen OT 1

meaning [ˈmiːnɪŋ] Sinn; Bedeutung OT 1

meaningful [ˈmiːnɪŋfl] sinnvoll OT 4

meantime [ˈmiːntaɪm] Zwischenzeit **WS 3**, 119

meanwhile [ˈmiːnwaɪl] inzwischen; mittlerweile OT 5

measles [ˈmiːzlz] Masern OT 5

measure [ˈmeʒə] Maßnahme OT 5

to **measure** [ˈmeʒə] messen; ausmessen; abschätzen OT 1

measurement [ˈmeʒəmənt] Maß; Maßeinheit OT 2

meat [miːt] Fleisch; Substanz OT 1

meatball [ˈmiːtbɔːl] Fleischklößchen; Hackfleischbällchen OT 1

meat loaf [ˈmiːt ləʊf] Hackbraten OT 3

mechanical [məˈkænɪkl] mechanisch OT 5

medal [ˈmedl] Medaille OT 2

median [ˈmiːdiən] Median; Durchschnitt OT 5

medical [ˈmedɪkl] ärztliche Untersuchung; medizinisch OT 2

medicine [ˈmedsn] Medizin OT 5

medieval [ˌmediˈiːvl] mittelalterlich OT 2

medium [ˈmiːdiəm] Mittel; Medium OT 2

medium-sized [ˈmiːdiəm saɪzd] mittelgroß OT 2

to **meet** [miːt] treffen; begegnen; kennenlernen OT 1

to **meet a demand** [miːt ə dɪˈmɑːnd] einen Anspruch befriedigen **WS 3**, 96

meeting [ˈmiːtɪŋ] Besprechung; Treffen; Begegnung OT 1

melody [ˈmelədi] Melodie **WS 2**, 66

to **melt** [melt] schmelzen OT 4

member [ˈmembə] Mitglied OT 1

membership [ˈmembəʃɪp] Mitgliedschaft **WS 2**, 62

memoir [ˈmemwɑː] Memoiren; Erinnerung OT 5

memorable [ˈmemərəbl] unvergesslich OT 3

memorial [məˈmɔːriəl] Denkmal OT 4

to **memorize** [ˈmeməraɪz] auswendig lernen; sich merken **WS 1**, 23

memory [ˈmeməri] Gedächtnis OT 2

to **mend** [mend] reparieren OT 3

menial [ˈmiːniəl] untergeordnet; nieder OT 5

mental [ˈmentl] mental; geistig OT 4

mentality [menˈtæləti] Geisteshaltung **WS 2**, 56

to **mention** [ˈmenʃn] erwähnen OT 2

menu [ˈmenjuː] Speisekarte; Menü OT 1

merchant [ˈmɜːtʃənt] Händler(in) OT 3

to **merge** [mɜːdʒ] verschmelzen **WS 2**, 60

merit [ˈmerɪt] Wert; Leistung OT 5

mermaid [ˈmɜːmeɪd] Nixe **WS 1**, 43

mesh [meʃ] Netz **WS 3**, 101

mess [mes] Unordnung OT 2

to **mess up** [ˌmesˈʌp] in Unordnung bringen; vergeigen OT 2

message [ˈmesɪdʒ] Nachricht; Botschaft; Botschaft OT 1

metal [ˈmetl] Metall; Heavy Metal OT 1

metaphor [ˈmetəfə] Metapher **WS 2**, 64

method [ˈmeθəd] Methode OT 1

metre [ˈmiːtə] Meter; Versmaß OT 1

metro [ˈmetrəʊ] U-Bahn OT 1

metronomic [ˌmetrəˈnɒmɪk] metronomisch **WS 1**, 29

microphone [ˈmaɪkrəfəʊn] Mikrofon OT 5

microwave [ˈmaɪkrəweɪv] Microwelle OT 4

middle [ˈmɪdl] Mitte; Taille OT 1

midnight [ˈmɪdnaɪt] Mitternacht OT 1

midst [mɪdst] Mitte **WS 2**, 58

mid-western [ˌmɪdˈwestən] des mittleren Westens OT 4

might [maɪt] könnte(n) OT 2

mighty [ˈmaɪti] sehr OT 3

migrant [ˈmaɪgrənt] Migrant(in) OT 4

to **migrate** [maɪˈgreɪt] migrieren OT 3

migration [maɪˈgreɪʃn] Migration OT 3

mild [maɪld] mild **WS 1**, 37

mile [maɪl] Meile (etwa 1,6 km) OT 1

milestone [ˈmaɪlstəʊn] Meilenstein OT 3

militant [ˈmɪlɪtənt] militant **WS 2**, 62

military [ˈmɪlətri] militärisch; Militär... OT 5

milk [mɪlk] Milch OT 1

mill [mɪl] Fabrik; Mühle **WS 3**, 114

millennial [mɪˈleniəl] Millennium-Generation; Millenial OT 5

million [ˈmɪljən] Million OT 1

millworker [mɪlwɜːkə] Fabrikarbeiter(in) **WS 2**, 69

minced [mɪnst] fein gehackt OT 2

mind [maɪnd] Verstand; Meinung; Sinn OT 1

   to **change one's mind** [tʃeɪndʒ wʌnz maɪnd] seine Meinung ändern OT 2

mind map [ˈmaɪnd mæp] Gedankenkarte; Mindmap OT 1

mindset [ˈmaɪndset] Mentalität **WS 3**, 94

mine [maɪn] Bergwerk OT 2

mine [maɪn] meine(r, -s); mein Haus/ meine Wohnung OT 1

miner [ˈmaɪnə] Bergarbeiter OT 3

mini [ˈmɪni] klein; winzig OT 5

miniature [ˈmɪnətʃə] Miniatur OT 2

minibus [ˈmɪnibʌs] Kleinbus OT 2

to **minimize** [ˈmɪnɪmaɪz] minimieren; verkleinern **WS 3**, 95

minimum [ˈmɪnɪməm] Mindest...;
Minimal... OT 1

mining [ˈmaɪnɪŋ] Bergbau... OT 3

minister [ˈmɪnɪstə] Minister(in) OT 4

minor [ˈmaɪnə] Minderjährige(r) OT 2

minority [maɪˈnɒrəti] Minderheit OT 4

mint [mɪnt] Minze; Pfefferminzbonbon;
Münzanstalt OT 1

minute [ˈmɪnɪt] Minute; Moment OT 1

mirror [ˈmɪrə] Spiegel OT 1

miserable [ˈmɪzrəbl] unglücklich OT 2

to **misplace** [ˌmɪsˈpleɪs] verlegen
WS 1, 22

Miss [mɪs] Frau; Fräulein OT 2

to **miss** [mɪs] vermissen OT 2

missing [ˈmɪsɪŋ] verschwunden;
vermisst OT 1

mission [ˈmɪʃn] Mission; Aufgabe
WS 2, 54

mist [mɪst] Nebel **WS 1**, 35

mistake [mɪˈsteɪk] Fehler OT 1

by mistake [baɪ mɪˈsteɪk]
versehentlich OT 2

to **make a mistake** [ˌmeɪk ə mɪˈsteɪk]
einen Fehler machen OT 2

misty [ˈmɪsti] neblig; dunstig **WS 1**, 13

to **misunderstand** [ˌmɪsʌndəˈstænd]
missverstehen OT 5

misunderstanding [ˌmɪsʌndəˈstændɪŋ]
Missverständnis OT 3

mitten [ˈmɪtn] Fausthandschuh OT 4

mix [mɪks] Mischung OT 2

mixed up [ˌmɪkst ˈʌp] durcheinander
OT 2

mixture [ˈmɪkstʃə] Mischung OT 2

mob [mɒb] Meute OT 5

mobile phone [ˈməʊbaɪl] Handy;
Mobiltelefon OT 1

to **mobilize** [ˈməʊbəlaɪz] mobilisieren
WS 1, 32

to **mock** [mɒk] verspotten **WS 2**, 64

mockingbird [ˈmɒkɪŋbɜːd]
(Spott)drossel **WS 2**, 64

modal [ˈməʊdl] Modalverb OT 2

model [ˈmɒdl] Modell; Fotomodell
OT 1

moderate [ˈmɒdərət] maßvoll;
moderat **WS 1**, 36

modern [ˈmɒdn] modern OT 1

modest [ˈmɒdɪst] bescheiden OT 2

module [ˈmɒdjuːl] Modul OT 4

to **mold** [məʊld] formen **WS 3**, 97

moment [ˈməʊmənt] Moment;
Augenblick OT 1

momentous [məˈmentəs] bedeutsam;
folgenschwer **WW**, 11

monarch [ˈmɒnək] Monarch(in);
Herrscher(in) OT 4

monarchy [ˈmɒnəki] Monarchie OT 4

Monday [ˈmʌndeɪ] Montag OT 1

money [ˈmʌni] Geld OT 1

to **monitor** [ˈmɒnɪtər] kontrollieren
WS 4, 135

monk [mʌŋk] Mönch OT 3

monograph [ˈmɒnəɡrɑːf] Monografie
WS 3, 96

monolingual [ˌmɒnəˈlɪŋɡwəl]
einsprachig OT 5

monopoly [məˈnɒpəli] Monopol OT 4

monotone [ˈmɒnətəʊn] monoton OT 5

monster [ˈmɒnstə] Monster;
Ungeheuer; Schlingel OT 1

month [mʌnθ] Monat OT 1

monument [ˈmɒnjumənt] Monument;
Denkmal OT 4

monumental [ˌmɒnjuˈmentl] riesig
WS 2, 58

mood [muːd] Stimmung OT 3

moody [ˈmuːdi] launisch OT 5

moon [muːn] Mond OT 1

moor [mɔː] Heidelandschaft OT 3

to **moor** [mɔː] vertäuen; anlegen OT 3

mooring [ˈmɔːrɪŋ] Anlegeplatz OT 3

moose [muːs] Elch OT 4

moped [ˈməʊped] Moped OT 4

moral [ˈmɒrəl] Moral OT 2

more [mɔː] mehr OT 1

moreover [mɔːˈrəʊvə] außerdem OT 4

morning [ˈmɔːnɪŋ] Morgen; Vormittag
OT 1

mortgage [ˈmɔːɡɪdʒ] Hypothek OT 4

mosaic [məʊˈzeɪɪk] Mosaik OT 2

mosquito [məˈskiːtəʊ] Stechmücke OT 2

most [məʊst] der/die/das meiste; die
meisten OT 1

motel [məʊˈtel] Motel OT 3

mother [ˈmʌðə] Mutter OT 1

motif [məʊˈtiːf] Motiv **WS 3**, 101

motion [ˈməʊʃn] Bewegung **WS 2**, 66

to **motivate** [ˈməʊtɪveɪt] motivieren;
anregen OT 5

motivated [ˈməʊtɪveɪtɪd] motiviert OT 4

motivation [ˌməʊtɪˈveɪʃn] Motivation;
Begründung OT 5

motivational [ˌməʊtɪˈveɪʃənl] anregend;
Motivations... OT 5

motive [ˈməʊtɪv] Beweggrund; Motiv
WS 3, 116

to **motor** [ˈməʊtə] fahren OT 3

motorized [ˈməʊtəraɪzd] motorisiert
OT 4

motto [ˈmɒtəʊ] Motto OT 4

mountain [ˈmaʊntən] Berg OT 1

mountain biking [ˈmaʊntən baɪkɪŋ]
Mountainbiken OT 2

mountain range [ˈmaʊntən reɪndʒ]
Gebirge OT 4

mouse [maʊs] Maus OT 1

mouth [maʊθ] Mund; Maul OT 1

mouthguard [ˈmaʊθɡɑːd] Mundschutz
OT 2

to **move** [muːv] bewegen; umziehen;
rühren OT 1

movement [ˈmuːvmənt] Bewegung OT 4

movie [ˈmuːvi] Film OT 2

to **mow** [məʊ] mähen OT 5

MP (member of parliament) [ˌem ˈpiː]
Abgeordnete(r) OT 4

Mr [ˈmɪstə] Herr OT 1

Mrs [ˈmɪsɪz] Frau OT 1

Ms [mɪz] Frau OT 2

much [mʌtʃ] viel; sehr; oft OT 1

to **muck around** [mʌk əˈraʊnd] Spaß
haben; vertrödeln OT 5

mud [mʌd] Schlamm OT 3

muddy [ˈmʌdi] schlammig; matschig
OT 4

mudslide [ˈmʌdslaɪd] Schlammlawine
OT 5

muesli [ˈmjuːzli] müsli OT 5

muffin [ˈmʌfɪn] Muffin; Hefegebäck,
das getoastet und mit Butter gegessen
wird OT 1

mule [mjuːl] Maultier OT 3

multicultural [ˌmʌltiˈkʌltʃərəl]
multikulturell OT 4

multiculturalism [ˌmʌltiˈkʌltʃərəlɪzəm]
Multikulturalismus OT 4

multi-functional [ˌmʌltiˈfʌŋkʃənl]
multi-funktional OT 4

multinational [ˌmʌltiˈnæʃnəl]
multinational OT 4

multiple [ˈmʌltɪpl] vielfach OT 2

to **multiply** [ˈmʌltɪplaɪ] multiplizieren;
vervielfachen **WS 4**, 136

mum [mʌm] Mama; Mama; Mami OT 1

mural [ˈmjʊərəl] Wandgemälde OT 2

murder [ˈmɜːdər] Mord OT 5

to **murder** [ˈmɜːdə] ermorden OT 2

murky [ˈmɜːki] trübe OT 4

muscle [ˈmʌsl] Muskel OT 2

museum [mjuːˈziːəm] Museum OT 1

mushroom [ˈmʌʃrʊm] Pilz OT 2

music [ˈmjuːzɪk] Musik; Noten OT 1

musical ['mjuːzɪkl] Musik…; musikalisch OT 2

musician [mjuːˈzɪʃn] Musiker(in) OT 2

must [mʌst] müssen OT 1

mustard ['mʌstəd] Senf OT 1

to mutter ['mʌtə] murmeln **WS 3**, 105

my [maɪ] mein OT 1

myself [maɪˈself] (ich) selbst OT 3

mysterious [mɪˈstɪəriəs] geheimnisvoll; rätselhaft **WS 2**, 82

mystery ['mɪstri] Geheimnis; Rätsel OT 5

myth [mɪθ] Mythos; Legende OT 4

mythical ['mɪθɪkl] mystisch; geheimnisvoll **WS 1**, 17

mythology [mɪˈθɒlədʒi] Mythologie OT 2

N

to nag [næg] an jemandem herumnörgeln **WW**, 11

name [neɪm] Name; Ruf OT 1

to nap [næp] ein Nickerchen machen OT 2

nappy ['næpi] Windel OT 3

narrative ['nærətɪv] Geschichte; Erzählung **WS 2**, 65

narrator [nəˈreɪtə] Erzähler(in) OT 2

narrow ['nærəʊ] eng OT 2

narrowboat ['nærəʊbəʊt] schmales Kanalboot; Hausboot OT 3

narrow-minded [ˌnærəʊ ˈmaɪndɪd] engstirnig OT 5

nasty ['nɑːsti] unangenehm OT 2

nation ['neɪʃn] Nation OT 2

national ['næʃnəl] national OT 1

nationalism ['næʃnəlɪzəm] Nationalismus **WS 2**, 60

nationality [ˌnæʃəˈnæləti] Staatsangehörigkeit OT 2

native ['neɪtɪv] Einheimische(r) OT 3

native ['neɪtɪv] einheimisch OT 3

natural ['nætʃrəl] natürlich; Natur…; normal OT 1

naturalist ['nætʃrəlɪst] Naturforscher(in) OT 2

nature ['neɪtʃə] Natur OT 2

naughty ['nɔːti] ungezogen OT 2

naval officer ['neɪvl ˈɒfɪsə] Marineoffizier(in) **WS 2**, 69

to navigate ['nævɪgeɪt] navigieren **WS 1**, 38

navigation [ˌnævɪˈgeɪʃn] Navigation **WS 1**, 15

navy ['neɪvi] Marine OT 3

near [nɪə] nahe; in der Nähe von; gegen OT 1

nearby [ˌnɪəˈbaɪ] in der Nähe OT 3

nearly ['nɪəli] fast; beinahe OT 2

neat [niːt] ordentlich OT 4

necessarily [ˌnesəˈserəli] unbedingt; notwendig OT 4

necessary ['nesəsəri] notwendig OT 3

necessity [nəˈsesəti] Notwendigkeit OT 4

neck [nek] Hals; Nacken; Genick OT 1

necklace ['nekləs] Halskette OT 3

to need [niːd] brauchen; nötig haben; erfordern OT 1

negative ['negətɪv] Verneinung; Negativ OT 1

negativity [ˌnegəˈtɪvəti] Negativität; negative Einstellung OT 4

neglect [nɪˈglekt] Vernachlässigung **WS 2**, 70

negro ['niːgrəʊ] Neger(in) **WS 2**, 64

neighbourhood ['neɪbəhʊd] Nachbarschaft OT 4

neighbour ['neɪbə] Nachbar OT 2

neither ['naɪðə] auch nicht OT 3

  neither … nor ['naɪðə 'nɔː] weder … noch OT 4

nephew ['nefjuː] Neffe OT 5

nerve [nɜːv] Nerv OT 3

nervous ['nɜːvəs] nervös OT 2

nest [nest] Nest OT 3

net [net] Netz OT 4

netball ['netbɔːl] Netzball OT 5

network ['netwɜːk] Netzwerk OT 4

neurological [ˌnjʊərəˈlɒdʒɪkl] neurologisch OT 5

neutral ['njuːtrəl] neutral OT 3

neutrality [njuːˈtræləti] Neutralität **WS 2**, 60

never ['nevə] nie; niemals; gar nicht OT 1

new [njuː] neu OT 1

  brand new [ˌbrænd ˈnjuː] brandneu OT 2

news [njuːz] Neuigkeit(en); Nachrichten OT 1

newsletter ['njuːzletə] Mitteilungsblatt; Newsletter OT 3

newspaper ['njuːzpeɪpə] Zeitung; Zeitungspapier OT 1

next [nekst] als Nächstes; nächste(r) OT 3

  next to ['nekst tuː] neben OT 1

nice [naɪs] schön; nett; gut OT 1

nickname ['nɪkneɪm] Spitzname OT 4

niece [niːs] Nichte OT 4

nigger ['nɪgər] Nigger **WS 2**, 65

night [naɪt] Nacht; Abend OT 1

nine [naɪn] neun OT 1

ninety ['naɪnti] neunzig OT 1

nobleman ['nəʊblmən] Adliger OT 3

nobody ['nəʊbədi] niemand; keiner OT 1

to nod [nɒd] nicken OT 3

noise [nɔɪz] Geräusch; Lärm; Krach OT 1

noisy ['nɔɪzi] laut; lärmend; laut OT 1

nomadic [nəʊˈmædɪk] nomadisch OT 3

to nominate ['nɒmɪneɪt] nominieren; aufstellen **WS 2**, 78

nomination [ˌnɒmɪˈneɪʃn] Nominierung; Aufstellung **WS 2**, 78

nominee [ˌnɒmɪˈniː] Kandidat(in) **WS 2**, 79

non-binary [ˌnɒn ˈbaɪnəri] nicht binär **WS 3**, 112

none [nʌn] keine(r, -s) OT 3

nonetheless [ˌnʌnðəˈles] trotzdem; nichtsdestoweniger **WS 2**, 57

nonsense ['nɒnsns] Unsinn; Quatsch OT 1

nonviolence [ˌnɒnˈvaɪələns] Gewaltlosigkeit **WS 2**, 60

nonviolent [ˌnɒnˈvaɪələnt] gewaltlos **WS 2**, 60

noodle ['nuːdl] Nudel OT 2

noon [nuːn] Mittag OT 4

norm [nɔːm] Regel; Standard OT 5

normal ['nɔːml] normal; üblich OT 1

normalization [ˌnɔːməlaɪˈzeɪʃn] Normalisierung **WS 3**, 114

Norman ['nɔːmən] normannisch OT 3

north [nɔːθ] Nord- OT 1

north-east [nɔːθ ˈiːst] Nordosten OT 1

northern [nɔːðən] nördlich OT 2

nose [nəʊz] Nase OT 2

nostalgia [nɒˈstældʒə] Nostalgie OT 4

notable ['nəʊtəbl] bemerkenswert OT 4

note [nəʊt] Notiz; Zettel OT 1

notebook ['nəʊtbʊk] Notizbuch OT 2

noteworthy ['nəʊtwɜːði] bemerkenswert **WS 2**, 62

nothing ['nʌθɪŋ] nichts OT 1

notice ['nəʊtɪs] Schild; Aushang; Bescheid OT 1

to notice ['nəʊtɪs] bemerken OT 4

noticeboard ['nəʊtɪsbɔːd] Anschlagbrett; Schwarzes Brett OT 1

notification [ˌnəʊtɪfɪˈkeɪʃn] Benachrichtigung **WS 3**, 108

to notify ['nəʊtɪfaɪ] benachrichtigen **WS 1**, 15

notion ['nəʊʃn] Idee; Vorstellung **WS 3**, 101

noun [naʊn] Substantiv; Nomen; Hauptwort OT 1

novel ['nɒvl] Roman OT 2

novelist ['nɒvəlɪst] Schriftsteller(in) OT 4

November [nəʊ'vembə] November OT 1

now [naʊ] jetzt; sofort; nun OT 1

nowadays ['naʊədeɪz] heutzutage OT 3

nowhere ['nəʊweə] nirgendwo OT 2

nuanced ['njuːɑːnst] differenziert WS 3, 116

nub [nʌb] Kernpunkt WS 3, 101

nuclear ['njuːkliə] Atom...; Nuklear... OT 3

number ['nʌmbə] Zahl; Nummer; Anzahl OT 1

numerical [njuː'merɪkl] numerisch OT 5

numerous ['njuːmərəs] zahlreich WS 1, 39

nun [nʌn] Nonne OT 3

nurse [nɜːs] Krankenschwester(-pfleger) OT 1

nursery ['nɜːsəri] Kindergarten; Kindertagesstätte OT 5

nursing ['nɜːsɪŋ] Krankenpflege OT 5

to **nurture** ['nɜːtʃə] pflegen; fördern WS 1, 12

nut [nʌt] Nuss; hier: Verrückte(r) OT 5

nutrient ['njuːtriənt] Nährstoff WS 1, 36

nutrition [njuː'trɪʃn] Ernährung WS 1, 36

nutritious [njuː'trɪʃəs] nahrhaft OT 4

O

o'clock [ə'klɒk] Uhr OT 1

obesity [əʊ'biːsəti] Fettleibigkeit WS 1, 37

object ['ɒbdʒɪkt] Gegenstand; Objekt OT 1

objection [əb'dʒekʃn] Einwand OT 3

obligation [ˌɒblɪ'geɪʃn] Pflicht OT 5

obliged: to be obliged (to) [bi 'ɒblɪɡeɪtɪd] müssen; verpflichtet sein OT 5

obscure [əb'skjʊə] unklar; rätselhaft WS 1, 43

observation [ˌɒbzə'veɪʃn] Beobachtung OT 3

to **observe** [əb'zɜːv] beobachten OT 4

observer [əb'zɜːvə] Beobachter(in) OT 5

obsession [əb'seʃn] Obsession; Besessenheit OT 5

obstacle ['ɒbstəkl] Hindernis OT 4

obtainable [əb'teɪnəbl] erreichbar WS 3, 97

obvious ['ɒbviəs] offensichtlich OT 3

obviously ['ɒbviəsli] offensichtlich OT 3

occasion [ə'keɪʒn] Gelegenheit OT 3

occasionally [ə'keɪʒnəli] hin und wieder; gelegentlich OT 4

occupation [ˌɒkju'peɪʃn] Tätigkeit; Beschäftigung OT 4

occupied: to be occupied [bi 'ɒkjupaɪd] beschäftigt sein OT 5

to **occupy** ['ɒkjupaɪ] einnehmen; besetzen WS 3, 122

to **occur** [ə'kɜːr] passieren WS 1, 28

ocean ['əʊʃn] Ozean OT 2

October [ɒk'təʊbə] Oktober OT 1

odd [ɒd] eigenartig OT 2

odds [ɒdz] Chancen; Widrigkeiten WS 1, 17

of [əv] von; aus; an OT 1

off [ɒf] von; aus; los; weg OT 1

to **be off beat** [ˌɒf'biːt] aus dem Takt kommen OT 4

offence [ə'fens] Straftat OT 5

to **offend** [ə'fend] beleidigen OT 3

offender [ə'fendə] Täter(in) OT 5

offensive [ə'fensɪv] beleidigend WS 1, 23

offer ['ɒfə] Angebot OT 2

to **offer** ['ɒfə] anbieten OT 2

offering ['ɒfərɪŋ] Angebot OT 4

office ['ɒfɪs] Büro OT 2

officer ['ɒfɪsə] Offizier(in) OT 2

official [ə'fɪʃl] Beamter; Beamtin OT 2

official [ə'fɪʃl] offiziell OT 2

officially [ə'fɪʃəli] offiziell OT 4

off-road ['ɒf rəʊd] geländetauglich OT 2

offshore ['ɒf ʃɔːr] küstennah; offshore WS 1, 12

offstage [ˌɒf'steɪdʒ] aus dem Off OT 2

often ['ɒfn] oft; häufig OT 1

oil [ɔɪl] Öl OT 3

OK [əʊ'keɪ] in Ordnung OT 1

old [əʊld] alt; ehemalig OT 1

old-fashioned [ˌəʊld'fæʃnd] altmodisch OT 2

Olympic [ə'lɪmpɪk] olympisch; Olympia... OT 2

on [ɒn] auf; an; am; in OT 1

once [wʌns] einmal OT 2

one [wʌn] eins; ein{e}; eine OT 1

onion ['ʌnjən] Zwiebel OT 2

online [ˌɒn'laɪn] online OT 3

only ['əʊnli] nur OT 1

onscreen [ˌɒn'skriːn] auf dem Bildschirm; auf der Leinwand OT 2

onto ['ɒntuː] auf OT 1

open ['əʊpən] offen; auf; frei OT 1

to **open** ['əʊpən] aufmachen; öffnen; aufgehen OT 1

opening times ['əʊpnɪŋ taɪmz] Öffnungszeiten OT 1

to **operate** ['ɒpəreɪt] bedienen; operieren OT 3

operation [ˌɒpə'reɪʃn] Verfahren; Vorgang OT 4

operator ['ɒpəreɪtə] Leitstellendisponent(in) OT 2

opinion [ə'pɪnjən] Meinung OT 3

opponent [ə'pəʊnənt] Gegner(in) OT 2

opportunity [ˌɒpə'tjuːnəti] Gelegenheit OT 2

to **oppose** [ə'pəʊz] ablehnen; sich widersetzen WS 2, 60

opposite ['ɒpəzɪt] Gegenteil; Gegensatz OT 1

opposition [ˌɒpə'zɪʃn] Opposition WS 1, 37

to **oppress** [ə'pres] unterdrücken WS 2, 63

oppression [ə'preʃn] Unterdrückung OT 5

oppressor [ə'presə] Unterdrücker(in) WS 2, 60

to **opt** [ɒpt] (sich) entscheiden (für/gegen) OT 5

optimistic [ˌɒptɪ'mɪstɪk] optimistisch OT 4

to **optimize** ['ɒptɪmaɪz] optimieren OT 5

option ['ɒpʃn] Wahl OT 2

optional ['ɒpʃənl] optional; freiwillig OT 4

or [ɔː] oder; noch OT 1

oral ['ɔːrəl] mündlich OT 1

orange ['ɒrɪndʒ] Apfelsine; Orange OT 1

orange ['ɒrɪndʒ] orange; orangefarben OT 1

oratory ['ɒrətri] Redekunst; Rhetorik WS 2, 60

orbit ['ɔːbɪt] Orbit; Umlaufbahn OT 4

orchard ['ɔːtʃəd] Obstgarten OT 4

orchestra ['ɔːkɪstrə] Orchester OT 1

order ['ɔːdə] Reihenfolge; Bestellung; Befehl OT 1

to **order** ['ɔːdə] befehlen; in eine Reihenfolge bringen; bestellen OT 1

ordinance ['ɔːdɪnəns] Verfügung WS 2, 54

ordinary ['ɔːdnri] normal OT 2

organ ['ɔːɡən] Organ OT 5

organic [ɔː'ɡænɪk] biologisch OT 4

organization [ˌɔːɡənaɪ'zeɪʃn] Organisation; Gesellschaft OT 3

organizational [ˌɔːɡənaɪ'zeɪʃənl] organisatorisch OT 4

to **organize** [ˈɔːgənaɪz] organisieren OT 1

organizer [ˈɔːgənaɪzə] Organisator(in) OT 4

orientated [ˈɔːriənteɪt] orientiert OT 5

orientation [ˌɔːriənˈteɪʃn] Orientierung; Ausrichtung **WS 3**, 111

origin [ˈɒrɪdʒɪn] Ursprung OT 3

original [əˈrɪdʒənl] ursprünglich; Original... OT 3

   originally [əˈrɪdʒənəli] ursprünglich OT 2

to **originate** [əˈrɪdʒɪneɪt] stammen **WS 1**, 17

osteoporosis [ˌɒstiəʊpəˈrəʊsɪs] Osteoporose **WS 1**, 37

other [ˈʌðə] andere(r, -s) OT 1

otherwise [ˈʌðəwaɪz] sonst; ansonsten OT 4

otter [ˈɒtə] Otter OT 4

ought to [ˈɔːt tə] sollte OT 5

our [ˈaʊə] unser OT 1

ours [ɑːz, ˈaʊəz] unsere(r, -s) OT 3

ourselves [ɑːˈselvz, ˌaʊəˈselvz] uns OT 3

out [aʊt] heraus; aus; draußen OT 1

outback [ˈaʊtbæk] Busch; Hinterland OT 5

outcome [ˈaʊtkʌm] Ergebnis **WS 1**, 33

outcropping [ˈaʊtkrɒpɪŋ] Felsvorsprung **WS 1**, 35

outcry [ˈaʊtkraɪ] Aufschrei; Protest **WS 2**, 54

outdoor [ˈaʊtdɔː] im Freien OT 2

outer space [ˌaʊtə ˈspeɪs] Weltraum OT 5

outfit [ˈaʊtfɪt] Verein; hier: Band **WS 1**, 29

outgoing [ˌaʊtˈgəʊɪŋ] kontaktfreudig OT 4

to **outline** [ˈaʊtlaɪn] umreißen; zusammenfassen OT 4

outlook [ˈaʊtlʊk] Einstellung **WS 3**, 97

outrage [ˈaʊtreɪdʒ] Empörung **WS 2**, 53

outraged [ˈaʊtreɪdʒd] entsetzt **WS 2**, 64

outreach [ˈaʊtriːtʃ] Reichweite **WS 3**, 111

outside [ˌaʊtˈsaɪd] draußen OT 1

outstanding [aʊtˈstændɪŋ] herausragend OT 3

to **outweigh** [ˌaʊtˈweɪ] aufheben; überwiegen **WS 2**, 62

oven [ˈʌvn] Ofen OT 2

over [ˈəʊvə] drüben OT 2

   over there [ˈəʊvə ˌðeə] dort drüben OT 2

overall [ˌəʊvərˈɔːl] allgemein OT 5

   overboard [ˈəʊvəbɔːd] über Bord OT 3

to **overcome** [ˌəʊvəˈkʌm] überwinden; bewältigen OT 4

overcrowded [ˌəʊvəˈkraʊdɪd] überfüllt **WS 1**, 36

to **overdo** [ˌəʊvəˈduː] übertreiben OT 5

to **overflow** [ˌəʊvəˈfləʊ] überlaufen OT 4

overly [ˈəʊvəli] übermäßig OT 5

overnight [ˌəʊvəˈnaɪt] über Nacht OT 2

to **overrate** [ˌəʊvəˈreɪt] überbewerten OT 5

overseas [ˌəʊvəˈsiːz] ausländisch OT 2

to **oversee** [ˌəʊvəˈsiː] überwachen; beaufsichtigen OT 4

to **oversleep** [ˌəʊvəˈsliːp] verschlafen OT 4

to **overstate** [ˌəʊvəˈsteɪt] überbewerten **WS 3**, 96

overt [əʊˈvɜːt] offen **WS 2**, 62

overtime [ˈəʊvətaɪm] Überstunden OT 5

to **overturn** [ˌəʊvəˈtɜːn] (um)stürzen; umwerfen **WS 2**, 53

overuse [ˌəʊvəˈjuːs] Überbeanspruchung **WS 3**, 107

overview [ˈəʊvəvjuː] Überblick; Übersicht OT 4

overweight [ˌəʊvəˈweɪt] übergewichtig **WS 3**, 105

own [əʊn] eigene(r, -s) OT 1

   on one's own [ɒn wʌnz əʊn] allein OT 2

to **own** [əʊn] besitzen OT 2

owner [ˈəʊnə] Besitzer(in) OT 2

oxygen [ˈɒksɪdʒən] Sauerstoff OT 5

P

PA (public address) system [ˌpiː ˈeɪ sɪstɪm] Beschallungsanlage OT 2

pace [peɪs] Geschwindigkeit; Tempo **WS 1**, 29

pack [pæk] Rudel OT 4

to **pack** [pæk] packen OT 2

package [ˈpækɪdʒ] Paket OT 3

packaging [ˈpækɪdʒɪŋ] Verpackung OT 3

packed lunch [ˈpækt lʌntʃ] Lunchpaket OT 1

packet [ˈpækɪt] Paket OT 2

to **paddle** [ˈpædl] paddeln OT 3

pad [pæd] Polster OT 2

page [peɪdʒ] Seite; Webseite OT 1

pain [peɪn] Schmerz; Nervensäge OT 2

painful [ˈpeɪnfl] schmerzhaft **WS 3**, 122

painkiller [ˈpeɪnkɪlə] Schmerzmittel OT 2

paint [peɪnt] Farbe OT 1

to **paint** [peɪnt] malen; anstreichen OT 1

painting [ˈpeɪntɪŋ] Malen; Gemälde OT 1

pair [peə] Paar OT 2

palace [ˈpæləs] Palast; Schloss OT 1

pale [peɪl] blass OT 3

pan [pæn] Pfanne OT 2

to **pan** [pæn] (eine Kamera) schwenken **WS 2**, 76

pandemic [pænˈdemɪk] Pandemie OT 5

panel [ˈpænl] Gremium; Forum OT 4

to **panic** [ˈpænɪk] in Panik geraten OT 2

panoramic [ˌpænəˈræmɪk] panoramisch; panoramaartig **WS 1**, 35

panther [ˈpænθə] Panther OT 2

pants [pænts] Hose OT 5

paper [ˈpeɪpə] Papier; Zeitung; Klausur OT 1

paperwork [ˈpeɪpəwɜːk] Schreibarbeit OT 5

par: on par [ɒn pɑː] gleichgestellt **WS 3**, 107

to **parachute** [ˈpærəʃuːt] Fallschirm springen OT 4

parade [pəˈreɪd] Umzug; Parade OT 2

paradise [ˈpærədaɪs] Paradies OT 5

paragliding [ˈpærəglaɪdɪŋ] Gleitschirmfliegen OT 5

paragraph [ˈpærəgrɑːf] Absatz; Abschnitt OT 1

parallelism [ˈpærəlelɪzəm] Parallelität **WS 2**, 64

paramedic [ˌpærəˈmedɪk] Rettungssanitäter(in) OT 1

paramount [ˈpærəmaʊnt] vorrangig; entscheidend **WS 2**, 55

to **paraphrase** [ˈpærəfreɪz] umschreiben OT 3

parasite [ˈpærəsaɪt] Parasit **WS 4**, 140

parcel [ˈpɑːsl] Paket OT 2

parent [ˈpeərənt] Elternteil OT 1

parental [pəˈrentl] elterlich **WS 3**, 112

park ranger [ˈpɑːk ˌreɪndʒə] Forstbeamter; -beamtin OT 2

park [pɑːk] Park OT 1

to **park** [pɑːk] parken OT 2

parking [ˈpɑːkɪŋ] Parken OT 2

parliament [ˈpɑːləmənt] Parlament; Abgeordnetenhaus OT 4

parlour [ˈpɑːlə] Salon **WS 3**, 114

part [pɑːt] Teil; Einzelteil; Folge OT 1

   part of speech [ˌpɑːt əv ˈspiːtʃ] Wortart OT 2

participant [pɑːˈtɪsɪpənt] Teilnehmer(in) OT 4

to **participate** [pɑːˈtɪsɪpeɪt] teilnehmen OT 4

participation [pɑːˌtɪsɪˈpeɪʃn] Beteiligung OT 5

participle [pɑːˈtɪsɪpl] Partizip OT 2

particular [pəˈtɪkjələ] bestimmt; besondere OT 4

particularly [pəˈtɪkjələli] besonders OT 4

partisan [ˈpɑːtɪzæn] parteiisch **WS 2**, 69

partly [ˈpɑːtli] teilweise OT 4

partner [ˈpɑːtnə] Partner(in); Gesellschafter(in); Teilhaber(in) OT 1

partnership [ˈpɑːtnəʃɪp] Partnerschaft; Kooperation OT 4

part-time [ˌpɑːt ˈtaɪm] nebenberuflich; teilzeitlich OT 5

party [ˈpɑːti] Party; Partei; Gruppe OT 1

to **pass** [pɑːs] zuspielen; an etw. vorbeifahren OT 2

passage [ˈpæsɪdʒ] Überfahrt; Passage **WS 1**, 19

passenger [ˈpæsɪndʒə] Passagier(in) OT 2

passion [ˈpæʃn] Leidenschaft OT 5

passionate [ˈpæʃənət] leidenschaftlich OT 4

passport [ˈpɑːspɔːt] Pass OT 2

past [pɑːst] nach; vorbei OT 1

pasta [ˈpæstə] Nudeln; Teigwaren OT 1

to **paste** [peɪst] kleben OT 2

pasture [ˈpɑːstʃə] Weide **WS 1**, 36

pat [pæt] Klaps OT 3

patch [pætʃ] Fleck; Flicken OT 5

patchy [ˈpætʃi] lückenhaft; ungleichmäßig OT 4

to **patent** [ˈpætnt] patentieren OT 4

paternal [pəˈtɜːnl] väterlich **WS 2**, 54

path [pɑːθ] Weg; Bahn OT 1

patient [ˈpeɪʃnt] Patient(in) OT 1

patriot [ˈpeɪtrɪət] Patriot OT 2

to **patrol** [pəˈtrəʊl] patrouillieren **WS 2**, 69

pattern [ˈpætn] Muster OT 4

to **pause** [pɔːz] eine Pause machen OT 3

to **pay** [ˈpeɪ] bezahlen; zahlen; sich lohnen OT 1

pay gap [ˈpeɪ gæp] Lohngefälle OT 5

PE (physical education) [ˌpiːˈiː] Sport; Sportunterricht OT 1

pea [piː] Erbse OT 1

peace [piːs] Frieden OT 3

peaceful [ˈpiːsfl] friedlich OT 3

peak [piːk] Gipfel; Spitzen... OT 4

pear [peə] Birne OT 1

peculiar [pɪˈkjuːlɪə] seltsam; eigen

WS 2, 54

peddler [ˈpedlə] Hausierer(in) **WS 2**, 69

pedigree [ˈpedɪgriː] Rasse... OT 3

to **peel** [piːl] schälen **WS 3**, 108

peer [pɪə] Peer OT 4

pen [pen] Stift; Pferch; Knast OT 1

penal [ˈpiːnl] strafrechtlich OT 5

penalty [ˈpenəlti] Strafe; Strafstoß OT 3

pencil [ˈpensl] Bleistift OT 1

pencil case [ˈpensl ˌkeɪs] Federtasche OT 1

penguin [ˈpeŋgwɪn] Pinguin OT 2

peninsula [pəˈnɪnsjələ] Halbinsel OT 5

penny [ˈpeni] Penny OT 1

pension [ˈpenʃn] Rente **WS 1**, 32

pensive [ˈpensɪv] nachdenklich **WS 3**, 97

people [ˈpiːpl] Leute; Menschen; Volk OT 1

pepper [ˈpepə] Pfeffer; Paprika OT 2

per [pə] per; je OT 4

to **perceive** [pəˈsiːv] wahrnehmen **WS 2**, 68

percent [pəˈsent] Prozent OT 3

percentage [pəˈsentɪdʒ] Prozentsatz; Anteil OT 4

perception [pəˈsepʃn] Wahrnehmung **WS 3**, 95

perfect [ˈpɜːfɪkt] perfekt OT 2

to **perform** [pəˈfɔːm] auftreten OT 2

performance [pəˈfɔːməns] Aufführung OT 2

perhaps [pəˈhæps] vielleicht OT 3

period [ˈpɪərɪəd] Zeit; Epoche OT 3

periodically [ˌpɪəriˈɒdɪkli] regelmäßig **WS 4**, 135

permanent [ˈpɜːmənənt] permanent; dauerhaft OT 4

  permanently [ˈpɜːmənəntli] permanent; immer OT 3

to **permeate** [ˈpɜːmieɪt] durchdringen **WS 2**, 82

permissible [pəˈmɪsəbl] erlaubt **WS 3**, 114

permission [pəˈmɪʃn] Erlaubnis OT 2

permit [ˈpɜːmɪt] Erlaubnis OT 3

to **permit** [pəˈmɪt] erlauben OT 4

perpetual [pəˈpetʃuəl] ständig **WS 2**, 72

to **perpetuate** [pəˈpetʃueɪt] aufrechterhalten **WS 2**, 73

perseverance [ˌpɜːsəˈvɪərəns] Ausdauer; Durchhaltevermögen OT 4

person [ˈpɜːsn] Person OT 1

personal [ˈpɜːsənl] persönlich; privat; Körper... OT 1

personality [ˌpɜːsəˈnæləti] Persönlichkeit; Prominente OT 4

to **personalize** [ˈpɜːsənəlaɪz] personalisieren OT 5

personification [pəˌsɒnɪfɪˈkeɪʃn] Personifizierung **WS 2**, 64

perspective [pəˈspektɪv] Sichtweise; Perspektive OT 5

to **persuade** [pəˈsweɪd] überreden; überzeugen OT 3

persuasive [pəˈsweɪsɪv] überzeugend OT 5

to **pertain to** [pəˈteɪn] zu etwas gehören **WS 3**, 94

pest [pest] Plage; Schädling OT 5

pet [pet] Haustier; Liebling; Schatz OT 1

to **pet** [pet] streicheln; Schatz OT 4

petition [pəˈtɪʃn] Antrag OT 3

petrochemical [ˌpetrəʊˈkemɪkl] Petrochemikalie OT 4

petrol [ˈpetrəl] Benzin OT 1

pharmacist [ˈfɑːməsɪst] Apotheker(in) OT 2

pharmacy [ˈfɑːməsi] Apotheke OT 2

phase [feɪz] Phase; Abschnitt **WS 3**, 122

phenomenon [fəˈnɒmɪnən] Phänomen OT 5

philosophy [fəˈlɒsəfi] Philosophie OT 4

phone [fəʊn] Telefon OT 1

to **phone** [fəʊn] telefonieren OT 1

photo [ˈfəʊtə] Foto OT 1

  to **take a photo** [ˌteɪk ə ˈfəʊtəʊ] ein Foto machen OT 1

photograph [ˈfəʊtəgrɑːf] Foto OT 1

photographer [fəˈtɒgrəfə] Fotograf(in) OT 2

phrase [freɪz] Wendung; Ausdruck OT 1

physical [ˈfɪzɪkl] körperlich OT 2

physics [ˈfɪzɪks] Physik OT 5

pianist [ˈpɪənɪst] Pianist(in) OT 2

piano [piˈænəʊ] Klavier OT 1

to **pick** [pɪk] pflücken; aussuchen OT 2

  to **pick a fight** [pɪk ə faɪt] einen Streit mit anzetteln OT 5

  to **pick up** [pɪk ʌp] aufheben; abholen OT 2

picker [ˈpɪkə] Pflücker(in) OT 4

picnic [ˈpɪknɪk] Picknick OT 1

picture [ˈpɪktʃə] Bild OT 1

picturesque [ˌpɪktʃəˈresk] malerisch OT 4

pie [paɪ] gedeckter Obstkuchen; Pastete OT 1

piece [piːs] Stück; Teil; Bestandteil OT 1

  in one piece [ɪn ˈwʌn ˌpiːs] heil OT 2

pie chart [ˈpaɪ tʃɑːt] Tortendiagramm OT 4

pier [pɪər] Kai OT 5

pierced [pɪəsd] durchstochen OT 3

pig [pɪg] Schwein; Sau; Bulle OT 1

pigeon [ˈpɪdʒɪn] Taube OT 5

pilates [pɪˈlɑːtiːz] Pilates **WS 1**, 37

to **pile** [paɪl] auftürmen OT 3

pill [pɪl] Tablette OT 5

pillow [ˈpɪləʊ] Kopfkissen OT 2

pillowcase [ˈpɪləʊkeɪs] Kopfkissenbezug OT 3

pin [pɪn] Stecknadel; Reißnagel; Anstecknadel OT 1

to **pin** [pɪn] heften; hängen; festsetzen OT 1

pineapple [ˈpaɪnæpl] Ananas OT 2

pinewood [ˈpaɪnwʊd] Kiefernholz **WS 1**, 22

ping-pong [ˈpɪŋ pɒŋ] Tischtennis OT 4

pink [pɪŋk] rosa; rosafarben OT 1

pioneer [ˌpaɪəˈnɪə] Pionier(in) OT 4

pipe [paɪp] Leitung OT 4

pipeline [ˈpaɪplaɪn] Pipeline OT 4

pit [pɪt] Grube OT 5

pitch [pɪtʃ] Spielfeld OT 3

to **pitch** [pɪtʃ] aufstellen **WS 1**, 16

pity: it's a pity [ɪts ə ˈpɪti] das ist schade OT 2

place [pleɪs] Ort; Stelle; Platz OT 1

to **place** [pleɪs] anbringen; vermitteln OT 5

placement [ˈpleɪsmənt] Platzierung OT 5

plagiarism [ˈpleɪdʒərɪzəm] Plagiat OT 2

to **plagiarize** [ˈpleɪdʒəraɪz] plagiieren OT 2

plague [pleɪg] Pest OT 3

plain [pleɪn] Ebene; Flachland OT 4

to **plan** [plæn] planen; vorhaben OT 1

plane [pleɪn] Flugzeug; Ebene; Hobel OT 1

planet [ˈplænɪt] Planet OT 2

plank [plæŋk] Planke; hier: Liegestütze **WS 1**, 37

planner [ˈplænə] Planer(in) OT 4

plant [plɑːnt] Pflanze OT 2

plantain [ˈplæntɪn] Kochbanane OT 4

plantation [plɑːnˈteɪʃn] Plantage **WS 2**, 54

plaster [ˈplɑːstə] Gips; Pflaster; Gips OT 1

plastic [ˈplæstɪk] Plastik OT 3

plastic [ˈplæstɪk] aus Plastik; Plastik... OT 3

plate [pleɪt] Teller; Platte; Schild OT 1

platform [ˈplætfɔːm] Bahnsteig; Plattform OT 1

platypus [ˈplætɪpəs] Schnabeltier OT 5

plausible [ˈplɔːzəbl] einleuchtend **WS 4**, 143

play [pleɪ] Theaterstück; Aufführung OT 1

to **play** [pleɪ] spielen; spielen gegen; aufgeführt werden OT 1

player [ˈpleɪə] Spieler(in); Spieler; Akteur OT 1

playground [ˈpleɪgraʊnd] Spielplatz; Schulhof; Tummelplatz OT 1

playwright [ˈpleɪraɪt] Dramatiker(in) OT 4

to **plead guilty** [pliːd ˈgɪlti] sich schuldig bekennen OT 5

pleasant [ˈpleznt] angenehm OT 3

pleasantry [ˈplezntri] Nettigkeit **WS 1**, 17

please [pliːz] bitte OT 1

pleased [pliːzd] zufrieden OT 1

pleasure [ˈpleʒə] Freude; Vergnügen OT 1

to **pledge** [pledʒ] geloben **WS 2**, 69

plenty [ˈplenti] reichlich; viel OT 2

plot [plɒt] Handlung OT 3

to **plug in** [plʌg] einstecken; zustopfen; einstöpseln OT 1

plum [plʌm] Pflaume; Zwetsche OT 1

plural [ˈplʊərəl] Plural; Mehrzahl OT 1

pocket [ˈpɒkɪt] Tasche OT 2

pocketknife [ˈpɒkɪtnaɪf] Taschenmesser OT 2

podcast [ˈpɒdkɑːst] Podcast OT 3

poem [ˈpəʊɪm] Gedicht OT 1

poet [ˈpəʊɪt] Dichter(in); Poet OT 1

poetry [ˈpəʊətri] Dichtung OT 4

point [pɔɪnt] Punkt; Argument; Sache OT 1

to **point (to)** [pɔɪnt] zeigen (auf); richten OT 1

poison [ˌpɔɪzn] Gift OT 1

poison ivy [ˌpɔɪzn ˈaɪvi] giftiger Efeu OT 2

poisonous [ˈpɔɪzənəs] giftig OT 5

to **poke** [pəʊk] stoßen **WS 1**, 42

polar bear [ˈpəʊlə beə] Eisbär OT 4

pole [pəʊl] Stange; Pol OT 4

police [pəˈliːs] Polizei; Polizisten OT 1

policy [ˈpɒləsi] Politik; politische Linie OT 5

Polish [ˈpəʊlɪʃ] polnisch OT 2

polite [pəˈlaɪt] höflich OT 1

political [pəˈlɪtɪkl] politisch OT 3

politician [ˌpɒləˈtɪʃn] Politiker(in) OT 3

politics [ˈpɒlətɪks] Politik OT 4

poll [pəʊl] Umfrage OT 5

pollen [ˈpɒlən] Pollen **WS 4**, 140

to **pollinate** [ˈpɒləneɪt] befruchten; bestäuben **WS 4**, 135

pollination [ˌpɒləˈneɪʃn] Bestäubung **WS 4**, 140

pollinator [ˈpɒləneɪtə] Bestäuber **WS 4**, 140

to **pollute** [pəˈluːt] verschmutzen; verseuchen OT 5

pollution [pəˈluːʃn] Verschmutzung OT 3

polo shirt [ˈpəʊləʊ ʃɜːt] Polohemd OT 5

polyp [ˈpɒlɪp] Polyp OT 5

polysexual [pɒlɪˈsekʃʊəl] polysexuell **WS 3**, 112

pond [pɒnd] Teich OT 1

ponderously [ˈpɒndərəsli] gemächlich OT 3

pony [ˈpəʊni] Pony OT 3

pool [puːl] Pfütze; Schwimmbecken; Fleck; Schwimmbecken OT 1

poor [pʊə] arm; schlecht; dürftig OT 1

pop [pɒp] Pop- OT 2

popcorn [ˈpɒpkɔːn] Popcorn OT 2

Pope [pəʊp] Papst OT 3

pope [pəʊp] Papst OT 2

popular [ˈpɒpjələ] beliebt; populär; weitverbreitet OT 1

popularity [ˌpɒpjuˈlærəti] Popularität OT 4

to **popularize** [ˈpɒpjələraɪz] populär machen **WS 2**, 60

populated [ˈpɒpjuleɪtɪd] bevölkert; besiedelt OT 5

population [ˌpɒpjəˈleɪʃən] Bevölkerung OT 3

pork [pɔːk] Schweinefleisch OT 2

porridge [ˈpɒrɪdʒ] Haferbrei OT 5

port [pɔːt] Hafen OT 2

portable [ˈpɔːtəbl] tragbar OT 4

portal [ˈpɔːtl] Portalseite OT 5

porter [ˈpɔːtə] Portier; Pförtner(in) **WS 1**, 35

to **portray** [pɔːˈtreɪ] darstellen; porträtieren **WS 1**, 18

to **pose** [pəʊz] posieren; darstellen **WS 3**, 109

posh [pɒʃ] schick; nobel **WS 1**, 15

position [pəˈzɪʃn] Position OT 3

positive [ˈpɒzətɪv] Positiv; positiver Befund; Positiv OT 1

positivity [ˌpɒzəˈtɪvəti] positive Einstellung **WS 3**, 119

to **possess** [pəˈzes] besitzen OT 4

possession [pəˈzeʃn] Besitz OT 4

possessive [pəˈzesɪv] besitzergreifend; besitzanzeigend; Possessivbegleiter OT 1

possibility [ˌpɒsəˈbɪləti] Möglichkeit OT 4

possible [ˈpɒsəbl] möglich OT 2

post [pəʊst] Post OT 2

post [pəʊst] Beitrag OT 3

to **post** [pəʊst] posten; verschicken OT 4

postcard [ˈpəʊstkɑːd] Postkarte; Ansichtskarte OT 1

poster [ˈpəʊstə] Plakat; Poster OT 1

postgraduate [ˌpəʊstˈgrædʒuət] Graduierten... **WS 3**, 116

postman [ˈpəʊstmən] Briefträger(in) OT 2

posture [ˈpɒstʃə] Körperhaltung OT 4

postwoman [ˈpəʊstwʊmən] Briefträgerin OT 2

pot [pɒt] Topf OT 2

potato [pəˈteɪtəʊ] Kartoffel OT 1

potential [pəˈtenʃl] möglich OT 4

pottery [ˈpɒtəri] Töpfern; Töpferwaren OT 3

poultry [ˈpəʊltri] Geflügel OT 2

pound [paʊnd] Pfund OT 1

to **pour** [pɔː] gießen OT 1

poverty [ˈpɒvəti] Armut OT 5

power [ˈpaʊə] Kraft; Macht OT 4

to **power** [ˈpaʊə] antreiben OT 4

powerful [ˈpaʊəfl] mächtig OT 2

powerhouse [ˈpaʊəhaʊs] Kraftzentrum **WS 3**, 119

practical [ˈpræktɪkl] praktisch OT 2

practice [ˈpræktɪs] Praxis; Übung OT 1

to **practise** [ˈpræktɪs] üben; trainieren; proben OT 1

to **praise** [preɪz] loben OT 4

prawn [prɔːn] Garnele OT 3

to **pray** [preɪ] beten OT 3

prayer [preə] Gebet OT 4

preacher [ˈpriːtʃə] Prediger(in) **WS 2**, 58

precarious [prɪˈkeəriəs] gefährlich **WS 3**, 109

to **precede** [prɪˈsiːd] vorangehen **WS 2**, 65

precisely [prɪˈsaɪsli] genau **WS 3**, 114

preconception [ˌpriːkənˈsepʃn] Vorurteil **WS 3**, 105

predator [ˈpredətə] Raubtier; Räuber OT 5

predecessor [ˈpriːdəsesə] Vorgänger(in) **WS 3**, 111

to **predict** [prɪˈdɪkt] vorhersagen OT 2

predictable [prɪˈdɪktəbl] vorhersehbar OT 5

predicting [prɪˈdɪktɪŋ] Vorhersagen OT 2

prediction [prɪˈdɪkʃn] Vorhersage OT 2

to **prefer** [prɪˈfɜː] vorziehen; etwas lieber tun OT 1

preference [ˈprefrəns] Vorliebe; Präferenz OT 4

pregnant [ˈpregnənt] schwanger OT 3

prejudice [ˈpredʒədɪs] Vorurteil **WS 3**, 116

premier [ˈpremiə] erste OT 2

preparation [ˌprepəˈreɪʃn] Vorbereitung OT 2

to **prepare** [prɪˈpeə] vorbereiten; zubereiten OT 1

preposition [ˌprepəˈzɪʃn] Präposition; Verhältniswort OT 1

to **presage** [ˈpresɪdʒ] vorhersagen **WS 2**, 69

preschool [ˈpriːskuːl] vorschulisch OT 5

to **prescribe** [prɪˈskraɪb] vorschreiben; festsetzen OT 5

prescription [prɪˈskrɪpʃn] Rezept **WS 2**, 69

presence [ˈprezns] Präsenz; Anwesenheit **WS 2**, 69

present [ˈpreznt] Geschenk; Gegenwart OT 1

to **present** [prɪˈzent] überreichen; vorstellen; vorlegen OT 1

presentation [ˌpreznˈteɪʃn] Präsentation; Vortrag; Überreichung OT 1

presenter [prɪˈzentə] Moderator(in) OT 4

to **preserve** [prɪˈzɜːv] erhalten OT 3

presidency [ˈprezɪdənsi] Präsidentschaft **WS 2**, 57

president [ˈprezɪdənt] Präsident(in) OT 3

presidential [ˌprezɪˈdenʃl] präsidentiell OT 4

to **press** [pres] drücken; pressen; auspressen OT 1

pressure [ˈpreʃə] Druck OT 3

prestigious [preˈstɪdʒəs] angesehen **WS 3**, 123

to **pretend** [prɪˈtend] vorgeben; so tun, als ob; so tun als ob OT 1

pretty [ˈprɪti] hübsch OT 1

to **prevail** [prɪˈveɪl] überwiegen **WS 2**, 65

to **prevent** [prɪˈvent] verhindern; abhalten OT 4

prevention [prɪˈvenʃn] Verhütung OT 2

previous [ˈpriːviəs] früher OT 5

previously [ˈpriːviəsli] vorher; früher OT 4

price [praɪs] Preis OT 1

pride [praɪd] Stolz OT 5

to **pride oneself** [praɪd wʌnˈself] stolz auf etwas sein OT 5

primary [ˈpraɪməri] Haupt...; primär OT 1

primary school [ˈpraɪməri ˌskuːl] Primärschule; Grundschule OT 1

primatologist [ˌpraɪməˈtɒlədʒɪst] Primatenforscher(in) **WW**, 11

prince [prɪns] Prinz OT 1

principal [ˈprɪnsəpl] Rektor(in) OT 2

principle [ˈprɪnsəpl] Prinzip OT 4

printed [ˈprɪntəd] gedruckt OT 5

prior to [ˈpraɪə tə] vor **WS 1**, 32

to **prioritize** [praɪˈɒrətaɪz] priorisieren **WS 4**, 138

priority [praɪˈɒrəti] Priorität OT 5

prison [ˈprɪzn] Gefängnis OT 4

privacy [ˈprɪvəsi] Privatsphäre OT 3

privacy settings [ˈprɪvəsi ˈsetɪŋz] Datenschutzeinstellungen OT 3

private [ˈpraɪvət] privat OT 3

to **privatize** [ˈpraɪvətaɪz] privatisieren **WS 1**, 31

privilege [ˈprɪvəlɪdʒ] Privileg; Recht OT 4

privileged [ˈprɪvəlɪdʒd] privilegiert **WS 3**, 105

prize [praɪz] Gewinn; Preis OT 1

pro [prəʊ] Vorteil OT 2

proactive [ˌprəʊˈæktɪv] proaktiv OT 4

proactively [ˌprəʊˈæktɪvli] proaktiv **WS 1**, 12

probability [ˌprɒbəˈbɪləti] Wahrscheinlichkeit **WS 3**, 106

probably [ˈprɒbəbli] wahrscheinlich OT 2

probation [prəˈbeɪʃn] Bewährung OT 5

problem [ˈprɒbləm] Problem; Aufgabe OT 1

problem-solver [ˈprɒbləm sɒlvə] Problemlöser(in) OT 4

procedure [prəˈsiːdʒə] Prozedur; Verfahren OT 4

process [ˈprəʊses] Prozess OT 4

procession [prəˈseʃn] Umzug OT 2

processor [ˈprəʊsesə] Prozessor **WS 3**, 99

to **produce** [prəˈdjuːs] erzeugen OT 3

product [ˈprɒdʌkt] Produkt OT 2

production [prəˈdʌkʃn] Produktion; Inszenierung OT 5

productive [prə'dʌktɪv] produktiv **WS 3**, 119

professional [prə'feʃənl] professionell OT 3

proficiency [prə'fɪʃnsi] Kompetenz OT 4

profile ['prəʊfaɪl] Profil OT 5

profiling ['prəʊfaɪlɪŋ] Profilierung; Profilerstellung **WS 1**, 34

profit ['prɒfɪt] Profit; Gewinn OT 4

profitable ['prɒfɪtəbl] profitabel **WS 3**, 99

program ['prəʊgræm] Programm; Kurs OT 3

programme ['prəʊgræm] Programm; Sendung OT 1

to **programme** ['prəʊgræm] programmieren OT 2

programming ['prəʊgræmɪŋ] Programmierung OT 2

progress ['prəʊgres] Fortschritt OT 4

to **progress** [prə'gres] fortschreiten OT 5

progression [prə'greʃn] Fortschreiten; Entwicklung OT 5

progressive [prə'gresɪv] fortschrittlich; progressiv; fortschreitend OT 1

project ['prɒdʒekt] Projekt; Vorhaben; Arbeit OT 1

projector [prə'dʒektə] Projektor; Beamer OT 1

proliferation [prə,lɪfə'reɪʃn] Verbreitung **WS 3**, 110

prolific [prə'lɪfɪk] produktiv; erfolgreich **WS 1**, 28

prolonged [prə'lɒŋd] anhaltend; verlängert OT 5

prom [prɒm] Schulball OT 3

promenade [,prɒmə'nɑːd] Promenade OT 5

prominence ['prɒmɪnəns] Bedeutung **WS 2**, 60

prominent ['prɒmɪnənt] bedeutend OT 4

promise ['prɒmɪs] Versprechen OT 2

to **promise** ['prɒmɪs] versprechen OT 2

to **promote** [prə'məʊt] fördern OT 4

prompt [prɒmpt] Hinweis OT 3

pronoun ['prəʊnaʊn] Pronomen; Fürwort OT 1

to **pronounce** [prə'naʊns] aussprechen OT 3

pronounced [prə'naʊnst] ausgesprochen OT 2

pronunciation [prə,nʌnsi'eɪʃn] Aussprache OT 2

proof [pruːf] …sicher; undurchdringlich OT 5

prop [prɒp] Stütze; Requisite OT 1

propaganda [,prɒpə'gændə] Propaganda **WS 2**, 54

proper ['prɒpə] richtig; anständig; angemessen OT 1

property ['prɒpəti] Eigentum; Immobilie OT 4

proportion [prə'pɔːʃn] Anteil OT 5

to **propose** [prə'pəʊz] vorschlagen **WS 1**, 30

proposition [,prɒpə'zɪʃn] Vorschlag **WS 4**, 134

prosecution [,prɒsɪ'kjuːʃn] Staatsanwaltschaft OT 5

prosecutor ['prɒsɪkjuːtə] Staatsanwalt/-anwältin OT 5

prospective [prə'spektɪv] zukünftig **WS 3**, 105

prospectus [prə'spektəs] Prospekt OT 4

to **prosper** ['prɒspə] florieren OT 2

prosperity [prɒ'sperəti] Wohlstand **WS 4**, 136

protagonist [prə'tægənɪst] Protagonist(in); Hauptfigur **WS 1**, 34

to **protect** [prə'tekt] schützen OT 2

protection [prə'tekʃn] Schutz **WS 4**, 135

protein ['prəʊtiːn] Protein OT 5

protest ['prəʊtest] Protest OT 4

to **protest** [prə'test] protestieren OT 4

Protestant ['prɒtɪstənt] protestantisch; Protestant OT 3

protester [prə'testə] Demonstrant(in); Protestierer(in) OT 4

prototype ['prəʊtətaɪp] Prototyp OT 4

proud [praʊd] stolz OT 2

to **prove** [pruːv] beweisen OT 4

provenance ['prɒvənəns] Herkunft **WS 4**, 143

to **provide** [prə'vaɪd] zur Verfügung stellen; versorgen (mit) OT 4

province ['prɒvɪns] Provinz OT 4

provision [prə'vɪʒn] Maßnahme OT 5

to **provoke** [prə'vəʊk] provozieren; auslösen **WS 2**, 57

psychologist [saɪ'kɒlədʒɪst] Psychologe/Psychologin OT 5

psychology [saɪ'kɒlədʒi] Psychologie OT 5

psychotherapist [,saɪkəʊ'θerəpɪst] Psychotherapeut(in) **WS 3**, 112

pub [pʌb] Kneipe OT 2

puberty ['pjuːbəti] Pubertät OT 5

public ['pʌblɪk] Öffentlichkeit OT 3

publication [,pʌblɪ'keɪʃn] Veröffentlichung OT 4

publicly ['pʌblɪkli] öffentlich **WS 2**, 63

to **publish** ['pʌblɪʃ] veröffentlichen OT 4

publisher ['pʌblɪʃə] Verleger(in) OT 5

puck [pʌk] Puck OT 4

pueblo ['pwebləʊ] Pueblo OT 3

to **pull** [pʊl] ziehen; ziehen an; drücken OT 1

pulse [pʌls] Hülsenfrucht OT 4

pump [pʌmp] Pumpe OT 2

pumpkin ['pʌmpkɪn] Kürbis OT 2

pun [pʌn] Witz; Wortspiel OT 4

to **punch** [pʌntʃ] schlagen OT 5

punctual ['pʌŋktʃuəl] pünktlich OT 4

to **punctuate** ['pʌŋktʃueɪt] mit Satzzeichen versehen OT 3

punctuation [,pʌŋktʃu'eɪʃn] Zeichensetzung OT 3

pundit ['pʌndɪt] Experte; Expertin **WS 2**, 69

to **punish** ['pʌnɪʃ] bestrafen OT 3

puppy ['pʌpi] Welpe OT 2

to **purchase** ['pɜːtʃəs] kaufen; beschaffen **WS 3**, 104

purity ['pjʊərəti] Reinheit **WS 1**, 20

purple ['pɜːpl] lila; violett **WS 1**, 13

purpose ['pɜːpəs] Zweck OT 5

on **purpose** [ɒn 'pɜːpəs] absichtlich OT 2

purposeful ['pɜːpəsfl] zielgerichtet **WS 3**, 116

to **pursue** [pə'sjuː] verfolgen OT 4

pursuit [pə'sjuːt] Beschäftigung; Verfolgung OT 4

to **push** [pʊʃ] stoßen OT 2

to **push one's luck** [pʊʃ wʌns lʌk] übertreiben **WS 3**, 98

pushy ['pʊʃi] aggressiv OT 5

to **put** [pʊt] setzen; stellen; legen OT 1

to **put on** [pʌt 'ɒn] sich anziehen; veranstalten OT 1

to **put up** [pʊt 'ʌp] errichten OT 1

puzzled ['pʌzld] verblüfft; verwirrt OT 5

pyjamas [pə'dʒɑːməz] Schlafanzug OT 3

Q

quack! [kwæk] Quak! (Ente) OT 2

qualification [,kwɒlɪfɪ'keɪʃn] Qualifikation; Eignung OT 4

qualified ['kwɒlɪfaɪd] qualifiziert OT 4

quality ['kwɒləti] Eigenschaft; Qualität OT 3

to **quantify** [ˈkwɒntɪfaɪ] messen;
quantifizieren **WS 4**, 146

quarter [ˈkwɔːtə] Viertel; Quartal; Seite
OT 1

quarter to [ˈkwɔːtə tə] viertel vor OT 1

quarterback [ˈkwɔːtəbæk] Quarterback
OT 2

queen [kwiːn] Königin OT 1

queer [kwɪər] schwul; queer OT 5

question [ˈkwestʃən] Frage OT 1

to **question** [ˈkwestʃən] fragen OT 4

questionnaire [ˌkwestʃəˈneə]
Fragebogen OT 1

queue [kjuː] Schlange; Warteschlange
OT 1

quick [kwɪk] schnell OT 3

quiet [ˈkwaɪət] still; ruhig; leise OT 1

to **quit** [kwɪt] kündigen OT 5

quite [kwaɪt] ziemlich OT 3

quiz [kwɪz] Quiz OT 2

quotation [kwəʊˈteɪʃn] Zitat OT 2

quotation mark [kwəʊˈteɪʃn maːk]
Anführungszeichen OT 2

to **quote** [kwəʊt] zitieren OT 2

R

rabbit [ˈræbɪt] Kaninchen OT 1

race [reɪs] Rennen OT 2

to **race** [reɪs] rasen OT 5

racial [ˈreɪʃl] rassisch **WS 2**, 78

racing [ˈreɪsɪŋ] Rennsport OT 2

racism [ˈreɪsɪzəm] Rassismus **WW**, 10

racist [ˈreɪsɪst] rassistisch **WS 2**, 56

racoon [rəˈkuːn] Waschbär OT 4

radar [ˈreɪdɑː] Radar **WS 2**, 82

radical [ˈrædɪkl] radikal; grundlegend
OT 4

radio [ˈreɪdiəʊ] Radio; Rundfunk;
Funkgerät OT 1

rag [ræg] Lumpen **WS 2**, 82

to **rage** [reɪdʒ] toben; rasen **WS 2**, 78

ragged [ˈrægɪd] zerklüftet **WS 1**, 15

raid [reɪd] Razzia OT 5

rail [reɪl] Bahn; Geländer OT 3

railroad [ˈreɪlrəʊd] Eisenbahn **WS 2**, 75

railway [ˈreɪlweɪ] Bahn; Eisenbahn;
Schiene OT 2

to **rain** [reɪn] regnen OT 1

rainbow [ˈreɪnbəʊ] Regenbogen OT 5

raincoat [ˈreɪnkəʊt] Regenmantel
WS 1, 38

rainfall [ˈreɪnfɔːl] Regen; Niederschlag
OT 4

rainforest [ˈreɪnfɒrɪst] Regenwald OT 2

rainstorm [ˈreɪnstɔːm] Regenschauer;
Gewitter OT 5

rainwater [ˈreɪnwɔːtə] Regenwasser
OT 4

rainy [ˈreɪni] regnerisch OT 4

to **raise** [reɪz] einwerben; erheben;
erhöhen OT 2

rally [ˈræli] Kundgebung;
Demonstration **WS 2**, 61

to **rally** [ˈræli] sich versammeln
WS 2, 58

ramp [ræmp] Rampe OT 2

random [ˈrændəm] zufällig; willkürlich
OT 5

range [reɪndʒ] Angebot; Palette OT 4

ranger [ˈreɪndʒə] Aufseher(in);
Förster(in) OT 3

rank [ræŋk] Position; Rang OT 4

to **rank** [ræŋk] in eine Reihenfolge
bringen OT 4

ranking [ˈræŋkɪŋ] Reihenfolge OT 4

rap [ræp] Rap OT 4

rapid [ˈræpɪd] schnell OT 3

rare [reə] selten OT 2

raspberry [ˈrɑːzbəri] Himbeere OT 1

rat [ræt] Ratte OT 3

rate [reɪt] Rate; Geschwindigkeit OT 4

to **rate** [reɪt] bewerten; beurteilen OT 5

rather [ˈrɑːðə] ziemlich OT 3

rationale [ˌræʃəˈnɑːl] Begründung
WS 1, 12

ratter [ˈrætə] Rattenfänger (Hund) OT 3

raven [ˈreɪvn] Rabe OT 2

to **reach** [riːtʃ] erreichen OT 3

to **react** [riˈækt] reagieren OT 3

reaction [riˈækʃn] Reaktion OT 3

to **read** [riːd] lesen; ablesen; anzeigen
OT 1

reader [ˈriːdə] Leser(in) OT 2

reading [ˈriːdɪŋ] Lesen; Lektüre; Lesung
OT 1

ready [ˈredi] bereit OT 1

real [rɪəl] echt OT 1

really [ˈriːəli] wirklich; sehr OT 1

realist [ˈriːəlɪst] Realist(in) **WS 2**, 78

realistic [ˌriːəˈlɪstɪk] realistisch OT 4

reality [riˈæləti] Realität OT 5

to **realize** [ˈriːəlaɪz] erkennen OT 2

to **rear** [rɪə] aufziehen **WS 1**, 35

to **rearrange** [ˌriːəˈreɪndʒ] umstellen
OT 2

reason [ˈriːzn] Grund; Vernunft;
Verstand OT 1

reasonable [ˈriːznəbl] vernünftig
WS 2, 73

rebel [ˈrebəl] Rebell(in) OT 4

to **rebel** [rɪˈbel] rebellieren; sich
auflehnen OT 4

rebellion [rɪˈbeljən] Aufstand OT 3

rebellious [rɪˈbeljəs] rebellisch;
rebellierend **WW**, 10

to **rebuild** [ˌriːˈbɪld] wieder aufbauen
OT 2

to **recant** [rɪˈkænt] zurückziehen
WS 2, 58

to **receive** [rɪˈsiːv] erhalten OT 2

receiver [rɪˈsiːvə] Empfänger(in) OT 4

recent [ˈriːsnt] neueste(r) OT 3

recently [ˈriːsntli] neulich OT 3

reception [rɪˈsepʃn] Rezeption;
Empfang; Aufnahme OT 1

receptionist [rɪˈsepʃənɪst]
Rezeptionist(in) OT 1

recess [ˈriːses] Pause OT 4

recipe [ˈresəpi] Rezept OT 2

to **reclaim** [rɪˈkleɪm] zurückgewinnen;
zurückfordern **WS 2**, 69

recognition [ˌrekəɡˈnɪʃn] Erkennung
WS 4, 140

recognizable [ˈrekəɡnaɪzəbl] erkennbar
OT 4

to **recognize** [ˈrekəɡnaɪz] erkennen OT 3

to **recommend** [ˌrekəˈmend] empfehlen
OT 3

recommendation [ˌrekəmenˈdeɪʃn]
Empfehlung OT 4

reconciliation [ˌrekənsɪliˈeɪʃn]
Versöhnung **WS 3**, 112

to **reconstruct** [ˌriːkənˈstrʌkt]
wiederaufbauen OT 3

reconstruction [ˌriːkənˈstrʌkʃn]
Wiederaufbau **WS 2**, 58

to **record** [rɪˈkɔːd] aufnehmen;
aufzeichnen; protokollieren OT 1

recording studio [rɪˈkɔːdɪŋ ˌstjuːdiəʊ]
Aufnahmestudio OT 3

to **recover** [rɪˈkʌvə] (sich) erholen OT 4

recovery [rɪˈkʌvəri] Rettung;
Wiederherstellung OT 3

to **recreate** [ˌriːkriˈeɪt] wiederherstellen
WS 3, 119

recreation [ˌriːkriˈeɪʃn] Modell OT 4

recreational [ˌrekriˈeɪʃnl] Freizeit...
OT 3

to **recruit** [rɪˈkruːt] einstellen;
rekrutieren **WS 1**, 14

rectangular [rekˈtæŋɡjələ] rechteckig
OT 2

to **recuperate** [rɪˈkjuːpəreɪt] sich
erholen **WS 1**, 12

to **recycle** [ˌriːˈsaɪkl] wiederverwerten OT 2

recycler [ˌriːˈsaɪklə] Wiederverwerter(in) OT 3

red [red] rot; Rotwein OT 1

to **reduce** [rɪˈdjuːs] reduzieren; verringern OT 4

reduction [rɪˈdʌkʃn] Verringerung; Reduzierung **WS 3**, 93

reef [riːf] Riff OT 5

reel [riːl] Reel; Rolle **WS 4**, 146

reenactment [ˌriː ɪˈnæktmənt] Nachstellung OT 4

to **refer** [rɪˈfɜː] sich beziehen OT 3

referee [ˌrefəˈriː] Schiedsrichter(in) OT 3

reference [ˈrefrəns] Referenz **WS 2**, 65

referendum [ˌrefəˈrendəm] Referendum; Volksabstimmung **WW**, 11

to **refine** [rɪˈfaɪn] verfeinern OT 4

to **reflect** [rɪˈflekt] spiegeln OT 2

reflective [rɪˈflektɪv] nachdenklich; reflektierend; hier: widerspiegelnd **WS 2**, 69

reform [rɪˈfɔːm] Reform **WS 2**, 62

reformation [ˌrefəˈmeɪʃn] Reformation OT 3

reformer [rɪˈfɔːmə] Reformator(in) **WS 2**, 57

to **reframe** [ˌriːˈfreɪm] umstrukturieren **WS 3**, 111

refreshment [rɪˈfreʃmənt] Erfrischung OT 4

refusal [rɪˈfjuːzl] Weigerung **WS 2**, 60

to **refuse** [rɪˈfjuːz] sich weigern OT 4

regal [ˈriːgəl] königlich; majestätisch **WS 2**, 76

to **regard** [rɪˈgɑːd] betrachten; ansehen OT 4

regardless [rɪˈgɑːdləs] unabhängig von OT 4

reggae [ˈregeɪ] Reggae OT 2

region [ˈriːdʒən] Region OT 3

regional [ˈriːdʒənl] regional OT 5

register [ˈredʒɪstə] Kasse OT 2

registration [ˌredʒɪˈstreɪʃn] Registrierung **WS 2**, 56

registration plate [ˌredʒɪˈstreɪʃnpleɪt] Nummernschild OT 4

to **regret** [rɪˈgret] bereuen OT 2

regular [ˈregjələ] regelmäßig; normal; ganz normal OT 1

rehearsal [rɪˈhɜːsl] Probe OT 2

to **rehearse** [rɪˈhɜːs] proben OT 3

to **reign** [reɪn] regieren; herrschen **WS 2**, 72

reindeer [ˈreɪndɪə] Rentier OT 3

to **reinforce** [ˌriːɪnˈfɔːs] verstärken; bekräftigen OT 5

to **reject** [rɪˈdʒekt] ablehnen **WS 3**, 105

rejection [rɪˈdʒekʃn] Zurückweisung; Ablehnung **WS 2**, 60

to **rejoin** [ˌriːˈdʒɔɪn] wieder beitreten OT 4

to **relate to** [rɪˈleɪt tə] mit etw. in Zusammenhang stehen; sich auf etw. beziehen OT 5

related [rɪˈleɪtɪd] verwandt OT 3

relation [rɪˈleɪʃn] Beziehung; Verhältnis OT 5

relationship [rɪˈleɪʃnʃɪp] Beziehung OT 3

relative [ˈrelətɪv] Verwandte(r) OT 3

relatively [ˈrelətɪvli] relativ; ziemlich OT 4

to **relax** [rɪˈlæks] sich entspannen OT 3

relaxing [rɪˈlæksɪŋ] erholsam OT 2

to **release** [rɪˈliːs] veröffentlichen; auf den Markt bringen OT 4

relentless [rɪˈlentləs] unerbittlich **WS 3**, 112

relevance [ˈreləvəns] Bedeutung **WS 3**, 110

relevancy [ˈreləvənsi] Relevanz; Bedeutung **WS 3**, 119

relevant [ˈreləvənt] wichtig OT 4

reliability [rɪˌlaɪəˈbɪləti] Zuverlässigkeit **WS 3**, 106

reliable [rɪˈlaɪəbl] verlässlich OT 4

reliant [rɪˈlaɪənt] angewiesen **WS 4**, 135

relief [rɪˈliːf] Erleichterung; Hilfe OT 2

relieved [rɪˈliːvd] erleichtert OT 3

religion [rɪˈlɪdʒən] Religion OT 3

religious [rɪˈlɪdʒəs] religiös; fromm OT 3

to **relocate** [ˌriːləʊˈkeɪt] umziehen; verlagern OT 4

reluctance [rɪˈlʌktəns] Abneigung OT 4

to **rely on** [rɪˈlaɪ ɒn] sich verlassen auf OT 4

to **remain** [rɪˈmeɪn] bleiben OT 4

remarriage [ˌriːˈmærɪdʒ] Wiederverheiratung OT 5

to **remember** [rɪˈmembə] sich erinnern an OT 1

to **remind** [rɪˈmaɪnd] erinnern OT 2

remnant [ˈremnənt] Überrest **WS 1**, 17

remorse [rɪˈmɔːs] Reue OT 5

remote [rɪˈməʊt] Fernbedienung OT 3

remote [rɪˈməʊt] entfernt; abgelegen OT 4

remotely [rɪˈməʊtli] aus der Ferne OT 4

removal [rɪˈmuːvl] Beseitigung; Entfernung **WS 2**, 56

removal van [rɪˈmuːvl væn] Umzugswagen OT 4

to **remove** [rɪˈmuːv] entfernen OT 2

to **render** [ˈrendə] machen **WS 4**, 138

renewable [rɪˈnjuːəbl] erneuerbar OT 4

renovation [ˌrenəˈveɪʃn] Renovierung **WS 1**, 24

renowned [rɪˈnaʊnd] renommiert; berühmt **WS 1**, 18

to **rent** [rent] mieten OT 3

repair [rɪˈpeə] Reparatur OT 2

to **repair** [rɪˈpeər] beheben; reparieren OT 5

to **repeat** [rɪˈpiːt] wiederholen; weitererzählen; sich wiederholen OT 1

repertoire [ˈrepətwɑː] Repertoire; Programm **WS 2**, 67

repetition [ˌrepəˈtɪʃn] Wiederholung OT 5

repetitive [rɪˈpetətɪv] repetitiv; sich wiederholend OT 5

to **rephrase** [ˌriːˈfreɪz] neu formulieren; umformulieren OT 5

to **replace** [rɪˈpleɪs] ersetzen OT 3

replica [ˈreplɪkə] Kopie OT 4

reply [rɪˈplaɪ] Antwort OT 1

to **reply** [rɪˈplaɪ] antworten; erwidern OT 1

to **report** [rɪˈpɔːt] berichten; melden; sich melden OT 1

reportedly [rɪˈpɔːtɪdli] angeblich **WS 2**, 66

reporter [rɪˈpɔːtə] Reporter(in) OT 1

to **represent** [ˌreprɪˈzent] vertreten OT 3

representation [ˌreprɪzenˈteɪʃn] hier: Darstellung **WS 4**, 141

representative [ˌreprɪˈzentətɪv] Vertreter(in); Abgeordnete(r) OT 4

to **reproduce** [ˌriːprəˈdjuːs] vervielfältigen **WS 4**, 135

reptile [ˈreptaɪl] Reptil OT 2

republic [rɪˈpʌblɪk] Republik OT 4

reputation [ˌrepjuˈteɪʃn] Ansehen; Reputation **WS 2**, 58

request [rɪˈkwest] Bitte; Musikwunsch OT 1

to **require** [rɪˈkwaɪə] benötigen OT 4

required [rɪˈkwaɪəd] erforderlich OT 3

requirement [rɪˈkwaɪəmənt] Voraussetzung OT 5

rescue [ˈreskjuː] Rettung OT 2

research [rɪˈsɜːtʃ] Forschung OT 2

to **research** [rɪˈsɜːtʃ] erforschen OT 4

researcher [rɪ'sɜːtʃə] Forscher(in) OT 2

to **resemble** [rɪ'zembl] ähneln **WS 1**, 24

reservation [ˌrezə'veɪʃn] Reservierung; Vorbehalt; Reservat OT 1

reserved [rɪ'zɜːvd] reserviert OT 2

reservoir ['rezəvwɑːr] Reservoir; Behälter OT 5

to **reshuffle** [riː'ʃʌfl] neu mischen **WS 3**, 118

residence ['rezɪdəns] Residenz; Wohnsitz **WS 1**, 25

resident ['rezɪdənt] Bewohner(in) OT 4

residential [ˌrezɪ'denʃl] Wohn- OT 4

to **resign** [rɪ'zaɪn] zurücktreten OT 4

resilience [rɪ'zɪliəns] Widerstandsfähigkeit **WS 1**, 14

to **resist** [rɪ'zɪst] widerstehen OT 5

resistance [rɪ'zɪstəns] Widerstand; hier: Resistenz OT 5

resolution [ˌrezə'luːʃn] hier: Auflösung; Beschluss **WS 3**, 122

resolve [rɪ'zɒlv] Entschlossenheit **WS 2**, 58

resort [rɪ'zɔːt] Urlaubsort OT 3

resource [rɪ'sɔːs] Ressource; Mittel OT 4

respect [rɪ'spekt] Respekt OT 5

to **respect** [rɪ'spekt] achten OT 3

respectful [rɪ'spektfl] respektvoll OT 3

to **respond** [rɪ'spɒnd] antworten; reagieren; ansprechen OT 1

respondent [rɪ'spɒndənt] Befragte(r) OT 5

response [rɪ'spɒns] Reaktion; Antwort OT 4

responsibility [rɪˌspɒnsə'bɪləti] Verantwortung OT 3

responsible [rɪ'spɒnsəbl] verantwortlich OT 3

rest [rest] Ruhe; Pause; Rest OT 1

restaurant ['restrɒnt] Restaurant; Gaststätte OT 1

to **restore** [rɪ'stɔː] wiederherstellen OT 3

to **restrict** [rɪ'strɪkt] einschränken OT 4

restriction [rɪ'strɪkʃn] Einschränkung OT 4

result [rɪ'zʌlt] Ergebnis OT 2

to **result** [rɪ'zʌlt] resultieren; als Ergebnis haben **WS 1**, 17

to **resume** [rɪ'zjuːm] übernehmen; wieder annehmen OT 5

retail ['riːteɪl] Einzelhandel OT 5

retailer ['riːteɪlə] Händler(in) **WS 3**, 106

to **retain** [rɪ'teɪn] behalten **WS 1**, 27

to **retire** [rɪ'taɪər] in Rente gehen OT 5

to **retreat** [rɪ'triːt] zurückweichen **WS 1**, 18

to **return** [rɪ'tɜːn] zurückkehren OT 2

reusable [ˌriː'juːzəbl] wiederverwendbar OT 3

to **reuse** [ˌriː'juːz] wiederverwenden OT 4

to **reveal** [rɪ'viːl] zeigen OT 4

revenue ['revənjuː] Einnahmen **WS 1**, 31

to **reverberate** [rɪ'vɜːbəreɪt] nachhallen **WS 1**, 17

reverse [rɪ'vɜːs] umgekehrt **WS 3**, 117

to **revert** [rɪ'vɜːt] zurückkehren **WS 2**, 64

review [rɪ'vjuː] Kritik; Review OT 5

to **review** [rɪ'vjuː] überprüfen; beurteilen OT 3

to **revise** [rɪ'vaɪz] revidieren OT 2

to **revisit** [ˌriː'vɪsɪt] wieder besuchen **WS 2**, 76

revival [rɪ'vaɪvl] Wiederbelebung OT 5

revolting [rɪ'vəʊltɪŋ] abstoßend OT 2

revolution [ˌrevə'luːʃn] Revolution OT 2

revolutionary [ˌrevə'luːʃənəri] revolutionär **WS 2**, 63

to **revolutionize** [ˌrevə'luːʃənaɪz] revolutionieren OT 4

to **reward** [rɪ'wɔːd] belohnen OT 5

rewarding [rɪ'wɔːdɪŋ] lohnend OT 5

to **rewrite** [ˌriː'raɪt] neu schreiben OT 2

rhetoric ['retərɪk] Rhetorik **WS 2**, 58

rhetorical [rɪ'tɒrɪkl] rhetorisch **WS 1**, 24

rhyme ['raɪm] Reim OT 2

rhythm ['rɪðəm] Rhythmus **WS 1**, 29

rhythmical ['rɪðmɪkl] rhythmisch **WS 2**, 67

rib [rɪb] Rippe OT 3

ribbon ['rɪbən] Band **WS 1**, 35

rice [raɪs] Reis OT 1

rich [rɪtʃ] reich; gehaltvoll; ertragreich OT 1

ride [raɪd] Ritt; Fahrt OT 1

to **ride** [raɪd] fahren OT 5

rifle ['raɪfl] Gewehr **WS 2**, 64

rig [rɪg] Bohrinsel **WS 1**, 16

right [raɪt] rechte(r, -s); richtig OT 1

to **right** [raɪt] wiedergutmachen; richtigstellen **WS 2**, 76

righteous ['raɪtʃəs] gerecht **WS 2**, 79

rights [raɪts] Rechte OT 3

rigid ['rɪdʒɪd] starr; rigide OT 5

to **rile up** [raɪl ʌp] reizen; ärgern **WS 2**, 72

rim [rɪm] Rand OT 3

to **ring** [rɪŋ] klingeln; klingen OT 1

rink [rɪŋk] Bahn; Eisbahn OT 4

riot ['raɪət] Aufruhr; Unruhen **WS 2**, 58

ripple ['rɪpl] Welle; Kräuselung WW, 11

to **rise** [raɪz] aufsteigen OT 3

risk [rɪsk] Risiko; Gefahr OT 4

risky ['rɪski] riskant **WS 2**, 68

ritual ['rɪtʃuəl] Ritual OT 4

rival ['raɪvl] Rivale; Rivalin **WS 1**, 13

rivalry ['raɪvlri] Konkurrenz OT 5

river ['rɪvə] Fluss OT 1

road [rəʊd] Straße OT 1

　　the open road [ðə ˈəʊpən ˌrəʊd] die freie Straße OT 2

to **roam** [rəʊm] herumschweifen; durchschweifen OT 5

roast [rəʊst] gebraten OT 1

robbery ['rɒbəri] Raubüberfall **WS 2**, 63

robotic [rəʊ'bɒtɪk] Roboter... **WS 4**, 140

robust [rəʊ'bʌst] solide; robust **WS 3**, 116

rock [rɒk] Stein OT 2

rocket ['rɒkɪt] Rakete OT 4

rocky ['rɒki] steinig **WS 1**, 35

role [rəʊl] Rolle OT 1

roleplay ['rəʊlpleɪ] Rollenspiel OT 2

to **role-play** ['rəʊlpleɪ] ein Rollenspiel machen OT 2

roller skate ['rəʊlə skeɪt] Rollschuh OT 5

roll [rəʊl] Rolle; Filmrolle OT 2

Roman ['rəʊmən] römisch OT 2

romance [rəʊ'mæns] Romantik; Liebesgeschichte **WS 1**, 34

roof ['ruːf] Dach OT 1

room ['ruːm] Raum; Zimmer; Platz OT 1

roommate ['ruːmˌmeɪt] Mitbewohner(in) OT 5

root [ruːt] Wurzel OT 3

rope [rəʊp] Seil OT 3

to **rot** [rɒt] verfaulen OT 5

rota ['rəʊtə] abwechselnder Dienst OT 5

rough [rʌf] rau OT 3

roughly ['rʌfli] ungefähr OT 3

round [raʊnd] rund OT 1

rounded ['raʊndɪd] rund **WS 1**, 35

route [ruːt] Strecke OT 2

routine [ruː'tiːn] Routine OT 5

to **row** [rəʊ] rudern **WS 1**, 37

row [rəʊ] Reihe OT 2

rowing boat ['rəʊɪŋ bəʊt] Ruderboot OT 1

royal ['rɔɪəl] königlich; Königs... OT 1

royalty ['rɔɪəlti] Tantieme; Lizenzgebühr **WS 2**, 66

to **rub** [rʌb] reiben OT 3

rubber [ˈrʌbə] Gummi; Radiergummi; Schwamm OT 1

rubbish [ˈrʌbɪʃ] Müll OT 4

rucksack [ˈrʌksæk] Rucksack OT 1

rude [ruːd] unhöflich OT 2

rugby [ˈrʌgbi] Rugby OT 1

rugged [ˈrʌgɪd] rau; schroff WS 1, 15

ruin [ˈruːɪn] Ruine OT 2

ruined [ˈruːɪnd] verfallen OT 3

rule [ruːl] Regel; Herrschaft OT 1

to **rule** [ruːl] herrschen OT 2

rulebook [ˈruːl bʊk] Regelwerk OT 2

ruler [ˈruːlə] Lineal; Herrscher(in) OT 1

rumble [ˈrʌmbl] Grollen; Schlägerei WS 2, 53

to **run** [rʌn] laufen; rennen; leiten OT 1

    to **run out** [rʌn aʊt] zu Ende gehen OT 2

runaway [ˈrʌnəweɪ] Ausreißer(in) OT 5

runner [ˈrʌnə] Läufer(in) OT 2

running [ˈrʌnɪŋ] Führung; Leitung OT 1

runway [ˈrʌnweɪ] Landebahn WS 1, 38

rural [ˈrʊərəl] ländlich WS 1, 26

to **rush** [rʌʃ] eilen OT 2

    to **rush off** [rʌʃ ɒf] loshasten OT 2

rush hour [ˈrʌʃ aʊə] Hauptverkehrszeit OT 1

S

sack [sæk] Sack OT 2

sack race [ˈsæk reɪs] Sackhüpfen OT 2

sacred [ˈseɪkrɪd] heilig OT 4

sacrifice [ˈsækrɪfaɪs] Opfer WS 2, 58

sad [sæd] traurig; langweilig OT 1

saddened [ˈsædnd] betrübt OT 5

safari [səˈfɑːri] Safari OT 2

safe [seɪf] sicher; ungefährlich; zuverlässig OT 1

safety [ˈseɪfti] Sicherheit OT 2

saga [ˈsɑːgə] Geschichte; Sage WS 2, 69

sail [seɪl] Segel OT 5

to **sail** [seɪl] (mit dem Schiff) fahren OT 2

sailing [ˈseɪlɪŋ] Segeln; Überfahrt OT 1

sailor [ˈseɪlə] Seemann OT 3

saint [seɪnt] Heilige(r) OT 3

salacious [səˈleɪʃəs] anzüglich WS 2, 72

salad [ˈsæləd] Salat OT 1

salary [ˈsæləri] Gehalt; Lohn OT 5

sale [seɪl] Verkauf OT 3

sales [seɪlz] Verkäufe OT 2

sales assistant [ˌseɪləˈsɪstənt] Verkäufer(in) OT 2

salmon [ˈsæmən] Lachs OT 1

salt [sɔːlt] Salz OT 2

salty [ˈsɔːlti] salzig OT 3

salute [səˈluːt] militärischer Gruß OT 3

to **salvage** [ˈsælvɪdʒ] Bergungs... OT 3

salvaged [ˈsælvɪdʒd] geborgen OT 3

same [seɪm] gleich OT 1

to **sample** [ˈsɑːmpl] probieren; eine Probe nehmen OT 4

to **sanction** [ˈsæŋkʃn] genehmigen WS 2, 79

sanctuary [ˈsæŋktʃuəri] Schutzgebiet OT 5

sand [sænd] Sand OT 1

sandstone [ˈsændstəʊn] Sandstein OT 4

sandwich [ˈsænwɪtʃ] Sandwich OT 1

sandy [ˈsændi] sandig OT 5

sanitation [ˌsænɪˈteɪʃn] Sanitär... WS 2, 58

sarcastic [sɑːˈkæstɪk] sarkastisch WS 1, 37

sash [sæʃ] Schärpe OT 4

sachet [ˈsæʃeɪ] kleine Tüte OT 3

satellite [ˈsætəlaɪt] Satellit OT 4

to **satisfy** [ˈsætɪsfaɪ] befriedigen WS 1, 36

Saturday [ˈsætədeɪ] Samstag OT 1

sauce [sɔːs] Soße OT 1

sauna [ˈsɔːnə] Sauna OT 2

sausage [ˈsɒsɪdʒ] Wurst; Würstchen OT 1

to **save** [seɪv] retten; sparen OT 2

savoury [ˈseɪvəri] pikant OT 3

savvy [ˈsævi] klug; schlau OT 5

saxophone [ˈsæksəfəʊn] Saxofon OT 2

to **say** [seɪ] sagen; aussprechen; sprechen OT 1

scale [skeɪl] Maßstab OT 2

    large scale [ˈlɑːdʒ skeɪl] großskalig OT 2

    small scale [ˈsmɔːl skeɪl] kleinskalig OT 2

scallop [ˈskɒləp] Kammmuschel; Jakobsmuschel WS 1, 12

to **scan** [skæn] überfliegen; scannen OT 2

to **scare** [skeə] Angst machen OT 2

scared [skeəd] verängstigt; erschrecken OT 1

scaremongering [ˈskeəmʌŋgərɪŋ] Panikmache WS 1, 32

scarf [skɑːf] Schal; Halstuch; Kopftuch OT 1

scary [ˈskeəri] unheimlich; beängstigend OT 2

to **scatter** [ˈskætə] verstreuen WS 1, 35

to **scavenge** [ˈskævɪndʒ] nach etw. suchen OT 5

scenario [səˈnɑːriəʊ] Szenario WS 4, 140

scene [siːn] Szene OT 2

    behind the scenes [bɪˌhaɪnd ðə ˈsiːnz] hinter den Kulissen OT 2

scenery [ˈsiːnəri] Landschaft; Kulisse OT 2

sceptical [ˈskeptɪkl] skeptisch WS 1, 32

schedule [ˈʃedjuːl] Stundenplan OT 2

scheme [skiːm] Programm WS 1, 14

scheme [skiːm] Programm OT 5

scholarship [ˈskɒləʃɪp] Stipendium OT 5

school [skuːl] Schule; College; Universität OT 1

school bag [ˈskuːl bæg] Schultasche; Schulranzen OT 1

school day [skuːl deɪ] Schultag OT 1

schoolmate [ˈskuːlmeɪt] Schulkamerad(in) OT 4

schoolwork [ˈskuːlwɜːk] Schulaufgaben OT 5

science [ˈsaɪəns] Wissenschaft; Naturwissenschaft OT 1

scientific [ˌsaɪənˈtɪfɪk] wissenschaftlich OT 3

scientist [ˈsaɪəntɪst] Naturwissenschaftler(in) OT 1

scissors [ˈsɪzəz] Schere OT 1

to **scold** [skəʊld] ausschimpfen WS 2, 64

scone [skəʊn] brötchenartiges, süßes Gebäck OT 1

scorching [ˈskɔːtʃɪŋ] glühend OT 5

score [skɔːr] Note OT 5

to **score** [skɔː] punkten; ein Tor schießen; bekommen OT 1

to **scorn** [skɔːn] verachten WS 3, 101

Scottish [ˈskɒtɪʃ] schottisch OT 2

scout [skaʊt] Scout; Kundschafter(in) OT 3

to **scramble** [ˈskræmbl] herumkriechen WS 1, 22

to **scrap** [skræp] verschrotten; abschaffen WS 2, 53

to **scrape** [skreɪp] kratzen; schrubben OT 2

scrapple [ˈskræpl] Scrapple OT 3

to **scratch** [skrætʃ] kratzen OT 2

to **scream** [skriːm] schreien OT 3

screen [skriːn] Bildschirm; Leinwand; Wandschirm OT 1

script [skrɪpt] Drehbuch OT 2

scroll [skrəʊl] Schriftrolle OT 2

to **sculpt** [skʌlpt] formen **WS 3**, 117

sculptor [ˈskʌlptə] Bildhauer(in) **WS 2**, 55

sculpture [ˈskʌlptʃə] Skulptur OT 2

sea [siː] Meer; See OT 1

seabed [ˈsiːbed] Meeresboden OT 3

seabird [ˈsiːbɜːd] Seevogel OT 5

seafaring [ˈsiːfeərɪŋ] seefahrend OT 3

seafloor [siːfloː] Meeresgrund **WS 4**, 135

seafood [ˈsiːfuːd] Meeresfrüchte OT 4

seal [siːl] Robbe; Seehund; Siegel OT 1

seaman [ˈsiːmən] Seemann OT 3

search [sɜːtʃ] Suche OT 2

to **search** [sɜːtʃ] (durch)suchen OT 4

seashell [ˈsiːʃel] Muschel OT 3

seashore [ˈsiːʃɔː] Strand OT 4

seasick [ˈsiːsɪk] seekrank OT 3

seaside [ˈsiːsaɪd] Meeresküste OT 3

season [ˈsiːzn] Jahreszeit OT 2

seasoning [ˈsiːzənɪŋ] Gewürz OT 2

seat [siːt] Sitzplatz OT 2

to **seat** [siːt] setzen OT 5

seating [ˈsiːtɪŋ] Sitzplätze OT 2

seaweed [ˈsiːwiːd] Seetang **WS 1**, 12

to **secede** [sɪˈsiːd] sich abspalten **WS 2**, 54

second [ˈsekənd] Sekunde; Zweite(r, -s); Moment OT 1

secondary [ˈsekəndri] weiterführend; sekundär OT 1

secondary school [ˈsekəndri ˌskuːl] Sekundarschule; weiterführende Schule OT 1

secondly [ˈsekəndli] zweitens OT 2

secret [ˈsiːkrət] Geheimnis OT 2

secretary [ˈsekrətri] Sekretär(in); Minister(in) OT 1

secretive [ˈsiːkrətɪv] geheimnisvoll **WS 3**, 96

section [ˈsekʃn] Teil OT 2

sector [ˈsektə] Bereich OT 5

secure [sɪˈkjʊə] sicher OT 3

to **secure** [sɪˈkjʊər] sichern; ergattern OT 5

security [sɪˈkjʊərəti] Sicherheit OT 5

to **see** [siː] sehen; sich vorstellen; verstehen OT 1

seed [siːd] Samen OT 2

to **seek** [siːk] suchen OT 5

to **seem** [siːm] scheinen OT 2

segment [ˈsegmənt] Segment; Abschnitt OT 5

segregation [ˌsegrɪˈgeɪʃn] Trennung; Segregation **WS 2**, 53

to **seize** [siːz] ergreifen **WS 1**, 18

seldom [ˈseldəm] selten OT 5

to **select** [sɪˈlekt] wählen; auswählen OT 4

selection [sɪˈlekʃn] Auswahl OT 4

selective [sɪˈlektɪv] getrennt OT 4

self-belief [ˌselfbɪˈliːf] Selbstwertgefühl; Selbstbewusstsein OT 5

self-employed [ˌself ɪmˈplɔɪd] selbständig OT 5

self-esteem [ˌself ɪˈstiːm] Selbstbewusstsein **WS 1**, 37

selfie [ˈselfi] Selfie OT 4

selfish [ˈselfɪʃ] egoistisch OT 3

self-service [ˌself ˈsɜːvɪs] Selbstbedienung OT 4

self-sufficient [ˌself səˈfɪʃnt] selbstständig; unabhängig OT 4

to **sell** [sel] verkaufen; sich verkaufen OT 1

semester [sɪˈmestə] Semester OT 4

semi- [ˈsemi] halb- OT 3

semi-detached house [ˌsemidɪtætʃt ˈhaʊs] Doppelhaushälfte OT 4

senator [ˈsenətə] Senator(in) OT 4

to **send** [send] schicken; verschicken; abschicken OT 1

senior [ˈsiːniə] Oberstufenschüler(in); Senior(in) OT 4

senior citizen [ˌsiːniəˈsɪtɪzn] Senior(in) OT 2

sensation [senˈseɪʃn] Sensation **WS 2**, 66

sense [sens] Sinn OT 2

sensible [ˈsensəbl] vernünftig OT 2

sensitive [ˈsensətɪv] einfühlsam OT 4

sensory [ˈsensəri] sensorisch OT 5

sentence [ˈsentəns] Satz; Strafe; Urteil OT 1

to **sentence** [ˈsentəns] verurteilen OT 5

separate [ˈseprət] getrennt OT 2

separation [ˌsepəˈreɪʃn] Trennung **WS 3**, 122

September [sepˈtembə] September OT 1

sequel [ˈsiːkwəl] Folge; Fortsetzung OT 4

sequence [ˈsiːkwəns] Aufeinanderfolge OT 3

to **sequence** [ˈsiːkwəns] in eine Reihenfolge bringen OT 3

sequencing [ˈsiːkwənsɪŋ] Sequenzierung; Reihenfolge OT 3

sequentially [sɪˈkwenʃəli] der Reihe nach OT 4

series [ˈsɪəriːz] Serie OT 4

serious [ˈsɪəriəs] ernst OT 2

seriousness [ˈsɪəriəsnəs] Ernsthaftigkeit OT 5

sermon [ˈsɜːmən] Predigt **WS 2**, 60

serpent [ˈsɜːpənt] Schlange OT 5

servant [ˈsɜːvənt] Diener(in) OT 3

to **serve** [sɜːv] servieren; bedienen OT 1

server [ˈsɜːvə] Kellner(in) OT 3

service [ˈsɜːvɪs] Dienst OT 2

session [ˈseʃn] Session ; Sitzung OT 4

to **set** [set] stellen OT 2

to **set off** [ˌsetˈɒf] aufbrechen OT 2

to **set the table** [set ðə teɪbl] den Tisch decken OT 2

setting [ˈsetɪŋ] Setting; Umgebung OT 5

to **settle** [ˈsetl] sich niederlassen; besiedeln OT 4

to **settle down** [ˈsetl daʊn] sich beruhigen OT 2

to **settle in** [ˈsetl ɪn] sich eingewöhnen OT 5

settlement [ˈsetlmənt] Siedlung OT 4

settler [ˈsetlə] Siedler(in) OT 3

seven [ˈsevn] sieben OT 1

seventeen [ˌsevnˈtiːn] siebzehn OT 1

seventy [ˈsevnti] siebzig OT 1

several [ˈsevrəl] mehrere; einige OT 1

severe [sɪˈvɪə] schwer; stark OT 4

to **sew** [səʊ] nähen OT 3

sex [seks] Geschlecht; Sex OT 5

shade [ʃeɪd] Schatten OT 5

shadow [ˈʃædəʊ] Schatten OT 3

to **shadow sb** [ˈʃædəʊ] bei jdm hospitieren OT 5

to **shake** [ʃeɪk] schütteln OT 2

shall [ʃæl] werden OT 2

shame [ʃeɪm] Schamgefühl OT 5

it's a shame [ɪts ə ˈʃeɪm] das ist schade OT 2

to **shame** [ʃeɪm] (be)schämen **WS 3**, 112

shampoo [ʃæmˈpuː] Shampoo OT 3

shape [ʃeɪp] Form; Gestalt; Zustand OT 1

to **shape** [ʃeɪp] formen OT 4

to **share** [ʃeə] teilen OT 2

shark [ʃɑːk] Hai OT 2

sharp [ʃɑːp] scharf OT 4

she [ʃi] sie OT 1

shed [ʃed] Schuppen; Stall OT 1

sheep [ʃiːp] Schaf OT 1

sheepdog [ˈʃiːpdɒg] Hütehund OT 2

to **sheer** [ʃɪə] sich losmachen OT 3

sheet [ʃiːt] Betttuch; Blatt OT 1

shelf [ʃelf] Regal OT 2

shellfish [ˈʃelfɪʃ] Meeresfrüchte OT 3

shelter [ˈʃeltə] Unterschlupf OT 2

shepherd [ˈʃepəd] Schäfer OT 2

shift [ʃɪft] Veränderung OT 5

to shift [ʃɪft] verändern; verlagern OT 5

to shine [ʃaɪn] leuchten; glänzen OT 1

shiny [ˈʃaɪni] glänzend; funkelnd
WS 3, 104

ship [ʃɪp] Schiff OT 1

shirt [ʃɜːt] Hemd; Oberhemd OT 1

to shiver [ˈʃɪvə] zittern OT 3

shock [ʃɒk] Überraschung OT 3

to shock [ʃɒk] überraschen;
schockieren OT 4

shoe [ʃuː] Schuh; Hufeisen OT 1

to shoot [ʃuːt] schießen OT 3

shop [ʃɒp] Laden; Geschäft; Einkauf
OT 1

to shop [ʃɒp] kaufen; einkaufen;
verpfeifen OT 1

shoplifting [ˈʃɒplɪftɪŋ] Ladendiebstahl
OT 5

shopper [ˈʃɒpə] Käufer(in) OT 4

shopping [ˈʃɒpɪŋ] Einkaufen OT 1

shopping centre [ˈʃɒpɪŋ sentə]
Einkaufszentrum OT 1

shopping trolley [ˈʃɒpɪŋ trɒli]
Einkaufswagen; Servierwagen;
Straßenbahn OT 1

shore [ʃɔː] Küste OT 2

shoreline [ˈʃɔːlaɪn] Küste OT 4

short [ʃɔːt] kurz; klein OT 1

shortage [ˈʃɔːtɪdʒ] Mangel OT 5

to shorten [ˈʃɔːtn] kürzen; abkürzen
OT 4

shorthand [ˈʃɔːthænd] Kurzform
WS 3, 96

shortlist [ˈʃɔːtlɪst] Auswahlliste OT 2

shorts [ʃɔːts] kurze Hosen OT 3

shot [ʃɒt] Schuss; Schnappschuss OT 2

should [ʃəd] sollte OT 2

shoulder [ˈʃəʊldə] Schulter;
Schulterstück; Standspur OT 1

to shout [ʃaʊt] laut rufen OT 1

to show [ʃəʊ] zeigen; vorzeigen; zu
sehen sein OT 1

show-and-tell [ʃəʊ ən ˈtel] Kurzvortrag
über einen mitgebrachten Gegenstand
OT 2

shower [ˈʃaʊə] Dusche; Schauer;
Regenschauer OT 1

showground [ˈʃəʊɡraʊnd]
Ausstellungsgelände OT 2

to shred [ʃred] zerfetzen OT 2

shredded [ˈʃredɪd] zerkleinert OT 2

to shrink [ʃrɪŋk] schrumpfen WS 1, 31

shrub [ʃrʌb] Busch WS 1, 22

shrubby [ˈʃrʌbi] buschig WS 1, 22

to shrug [ʃrʌɡ] mit den Schultern
zucken WS 3, 113

to shut [ʃʌt] zumachen; schließen OT 2

to shut up [ʃʌt ʌp] den Mund halten
OT 2

shy [ʃaɪ] schüchtern OT 2

sibling [ˈsɪblɪŋ] Geschwister(kind);
Bruder; Schwester OT 5

sick [sɪk] krank; übel; geschmacklos
OT 1

side [saɪd] Seite; Partei; Mannschaft
OT 1

sideline [ˈsaɪdlaɪn] Nebenberuf OT 5

to sigh [saɪ] seufzen OT 5

sight [saɪt] Sehenswürdigkeit;
Sehvermögen; Anblick OT 1

sighting [ˈsaɪtɪŋ] Sichtung WS 1, 38

sightseeing [ˈsaɪtsiːɪŋ] Besichtigungen;
Sightseeing OT 1

sign [saɪn] Schild; Zeichen; Anzeichen
OT 1

to sign [saɪn] unterschreiben OT 2

to sign up [saɪn ʌp] sich anmelden
OT 2

signal [ˈsɪɡnəl] Signal OT 2

signature [ˈsɪɡnətʃə] Unterschrift
WS 2, 78

significance [sɪɡˈnɪfɪkəns] Bedeutung;
Wichtigkeit OT 5

to signify [ˈsɪɡnɪfaɪ] bedeuten OT 4

signpost [ˈsaɪnpəʊst] Wegweiser; Schild
OT 5

silence [ˈsaɪləns] Schweigen; Ruhe OT 5

silent [ˈsaɪlənt] stumm; still WS 1, 24

silly [ˈsɪli] dumm; albern OT 1

silver [ˈsɪlvə] Silber...; silbern;
silberfarben OT 1

similar [ˈsɪmələ] ähnlich OT 1

similarity [ˌsɪməˈlærəti] Ähnlichkeit OT 3

to simmer [ˈsɪmə] köcheln OT 2

simple [ˈsɪmpl] einfach; schlicht;
einfältig OT 1

simplicity [sɪmˈplɪsəti] Einfachheit
WS 2, 67

to simplify [ˈsɪmplɪfaɪ] vereinfachen
WS 2, 68

simultaneous [ˌsɪmlˈteɪniəs]
gleichzeitig; simultan OT 5

sin [sɪn] Sünde WS 2, 64

since [sɪns] seit OT 2

sincerely [sɪnˈsɪəli] aufrichtig; mit
freundlichen Grüßen OT 3

sincerity [sɪnˈserəti] Ernsthaftigkeit
WS 2, 69

to sing [sɪŋ] singen OT 1

singer [ˈsɪŋə] Sänger(in) OT 1

single [ˈsɪŋɡl] Einzel... OT 3

sinister [ˈsɪnɪstə] unheimlich WS 1, 35

sink [sɪŋk] Spülbecken OT 3

to sink [sɪŋk] sinken OT 3

sir [sɜː] (mein) Herr OT 1

siren [ˈsaɪrən] Sirene OT 3

sister [ˈsɪstə] Schwester;
Ordensschwester; Stationsschwester
OT 1

to sit [sɪt] sitzen; liegen; tagen OT 1

site [saɪt] Platz OT 2

situated [ˈsɪtʃueɪtɪd] gelegen OT 4

situation [ˌsɪtʃuˈeɪʃn] Lage; Situation;
Schlamassel OT 1

six [sɪks] sechs OT 1

sixteen [ˌsɪksˈtiːn] sechzehn OT 1

sixty [ˈsɪksti] sechzig OT 1

size [saɪz] Größe OT 2

to skate [skeɪt] Schlittschuh laufen OT 2

skateboard [ˈskeɪtbɔːd] Skateboard
OT 1

skeletal [ˈskelətl] Skelett... OT 3

skeleton [ˈskelɪtn] Skelett; Gerippe OT 2

sketch [sketʃ] Skizze; Sketch OT 2

to ski [skiː] Ski laufen OT 3

skiing [ˈskiːɪŋ] Skifahren OT 3

skill [skɪl] Fertigkeit; Fähigkeit OT 1

skilled [skɪld] geschickt; ausgebildet
OT 4

to skim [skɪm] querlesen; überfliegen
OT 2

skin [skɪn] Haut OT 2

skinny [ˈskɪni] mager; dünn OT 5

to skip [skɪp] auslassen OT 3

skirt [skɜːt] Rock OT 1

skit [skɪt] Sketch OT 2

skull [skʌl] Schädel OT 2

sky [skaɪ] Himmel OT 1

skydiver [ˈskaɪdaɪvər]
Fallschirmspringer(in) OT 5

skyline [ˈskaɪlaɪn] Skyline OT 4

to skyrocket [ˈskaɪrɒkɪt] in die Höhe
schießen WS 3, 96

skyscraper [ˈskaɪskreɪpə] Wolkenkratzer
OT 3

slang [slæŋ] Slang OT 4

slangy [ˈslæŋi] salopp WS 2, 67

to slap on [slæp ɒn] draufklatschen OT 5

to slash [slæʃ] zerschneiden;
reduzieren WS 1, 36

slave [sleɪv] Sklave(-in) OT 3

slavery [ˈsleɪvəri] Sklaverei WW, 10

to slay [sleɪ] töten WS 2, 79

sled [sled] Schlitten OT 4

sleep [sliːp] Schlaf OT 5

to **go to sleep** [ˌɡəʊ tə ˈsliːp] einschlafen OT 1

to **sleep** [sliːp] schlafen OT 1

sleepover [ˈsliːpoʊvə] Pyjama-Party OT 1

sleeve [sliːv] Ärmel **WS 2**, 59

sleeved [sliːvd] mit Ärmeln OT 3

slice [slaɪs] Scheibe; Stück; Anteil OT 1

slick [slɪk] clever; glatt **WS 3**, 93

slide [ˈslaɪd] Folie OT 1

to **slide on** [slaɪd ɒn] aufschieben OT 5

slideshow [ˈslaɪdʃəʊ] Diaschau OT 5

slightly [ˈslaɪtli] etwas; ein bisschen OT 3

slim [slɪm] schlank **WS 3**, 117

to **slip on** [ˈslɪp ɒn] rasch anziehen OT 5

slipper [ˈslɪpə] Pantoffel OT 4

slippery [ˈslɪpəri] glatt OT 3

slogan [ˈsləʊɡən] Slogan OT 2

to **slop on** [ˈslɒp ɒn] schwappen OT 5

slot machine [ˈslɒt məʃiːn] Spielautomat **WS 4**, 135

slow [sləʊ] langsam OT 2

to **slow down** [sləʊˈdaʊn] verlangsamen OT 4

slum [slʌm] Slum; Elendsviertel OT 5

to **slump** [slʌmp] abrutschen; zusammensacken OT 5

small [smɔːl] klein OT 1

smallpox [ˈsmɔːlpɒks] Pocken OT 5

smart [smɑːt] schlau OT 5

smartly [ˈsmɑːtli] schick; klug OT 4

smartphone [ˈsmɑːtfəʊn] Smartphone OT 3

to **smell** [smel] riechen; stinken OT 1

smelly [ˈsmeli] übel riechend OT 3

to **smile** [smaɪl] lächeln OT 1

smoke [sməʊk] Rauch OT 2

smooth [smuːð] glatt OT 4

smoothly [ˈsmuːði] glatt OT 3

to **smuggle** [ˈsmʌɡl] schmuggeln OT 5

snack [snæk] Snack; Imbiss OT 1

snail mail [ˈsneɪl meɪl] Schneckenpost OT 4

snake [sneɪk] Schlange; falsche Schlange; heimtückische Person OT 1

to **snap** [snæp] zerbrechen OT 3

sneaker [ˈsniːkə] Turnschuh OT 5

snow [snəʊ] Schnee OT 1

to **snow** [snəʊ] schneien OT 1

snowboarding [ˈsnəʊbɔːdɪŋ] Snowboardfahren OT 3

snow-capped [ˈsnəʊ kæpt] schneebedeckt OT 4

snowmobile [ˈsnəʊməbiːl] Schneemobil OT 4

snowy [ˈsnəʊi] verschneit OT 4

so [səʊ] also; so OT 1

to **soak** [səʊkd] naß werden; durchnässen OT 3

to **soak up** [səʊk ʌp] aufnehmen; hier: (Sonne) tanken OT 5

soap [səʊp] Seife OT 2

to **soar** [sɔː] schweben OT 3

soccer [ˈsɒkə] Fußball OT 2

sociable [ˈsəʊʃəbl] gesellig; kontaktfreudig **WS 3**, 98

social [ˈsəʊʃl] gesellschaftlich OT 3

socialization [ˌsəʊʃəlaɪˈzeɪʃn] Sozialisierung **WS 3**, 122

to **socialize** [ˈsəʊʃəlaɪz] Kontakte pflegen OT 4

social media [ˌsəʊʃl ˈmiːdiə] soziale Medien OT 2

societal [səˈsaɪətl] gesellschaftlich **WS 3**, 112

society [səˈsaɪəti] Gesellschaft OT 3

socio-economic [ˌsəʊsiəʊ ˌiːkəˈnɒmɪk] sozioökonomisch **WS 2**, 83

sock [sɒk] Socke OT 1

soda [ˈsəʊdə] Limo; Sprudel OT 5

sofa [ˈsəʊfə] Sofa OT 1

soft [sɒft] weich; gedämpft; zart OT 1

soil [sɔɪl] Erde; Erdreich OT 4

solar [ˈsəʊlə] Sonnen... OT 3

soldier [ˈsəʊldʒə] Soldat(in) OT 1

sole [səʊl] einzig **WS 1**, 17

solemn [ˈsɒləm] feierlich; getragen **WS 2**, 69

solid [ˈsɒlɪd] fest; massiv OT 4

solidarity [ˌsɒləˈdærəti] Solidarität; Verbundenheit **WS 2**, 77

solitary [ˈsɒlətri] einsam **WS 2**, 55

solo [ˈsəʊləʊ] solo OT 2

solution [səˈluːʃn] Lösung OT 3

to **solve** [sɒlv] lösen OT 4

some [sʌm] etwas; einige; manche(r, -s) OT 1

somebody [ˈsʌmbədi] jemand OT 1

someday [ˈsʌmdeɪ] eines Tages; irgendwann OT 5

somehow [ˈsʌmhaʊ] irgendwie OT 4

someone [ˈsʌmwʌn] jemand; irgendjemand OT 1

something [ˈsʌmθɪŋ] etwas OT 1

sometime [ˈsʌmtaɪm] irgendwann OT 3

sometimes [ˈsʌmtaɪmz] manchmal OT 1

somewhat [ˈsʌmwɒt] irgendwie **WS 1**, 27

somewhere [ˈsʌmweə] irgendwo; irgendwohin OT 1

son [sʌn] Sohn OT 1

to **have a son** [hæv ə ˈsʌn] einen Sohn bekommen OT 1

song [sɒŋ] Lied; Gesang OT 1

songwriter [ˈsɒŋraɪtər] Texter(in); Liederkomponist(in) OT 5

soon [suːn] bald OT 1

sophisticated [səˈfɪstɪkeɪtɪd] anspruchsvoll; gebildet **WS 4**, 135

sophomore [ˈsɒfəmɔːr] Student im 2. Studienjahr OT 5

sorry [ˈsɒri] Entschuldigung; Es tut mir leid OT 1

sort [sɔːt] Art OT 2

to **sort** [sɔːt] sortieren OT 4

to **sort out** [sɔːt ˈaʊt] klären; aussortieren OT 4

soul [səʊl] Seele OT 2

sound [saʊnd] Geräusch; Ton; Klang OT 1

to **sound** [saʊnd] klingen OT 4

soundtrack [ˈsaʊndtræk] Tonspur **WS 2**, 82

sound wave [ˈsaʊnd weɪv] Schallwelle **WS 3**, 96

soup [suːp] Suppe OT 1

source [sɔːs] Quelle OT 2

south [saʊθ] Süd- OT 2

southern [ˈsʌðən] südlich OT 4

southwest [ˌsaʊθˈwest] südwestlich OT 3

souvenir [ˌsuːvəˈnɪə] Andenken OT 3

soya [ˈsɔɪə] Soja **WS 4**, 135

spa [spɑː] Heilbad OT 2

space [speɪs] Platz; Weltraum; Feld OT 1

spacecraft [ˈspeɪskrɑːft] Raumfahrzeug OT 4

spacewalker [ˈspeɪswɔːkə] Spacewalker; jemand, der im Weltraum spazieren geht OT 5

spacious [ˈspeɪʃəs] geräumig **WS 1**, 25

spaghetti [spəˈɡeti] Spaghetti OT 1

span [spæn] Spanne **WS 3**, 108

spaniel [ˈspænjəl] Spaniel OT 2

Spanish [ˈspænɪʃ] spanisch OT 1

spare [speə] übrig; zusätzlich OT 3

spark [spɑːk] Funke OT 4

to **speak** [spiːk] sprechen; reden; eine Rede halten OT 1

speaker [ˈspiːkə] Redner(in) OT 2

spear [spɪə] Speer OT 4

to **spear** [spɪər] aufspießen OT 5

special [ˈspeʃl] besondere(r, -s); speziell; Spezial... OT 1

specialist [ˈspeʃəlɪst] Spezialist(in); Expert(in) OT 5

to **specialize** [ˈspeʃəlaɪz] sich spezialisieren OT 3

species [ˈspiːʃiːz] Spezies; Art OT 5

specific [spəˈsɪfɪk] bestimmt; konkret; spezifisch OT 2

specifically [spəˈsɪfɪkli] speziell **WS 2**, 79

spectacle [ˈspektəkl] Spektakel; Sensation **WS 1**, 35

spectacular [spekˈtækjələ] spektakulär OT 2

spectator [spekˈteɪtə] Zuschauer(in) OT 2

to **speculate** [ˈspekjuleɪt] spekulieren; nachdenken OT 4

speculation [ˌspekjuˈleɪʃn] Spekulation **WS 1**, 32

speech [spi:tʃ] Rede OT 2

speed [spi:d] Geschwindigkeit OT 2

to **spell** [spel] buchstabieren; orthografisch richtig schreiben; ergeben OT 1

spelling [ˈspelɪŋ] Rechtschreibung; Schreibweise OT 1

to **spend** [spend] ausgeben; verbringen OT 1

to **spice** [spaɪs] würzen OT 4

spice [spaɪs] Gewürz OT 2

spicy [ˈspaɪsi] scharf; würzig OT 4

spider [ˈspaɪdə] Spinne OT 1

spiky [ˈspaɪki] stachelig; spitz OT 5

to **spill** [spɪl] verschütten OT 2

spin master [spɪn ˈmɑːstə] Imageberater(in); Spindoktor **WS 2**, 69

to **spiral** [ˈspaɪrəl] sich drehen **WS 1**, 24

spire [ˈspaɪə] Kirchturm; Turmspitze **WS 1**, 35

spirit [ˈspɪrɪt] Geist OT 2

spirited [ˈspɪrɪtɪd] lebendig **WS 1**, 17

spirit level [ˈspɪrɪt levl] Wasserwaage OT 5

spiritual [ˈspɪrɪtʃuəl] spirituell; geistig **WS 2**, 60

spite: in spite of [ɪn spaɪt əv] trotz OT 5

to **splash** [splæʃ] platschen OT 2

to **split** [splɪt] trennen OT 3

to **split up** [ˌsplɪtˈʌp] sich trennen OT 2

to **spoil** [spɔɪl] verderben OT 2

spoilage [ˈspɔɪlɪdʒ] Verderben OT 4

sponsor [ˈspɒnsə] Sponsor(in) OT 2

to **sponsor** [ˈspɒnsə] finanziell unterstützen OT 2

sponsorship [ˈspɒnsəʃɪp] finanzielle Unterstützung OT 2

spooky [ˈspuːki] gruselig **WS 1**, 43

spoon [spuːn] Löffel OT 2

sport [spɔːt] Sport; Sportart OT 1

   good sport [gʊd spɔːt] kein(e) Spielverderber(in) OT 2

sporting [ˈspɔːtɪŋ] sportlich; Sport... OT 5

sportswoman [ˈspɔːtswʊmən] Sportler(in) OT 2

sporty [ˈspɔːti] sportlich OT 3

to **spot** [spɒt] erspähen OT 1

sprain [spreɪn] Verstauchung OT 2

to **sprain** [spreɪn] verstauchen OT 2

sprawling [ˈsprɔːlɪŋ] ausgedehnt **WS 1**, 34

to **spray** [spreɪ] sprühen OT 3

to **spread** [spred] verbreiten OT 4

spring [sprɪŋ] Frühling; Quelle OT 2

   hot spring [ˈhɒt sprɪŋ] Thermalquelle OT 2

to **sprinkle** [ˈsprɪŋkl] streuen OT 2

to **spur** [spɜːr] anspornen **WS 1**, 32

spy [spaɪ] Spion(in) **WS 2**, 57

square [skweə] Quadrat; Feld; Kästchen; Platz OT 1

to **squeeze** [skwiːz] quetschen **WS 1**, 25

squirrel [ˈskwɪrəl] Eichhörnchen OT 1

stability [stəˈbɪləti] Stabilität OT 5

stable [ˈsteɪbl] Stall OT 4

to **stack** [stæk] stapeln OT 4

stadium [ˈsteɪdiəm] Stadion OT 1

staff [stɑːf] Personal; Stab OT 1

stage [steɪdʒ] Phase; Bühne OT 2

to **stage** [steɪdʒ] veranstalten; inszenieren **WS 2**, 53

staggering [ˈstægərɪŋ] erschreckend; atemberaubend OT 4

stairs [ˈsteəz] Treppe, Treppenstufen OT 1

to **stake** [steɪk] abstecken **WS 3**, 96

stall [stɔːl] Stand OT 4

stamp [stæmp] Briefmarke; Rabattmarke; Stempel OT 1

stance [stæns] Haltung **WS 2**, 60

to **stand** [stænd] stehen; stellen; gelten OT 1

   to **stand out** [ˈstænd aʊt] hervorstechen **WS 3**, 96

standard [ˈstændəd] Standard OT 5; Flagge **WS 1**, 13

standard [ˈstændəd] standardmäßig; normal OT 5

star [stɑː] Stern; Star OT 1

to **stare** [steə] starren OT 2

stark [stɑːk] krass; deutlich **WS 2**, 83

start [stɑːt] Anfang OT 1

to **start** [stɑːt] anfangen; beginnen; aufbrechen OT 1

starter [ˈstɑːtə] Vorspeise; Teilnehmer(in); Teilnehmer(in) OT 1

start-up [ˈstɑːtʌp] junges Unternehmen OT 5

to **starve** [stɑːv] hungern(lassen); verhungern; verhungern lassen OT 1

state [steɪt] Staat; Bundesstaat OT 1

to **state** [steɪt] erklären; festlegen OT 5

statement [ˈsteɪtmənt] Aussage; Erklärung; Kontoauszug OT 1

station [ˈsteɪʃn] Station; Bahnhof; Sender OT 1

statistic [stəˈtɪstɪk] Statistik OT 3

statue [ˈstætʃuː] Statue; Standbild OT 1

status [ˈsteɪtəs] Status OT 5

staunch [stɔːntʃ] standhaft; treu **WS 1**, 13

to **stay** [steɪ] bleiben; wohnen OT 1

staycation [ˌsteɪˈkeɪʃn] Ferien zuhause **WS 1**, 12

steady [ˈstedi] ruhig; stabil OT 3

steak [steɪk] Steak; Rindfleisch OT 1

to **steal** [stiːl] klauen OT 2

steam [stiːm] Dampf OT 2

steel [stiːl] Stahl OT 2

steely [ˈstiːli] stahlhart; stählern **WS 1**, 35

steep [stiːp] steil OT 2

to **steer** [stɪə] steuern OT 3

to **stem from** [stem frəm] von etwas kommen **WS 1**, 17

step [step] Schritt; Stufe OT 1

to **step** [step] treten OT 4

   to **step in** [step ˈɪn] eintreten OT 4

   to **step up** [step ʌp] vortreten OT 5

stepping-stone [ˈstepɪŋ stəʊn] Trittstein **WS 1**, 16

stereotype [ˈsteriətaɪp] Stereotype; Klischee OT 5

stereotypical [ˌsteriəˈtɪpɪkl] stereotypisch OT 5

steroid [ˈsterɔɪd] Steroid OT 5

stew [stjuː] Eintopf OT 3

stick [stɪk] Zweig OT 2

to **stick** [stɪk] stecken; kleben; stoßen OT 1

   to **stick to** [stɪk tə] dabei bleiben OT 5

sticky note [ˌstɪki ˈnəʊt] Haftnotiz OT 5

stiff [stɪf] steif; starr OT 5

stigma [ˈstɪgmə] Stigma OT 5

still [stɪl] immer noch; noch immer; trotzdem OT 1

still [stɪl] still OT 1

stilted [ˈstɪltɪd] gekünstelt **WS 3**, 114

to **sting** [stɪŋ] stechen OT 2

stingray [ˈstɪŋreɪ] Stachelrochen OT 5

to **stir** [stɜː] rühren OT 2

to **stock up** [stɒk 'ʌp] sich bevorraten; auffüllen OT 4

to **stoke** [stəʊk] schüren **WS 2**, 58

stomach ['stʌmək] Magen; Bauch OT 1

stone [stəʊn] Stein; britische Gewichtseinheit: 6,35 kg OT 1

stop [stɒp] Halt; Aufenthalt; Haltestelle OT 1

to **stop** [stɒp] anhalten; aufhören; stehen bleiben OT 1

storage ['stɔːrɪdʒ] Lagerung OT 3

to **store** [stɔː] aufbewahren OT 2

storey ['stɔːri] Etage **WS 2**, 66

storm [stɔːm] Sturm OT 2

story ['stɔːri] Geschichte; Bericht; Story OT 1

storyboard ['stɔːribɔːd] Storyboard; Szenenbuch OT 4

storybook ['stɔːribʊk] Geschichtenbuch OT 2

storyteller ['stɔːritelə] Geschichtenerzähler(in) OT 2

storytelling ['stɔːritelɪŋ] Geschichtenerzählen OT 4

stove [stəʊv] Ofen OT 3

straight away ['streɪt ə,weɪ] sofort OT 2

straight [streɪt] gerade; direkt OT 3

straight [streɪt] heterosexuell OT 5

straightforward [,streɪt'fɔːwəd] direkt; gradlinig **WS 1**, 32

strange [streɪndʒ] seltsam; merkwürdig; fremd OT 1

stranger ['streɪndʒə] Fremde(r) OT 3

strategy ['strætədʒi] Strategie OT 5

straw [strɔː] Trinkhalm; Strohhalm; Stroh OT 4

strawberry ['strɔːbəri] Erdbeere OT 1

stream [striːm] Bach OT 2

streaming ['striːmɪŋ] Streaming OT 5

street [striːt] Straße OT 1

strength [streŋkθ] Stärke OT 4

to **strengthen** ['streŋkθn] stärker werden; stärker machen OT 4

stress [stres] Stress; Betonung; Gewicht OT 1

stressed [strest] gestresst; angestrengt OT 2

stressful ['stresfl] stressig OT 4

stressor ['stresə] Stressfaktor **WS 4**, 146

to **stretch** [stretʃ] sich erstrecken OT 3

strict [strɪkt] streng OT 2

strike [straɪk] Streik OT 4

to **strike** [straɪk] streiken; zuschlagen; treffen OT 4

striking ['straɪkɪŋ] auffallend OT 4

string [strɪŋ] Schnur; Saite OT 2

strip [strɪp] Streifen OT 2

to **strive** [straɪv] sich bemühen **WS 3**, 112

to **stroke** [strəʊk] streicheln OT 3

stroll [strəʊl] Spaziergang **WS 1**, 15

strong [strɒŋ] stark OT 2

structure ['strʌktʃə] Struktur; Aufbau; Gebäude OT 1

to **structure** ['strʌktʃə] strukturieren; aufbauen OT 5

to **struggle** ['strʌgl] sich anstrengen; sich bemühen OT 5

student ['stjuːdnt] Student(in); Schüler(in); Kursteilnehmer(in) OT 1

studies ['stʌdiz] Studium; Wissenschaft OT 1

  religious studies [rɪ'lɪdʒəs stʌdiz] Religionsunterricht OT 1

studio ['stjuːdiəʊ] Studio OT 5

study ['stʌdi] Studie; Untersuchung; das Lernen OT 1

to **study** ['stʌdi] studieren; lernen; prüfen OT 1

stuff [stʌf] Zeug OT 2

stuffing ['stʌfɪŋ] Füllung OT 3

stunning ['stʌnɪŋ] toll; atemberaubend OT 5

stupid ['stjuːpɪd] dumm OT 2

sturdy ['stɜːdi] kräftig **WS 4**, 142

style [staɪl] Stil OT 2

stylish ['staɪlɪʃ] schick OT 4

subculture ['sʌbkʌltʃə] Subkultur **WS 3**, 94

subgroup ['sʌbgruːp] Untergruppe **WS 3**, 96

subheading ['sʌb,hedɪŋ] Unterüberschrift OT 2

subject ['sʌbdʒɪkt] Thema; Fach; Subjekt OT 1

  to **change the subject** [,tʃeɪndʒ ðə 'sʌbdʒekt] das Thema wechseln OT 2

submarine [,sʌbmə'riːn] U-Boot **WS 1**, 31

to **subscribe to** [səb'skraɪb] abonnieren; anmelden OT 5

subsequently ['sʌbsɪkwəntli] folglich; darauf folgend **WS 1**, 12

substance ['sʌbstəns] Substanz OT 3

substantial [səb'stænʃl] reichlich OT 5

substitute ['sʌbstɪtjuːt] Ersatz OT 3

substitution [,sʌbstɪ'tjuːʃn] Ersatz; Ersetzen OT 3

subtle ['sʌtl] dezent; subtil **WS 1**, 29

subway ['sʌbweɪ] U-Bahn; Unterführung OT 1

to **succeed** [sək'siːd] Erfolg haben OT 2

success [sək'ses] Erfolg OT 3

successful [sək'sesfl] erfolgreich OT 2

such [sʌtʃ] so OT 2

to **suck** [sʌk] saugen OT 4

sudden ['sʌdn] plötzlich OT 3

  suddenly ['sʌdənli] plötzlich; auf einmal OT 2

to **suffer** ['sʌfə] leiden OT 4

sugar ['ʃʊgə] Zucker OT 1

sugary ['ʃʊgəri] zuckerhaltig **WS 1**, 36

to **suggest** [sə'dʒest] vorschlagen; hindeuten auf; andeuten OT 1

suggestion [sə'dʒestʃən] Vorschlag; Andeutung OT 1

suicide ['suːɪsaɪd] Suizid; Selbstmord **WS 1**, 12

suit [suːt] Anzug; Kostüm OT 1

to **suit** [suːt] passen; sich eignen (für) OT 5

suitable ['suːtəbl] geeignet OT 4

sum [sʌm] Rechenaufgabe OT 2

to **summarize** ['sʌməraɪz] zusammenfassen OT 2

summary ['sʌməri] Zusammenfassung OT 1

summer ['sʌmə] Sommer OT 1

summit ['sʌmɪt] Gipfel **WS 1**, 12

sun [sʌn] Sonne OT 1

to **sunbathe** ['sʌnbeɪð] sonnenbaden **WS 1**, 43

sunburn ['sʌnbɜːn] Sonnenbrand OT 2

Sunday ['sʌndeɪ] Sonntag OT 1

sundial ['sʌndaɪəl] Sonnenuhr OT 3

sunlit ['sʌnlɪt] sonnig; sonnenbestrahlt **WS 1**, 13

sunny ['sʌni] sonnig; fröhlich; glücklich OT 1

sunscreen ['sʌnskriːn] Sonnenschutzmittel OT 2

sunset ['sʌnset] Sonnenuntergang OT 3

sunshine ['sʌnʃaɪn] Sonnenschein OT 3

sunstroke ['sʌnstrəʊk] Sonnenstich OT 2

super ['suːpər] super; besonders OT 5

superhero ['suːpəhɪərəʊ] Superheld OT 5

superlative [suː'pɜːlətɪv] unübertrefflich OT 2

supermarket ['suːpəmɑːkɪt] Supermarkt OT 1

to **supervise** ['suːpəvaɪz] beaufsichtigen OT 3

supervision [,suːpə'vɪʒn] Überwachung; Aufsicht OT 5

supervisor ['suːpəvaɪzə] Leiter(in) OT 5

supply [sə'plaɪ] Vorrat; Lieferung OT 3

to **support** [sə'pɔːt] unterstützen; unterhalten; für Lebensunterhalt aufkommen OT 1

supporter [sə'pɔːtə] Anhänger(in) OT 3

supportive [sə'pɔːtɪv] unterstützend OT 5

to **suppose** [sə'pəʊz] vermuten; annehmen OT 1

supposedly [sə'pəʊzɪdli] angeblich **WS 1**, 20

suppression [sə'preʃn] Unterdrückung **WS 2**, 56

sure [ʃʊə] sicher; klar; wirklich OT 1

surely ['ʃʊəli] sicherlich OT 4

to **surface** ['sɜːfɪs] auftauchen **WS 1**, 12

surface ['sɜːfɪs] Oberfläche OT 3

surfing ['sɜːfɪŋ] Surfen; Wellenreiten OT 1

to **surge** [sɜːdʒ] ansteigen; wogen **WS 1**, 36

surgeon ['sɜːdʒən] Chirurg(in) OT 3

surgery ['sɜːdʒəri] Sprechstunde; Praxis OT 5

to **surpass** [sə'pɑːs] übertreffen OT 5

surprise [sə'praɪz] Überraschung OT 1

to **surprise** [sə'praɪz] überraschen OT 5

surprised [sə'praɪzd] überrascht OT 2

surprising [sə'praɪzɪŋ] überraschend OT 2

to **surrender** [sə'rendə] aufgeben; übergeben OT 4

to **surround** [sə'raʊnd] umgeben OT 4

surroundings [sə'raʊndɪŋz] Umwelt; Umgebung **WS 1**, 26

survey ['sɜːveɪ] Umfrage; Studie OT 1

to **survey** ['sɜːveɪ] befragen OT 5

survival [sə'vaɪvl] Überleben OT 2

to **survive** [sə'vaɪv] überleben OT 3

survivor [sə'vaɪvə] Überlebende(r) OT 3

to **suspect** [sə'spekt] vermuten **WS 1**, 25

to **suspend** [sə'spend] unterbrechen; aussetzen **WS 2**, 57

suspense [sə'spens] Anspannung OT 3

suspicious [sə'spɪʃəs] misstrauisch; verdächtig OT 3

to **sustain** [sə'steɪn] erhalten OT 4

sustainability [sə,steɪnə'bɪləti] Nachhaltigkeit OT 3

sustainable [sə'steɪnəbl] nachhaltig OT 3

sustainably [sə'steɪnəbli] nachhaltig OT 3

to **swap** [swɒp] tauschen OT 3

to **sway** [sweɪ] beeinflussen; schwanken **WS 3**, 116

to **sweat** ['swet] schwitzen OT 2

sweatshirt ['swetʃɜːt] Sweatshirt OT 1

to **sweep** [swiːp] fegen OT 4

sweet [swiːt] süß OT 1

sweet [swiːt] Bonbon; Nachtisch OT 1

sweetheart ['swiːthɑːt] Liebste(r); Liebes OT 5

swelling ['swelɪŋ] Schwellung OT 2

to **swim** [swɪm] schwimmen; durchschwimmen; verschwimmen OT 1

swimmer ['swɪmə] Schwimmer(in) OT 3

swimming ['swɪmɪŋ] Schwimmen OT 1

swimwear ['swɪmweər] Badebekleidung OT 5

switch [swɪtʃ] Umstellung; Umstieg OT 5

to **switch on** [swɪtʃ ɒn] anmachen OT 3

swollen ['swəʊln] geschwollen OT 2

sword [sɔːd] Schwert OT 1

syllable ['sɪləbl] Silbe OT 3

symbol ['sɪmbl] Symbol; Zeichen OT 1

symbolic [sɪm'bɒlɪk] symbolisch **WS 2**, 57

to **symbolize** ['sɪmbəlaɪz] symbolisieren **WS 1**, 12

sympathetic [,sɪmpə'θetɪk] mitfühlend OT 2

to **sympathize (with)** ['sɪmpəθaɪz] mitfühlen (mit jmd) OT 5

sympathizer ['sɪmpəθaɪzə] Sympathisant(in) **WS 2**, 53

symptom ['sɪmptəm] Symptom; Anzeichen **WS 3**, 108

synaesthesia [,sɪnəs'θiːziə] Synästhesie OT 2

synonym ['sɪnənɪm] Synonym OT 2

to **synthesize** ['sɪnθəsaɪz] synthetisieren **WS 3**, 116

synthetic [sɪn'θetɪk] synthetisch; künstlich **WS 3**, 104

syrup ['sɪrəp] Sirup OT 3

system ['sɪstəm] System OT 2

systematically [,sɪstə'mætɪkli] systematisch OT 5

systemic [sɪ'stiːmɪk] systembedingt **WS 2**, 68

T

tab [tæb] Tab; Tabulator OT 4

table ['teɪbl] Tisch; Tabelle OT 1

tablecloth ['teɪblklɒθ] Tischdecke OT 2

tablespoon ['teɪblspuːn] Esslöffel OT 2

tablet ['tæblət] Tafel; Tablet OT 2

to **tackle** ['tækl] tackeln; angreifen OT 2

tacky ['tæki] kitschig; hässlich **WS 1**, 27

taco ['tækəʊ] Taco OT 3

tag [tæg] Etikett; kurze Schnur, die gelochte Blätter zusammenhält OT 2

tail [teɪl] Schwanz OT 2

to **tailor** ['teɪlə] schneidern OT 4

to **take** [teɪk] nehmen; machen; annehmen OT 1

to **take a day off** [teɪk ə deɪ ɒf] einen Tag freimachen OT 2

to **take apart** [teɪk ə'pɑːt] zerlegen; auseinandernehmen OT 4

to **take for granted** [teɪk fə 'grɑːntɪd] als selbstverständlich ansehen OT 4

to **take part** [teɪk 'pɑːt] teilnehmen OT 2

to **take turns** [teɪk 'tɜːnz] sich abwechseln OT 1

tale [teɪl] Geschichte OT 2

talent ['tælənt] Talent OT 5

talented ['tæləntɪd] begabt; talentiert OT 5

to **talk** [tɔːk] reden; sprechen; sich unterhalten OT 1

tall [tɔːl] groß; hoch OT 1

tally ['tæli] Gesamtliste OT 4

tank [tæŋk] Tank OT 3

tap [tæp] Wasserhahn OT 3

to **tap** [tæp] tippen OT 5

to **taper off** ['teɪpər ɒf] abnehmen **WS 2**, 56

target ['tɑːgɪt] Ziel OT 4

to **target** ['tɑːgɪt] zielen auf OT 5

tartan ['tɑːtn] Tartan; Schottenstoff **WS 1**, 12

task [tɑːsk] Aufgabe OT 1

taste [teɪst] Geschmack OT 5

to **taste** [teɪst] schmecken; probieren OT 1

tasty ['teɪsti] schmackhaft OT 2

tattoo [tə'tuː] Tätowierung OT 3

tax [tæks] Steuer OT 4

tea [tiː] Tee; Abendessen; Nachmittagstee mit belegten Broten und Kuchen OT 1

to **teach** [tiːtʃ] unterrichten; lehren; zeigen OT 1

teacher ['tiːtʃə] Lehrer(in) OT 1

team [tiːm] Mannschaft; Team; Gruppe OT 1

teammate ['tiːmmeɪt] Manschaftskollege(-in) OT 2

tear [tɪə] Träne OT 2

to **tear** [teə] reißen **WS 2**, 72

to **tease** [tiːz] ärgern; heiß machen OT 2

tech [tek] technisch OT 2

technical ['teknɪkl] technisch OT 2

technique [tek'niːk] Technik OT 4

technological [ˌteknə'lɒdʒɪkl] technisch; technologisch OT 4

technology [tek'nɒlədʒi] Technologie OT 1

tech-savvy [ˌtek 'sævi] technikerfahren; computererfahren **WS 3**, 99

teen [tiːn] Teenager OT 2

teenage ['tiːneɪdʒ] Teenager... OT 3

teenager ['tɪːneɪdʒə] Teenager OT 2

teenocratic ['tiːnə'krætɪk] teenokratisch **WS 3**, 114

tooth [tuːθ] Zahn OT 2

telegram ['telɪɡræm] Telegramm **WS 2**, 61

telenovela [ˌtələnə'velə] Seifenoper **WS 3**, 95

telescope ['telɪskəʊp] Teleskop **WS 3**, 105

television ['telɪvɪʒn] Fernseher OT 2

to tell [tel] erzählen; sagen; erkennen OT 1

to tell off [tel ɒf] ausschimpfen OT 2

temperature ['temprətʃə] Temperatur OT 2

template ['templeɪt] Vorlage OT 4

temple ['templ] Tempel; Schläfe OT 1

temporary ['temprəri] befristet; temporär OT 4

tempt [tempt] locken OT 4

temptation [temp'teɪʃn] Versuchung **WS 3**, 108

ten [ten] zehn OT 1

to tend to [tend tə] zu etwas neigen **WW**, 11

tendency ['tendənsi] Tendenz **WS 3**, 96

tender ['tendə] zart **WS 1**, 31

tenement ['tenəmənt] Mietshaus **WS 1**, 35

tennis ['tenɪs] Tennis OT 1

tense [tens] Zeitform; Tempus OT 1

tension ['tenʃn] Anspannung OT 3

tent [tent] Zelt OT 1

tentative ['tentətɪv] zaghaft; vorsichtig **WS 3**, 107

term [tɜːm] Semester OT 2

terrain [tə'reɪn] Gelände **WS 1**, 15

terrible ['terəbl] schrecklich; furchtbar OT 1

terrier ['teriə] Terrier OT 2

terrified ['terɪfaɪd] verängstigt OT 3

territory ['terətri] Gebiet OT 4

test [test] Test; Untersuchung OT 1

text [tekst] SMS; Text OT 2

to text [tekst] simsen OT 2

textbook ['tekstbʊk] Lehrbuch OT 3

than [ðən] als OT 1

thankfully ['θæŋkfəli] zum Glück OT 5

thanks [θæŋks] Danke! OT 1

Thanksgiving [ˌθæŋks'ɡɪvɪŋ] amerikanisches Erntedankfest OT 2

that [ðæt] dieser/diese/dieses OT 1

theatre ['θɪətə] Theater OT 1

theft [θeft] Diebstahl OT 5

their [ðeə] ihr OT 1

theirs [ðeəz] ihre(r, -s) OT 3

theme [θiːm] Thema OT 2

themed [θiːmd] thematisch OT 4

themselves [ðəm'selvz] sich (selbst) OT 3

then [ðen] dann; damals OT 1

theoretical [ˌθɪə'retɪkl] theoretisch OT 4

to theorize ['θɪəraɪz] theoretisieren **WS 3**, 95

therapy ['θerəpi] Therapie OT 5

there [ðeə] da; dort; dahin OT 1

therefore ['ðeəfɔːr] daher; deshalb; darum OT 5

thermostat ['θɜːməstæt] Thermostat; Temperaturregler OT 5

these [ðiːz] diese; die(hier); so OT 1

thick [θɪk] dick; dicht; stark OT 1

thigh [θaɪ] Oberschenkel; Schenkel; Keule OT 1

thin [θɪn] dünn; schwach OT 1

thing [θɪŋ] Ding; Sache OT 1

to think [θɪŋk] denken; glauben OT 1

to think about ['θɪŋk əbaʊt] denken an; nachdenken über OT 1

to think of ['θɪŋk əv] denken an; halten von OT 1

third [θɜːd] Dritte(r, -s); Drittel OT 1

thirsty ['θɜːsti] durstig OT 1

thirteen [ˌθɜː'tiːn] dreizehn OT 1

thirty ['θɜːti] dreißig OT 1

this [ðɪs] diese(r, -s); so'n; so OT 1

thoroughly ['θʌrəli] völlig; durchaus OT 5

those [ðəʊz] diese da; jene dort OT 1

though [ðəʊ] obwohl; jedoch OT 2

thought [θɔːt] Gedanke OT 4

thoughtful ['θɔːtfl] aufmerksam; rücksichtsvoll OT 5

thought-provoking ['θɔːt prəvəʊkɪŋ] zum Nachdenken anregend OT 5

threat [θret] Gefahr OT 4

to threaten ['θretn] gefährden OT 4

three [θriː] drei OT 1

thriller ['θrɪlə] Thriller; Krimi **WS 2**, 53

thrilling ['θrɪlɪŋ] aufregend; spannend **WS 1**, 24

throat [θrəʊt] Kehle; Hals OT 4

throne [θrəʊn] Thron OT 4

throng [θrɒŋ] Menschenmenge OT 2

through [θruː] durch; hindurch OT 1

throughout [θruː'aʊt] während OT 3

to throw [θrəʊ] werfen; durcheinanderbringen; aus dem Konzept bringen OT 1

to throw up [θrəʊ ʌp] sich übergeben OT 2

to thrust [θrʌst] stoßen **WS 2**, 58

thumbs up [θʌmz 'ʌp] Daumen hoch OT 4

to thunder ['θʌndə] donnern OT 4

thunderstorm ['θʌndəstɔːm] Gewitter OT 2

Thursday ['θɜːzdeɪ] Donnerstag OT 1

tick [tɪk] Haken; Häkchen; Ticken OT 1

ticket ['tɪkɪt] Eintrittskarte; Fahrschein; Fahrkarte OT 1

to tidy ['taɪdi] aufräumen OT 1

tie [taɪ] Verbindung OT 5

tie [taɪ] Krawatte; Band; Schnur OT 1

to tie [taɪ] binden; zubinden OT 5

tiger ['taɪɡə] Tiger OT 1

tight-knit [ˌtaɪt 'nɪt] eng verbunden OT 4

tightly ['taɪtli] fest OT 3

tights [taɪts] Strumpfhose OT 2

tile [taɪl] Fliese OT 2

till [tɪl] bis OT 2

tiller ['tɪlər] Ruderpinne OT 3

to tilt [tɪlt] sich neigen OT 3

time [taɪm] Zeit; Zeitpunkt; Mal OT 1

full time [ˌfʊl 'taɪm] vollzeit OT 2

in (two) months' time [ɪn 'tuː mʌnθs taɪm] in (zwei) Monaten OT 2

some of the time [səm əv ðə taɪm] manchmal OT 2

timeline ['taɪmlaɪn] Zeitachse OT 2

timely ['taɪmli] rechtzeitig; passend OT 3

timer ['taɪmər] Timer; Zeituhr OT 5

times [taɪmz] mal OT 5

timetable ['taɪmteɪbl] Fahrplan; Stundenplan; Zeitplan OT 1

timing ['taɪmɪŋ] Zeitpunkt OT 3

tin [tɪn] Zinn; Dose OT 2

tinder ['tɪndə] Zunder OT 2

tiny ['taɪni] winzig OT 1

tip [tɪp] Spitze; Tipp; Trinkgeld OT 1

to tip over [tɪp 'əʊvə] umkippen OT 5

tipping point ['tɪpɪŋ pɔɪnt] Kipppunkt; Trendwende OT 5

tiring ['taɪərɪŋ] ermüdend OT 4

tired ['taɪəd] müde; abgedroschen OT 1

tirelessly ['taɪələsli] unermüdlich **WS 4**, 146

tissue [ˈtɪʃuː] Papiertaschentuch **WS 3**, 119

titan [ˈtaɪtn] Titan; Riese **WS 2**, 82

title [ˈtaɪtl] Titel; Rechtsanspruch OT 1

to [tuː] zu OT 1

toast [təʊst] Toast; Trinkspruch OT 2

tobacco [təˈbækəʊ] Tabak OT 4

today [təˈdeɪ] heute OT 1

toe [təʊ] Zehe; Spitze OT 1

together [təˈɡeðə] zusammen OT 1

to toil [tɔɪl] schuften **WS 3**, 114

toilet [ˈtɔɪlət] Toilette OT 2

toiletry [ˈtɔɪlətri] Toilettenartikel **WS 1**, 25

tolerance [ˈtɒlərəns] Toleranz OT 5

tolerant [ˈtɒlərənt] tolerant OT 5

toll [təʊl] Tribut; Zoll **WS 3**, 119

tomato [təˈmɑːtəʊ] Tomate OT 1

tomboy [ˈtɒmbɔɪ] burschikoses Mädchen; Wildfang OT 5

tomorrow [təˈmɒrəʊ] morgen OT 1

ton [tʌn] Tonne OT 4

tone [təʊn] Ton OT 4

toner cartridge [ˈtəʊnə ˈkɑːtrɪdʒ] Tonerkartusche OT 5

tongue [tʌŋ] Zunge OT 3

tonight [təˈnaɪt] heute Abend; heute Nacht OT 1

too [tuː] zu; auch; obendrein OT 1

tool [tuːl] Werkzeug OT 2

toolkit [ˈtuːlkɪt] Toolkit; Werkzeugkiste OT 5

toothbrush [ˈtuːθbrʌʃ] Zahnbürste OT 4

top [tɒp] obere(r, -s) OT 1

topic [ˈtɒpɪk] Thema OT 1

to topple [ˈtɒpl] stürzen; kippen **WS 2**, 56

tor [tɔːr] schroffer Fels **WS 1**, 22

torch [tɔːtʃ] Taschenlampe; Fackel OT 1

to take the torch [ˌteɪk ðə ˈtɔːtʃ] den Staffelstab übernehmen **WS 3**, 99

torchlight [ˈtɔːtʃlaɪt] Fackelschein; Taschenlampenlicht **WS 1**, 16

tornado [tɔːˈneɪdəʊ] Tornado OT 4

tortoise [ˈtɔːtəs] Schildkröte OT 1

to toss [tɒs] werfen; schwenken OT 1

total [ˈtəʊtl] Gesamtmenge OT 3

total [ˈtəʊtl] gesamt OT 3

totally [ˈtəʊtəli] völlig OT 3

touch [tʌtʃ] Kontakt; Berührung OT 2

in touch [ɪn tʌtʃ] in Verbindung; in Kontakt OT 2

to touch [tʌtʃ] berühren; anfassen; angreifen OT 1

touchdown [ˈtʌtʃdaʊn] Touchdown OT 2

tough [tʌf] hart OT 3

tour [tʊə] Reise; Tour; Rundgang OT 1

to tour [tʊə] besuchen; besichten OT 5

tourism [ˈtʊərɪzm, ˈtɔːrɪzm] Tourismus OT 3

tourist [ˈtʊərɪst] Tourist(in) OT 1

tournament [ˈtɔːnəmənt] Turnier OT 3

toward(s) [təˈwɔːdz] in Richtung OT 2

towel [ˈtaʊəl] Handtuch OT 2

tower [ˈtaʊə] Turm OT 1

to tower [ˈtaʊə] ragen; sich erheben **WS 1**, 13

town [taʊn] Stadt OT 1

townspeople [ˈtaʊnzpiːpl] Stadtbewohner(innen) OT 4

towpath [ˈtəʊpɑːθ] Treidelpfad OT 3

toxic [ˈtɒksɪk] giftig **WS 4**, 138

to trace [treɪs] folgen; zurückverfolgen OT 3

track [træk] Weg OT 2

tracksuit [ˈtræksuːt] Trainingsanzug **WS 3**, 102

tract [trækt] Gebiet **WS 4**, 138

tractor [ˈtræktə] Traktor OT 2

trade [treɪd] Handwerk; Handel OT 4

to trade [treɪd] handeln OT 5

trader [ˈtreɪdə] Händler(in) **WS 1**, 21

tradition [trəˈdɪʃn] Tradition OT 2

traditional [trəˈdɪʃənl] traditionell; konservativ OT 2

traffic [ˈtræfɪk] Verkehr OT 1

tragic [ˈtrædʒɪk] tragisch OT 3

trail [treɪl] Pfad; Spur OT 2

trailblazer [ˈtreɪlbleɪzə] Vorreiter(in); Bahnbrecher(in) **WS 2**, 74

trailer [ˈtreɪlər] Trailer OT 5

train [treɪn] Zug; Folge; Kette OT 1

to train [treɪn] ausbilden; trainieren OT 2

traineeship [ˌtreɪˈniːʃɪp] Praktikumsplatz OT 5

trainer [ˈtreɪnər] Turnschuh OT 5

training [ˈtreɪnɪŋ] Ausbildung OT 2

trait [treɪt] Charakterzug **WS 4**, 146

tram [træm] Straßenbahn OT 2

trans [trænz] trans... OT 5

transaction [trænˈzækʃn] Transaktion; Geschäft **WS 4**, 146

transatlantic [ˌtrænzətˈlæntɪk] transatlantisch OT 3

to transcribe [trænˈskraɪb] abschreiben; transkribieren OT 5

transcriber [trænˈskraɪbə] Transkribierer(in) OT 5

transcript [ˈtrænskrɪpt] Abschrift; Niederschrift OT 5

to transfer [trænsˈfɜːr] übertragen OT 5

transferable [trænsˈfɜːrəbl] übertragbar OT 5

to transform [trænsˈfɔːm] verändern OT 4

transformation [ˌtrænsfəˈmeɪʃn] Veränderung **WS 2**, 60

transgender [trænzˈdʒendər] transsexuell OT 5

transition [trænˈzɪʃn] Wechsel; Übergang OT 5

translation [trænsˈleɪʃn] Übersetzung OT 2

translator [trænzˈleɪtə] Übersetzer(in) OT 5

to transport [trænˈspɔːt] transportieren OT 3

trap [træp] Falle OT 4

to trap [træp] fangen OT 5

trapper [ˈtræpə] Fallensteller(in) **WS 1**, 21

trash [træʃ] Abfall OT 2

to travel [ˈtrævl] reisen; fahren; bereisen OT 1

travel agent [ˈtrævl eɪdʒənt] Reisekaufmann, -kauffrau OT 3

traveller [ˈtrævələ] Reisende(r) OT 3

to traverse [trəˈvɜːs] durchqueren **WS 1**, 16

tray [treɪ] Tablett OT 2

treacherous [ˈtretʃərəs] verräterisch; tückisch **WS 1**, 18

treasure [ˈtreʒə] Schatz OT 3

treasurer [ˈtreʒərə] Schatzmeister(in) OT 3

treat [triːt] Genuss; Vergnügen OT 5

to treat [triːt] behandeln OT 2

treatment [ˈtriːtmənt] Behandlung OT 4

treaty [ˈtriːti] Vertrag OT 4

tree [triː] Baum OT 1

tremor [ˈtremə] Zittern OT 3

trend [trend] Trend OT 4

trendy [ˈtrendi] modern OT 2

trial [ˈtraɪəl] Prozess OT 2

tribal [ˈtraɪbl] Stammes... OT 3

tribe [traɪb] Stamm OT 2

tribunal [traɪˈbjuːnl] Tribunal; Gericht OT 5

trick [trɪk] Trick OT 5

to trickle [ˈtrɪkl] rinnen OT 3

tricky [ˈtrɪki] kompliziert OT 4

to trigger [ˈtrɪɡə] auslösen OT 5

trillion [ˈtrɪljən] Billion **WS 4**, 144

trilogy [ˈtrɪlədʒi] Trilogie OT 5

trip [trɪp] Reise; Ausflug; Fahrt OT 1

to **trip** [trɪp] stolpern OT 2

triple [ˈtrɪpl] dreifach **WS 2**, 53

triumphant [traɪˈʌmfənt] triumphierend OT 3

troll [trɒl] Troll **WS 2**, 72

trolley [ˈtrɒli] Wagen; Straßenbahn (AmE) OT 2

troop [truːp] Truppe OT 3

trooper [ˈtruːpə] Soldat(in) **WS 2**, 53

trophy [ˈtrəʊfi] Pokal OT 2

tropical [ˈtrɒpɪkl] Tropen- OT 4

trouble [ˈtrʌbl] Schwierigkeit; Ärger OT 2

    to **be in trouble** [ˌbi ɪn ˈtrʌbl] Ärger bekommen OT 2

trough [trɒf] Trog OT 3

trousers [ˈtraʊzəz] Hose OT 2

trout [traʊt] Forelle OT 4

truant [ˈtruːənt] Schulschwänzer(in) **WS 2**, 76

truck [trʌk] LKW OT 1

true [truː] wahr; richtig; treu OT 1

    truly [ˈtruːli] wirklich OT 4

trumpet [ˈtrʌmpɪt] Trompete OT 4

trunk [trʌŋk] Kofferraum OT 2

to **trust** [trʌst] vertrauen OT 2

trustworthy [ˈtrʌstwɜːði] vertrauenswürdig **WS 4**, 140

truth [truːθ] Wahrheit OT 3

to **try** [traɪ] versuchen; ausprobieren OT 1

T-shirt [ˈtiːʃɜːt] Hemd; T-Shirt OT 1

tube [tjuːb] Schlauch; Londoner U-Bahn; Tube OT 1

to **tuck in** [tʌk ˈɪn] einstecken OT 4

tuck shop [tʌk ʃɒp] Laden; Kiosk OT 5

Tuesday [ˈtjuːzdeɪ] Dienstag OT 1

tuition [tjuˈɪʃn] Studiengebühr(en) OT 5

tune [tjuːn] Melodie OT 4

    to **change one's tune** [tʃeɪndʒ wʌnz tjuːn] eine andere Tonlage anschlagen; seine Meinung ändern **WS 3**, 98

tunic [ˈtjuːnɪk] Tunika OT 2

tunnel [ˈtʌnl] Tunnel OT 3

tup [tʌp] Widder OT 2

turbulent [ˈtɜːbjələnt] turbulent; unruhig **WS 3**, 94

turkey [ˈtɜːki] Truthahn OT 3

turn [tɜːn] Wende; Drehung; Kurve OT 1

    It's your turn. [ɪts ˈjɔː tɜːn] Du bist dran! OT 1

to **turn** [tɜːn] drehen; s. drehen OT 2

turnout [ˈtɜːnaʊt] Beteiligung **WS 1**, 32

turntable [ˈtɜːnteɪbl] Drehscheibe OT 2

turtle [ˈtɜːtl] Wasserschildkröte OT 2

tutor [ˈtjuːtə] Tutor(in) OT 2

to **tutor** [ˈtjuːtə] unterrichten; Nachhilfe geben OT 5

tutorial [tjuːˈtɔːriəl] Lernprogramm OT 4

TV [ˌtiːˈviː] Fernsehen; Fernseher OT 1

tweed [twiːd] Tweed(stoff) **WS 1**, 17

twelve [twelv] zwölf OT 1

twenty [ˈtwenti] zwanzig OT 1

twice [twaɪs] zweimal OT 2

twig [twɪg] Zweig OT 2

twin [twɪn] Zwilling OT 1

to **twist** [twɪst] Drehung OT 3

two [tuː] zwei OT 1

type [taɪp] Art OT 2

to **type** [taɪp] tippen OT 5

typewriter [ˈtaɪpraɪtə] Schreibmaschine OT 5

typical [ˈtɪpɪkl] typisch OT 2

typist [ˈtaɪpɪst] Schreibkraft OT 5

tyranny [ˈtɪrəni] Tyrannei **WS 3**, 94

U

ubiquity [juːˈbɪkwəti] Allgegenwart **WS 3**, 112

ugly [ˈʌgli] hässlich OT 1

ukulele [ˌjuːkəˈleɪli] Ukulele **WS 3**, 111

ulterior [ʌlˈtɪəriə] versteckt **WS 3**, 116

ultimately [ˈʌltɪmətli] schlussendlich **WS 1**, 17

umbrella [ʌmˈbrelə] Regenschirm; Schutz OT 1

unable [ʌnˈeɪbl] unfähig; nicht imstande OT 4

unacceptable [ˌʌnəkˈseptəbl] inakzeptabel OT 5

unaccompanied [ˌʌnəˈkʌmpənid] unbegleitet OT 2

unacknowledged [ˌʌnəkˈnɒlɪdʒd] uneingestanden **WS 2**, 68

unanimously [juːˈnænɪməsli] einstimmig **WS 2**, 78

unattended [ˌʌnəˈtendɪd] unbeaufsichtigt OT 4

unavoidable [ˌʌnəˈvɔɪdəbl] unvermeidlich **WS 2**, 54

unbeknownst [ˌʌnbɪˈnəʊnst] unbekannt **WS 1**, 17

unbelievable [ˌʌnbɪˈliːvəbl] unglaublich OT 4

unborn [ˌʌnˈbɔːn] Ungeborene(r) **WS 4**, 138

unbreakable [ʌnˈbreɪkəbl] unzerbrechlich **WS 1**, 20

uncaring [ʌnˈkeərɪŋ] gefühllos OT 5

uncertainty [ʌnˈsɜːtnti] Unsicherheit OT 5

unchaperoned [ʌnˈʃæpərəʊnd] ohne Begleitung **WS 4**, 135

uncle [ˈʌŋkl] Onkel OT 1

uncomfortable [ʌnˈkʌmftəbl] unbequem OT 2

uncommon [ʌnˈkɒmən] ungewöhnlich; selten OT 5

unconstitutional [ˌʌnˌkɒnstɪˈtjuːʃənl] verfassungswidrig **WS 2**, 59

uncontracted [ʌnkənˈtræktɪd] nicht zusammengezogen **WS 4**, 138

unconventional [ˌʌnkənˈvenʃənl] unkonventionell OT 5

undecided [ˌʌndɪˈsaɪdɪd] unentschieden; unentschlossen OT 5

undeniable [ˌʌndɪˈnaɪəbl] unbestreitbar **WS 1**, 30

under [ˈʌndə] unter; darunter; nach OT 1

to **undergo** [ˌʌndəˈgəʊ] durchmachen OT 5

undergraduate [ˌʌndəˈgrædʒuət] Student(in) (ohne Abschluss) OT 5

underground [ˈʌndəgraʊnd] U-Bahn OT 1

underneath [ˌʌndəˈniːθ] unterhalb; darunter OT 5

to **understand** [ˌʌndəˈstænd] verstehen; gehört haben OT 1

underway [ˌʌndəˈweɪ] im Gange; in Bearbeitung **WS 3**, 99

underwhelming [ˌʌndəˈwelmɪŋ] enttäuschend **WS 1**, 29

underworld [ˈʌndəwɜːld] Unterwelt OT 5

undesirable [ˌʌndɪˈzaɪərəbl] unerwünscht **WS 2**, 68

undisturbed [ˌʌndɪˈstɜːbd] ungestört **WS 2**, 53

undocumented [ˌʌnˈdɒkjumentɪd] nicht erfasst OT 4

undrained [ʌnˈdreɪnd] nicht abgetropft OT 2

undrinkable [ʌnˈdrɪŋkəbl] untrinkbar OT 5

unelected [ˌʌnɪˈlektɪd] nicht gewählt OT 4

unemployed [ˌʌnɪmˈplɔɪd] arbeitslos OT 5

unemployment [ˌʌnɪmˈplɔɪmənt] Arbeitslosigkeit OT 3

unexpected [ˌʌnɪkˈspektɪd] unerwartet OT 5

unexpectedly [ˌʌnɪkˈspektɪdli] unerwarteterweise OT 3

unfair [ˌʌnˈfeə] nicht fair OT 2

unfamiliar [ˌʌnfəˈmɪliə] unbekannt OT 2

unfit [ʌnˈfɪt] ungeeignet; nicht in Form OT 2

to unfold [ʌnˈfəʊld] entfalten WS 1, 35

unforgettable [ˌʌnfəˈgetəbl] unvergesslich OT 5

unfortunately [ʌnˈfɔːtʃənətli] leider OT 2

unhappy [ʌnˈhæpi] unglücklich; traurig; unzufrieden OT 1

unhealthy [ʌnˈhelθi] nicht gesund OT 3

uni [ˈjuːni] Uni OT 3

unicorn [ˈjuːnɪkɔːn] Einhorn WS 1, 13

uniform [ˈjuːnɪfɔːm] Uniform OT 1

to unify [ˈjuːnɪfaɪ] vereinigen WS 2, 66

uninhabitable [ˌʌnɪnˈhæbɪtəbl] unbewohnbar OT 4

uninhabited [ˌʌnɪnˈhæbɪtɪd] unbewohnt WS 1, 39

uninterested [ʌnˈɪntrəstɪd] desinteressiert OT 5

union [ˈjuːniən] Union; Bund OT 4

unionized [ˈjuːniənaɪzd] gewerkschaftlich organisiert WS 3, 114

unique [juˈniːk] einzigartig OT 2

unisex [ˈjuːnɪseks] Unisex...; nicht geschlechtsspezifisch OT 5

unit [ˈjuːnɪt] Einheit OT 4

to unite [juˈnaɪt] sich vereinigen OT 5

unity [ˈjuːnəti] Einheit OT 4

universe [ˈjuːnɪvɜːs] Universum OT 4

university [juːnɪˈvɜːsəti] Universität; Hochschule OT 1

unjust [ʌnˈdʒʌst] ungerecht WS 2, 60

unkind [ʌnˈkaɪnd] unfreundlich OT 3

unknown [ʌnˈnəʊn] unbekannt OT 3

unless [ənˈles] außer wenn OT 4

unlike [ʌnˈlaɪk] anders als WS 1, 20

to unlock [ʌnˈlɒk] entriegeln WS 4, 136

unmarried [ʌnˈmærid] unverheiratet OT 5

unmistakeable [ˌʌnmɪˈsteɪkəbl] unverwechselbar WS 2, 66

unnatural [ʌnˈnætʃrəl] unnatürlich OT 5

unnecessary [ʌnˈnesəsəri] unnötig; überflüssig OT 5

unofficial [ˌʌnəˈfɪʃl] inoffiziell OT 5

unpaid [ˌʌnˈpeɪd] unbezahlt OT 5

unpalatable [ʌnˈpælətəbl] ungenießbar WS 1, 12

unpleasant [ʌnˈpleznt] unangenehm OT 5

unrest [ʌnˈrest] Unruhe(n) WS 1, 18

unspoilt [ˌʌnˈspɔɪlt] unberührt OT 3

unsurprisingly [ˌʌnsəˈpraɪzɪŋli] erwartungsgemäß OT 3

unthinkingly [ʌnˈθɪŋkɪŋli] ohne nachzudenken WS 3, 105

until [ʌnˈtɪl] bis OT 3

untold [ˌʌnˈtəʊld] unermesslich WS 4, 138

untrustworthy [ʌnˈtrʌstwɜːði] unglaubwürdig WS 3, 105

unusual [ʌnˈjuːʒuəl] ungewöhnlich OT 2

unwilling [ʌnˈwɪlɪŋ] widerwillig OT 4

to unwrap [ʌnˈræp] auspacken OT 5

to unzip [ˌʌnˈzɪp] Reißverschluss aufmachen WS 1, 42

up [ʌp] hinauf; nach oben OT 1

upbeat [ˈʌpbiːt] optimistisch WS 2, 67

upcycling [ˈʌpsaɪklɪŋ] Abfallveredlung; Wiederverwertung OT 4

to update [ˈʌpdeɪt] aktualisieren OT 3

to upend [ʌpˈend] umdrehen WS 3, 114

to upload [ˈʌpləʊd] hochladen OT 3

upon [əˈpɒn] auf; an WS 1, 29

upper [ˈʌpə] obere OT 4

upset [ʌpˈset] verärgert; traurig OT 2

upstairs [ʌpˈsteəz] oben; im oberen Stockwerk OT 1

upstart [ˈʌpstɑːt] Aufsteiger(in) WS 2, 69

upstream [ˌʌpˈstriːm] flussaufwärts OT 3

uptight [ʌpˈtaɪt] verklemmt OT 5

upwards [ˈʊpwədz] aufwärts; nach oben OT 3

urban [ˈɜːbən] städtisch; urban OT 4

urge [ɜːdʒ] Drang WS 1, 21

urgent [ˈɜːdʒənt] dringend WS 3, 112

urgently [ˈɜːdʒəntli] dringend OT 4

us [ʌs] uns; wir OT 1

usable [ˈjuːzəbl] nutzbar; verwendbar OT 5

usage [ˈjuːsɪdʒ] Gebrauch WS 4, 135

to use [juːz] gebrauchen; verwenden OT 1

useful [ˈjuːsfl] nützlich; hilfreich OT 1

user [ˈjuːzə] Benutzer(in) OT 2

usual [ˈjuːʒuəl] üblich OT 2

usually [ˈjuːʒuəli] normalerweise; gewöhnlich OT 1

to utilize [ˈjuːtəlaɪz] verwenden; nutzen WS 2, 77

utopia [juːˈtəʊpiə] Utopie WS 4, 146

V

vacation [veɪˈkeɪʃn] Urlaub OT 2

to vacuum [ˈvækjuːm] staubsaugen OT 5

vacuum cleaner [ˈvækjuːm kliːnə] Staubsauger OT 4

vague [veɪg] unbestimmt; vage OT 5

valid [ˈvælɪd] valid; korrekt WS 2, 68

validity [vəˈlɪdəti] Gültigkeit WS 3, 116

valley [ˈvæli] Tal OT 1

valuable [ˈvæljuəbl] wertvoll OT 2

value [ˈvæljuː] Wert OT 4

to value [ˈvæljuː] wertschätzen OT 5

vampire [ˈvæmpaɪə] Vampir(in) OT 2

van [væn] Lieferwagen OT 2

to vandalize [ˈvændəlaɪz] mutwillig beschädigen OT 5

vanilla [vəˈnɪlə] Vanille OT 1

to vanish [ˈvænɪʃ] verschwinden OT 4

variant [ˈveəriənt] Variante WS 2, 68

variation [ˌveəriˈeɪʃn] Variante; Variation OT 5

varied [ˈveərid] unterschiedlich OT 4

variety [vəˈraɪəti] Vielfalt; Auswahl OT 4

various [ˈveəriəs] verschiedene OT 4

to vary [ˈveəri] variieren OT 5

vast [vɑːst] enorm; groß OT 4

vaulting horse [ˈvɔːltɪŋ hɔːs] Pferd (Geräteturnen) OT 3

vegan [ˈviːgən] vegan; Veganer(in) OT 4

vegetable [ˈvedʒtəbl] Gemüse OT 1

vegetarian [ˌvedʒəˈteəriən] vegetarisch OT 2

vegetation [ˌvedʒəˈteɪʃn] Vegetation; Pflanzenwelt WS 1, 22

veggie [ˈvedʒi] Gemüse OT 5

veggie [ˈvedʒi] vegetarisch OT 2

vehicle [ˈviːəkl] Fahrzeug; Medium OT 2

velvety [ˈvelvəti] samtartig OT 2

vending machine [ˈvendɪŋ məʃiːn] Automat OT 1

venture [ˈventʃə] Unternehmen OT 5

venue [ˈvenjuː] Veranstaltungsort WS 1, 29

verb [vɜːb] Verb; Zeitwort OT 1

verbal [ˈvɜːbl] verbal; mündlich OT 5

verdict [ˈvɜːdɪkt] Urteil WS 2, 70

to verify [ˈverɪfaɪ] überprüfen; belegen WS 3, 117

vernacular [vəˈnækjələ] (Landes-)Sprache; Mundart WS 2, 68

verse [vɜːs] Vers OT 3

version [ˈvɜːʒn] Version OT 2

versus [ˈvɜːsəs] gegen WS 2, 58

very [ˈveri] sehr OT 1

vessel [ˈvesl] Schiff OT 3

vested interest [ˌvestɪd ˈɪntrəst] persönliches Interesse WS 3, 116

via [ˈviːə] über OT 2

vibrant [ˈvaɪbrənt] dynamisch; lebhaft OT 5

vice-president [ˌvaɪs ˈprezɪdənt] Vizepräsident(in) OT 4

vice versa [ˈvaɪs ˈvɜːsə] vice versa; umgekehrt **WS 2**, 70

victim [ˈvɪktɪm] Opfer OT 5

victory [ˈvɪktəri] Sieg OT 4

video [ˈvɪdiəʊ] Videokassette; Video; Videorekorder OT 1

video game [ˈvɪdiəʊ ɡeɪm] Videospiel OT 2

view [vjuː] Sicht; Blick; Aussicht OT 1

to view [vjuː] betrachten; besichtigen OT 1

viewer [ˈvjuːə] Zuschauer(in) OT 3

viewpoint [ˈvjuːpɔɪnt] Aussichtspunkt; Standpunkt OT 3

vigorous [ˈvɪɡərəs] kraftvoll; energisch **WS 1**, 37

village [ˈvɪlɪdʒ] Dorf; Dorfbewohner OT 1

vindication [ˌvɪndɪˈkeɪʃn] Rechtfertigung **WS 3**, 105

vine [vaɪn] Weinrebe OT 4

vintage [ˈvɪntɪdʒ] alt; klassisch; Vintage OT 5

violence [ˈvaɪələns] Gewalt OT 4

violent [ˈvaɪələnt] gewalttätig OT 5

violet [ˈvaɪələt] violett OT 2

violin [ˌvaɪəˈlɪn] Geige OT 1

viral [ˈvaɪrəl] viral OT 4

virtual [ˈvɜːtʃuəl] virtuell OT 5

virus [ˈvaɪrəs] Virus **WS 4**, 140

visibility [ˌvɪzəˈbɪləti] Sichtbarkeit **WS 2**, 58

visible [ˈvɪzəbl] sichtbar OT 4

visit [ˈvɪzɪt] Besuch OT 1

to visit [ˈvɪzɪt] besuchen; Besuch abstatten; besichtigen OT 1

visitor [ˈvɪzɪtə] Besucher(in) OT 1

vista [ˈvɪstə] Aussicht **WS 1**, 35

visual [ˈvɪʒuəl] visuell OT 2

visualization [ˌvɪʒuəlaɪˈzeɪʃn] Visualisierung OT 3

to visualize [ˈvɪʒuəlaɪz] veranschaulichen OT 4

vital [ˈvaɪtl] lebenswichtig OT 3

to vlog [vlɒɡ] vloggen; einen Vlog erstellen OT 3

vlog [vlɒɡ] Vlog; Video-Blog OT 3

vlogger [ˈvlɒɡə] Vlogger(in) OT 3

vocalist [ˈvəʊkəlɪst] Sänger(in) OT 2

vocals [ˈvəʊklz] Gesang OT 2

vocational [vəʊˈkeɪʃənl] beruflich OT 5

voice [vɔɪs] Stimme OT 2

volcanic [vɒlˈkænɪk] vulkanisch **WS 1**, 25

volcano [vɒlˈkeɪnəʊ] Vulkan OT 2

volleyball [ˈvɒlibɔːl] Volleyball OT 5

volume [ˈvɒljuːm] Lautstärke OT 3

voluntary [ˈvɒləntri] freiwillig OT 4

to volunteer [ˌvɒlənˈtɪə] sich freiwillig melden; ein Ehrenamt haben OT 2

vote [vəʊt] Wahlstimme; Stimme; Wahlrecht OT 5

to vote [vəʊt] wählen; abstimmen OT 1

voter [ˈvəʊtə] Wähler(in) OT 4

to vouch [vaʊtʃ] bürgen; sich verbürgen **WS 3**, 93

voucher [ˈvaʊtʃə] Gutschein **WS 1**, 25

to vow [vaʊ] schwören **WS 2**, 57

vowel [ˈvaʊəl] Vokal; Selbstlaut OT 1

voyage [ˈvɔɪɪdʒ] Reise OT 3

to voyage [ˈvɔɪɪdʒ] reisen **WS 1**, 21

VR, virtual reality [ˌviː ˈɑː, ˈvɜːtʃuəl riˈæləti] VR; virtuelle Realität **WS 3**, 99

vulnerable [ˈvʌlnərəbl] verletzlich; gefährdet **WS 2**, 73

W

waffle [ˈwɒfl] Waffel OT 3

wage [weɪdʒ] Gehalt OT 3

wagon [ˈwæɡən] Wagen OT 4

wail [weɪl] Klagen; Jammern; Klagelaut **WS 1**, 12

waist [weɪst] Taille **WS 1**, 16

to wait [weɪt] warten OT 1

waiter [ˈweɪtə] Kellner(in) OT 1

to wake up [ˈweɪk ʌp] aufwachen OT 1

to walk [wɔːk] laufen; gehen (zu Fuß); spazieren gehen OT 1

walker [ˈwɔːkər] Wanderer; Wanderin **WS 1**, 12

wall [wɔːl] Wand; Mauer OT 1

wallet [ˈwɒlɪt] Brieftasche OT 1

walrus [ˈwɔːlrəs] Walross OT 4

waltz [wɔːls] Walzer **WS 1**, 26

to wander [ˈwɒndə] wandern **WS 1**, 16

to want [wɒnt] wollen; mögen; brauchen OT 1

war [wɔː] Krieg OT 2

wardrobe [ˈwɔːdrəʊb] Kleiderschrank; Garderobe OT 1

warm [wɔːm] warm; herzlich OT 1

warmth [wɔːmθ] Wärme OT 4

to warn [wɔːn] warnen OT 2

warning [ˈwɔːnɪŋ] Warnung OT 2

warrior [ˈwɒriə] Krieger(in) OT 2

warship [ˈwɔːʃɪp] Kriegsschiff OT 3

wartime [ˈwɔːtaɪm] Kriegszeit; im Krieg OT 3

to wash [wɒʃ] waschen OT 2

washer [ˈwɒʃə] Wäscher(in) OT 4

washing up [ˌwɒʃɪŋ ˈʌp] Geschirrspülen OT 2

wasp [wɒsp] Wespe OT 3

waste [weɪst] Abfall OT 3

to waste [weɪst] verschwenden OT 3

to watch [wɒtʃ] beobachten; zuschauen; beobachten OT 1

watchful [ˈwɒtʃfl] wachsam **WS 3**, 114

water [ˈwɔːtə] Wasser OT 1

waterfall [ˈwɔːtəfɔːl] Wasserfall OT 1

water fountain [ˈwɔːtə faʊntən] Trinkwasserbrunnen OT 2

waterhole [ˈwɔːtəhəʊl] Wasserloch OT 5

watering hole [ˈwɔːtərɪŋ həʊl] Wasserstelle OT 5

waterproof [ˈwɔːtəpruːf] wasserdicht OT 2

watershed [ˈwɔːtəʃed] Wasserscheide **WS 1**, 34

wave [weɪv] Welle OT 1

to wave [weɪv] winken; schwenken **WS 2**, 53

way [weɪ] Weg; Richtung; Entfernung OT 1

  all the way [ˈɔːl ðə weɪ] der ganze Weg OT 2

  Way to go! [ˈweɪ tə ɡəʊ] Gut gemacht! OT 2

waymarking [ˈweɪmɑːkɪŋ] Wegmarkierung **WS 1**, 15

waypoint [ˈweɪpɔɪnt] Zwischenstation OT 2

we [wi] wir OT 1

weak [wiːk] schwach OT 4

to weaken [ˈwiːkən] schwächer werden; schwächen OT 4

weakness [ˈwiːknəs] Schwäche OT 4

wealth [welθ] Reichtum OT 5

wealthy [ˈwelθi] reich OT 4

weapon [ˈwepən] Waffe OT 3

to wear [weə] tragen; sich abnutzen OT 1

weather [ˈweðə] Wetter OT 1

to weave [wiːv] weben **WS 1**, 17

to wed [wed] heiraten OT 3

wedding [ˈwedɪŋ] Hochzeit **WS 1**, 26

Wednesday [ˈwenzdeɪ] Mittwoch OT 1

weed [wiːd] Unkraut OT 5

week [wiːk] Woche OT 1

weekend [ˈwiːkˌend] Wochenende OT 1

weekly [ˈwiːkli] wöchentlich OT 4

to weigh [weɪ] wiegen OT 3

weight [weɪt] Gewicht OT 2

weird [wɪəd] seltsam; schräg; verrückt OT 1

welcome [ˈwelkəm] Willkommen! OT 1

to welcome [ˈwelkəm] begrüßen; willkommen heißen OT 1

welfare [ˈwelfeər] Wohlfahrt **WS 1**, 31

well [wel] also; nun; nun ja OT 1

  well done [wel ˈdʌn] gut gemacht OT 1

well-being [ˈwel biːɪŋ] Wohlbefinden OT 5

wellness [ˈwelnəs] Wohlbefinden OT 5

Welsh [welʃ] walisisch OT 1

west [west] West...; westlich OT 1

wet [wet] nass; feucht; regnerisch OT 1

wetsuit [ˈwetsuːt] Taucheranzug; Neoprenanzug OT 1

whale [weɪl] Wal OT 2

whaling [ˈweɪlɪŋ] Walfang OT 2

what [wɒt] was OT 1

whatever [wɒˈtevə] Was auch immer. OT 2

wheat [wiːt] Weizen OT 5

wheel [wiːl] Rad OT 1

wheelbarrow [ˈwiːlbærəʊ] Schubkarre OT 4

wheelchair [ˈwiːltʃeə] Rollstuhl OT 2

wheelchair user [ˈwiːltʃeə ˌjuːzə] Rollstuhlfahrer(in) OT 2

when [wen] wann; wenn; als OT 1

whenever [wenˈevə] jedes Mal, wenn OT 3

where [weə] wo; wenn OT 1

whereas [ˌweərˈæz] während OT 5

wherever [weərˈevə] wo (auch) immer OT 3

whether [ˈweðə] ob OT 2

which [wɪtʃ] welche(r, -s) OT 1

while [waɪl] während OT 2

whilst [waɪlst] wenn **WS 1**, 17

whipped cream [ˌwɪptˈkriːm] Schlagsahne OT 3

whirlpool [ˈwɜːlpuːl] Whirlpool; hier: Strudel **WS 1**, 20

whisky [ˈwɪski] Whisky **WS 1**, 17

to **whisper** [ˈwɪspə] flüstern **WS 1**, 19

whistle [ˈwɪsl] Pfeife OT 2

white [waɪt] weiß; blass; bleich OT 1

whiteboard [ˈwaɪtbɔːd] Weißwandtafel; Whiteboard; weiße Tafel OT 1

to **whizz** [wɪz] zischen OT 2

who [huː] wer, wen, wem; der/die/das OT 1

whoever [huːˈevə] egal wer OT 4

whole [həʊl] ganz OT 1

wholegrain [ˈhəʊlɡreɪn] Vollkorn... **WS 1**, 36

whopping [ˈwɒpɪŋ] hier: überwältigend **WS 3**, 108

whose [huːz] wessen; dessen/deren OT 1

why [waɪ] warum; weshalb OT 1

wicked [ˈwɪkɪd] böse; krass OT 2

wide [waɪd] weit OT 2

widespread [ˈwaɪdspred] weitverbreitet **WS 1**, 36

wife [waɪf] Frau; Ehefrau OT 1

wild [waɪld] wild OT 2

wilderness [ˈwɪldənəs] Wildnis OT 2

wildfire [ˈwaɪldfaɪə] Großfeuer OT 2

wildlife [ˈwaɪldlaɪf] Tierwelt OT 2

willing: to be willing [bi ˈwɪlɪŋ] bereit sein OT 4

to **win** [wɪn] gewinnen OT 1

winch [wɪntʃ] Winde OT 3

wind [wɪnd] Wind OT 2

winding [ˈwaɪndɪŋ] gewunden OT 3

windlass [ˈwɪndləs] Winsch OT 3

window [ˈwɪndəʊ] Fenster; Schaufenster; Schalter OT 1

to **windsurf** [ˈwɪndsɜːf] windsurfen OT 1

windsurfing [ˈwɪndsɜːfɪŋ] Windsurfen OT 1

windturbine [ˈwɪnd tɜːbaɪn] Windrad OT 4

wind-up radio [ˈwaɪnd ʌp ˈreɪdiəʊ] Radio mit Kurbel OT 4

windy [ˈwɪndi] windig OT 2

wing [wɪŋ] Flügel OT 2

winner [ˈwɪnə] Gewinner(in); Sieger(in); Siegtreffer OT 1

winning [ˈwɪnɪŋ] gewinnend OT 2

winter [ˈwɪntə] Winter OT 1

to **wipe** [waɪp] wischen OT 5

  to **wipe out** [ˈwaɪp aʊt] vernichten OT 5

wisdom [ˈwɪzdəm] Weisheit **WS 3**, 105

wise [waɪz] weise; klug **WW**, 11

wish [wɪʃ] Wunsch OT 2

to **wish** [wɪʃ] wünschen OT 2

witch [wɪtʃ] Hexe OT 2

with [wɪð] mit; bei; vor OT 1

to **withdraw** [wɪðˈdrɔː] sich zurückziehen **WS 1**, 18

withdrawal [wɪðˈdrɔːəl] Entzug **WS 4**, 146

within [wɪˈðɪn] innerhalb OT 4

without [wɪˈðaʊt] ohne OT 1

witness [ˈwɪtnəs] ohne OT 1

to **witness** [ˈwɪtnəs] Zeuge sein von OT 3

wolf [wʊlf] Wolf OT 4

woman [ˈwʊmən] Frau OT 1

to **woman up** [ˌwʊmən ˈʌp] *in Anlehnung an* ‚to man up': ihre Frau stehen **WS 2**, 76

wombat [ˈwɒmbæt] Wombat OT 5

wonder [ˈwʌndə] Wunder OT 4

to **wonder** [ˈwʌndə] sich fragen; sich wundern OT 4

wonderful [ˈwʌndəfl] wunderbar OT 1

wood [wʊd] Holz OT 2

wooded [ˈwʊdɪd] bewaldet OT 4

wooden [ˈwʊdn] hölzern; Holz...; steif OT 2

woodland [ˈwʊdlənd] Wald; Waldfläche OT 4

woods [wʊdz] Wald OT 2

wool [wʊl] Wolle OT 3

woolly [ˈwʊli] wollig OT 2

word [wɜːd] Wort; Nachricht OT 1

wordlist [ˈwɜːdlɪst] Wortliste OT 2

work [wɜːk] Arbeit OT 2

  at work [ət wɜːk] bei der Arbeit OT 2

to **work** [wɜːk] arbeiten; bedienen; funktionieren OT 1

worker [ˈwɜːkə] Arbeiter(in) OT 2

workforce [ˈwɜːkfɔːs] Arbeitskräfte OT 5

workout [ˈwɜːkaʊt] Fitnesstraining OT 3

workplace [ˈwɜːkpleɪs] Arbeitsplatz OT 5

worksheet [ˈwɜːkʃiːt] Arbeitsblatt OT 2

workshop [ˈwɜːkʃɒp] Werkstatt; Workshop OT 1

world [wɜːld] Welt OT 1

  from around the world [frəm əˈraʊnd ði ˌwɜːld] aus aller Welt OT 1

worldwide [ˌwɜːldˈwaɪd] weltweit OT 3

worm [wɜːm] Wurm OT 1

worried [ˈwʌrid] besorgt; beunruhigt OT 1

worry [ˈwʌri] Sorge OT 5

to **worry** [ˈwʌri] sich Sorgen machen OT 1

to **worship** [ˈwɜːʃɪp] verehren OT 5

worth [wɜːθ] wert OT 4

worthwhile [ˌwɜːθˈwaɪl] lohnend OT 2

worthy [ˈwɜːði] würdig; wert **WS 3**, 97

to **wrap** [ræp] einwickeln OT 2

wreath [riːθ] Kranz OT 3

wreck [rek] Wrack OT 3

to **wrestle** [ˈresl] ringen OT 2

wrestling [ˈreslɪŋ] Ringen OT 2

to **wrinkle** [ˈrɪŋkl] rümpfen; runzeln **WS 3**, 101

wrist [rɪst] Handgelenk OT 1

to **write** [raɪt] schreiben OT 1

writer [ˈraɪtə] Schriftsteller(in); Verfasser(in) OT 1

writing [ˈraɪtɪŋ] Schreiben; Inschrift; Schrift OT 1

wrong [rɒŋ] Unrecht **WS 2**, 76

wrong [rɒŋ] falsch OT 1

  What's wrong? [wɒts rɒŋ] Was ist los? OT 2

X

X-ray [ˈeks reɪ] Röntgen OT 1

Y

yacht [jɒt] Jacht; Yacht OT 5
yard [jɑːd] Yard (= 91,44 cm) OT 2
yawn [jɔːn] Gähnen OT 2
year [jɪə] Jahr; Jahrgang OT 1
yearbook [ˈjɪəbʊk] Jahrbuch OT 4
to yearn for [jɜːn fə] verlangen nach; schmachten WS 1, 13
yellow [ˈjeləʊ] gelb OT 1
yesterday [ˈjestədeɪ] gestern OT 1
yet [jet] noch; schon OT 2
yew [juː] Eibe WS 1, 38
yoga [ˈjəʊɡə] Yoga OT 5

yoghurt [ˈjɒɡət] Joghurt OT 1
yolk [jəʊk] Eigelb WS 1, 24
you [ju] du/Sie; man; dich/Sie OT 1
young [jʌŋ] jung OT 1
youngster [ˈjʌŋstə] Jugendliche OT 5
your [jɔː] dein/Ihr; euer/Ihr OT 1
yours [jɔːz] deine(r, -s)/Ihre(r, -s) OT 3
yourself [jɔːˈself] dich/sich; dich/sich (selbst); selbst OT 2
yourselves [jɔːˈselvz, jəˈselvz] euch (selbst) OT 3
youth [juːθ] Jugend OT 2

youth hostel [ˈjuːθ hɒstl] Jugendherberge OT 2
yuck [jʌk] Igitt! OT 3
yummy [ˈjʌmi] lecker OT 5

Z

zebra [ˈzebrə] Zebra OT 1
zip line [ˈzɪp laɪn] Seilrutsche OT 1
zone [zəʊn] Zone OT 2
  end zone [ˈend zəʊn] Endzone OT 2
zoo [zuː] Zoo OT 1
to zoom [zuːm] einzoomen OT 2
zucchini [zuˈkiːni] Zucchini OT 3

Dictionary: German – English

A

Aal eel WS 1, 12
abbauen to dismantle WS 2, 78
Abbrecher(in) dropout WS 3, 119
abdecken to cover OT 2
Abend evening OT 1
Abendessen dinner OT 1; supper OT 2
Abenteuer adventure OT 1
abenteuerlustig adventurous OT 2
Abfahrt exit OT 2; departure OT 2
Abfall garbage OT 2; trash OT 2; waste OT 3
Abfalleimer litter bin OT 2
abfällig derogative WS 2, 65
Abfallveredlung upcycling OT 4
abflachen to level off OT 5
Abflug departure OT 2
abgekürzt abbreviated OT 5
abgelegen remote OT 4
Abgeordnetenhaus parliament OT 4
Abgeordnete(r) delegate OT 4; representative OT 4; MP (member of parliament) OT 4
abgesehen von apart from OT 3
abgetropft drained OT 2
abgießen to drain OT 2
abhalten to prevent OT 4; to deter WS 2, 73
abhängen to depend OT 2
  abhängen von to hinge on WS 3, 112
abhängig addicted WS 2, 73
  abhängig von dependent on WS 4, 135
abholen to pick up OT 2
Abholzung deforestation OT 5
abkippen to dump OT 2
Abklärung clarification OT 4
abkühlen to cool OT 5

abkürzen to shorten OT 4
Abkürzung abbreviation OT 2
ablehnen to oppose WS 2, 60; to dismiss WS 3 105; to reject WS 3 105
Ablehnung rejection WS 2, 60
ablenken to distract WS 3, 108
Abmessung dimension OT 2
abnehmen to taper off WS 2, 56
Abneigung reluctance OT 4
Abolitionist(in) abolitionist WS 2, 57
abonnieren to subscribe to OT 5
abreißen to demolish OT 5
abrutschen to slump OT 5
Absatz paragraph OT 1; heel WS 3, 119
abschaffen to abolish WW, 10; to scrap WS 2, 53
Abschaffung abolition WS 2, 54
abschalten to disconnect WS 3, 108
Abschieds... leaving OT 2
abschließen to finalize OT 4
Abschnitt segment OT 5; phase WS 3, 122
abschrecken to deter WS 2, 73
abschreiben to transcribe OT 5
Abschrift transcript OT 5
abschwächen to diminish WS 2, 73
(sich) abseilen to abseil OT 2
Absicht intention OT 5; aim OT 5
absichtlich on purpose OT 2; deliberate WS 2, 58
absolut absolute WS 1, 29
  absolut absolutely OT 2
sich abspalten to secede WS 2, 54
abstammen (von) to be descended (from) OT 3; to descend (from) OT 5
Abstammung ancestry OT 3; descent OT 5
abstauben to dust WS 1, 20

abstecken to stake WS 3, 96
Abstimmung ballot WS 1, 32
abstoßend revolting OT 2
abstürzen to crash OT 3
Abteilung department OT 4; division WS 2, 53
(ab)warten to hang on OT 4
sich abwechseln to take turns OT 1
Abwechslung variation WS 1, 21
abwertend derogative WS 2, 65
Abwesenheit absence WS 3, 101
Abzeichen badge OT 5
sich abzeichnen to loom WS 1, 35
acht eight OT 1
achten to respect OT 3
achtzehn eighteen OT 1
achtzig eighty OT 1
Ackerland farmland OT 4
Adaptierung adaptation OT 4
Adjektiv adjective OT 2
Adler eagle OT 2
Adliger nobleman OT 3
Adoption adoption WS 2, 68
Adresse address OT 1
aerobisch aerobic WS 1, 37
Affäre affair OT 4
afrikanisch African OT 2
Agentur agency OT 4
Aggression aggression WS 2, 60
aggressiv pushy OT 5; aggressive WS 1, 37
Ahne forefather OT 4
ähneln to resemble WS 1, 24
ähnlich similar OT 1
Ähnlichkeit similarity OT 3
ahnungslos clueless WS 3, 113
akademisch academic OT 4

Akkord chord **WS 3**, 111
Akkordeon accordion OT 2
akquirieren to acquire **WS 3**, 106
Akronym acronym **WS 3**, 108
Aktion action OT 2; campaign OT 3
aktiv energetic OT 2; actively OT 4
aktivieren to activate **WS 4**, 135
Aktivismus activism OT 5
Aktivist(in) activist OT 5
Aktivität activity OT 1
aktualisieren to update OT 3
aktuell current OT 2
Akustik acoustics **WS 1**, 39
akustisch acoustic OT 2
Akzent accent OT 2
akzeptabel acceptable **WS 3**, 96
Akzeptanz acceptance OT 5
akzeptieren to embrace **WS 2**, 69
Alarm alarm OT 2
alarmieren to alert OT 2
alaskisch Alaskan OT 2
albern silly OT 1
Album album OT 3
Algorithmus algorithm OT 5
Alien alien OT 2
Alkohol alcohol OT 3
alkoholisch alcoholic OT 3
alle everybody OT 1; all OT 1
Allee avenue **WS 3**, 97
allein alone OT 2; on one's own OT 2;
    lone **WS 1**, 25
alles everything OT 1; all OT 1
Allgegenwart ubiquity **WS 3**, 112
allgemein general OT 4; overall OT 5
    im Allgemeinen generally OT 4
Alliteration alliteration **WS 2**, 64
allmählich gradually **WS 2**, 56
alltäglich everyday OT 3
Alpaka alpaca OT 2
Alphabet alphabet OT 1
alphabetisch alphabetical OT 2
als as OT 1; than OT 1
    als Nächstes next OT 3
also well OT 1; so OT 1
alt old OT 1; vintage OT 5
Alter age OT 1
älter elderly OT 4
alternativ alternative OT 4
Älteste(r) elder OT 4
altmodisch old-fashioned OT 2
Ambition ambition OT 5
amerikanisch American OT 1
    amerikanisches Erntedankfest
        Thanksgiving OT 2
Amsel blackbird OT 1

Amtsbruder fellow minister **WS 2**, 58
Amtsschwester fellow minister
    WS 2, 58
amüsiert amused OT 3
an at OT 1; upon **WS 1**, 29
analphabetisch illiterate OT 4
Analyse analysis OT 5
analysieren to analyse OT 3
Analyst(in) analyst OT 5
Analytiker(in) analyst OT 5
Ananas pineapple OT 2
anbauen to grow OT 1
anbeten to adore OT 4
anbieten to offer OT 2
anbringen to place OT 5
andauernd everlasting **WS 4**, 146
Andenken souvenir OT 3
andere(r, -s) other OT 1
    ein(e) andere(r, -s) another OT 1
ändern to change OT 1
anders als unlike **WS 1**, 20
andeuten to hint OT 4
andeuten to foreshadow **WS 2**, 60
Aneignung appropriation **WS 2**, 68
Anekdote anecdote OT 4
anerkannt certified OT 5
anerkennen to appreciate OT 4;
    to acknowledge OT 5
Anerkennung appreciation **WS 2**, 68
Anfang start OT 1; beginning OT 1
anfangen to start OT 1; to begin OT 2
anfänglich initial OT 5
anfangs at first OT 2; initially OT 5
Anfangs… introductory OT 5
anfassen to touch OT 1; to feel OT 1
anfechten to dispute **WS 1**, 20
anführen to cite OT 2
Anführungszeichen quotation mark
    OT 2; inverted commas OT 3
angeben to indicate OT 4
angeblich supposedly **WS 1**, 20;
    reportedly **WS 2**, 66
Angebot offer OT 2; range OT 4;
    offering OT 4
    ein Angebot machen to bid for OT 5
angegliedert affiliated **WS 2**, 71
Angelegenheit matter OT 2; affair OT 4
angelsächsisch Anglo-Saxon OT 3
angemessen appropriate OT 4
angenehm enjoyable OT 2; pleasant OT 3
angesehen prestigious **WS 3**, 123
Angestellte(r) employee OT 5
angestrengt stressed OT 2
angewidert disgusted OT 5
angewiesen reliant **WS 4**, 135

Angewohnheit habit OT 4
anglikanisch Anglican OT 3
angreifen to tackle OT 2; to attack OT 4
    angreifend attacking OT 3
Angreifer(in) invader OT 3
angrenzen to border OT 4
Angriff attack OT 2; assault OT 5;
    aggression **WS 2**, 60
Angst fear OT 3
    Angst machen to scare OT 2
ängstlich afraid OT 2; anxious OT 5
Ängstlichkeit anxiety OT 5
anhalten to stop OT 1; to last OT 2
anhaltend prolonged OT 5
Anhänger(in) supporter OT 3;
    follower OT 3
anheben to elevate **WS 2**, 68
Animation animation **WS 4**, 135
animiert animated OT 4
ankern to anchor OT 4
anklagen (wegen) to charge (with) OT 5;
    to accuse OT 5
ankommen to arrive OT 1; to get to OT 2
Ankunft arrival OT 2
    geschätzte Ankunftszeit ETA
        (estimated time of arrival) OT 2
Anlage facility OT 3; complex OT 4
anlegen to moor OT 3
Anlegeplatz mooring OT 3
Anleitung guidance OT 4
anmachen to switch on OT 3
(sich) anmelden to sign up OT 2;
    to subscribe to OT 5; to enroll **WS 3**, 105
Anmelder(in) applicant OT 5
Annahme assumption **WS 1**, 32
annehmen to suppose OT 1; to accept
    OT 2; to adopt OT 5; to assume
    WS 2, 57
annotieren to annotate **WS 2**, 65
Anonymität anonymity **WS 2**, 72
sich anpassen to adapt **WS 2**, 67;
    to adjust **WS 3**, 11
Anpassung assimilation OT 4;
    conformity **WS 3**, 95
    anregend motivational OT 5
anregen to inspire OT 4; to motivate OT 5
Anreiz incentive OT 5
anrufen to call OT 1
Anrufer(in) caller OT 2
Ansage announcement OT 2
ansagen to announce OT 2
Ansager(in) announcer OT 2
Ansammlung cluster **WS 4**, 140
Ansatz approach OT 5
anschauen to behold OT 3

anscheinend apparently OT 3
Anschlagbrett noticeboard OT 1
Ansehen reputation **WS 2**, 58
ansehen to look OT 1; to regard OT 4
Ansicht attitude OT 4
ansonsten otherwise OT 4
Anspannung suspense OT 3;
   tension OT 3
Anspielung allusion **WS 2**, 64
anspornen to spur **WS 1**, 32
ansprechen to address OT 5; to appeal
   WS 1, 24
Anspruch: einen Anspruch befriedigen
   to meet a demand **WS 3**, 96
anspruchsvoll demanding OT 4;
   exacting **WS 3**, 101; sophisticated
   WS 4, 135
anständig proper OT 1; decent **WS 2**, 63
ansteigen to surge **WS 1**, 36
Anstoß impulse **WS 1**, 21
anstoßen to bump into OT 4; to initiate
   WS 2, 71
sich anstrengen to struggle OT 5
Anstrengung effort OT 3; endeavour
   WS 1, 13
Anteil percentage OT 4; proportion OT 5
Anteilnahme compassion **WS 1**, 14
Antidot antidote **WS 2**, 69
antik ancient OT 2
Antilope antelope OT 4
Antithese antithesis **WS 2**, 69
Antrag petition OT 3
antreiben to power OT 4
Antrieb incentive OT 5
Antritts... inaugural **WS 2**, 55
Antropologie anthropology OT 4
Antwort answer OT 1; reply OT 1;
   response OT 4
antworten to answer OT 1; to respond
   OT 1; to reply OT 1
Anwalt, Anwältin advocate **WS 2**, 58
Anweisung instruction OT 1; direction
   OT 2
anwendbar applicable **WS 2**, 82
Anwendung application OT 4
Anwesen estate **WS 1**, 15
Anwesenheit presence **WS 2**, 69
Anzeichen symptom **WS 3**, 108
Anzeige indicator **WS 3**, 94
(sich) anziehen to put on OT 1;
   to dress OT 3; to attract OT 4
Anzug suit OT 1
anzüglich salacious **WS 2**, 72
anzünden to light OT 2
apathisch apathetic **WS 1**, 32

Apfel apple OT 1
Apfelsine orange OT 1
Apotheke pharmacy OT 2
Apotheker(in) pharmacist OT 2
App app OT 3
appellieren to appeal **WS 1**, 24
appetitlich appetizing OT 3
applaudieren to applaud OT 2
Applaus applause OT 2
Aquädukt aqueduct OT 3
Aquarium aquarium OT 2
Äquator equator OT 5
Arbeit employment OT 4
arbeiten to work OT 1
Arbeiter(in) worker OT 2
Arbeitgeber(in) employer OT 3
Arbeits... labour OT 5
Arbeitsblatt worksheet OT 2
Arbeitskräfte workforce OT 5
arbeitslos unemployed OT 5
Arbeitslosigkeit unemployment OT 3
Arbeitsplatz workplace OT 5
Archäologe(-in) archaeologist OT 2
archäologisch archaeological OT 2
archetypisch archetypal **WS 3**, 106
Architekt(in) architect OT 4
Architektur architecture OT 4
Archiv archive OT 5
Arena arena OT 1
Ärger trouble OT 2
ärgerlich annoying OT 2
ärgern to tease OT 2; to annoy OT 5;
   to rile up **WS 2**, 72
argumentativ argumentative
   WS 3, 109
Arktis arctic OT 4
arktisch arctic OT 4
Arm arm OT 1
arm poor OT 1
   arm an low **WS 1**, 36
Armee army OT 4
Ärmel sleeve **WS 2**, 59
Armut poverty OT 5
Art kind OT 1; type OT 2; sort OT 2;
   species OT 5
   Art und Weise manner OT 3
Artefakt artefact OT 2
artenreich biodiverse **WS 1**, 12
Artenvielfalt biodiversity **WS 3**, 104
Artikel article OT 1
Arzt, Ärztin doctor OT 1
   ärztliche Untersuchung medical OT 2
Asche ash OT 2
asexuell asexual OT 5
Aspekt aspect OT 4

Assimilation assimilation OT 4
Assistent(in) assistant OT 4
assoziieren to associate (with) OT 5
Ast branch OT 2
Astronaut(in) astronaut OT 3
Astronom(in) astronomer **WS 3**, 105
atemberaubend breathtaking OT 2;
   staggering OT 4; stunning OT 5
atemlos breathless OT 3
Atem(zug) breath OT 2
atmen to breathe OT 2
Atmosphäre atmosphere OT 3
Atom... nuclear OT 3
Attentat assassination **WS 2**, 58
Attentäter(in) assassin **WS 2**, 57
ätzend gross OT 3
auch also OT 1; too OT 1
   auch nicht either OT 2; neither OT 3
Audio... audio OT 2
auf on OT 1; onto OT 1; upon **WS 1**, 29
aufbauen to structure OT 5
   wieder aufbauen to rebuild OT 2
aufbewahren to store OT 2
aufbieten to exert **WS 3**, 105
(auf)blühen to flourish **WS 1**, 12
aufbrechen to set off OT 2
aufdecken to expose **WS 2**, 63
Aufdeckung exposure OT 4
Aufeinanderfolge sequence OT 3
Aufenthaltsraum lounge OT 4
Auffahrt driveway OT 4
auffallend striking OT 4
Aufführung performance OT 2
auffüllen to stock up OT 4
Aufgabe job OT 1; task OT 1; assignment
   OT 4; mission **WS 2**, 54
aufgeben to give up OT 2; to surrender
   OT 4
aufgeregt excited OT 1; frantic OT 3
aufgeschlossen approachable OT 4
hier: Aufgliederung breakdown
   WS 3, 105
Aufhänger hook **WS 2**, 66
aufheben to pick up OT 2; to outweigh
   WS 2, 62
aufhören to finish OT 1; to stop OT 1
aufladen to charge OT 2
sich auflehnen to rebel OT 4
auflisten to list OT 5
Auflösung resolution **WS 3**, 122
aufmachen to open OT 1
aufmerksam thoughtful OT 5
Aufmerksamkeit attention OT 2
Aufmerksamkeitsdefizit-
   Hyperaktivitätsstörung attention

deficit hyperactivity disorder (ADHD) OT 5

aufmuntern to cheer up OT 1

Aufnahmestudio recording studio OT 3

aufnehmen to record OT 1; to soak up OT 5

aufpassen to pay attention OT 2

  auf jdn. aufpassen to look after OT 1

aufräumen to tidy OT 1

aufrechterhalten to maintain OT 4; to perpetuate **WS 2**, 73

aufregen to annoy OT 5

aufregend exciting OT 1; thrilling **WS 1**, 24

Aufregung excitement **WS 1**, 29

aufrichtig sincerely OT 3; heartfelt **WS 3**, 101

Aufruf appeal OT 2

Aufruhr riot **WS 2**, 58

Aufsatz essay OT 3

aufsaugen to soak up **WS 1**, 17

aufschlüsseln to break down OT 5

aufschlussreich insightful **WS 1**, 35

Aufschrei outcry **WS 2**, 54

Aufseher(in) attendant OT 2; ranger OT 3

Aufsicht supervision OT 5

aufspießen to spear OT 5

Aufstand rebellion OT 3; insurrection **WS 2**, 73

aufstehen to get up OT 1

aufsteigen to rise OT 3

Aufsteiger(in) upstart **WS 2**, 69

aufstellen to pitch **WS 1**, 16; to nominate **WS 2**, 78

Aufstellung nomination **WS 2**, 78

auftauchen to appear OT 3; to surface **WS 1**, 12

Auftrag mandate **WS 1**, 30

  im Auftrag on behalf of **WS 3**, 111

Auftragnehmer(in) contractor OT 5

Auftreten debut OT 4

auftreten to perform OT 2

Auftrieb geben to buoy OT 3

Auftritt gig OT 5

auftürmen to pile OT 3

aufwachen to wake up OT 1

aufwärts upwards OT 3

aufziehen to rear **WS 1**, 35

Auge eye OT 1

Augenbraue eyebrow OT 5

Augenlid eyelid OT 2

August August OT 1

Auktionator(in) auctioneer **WS 1**, 35

Aula assembly hall OT 1

aus from OT 1

ausbauen to expand OT 5

ausbeuten to exploit OT 3

Ausbeutung exploitation **WS 2**, 68

ausbilden to train OT 2

Ausbildung training OT 2; education OT 3; apprenticeship OT 5

ausbrechen to erupt OT 2

Ausdauer perseverance OT 4

Ausdehnung expansion **WS 3**, 114

Ausdruck expression OT 1

ausdrücken to express OT 4

auseinander apart OT 5

auseinandernehmen to take apart OT 4

Auseinandersetzung argument OT 1

Ausflug trip OT 1; excursion **WS 1**, 22

ausführen to carry out **WS 1**, 19

ausführen: weiter ausführen to elaborate **WS 3**, 122

ausführend executive OT 4

ausführlich detailed OT 4

Ausgabe issue OT 2; expense OT 4

Ausgang exit OT 2

Ausgangssperre curfew OT 3

ausgebildet skilled OT 4

ausgedehnt sprawling **WS 1**, 34

ausgefallen fancy **WS 3**, 105

ausgemergelt emaciated OT 3

ausgeprägt distinctive OT 5

ausgerichtet sein to be geared towards OT 5

ausgesprochen pronounced OT 2

ausgestellt flared **WS 3**, 102

ausgestorben extinct OT 2

ausgesucht exquisite **WS 1**, 25

ausgezeichnet excellent OT 2

ausgleichen to balance OT 5

ausgraben to excavate OT 2

Ausgrabung excavation OT 2

ausgrenzen to marginalize **WS 2**, 68

ausgrenzend exclusionary **WS 2**, 66

Ausgrenzung discrimination OT 5

Aushang notice OT 1

auslachen to laugh at OT 2

Ausland: im Ausland abroad OT 2

ausländisch foreign OT 1; overseas OT 2

auslassen to skip OT 3

ausleeren to empty out OT 3

ausleihen to borrow OT 2

auslöschen to erase **WS 1**, 12

auslösen to trigger OT 5; to provoke **WS 2**, 57; to activate **WS 4**, 135

ausmachen to determine OT 4; to account for OT 5; to constitute **WS 2**, 56

Ausmaß extent OT 3

Ausnahme exception OT 5

auspacken to unwrap OT 5

ausrangieren to discard **WS 3**, 104

ausreichend ample **WS 1**, 15

Ausreißer(in) runaway OT 5

ausrichten to host OT 3

Ausrichtung orientation **WS 3**, 111

ausrufen to declare OT 4

ausrüsten to equip **WS 1**, 25

Ausrüstung equipment OT 2; kit OT 2; gear **WS 1**, 12

Aussage statement OT 1

ausschimpfen to tell off OT 2; to scold **WS 2**, 64

ausschließen to exclude **WS 2**, 54

Ausschluss exclusion **WS 4**, 135

Ausschnitt clip OT 2; excerpt OT 4

Aussehen appearance OT 2

außer except OT 2

  außer wenn unless OT 4

außerdem moreover OT 4; besides OT 5

Außerirdische(r) alien OT 2

äußern to express OT 4

äußerst highly OT 4

aussetzen to suspend **WS 2**, 57

Aussicht view OT 1; vista **WS 1**, 35

Aussichtspunkt viewpoint OT 3

aussortieren to sort out OT 4

ausspielen to act out OT 2

Aussprache pronunciation OT 2

aussprechen to pronounce OT 3

aussteigen to get out OT 1; to get off OT 2; to disembark **WS 2**, 59

Aussteiger(in) dropout **WS 3**, 119

ausstellen to exhibit OT 2

Aussteller(in) exhibitor **WS 4**, 140

Ausstellung exhibition OT 1; display OT 2

Ausstellungsgelände showground OT 2

Aussterben extinction OT 4

Ausstoss emission OT 4

Ausstrahlung charisma **WS 2**, 60

Austausch exchange OT 1

austauschen to exchange OT 5

Auswahl selection OT 4; variety OT 4

auswählen to choose OT 1; to elect OT 4; to select OT 4; to pick **WW**, 11

Auswahlfach elective OT 4

Auswahlliste shortlist OT 2

auswandern to emigrate OT 4

Ausweis ID card (identification card) OT 5

auswendig lernen to memorize **WS 1**, 23

sich auswirken auf to affect OT 3

Auswirkung impact OT 3

Auszeichnung award OT 2

Auszubildende(r) apprentice OT 5

Auszug extract OT 3; abstract OT 4; excerpt OT 4

authentisch authentic OT 4

Autismus autism OT 5

Auto car OT 1

Autobiografie autobiography WS 2, 54

Automat vending machine OT 1

Automobil automobile OT 4

autonom autonomous OT 4

Autor(in) author OT 2

Autorität authority OT 3

Avatar avatar OT 3

Avocado avocado OT 5

B

Baby baby OT 1

Bach stream OT 2

Backe cheek OT 4

backen to bake OT 1

Bäcker(in) baker OT 4

Bad bath OT 1

Badebekleidung swimwear OT 5

Badehaus bathhouse OT 2

baden to bathe WS 1, 29

Badewanne bath OT 1

Badezimmer bathroom OT 1

Badminton badminton OT 1

Bahn railway OT 2; rail OT 3; rink OT 4

Bahnbrecher(in) trailblazer WS 2, 74

Bahnhof station OT 1

Bahnsteig platform OT 1

Balance balance OT 3

bald soon OT 1

Balken beam OT 3

Balkon balcony WS 2, 58

Ball ball OT 1

Ballade ballad WS 1, 28

Ballett ballet OT 4

Ballsaal ballroom WS 1, 26

Banane banana OT 1

Band, das ribbon WS 1, 35

Band, die band OT 1; outfit WS 1, 29

Bande gang OT 5

Bank bench OT 3; bank OT 3

Banking banking OT 5

Bankwesen banking OT 5

Bar bar OT 1

Bär bear OT 1

Barde bard WS 1, 17

Bargeld cash OT 1

Barriere barrier OT 3

barrierefrei accessible OT 2

Bart beard OT 1

Baseball baseball OT 1

basierend auf based on OT 4

Basis basis OT 4; base OT 5

Basketball basketball OT 3

Bass bass WS 2, 67

Batterie battery OT 2

Bau construction OT 4

bauen to build OT 1; to construct OT 4

Bauer, Bäuerin farmer OT 2

Bauernhaus farmhouse OT 2

Bauernhof farm OT 1

Bauherr(in) builder OT 5

Baum tree OT 1

Baumeister(in) builder OT 5

Baumwolle cotton OT 4

Baumwollentkörnungsmaschine cotton gin WS 2, 54

beabsichtigen to intend OT 4; to aim OT 4

beachtlich formidable WS 1, 12

Beachtung consideration WS 3, 114

Beamer projector OT 1

Beamter, Beamtin official OT 2

beängstigend scary OT 2

beantworten to answer OT 1

bearbeiten to edit OT 4

Bearbeitung: in Bearbeitung underway WS 3, 99

beaufsichtigen to supervise OT 3; to oversee OT 4

Becken basin OT 3

bedeckt covered OT 2

Bedenken concern OT 5

bedeuten to mean OT 1; to signify OT 4

bedeutend prominent OT 4

bedeutsam momentous WW, 11

Bedeutung meaning OT 1; importance OT 3; significance OT 5; prominence WS 2, 60; relevance WS 3, 110; relevancy WS 3, 119

  von Bedeutung sein to matter OT 2

bedienen to serve OT 1; to operate OT 3

sich beeilen to hurry OT 1; to hurry up OT 2

beeindrucken to impress OT 4

  beeindruckend impressive OT 2

beeinflussen to influence OT 3; to impact WS 2, 82; to sway WS 3, 116

beeinträchtigt impaired OT 5

beenden to finish OT 1; to conclude OT 3

beengt cramped OT 3

Beerdigung funeral OT 4

Beere berry OT 4

Beet bed OT 1

sich befassen mit to engage with OT 4

Befehlsform imperative OT 1

befehlshabend commanding OT 2

befestigt fortified WS 1, 25

befolgen to abide by WS 2, 65

befragen to survey OT 5

Befragte(r) respondent OT 5

befreien to liberate WS 2, 62

Befreiung liberation WS 2, 62

befriedigen to satisfy WS 1, 36

befristet temporary OT 4

befruchten to pollinate WS 4, 135

befürchten to fear OT 5

begabt talented OT 5; giftet OT 5

begegnen to encounter OT 3; to face OT 4

begehen to commit OT 3

begeisternd inspirational WS 2, 62

begeistert excited OT 1; enthusiastic OT 3

Beginn beginning OT 1; advent OT 5

beginnen to start OT 1; to embark WS 1, 33

beglaubigt certified OT 5

begleiten to escort OT 4; to accompany WS 2, 67

Begleitung: in Begleitung accompanied OT 3

  ohne Begleitung unchaperoned WS 4, 135

begraben to bury WS 2, 60

begrenzen to limit OT 4; to border OT 4

Begriff concept OT 4

Begründung motivation OT 5; rationale WS 1, 12

begrüßen to welcome OT 1

behalten to keep OT 2; to retain WS 1, 27

Behälter container OT 4; reservoir OT 5

behandeln to treat OT 2

Behandlung treatment OT 4

behaupten to claim OT 3; to assert WS 3, 95

Behauptung claim OT 5; assertion WS 3, 119

Behausung dwelling OT 4

beheben to repair OT 5

beherrschen to master OT 4; to dominate WS 1, 35

behilflich instrumental WS 2, 56

Behinderte(r) disabled OT 4

Behinderung disability OT 2

Behörde authority OT 3

bei at OT 1; by OT 1

beide both OT 1

Beiklang connotation WS 3, 110

Bein leg OT 1

beinhalten to entail OT 4

beiseite aside OT 5

Beispiel example OT 1

  zum Beispiel for instance OT 4

beißen to bite **WS 3**, 112

Beitrag post OT 3; contribution **WS 1**, 29

beitragen (zu) to contribute (to) OT 5

bekannt familiar OT 2

   bekannt geben to announce OT 2

Bekannte(r) acquaintance OT 3

Bekanntgabe announcement OT 2

Bekanntschaft acquaintance OT 3

sich beklagen to complain OT 3

bekommen to get OT 1; to gain OT 4

bekräftigen to reinforce OT 5

beladen to load OT 3

belegen to verify **WS 3**, 117

beleidigen to offend OT 3; to insult OT 5

beleidigend offensive **WS 1**, 23

beliebt popular OT 1

bellen to bark OT 2

belohnen to reward OT 5

bemängeln to fault OT 2

bemerken to comment OT 3; to notice OT 4

bemerkenswert notable OT 4; noteworthy **WS 2**, 62

Bemerkung comment OT 3

Bemühen endeavour **WS 1**, 13

sich bemühen to struggle OT 5; to strive **WS 3**, 112

benachrichtigen to notify **WS 1**, 15

Benachrichtigung notification **WS 3**, 108

benachteiligt disadvantaged OT 5

Benehmen behaviour OT 2

sich benehmen to behave OT 2

beneiden to envy OT 5

beneidenswert enviable **WS 3**, 112

benötigen to require OT 4

benutzen to use OT 1

Benutzer(in) user OT 2

Benzin petrol OT 1

beobachten to watch OT 1; to observe OT 4

Beobachter(in) observer OT 5

Beobachtung observation OT 3

bequem comfortable OT 1

Bequemlichkeit convenience OT 4

Berater(in) consultant OT 5; advisor OT 5

Beratung counselling OT 5

Beratungslehrer(in) guidance counsellor OT 3

Berechnung calculation **WS 1**, 36

berechtigt eligible **WS 1**, 32; entitled **WS 2**, 65

Bereich sector OT 5; division **WS 2**, 53

bereichern to enrich OT 4

Bereicherung enrichment **WS 3**, 114

bereit ready OT 1

bereuen to regret OT 2

Berg mountain OT 1

bergab downhill OT 5

Bergarbeiter miner OT 3

Bergbau... mining OT 3

Bergsteigen climbing OT 1

Bergungs... to salvage OT 3

Bergwerk mine OT 2

berichten to report OT 1

berüchtigt infamous OT 4

beruflich vocational OT 5

(sich) beruhigen to settle down OT 2; to calm down OT 2

beruhigen to lull **WS 1**, 34

berühmt famous OT 1; renowned **WS 1**, 18

Berühmtheit fame **WS 2**, 74

berühren to touch OT 1

beschädigen to damage OT 3

beschädigt damaged OT 2

Beschädigung damage OT 3

beschaffen to purchase **WS 3**, 104

beschäftigen to employ OT 4

beschäftigt busy OT 1; occupied OT 5

Beschäftigung pursuit OT 4; employment OT 4; occupation OT 4

Beschallungsanlage PA (public address) system OT 2

beschämen to shame **WS 3**, 112

beschämt ashamed OT 3

bescheiden modest OT 2

beschleunigen to accelerate **WS 4**, 135

Beschluss resolution **WS 3**, 122

beschreiben to describe OT 1; to depict **WS 2**, 77

beschreibend descriptive OT 4

Beschreibung description OT 1

beschriften to label OT 1

beschuldigen to accuse OT 5

Beschwerde complaint OT 2

sich beschweren to complain OT 3

beseitigen to eliminate OT 3

Beseitigung removal **WS 2**, 56

Besen broom OT 4

Besessenheit obsession OT 5

besetzen to occupy **WS 3**, 122

Besetzung cast OT 3

besichtigen to tour OT 5

Besichtigungen sightseeing OT 1

besiedelt populated OT 5

besiegen to defeat **WW**, 10

Besitz possession OT 4

besitzen to own OT 2; to possess OT 4

besitzergreifend possessive OT 1

Besitzer(in) owner OT 2

besondere(r, -s) special OT 1; particular OT 4

besonders especially OT 2; particularly OT 4

besorgt worried OT 1; concerned OT 3; anxious OT 5

   besorgt sein to care OT 2

Besorgung errand OT 4

besprechen to discuss OT 1

Besprechung discussion OT 1; meeting OT 1

besser better OT 1

Bestandteil component **WS 3**, 96

bestätigen to confirm OT 4; to acknowledge OT 5; to certify **WS 2**, 83

Bestätigung confirmation **WS 3**, 116; approval **WS 3**, 116

bestäuben to pollinate **WS 4**, 135

Bestäuber pollinator **WS 4**, 140

Bestäubung pollination **WS 4**, 140

Besteck cutlery OT 3

bestehen to consist OT 3

   bestehen auf to insist **WS 1**, 22

bestellen to order OT 1

Bestellung order OT 1

beste(r, -s) best OT 1

bestimmen to define OT 4; to determine OT 4; to dictate OT 5

bestimmt definitely OT 2; specific OT 2; particular OT 4; destined **WS 2**, 76

   bestimmter Artikel definite article OT 1

Bestimmungswort determiner OT 1

bestrafen to punish OT 3

bestreiten to dispute **WS 1**, 20

besuchen to visit OT 1; to attend OT 2; to tour OT 5

   wieder besuchen to revisit **WS 2**, 76

Besucher(in) visitor OT 1

beteiligt sein to be involved OT 3

Beteiligung participation OT 5; involvement **WS 1**, 32

beten to pray OT 3

Beton concrete OT 2

betonen to emphasize OT 4

Betonung stress OT 1; emphasis (on) OT 5

betrachten to regard OT 4

Betrag amount OT 2

betreffend concerning OT 5

Betreuer(in) guardian OT 2; carer OT 5

Betreuung care OT 2

betrübt saddened OT 5

Bett bed OT 1

Bettdecke duvet OT 2

betteln to beg OT 5

Betttuch sheet OT 1

Beule dent **WS 3**, 104

beunruhigt alarmed OT 3

Beurteilen judging OT 2

beurteilen to review OT 3; to assess
    OT 4; to rate OT 5

bevölkert populated OT 5

Bevölkerung population OT 3

sich bevorraten to stock up OT 4

bevorstehend forthcoming **WS 1**, 29

bevorzugt favoured OT 4

bewaffnet armed OT 5

Bewährung probation OT 5

bewaldet forested OT 4; wooded OT 4

bewältigen to overcome OT 4

bewegen to move OT 1

Beweggrund motive **WS 3**, 116

beweglich agile OT 3

Beweglichkeit flexibility **WS 1**, 37

Bewegung movement OT 4; motion
    WS 2, 66

Beweis evidence OT 4

beweisen to prove OT 4

sich bewerben (um) to apply (for) OT 3;
    to bid (for) OT 5

Bewerber(in) applicant OT 5

bewerten to evaluate OT 4; to rate OT 5

Bewerter(in) assessor **WS 1**, 16

Bewertung evaluation OT 5; assessment
    WS 3, 105

bewohnbar habitable OT 4

bewohnen to inhabit OT 4

Bewohner(in) resident OT 4

Bewunderer, Bewunderin admirer
    WS 2, 60

bewundern to admire OT 4; to adore
    OT 4

bewundernswert admirable **WS 3**, 119

bewusst aware OT 5; conscious **WS 3**, 93

    sich bewusst sein to be aware OT 4

Bewusstsein awareness OT 4

bezahlen to pay OT 1

bezaubern to charm **WS 1**, 17

beziehen: sich auf etw. beziehen to
    refer to OT 3; to relate to OT 5

Beziehung relationship OT 3; relation
    OT 5

Bezirk district OT 5

bezogen auf based on OT 4

bezüglich concerning OT 5

Biber beaver OT 4

Bibliothek library OT 1

Biene bee OT 1

Bier beer OT 1

bikulturell bicultural OT 4

Bild picture OT 1; image OT 3

Bildhauer(in) sculptor **WS 2**, 55

Bildroman graphic novel OT 5

Bildschirm screen OT 1

Bildsprache imagery **WS 2**, 64

Bildungs- educational OT 4

Bildunterschrift caption OT 2

billig cheap OT 2

billigen to condone **WS 2**, 73

Billion trillion **WS 4**, 144

binär binary **WS 3**, 112

binden to tie OT 5

Binnenland interior OT 5

Biografie biography OT 4

Biokraftstoff biofuel OT 3

Biologie biology OT 1

biologisch organic OT 4; biological
    OT 5

bipolar bipolar OT 5

Birne pear OT 1

bis till OT 2; until OT 3

bisexuell bisexual OT 5

Bison bison OT 4

Biss bite OT 2

bisschen: ein bisschen a bit OT 1

Bitte request OT 1

bitte please OT 1

bitter bitter **WS 3**, 97

bitterlich bitterly OT 5

blamieren to disgrace **WS 2**, 64

Blase bubble OT 2; bladder OT 4

blasen to blow OT 2

blass pale OT 3

Blatt sheet OT 1

blattreich leafy **WS 1**, 36

Blauhäher blue jay **WS 2**, 64

Blazer blazer OT 5

bleiben to stay OT 1; to keep OT 2;
    to remain OT 4

Bleistift pencil OT 1

Blick glance **WS 2**, 82

    flüchtiger Blick glimpse OT 5

blicken to gaze OT 5

blind blind **WS 2**, 60

    blind machen to blind **WS 2**, 60

Blindenführhund guide dog OT 2

Blitz flash OT 4

Block block OT 4

Blockade blockade **WS 2**, 53

Blockbuster blockbuster **WS 1**, 17

Blocker blocker OT 5

blockieren to block OT 5

blöd dumb OT 5

Blog blog OT 1

Blogeintrag blogpost OT 4

Blogger(in) blogger OT 3

blond blonde OT 1

Blues blues **WW**, 10

blühen to bloom **WS 3**, 99

Blume flower OT 1

Blut blood OT 2

bluten to bleed **WS 2**, 76

blutig bloody **WS 1**, 13

Blutvergießen bloodshed OT 5

BMX-Rad fahren BMXing OT 5

Boden bottom OT 1; ground OT 2

Bogen bow OT 2; arch OT 3

Bogenschütze(-in) archer OT 3

Bohne bean OT 1

Bohrinsel rig **WS 1**, 16

bombadieren to blast OT 5; to bombard
    WS 3, 122

Bonbon sweet OT 1

Boot boat OT 1

    mit dem Boot fahren to cruise OT 3

Bootfahren boating OT 3

Bootsfahrer(in) boater OT 3

Bord to board OT 4

    an Bord aboard OT 4

    über Bord overboard OT 3

Bordkarte boarding pass OT 2

Bordstein curb OT 5

Böse evil OT 5

böse angry OT 1; wicked OT 2; mad (AE)
    OT 2

Bot bot **WS 2**, 73

botanisch botanical OT 4

Boxer(in) boxer **WS 2**, 53

Boygroup boyband OT 2

boykottieren to boycott **WS 2**, 59

Brachvogel curlew OT 2

brainstormen to brainstorm OT 2

Brandbekämpfung firefighting OT 2

brandneu brand new OT 2

Bratensoße gravy OT 1

brauchen to need OT 1

braun brown OT 1

brechen to break OT 1

Brei mash **WS 4**, 141

brennen to burn OT 2

Brennholz firewood OT 4

Brennofen kiln OT 3

Brennstoff fuel OT 2

Brief letter OT 1

Briefkasten letterbox OT 1; mailbox OT 4

Briefmarke stamp OT 1

Brieftasche wallet OT 1
Briefträger(in) postman OT 2
Briefumschlag envelope OT 2
Brigade brigade **WS 1**, 38
bringen to bring OT 1
Brise breeze OT 3
Brite Briton OT 2
britisch British OT 1
Brokkoli broccoli OT 1
Brombeere blackberry OT 1
Broschüre brochure OT 1; booklet OT 2
Brot bread OT 1
Brötchen bread roll OT 1
Brotlaib loaf OT 1
Brotverdiener(in) breadwinner OT 5
Brücke bridge OT 1
Bruder brother OT 1
Brüderschaft brotherhood **WS 2**, 60
Brutalität brutality **WS 2**, 58
brüten to breed OT 5
Buch book OT 1
buchen to book OT 4
Bücherei library OT 1
Bücherregal bookcase OT 1
Buchstabe letter OT 1
buchstabieren to spell OT 1
buchstäblich literally **WS 3**, 101
Bucht bay OT 4; inlet **WS 1**, 35
Buchung booking OT 2
Büffel buffalo OT 4
Buffet buffet OT 4
Bügeln ironing OT 5
Bühne stage OT 2
Bund union OT 4
Bündel bundle OT 2
Bundes... federal OT 4
Bundesstaat state OT 1
bunt coloured OT 1
Burg castle OT 1
bürgen to vouch **WS 3**, 93
Bürger... civil **WW**, 10
bürgerlich civil **WW**, 10; civic **WS 3**, 110
Bürgermeister(in) mayor OT 3
Büro office OT 2
Bursche lad OT 5
Bürste brush OT 2
bürsten to brush OT 4
Bus bus OT 1
Busch bush OT 5; outback OT 5; shrub **WS 1**, 22
Buschfeuer bushfire OT 5
buschig shrubby **WS 1**, 22
Buschland bush OT 5; bushland OT 5
Busladung busload OT 5
Bussard buzzard OT 2

Butter butter OT 1

C
Caddie caddie OT 4
Café café OT 1
Cafeteria cafeteria OT 2
Camp camp OT 1
Camper(in) camper OT 2
Campingplatz campsite OT 2
Campus campus OT 4
Canyon canyon OT 3
Cartoonist cartoonist OT 4
Catering catering OT 3
Cello cello OT 1
Cerealien cereal OT 1
Champion champion OT 4
Chancen odds **WS 1**, 17
Chaos chaos OT 4
chaotisch disorganized OT 2
Charakter character OT 2
charakterisieren to characterize **WS 2**, 67
Charakterzug trait **WS 4**, 146
Charisma charisma **WS 2**, 60
charismatisch charismatic **WS 2**, 58
charmant charming OT 3
Chart chart OT 4
Checkliste checklist OT 2
Cheerleader(in) cheerleader OT 3
Chef(in) boss OT 2
Chemie chemistry OT 5
Chemikalie chemical OT 3
Chili chili OT 2
chillen to chill (out) **WS 1**, 25
chinesisch Chinese OT 1
Chirurg(in) surgeon OT 3
Cholera cholera OT 4
Chor choir OT 1
Christ(in) Christian **WS 2**, 58
christlich Christian **WS 2**, 58
Chromosom chromosome OT 5
chronologisch chronological OT 4
clever slick **WS 3**, 93
CO2-Ausstoß carbon emission OT 3
CO2-Bilanz carbon footprint OT 3
Comicheft comic OT 1
Computer computer OT 5
computererfahren tech-savvy **WS 3**, 99
Computerraum computer lab OT 2
Condor condor OT 3
cool cool OT 1
Cousin(e) cousin OT 1
Cracker cracker OT 3
Credo creed **WS 2**, 58

Curling curling OT 4
Curriculum curriculum OT 4
Currygericht curry OT 1
Cyber-Mobbing cyberbullying OT 5; cyberthreat OT 5
D
da there OT 1
dabei bleiben to stick to OT 5
Dach roof OT 1
Dachboden attic OT 2
daher therefore OT 5; hence **WS 3**, 110
dahinter beyond OT 3
Dame lady OT 2
Dampf steam OT 2
danach afterward(s) OT 4
daneben gehen to backfire OT 4
dankbar grateful OT 3
Danke! thanks OT 1
dann then OT 1
Darlehen loan OT 4
darstellen to portray **WS 1**, 18; to pose **WS 3**, 109
hier: Darstellung representation **WS 4**, 141
darum therefore OT 5
darunter underneath OT 5
Datei file OT 2
Daten data OT 5
Datenschutzeinstellungen privacy settings OT 3
Dauer duration **WS 3**, 108
dauerhaft permanent OT 4
dauern to last OT 2
Daumen thumb OT 4
Daumen hoch thumbs up OT 4
Debatte debate OT 4
Debüt debut OT 4
Deck deck OT 3
Decke ceiling OT 2; blanket OT 2
Deckel lid OT 2
definieren to define OT 4
Definition definition OT 1
definitiv definitely OT 2
dehydriert dehydrated OT 2
Deich levee OT 4
dein/Ihr your OT 1
deine(r, -s)/Ihre(r, -s) yours OT 3
Dekade decade OT 4
dekadent decadent **WS 2**, 63
Dekoration decoration OT 3
dekorieren to decorate OT 2
Delfin dolphin OT 1
Delle dent **WS 3**, 104
Demokratie democracy OT 3

Demonstrant(in) protester OT 4;
demonstrator **WS 2**, 53

Demonstration demonstration OT 5;
rally **WS 2**, 61

Demonstrativbegleiter demonstrative
OT 1

demütigend humiliating **WS 3**, 113

denken to think OT 1

denken an to think about OT 1;
to think of OT 1

Denkmal memorial OT 4; monument
OT 4

Depression depression OT 5

depressiv depressive **WS 3**, 108

derzeit currently OT 4

desensibilisieren to desensitize **WS 2**, 79

deshalb therefore OT 5

Design design OT 1

Designer(in) designer OT 3

Desinfektionsmittel disinfectant OT 3

desinteressiert uninterested OT 5

Detail detail OT 2

detailliert detailed OT 4

deutlich clearly OT 3; stark **WS 2**, 83

deutsch German OT 1

dezent subtle **WS 1**, 29

dezentralisieren to devolve **WS 1**, 30

Diabetes diabetes **WS 1**, 37

Diagramm diagram OT 1; chart OT 4;
graph OT 5

Dialekt dialect OT 4

Dialog dialogue OT 1

Diaschau slideshow OT 5

Diaspora diaspora **WS 1**, 35

Diät diet OT 3

Diäten dieting OT 5

diätetisch dietary OT 5

dich/sich (selbst) yourself OT 2

Dichter(in) poet OT 1

Dichtung poetry OT 4

dick thick OT 1

Didgeridoo didgeridoo OT 5

Diebstahl theft OT 5; larceny **WS 2**, 60

Diener(in) attendant OT 2; servant OT 3

Dienst service OT 2

Dienstag Tuesday OT 1

Diesel diesel OT 3

differenziert nuanced **WS 3**, 116

diffus diffused **WS 3**, 122

digital digital OT 1

Digitalisierung digitalization **WS 3**, 106

Dilemma dilemma OT 5

Ding thing OT 1

Dingo dingo OT 5

Dinosaurier dinosaur OT 1

Diplom diploma OT 4

direkt straight OT 3; directly OT 3;
straightforward **WS 1**, 32

diskreditieren to discredit **WS 3**, 97

diskriminieren to discriminate OT 5

Diskriminierung discrimination OT 5

Diskussion discussion OT 1

sich distanzieren to distance oneself
OT 4

Disziplin discipline **WS 3**, 116

Dokument document OT 4

Dokumentation documentary OT 2

Dollar dollar OT 1

Dolmetscher(in) interpreter OT 3

dominieren to dominate **WS 1**, 35

donnern to thunder OT 4

Donnerstag Thursday OT 1

Dopamin dopamine **WS 4**, 135

Doppel... double OT 1

Doppelhaushälfte semi-detached
house OT 4

doppelt double OT 1

Doppelung duplication **WS 4**, 141

Dorf village OT 1

dort there OT 1

dort drüben over there OT 2

Dose can OT 2; tin (AE) OT 2

Dosen... canned OT 2

Downsyndrom Down syndrome OT 5

Dozent(in) lecturer **WS 3**, 93

Drama drama OT 1

Dramatiker(in) playwright OT 4

dramatisch dramatic OT 4

Drang urge **WS 1**, 21

drastisch drastic OT 5

Draufgängertum bravado **WS 2**, 82

draufklatschen to slap on OT 5

draußen outside OT 1; afield **WS 1**, 15

Dreck dirt OT 4

dreckig filthy **WS 1**, 36

Drehbuch script OT 2

drehen to turn OT 2; to film OT 5

sich drehen to spiral **WS 1**, 24

Drehscheibe turntable OT 2

Drehung to twist OT 3

drei three OT 1

dreifach triple **WS 2**, 53

dreißig thirty OT 1

dreizehn thirteen OT 1

dringend urgent OT 4

drinnen indoors OT 3

Dritte(r, -s) third OT 1

Droge drug OT 3

drohen to loom **WS 1**, 35

Drone drone OT 4

drüben over OT 2

Druck pressure OT 3

drücken to press OT 1

Dschungel jungle **WS 2**, 53

du/Sie you OT 1

dual dual OT 4

Dualität duality OT 4

Dudelsack bagpipe **WS 1**, 12

dulden to condone **WS 2**, 73

dumm silly OT 1; stupid OT 2; dumb OT 5

Dung manure OT 3

Dünger fertilizer OT 3

dunkel dark OT 1

dunkelhaarig dark-haired OT 3

Dunkelheit darkness OT 5

dünn thin OT 1; skinny OT 5

dunstig misty **WS 1**, 13

durch through OT 1

durchaus thoroughly OT 5

Durchbruch breakthrough OT 4

durchdringen to permeate **WS 2**, 82

durcheinander mixed up OT 2

durchführen to conduct OT 3;
to implement OT 4

Durchhaltevermögen perseverance
OT 4

durchmachen to undergo OT 5

durchnässt soaked OT 3

durchqueren to traverse **WS 1**, 16

Durchschnitt median OT 5

im Durchschnitt on average OT 5

durchschnittlich average OT 3

durchschweifen to roam OT 5

durchsetzen to enforce OT 4; to impose
WS 1, 30; to assert **WS 3**, 95

durchstochen pierced OT 3

dürr arid OT 5

Dürre drought OT 5

durstig thirsty OT 1

Dusche shower OT 1

düster bleak OT 4

Dutzend dozen OT 4

Dynamik dynamic OT 5

dynamisch vibrant OT 5

Dyskalkulie dyscalculia OT 5

Dyspraxie dyspraxia OT 5

dystopisch dystopian OT 5

E

Ebene plain OT 4; lowland **WS 1**, 17

ebenso alike OT 4

(sich) ebnen to level off OT 5

echt real OT 1; authentic OT 4; genuine
OT 5

Ecke corner OT 1

Edelstein jewel OT 3; gem **WS 3**, 104

Efeu poison ivy OT 2

effizient efficient OT 3

egal (wie) no matter OT 5

   egal wer whoever OT 4

egoistisch selfish OT 3

Ehe marriage OT 3

Ehefrau wife OT 1

Ehemann husband OT 2

Ehre glory **WS 2**, 76

ehren to honour OT 4

Ehrenamt volunteering OT 2

   ein Ehrenamt haben to volunteer OT 2

Ehrfurcht awe **WS 1**, 25

Ehrgeiz ambition OT 5

ehrgeizig ambitious OT 3

ehrlich honest OT 2

Ei egg OT 1

Eibe yew **WS 1**, 38

Eichhörnchen squirrel OT 1

Eifer fervour **WS 2**, 58

eifersüchtig jealous OT 2

eifrig eager OT 2

Eigelb yolk **WS 1**, 24

eigen peculiar **WS 2**, 54

eigenartig odd OT 2

eigene(r, -s) own OT 1

Eigenschaft quality OT 3

eigenständig distinct OT 5

eigentlich actually OT 3

Eigentum property OT 4

sich eignen (für) to suit OT 5

Eignung qualification OT 4

eilen to rush OT 2

Eimer bucket OT 3

einbauen to incorporate **WS 1**, 34

einbetten to embed **WS 1**, 12

einbeziehen to involve OT 4

eindeutig definite OT 1; distinct OT 5

Eindruck impression OT 5

einfach simple OT 1; easy OT 1; basic OT 4

Einfachheit simplicity **WS 2**, 67

einfangen to capture OT 4

Einfluss influence OT 5

einflussreich influential **WS 2**, 75

einfühlsam sensitive OT 4; empathetic
   WS 3, 111

Einführung introduction OT 2; advent
   OT 5; induction OT 5; inception
   WS 1, 14

Einführungs... introductory OT 5

Eingang entrance OT 1

Eingangsbereich entrance hall OT 1

Eingangshalle entrance hall OT 1

Eingebung inspiration OT 4;
   epiphany **WS 2**, 76

sich eingewöhnen to settle in OT 5

eingravieren to engrave OT 4

eingreifen to intervene OT 5;
   to encroach **WS 3**, 112

Eingriff intervention OT 5

einheimisch local OT 2

Einheimische(r) local OT 2; native OT 3

Einheit unity OT 4; unit OT 4; entity
   WS 2, 54

Einhorn unicorn **WS 1**, 13

einig: sich einig sein to agree OT 1

einige some OT 1; several OT 1

Einkaufen shopping OT 1

einkaufen to shop OT 1

Einkaufswagen shopping trolley OT 1

Einkaufszentrum shopping centre OT 1;
   mall OT 3

Einkommen income OT 5

einladen to invite OT 2

Einladung invitation OT 1

einleuchtend plausible **WS 4**, 143

(sich) einloggen to log on OT 3

einlullen to lull **WS 1**, 34

einmal once OT 2

einmarschieren to invade OT 3

Einnahmen revenue **WS 1**, 31

   jdn. einnehmen to charm s. o. **WS 1**, 17

einplanen to budget OT 3

einreichen to hand in OT 2

Einrichtung institution OT 4; amenity
   OT 4; establishment **WS 2**, 63

eins one OT 1

einsam lonely OT 3; solitary **WS 2**, 65

einsammeln to collect OT 5

Einsatz engagement OT 4; dedication
   WS 2, 57

einschätzen to judge OT 2

Einschätzung assessment **WS 3**, 105

einschlafen to go to sleep OT 1

einschließen to include OT 2

einschließlich including OT 1

einschränken to restrict OT 4

   sich einschränken to downsize OT 3

Einschränkung restriction OT 4

einschüchtern to intimidate **WS 1**, 35

Einsendung entry OT 2

sich einsetzen (für) to campaign (for)
   OT 5; to champion **WS 2**, 54; to lobby
   WS 2, 70

einsperren to imprison **WS 1**, 18

einsprachig monolingual OT 5

einstecken to plug in OT 1

einsteigen to get in OT 1

einstellen to recruit **WS 1**, 14

Einstellung attitude OT 4; outlook
   WS 3, 97

einstimmig unanimously **WS 2**, 78

einstufen to classify OT 4

Einstufung classification **WS 4**, 135

eintauchen to immerse **WS 1**, 17

Eintopf stew OT 3

Eintrag entry OT 2

eintragen to enter OT 2

einträufeln to instil **WS 2**, 64

eintreten to enter OT 2; to step in OT 4

   eintreten in to join OT 1

Eintritt admission OT 2

Eintrittskarte ticket OT 1

einverstanden sein to be willing OT 4

Einwand objection OT 3

Einwanderer(in) immigrant OT 4

einwandern to immigrate OT 5

Einwanderung immigration OT 2

Einweckglas jar OT 2

einwerben to raise OT 2

einwickeln to wrap OT 2

Einwohner(in) citizen OT 2

Einzel... single OT 3

Einzelhandel retail OT 5

einzeln individually OT 5

einzig sole **WS 1**, 17

einzigartig unique OT 2

Eis ice OT 1; ice cream OT 1

Eisbahn rink OT 4

Eisbär polar bear OT 4

Eiscreme ice cream OT 1

Eisenbahn railway OT 2; railroad
   WS 2, 75

eisig icy OT 5

ekelhaft disgusting OT 2

Elch moose OT 4

Elefant elephant OT 1

Elektriker(in) electrician OT 5

elektrisch electric OT 1; electrical OT 5

elektrisieren to electrify **WS 2**, 69

elektronisch electronic OT 2

Element element OT 4

Elend hardship **WS 2**, 67

Elendsviertel slum OT 5

elf eleven OT 1

Elfenbein ivory OT 4

Elite elite **WS 3**, 100

Ellbogen elbow OT 1

Elster magpie OT 1

elterlich parental **WS 3**, 112

Elternteil parent OT 1

emailen to email OT 3

Emanzipation emancipation **WS 2**, 57

sich emanzipieren to emancipate **WS 3**, 114

Emission emission OT 4

Emoji emoji OT 2

Emotion emotion OT 5

emotional emotional OT 4; emotive **WS 1**, 24

Empathie empathy **WS 1**, 35

Empfang reception OT 1

Empfänger(in) receiver OT 4

Empfangschef(in) receptionist OT 1

empfehlen to recommend OT 3

Empfehlung recommendation OT 4

Empfehlungsschreiben letter of reference OT 5

emphatisch emphatic OT 5

empört disgusted OT 5

Empörung outrage **WS 2**, 53

Ende ending OT 1; end OT 1; finish **WS 2**, 76

    zu Ende gehen to run out OT 2

enden to end OT 1

endgültig final OT 2

endlich at last OT 2

endlos endless OT 4

Endung ending OT 1

Endzone end zone OT 2

Energie energy OT 2

energisch vigorous **WS 1**, 37

eng narrow OT 2; closely OT 3

    eng verbunden tight-knit OT 4

Engagement engagement OT 4

engagieren to engage OT 5

engagiert dedicated **WS 3**, 119

englisch English OT 1

engstirnig narrow-minded OT 5

Enkel grandson OT 1

Enkel(in) grandchild OT 1

enorm vast OT 4

entdecken to discover OT 2; to detect **WS 1**, 27

Entdeckung discovery OT 4

Ente duck OT 2

entfalten to unfold **WS 1**, 35

entfernen to remove OT 2

entfernt remote OT 4

Entfernung distance OT 2; removal **WS 2**, 56

entführen to kidnap OT 3

Entführer(in) kidnapper OT 2

entgegentreten to confront **WS 1**, 20

Entgiftung detox **WS 3**, 108

enthalten to contain OT 4

Enthusiasmus enthusiasm **WS 1**, 32

entkommen to escape OT 2

entlang along OT 2

entlarven to expose **WS 2**, 63

entlassen to dismiss **WS 3**, 105

entrechtet disenfranchised **WS 2**, 62

entriegeln to unlock **WS 4**, 136

Entschädigung compensation OT 5

entscheiden to decide OT 1; to opt OT 5

entscheidend paramount **WS 2**, 55; decisive **WS 2**, 57

Entscheidung decision OT 1

Entscheidungsträger(in) decision maker **WS 4**, 136

entschlossen determined OT 5

Entschlossenheit determination OT 4; resolve **WS 2**, 58

entschuldigen to excuse OT 1

    sich entschuldigen to apologize OT 2

Entschuldigung sorry OT 1; apology OT 3; excuse OT 5

entsetzlich dire **WS 4**, 140

entsetzt aghast OT 3; horrified OT 5; outraged **WS 2**, 64

sich entspannen to relax OT 3

entsprechend equivalent (to) OT 5

entstehen to arise **WS 2**, 65

enttäuschend disappointingly OT 3; disappointing OT 4; underwhelming **WS 1**, 29

enttäuscht disappointed OT 2; disenchanted **WS 3**, 46

Enttäuschung disappointment **WS 1**, 32

Entvölkerung depopulation **WS 1**, 35

entwerfen to draft OT 5

entwickeln to develop OT 2

    sich entwickeln to evolve OT 4

Entwickler(in) developer OT 5

Entwicklung development OT 4; evolution OT 5; progression OT 5

entwicklungsbedingt developmental **WS 3**, 95

Entwurf draft OT 2

Entzug detox **WS 3**, 108; withdrawal **WS 4**, 146

Entzündung infection OT 2

Enzyklopädie encyclopedia OT 4

epidemisch epidemic OT 5

Episode episode **WS 3**, 95

Epoche period OT 3

Erbe heritage OT 4; legacy OT 4

erben to inherit OT 4

Erbse pea OT 1

Erdbeben earthquake OT 2

Erdbeere strawberry OT 1

Erde Earth OT 1; ground OT 2; soil OT 4

Erdkugel globe OT 5

Erdkunde geography OT 1

Erdreich soil OT 4

erdrücken to crush **WS 1**, 32

Ereignis event OT 1; incident OT 5

erfahren to come to know OT 5; to experience OT 5

erfahren experienced OT 3

Erfahrung experience OT 2; expertise **WS 1**, 34

erfahrungsmäßig experiential OT 4

erfinden to invent OT 2

Erfinder(in) inventor OT 2

Erfindung invention OT 2

Erfolg success OT 3

    Erfolg haben to succeed OT 2

erfolgreich successful OT 2; prolific **WS 1**, 28

erforderlich required OT 3

erforschen to explore OT 1; to research OT 4

Erforschung exploration OT 5

Erfrischung refreshment OT 4

erfüllen to comply with **WS 1**, 22

Erfüllung completion OT 4; accomplishment **WS 1**, 37

erfunden fictional OT 2; imaginary OT 4

ergänzen to complement **WS 1**, 29

ergänzend additional OT 5

Ergänzung amendment OT 4; addition OT 4

ergattern to secure OT 5

Ergebnis result OT 2; finding OT 4; outcome **WS 1**, 33

    als Ergebnis haben to result **WS 1**, 17

ergreifen to seize **WS 1**, 18

erhalten to receive OT 2; to preserve OT 3; to sustain OT 4

erhältlich available OT 4

erheben to raise OT 2

    sich erheben to tower **WS 1**, 13

erheblich appreciable **WS 4**, 146

erhöhen to raise OT 2; to increase OT 5

erhöht increased OT 5

sich erholen to recover OT 4; to recuperate **WS 1**, 12

erholsam relaxing OT 2

erinnern to remind OT 2

    erinnern an to commemorate **WS 2**, 78

    sich erinnern an to think of OT 1; to remember OT 1

Erinnerung memoir OT 5

erkennbar recognizable OT 4; apparent **WS 3**, 112

erkennen to realize OT 2; to recognize OT 3

Erkenntnis finding OT 4
Erkennung recognition **WS 4**, 140
erklären to explain OT 1; to state OT 5
erklärend explanatory **WS 4**, 138
Erklärung explanation OT 1
erkunden to explore OT 1
erlauben to allow OT 3; to permit OT 4
Erlaubnis permission OT 2; permit OT 3;
　licence OT 3
erlaubt allowed OT 2
erläuternd explanatory **WS 4**, 138
erleben to experience OT 5
erleichtern to alleviate OT 5
erleichtert relieved OT 3
Erleichterung relief OT 2
Erleuchtung epiphany **WS 2**, 76
ermächtigen to empower OT 5
ermöglichen to enable OT 4
ermorden to murder OT 2;
　to assassinate **WS 2**, 58
Ermordung assassination **WS 2**, 58
ermüdend tiring OT 4
ermutigen to encourage OT 4
Ernährer(in) breadwinner OT 5
Ernährung nutrition **WS 1**, 36
Ernährungswissenschaftler(in)
　dietician OT 5
ernennen to appoint OT 4
erneuerbar renewable OT 4
ernst serious OT 2
ernsthaft intense OT 5; in earnest
　WS 3, 114
Ernsthaftigkeit seriousness OT 5;
　sincerity **WS 2**, 69
Ernte harvest OT 3
ernten to harvest OT 4
erobern to conquer OT 2
E-Roller e-scooter OT 5
erratisch erratic OT 5
erreichbar achievable **WS 1**, 12;
　obtainable **WS 3**, 97
erreichen to reach OT 3; to gain OT 4;
　to achieve OT 4; to attain **WS 2**, 58;
　to accomplish **WS 3**, 111
errichten to put up OT 1; to construct
　OT 4; to erect OT 4
Errungenschaft achievement OT 4
Ersatz substitution OT 3; substitute OT 3
Erschaffer(in) creator OT 5
erscheinen to appear OT 3
erschöpft exhausted OT 2
erschreckend frightening OT 1; alarming
　OT 4; staggering OT 4
erschwinglich affordable **WS 3**, 112
Ersetzen substitution OT 3

ersetzen to replace OT 3
erspähen to spot OT 1
erstaunlich amazing OT 1
erstaunlicherweise astonishingly OT 3
erstaunt amazed OT 3
erste(r, -s) first OT 1; premier OT 2
　Erste Hilfe first aid OT 2
ersticken to choke **WS 4**, 134
sich erstrecken to stretch OT 3
erteilen to issue OT 4
ertragen to bear OT 5
ertrinken to drown OT 3
erwachsen grown up OT 2; mature
　WS 3, 105
Erwachsenenalter adulthood **WS 3**, 111
Erwachsene(r) adult OT 1
erwähnen to mention OT 2
erwarten to expect OT 2; to anticipate
　WS 1, 37
Erwartung expectation OT 4
erwartungsgemäß unsurprisingly OT 3
erweitert extended OT 5
erwerben to acquire **WS 3**, 106
erzählen to tell OT 1
Erzähler(in) narrator OT 2
Erzählung narrative **WS 2**, 65
Erzbischof archbishop **WS 2**, 60
erzeugen to produce OT 3; to generate
　OT 4
erziehen to educate **WS 2**, 57
erzielen to attain **WS 2**, 58
es it OT 1
Esel donkey OT 4
essbar edible **WS 4**, 142
Essen food OT 1
essen to eat OT 1
Essensausgabe food bank OT 5
Esser(in) eater **WS 1**, 36
Esslöffel tablespoon OT 2
Esszimmer dining room OT 1
Etage storey **WS 2**, 66
Ethik ethic **WS 3**, 122
ethisch ethical OT 3
ethnisch ethnic OT 5
Ethnizität ethnicity **WS 3**, 105
Etikett tag OT 2; label OT 5
Etikette etiquette **WS 3**, 101
etwa approximately OT 5
etwas some OT 1; something OT 1;
　slightly OT 3
euch (selbst) yourselves OT 3
euer/Ihr your OT 1
Europäer(in) European OT 3
evakuieren to evacuate OT 4
Evakuierung evacuation OT 4

Evolution evolution OT 5
ewig eternal **WS 3**, 104
Exekutive executive OT 4
Existenz existence OT 4
existieren to exist OT 3
exklusiv exclusive **WS 2**, 71
exotisch exotic **WS 1**, 12
Expansion expansion **WS 3**, 114
Expedition expedition OT 2
Experiment experiment OT 2
experimentieren to experiment OT 4
Experte, Expertin expert OT 3;
　specialist OT 5; pundit **WS 2**, 69
Expertise expertise **WS 1**, 34
explodieren to explode OT 5
Exploration exploration OT 5
exploratisch exploratory **WS 3**, 122
Explosion explosion **WS 1**, 43
Exporteur(in) exporter OT 5
exquisit exquisite **WS 1**, 25
Extra... extra OT 1
Extrem extreme OT 4
extrem extremely OT 3; extreme OT 4;
　drastic OT 5

F
fabelhaft fabulous OT 2
Fabrik factory OT 2; mill **WS 3**, 114
Fabrikarbeiter(in) millworker
　WS 2, 69
Fach subject OT 1
Facharbeit coursework OT 4
Fachrichtung discipline **WS 3**, 116
Fachzeitschrift journal OT 3
Fackelschein torchlight **WS 1**, 16
fähig capable OT 4
　fähig sein to be able OT 2
Fähigkeit ability OT 4; capacity OT 5
Fahne flag OT 5
Fahranfänger{in} learner OT 3
Fahrbahn lane OT 4
fahren to go OT 1; to drive OT 1;
　to motor OT 3; to ride OT 5
Fahrer(in) driver OT 2
Fahrgeld fare **WS 2**, 59
Fahrplan timetable OT 1
Fahrrad bike OT 1; bicycle OT 3
　mit dem Fahrrad fahren to cycle OT 1
Fahrt journey OT 1; ride OT 1; drive OT 5
Fahrtenbuch logbook **WS 1**, 23
Fahrzeug vehicle OT 2
Fakt fact OT 1
Faktor factor OT 3
Fall case OT 1
Falle trap OT 4

fallen to fall OT 1; drop OT 4; to decrease OT 5

   fallen lassen to drop OT 1

Fallensteller(in) trapper **WS 1**, 21

falls if OT 1

Fallschirm springen to parachute OT 4

Fallschirmspringer(in) skydiver OT 5

falsch incorrectly OT 5; fake **WS 1**, 18

Falschmeldung hoax **WS 1**, 20

falten to fold **WS 2**, 69

Familie family OT 1

Fan fan OT 1

Fanatiker(in) fanatic OT 5

fangen to catch OT 1; to trap OT 5

Fantasie fantasy OT 2

fantastisch fantastic OT 1; fanciful **WS 3**, 101

Fantasy fantasy OT 2

FAQ FAQ OT 3

Farbe colour; paint OT 1

färben to dye OT 3

farbenfroh colourful OT 3

farbig coloured OT 1

Fassade façade **WS 3**, 111

fast almost OT 2; nearly OT 2

Faszination fascination OT 3

faszinieren to fascinate OT 4; to intrigue **WS 2**, 54

faszinierend fascinating OT 2; intriguing OT 5

faul lazy OT 2

Fausthandschuh mitten OT 4

favorisiert favoured OT 4

Feder feather OT 2

Federtasche pencil case OT 1

Feedback feedback OT 2

fegen to sweep OT 4

fehlend missing OT 1

Fehler mistake OT 1

fehlerhaft incorrectly OT 5

fehlschlagen to backfire OT 4

Feier party OT 1; celebration OT 2; ceremony OT 2

feierlich ceremonial OT 3; celebratory **WS 1**, 26; solemn **WS 2**, 69

feiern to celebrate OT 3

Feigling coward **WS 2**, 83

Feind(in) enemy OT 3

Feinkostladen deli OT 5

Feld field OT 1; square OT 1; space OT 1

Feldfrüchte crop OT 3

Fell fur OT 4

Fels(en) cliff OT 5

   schroffer Fels tor **WS 1**, 22

Felsvorsprung outcropping **WS 1**, 35

Feminismus feminism **WS 3**, 110

Fenster window OT 1

Ferienlager camp OT 1

fern far-off OT 2; faraway OT 5

Fernbedienung remote OT 3

   Ferne: aus der Ferne remotely OT 4

Fernglas binoculars OT 2

Fernsehen, Fernseher TV OT 1; television OT 2

Ferse heel **WS 3**, 119

fertigstellen to finalize OT 4

fesseln to engage OT 5

fest tightly OT 3; firm OT 4; solid OT 4

Fest festival OT 1; feast OT 3

festhalten to grasp OT 5

festigen to cement **WS 2**, 58

Festival festival OT 1

Festivalbesucher(in) festival-goer OT 4

Festland mainland OT 3

festlegen to state OT 5

festmachen to fasten **WS 4**, 141

festnehmen to capture OT 4

Festnetz landline OT 4

festsetzen to prescribe OT 5

Festung fort OT 2; fortification **WS 1**, 18; fortress **WS 1**, 25

Festzelt marquee OT 2

Fett fat OT 2

fett fatty **WS 1**, 36

fetten to grease **WS 1**, 24

fettgedruckt bold OT 1

Fettleibigkeit obesity **WS 1**, 37

feucht humid OT 4

Feuer fire OT 2

Feuerlöscher fire extinguisher OT 5

Feuermacher(in) fire-builder OT 2

Feuerwehrfrau, -mann firefighter OT 2

Feuerwerk fireworks OT 3

Fiedel fiddle **WS 1**, 26

Figur figure OT 3

fiktiv imaginary OT 4

Film film OT 1; movie OT 2

Filmaufnahmen footage OT 4

Filmemacher(in) filmmaker OT 4

filmen to film OT 5

Filmmaterial footage OT 4

Filmrolle roll OT 2

Filter filter OT 4

filtern to filter **WS 2**, 72

Filzstift marker OT 1

Finalist(in) finalist OT 5

finanziell financial OT 4

   finanziell unterstützen to sponsor OT 2

finanzieren to finance OT 4

finden to find OT 1; to locate **WS 4**, 140

Finger finger OT 1

Fingerabdruck fingerprint **WS 2**, 82

Fingernagel fingernail OT 2

Fingerspitze fingertip **WS 3**, 97

Fisch fish OT 1

Fischer fisherman OT 2

Fischerei fishing OT 3

Fischstäbchen fish finger OT 1

fit: sich fit halten to keep fit OT 2

Fitness fitness OT 5

Fitnesstraining workout OT 3

Flachland plain OT 4

Flagge standard **WS 1**, 13

Flaggschiff flagship OT 3

Flamingo flamingo OT 2

Flasche bottle OT 1

flauschig fluffy OT 2

Fleck patch OT 5

Fledermaus bat OT 1

Fleisch meat OT 1

Fleischklößchen meatball OT 1

flexibel flexible OT 5

Flexibilität flexibility **WS 1**, 37

Flicken patch OT 5

fliegen to fly OT 1

Fliese tile OT 2

fließend fluent OT 3; flowing OT 5; fluid **WS 3**, 110

Floh flea OT 5

Flora flora OT 4

florieren to prosper OT 2

Flotte fleet OT 3

Fluchtweg fire escape OT 5

Flug flight OT 1

Flugblatt handout OT 4

Flügel wing OT 2

Fluggesellschaft airline OT 5

Flughafen airport OT 1

Flugzeug plane OT 1; airplane OT 2; aeroplane OT 4

Fluss river OT 1; flow **WS 3**, 122

flussaufwärts upstream OT 3

flüssig liquid OT 2

Flußmündung delta **WS 2**, 67

flüstern to whisper **WS 1**, 19

Flut flood OT 2; flooding OT 5

Flyer flyer OT 4

fokusieren to focus OT 2

Folge consequence OT 4; sequel OT 4

Fortsetzung sequel OT 4

folgen to follow OT 2; to trace OT 3

folgenschwer momentous **WW**, 11

folgerichtig logical OT 5

folglich subsequently **WS 1**, 12

Folie slide OT 1; foil OT 2

Folklore folklore OT 5

fördern to promote OT 4; to nurture
WS 1, 12; to further WS 2, 62

Förderung grant OT 4

Forelle trout OT 4

Form form OT 1; shape OT 1

Format format OT 5

Formation formation OT 5

Formel formula OT 2

formell formal OT 3

formen to shape OT 4; to mold WS 3, 97;
to sculpt WS 3, 117

förmlich formal OT 3

Formular form OT 4

forschend exploratory WS 3, 122

Forscher(in) researcher OT 2;
explorer OT 3

Forschung research OT 2

Forstbeamter, Forstbeamtin park
ranger OT 2

Förster(in) ranger OT 3

Fortschreiten progression OT 5

fortschreiten to progress OT 5

Fortschritt advance OT 4; progress OT 4

fortschrittlich progressive OT 1

Forum forum OT 2; panel OT 4

fossil fossil OT 3

Foto photograph OT 1

Fotoapparat camera OT 1

Fotograf(in) photographer OT 2

Foul foul OT 3

foulen to foul OT 3

Fracht freight OT 2

Frachtkahn barge OT 3

fracken to frack OT 5

Frage question OT 1

Fragebogen questionnaire OT 1

fragen to ask OT 1; to question OT 4
sich fragen to wonder OT 4

fransig fringed WS 3, 94

französisch French OT 1

Frau Mrs, Ms OT 1; woman OT 1; wife OT 1
ihre Frau stehen to woman up
WS 2, 76
unverheiratete Frau maiden WS 1, 13

Fräulein Miss OT 2

frech cheeky OT 3

frei free OT 1
im Freien outdoor OT 2

Freiberufler(in) freelancer OT 5

freiberuflich freelance OT 5

Freiheit liberty OT 2; freedom OT 3

Freiheitsstrafe custodial sentence OT 5

Freitag Friday OT 1

freiwillig optional OT 4; voluntary OT 4
sich freiwillig melden to volunteer
OT 2

Freizeit leisure OT 3

Freizeit... recreational OT 3

fremd foreign OT 1

Fremde(r) stranger OT 3

Freude pleasure OT 1; happiness OT 5;
joy WS 1, 29
sich auf etwas freuen to look forward
to OT 1

Freund(in) friend OT 1

freundlich friendly OT 1; kind OT 1

Freundlichkeit friendliness OT 4

Frieden peace OT 3

Friedhof cemetery WS 2, 57

friedlich peaceful OT 3

frisch fresh OT 3

Frisur hairstyle WS 2, 68

Fritte chip OT 1

frittiert fried OT 2

froh glad OT 2

fröhlich cheerful OT 2

fromm religious OT 3

fruchtbar fertile WS 1, 34

früh early OT 1

früher previous OT 4

frühere(r) former OT 5

fröhlich joyful WS 3, 105

Frühling spring OT 2

Frühstück breakfast OT 1

Frühstücksflocken cereal OT 1

frustriert frustrated OT 4

Fuchs fox OT 1

sich fühlen to feel OT 1

führen to guide OT 1; to lead OT 3

führend leading OT 2

Führer(in) guide OT 1

Führung leadership OT 2

füllen to fill OT 1

Füllung stuffing OT 3

Fundament foundation OT 4; bedrock
WS 2, 82

fünf five OT 1

fünfzehn fifteen OT 1

fünfzig fifty OT 1

Funke spark OT 4

funkelnd shiny WS 3, 104

Funktion function OT 4

für for OT 1; in favour OT 4

Furcht fear OT 3

furchtbar horrible OT 2; dire WS 4, 140

fürchten to dread WS 1, 22

furchtlos fearless WS 1, 13; gallant
WS 1, 13

Fürsprecher(in) advocate (for) OT 5

Fürwort pronoun OT 1

Fuß foot OT 1; base OT 5

Fußabdruck footprint OT 2

Fußball football OT 1; soccer OT 2

Fußboden floor OT 1

Fussel fuzz OT 4

Fußknöchel ankle OT 1

Fußstapfen footstep OT 5

Fußweg footpath WS 1, 12

Füttern feeding OT 2

füttern to feed OT 2

G

Gabelstapler forklift OT 5

Gähnen yawn OT 2

Galerie gallery OT 1

Gallone gallon OT 3

Gamer(in) gamer OT 4

Gange: im Gange underway WS 3, 99

ganz whole OT 1; completely OT 4

ganze(r, -s) entire OT 3

ganztags full-time OT 5

Garage garage OT 4

garantieren to guarantee OT 4

Garderobe cloakroom OT 4

Garnele prawn OT 3

Garnison garrison WS 1, 25

Garten garden OT 1

Gartenarbeit gardening OT 1

Gärtner(in) gardener OT 4

Gas gas OT 4

Gaskocher gas cooker OT 3

Gasse lane OT 4

Gast guest OT 2

Gästebuch guestbook OT 2

Gastfreundlichkeit hospitality OT 2

Gastgeber(in) host OT 3

Gasthaus inn OT 2

Gebäude building OT 1

geben to give OT 1

Gebet prayer OT 4

Gebiet area OT 1; territory OT 4; trackt
WS 4, 138

gebildet sophisticated WS 4, 135

Gebildetsein literacy WS 3, 106

Gebirge mountain range OT 4

geboren: geboren sein to be born OT 2

Geborgenheit comfort WS 3, 111

gebraten roast OT 1

Gebrauch usage WS 4, 135

Gebühr fee OT 3

Geburt birth OT 2

Geburtsdatum date of birth OT 2

Geburtsort birthplace OT 4

Geburtstag birthday OT 1

Gebüsch bush OT 5

Gedächtnis memory OT 2

Gedanke thought OT 4

Gedicht poem OT 1

gedruckt printed OT 5

geeignet fit OT 2; suitable OT 4

Gefahr danger OT 2; threat OT 4;
risk OT 4

gefährden to threaten OT 4;
to endanger OT 5

gefährdet endangered OT 2; vulnerable
WS 2, 73

gefährlich dangerous OT 1; hazardous
OT 4; precarious **WS 3**, 109

Gefährte, Gefährtin fellow **WS 2**, 60

gefallen to appeal **WS 1**, 24

gefangen: gefangen nehmen to arrest
OT 4

Gefangene(r) captive **WS 2**, 54

Gefangenschaft captivity **WS 1**, 18

Gefängnis prison OT 4; jail **WS 2**, 60

Geflügel poultry OT 2

Gefrierschrank freezer OT 3

gefroren frozen OT 4

Gefühl feeling OT 2; emotion OT 5

gefühllos uncaring OT 5

gefühlvoll emotive **WS 1**, 24

gegen against OT 1; contrary to **WS 1**, 37;
versus **WS 2**, 58

Gegen... counter- **WS 2**, 75

Gegenargument counterargument
WS 1, 37

Gegenbewegung countermovement
WS 3, 114

Gegend area OT 1

Gegenmittel antidote **WS 2**, 69

Gegenreaktion backlash **WS 2**, 56

Gegensatz antithesis **WS 2**, 69

gegenseitig each other OT 3

Gegenstand object OT 1; item OT 3

Gegenteil opposite OT 1; contrast OT 3

Gegenüberstellung juxtaposition
WS 2, 76

Gegner(in) opponent OT 2

gehackt chopped OT 2

Gehalt wage OT 3; salary OT 5

Geheimnis secret OT 2; mystery OT 5

geheimnisvoll mythical **WS 1**, 17;
mysterious **WS 2**, 82; enigmatic
WS 2, 82; secretive **WS 3**, 96

gehen to go OT 1; to walk OT 1

Geheul howl OT 5

Gehirn brain OT 2

gehorchen to obey OT 3

nicht gehorchen to disobey OT 3

gehören to belong OT 2

zu etwas gehören to pertain to
WS 3, 94

Geige violin OT 1; fiddle **WS 1**, 26

Geist spirit OT 2; ghost OT 2

Geisteshaltung mentality **WS 2**, 56

Geisteswissenschaften humanities OT 4

geistig mental OT 4; spiritual **WS 2**, 60;
intellectual **WS 3**, 116

gekehrt: in sich gekehrt introverted
WS 3, 111

Gekritzel doodle **WS 4**, 142

gekünstelt stilted **WS 3**, 114

Gel gel OT 2

Gelände terrain **WS 1**, 15

Geländer rail OT 3

geländetauglich off-road OT 2

gelangweilt bored OT 1

gelb yellow OT 1

Geld money OT 1

Geldgeber(in) investor OT 4

Geldmittel fund OT 4

gelegen located OT 4; situated OT 4

Gelegenheit opportunity OT 2; occasion
OT 3

gelegentlich occasionally OT 4

geloben to pledge **WS 2**, 69

gemächlich ponderously OT 3

Gemälde painting OT 1

gemäß according to OT 4

Gemeindeland common OT 2

Gemeinschaft community OT 2

gemeinschaftlich collaborative
WS 3, 107

gemischt blended OT 5

gemischtgeschlechtlich co-ed,
co-educational OT 2

Gemüse vegetable OT 1; veggie OT 5

gemütlich leisurely **WS 1**, 25

genannt: zuvor genannt
aforementioned **WS 3**, 99

genau just OT 1; exact OT 2; accurate
OT 4; precisely **WS 3**, 114

genehmigen to approve OT 4;
to sanction **WS 2**, 79

Generalisierung generalization OT 5

Generation generation OT 3

generell general OT 4

genetisch genetic OT 5

genial brilliant OT 1

genießen to enjoy OT 1

Genre genre OT 5

genug enough OT 1

Genuss treat OT 5

Geocache geocache OT 2

Geocaching geocaching OT 2

Geografie geography OT 1

geografisch geographical OT 4

Geologie geology OT 2

Gepäck luggage OT 4; baggage **WS 3**, 105

Gepard cheetah OT 3

gerade straight OT 3; currently OT 4

Gerät appliance OT 3; device OT 3;
gadget OT 4

geräumig spacious **WS 1**, 25

Geräusch sound OT 1; noise OT 1

gerecht fair OT 1; righteous **WS 2**, 79

Gericht dish OT 2; court OT 4;
tribunal OT 5

geriffelt fluted **WS 2**, 55

gernhaben to like OT 1

gerontokratisch gerontocratic **WS 3**, 114

Gesamtliste tally OT 4

Gesamtmenge total OT 3

Gesang vocals OT 2

gesäumt lined **WS 1**, 35

Geschäft(e) business OT 3; deal OT 5;
transaction **WS 4**, 146

Geschäftsführer(in) manager OT 1;
Chief Executive Officer (CEO) OT 5

Geschäftsführung management OT 4

Geschäftsfrau, -mann businesswoman,
-man OT 4

geschehen to happen OT 1

Geschenk gift OT 1; blessing **WS 2**, 76

Geschichte history OT 1; story OT 1;
narrative **WS 2**, 56; saga **WS 2**, 69

Geschichtenbuch storybook OT 2

Geschichtenerzählen storytelling OT 4

Geschichtenerzähler(in) storyteller OT 2

geschichtlich historical OT 2

Geschick skill OT 1

geschickt skilled OT 4

Geschirr dishes OT 2

Geschirrspülen washing up OT 2

Geschlecht gender OT 4; sex OT 5

geschlechtslos genderless OT 5

geschlechtsneutral gender-neutral OT 5

geschlechtsspezifisch gendered OT 5

Geschlechtswort article OT 1

Geschmack taste OT 5

Geschöpf creature OT 5

Geschrei hue and cry **WS 1**, 35

Geschwindigkeit speed OT 2; rate OT 4;
pace **WS 1**, 29

Geschwister(kind) sibling OT 5

geschwollen swollen OT 2

gesellig sociable **WS 3**, 98

Gesellschaft society OT 3; organization OT 3; establishment **WS 2**, 63

gesellschaftlich social OT 3; societal **WS 3**, 112

Gesetz law OT 3; bill OT 4; act OT 5

gesetzgebend legislative OT 4

Gesetzgebung legislation **WS 1**, 17; legislature **WS 2**, 57

Gesicht face OT 1

Gesichts- facial OT 4

gespannt curious OT 4

Gespräch conversation OT 1

gesprächig chatty OT 5

Gesprächs... conversational OT 5

Geständnis confession **WS 2**, 58

Geste gesture OT 5

gestern yesterday OT 1

gestikulieren to gesticulate **WS 4**, 146

gestresst stressed OT 2

gesund healthy OT 2

Gesundheit health OT 3

Gesundheitsfürsorge healthcare OT 4

getragen solemn **WS 2**, 69

Getränk drink OT 1

Getreide crop OT 3; grain OT 5

getrennt separate OT 2; selective OT 4

getrocknet dried OT 3

Gewalt violence OT 4

gewaltig formidable **WS 1**, 12

gewaltlos nonviolent **WS 2**, 60

Gewaltlosigkeit nonviolence **WS 2**, 60

gewalttätig violent OT 5

Gewehr rifle **WS 2**, 64

gewerkschaftlich organisiert unionized **WS 3**, 114

Gewicht weight OT 2

Gewinn prize OT 1; profit OT 4

gewinnen to win OT 1

Gewinner(in) winner OT 1

Gewissen conscience **WS 2**, 65

Gewissheit certainty OT 4

Gewitter thunderstorm OT 2; rainstorm OT 5

gewöhnlich common OT 5; habitual **WS 2**, 68

gewunden winding OT 3

Gewürz spice OT 2; seasoning OT 2

gewürzt spicy OT 4

Giebel gable **WS 1**, 35

gießen to pour OT 1

giftig poisonous OT 5; toxic **WS 4**, 138

Gig gig OT 5

Gipfel peak OT 4; summit **WS 1**, 12

gipfeln to culminate **WS 2**, 58

Gips plaster OT 1

Giraffe giraffe OT 1

Gitarre guitar OT 1

Gitarrist(in) guitarist OT 4

Gladiator(in) gladiator OT 2

glamourös glamorous OT 4

glamouröses Zelten glamping OT 4

glänzen to beam **WS 1**, 13

glänzend shiny **WS 3**, 104

Glas glass OT 1

glatt slippery OT 3; smooth OT 4; slick **WS 3**, 93

Glaube faith OT 3; belief OT 3; ideology **WS 1**, 32; creed **WS 2**, 58

glauben to believe OT 2

gleich same OT 1; equal OT 4

gleichberechtigt equal OT 4

Gleichberechtigung equality OT 5

gleichgesinnt like-minded **WS 3**, 99

gleichgestellt par: on par **WS 3**, 107

gleichzeitig simultaneous OT 5

Gleitschirmfliegen paragliding OT 5

Gletscher glacier **WS 1**, 22

global global OT 4

Globalisierung globalization **WS 3**, 110

Globus globe OT 5

Glocke bell OT 1

glorreich glorious **WS 2**, 66

Glück luck OT 1; fortune OT 3; happiness OT 5

Glück haben to be lucky OT 3

zum Glück thankfully OT 5

glücklich happy OT 1; fortunate OT 3; lucky OT 4

glücklicherweise luckily OT 3

Glückwünsche congratulations OT 2

Glühbirne light bulb OT 4

glühen to glow **WS 1**, 35

glühend scorching OT 5

Gold gold OT 2

golden golden OT 2

Goldrausch gold rush OT 5

Golf golf OT 4

Golfer(in) golfer OT 4

Gott God OT 3

Gouverneur(in) governor OT 3

graben to dig OT 5

Grad degree OT 5

gradlinig straightforward **WS 1**, 32

Graduierten... postgraduate **WS 3**, 116

Grafiken graphics OT 3

Grafschaft county **WS 1**, 34

Gramm gram OT 2

Grammatik grammar OT 1

Granit granite **WS 1**, 22

Gras grass OT 1

grasen to graze **WS 1**, 36

Grasland grassland OT 4

Gräte fishbone **WS 4**, 142

gratulieren to congratulate OT 2

grau grey OT 1

grausam cruel OT 3

gravieren to engrave OT 4

greifen to grab OT 3; to grasp OT 5

Gremium panel OT 4

Grenze border OT 3; limit OT 4; boundary OT 4

grenzenlos limitless **WS 2**, 82

Grieche(-in) Greek OT 2

griesgrämig grouchy OT 2

Griff handle OT 2

in den Griff bekommen to get to grips **WS 3**, 97

Grillen barbecue OT 2

grinsen to grin OT 2

Grippe influenza OT 5

Grizzlybär grizzly OT 2

Grollen rumble **WS 2**, 53

groß big, tall, large OT 1; great OT 1; vast OT 4

großartig magnificent OT 5

Größe size OT 2

Großeltern grandparents OT 1

Großgrundbesitzertum landlordism **WS 1**, 17

Großmutter grandmother OT 1

Großvater grandfather OT 1

großzügig lavish **WS 1**, 26

Grube pit OT 5

grün green OT 1

Grund reason OT 1

Grund... basic OT 4

Grundbesitzer landlord **WS 1**, 19

gründen to found OT 4; to form OT 4; to establish OT 5

Grundlage basis OT 4; foundation OT 4

grundlegend radical OT 4

gründlich exhaustive **WS 3**, 114; in-depth **WS 4**, 135

grundsätzlich basic OT 4; fundamental **WS 2**, 62

Grundschule primary school OT 1; elementary school OT 2

Grunge grunge WW, 11

Grünland grassland OT 4

Grunzen grunt **WS 3**, 108

Gruppe group OT 1; cluster **WS 4**, 140

Gruppenfläche breakout area OT 5

gruppieren to group OT 4

gruselig creepy OT 5; spooky **WS 1**, 43

Gruß greeting OT 2

militärischer Gruß salute OT 3

mit freundlichen Grüßen sincerely OT 3

grüßen to greet OT 2; to hail OT 2

Gültigkeit validity WS 3, 116

Gummi rubber OT 1

günstig convenient OT 4

Gurke cucumber OT 1

gut good OT 1

gut aussehend handsome OT 1

gut gemacht well done OT 1

Gutacher(in) assessor WS 1, 16

Güte kindness WS 3, 95

Güter goods OT 3

Gutschein coupon OT 2; voucher WS 1, 25

Gymnastik gymnastics OT 1

H

Haare hair OT 1

Haarschnitt haircut OT 2

haben to have got OT 1; to feature OT 2

Habitat habitat OT 5

Hackbraten meat loaf OT 3

Hackfleischbällchen meatball OT 1

Hafen port OT 2; harbour OT 4

Haferbrei porridge OT 5

Haftnotiz sticky note OT 5

Hähnchen chicken OT 1

Hai shark OT 2

Häkchen tick OT 1

Haken tick OT 1; hook WS 2, 66

halb half OT 1; halfway OT 4

halb- semi- OT 3

halbieren to halve WS 4, 136

Halbinsel peninsula OT 5

halbwegs halfway OT 4

Halle hall OT 1

Hallo! hello OT 1

Halloween Halloween OT 2

Hals neck OT 1; throat OT 4

Halsband collar OT 2

Halskette necklace OT 3

Halt stop OT 1

halten to hold OT 1

Haltestelle halt OT 2

Haltung stance WS 2, 60

Hamburger burger OT 1

Hamster hamster OT 1

mit der Hand schreiben to handwrite OT 5

Hand hand OT 1

Handapparat handset OT 2

Handarbeit handicraft OT 4

Hand-Auge-Koordination hand-eye coordination WS 3, 98

Handbuch handbook OT 3; manual OT 3

Handel trade OT 5; commerce OT 5

handeln to trade OT 5

Handgelenk wrist OT 1

handgewebt handwoven WS 1, 17

handhaben to handle OT 4

Händler(in) merchant OT 3; trader WS 1, 21; retailer WS 3, 106

Handlung plot OT 3

Handout handout OT 4

Handschrift handwriting OT 2

Handschuh glove OT 1

Handtasche handbag OT 3

Handtuch towel OT 2

Handvoll handful OT 4

Handwerk handicraft OT 4; trade OT 4; craft OT 4

Handy mobile phone OT 1; cell phone OT 4

Hanf hemp WS 1, 20

Harpune harpoon OT 4

hart hard OT 2; tough OT 2

hassen to hate OT 1; to loath OT 5

Hasser(in) hater WS 2, 72

hässlich ugly OT 1; tacky WS 1, 27

Haufen heap OT 5

häufig frequent OT 3; common OT 5

Häufigkeit frequency OT 3

Haupt primary OT 1; main OT 1; core OT 4

Hauptfigur protagonist WS 1, 34

Hauptgang main course OT 1

Hauptpunkt gist WS 3, 122

Hauptrichtung mainstream WS 2, 66

hauptsächlich generally OT 4

Hauptstadt capital OT 1

Hauptverkehrszeit rush hour OT 1

Hauptwort noun OT 1

Haus house OT 1

Hausarbeit housework OT 1; chore OT 4

Hausaufgaben homework OT 1

Hausboot narrowboat OT 3

Häuschen cottage OT 3

Hausfrau housewife OT 5

Haushälter(in) housekeeper OT 3

Haushalts… household OT 4

Hausierer(in) peddler WS 2, 69

häuslich household OT 4

Hausmeister(in) caretaker OT 1

Haustier pet OT 1

Haut skin OT 2

heben to lift OT 3

heften to pin OT 1

heftig fiercely WS 1, 15

Heide heather WS 1, 15

Heidelandschaft moor OT 3

heil in one piece OT 2

Heilbad spa OT 2

heilen to cure WS 3, 117; to heal WS 3, 117

heilig sacred OT 4

Heilige(r) saint OT 3

Heilkraut herb OT 3

Heimat homeland OT 5

Heimweh homesickness OT 5

voll Heimweh homesick OT 2

heiraten to marry OT 1; to wed OT 3

heiß hot OT 1

heizen to heat OT 2

hektisch frantic OT 3; hectic OT 4

Held(in) hero OT 4

helfen to help OT 1

Helfer(in) helper OT 5

Helm helmet OT 1

Hemd shirt OT 1

Hemisphäre hemisphere OT 5

Henne hen OT 4

heraus out OT 1

sich herausbilden to crystallize WS 4, 141

herausfinden to find out OT 2

herausfließen to empty out OT 3

herausfordern to challenge OT 4

Herausforderung challenge OT 3

Herausgeber(in) editor OT 2

herausplatzen to blurt WS 1, 20

herausragend outstanding OT 3

Herbst autumn OT 2

Herd cooker OT 3

Herde herd OT 5

Herkunft provenance WS 4, 143

Herr Mr OT 1; lord OT 2

herrisch bossy OT 3

herrlich magnificent OT 5; glorious

herrschen to rule OT 2; to reign WS 2, 72

Herrscher(in) monarch OT 4

herstellen to manufacture OT 4

herumhängen to hang out OT 3

herumkriechen to scramble WS 1, 22

herumnörgeln to nag WW, 11

herumschweifen to roam OT 5

herunterladen to download OT 3

hervorstechen to stand out WS 3, 96

sich hervortun to excel OT 4

Herz heart OT 2

herzlich heartfelt WS 3, 101

heterosexuell heterosexual OT 5; straight OT 5

Heureka-Erlebnis eureka moment OT 4

heute today OT 1

   heute Abend tonight OT 1

heutzutage nowadays OT 3

hexagonal hexagonal **WS 1**, 39

Hexe witch OT 2

Hi-Fi-Anlage hi-fi OT 3

hier here OT 1

Highway highway OT 3

Hilfe relief OT 2; aid OT 5

hilfreich helpful OT 1

Himbeere raspberry OT 1

Himmel sky OT 1; heaven **WS 1**, 16

hinauf up OT 1

Hindernis obstacle OT 4

hinduistisch Hindu OT 1

hineinspringen to dive OT 3

hinfallen to fall over OT 2

hinrichten to execute OT 3

hinten at the back OT 3

   nach hinten backwards OT 3

hinter behind OT 1

   hinter der Bühne backstage OT 3

Hintergrund... background OT 3

Hinterhof backyard OT 5

Hinterland outback OT 5

hinterlassen to leave behind OT 2

hinüber across OT 1

hin und wieder occasionally OT 4

hinunter down OT 1

Hinweis tip OT 1; clue OT 1; prompt OT 3

hinzufügen to add OT 1

Hirsch deer OT 1

Hirschleder deerskin OT 3

Hirte, Hirtin herder OT 3

hispanisch Hispanic OT 3

Historiker(in) historian OT 2

historisch historic OT 2

Hit blockbuster **WS 1**, 17

Hitzewelle heatwave OT 5

Hobby hobby OT 1

hoch high OT 1; tall OT 1

hochhackig high-heeled OT 3

hochladen to upload OT 3

Hochschule college OT 2

höchst highly OT 4

höchste(r, -s) highest OT 1

Hochwasser flood OT 2

Hochzeit wedding **WS 1**, 26

hocken to huddle **WS 1**, 19

Hockey hockey OT 1

Hof farmyard OT 2

   kleiner Hof croft **WS 1**, 19

hoffen to hope OT 1

hoffentlich hopefully OT 3

hoffnungslos hopeless OT 4

hoffnungsvoll hopeful OT 4

höflich polite OT 1; gallant **WS 1**, 13

Höhe height OT 1

   in die Höhe schießen to skyrocket **WS 3**, 96

Höhepunkt high OT 1; climax **WS 2**, 64

Höhle cave OT 3

Hölle hell OT 5

Hologramm hologram OT 2

holprig bumpy OT 4

Holz wood OT 2

hölzern wooden OT 2

Holzhacken wood cutting OT 2

Holzscheit log OT 3

Honig honey OT 2

Hookline hook **WS 2**, 66

hören to listen OT 1; to hear OT 1

Hörer(in) listener OT 3

Horizont horizon OT 5

horizontal horizontal OT 5

Hormon hormone OT 5

Horn horn OT 3

Horror horror OT 4

Hose trousers OT 2; pants OT 5

   kurze Hosen shorts OT 3

hospitieren: bei jdm hospitieren to shadow sb OT 5

Hotel hotel OT 1

Hotline helpline OT 2

hübsch pretty OT 1; lovely OT 1

Hüfte hip OT 1

Hügel hill OT 1

Huhn chicken OT 1; hen OT 4

Hülsenfrucht pulse OT 4

humid humid OT 4

Humor humour OT 4

Hund dog OT 1

hundert hundred OT 1

Hunger hunger OT 3

hungern (lassen) to starve OT 1

Hungersnot famine OT 2

hungrig hungry OT 1

Hupe horn OT 3

Hurrikan hurricane OT 4

Hut hat OT 1

Hütehund sheepdog OT 2

Hüter(in) keeper OT 4

Hymne anthem OT 5

hyperaktiv hyperactive OT 5

Hypothek mortgage OT 4

I

ich me OT 1

   (ich) selbst myself OT 3

ideal ideal OT 4

Idee idea OT 1; notion **WS 3**, 101

identifizieren to identify OT 4

Identifizierung identification **WS 2**, 56

identisch identical **WS 3**, 122

Identität identity OT 3

Ideologie ideology **WS 1**, 32

Idiot(in) fool **WS 3**, 105

Idol idol OT 5

Igel hedgehog OT 1

Igitt! yuck OT 3

Iglu igloo OT 4

ignorieren to ignore OT 4

ihm, ihn him OT 1

ihre(r, -s) hers OT 3; theirs OT 3

ikonisch iconic OT 3

illegal illegal OT 3

Illustration illustration OT 2

illustrieren to illustrate OT 4

Imageberater(in) spin master **WS 2**, 69

immer always OT 1; permanently OT 3

   für immer forever OT 2

   immer noch still OT 1

Immobilie property OT 4

immun immune **WS 3**, 113

Imperativ imperative OT 1

Impuls impulse **WS 1**, 21

impulsiv impulsive **WS 4**, 135

in in, on, at OT 1

inakzeptabel unacceptable OT 5

Indikator indicator **WS 3**, 94

Individualisierung individuation **WS 3**, 122

Individualismus individualism **WS 2**, 69

individuell individual OT 3

Industrie industry OT 2

Industrie... industrial OT 2

Infinitiv infinitive OT 1

Influencer(in) influencer OT 5

Influenza influenza OT 5

Infografik infographic OT 3

Informatikunterricht ICT (information and communications technology) OT 1

Informationen information OT 1

   Informations- und Kommunikationstechnologie ICT (information and communications technology) OT 1

informativ informative OT 4

informell informal OT 5

informieren to inform OT 4; to brief **WS 1**, 38

Infrastruktur infrastructure OT 4

Ingenieur(in) engineer OT 2

Ingenieurwesen engineering OT 2

Ingwer ginger OT 1

Inhalt content(s) OT 2

Initiative initiative OT 4
initiieren to initiate **WS 2**, 71
Inklusion inclusion **WS 3**, 112
Inklusivität inclusiveness **WS 3**, 95
Inkubator incubator OT 5
Innen… indoor OT 2
Innenstadt downtown OT 4
Innere: das Innere interior OT 5
innerhalb inside OT 1; within OT 4
Innovation innovation OT 4
innovativ innovative OT 4
Innovator(in) innovator OT 4
innovieren to innovate OT 4
inoffiziell unofficial OT 5
Inschrift inscription **WS 2**, 55
Insekt insect OT 2
Insel island OT 1
insgesamt collectively **WS 2**, 67
Inspiration inspiration OT 4
inspirieren to inspire OT 4
instabil insecure OT 5
Installation installation OT 4
installieren to install OT 3
instinktiv instinctive **WS 3**, 105
instruieren to brief **WS 1**, 38
instruktiv instructive OT 5
Instrument instrument OT 1
instrumentell instrumental **WS 2**, 56
Insulaner(in) islander OT 4
inszenieren to stage **WS 2**, 53
Inszenierung production OT 5
Integration integration OT 5
integrativ inclusive OT 4
integrieren to integrate OT 4;
    to incorporate **WS 1**, 34
integrieren to incorporate **WS 1**, 34
intellektuell intellectual **WS 3**, 116
intelligent clever OT 2; intelligent OT 3
Intelligenz intelligence OT 4
    künstliche Intelligenz AI, artificial
        intelligence **WS 3**, 99
interagieren to interact OT 4
Interaktion interaction OT 4
interaktiv interactive OT 4
interessant interesting OT 1
Interesse interest OT 1
    persönliches Interesse vested
        interest **WS 3**, 116
Interessengemeinschaft constituency
    OT 4
interessiert interested OT 1
international international OT 1
Internet internet OT 3
interpersonell interpersonal OT 5
Interpretation interpretation **WS 3**, 122

interpretieren to interpret OT 4
Interview interview OT 1
interviewen to interview OT 1
Interviewer(in) interviewer OT 5
Interviewte(r) interviewee OT 3
intolerant intolerant OT 5
Intonation intonation OT 5
invasiv invasive OT 5
investieren to invest OT 4
Investition investment OT 4
Investor(in) investor OT 4
inzwischen meanwhile OT 5
irgendein(e) any OT 1
irgend etwas anything OT 1
irgend jemand anybody OT 1;
    anyone OT 1
irgendwann sometime OT 3;
    someday OT 5
irgendwie somehow OT 4
irgendwie somewhat **WS 1**, 27
irgendwo somewhere OT 1;
    anywhere OT 1
irisch Irish OT 1
Ironie irony **WS 2**, 64
irrational irrational **WS 4**, 146
Irrgarten maze OT 3
Isolation isolation **WS 3**, 111
isoliert isolated **WS 1**, 28
ist nicht ain't **WS 2**, 76
italienisch Italian OT 2

J
ja aye OT 2
Jacht yacht OT 5
Jacke jacket OT 1
jagen to hunt OT 2; to chase OT 2
Jäger(in) hunter OT 3
    Jäger und Sammler hunter-gatherer
        OT 5
Jahr year OT 1
Jahrbuch yearbook OT 4
Jahreszeit season OT 2
Jahrgang cohort **WS 1**, 32
Jahrhundert century OT 2
jährlich annual OT 5
Jahrmarkt fairground OT 2; fair OT 2
Jahrzehnt decade OT 4
Jakobsmuschel scallop **WS 1**, 12
Jammern wail **WS 1**, 12
japanisch Japanese OT 1
Jazz jazz OT 2
je ever OT 1; per OT 4
Jeansstoff denim **WS 3**, 101
jede(r, -s) every OT 1; each OT 1;
    everyone, everybody OT 1

jederzeit anytime OT 3
jedoch though OT 2; however
jemand someone OT 1; somebody
    OT 1
jetzt now OT 1
Job job OT 1
Joghurt yoghurt OT 1
Journal journal OT 3
Journalismus journalism OT 4
Journalist(in) journalist OT 2
jubeln to cheer up OT 1
jucken to itch OT 2
juckend itchy OT 2
Judo judo OT 1
Jugend youth OT 2
    Jugend(alter) adolescence **WS 3**, 94
Jugend… adolescent OT 5
Jugendbetreuer(in) counselor OT 2
Jugendherberge youth hostel OT 2
Jugendliche(r) adolescent OT 5;
    youngster OT 5
Juli July OT 1
jung young OT 1
Junge boy OT 1
Junge(s) cub OT 2
Junior(in) junior OT 2
Jury jury **WS 2**, 63
Justiz justice OT 5
Justiz… judicial OT 4

K
Kabarett cabaret **WS 1**, 43
Kabel cable OT 3
Kabine cabin OT 2; booth **WS 1**, 32
Kabinett cabinet OT 5
Kabinettsminister(in) cabinet minister
    OT 4
Kaffee coffee OT 1
Käfig cage OT 5
kahl bald OT 3; bare **WS 1**, 13
Kai pier OT 5
Kaiser emperor OT 2
Kajak kayak OT 4
Kakao cocoa OT 4
Kaktus cactus OT 4
Kalender calendar OT 1
Kalkulation calculation **WS 1**, 36
Kalorie calorie OT 5
kalt cold OT 1; freezing OT 2
kaltblütig cold-blooded **WS 1**, 18
Kamel camel OT 5
Kamera camera OT 1
Kameramann cameraman OT 5
Kamin fireplace OT 1
Kamm comb OT 2

Kammer chamber OT 2
Kammmuschel scallop WS 1, 12
Kampagne campaign OT 3; initiative OT 4
Kampf fight OT 1
kämpfen (um) to fight OT 1; to campaign (for) OT 5
Kämpfer(in) fighter OT 2
Kanal canal OT 3; channel OT 3
Kanarienvogel canary OT 2
Kandidat(in) candidate OT 4; nominee WS 2, 79
Känguru kangaroo OT 3
Kaninchen rabbit OT 1
Kantine canteen OT 1
Kanu canoe OT 2
Kapitalist(in) capitalist WS 2, 63
Kapitel chapter OT 1
Kapitol capitol WS 2, 56
kaputt busted OT 4
Kapuzenpullover hoodie OT 1
Karate karate WS 1, 37
Karibu caribou OT 4
Karneval carnival OT 4
Karotte carrot OT 1
Karre barrow OT 4
Karriere career OT 3
Karte card OT 1
Karteikarte file card OT 2
Kartoffel potato OT 1
Kartoffelbrei mashed potato OT 1
Kartoffelchip crisp OT 1
Karussell carousel WS 1, 29
Käse cheese OT 1
kaskadierend cascading WS 4, 138
Kasse register OT 2; check-out OT 4
Kassierer(in) cashier OT 4
katastrophal catastrophic WS 1, 36
Katastrophe disaster OT 2
Kate croft WS 1, 19
Kategorie category OT 3
Kathedrale cathedral OT 1
Katholik(in) Catholic OT 3
katholisch Catholic OT 3
Katze cat OT 1
Katzenhai catshark WS 1, 12
kaufen to shop OT 1; to buy OT 1; to purchase WS 3, 104
Käufer(in) shopper OT 4; buyer OT 5
Kaufhaus department store OT 4
kaum hardly OT 4; barely WS 2, 82
Kavallerie cavalry OT 3
Kehle throat OT 4
keine(r, -s) none OT 3
Keks biscuit OT 1; cookie (AE) OT 3

Kellner(in) waiter OT 1; server (AE) OT 3
Keltisch Celtic OT 2
kennen to know OT 1
kennenlernen to come to know OT 5
kenntnisreich knowledgeable OT 3
kennzeichnen to characterize WS 2, 67
Kerl guy OT 5; lad OT 5
Kern core OT 4
Kernpunkt nub WS 3, 101
Kerze candle OT 2
Kerzenlicht candlelight OT 4
Kessel kettle OT 2
Ketchup ketchup OT 3
Kette chain OT 3
Keulen cull OT 5
keulen to cull OT 5
Keyboard keyboard OT 1
KI AI, artificial intelligence WS 3, 99
Kidneybohne kidney bean OT 2
Kiefernholz pinewood WS 1, 22
Kilo kilo OT 2
Kilometer kilometre OT 1
Kilt kilt OT 2
Kind child OT 1; kid OT 1
Kindergarten nursery OT 5
Kindertagesstätte nursery OT 5
Kindheit childhood OT 3; infancy WS 3, 96
kindisch childish OT 3
Kino cinema OT 1
Kiosk tuck shop OT 5
kippen to topple WS 2, 56
Kirche church OT 1
Kirchturm spire WS 1, 35
Kirsche cherry OT 4
Kissen cushion OT 1
Kiste box OT 1; crate OT 4
kitschig tacky WS 1, 27
Kiwi kiwi OT 1
Klagelaut wail WS 1, 12
Klagen wail WS 1, 12
Klammer bracket OT 2
Klaps pat OT 3
klar clear OT 2
klären to clarify OT 4; to sort out OT 4
Klarinette clarinet OT 2
Klasse class OT 1
Klassenkamerad(in) classmate OT 3
Klassenstufe grade OT 2
Klassenzimmer classroom OT 1
klassisch classic OT 2; classical OT 2; vintage OT 5
klatschen to clap OT 1
klauen to steal OT 2
Klavier piano OT 1

kleben to stick OT 1; to paste OT 2
Klebstoff glue OT 1
Kleid dress OT 5
Kleider clothes OT 1
Kleiderschrank wardrobe OT 1
Kleidung clothes OT 1; clothing OT 4
klein small OT 1; little OT 1; mini WS 2, 55
klein scheinen lassen to dwarf WS 2, 55
Kleinbus minibus OT 2
Kleingeld cash OT 1
Kleinholz kindling OT 2
klemmen an to clip to OT 5
Kletterer(in) climber OT 2
klettern to climb OT 1
klicken to click OT 3
Klima climate OT 2
Klingel doorbell OT 2
klingeln to ring OT 1
klingen to sound OT 4
Klinik clinic OT 5
Klippe cliff OT 5
Klischee stereotype OT 5
Klo loo OT 2
klopfen to knock OT 2
Kloster abbey WS 1, 17
klug smart OT 4; savvy OT 5; wise WW, 11
Kneipe pub OT 2
Knie knee OT 1
Kniehose breeches OT 3
knien to kneel WS 2, 70
Knirschen crunch WS 1, 37
Knöchel ankle OT 1
Knochen bone OT 1
Knopf button OT 1
knuddelig cuddly OT 3
Koala koala OT 5
Koch, Köchin chef OT 1
köcheln to simmer OT 2
Kochen cooking OT 1; cookery OT 2
kochen to cook OT 1; to boil OT 1; to make OT 1
Kochfeld hob OT 3
ködern to entice WS 3, 114
kodieren to code OT 5
Koffein caffeine OT 5
Kofferraum trunk OT 2
Kohl cabbage OT 1
Kohle coal OT 2
Kohlendioxid carbon dioxide OT 3
Kohlenhydrat carbohydrate OT 5
kohlensäurehaltig fizzy OT 2
Kohlenstoff carbon OT 4
Kohorte cohort WS 3, 99
Kojote coyote OT 5

Kollaboration collaboration OT 4
Kollege, Kollegin colleague OT 4;
   counterpart OT 5
kolonial colonial OT 3
Kolonialisierung colonization OT 5
Kolonialismus colonialism OT 5
Kolonie colony OT 3
kolonisieren to colonize OT 3
Kolonist(in) colonist OT 4
Kombination combination OT 4
kombinieren to combine OT 4
Kombüse galley OT 3
Komitee committee OT 4
Komma comma OT 3
Kommandant(in) commander OT 2
kommen to come OT 1
   von etwas kommen to stem from
     WS 1, 17
Kommentator(in) commentator
   WS 2, 69
kommentieren to comment OT 3;
   to annotate **WS 2**, 65
Kommerz commerce OT 5
kommerziell commercial OT 4
Kommission committee OT 4;
   commission **WS 2**, 65
Kommode chest of drawers OT 1
Kommunikation communication OT 1
kommunizieren to communicate OT 4
Komödie comedy OT 4
Komparativ comparative OT 2
Kompass compass OT 2
kompatibel compatible OT 5
kompetent competent OT 4
Kompetenz proficiency OT 4;
   competency **WS 3**, 107
komplett completely OT 4
Komplex complex OT 4
Kompliment compliment OT 3
kompliziert complicated OT 3; tricky
   OT 4
komponieren to compose OT 3
Komponist(in) composer OT 2
Kompost compost OT 3
Kompostierungs- composting OT 4
Kompromiss compromise **WS 2**, 54
Konferenz conference OT 3
Konflikt conflict OT 4
Konformität conformity **WS 3**, 95
konfrontieren to confront **WS 1**, 20
Kongress congress **WS 2**, 54
König king OT 1
Königin queen OT 1
königlich royal OT 1; regal **WS 2**, 76
Konjunktion conjunction OT 2

konkret specific OT 2
Konkurrent(in) competitor OT 4
Konkurrenz competition OT 1; rivalry
   OT 5
konkurrenzorientiert competitive OT 3
konkurrieren to compete OT 2
konkurrierend competitively OT 4
können can OT 1; to be able OT 2
Konnotation connotation **WS 3**, 110
konnte could OT 1
könnte(n) could OT 1; might OT 2
konsequent consistent OT 5
Konsequenz consequence OT 4
konservativ conservative **WS 1**, 31
Konsonant consonant OT 1
konstant constantly OT 4
konstitutionell constitutional OT 4
konstruktiv constructive **WS 1**, 23
konsumieren to consume OT 4
Kontakt contact OT 1
   Kontakte pflegen to socialize OT 4
   in Kontakt in touch OT 2
kontaktfreudig outgoing OT 4; sociable
   WS 3, 98
kontaktieren to contact OT 2
kontaminieren to contaminate OT 5
Kontext context OT 4
Kontinent continent OT 5
kontinuierlich continuous OT 4
Konto account OT 3
Kontostand bank balance **WS 3**, 104
Kontrabass double bass OT 2
Kontrast contrast OT 3
kontrastieren to contrast OT 4
Kontrolle control OT 2
kontrollieren to control OT 4;
   to monitor **WS 4**, 135
Kontroverse controversy OT 4
Konvention convention **WS 1**, 21
konvertieren to convert **WS 2**, 61
sich konzentrieren to concentrate OT 3;
   to focus on OT 5
Konzept concept OT 4
Konzert concert OT 1
Kooperation partnership OT 4
Kopf head OT 1
Kopfball header OT 3
köpfen to behead OT 3
Kopfhörer headphones OT 2; headset
   OT 5
Kopfkissen pillow OT 2
Kopfkissenbezug pillowcase OT 3
Kopfsalat lettuce OT 2
Kopfschmerzen headache OT 1
kopfüber headfirst **WS 3**, 119

Kopie replica OT 4
kopieren to copy OT 1
Korallen... coral **WS 1**, 12
Korb basket OT 4
Kordel lanyard OT 5
koreanisch Korean OT 1
Körper body OT 1
Körperhaltung posture OT 4
körperlich physical OT 2
   körperliche Bewegung exercise OT 1
Körperverletzung: (schwere)
   Körperverletzung aggravated assault
   OT 5
korrekt valid **WS 2**, 68
Korrektur correction OT 4
Korrespondent(in) correspondent OT 4
Korridor corridor OT 2
korrigieren to correct OT 1
Korruption corruption **WS 2**, 60
Korsett corset OT 3
Kosten cost OT 1; expense OT 4
kosten to cost OT 1
kostenlos free OT 1; complimentary
   WS 1, 25
Kostüm costume OT 2
krabbeln to crawl OT 5
Krabbeltier creepy-crawly OT 2
Kraft force OT 2; power OT 4
   unbändige Kraft juggernaut **WS 1**, 31
kräftig sturdy **WS 4**, 142
kraftvoll vigorous **WS 1**, 37
Kraftzentrum powerhouse **WS 3**, 119
Krähe crow OT 3
Krampf cramp OT 2
krank sick OT 1; ill OT 2
Krankenhaus hospital OT 1
Krankenpflege nursing OT 5
Krankenpfleger(in) nurse OT 1
Krankenschwester nurse OT 1
Krankenwagen ambulance OT 1
Krankheit disease OT 2; illness OT 2
Kranz wreath OT 3
Krapfen doughnut OT 2
krass wicked OT 2; stark **WS 2**, 83
kratzen to scrape OT 2; to scratch OT 2
kraus frizzy OT 3
Kräuselung ripple **WW**, 11
Kraut herb OT 3
Krawatte tie OT 1
kreativ creative OT 2
Kreativität creativity OT 3
Krebs cancer **WS 3**, 117
Kreditkarte credit card OT 1
kreieren to create OT 2
Kreis circle OT 2

Kreuzfahrtschiff cruise ship OT 2
Kreuzung intersection **WS 2**, 82
Kricket cricket OT 1
kriechen to crawl OT 5
Krieg war OT 2
Krieger(in) warrior OT 2
kriegerisch martial **WS 1**, 37
Kriegsschiff warship OT 3
Kriegszeit wartime OT 3
Krimi thriller **WS 2**, 53
Kriminelle(r) criminal OT 3
Krise crisis OT 4
Kriterium criterion OT 5
Kritik criticism OT 3; review OT 5
Kritiker(in) critic OT 5
kritisch critical OT 4
kritisieren to criticize OT 3
Krone crown OT 1
krönen to crown OT 1
Kronleuchter chandelier OT 2
Krönung coronation OT 3
Krücke crutch OT 2
Küche kitchen OT 1; cuisine OT 3
Kuchen cake OT 1
Küchenchef(in) chef OT 1
Kugel bullet OT 2
Kuh cow OT 1
kühl cool OT 1; chilly **WS 2**, 59
Kühlschrank fridge OT 1
Kühlsystem cooling system OT 3
Kühnheit audacity **WS 2**, 69
kulminieren to culminate **WS 2**, 58
Kult... iconic OT 3
kultiviert civilized OT 5
Kultur culture OT 1
kulturell cultural OT 4
Kummer heartbreak **WS 2**, 58
Kumpel buddy OT 2; mate OT 4
Kunde, Kundin customer OT 2; client OT 5
Kundgebung rally **WS 2**, 61
kündigen to quit OT 5
Kundschafter(in) scout OT 3
Kunst art OT 1
Kunsthandwerk craft OT 4
Kunsthandwerker(in) artisan **WS 2**, 54
Künstler(in) artist OT 1
künstlerisch artistic **WS 1**, 18
künstlich artificial OT 4; synthetic **WS 3**, 104
   künstliche Intelligenz artificial intelligence OT 5
künstlich synthetic **WS 3**, 104
Kuppel dome OT 4
Kürbis pumpkin OT 2

Kurier(in) courier OT 2
Kurs program OT 3; course OT 3
kursieren to circulate OT 4
kurz short OT 1; brief OT 3
kürzen to shorten OT 4
Kurzform shorthand **WS 3**, 96
Kuss kiss OT 2
Küste coastline OT 5
Küste coast OT 1; shore OT 2; shoreline OT 4
Küsten... coastal OT 4
Küstenlinie coastline OT 5
küstennah offshore **WS 1**, 12
Küstenwache coastguard OT 2

L

Labor lab OT 4
Lache pool OT 1
lächeln to smile OT 1
lachen to laugh OT 1
Lachnummer laughing stock **WS 3**, 113
Lachs salmon OT 1
Lacrosse lacrosse OT 4
Laden shop OT 1
Ladendiebstahl shoplifting OT 5
Ladesymbol loader **WS 4**, 135
Ladung cargo OT 3
Lage situation OT 1; circumstance OT 5
Lagerfeuer campfire OT 2
Lagerung storage OT 3
Lamm lamb OT 2
Lampe lamp OT 1
Land country OT 1; countryside OT 1; land OT 2
Landbesitzer(in) landowner **WS 1**, 35
Landebahn runway **WS 1**, 38
landen to land OT 2
(Landes-)Sprache vernacular **WS 2**, 68
Landform landform **WS 1**, 22
Landkarte map OT 1
ländlich rural **WS 1**, 26
Landschaft landscape OT 2; scenery OT 2; landform **WS 1**, 22
Landstrasse highway OT 3
Landwirtschaft farming OT 2; agriculture OT 2
landwirtschaftlich agrarian OT 5
lang long OT 1
Länge length OT 3
Langlaufen cross-country skiing OT 5
langsam slow OT 2
langweilen to bore **WS 2**, 69
langweilig boring OT 1; dull **WS 1**, 16
Laptop laptop OT 3
Lärm noise OT 1

lassen to let OT 1
lässig casual OT 5
Last burden OT 3
Lastzug juggernaut **WS 1**, 31
Latein Latin OT 2
lateinamerikanisch Latino OT 2
Laterne lantern OT 2
Laufen running OT 1
laufen to walk OT 1; to run OT 1
laufend continuous OT 4
Läufer(in) runner OT 2
launisch moody OT 5
laut loud OT 1; noisy OT 1; aloud OT 2
   laut rufen to shout OT 1
Lautsprecher loudspeaker OT 2
Lautstärke volume OT 3
Lava lava OT 5
Leben life OT 1
   Leben nach dem Tod afterlife OT 5
leben to live OT 1
lebendig alive OT 2; spirited **WS 1**, 17
lebensbedrohlich life-threatening OT 2
Lebensdauer lifetime OT 3
lebenslang lifelong **WS 1**, 21
Lebenslauf CV (curriculum vitae) OT 4
Lebensmittel grocery OT 4
Lebensmittelsammelstelle food bank OT 5
Lebensmittelvergiftung food poisoning OT 2
Lebensstil lifestyle OT 4
lebenswichtig vital OT 3
Lebenszeit lifetime OT 3
Leber liver OT 5
Lebewesen creature OT 5
lebhaft lively OT 2; vibrant OT 5
lecker delicious OT 1; yummy OT 5
Leder leather OT 3
leer empty OT 1; blank OT 4
legal legal OT 3
legalisieren to legalize OT 5
Legasthenie dyslexia OT 5
legasthenisch dyslexic OT 5
legendär legendary **WS 1**, 16
Legende legend OT 4; myth OT 4
Legion legion OT 2
Legislative legislative OT 4; legislature **WS 2**, 57
lehnen to lean OT 3
Lehrbuch textbook OT 3
Lehrer(in) teacher OT 1; instructor OT 2
Lehrling apprentice OT 5
Lehrplan curriculum OT 4
lehrreich instructive OT 5

Lehrstelle apprenticeship OT 5

leicht easy OT 1; lightly **WS 1**, 32

Leichtathletik athletics OT 1

Leid distress **WS 3**, 112

leiden to suffer OT 4

Leidenschaft passion OT 5; fervour **WS 2**, 58

leidenschaftlich keen OT 2; passionate OT 4; ardent **WS 1**, 32

leider unfortunately OT 2

leihen to lend OT 2

Leihgabe loan OT 4

Leinen canvas OT 3; linen OT 3

Leinwand screen OT 1

sich leisten to afford OT 2

Leistung merit OT 5

Leistungen attainment OT 5

leiten to run OT 1; to manage OT 1; to guide OT 1

Leiter ladder OT 3

Leiter(in) manager OT 1; leader OT 2; director OT 2; supervisor OT 5

Leitung pipe OT 4

lernen to learn OT 1

Lernende(r) learner OT 3

Lernprogramm tutorial OT 4

Lesbe lesbian OT 5

Lesekompetenz literacy **WS 3**, 106

lesen to read OT 1

Leser(in) reader OT 2

letzte(r, -s) last OT 1; last OT 2

leuchtend bright OT 1

leugnen deny OT 4

Leute people OT 1; folks OT 2; guys OT 2

Leutnant lieutenant **WS 2**, 69

Lexikon encyclopedia OT 4

liberal liberal **WS 2**, 69

Licht light OT 1

ans Licht kommen to emerge OT 3

Lichtung clearing **WS 1**, 16

lieben to love OT 1

Liebes sweetheart OT 5

Liebesgeschichte romance **WS 1**, 34

liebevoll affectionate **WS 2**, 82

Liebhaber(in) enthusiast **WS 3**, 101

Lieblings... favourite OT 1

Liebste(r) sweetheart OT 5

Lied song OT 1

Liedtext lyrics **WS 1**, 13

liefern to deliver OT 3

Lieferung supply OT 3

Lieferwagen van OT 2

liegen to lie OT 1

Liegestütze plank **WS 1**, 37

Lifestyle lifestyle OT 4

Lift lift OT 3

Liga league OT 2

lila purple **WS 1**, 13

Limo soda OT 5

lindern to alleviate OT 5

Lineal ruler OT 1

Linguist(in) linguist OT 5

Linguistik linguistics OT 5

Linie line OT 1

Linse lens OT 2

Lippe lip OT 2

Liste list OT 1

listen to list OT 5

Liter litre OT 4

literarisch literary **WS 2**, 64

Lizenzgebühr royalty **WS 2**, 66

LKW truck OT 1

loben to compliment OT 3; to praise OT 4

Loch hole OT 1; loch **WS 1**, 12

locken to tempt OT 4; to entice **WS 3**, 114

locker casual OT 5

Löffel spoon OT 2

Logbuch logbook **WS 1**, 23

logisch logical OT 4

Logline logline OT 4

Logo logo OT 1

Lohn salary OT 5

lohnend worthwhile OT 2; rewarding OT 5

Lohngefälle pay gap OT 5

lokalisieren to localize **WS 3**, 114

Lokführer(in) engineer OT 2

Lokomotive engine OT 2

löschen to delete **WS 4**, 141

lösen to solve OT 4

(sich) lösen to sheer off OT 3

loshasten to rush off OT 2

Lösung solution OT 3

loswerden to get rid of OT 3

Löwe lion OT 1

Loyalität loyalty OT 5

Luchs lynx OT 2

Lücke gap OT 1

lückenhaft patchy OT 4

Luft air OT 2

Luftfahrt aerospace OT 4

Lumpen rag **WS 2**, 82

Lunchpaket packed lunch OT 1

Lunge lung OT 3

Lupe magnifying glass OT 2

lustig funny OT 1

luxuriös luxurious OT 2

M

machen to do OT 1; to make OT 1; to render **WS 4**, 138

machen to render **WS 4**, 138

selbst gemacht homemade OT 1

Macht power OT 4

mächtig powerful OT 2

Mädchen girl OT 1

Magen stomach OT 1

mager lean OT 5; skinny OT 5

magisch magical OT 2

Magnet magnet OT 4

magnetisch magnetic OT 2

mähen to mow OT 5

Mahlzeit meal OT 1

Maid (altmodisch) maiden **WS 1**, 13

Mailbox mailbox OT 4

Mainstream mainstream **WS 2**, 66

Mais corn OT 3

Maisscheune corn crib **WS 2**, 64

majestätisch majestic OT 4; regal **WS 2**, 76

mal times OT 5

Malaria malaria OT 5

malen to paint OT 1

malerisch picturesque OT 4

man you OT 1

Management management OT 4

managen to manage OT 1

Manager(in) manager OT 1

manchmal sometimes OT 1

Mandant(in) client OT 5

Mandat mandate **WS 1**, 30

Mandel almond **WS 1**, 24

Mangel lack OT 3; shortage OT 5; absence **WS 3**, 105; deficit **WS 3**, 105

Manifest manifesto OT 4

manipulieren to manipulate **WS 2**, 73

Mann man OT 1; husband OT 2

seinen Mann stehen to man up **WS 2**, 76

männlich male OT 2

Mannschaft team OT 1; crew OT 2

Manschaftskollege(-in) teammate OT 2

Mantel coat OT 2

Marathon marathon OT 2

Märchen fairy tale OT 1

marginalisieren to marginalize **WS 2**, 68

Marine navy OT 3

Marineoffizier(in) naval officer **WS 2**, 69

Marke brand OT 5

Marketing marketing OT 5

markieren to bookmark OT 4

Markierung marker OT 1

Markt market OT 1

   auf den Markt bringen to release OT 4; to launch OT 4

Marmelade jam OT 1

Marsch march OT 5

marschieren to march OT 4

Marschierer(in) marcher **WS 2**, 53

martialisch martial **WS 1**, 37

Maschine machine OT 2

   Maschinen machinery OT 2

Masern measles OT 5

Maske mask OT 3

Maskottchen mascot OT 2

Maß measurement OT 2

Massage massage OT 2

Massaker massacre OT 5

Masse mass OT 5

Maßeinheit measurement OT 2

Massen... mass OT 4

massiv solid OT 4

maßlos decadent **WS 2**, 63

Maßnahme measure OT 5; provision OT 5

Maßstab scale OT 2

maßvoll moderate **WS 1**, 36

Material material OT 4

Mathematik maths OT 1

Matratze mattress OT 4

matschig muddy OT 4; boggy **WS 1**, 16

Maultier mule OT 3

Maus mouse OT 1

Maximum maximum OT 2

Mayonnaise mayonnaise OT 1

MBA MBA (Masters of Business Administration) OT 5

mechanisch mechanical OT 5

Medaille medal OT 2

Median median OT 5

Medium medium OT 2

   soziale Medien social media OT 2

Medizin medicine OT 5

medizinisch medical OT 2

Meer sea OT 1

Meeres... marine OT 5

Meeresboden seabed OT 3

Meeresfrüchte shellfish OT 3; seafood OT 4

Meeresgrund seafloor **WS 4**, 135

Meeresküste seaside OT 3

Mehl flour OT 2

mehr more OT 1

   nicht mehr anymore OT 4

Mehrheit majority OT 4

Mehrzahl plural OT 1

Meile (etwa 1,6 km) mile OT 1

Meilenstein milestone OT 3

mein my, mine OT 1

meinen to deem **WS 3**, 93

Meinung opinion OT 3

   anderer Meinung sein to disagree OT 1

   seine Meinung wechseln to change one's tune **WS 3**, 98

Meisterleistung feat OT 2

Meisterschaft cup OT 5; championship **WS 2**, 75

Meisterstück masterpiece OT 4

sich melden to report OT 1

Melodie tune OT 4; melody **WS 2**, 66

Memoiren memoir OT 5

Menge crowd OT 1

   eine Menge a lot OT 1

   jede Menge loads of OT 3

Mensch person OT 1; human being OT 2

Menschenmenge crowd OT 1; throng OT 2

Menschenrecht human right OT 5

Menschheit humanity **WS 4**, 138

menschlich human OT 2

mental mental OT 4

Mentalität mindset **WS 3**, 94

sich merken to memorize **WS 1**, 23

merkwürdig funny OT 1

messen to measure OT 1; to quantify **WS 4**, 146

Messer knife OT 2

Metall metal OT 1

Metapher metaphor **WS 2**, 64

Meter metre OT 1

Methode method OT 1

metronomisch metronomic **WS 1**, 29

Meute mob OT 5

mich me OT 1

mieten to hire OT 3; to rent OT 3

Mietshaus tenement **WS 1**, 35

Migrant(in) migrant OT 4

Migration migration OT 3

migrieren to migrate OT 3

Mikrofon microphone OT 5

Mikrowelle microwave OT 4

Milch milk OT 1

Milchprodukte dairy OT 4

mild mild **WS 1**, 37

militant militant **WS 2**, 62

Militär... military OT 5

militärisch military OT 5

Millenial millennial OT 5

Millennium-Generation millennial OT 5

Milliarde billion OT 4

Million million OT 1

Minderheit minority OT 4

Minderjährige(r) minor OT 2

mindern to lessen **WS 3**, 122

Mindest... minimum OT 1

mindestens at least OT 1

Mindmap mind map OT 1

Mini-Job gig OT 5

Miniatur miniature OT 2

minimieren to minimize **WS 3**, 95

Minister(in) minister OT 4

Minute minute OT 1

Minze mint OT 1

mir me OT 1

mischen to combine OT 4; to blend **WS 2**, 68

   neu mischen to reshuffle **WS 3**, 118

Mischung mixture OT 2; mix OT 2; assortment **WS 1**, 26

Misserfolg failure OT 4

Mission mission **WS 2**, 54

misstrauisch suspicious OT 3

Missverständnis misunderstanding OT 3

missverstehen to misunderstand OT 5

mit with OT 1

mitarbeiten (an) to contribute (to) OT 5

Mitarbeiter(in) colleague OT 4

Mitbewohner(in) roommate OT 5

Mitfahrgelegenheit lift OT 3

mitfühlen (mit jmd) to sympathize (with) OT 5

mitfühlend sympathetic OT 2; compassionate **WS 1**, 29

Mitgefühl compassion **WS 1**, 14

Mitglied member OT 1

   Mitglied werden in to join OT 1

Mitgliedschaft membership **WS 2**, 62

Mitlaut consonant OT 1

Mittag noon OT 4

Mittagessen lunch OT 1

Mittagspause lunch break OT 1

Mittagszeit lunchtime OT 1

Mitte centre OT 1; middle OT 1; midst **WS 2**, 58

Mitteilungsblatt newsletter OT 3

Mittel medium OT 2; resource OT 4; agent OT 5

mittelalterlich medieval OT 2

mittelgroß medium-sized OT 2

Mitternacht midnight OT 1

mittlerweile meanwhile OT 5

Mittwoch Wednesday OT 1

mobben to bully OT 3

Möbel furniture OT 1

mobilisieren to mobilize **WS 1**, 32

möchte(n) would like OT 1

Mode fashion OT 1
Modell model OT 1; recreation OT 4
moderat moderate **WS 1**, 36
Moderator(in) presenter OT 4
modern modern OT 1; trendy OT 2
modisch fashionable OT 2
Modul module OT 4
mogeln to cheat OT 4
mögen to like OT 1
   nicht mögen to dislike OT 2
möglich possible OT 2; potential OT 4
Möglichkeit chance OT 2; possibility OT 4
Moment moment OT 1
Monarchie monarchy OT 4
Monarch(in) monarch OT 4
Monat month OT 1
Mönch monk OT 3
Mond moon OT 1
Monografie monograph **WS 3**, 96
Monopol monopoly OT 4
monoton monotone OT 5
Monster monster OT 1
Montag Monday OT 1
Monument monument OT 4
Moor bog **WS 1**, 16
Moorhuhn grouse **WS 1**, 22
Moped moped OT 4
Moral moral OT 2
Mord murder OT 5
Morgen morning OT 1; acre (Fläche) OT 4
morgen tomorrow OT 1
Morgendämmerung dawn OT 3
Mosaik mosaic OT 2
Motel motel OT 3
Motiv motif **WS 3**, 101; motive **WS 3**, 116
Motivation motivation OT 5
Motivations… motivational OT 5
motivieren to motivate OT 5
Motor engine OT 2
motorisiert motorized OT 4
Motto motto OT 4
Mountainbiken mountain biking OT 2
müde tired OT 1
Müdigkeit fatigue **WS 4**, 140
Muffin muffin OT 1
Mühe effort OT 3
Mühle mill **WS 3**, 114
Müll rubbish OT 4
Müllcontainer dumpster OT 4
Mülldeponie landfill OT 3
multi-ethnisch biracial **WS 2**, 71
multi-funktional multi-functional OT 4
Multikulturalismus multiculturalism OT 4
multikulturell multicultural OT 4

multinational multinational OT 4
multiplizieren to multiply **WS 4**, 136
Mund mouth OT 1
Mundharmonika harmonica **WS 2**, 67
mündlich oral OT 1; verbal OT 5
Mundschutz mouthguard OT 2
Münze coin OT 1
murmeln to mutter **WS 3**, 105
mürrisch crossly OT 3
Muschel seashell OT 3
Museum museum OT 1
Musik music OT 1
Musik… musical OT 2
musikalisch musical OT 2
Musiker(in) musician OT 2
Muskel muscle OT 2
Müsli muesli OT 5
müssen must OT 1; to be obliged to OT 5
Muster pattern OT 4
Mut bravery OT 2; courage **WS 1**, 14; audacity **WS 2**, 69
mutig bold OT 1
Mutter mother OT 1
Mutterschaf ewe OT 2
Mutti mum OT 1
mutwillig: mutwillig beschädigen to vandalize OT 5
Mütze cap OT 1
mystisch mythical **WS 1**, 17
Mythologie mythology OT 2
Mythos myth OT 4

N
nach after OT 1; past OT 1; according to OT 4
Nachbar neighbour OT 2
Nachbarschaft neighbourhood OT 4
nachdenken to speculate OT 4
   nachdenken über to think about OT 1; consider OT 3
   ohne nachzudenken unthinkingly **WS 3**, 105
nachdenkenswert thought-provoking **WS 3**, 113
nachdenklich reflective **WS 2**, 69; pensive **WS 3**, 97
Nachfrage demand OT 5
nachhallen to echo OT 5; to reverberate **WS 1**, 17
nachhaltig sustainable OT 3
Nachhaltigkeit sustainability OT 3
Nachhilfe tutoring OT 5
nachklingen to echo OT 5
Nachkomme descendant OT 3
Nachlass discount OT 4

nachlassen to lessen **WS 3**, 122
Nachmittag afternoon OT 1
Nachricht message OT 1
Nachstellung reenactment OT 4
nächste(r) next OT 3
Nacht night OT 1
   über Nacht overnight OT 2
Nachteil con OT 2; downside OT 3; disadvantage OT 4
nachteilig adverse **WS 1**, 36
Nachtisch dessert OT 1
Nachttopf chamber pot OT 3
Nachweis evidence OT 4
Nachwirkungen aftermath **WS 3**, 109
nackt bare **WS 1**, 13
Nadelbaum conifer **WS 1**, 35
nah near OT 1; close OT 1; nearby OT 3
   näher kommen to approach OT 3
nähen to sew OT 3
sich nähern to approach OT 3
nahrhaft nutritious OT 4
Nährstoff nutrient **WS 1**, 36
Nahrungsergänzungsmittel food supplement OT 5
Name name OT 1
   im Namen von on behalf of **WS 3**, 111
namens called OT 1
Nase nose OT 2
nass wet OT 1
Nation nation OT 2
national national OT 1
Nationalhymne anthem OT 5
Nationalismus nationalism **WS 2**, 60
Natur nature OT 2
Naturforscher(in) naturalist OT 2
natürlich of course OT 1; natural OT 1
Naturwissenschaften science OT 1
Naturwissenschaftler(in) scientist OT 1
Navigation navigation **WS 1**, 15
Navigationssystem GPS (global positioning system) OT 2
navigieren to navigate **WS 1**, 38
Nebel fog **WS 1**, 16; mist **WS 1**, 35
nebelig foggy OT 3
neben next to OT 1; by OT 1; beside OT 2; alongside **WS 1**, 36
Nebenberuf sideline OT 5
nebenberuflich part-time OT 5
Nebeneinander juxtaposition **WS 2**, 76
neblig misty **WS 1**, 13
Neffe nephew OT 5
Negativ negative OT 1
negativ adverse **WS 1**, 36
Negativität negativity OT 4
Neger(in) (rassistisch) negro **WS 2**, 64

nehmen to take OT 1

(sich) neigen to tilt OT 3

   zu etw. neigen to tend to OT 5

nennen to call OT 1

Neoprenanzug wetsuit OT 1

Nerv nerve OT 3

Nervensäge pain OT 2

nervös nervous OT 2

Nest nest OT 3

nett kind OT 1; nice OT 1

Nettigkeit pleasantry **WS 1**, 17

Netz net OT 4; mesh **WS 3**, 101

Netzball netball OT 5

Netzwerk network OT 4

neu new OT 1

neueste(r) recent OT 3

Neugier curiosity **WS 3**, 105

neugierig curious OT 4

   neugierig machen to intrigue **WS 2**, 54

Neuheit innovation OT 4

Neuigkeit(en) news OT 1

neulich recently OT 3

neun nine OT 1

neunzig ninety OT 1

neurologisch neurological OT 5

neutral neutral OT 3

Neutralität neutrality **WS 2**, 60

Newsletter newsletter OT 3

nicht not OT 1

Nichte niece OT 4

nichts nothing OT 1

nichtsdestoweniger nonetheless **WS 2**, 57

nicken to nod OT 3

nie never OT 1

nieder menial OT 5

Niedergang demise **WS 1**, 12

Niederschlag rainfall OT 4

Niederschrift transcript OT 5

niedlich cute OT 3

niemand nobody, no one OT 1

nirgendwo nowhere OT 2

Niveau level OT 1

Nixe mermaid **WS 1**, 43

nobel posh **WS 1**, 15

noch yet OT 2

   noch ein(e, -r) another OT 1

nomadisch nomadic OT 3

Nomen noun OT 1

nominieren to nominate **WS 2**, 78

Nominierung nomination **WS 2**, 78

Nonne nun OT 3

Nord- north OT 1

nördlich northern OT 2

Nordosten north-east OT 1

normal normal OT 1; ordinary OT 2; standard OT 5

normalerweise usually OT 1

Normalisierung normalization **WS 3**, 114

normannisch Norman OT 3

Nostalgie nostalgia OT 4

Not hardship **WS 2**, 67; distress **WS 3**, 112

Notaufnahme Accident and Emergency OT 1

Note score OT 5

Noten... grading OT 5

Notenpunkt credit OT 5

Notfall emergency OT 1

Notiz note OT 1

Notizbuch notebook OT 2

notwendig necessary OT 3; necessarily OT 4

Notwendigkeit necessity OT 4

Nudel noodle OT 2

   Nudeln pasta OT 1

Nuklear... nuclear OT 3

numerisch numerical OT 5

Nummer number OT 1

Nummernschild registration plate OT 4

nun well OT 1

nur just OT 1; only OT 1

Nuss nut OT 5

nutzbar usable OT 5

Nutzen avail **WS 2**, 82

nutzen to utilize **WS 2**, 77; to harness **WS 4**, 135

nützlich useful OT 1

Nutzung exploitation **WS 2**, 68

O

ob whether OT 2

obdachlos homeless OT 4

Obdachlose(r) homeless OT 4

oben upstairs OT 1; above OT 2

   nach oben up OT 1; upwards OT 3

obenauf atop **WS 2**, 56

Oberbefehlshaber Commander-in-Chief OT 4

obere(r, -s) top OT 1; upper OT 1

Oberfläche surface OT 3

oberhalb above OT 2

Oberschenkel thigh OT 1

Oberschicht elite **WS 3**, 100

Oberstufenschüler(in) senior OT 4

Objekt object OT 1

Objektiv lens OT 2

obligatorisch compulsory **WS 3**, 115

Obsession obsession OT 5

Obst fruit OT 1

Obstgarten orchard OT 4

obwohl though OT 2; although OT 2; despite OT 4

öde dull **WS 1**, 16

oder or OT 1

Ofen oven OT 2; heater OT 2; stove OT 3

offen open OT 1; overt **WS 2**, 62

   offen gesagt frankly OT 4

Offenbarung epiphany **WS 2**, 76

offenkundig evident **WS 2**, 58

offensichtlich obvious OT 3; evident **WS 2**, 58; apparent **WS 3**, 112

öffentlich publicly **WS 2**, 63

Öffentlichkeit public OT 3

offiziell official OT 2

Offizier(in) officer OT 2

öffnen to open OT 1

Öffnungszeiten opening times OT 1

offshore offshore **WS 1**, 12

oft often OT 1

ohne without OT 1

ohnmächtig werden to faint OT 2

Ohr ear OT 1

Ohrring earring OT 3

ökologisch ecological OT 5

   ökologischer Fußabdruck carbon footprint OT 3

Ökonomie economy OT 5

Ökosystem ecosystem **WS 1**, 12

Ökotourismus ecotourism OT 3

Okular eyepiece OT 2

Öl oil OT 3

olympisch Olympic OT 2

Oma grandma OT 1

Onkel uncle OT 1

online online OT 3

Opa grandpa OT 1

operieren to operate OT 3

Opfer victim OT 5; sacrifice **WS 2**, 58

Opposition opposition **WS 1**, 37

optimieren to optimize OT 5

optimistisch optimistic OT 4; upbeat **WS 2**, 67

optional optional OT 4

Orange orange OT 1

orange orange OT 1

Orbit orbit OT 4

Orchester orchestra OT 1

ordentlich neat OT 4

Ordnung order OT 1

   in Ordnung OK OT 1; alright OT 1

Organ organ OT 5

Organisation organization OT 3; agency OT 4

Organisator(in) organizer OT 4
organisatorisch organizational OT 4
organisieren to organize OT 1
orientiert orientated OT 5
Orientierung orientation **WS 3**, 111
Original... original OT 3
Orkan hurricane OT 4
Ort place OT 1
orten to locate **WS 4**, 140
örtlich locally OT 4
Ost- east OT 2
Osteoporose osteoporosis **WS 1**, 37
östlich eastern OT 2
Otter otter OT 4
Ozean ocean OT 2

P
Paar couple OT 2; pair OT 2
packen to pack OT 2
packend catchy **WS 1**, 25
Packer(in) bagger OT 4
paddeln to paddle OT 3
Paket packet OT 2
Palast palace OT 1
Palette range OT 4
Pandemie pandemic OT 5
Panik: in Panik geraten to panic OT 2
Panikmache scaremongering **WS 1**, 32
panoramaartig panoramic **WS 1**, 35
panoramisch panoramic **WS 1**, 35
Panther panther OT 2
Pantoffel slipper OT 4
Papa dad OT 1
Papier paper OT 1
Papiertaschentuch tissue **WS 3**, 119
Paprika pepper OT 2
Papst pope OT 2
Parade parade OT 2
Paradies paradise OT 5
Parallelität parallelism **WS 2**, 64
Parasit parasite **WS 4**, 140
Park park OT 1
parken to park OT 2
Parkplatz car park OT 2
Parlament parliament OT 4
parteiisch biased OT 5; partisan **WS 2**, 69
Partizip participle OT 2
Partner(in) partner OT 1
Partnerschaft partnership OT 4
Party party OT 1
Pass passport OT 2
Passage passage **WS 1**, 19
Passagier(in) passenger OT 2
passen to suit OT 5
passend timely OT 3; fitting **WS 1**, 17

passieren to happen OT 1; to occur
   WS 1, 28
Patentante godmother OT 5
patentieren to patent OT 4
Patient(in) patient OT 1
Patriot(in) patriot OT 2
patrouillieren to patrol **WS 2**, 69
Pause break OT 1; rest OT 1; recess OT 4
   eine Pause machen to pause OT 3
peinlich embarrassing OT 2; awkward
   WS 3, 114
pendeln to commute OT 5
Pendler(in) commuter OT 2
Pendlerbahn commuter rail OT 2
Penny penny OT 1
Pension lodge OT 2
per per OT 4
perfekt perfect OT 2
Periode cycle OT 4
permanent permanent OT 4
Personal staff OT 1; crew OT 2
personalisieren to personalize OT 5
Personifizierung personification
   WS 2, 64
persönlich personal OT 1
Persönlichkeit personality OT 4
Perspektive perspective OT 5
Pest plague OT 3
Petrochemikalie petrochemical OT 4
Pfad trail OT 2; footpath **WS 1**, 12
Pfadfinder(in) Scout OT 3
Pfanne pan OT 2
Pfeffer pepper OT 2
Pfeife whistle OT 2
pfeifen to blow OT 2
Pfeil arrow OT 3
Pferd horse OT 1
   zu Pferde on horseback OT 3
Pflanze plant OT 2
Pflanzenkunde botany **WS 1**, 21
Pflanzenwelt vegetation **WS 1**, 22
Pflaster plaster OT 1
Pflaume plum OT 1
pflegen to maintain OT 4; to nurture
   WS 1, 12
Pflicht obligation OT 5
Pflücker(in) picker OT 4
Pförtner(in) porter **WS 1**, 35
Pfund pound OT 1
Phänomen phenomenon OT 5
Phase stage OT 2; phase **WS 3**, 122
Philosophie philosophy OT 4
Physik physics OT 5
Pianist(in) pianist OT 2
Picknick picnic OT 1

pikant savoury OT 3
Pilates pilates **WS 1**, 37
Pilz mushroom OT 2; fungus **WS 4**, 140
Pinguin penguin OT 2
Pinsel brush OT 2
Pionier(in) pioneer OT 4
Pipeline pipeline OT 4
Plage pest OT 5
Plagiat plagiarism OT 2
plagiieren to plagiarize OT 2
Plakat poster OT 1
Plakette badge OT 5
planen to plan OT 1; to arrange OT 2;
   to design OT 4
Planer(in) planner OT 4
Planet planet OT 2
Planke plank **WS 1**, 37
Plantage plantation **WS 2**, 54
Plastik plastic OT 3
Plastik... plastic OT 3
platschen to splash OT 2
Platz square OT 1; space OT 1; site,
   ground OT 2
platzen to burst **WS 1**, 29
Platzierung placement OT 5
plaudern to chatter OT 2; to chat OT 3
plötzlich suddenly OT 2; sudden OT 3
Plural plural OT 1
Pocken smallpox OT 5
Podcast podcast OT 3
Pokal trophy OT 2
Pol pole OT 4
Politik politics OT 4; policy OT 5
Politiker(in) politician OT 3
politisch political OT 3
Polizei police OT 1
Pollen pollen **WS 4**, 140
polnisch Polish OT 2
Polohemd polo shirt OT 5
Polster pad OT 2
Polyp polyp OT 5
polysexuell polysexual **WS 3**, 112
Pommes frites French fries OT 2
Pony pony OT 3
Popcorn popcorn OT 2
populär machen to popularize
   WS 2, 60
Popularität popularity OT 4
Portalseite portal OT 5
Portier porter **WS 1**, 35
Portraitfoto headshot OT 5
porträtieren to portray **WS 1**, 18
posieren to pose **WS 3**, 109
Position position OT 3; rank OT 4
Positiv positive OT 1

Post post OT 2; mail OT 4
Postbote, -botin mail carrier OT 4
posten to post OT 4
Postkarte postcard OT 1
Prachtstück gem WS 3, 104
Präferenz preference OT 4
Praktikant(in) intern OT 5
Praktikum internship OT 4
Praktikumsplatz traineeship OT 5
praktisch practical OT 2; convenient OT 4
Präposition preposition OT 1
Präsentation presentation OT 1
präsentieren to feature OT 2
Präsenz presence WS 2, 69
präsidentiell presidential OT 4
Präsident(in) president OT 3
Präsidentschaft presidency WS 2, 57
Praxis practice OT 1; surgery OT 5
präzise accurate OT 4
Prediger(in) preacher WS 2, 58
Predigt sermon WS 2, 60
Preis price OT 1; prize OT 1
Preiselbeere cranberry OT 3
prima fine OT 1
primär primary OT 1
Primatenforscher(in) primatologist
   WW, 11
Prinz prince OT 1
Prinzip principle OT 4
priorisieren to prioritize WS 4, 138
Priorität priority OT 5
privat private OT 3
privatisieren to privatize WS 1, 31
Privatsphäre privacy OT 3
Privileg privilege OT 4
privilegiert privileged WS 3, 105
proaktiv proactive OT 4
Probe rehearsal OT 2
   eine Probe nehmen to sample
      WS 1, 12
proben to rehearse OT 3
probieren to sample OT 4
Problem problem OT 1; matter OT 2
Problemlöser(in) problem-solver OT 4
Produkt product OT 2
Produktion production OT 5
produktiv prolific WS 1, 28; productive
   WS 3, 119
professionell professional OT 3
Profil profile OT 5
Profilerstellung profiling WS 1, 34
Profilierung profiling WS 1, 34
Profit profit OT 4
profitabel profitable WS 3, 99
profitieren to benefit OT 4

Prognose forecast OT 2
Programm programme OT 1; program
   OT 3; scheme OT 5; repertoire WS 2, 67
programmieren to programme OT 2;
   to code OT 5
progressiv progressive OT 1
Projekt project OT 1
Projektor projector OT 1
Promenade promenade OT 5
Prominente(r) personality OT 4;
   celebrity OT 5
Pronomen pronoun OT 1
Propaganda propaganda WS 2, 54
Prospekt prospectus OT 4
Protagonist(in) protagonist WS 1, 34
Protein protein OT 5
Protest protest OT 4; outcry WS 2, 54
Protestantisch Protestant OT 3
protestieren to protest OT 4
Protestierer(in) protester OT 4
Prototyp prototype OT 4
Provinz province OT 4
provozieren to provoke WS 2, 57
Prozedur procedure OT 4
Prozent percent OT 3
Prozentsatz percentage OT 4
Prozess trial OT 2; process OT 4
Prozessor processor WS 3, 99
Prüfung exam OT 1
Psychologe, -login psychologist OT 5
Psychologie psychology OT 5
Psychotherapeut(in) psychotherapist
   WS 3, 112
Pubertät puberty OT 5
Publikum audience OT 1
Pueblo pueblo OT 3
Pullover jumper OT 1
Puma cougar OT 2
Pumpe pump OT 2
Punkt point OT 1; item OT 3;
   dot WS 3, 123
punkten to score OT 1
pünktlich punctual OT 4
Puppe doll OT 2
putzen to clean OT 1; to brush OT 4
Pyjama-Party sleepover OT 1

Q

Quadrat square OT 1
quälend agonizingly OT 3
Qualifikation qualification OT 4
qualifiziert qualified OT 4
Qualität quality OT 3
quantifizieren to quantify WS 4, 146
Quarterback quarterback OT 2

Quelle spring OT 2; source OT 2
Querfeldein... cross country OT 2
Querflöte flute OT 1
querlesen to skim OT 2
quetschen to squeeze WS 1, 25
Quiz quiz OT 2

R

Rabatt discount OT 4
Rabe raven OT 2
Rad wheel OT 1
Radar radar WS 2, 82
Radfahrer(in) cyclist OT 3
Radiergummi rubber OT 1
radikal radical OT 4
Radio radio OT 1
ragen to tower WS 1, 13
Rahmen frame OT 3; framework OT 4
Rakete rocket OT 4
Rampe ramp OT 2
Rampenlicht limelight WS 2, 58
Rand rim OT 3; edge OT 3; margin OT 5
Rang rank OT 4
Rasen lawn OT 5
rasen to race OT 5; to rage WS 2, 76
Rasse... pedigree OT 3
Rassentrennung desegregation
   WS 2, 58
rassisch racial WS 2, 78
Rassismus racism WW, 10
rassistisch racist WS 2, 56
Rat advice OT 2; council OT 3
Rate rate OT 4
raten to advise OT 4
Rathaus city hall OT 5
Rätsel mystery OT 5
rätselhaft obscure WS 1, 43; enigmatic
   WS 2, 82; mysterious WS 2, 82
Ratte rat OT 3
Rattenfänger ratter OT 3
rau rough OT 3; harsh OT 3
rau rugged WS 1, 15
Räuber predator OT 5
Raubtier predator OT 5
Raubüberfall robbery WS 2, 63
Rauch smoke OT 2
Raum room OT 1
Raumfahrzeug spacecraft OT 4
Razzia raid OT 5
reagieren to react OT 3
Reaktion reaction OT 3; response OT 4
Realist(in) realist WS 2, 78
realistisch realistic OT 4
Realität reality OT 5
rebellieren to rebel OT 4

Rebell(in) rebel OT 4

rebellisch rebellious **WW**, 10

Rechenaufgabe sum OT 2

Rechenschaft: zur Rechenschaft ziehen to hold accountable OT 5

Rechnung bill OT 4

Recht privilege OT 4

rechteckig rectangular OT 2

rechte(r, -s) right OT 1

rechtfertigen to justify OT 4

Rechtfertigung vindication **WS 3**, 105

rechtlich legal OT 3

rechts right OT 4

Rechtsanwalt, -anwältin lawyer OT 4

Rechtschreibung spelling OT 1

rechtzeitig timely OT 3

Redakteur(in) editor OT 2

Rede speech OT 2

Redekunst oratory **WS 2**, 60

reden to talk OT 1

Redner(in) speaker OT 2

reduzieren to downsize OT 3; to reduce OT 4; to slash **WS 1**, 36

Reduzierung reduction **WS 3**, 93

Reel reel **WS 4**, 146

Referendum referendum **WW**, 11

Referenz reference **WS 2**, 65

Referenzschreiben letter of reference OT 5

reflektierend reflective **WS 2**, 69

Reform reform **WS 2**, 62

Reformation Reformation OT 3

Reformator(in) reformer **WS 2**, 57

Regal shelf OT 2

Regel rule OT 1; guideline OT 3; norm OT 5

regelmäßig regular OT 1; periodically **WS 4**, 135

Regelschule mainstream school OT 5

Regelwerk rulebook OT 2

Regen rainfall OT 4

Regenbogen rainbow OT 5

Regenmantel raincoat **WS 1**, 38

Regenschauer rainstorm OT 5

Regenschirm umbrella OT 1

Regenwald rainforest OT 2

Regenwasser rainwater OT 4

Reggae reggae OT 2

Regie führen to direct OT 3

regieren to govern OT 3; to reign **WS 2**, 72

Regierung government OT 2

Regierungs... governmental OT 4

Region region OT 3

regional regional OT 5

Registrierung registration **WS 2**, 56

regnen to rain OT 1

regnerisch rainy OT 4

reiben to rub OT 3

Reich empire OT 2

reich rich OT 1; wealty OT 4

reichlich plenty OT 2; substantial OT 5

Reichtum fortune OT 3; wealth OT 5

Reichweite outreach **WS 3**, 111

reif mature **WS 3**, 105

Reihe row OT 2

der Reihe nach sequentially OT 4

Reihenfolge order OT 1; sequencing OT 3; ranking OT 4

in eine Reihenfolge bringen to sequence OT 3; to rank OT 4

Reim rhyme OT 2

Reinheit purity **WS 1**, 20

Reinigungsmittel cleaner OT 3

Reis rice OT 1

Reise journey OT 1; trip, tour OT 1; voyage OT 3

Reisebus coach OT 1

Reiseführer guidebook OT 3

Reisekaufmann, -kauffrau travel agent OT 3

reisen to travel OT 1; to voyage **WS 1**, 21

Reisende(r) traveller OT 3

Reiseziel destination OT 4

reißen to tear **WS 2**, 72

Reißverschluss zip **WS 1**, 42

Reißverschluss aufmachen to unzip **WS 1**, 42

Reiten horse riding OT 1

reizen to rile up **WS 2**, 72

reizvoll attractive OT 5

Reklamezettel leaflet OT 2

rekrutieren to recruit **WS 1**, 14

Rektor(in) principal OT 2

relativ relatively OT 4

Relativsatz relative clause OT 2

relaxen to chill (out) **WS 1**, 25

Relevanz relevancy **WS 3**, 119

Religion religion OT 3

Religionsunterricht religious studies OT 1

religiös religious OT 3

Rennen race OT 2

rennen to run OT 1

Rennsport racing OT 2

renommiert renowned **WS 1**, 18

Renovierung renovation **WS 1**, 24

Rente pension **WS 1**, 32

in Rente gehen to retire OT 5

Rentier reindeer OT 3

Reparatur repair OT 2

reparieren to mend OT 3; to repair OT 5

Repertoire repertoire **WS 2**, 67

repetitiv repetitive OT 5

Reporter(in) reporter OT 1; correspondent OT 4

Reptil reptile OT 2

Republik republic OT 4

Reputation reputation **WS 2**, 58

Requisite prop OT 1

reserviert reserved OT 2

Reservierung reservation OT 1

Reservoir reservoir OT 5

Residenz residence **WS 1**, 25

Respekt respect OT 5

respektlos disrespectful OT 3

respektvoll respectful OT 3

Ressource resource OT 4

Restaurant restaurant OT 1

resultieren to result **WS 1**, 17

retten to save OT 2

Rettung rescue OT 2; recovery OT 3

Rettungsleine lifeline OT 3

Rettungsring lifebuoy OT 3

Rettungssanitäter(in) paramedic OT 1

Rettungsschwimmer(in) lifeguard OT 4

Reue remorse OT 5

revidieren to revise OT 2

Review review OT 5

Revolte insurrection **WS 2**, 73

Revolution revolution OT 2

revolutionär revolutionary **WS 2**, 63

revolutionieren to revolutionize OT 4

Rezept recipe OT 2; prescription **WS 2**, 69

Rezeption reception OT 1

Rezeptionist(in) receptionist OT 1

Rhetorik rhetoric **WS 2**, 58; oratory **WS 2**, 60

rhetorisch rhetorical **WS 1**, 24

rhetorische Figur figue of speech **WS 2**, 76

rhetorisches Stilmittel figue of speech **WS 2**, 76

rhythmisch rhythmical **WS 2**, 67

Rhythmus rhythm **WS 1**, 29

Richter(in) judge OT 2

richtig right, correct, true OT 1; proper OT 1; actual OT 4

richtigstellen to right **WS 2**, 76

Richtlinie guideline OT 3

Richtung direction OT 2

in Richtung toward(s) OT 2

riechen to smell OT 1

übel riechend smelly OT 3

Riegel bar OT 1

Riese titan **WS 2**, 82

riesig enormous OT 1; huge, giant OT 2; massive OT 3; gigantic **WS 2**, 56; monumental **WS 2**, 58; immense **WS 3**, 122

Riff reef OT 5

rigide rigid OT 5

Rinder cattle OT 4

Rindfleisch beef OT 2

Ringen wrestling OT 2

ringen to wrestle OT 2

rinnen to trickle OT 3

Rippe rib OT 3

Risiko risk OT 4

riskant risky **WS 2**, 68

Ritt ride OT 1

Ritter knight **WS 1**, 20

Ritual ritual OT 4

Rivale rival **WS 1**, 13

Rivalin rival **WS 1**, 13

Robbe seal OT 1

Roboter... robotic **WS 4**, 140

robust robust **WS 3**, 116

Rock skirt OT 1

Rolle role OT 1; roll OT 2; reel **WS 4**, 146

Rollenspiel roleplay OT 2

Rollschuh roller skate OT 5

Rollstuhl wheelchair OT 2

Rollstuhlfahrer(in) wheelchair user OT 2

Rolltreppe escalator OT 1

Roman novel OT 2

Romantik romance **WS 1**, 34

römisch Roman OT 2

Röntgen X-ray OT 1

rosa pink OT 1

rot red OT 1

Rotbuche copper beech **WS 2**, 82

Rotwein red OT 1

Routine routine OT 5

Rücken back OT 1

Rückgang decline OT 5

Rückgrat backbone OT 2

Rucksack rucksack OT 1; backpack OT 2

   mit dem Rucksack reisen to backpack OT 3

rücksichtsvoll thoughtful OT 5

rückwärts backwards OT 3

Rudel pack OT 4

Ruder helm **WS 1**, 31

Ruderboot rowing boat OT 1

rudern to row **WS 1**, 37

Ruderpinne tiller OT 3

rufen to exclaim OT 3

Rugby rugby OT 1

Ruhe rest OT 1; silence OT 5

   in Ruhe lassen to leave alone OT 2

   Ruhe bewahren to keep calm OT 2

Ruhe silence OT 5

ruhig quiet OT 1; calm OT 2; steady OT 3

Ruhm fame **WS 2**, 74; glory **WS 2**, 76

sich rühmen to boast **WS 1**, 17

rühren to stir OT 2

Ruine ruin OT 2

Rumpf hull OT 3

rümpfen to wrinkle **WS 3**, 101

rund round OT 1; rounded **WS 1**, 35

Rundgang tour OT 1

runzeln to wrinkle **WS 3**, 101

S

sachlich factual OT 4

sachte gently OT 3

Sack sack OT 2

Sackhüpfen sack race OT 2

Safari safari OT 2

Saft juice OT 1

Sage legend OT 4; saga **WS 2**, 69

sagen to say OT 1

Sahne cream OT 1

Saite string OT 2

Salat salad OT 1

Salon parlour **WS 3**, 114

salopp slangy **WS 2**, 67

Salz salt OT 2

salzig salty OT 3

Samen seed OT 2

sammeln to collect OT 1; to gather OT 4; to collate **WS 1**, 22

Sammlung collection OT 2

Samstag Saturday OT 1

samtartig velvety OT 2

Sand sand OT 1

sandig sandy OT 5

Sandstein sandstone OT 4

Sandwich sandwich OT 1

sanft gentle **WS 1**, 15

Sänger(in) singer OT 1; vocalist OT 2

Sanitär... sanitation **WS 2**, 58

Sarg coffin OT 4

sarkastisch sarcastic **WS 1**, 37

Satellit satellite OT 4

satthaben to be fed up OT 1

Satz sentence OT 1

sauer acidic OT 5

Sauerstoff oxygen OT 5

saugen to suck OT 4

Säugetier mammal OT 2

Säugling baby OT 1

Säule column OT 1

Sauna sauna OT 2

Saxofon saxophone OT 2

scannen to scan OT 2

Schach chess OT 1

Schädel skull OT 2

Schaden harm OT 3

Schadenersatz amends OT 5

schädlich harmful OT 5

Schädling pest OT 5

Schaf sheep OT 1

Schäfer(in) shepherd OT 2

schaffen to create OT 2; to achieve OT 4; to accomplish **WS 3**, 111

Schal scarf OT 1

Schale dish OT 2

schälen to peel **WS 3**, 108

Schallwelle sound wave **WS 3**, 96

Schamgefühl shame OT 5

scharf hot OT 1; spicy OT 4; sharp OT 4

Schärpe sash OT 4

Schatten shadow OT 3; shade OT 5

Schatz treasure OT 3

schätzen to guess OT 1; to estimate OT 4; to appreciate OT 4

Schatzmeister(in) treasurer OT 3

Schätzung guess OT 1

Schau: Schau stellen to flaunt **WS 3**, 101

Schaubild diagram OT 1

Schauspieler(in) actor OT 1

Scheck cheque OT 4

Scheibe slice OT 1

scheiden: sich scheiden lassen to get divorced OT 3

Scheidung divorce OT 3

Schein note OT 1

scheinen to shine OT 1; to seem OT 2; to appear OT 3; to glow **WS 1**, 35

scheitern to fail OT 4

Scherbe fragment **WS 1**, 35

Schere scissors OT 1

sich scheuen to dread **WS 1**, 22

Scheune barn OT 2

schick smartly OT 4; stylish OT 4; glam OT 4; posh **WS 1**, 15

schicken to send OT 1

Schicksal destiny **WS 1**, 25

Schiedsrichter(in) referee OT 3

schießen to shoot OT 3; to fire OT 4

Schießerei gunfire OT 3

Schiff ship OT 1; vessel OT 3

   mit dem Schiff fahren to sail OT 2

Schild sign OT 1; notice OT 1; signpost OT 5

schildern to depict **WS 2**, 77

Schildkröte tortoise OT 1

Schinken ham OT 1

Schlacht battle OT 4

schlachten to cull OT 5

Schlachtschiff battleship OT 3

Schlaf sleep OT 5

Schlafanzug pyjamas OT 3

schlafen to sleep OT 1

schlafend asleep OT 2

Schlafenszeit bedtime OT 2

Schlaflosigkeit insomnia **WS 3**, 108

Schlafzimmer bedroom OT 1

Schlag beat OT 4

schlagen to hit OT 1; to beat OT 4;
to batter OT 4; to punch OT 5

Schlägerei rumble **WS 2**, 53

Schlagsahne whipped cream OT 3

Schlagzeile headline OT 2

Schlagzeug drums OT 1

Schlagzeuger(in) drummer OT 2

Schlamm mud OT 3

schlammig muddy OT 4

Schlammlawine mudslide OT 5

Schlange snake OT 1; queue OT 1;
serpent OT 5

schlank slim **WS 3**, 117

Schlankheitskuren dieting OT 5

schlau smart OT 5; savvy OT 5

Schlauch tube OT 1

schlecht bad OT 1

schlechtgelaunt gloomy **WS 1**, 16

Schleife loop **WS 4**, 142

schleppen to drag **WS 1**, 20

Schlepper(in) coyote OT 5

schleudern to hurl **WS 3**, 119

Schleuse lock OT 3

Schleusenwärter(in) lock keeper OT 3

schließen to close OT 1; to shut OT 2;
to conclude OT 3

Schließfach locker OT 2

schließlich finally OT 1; eventually OT 3

Schlitten sled OT 4

Schlittschuh laufen to skate OT 2

Schlucht canyon OT 3

Schlüpfer knickers **WS 3**, 101

Schluss conclusion OT 3

Schlüssel key OT 1

schlussendlich ultimately **WS 1**, 17

schlüssig coherent **WS 4**, 141

schmachten to yearn for **WS 1**, 13

schmackhaft tasty OT 2

schmecken to taste OT 1

schmelzen to melt OT 4

Schmerz pain OT 2; ache OT 3

schmerzen to hurt OT 1

schmerzend aching **WS 1**, 12

schmerzhaft aching **WS 1**, 12;
painful **WS 3**, 122

Schmerzmittel painkiller OT 2

Schmetterling butterfly **WS 2**, 53

schmieden to forge **WS 1**, 18

Schminke makeup OT 5

Schmuck jewelry OT 2

schmücken to decorate OT 2; to grace
WS 1, 17

Schmuckstück jewel OT 3

schmuggeln to smuggle OT 5

Schmutz dirt OT 4

schmutzig dirty OT 1

Schnabel beak **WS 1**, 36

Schnabeltier platypus OT 5

Schnappschuss shot OT 2

Schneckenpost snail mail OT 4

Schnee snow OT 1

schneebedeckt snow-capped OT 4

Schneemobil snowmobile OT 4

Schneide blade **WS 1**, 24

schneiden to cut OT 2; to chop OT 3

schneidern to tailor OT 4

schnell fast OT 1; quick OT 3; rapid OT 3

Schnitt edit OT 4; cut **WS 2**, 76

Schnittpunkt intersection **WS 2**, 82

schnitzen to carve OT 2

Schnitzer(in) carver OT 4

Schnitzerei carving OT 4

Schnur string OT 2

schnüren to lace **WS 3**, 119

schockieren to shock OT 4

Schokolade chocolate OT 1

Schokoladensplitter choc-chip OT 1

Schokoladensüchtige(r) chocoholic
OT 3

schon already OT 2; yet OT 2

schön lovely OT 1; beautiful OT 1; nice
OT 1; fair **WS 1**, 13

Schönheit beauty OT 3

Schöpfer(in) creator OT 5

Schöpfung creation OT 5

Schornstein chimney OT 3

Schottenrock kilt OT 2

Schottenstoff tartan **WS 1**, 12

schottisch Scottish OT 2

Schrank cupboard OT 1; cabinet OT 5

Schrecken horror OT 4

schrecklich awful OT 1; terrible OT 1;
dreadful OT 2; horrendous **WS 1**, 16

Schreibarbeit paperwork OT 5

Schreibblock pad OT 5

schreiben to write OT 1

neu schreiben to rewrite OT 2

Schreibkraft typist OT 5

Schreibmaschine typewriter OT 5

Schreibtisch desk OT 1

Schreibweise spelling OT 1

schreien to scream OT 3

Schriftrolle scroll OT 2

Schriftsteller(in) writer OT 1; novelist
OT 4

Schritt step OT 1

schroff rugged **WS 1**, 15

schrubben to scrape OT 2

schrumpfen to shrink **WS 1**, 31

Schubkarre wheelbarrow OT 4

Schublade drawer OT 1

schüchtern shy OT 2

schuften to toil **WS 3**, 114

Schuh shoe OT 1

Schulabgänger(in) leaver OT 5

Schulaufgaben schoolwork OT 5

Schulausflug field trip OT 2

Schulball prom OT 3

Schuld fault OT 2; blame OT 4

Schulden debt **WS 2**, 69

schuldfrei guilt-free **WS 3**, 104

schuldig guilty OT 4

sich schuldig bekennen to plead
guilty OT 5

Schuldige(r) culprit **WS 4**, 134

Schule school OT 1

Schüler(in) student OT 1

Schulhof playground OT 1

Schulkamerad(in) schoolmate OT 4

Schulleiter(in) head teacher OT 1

Schulschwänzer(in) truant **WS 2**, 76

Schultag school day OT 1

Schultasche school bag OT 1

Schulter shoulder OT 1

mit den Schultern zucken to shrug
WS 3, 113

schummeln to cheat OT 4

Schuppen shed OT 1

schüren to stoke **WS 2**, 58

Schuss shot OT 2

Schüsse gunfire OT 3

Schüssel bowl OT 1

Schusswaffe gun OT 3

schütteln to shake OT 2

Schutz conservation OT 2; custody OT 5;
protection **WS 4**, 135

Schütze gunman OT 4

schützen to protect OT 2

Schutzgebiet sanctuary OT 5

Schutzhütte bothy **WS 1**, 15

schwach weak OT 4

Schwäche weakness OT 4

schwächen to weaken OT 4

schwanger pregnant OT 3

schwanken to sway WS 3, 116

Schwanz tail OT 2

schwappen to slop on OT 5

schwarz black OT 1

schweben to float OT 3; to soar OT 3

Schweigen silence OT 5

Schwein pig OT 1

Schweinefleisch pork OT 2

Schwellung swelling OT 2

schwenken to wave WS 2, 53

   (eine Kamera) schwenken to pan
WS 2, 76

schwer difficult OT 1; heavy OT 1;
severe OT 4

Schwergewicht heavyweight
WS 2, 53

Schwert sword OT 1

Schwester sister OT 1

schwierig difficult OT 1; challenging
OT 1; gruelling WS 1, 22

Schwierigkeit difficulty OT 2;
trouble OT 2

Schwimmbecken pool OT 1

schwimmen to swim OT 1

Schwimmer(in) swimmer OT 3

Schwimmweste life jacket OT 3

Schwindel hoax WS 1, 20

schwindlig faint OT 2; dizzy OT 3

schwirren to buzz WS 4, 140

schwitzen to sweat OT 2

schwören to vow WS 2, 57

schwul gay OT 5; queer OT 5

Scout scout OT 3

sechs six OT 1

sechseckig hexagonal WS 1, 39

Sechstklässler(in) sixth grader OT 2

sechzehn sixteen OT 1

sechzig sixty OT 1

See lake OT 1; loch WS 1, 12

seefahrend seafaring OT 3

seekrank seasick OT 3

Seele soul OT 2

Seemann sailor OT 3; seaman OT 3

Seetang seaweed WS 1, 12

Seevogel seabird OT 5

Segel sail OT 5

segeln to sail OT 1

Segen blessing WS 2, 76

Segment segment OT 5

segnen to bless WS 2, 69

Segregation segregation WS 2, 53

sehen to look OT 1; to see OT 1

Sehenswürdigkeit sight OT 1; attraction
OT 2

sehnen: sich sehnen nach to long for
WS 1, 13

sehr very OT 1; really OT 1; agonizingly
OT 3

Sehvermögen sight OT 1

Seife soap OT 2

Seifenoper telenovela WS 3, 95

Seil rope OT 3

Seilrutsche zip line OT 1

sein to be OT 1

seine(r, -s) his OT 1

seit since OT 2

Seite side OT 1; page OT 1

   an der Seite von alongside WS 1, 36

   auf der anderen Seite across OT 1

Sekretär(in) secretary OT 1

sekundär secondary OT 1

Sekundarschule secondary school OT 1

Sekunde second OT 1

selbständig self-employed OT 5

Selbstbedienung self-service OT 4

Selbstbewusstsein self-belief OT 5;
self-esteem WS 1, 37

Selbstlaut vowel OT 1

Selbstmord suicide WS 1, 12

selbstsicher confident OT 3

selbstständig self-sufficient OT 4

Selbstvertrauen confidence OT 5

Selbstwertgefühl self-belief OT 5

Selfie selfie OT 4

selten rare OT 2; uncommon OT 5;
seldom OT 5

seltsam strange OT 1; weird OT 1;
peculiar WS 2, 54

Semester term OT 2; semester OT 4

Senator(in) senator OT 4

Sendung programme OT 1; broadcast
OT 3

Senf mustard OT 1

Senior(in) senior citizen OT 2

Sensation spectacle WS 1, 35; sensation
WS 2, 66

sensorisch sensory OT 5

Serie series OT 4

servieren to serve OT 1

Sessel armchair OT 1

Sessellift chairlift OT 5

Session session OT 4

Setting setting OT 5

setzen to seat OT 5

seufzen to sigh OT 5

Sex sex OT 5

Shampoo shampoo OT 3

sicher sure, safe OT 1; secure OT 3;
certain OT 3

   ... sicher proof OT 5

Sicherheit safety OT 2; security OT 5

Sicherheitsbeamter(in) guard OT 5

sicherlich certainly OT 2; surely OT 4

sichern to secure OT 5

sicherstellen to ensure OT 4

Sicht view OT 1

sichtbar visible OT 4

Sichtbarkeit visibility WS 2, 58

Sichtung sighting WS 1, 38

Sichtweise perspective OT 5

sie she OT 1; her OT 1

sieben seven OT 1

Siebenkampf heptathlon OT 2

siebzehn seventeen OT 1

siebzig seventy OT 1

Siedler(in) settler OT 3

Siedlung settlement OT 4

Sieg victory OT 4

Sieger(in) winner OT 1

Signal signal OT 2

Silbe syllable OT 3

Silber silver OT 1

silbern silver OT 1

simultan simultaneous OT 5

singen to sing OT 1

sinken to sink OT 3

Sinn sense OT 2

sinnvoll meaningful OT 4

Sirene siren OT 3

Sirup syrup OT 3

Sit-up crunch WS 1, 37

Situation situation OT 1

sitzen to sit OT 1

Sitzplatz seat OT 2

Sitzung session OT 4

Skateboard skateboard OT 1

Skelett skeleton OT 2

Skelett... skeletal OT 3

skeptisch sceptical WS 1, 32

Sketch sketch OT 2; skit OT 2

Skifahren skiing OT 3

Skilanglauf cross-country skiing OT 5

Ski laufen to ski OT 3

Skizze sketch OT 2

Sklave, Sklavin slave OT 3

Sklaverei slavery WW, 10

Sklavereigegner(in) abolitionist
WS 2, 57

Skulptur sculpture OT 2

Skyline skyline OT 4

Slang slang OT 4

Slogan slogan OT 2

Slum slum OT 5
Smartphone smartphone OT 3
SMS text OT 2
Snack snack OT 1
Snowboardfahren snowboarding OT 3
so such OT 2
Socke sock OT 1
Sofa sofa OT 1
sofort straight away OT 2; immediately
   OT 3; instantly **WS 3**, 106
sogar even OT 1
Sohn son OT 1
Soja soya **WS 4**, 135
Soldat(in) soldier OT 1; trooper **WS 2**, 53
Solidarität solidarity **WS 2**, 77
solide robust **WS 3**, 116
sollte ought to OT 5
solo solo OT 2
Sommer summer OT 1
Sommersprossen freckles OT 3
Sonne sun OT 1
Sonnen... solar OT 3
sonnenbaden to sunbathe **WS 1**, 43
sonnenbestrahlt sunlit **WS 1**, 13
Sonnenbrand sunburn OT 2
Sonnenschein sunshine OT 3
Sonnenschutzmittel sunscreen OT 2
Sonnenstich sunstroke OT 2
Sonnenuhr sundial OT 3
Sonnenuntergang sunset OT 3
sonnig sunny OT 1; sunlit **WS 1**, 13
Sonntag Sunday OT 1
sonst otherwise OT 4
   sonst noch else OT 1
Sorge care OT 2; worry OT 5; anxiety
   OT 5; concern OT 5
   sich Sorgen machen to worry OT 1
Sorgerecht custody OT 5
sorgfältig careful OT 1
sorglos careless OT 2
Soße sauce OT 1
sozial social OT 5
Sozialisierung socialization **WS 3**, 122
sozioökonomisch socio-economic
   WS 2, 83
Spacewalker spacewalker OT 5
Spaghetti spaghetti OT 1
Spalte column OT 1
spaltend divisive **WS 2**, 62
Spaniel spaniel OT 2
spanisch Spanish OT 1
Spanne span **WS 3**, 108
spannend thrilling **WS 1**, 24
Spannung excitement **WS 1**, 29
sparen to save OT 2

Spaß fun OT 1
   Spaß verstehen to take a joke OT 2
spät late OT 1
   später einmal one day OT 2
Spaziergang stroll **WS 1**, 15
Speck bacon OT 1
Speer spear OT 4
Speisekarte menu OT 1
Spektakel spectacle **WS 1**, 35
spektakulär spectacular OT 2
Spekulation speculation **WS 1**, 32
spekulieren to speculate OT 4
Spende donation OT 2
spenden to donate OT 2
Spendensammlung fundraising OT 2
Spender dispenser OT 5
Sperre ban OT 5
Spezialeffekte special effects OT 2
sich spezialisieren to specialize OT 3
Spezialist(in) specialist OT 5; geek OT 5
speziell specifically **WS 2**, 79
Spezies species OT 5
spezifisch specific OT 2
Spiegel mirror OT 1
spiegeln to reflect OT 2
Spiel match OT 1; game OT 1
Spielautomat slot machine **WS 4**, 135
Spielekonsole game console OT 4
spielen to play OT 1
Spieler(in) player OT 1; gamer OT 4
Spielfeld pitch OT 3
Spielplatz playground OT 1
Spind locker OT 2
Spindoktor spin master **WS 2**, 69
Spinne spider OT 1
Spion(in) spy **WS 2**, 57
spirituell spiritual **WS 2**, 60
Spirituosen liquor **WS 1**, 29
spitz spiky OT 5
Spitze tip OT 1; top OT 1; forefront
   WS 1, 32
Spitzen ... peak OT 4
Spitzname nickname OT 4
Sponsor(in) sponsor OT 2
spontan impromptu **WS 1**, 26; impulsive
   WS 4, 135
Sport sport OT 1; athletics OT 1; PE OT 1
Sport... sporting OT 5
Sporthalle gymnasium OT 4
Sportler(in) athlete OT 2
sportlich sporty OT 3; sporting OT 5
Sportunterricht PE (physical education)
   OT 1
(Spott)drossel mockingbird **WS 2**, 64
Sprache language OT 1

sprachlich linguistic OT 4
Sprachwissenschaftler(in) linguist
   OT 5
sprechen to speak OT 1
Sprechstunde surgery OT 5
sprenkeln to dot **WS 1**, 38
Springbrunnen fountain OT 1
springen to jump OT 2; to leap **WS 1**, 13
Spritztour joyride OT 5
Sprudel soda OT 5
sprühen to spray OT 3
sprunghaft erratic OT 5
Spülbecken sink OT 3
Spur trail OT 2
spürbar appreciable **WS 4**, 146
Spürhund hound OT 2
Staatsangehörigkeit nationality OT 2
Staatsanwalt, -anwältin prosecutor
   OT 5
Staatsanwaltschaft prosecution OT 5
Staatsbürgerschaft citizenship
   WS 2, 83
stabil steady OT 3
Stabilität stability OT 5
stachelig spiky OT 5
Stachelrochen stingray OT 5
Stadion stadium OT 1
Stadt town OT 1; city OT 1
Stadtbewohner(innen) townspeople
   OT 4
städtisch urban OT 4
Staffelstab: den Staffelstab
   übernehmen to take the torch
   WS 3, 99
Stahl steel OT 2
stählern steely **WS 1**, 35
stahlhart steely **WS 1**, 35
Stall stable OT 4
Stamm tribe OT 2; clan OT 5
stammen aus to date back OT 4;
   to originate OT 4
Stammes... tribal OT 3
Stand stall OT 4; booth **WS 1**, 32
Standard default OT 3; standard OT 5;
   norm OT 5
standardmäßig standard OT 5
standhaft staunch **WS 1**, 13
ständig constant OT 4; habitual **WS 2**,
   68; continually **WS 2**, 70; perpetual
   WS 2, 72
Standort location OT 2; garrison **WS 1**, 25
Standpunkt viewpoint OT 3
Stange pole OT 4
stapeln to stack OT 4
Star star OT 1

stark strong OT 2; severe OT 4; intense OT 5

   stärker machen to strengthen OT 4

Stärke strength OT 4

stärken to empower OT 5

starr stiff OT 5; rigid OT 5

starren to stare OT 2

starten to launch OT 4

Station station OT 1

Statistik statistic OT 3

stattdessen instead OT 2

Statue statue OT 1

Status status OT 5

Stau congestion OT 4

Staub dust OT 2

staubsaugen to vacuum OT 5

Staubsauger vacuum cleaner OT 4

Steak steak OT 1

stechen to sting OT 2

Stechmücke mosquito OT 2

stecken to stick OT 1

Stecknadel pin OT 1

stehen to stand OT 1

   auf etwas stehen to be into OT 2

steif stiff OT 5

steigen to climb OT 1

steil steep OT 2

Stein stone OT 1; rock OT 2

steinig rocky WS 1, 35

stellen to put OT 1; to set OT 2

Stellvertreter(in) deputy WS 2, 61

sterben to die OT 1

Stereotype stereotype OT 5

stereotypisch stereotypical OT 5

Stern star OT 1

Steroid steroid OT 5

Steuer, das helm WS 1, 31

Steuer, die tax OT 4

steuern to steer OT 3

Stichwort headword OT 2; keyword OT 2

Stiefel boot OT 1

Stift pen OT 1

Stigma stigma OT 5

Stil style OT 2

still quiet OT 1; still OT 1; silent WS 1, 24

Stimme voice OT 2; vote OT 5

Stimmung mood OT 3

Stipendium scholarship OT 5

Stirn forehead OT 3

   die Stirn runzeln to frown OT 3

Stockwerk floor OT 1

   im oberen Stockwerk upstairs OT 1

   im unteren Stockwerk downstairs OT 1

Stoff cloth OT 2; fabric WS 2, 82

stolpern to trip OT 2

Stolz pride OT 5

   Stolz auf etwas sein to pride oneself OT 5

stolz proud OT 2

stören to disturb OT 3; to bother OT 4

Störung disruption OT 4; disorder OT 5

Storyboard storyboard OT 4

stoßen to knock OT 2; to push OT 2; to poke WS 1, 42; to thrust WS 2, 58

Strafe penalty OT 3; sentence OT 5

strafrechtlich penal OT 5

Strafstoß penalty OT 3

Straftat offence OT 5

strahlen to beam WS 1, 13

Strahlenkranz halo WS 1, 12

Strand beach OT 1; seashore OT 4

Sträßchen laneway OT 5

Straße road OT 1; street OT 1

Straßenbahn tram OT 2; trolley (AE) OT 2

Straßenmusiker(in) busker OT 5

Strategie strategy OT 5

Streaming streaming OT 5

Strecke route OT 2

streicheln to stroke OT 3; to pet OT 4

Streichholz match OT 2

Streifen strip OT 2

Streik strike OT 4

streiken to strike OT 4

Streit argument OT 1

(sich) streiten to quarrel OT 2; to argue OT 3

Streitkräfte armed forces OT 4

streng strict OT 2

Stress stress OT 1

Stressfaktor stressor WS 4, 146

stressig stressful OT 4

streuen to sprinkle OT 2

Stroh straw OT 4

Strohhalm straw OT 4

Strom electricity OT 2; flow WS 3, 122

strömen to flock WS 1, 43

Strudel whirlpool WS 1, 20

Struktur structure OT 1

strukturieren to structure OT 5

Strumpfhose tights OT 2

Stück piece OT 1; bit OT 2

Student(in) student OT 1

Studie study OT 1

Studienanfänger freshman OT 4

Studiengebühr(en) tuition OT 5

studieren to study OT 1

Studio studio OT 5

Studium studies OT 1

Stufe step OT 1; level OT 1

Stuhl chair OT 1

stumm silent WS 1, 24

Stunde hour OT 1; class OT 1

Stundenplan timetable OT 1; schedule (AE) OT 2

Sturm storm OT 2

stürzen to fall OT 1; to topple WS 2, 56

Stütze prop OT 1

Subkultur subculture WS 3, 94

Substantiv noun OT 1

Substanz substance OT 3

substanzlos insubstantial WS 1, 35

subtil subtle WS 1, 29

Suche search OT 2

   nach etw. suchen to scavenge OT 5

suchen to search OT 4; to seek OT 5

Sucht addiction OT 5

süchtig addicted WS 2, 73

   süchtig machend addictive WS 4, 134

Süchtigkeit addiction OT 5

Süden south OT 2

südlich southern OT 4

südwestlich southwest OT 3

Suizid suicide WS 1, 12

summen to hum OT 4

Sumpf bog WS 1, 16

Sünde sin WS 2, 64

super super OT 5

Superheld superhero OT 5

Supermarkt supermarket OT 1

Suppe soup OT 1

Surfen surfing OT 1

Süßwaren confectionary WS 1, 36

Süßwasser freshwater WS 1, 13

Sweatshirt sweatshirt OT 1

Symbol symbol OT 1

symbolisch symbolic WS 2, 57

symbolisieren to symbolize WS 1, 12

Sympathisant(in) sympathizer WS 2, 53

Symptom symptom WS 3, 108

Synästhesie synaesthesia OT 2

Synonym synonym OT 2

synthetisch synthetic WS 3, 104

synthetisieren to synthesize WS 3, 116

System system OT 2

systematisch systematically OT 5

systembedingt systemic WS 2, 68

Szenario scenario WS 4, 140

Szene scene OT 2

Szenenbuch storyboard OT 4

T

Tabak tobacco OT 4

Tablet tablet OT 2

Tablett tray OT 2

Tablette pill OT 5

Tabulator tab OT 4

Tafel blackboard OT 1; tablet OT 2; board OT 2

Tag day OT 1

   helllichter Tag broad daylight WS 2, 79

Tagesausflug day out OT 2

Tagesordnung agenda OT 3

täglich daily OT 2

Taille waist WS 1, 16

Takt beat OT 4

   aus dem Takt kommen to be off beat OT 4

Tal valley OT 1; glen WS 1, 15

Talent talent OT 5

talentiert talented OT 5

Tank tank OT 3

Tante aunt OT 1

Tantieme royalty WS 2, 66

Tanz dance OT 5

tanzbar danceable WS 2, 67

Tanzen dancing OT 1

tapfer brave OT 1

Tartan tartan WS 1, 12

Tasche case OT 1; pocket OT 2

Taschenlampe torch OT 1; flashlight OT 2

Taschenlampenlicht torchlight WS 1, 16

Taschenmesser pocketknife OT 2

Tasse cup OT 1

Tastatur keyboard OT 1

Täter(in) offender OT 5

Tätigkeit occupation OT 4

Tätowierung tattoo OT 3

Tatsache fact OT 1

taub deaf OT 3

Taube pigeon OT 5

tauchen to dive OT 3; to dip OT 4

Taucheranzug wetsuit OT 1

Taucher(in) diver OT 3

tauschen to swap OT 3

Täuschung bluff WS 4, 143

Taxi cab OT 1

Technik technique OT 4

technikerfahren tech-savvy WS 3, 99

technisch technical OT 2; tech OT 2; technological OT 4

Technologie technology OT 1

technologisch technological OT 4

Tee tea OT 1

Teenager teen OT 2; teenager OT 2

teenokratisch teenocratic WS 3, 114

Teich pond OT 1

Teil part OT 1; piece OT 1; section OT 2

Teil... semi... OT 5

teilen to share OT 2

   sich teilen to divide OT 2

teilnahmslos apathetic WS 1, 32

teilnehmen to take part OT 2; to participate OT 4

Teilnehmer(in) participant OT 4

teilweise partly OT 4

teilzeitlich part-time OT 5

Telefon phone OT 1

Telegramm telegram WS 2, 61

Teleskop telescope WS 3, 105

Teller plate OT 1

Tempel temple OT 1

Temperatur temperature OT 2

Temperaturregler thermostat OT 5

Tempo pace WS 1, 29

temporär temporary OT 4

Tempus tense OT 1

Tendenz tendency WS 3, 96

Tennis tennis OT 1

Termin appointment OT 3

Terminkalender diary OT 1

Terrier terrier OT 2

Test test OT 1

teuer expensive OT 1

Teufel devil WS 2, 60

Text text OT 2

Texter(in) songwriter OT 5

Theater theatre OT 1

   Theater spielen to act OT 1

Theaterstück play OT 1

Thema topic OT 1; subject OT 1; issue OT 2

thematisch themed OT 4

theoretisch theoretical OT 4

theoretisieren to theorize WS 3, 95

Therapie therapy OT 5

Thermalquelle hot spring OT 2

Thermostat thermostat OT 5

Thriller thriller WS 2, 53

Thron throne OT 4

tief deep OT 1; low OT 2

Tier animal OT 1; beast OT 2

Tierwelt wildlife OT 2

Tiger tiger OT 1

Timer timer OT 5

tippen to key OT 2; to type OT 5; to tap OT 5

Tisch table OT 1

Tischdecke tablecloth OT 2

Tischler(in) carpenter OT 3

Tischtennis ping-pong OT 4

Titan titan WS 2, 82

Titel title OT 1

Toast toast OT 2

toben to rage WS 2, 78

Tochter daughter OT 1

Tod death OT 2

Todesdatum date of death OT 2

tödlich deadly OT 5; fatal WS 2, 58; lethal WS 2, 76

Toilette toilet OT 2

Toilettenartikel toiletry WS 1, 25

tolerant tolerant OT 5

Toleranz tolerance OT 5

toll great OT 1; awesome OT 2; stunning OT 5

Tomate tomato OT 1

Ton tone OT 4

Tonerkartusche toner cartridge OT 5

Tonne bin OT 4; ton OT 4

Tonspur soundtrack WS 2, 82

Toolkit toolkit OT 5

Topf pot OT 2

Töpfern pottery OT 3

Tor goal OT 1; gate OT 1

Tornado tornado OT 4

Tortendiagramm pie chart OT 4

Torwart goalkeeper OT 4

tot dead OT 1

töten to kill OT 1; to slay WS 2, 79

Touchdown touchdown OT 2

Tourismus tourism OT 3

Tourist(in) tourist OT 1

Tradition tradition OT 2; heritage OT 4

traditionell traditional OT 2

tragbar portable OT 4

Trage... carrier OT 5

tragen to wear OT 1; to carry OT 1

tragend bearing WS 1, 37

Träger(in) holder WS 1, 14

tragisch tragic OT 3

Trailer trailer OT 5

Trainer(in) coach OT 1

trainieren to train OT 2

Trainingsanzug tracksuit WS 3, 102

Traktor tractor OT 2

Träne tear OT 2

trans... trans OT 5

Transaktion transaction WS 4, 146

transatlantisch transatlantic OT 3

transkribieren to transcribe OT 5

Transkribierer(in) transcriber OT 5

Transparent banner OT 4

transportieren to transport OT 3

transsexuell transgender OT 5

Traum dream OT 2

Traumzeit dreamtime OT 5

traurig sad OT 1; upset OT 2
Treffen meeting OT 1
treffen to meet OT 1
Treffer dunk OT 3
treiben to herd OT 2; to float OT 3; to drive OT 5
Treidelpfad towpath OT 3
Trend fashion OT 1; trend OT 4
Trendwende tipping point OT 5
trennen to disconnect **WS 3**, 108
trennend divisive **WS 2**, 62
Trennung segregation **WS 2**, 53; separation **WS 3**, 122
Treppe stairs OT 1
treten to kick OT 1
treu loyal OT 4; staunch **WS 1**, 13
Treue loyalty **WS 1**, 13; allegiance **WS 2**, 69
Tribunal tribunal OT 5
Tribut toll **WS 3**, 119
Trick trick OT 5
Trilogie trilogy OT 5
trinken to drink OT 1
Trinkhalm straw OT 4
Trinkspruch toast OT 2
Trinkwasserbrunnen water fountain OT 2
Trittstein stepping-stone **WS 1**, 16
triumphierend triumphant OT 3
trocken dry OT 2; arid OT 5
Trog trough OT 3
Troll (Computer) troll **WS 2**, 72
Trompete trumpet OT 4
Tropen... tropical OT 4
tropfen to drip OT 3
trotz in spite of OT 5
trotzdem anyway OT 1; nonetheless **WS 2**, 57
trotzen to defy **WS 1**, 21
trübe murky OT 4; gloomy **WS 1**, 16
Truhe chest OT 1
Truppe troop OT 3
Truthahn turkey OT 3
Tschüss! bye OT 1
T-Shirt T-shirt OT 1
tückisch treacherous **WS 1**, 18
tun to do OT 1; to put OT 1
   so tun, als ob to pretend OT 1
Tunika tunic OT 2
Tunnel tunnel OT 3
Tür door OT 1
turbulent turbulent **WS 3**, 94
Turm tower OT 1
Turmspitze spire **WS 1**, 35
Turnen gym OT 1

Turnhalle gym OT 1; gymnasium OT 4
Turnier joust OT 2; tournament OT 3
Turnschuh sneaker OT 5; trainer OT 5
Türschwelle doorstep OT 5
Tüte bag OT 1
Tuten blast OT 3
Tutor(in) tutor OT 2
Tweed(stoff) tweed **WS 1**, 17
Typ guy OT 5
typisch typical OT 2
Tyrannei tyranny **WS 3**, 94

U
U-Bahn metro OT 1; subway OT 1; underground OT 1
Übel evil OT 5
üben to practise OT 1
über about OT 1; via OT 2
über... hyper OT 4
überall everywhere OT 1
Überarbeitung edit OT 4
Überbeanspruchung overuse **WS 3**, 107
überbewerten to overrate OT 5; to overstate **WS 3**, 96
Überblick overview OT 4
übereinstimmen (mit) to conform (to) OT 5; to correspond (to) **WS 3**, 106
Überfahrt passage **WS 1**, 19
Überfall assault OT 5
überfliegen to scan OT 2; to skim OT 5
überflüssig unnecessary OT 5
überfüllt crowded OT 2; overcrowded **WS 1**, 36
Übergang transition OT 5
übergeben to surrender OT 4
   sich übergeben to throw up OT 2
übergewichtig overweight **WS 3**, 105
überlaufen to overflow OT 4
Überleben survival OT 2
überleben to survive OT 3
Überlebende(r) survivor OT 3
Überlegung consideration **WS 3**, 114
übermäßig overly OT 5; excessive **WS 1**, 36
Übernahme adoption **WS 2**, 68
übernehmen to resume OT 5
überprüfen to check OT 1; to review OT 3; to verify **WS 3**, 117
überqueren to cross OT 1
überraschen to shock OT 4; to surprise OT 5
überrascht surprised OT 2; amazed OT 3
Überraschung surprise OT 1; shock OT 3
überreden to persuade OT 3
überreichen to present OT 1

Überrest remnant **WS 1**, 17
Überschrift heading OT 3
Übersetzer(in) translator OT 5
Übersetzung translation OT 2
Übersicht overview OT 4
Überstunden overtime OT 5
übertragbar transferable OT 5
übertragen to transfer OT 5
übertreffen to beat OT 4; to surpass OT 5
   sich selbst übertreffen to excel OT 4
übertreiben to overdo OT 5; to push one's luck **WS 3**, 98
Übertreibung exaggeration OT 4; hyperbole **WS 4**, 139
übertreten to convert **WS 2**, 61
übertrieben exaggerated OT 5
überwachen to oversee OT 4
Überwachung supervision OT 5
überwältigend whopping **WS 3**, 108
überwiegen to outweigh **WS 2**, 62; to prevail **WS 2**, 65
überwiegend dominant OT 4
überwinden to overcome OT 4
überzeugen to persuade OT 3; to convince OT 5
überzeugend persuasive OT 5
üblich usual OT 2
U-Boot submarine **WS 1**, 31
übrig spare OT 3
übriggeblieben leftover OT 4
Übung practice OT 1; exercise OT 1
Übungsheft exercise book OT 1
Ufer bank OT 3
Uhr clock OT 1; o'clock OT 1
Ukulele ukulele **WS 3**, 111
   um ... herum about OT 1
um around OT 1
umarmen to embrace **WS 2**, 69
Umarmung hug OT 1
(um)blättern to flick **WS 3**, 101
umdrehen to flip OT 5; to upend **WS 3**, 114
umfallen to fall over OT 2
umfangreich extensive **WS 3**, 106
umfassen to involve OT 4
umfassend comprehensive **WS 3**, 105
Umfeld environment OT 2
umformulieren to rephrase OT 5
Umfrage survey OT 1; poll OT 5
umgangssprachlich colloquial **WS 1**, 23
umgeben to surround OT 4
Umgebung setting OT 5; surroundings **WS 1**, 26
umgehen to deal with OT 2
umgehend immediate OT 5

umgekehrt vice versa **WS 2**, 70; reverse **WS 3**, 117

Umhang cloak OT 2

Umhängeband lanyard OT 5

umkehren to invert OT 5

umkippen to tip over OT 5

Umlaufbahn orbit OT 4

umreißen to outline OT 4

umschreiben to paraphrase OT 3

umsetzen to implement OT 4

Umstand circumstance OT 5

umständlich awkward **WS 3**, 114

umstellen to rearrange OT 2; to invert OT 5

Umstellung switch OT 5

Umstieg switch OT 5

umstoßen to knock over OT 2

umstritten controversial OT 3; contentious **WS 2**, 82

umstrukturieren to reframe **WS 3**, 111

(um)stürzen to overturn **WS 2**, 53

umwandeln to convert **WS 4**, 142

Umwelt environment OT 2; surroundings **WS 1**, 26

Umwelt… environmental OT 4

umweltfreundlich eco-friendly OT 3

Umweltschützer(in) environmentalist OT 3

umziehen to move OT 1; to relocate OT 4

Umzug parade OT 2; procession OT 2

Umzugswagen removal van OT 4

unabhängig independent OT 4; autonomous OT 4; self-sufficient OT 4

unabhängig von regardless OT 4

Unabhängigkeit independence OT 2

unangemessen improper **WS 2**, 68

unangenehm nasty OT 2; unpleasant OT 5

unbeaufsichtigt unattended OT 4

unbedingt necessarily OT 4

unbegleitet unaccompanied OT 2

unbekannt unfamiliar OT 2; unknown OT 3

unbequem uncomfortable OT 2

unberührt unspoilt OT 3

unbeschwert lightheartedly OT 4

unbestimmt vague OT 5

unbestreitbar undeniable **WS 1**, 30

unbestritten indisputable **WS 3**, 107

unbewohnbar uninhabitable OT 4

unbewohnt uninhabited **WS 1**, 39

unbezahlt unpaid OT 5

und and OT 1

uneben bumpy OT 4

uneingestanden unacknowledged **WS 2**, 68

Uneinigkeit disagreement OT 3

unendlich endless OT 4

unentschieden undecided OT 5

unentschlossen undecided OT 5

unerbittlich relentless **WS 3**, 112

unerheblich insubstantial **WS 1**, 35

unermesslich untold **WS 4**, 138

unermüdlich tirelessly **WS 4**, 146

unerschöpflich inexhaustible **WS 3**, 114

unerwartet unexpected OT 5

unerwarteterweise unexpectedly OT 3

unerwünscht undesirable **WS 2**, 68

unfähig unable OT 4

Unfall accident OT 1

unfreundlich unkind OT 3

ungarisch Hungarian OT 2

Ungeborene(r) unborn **WS 4**, 138

ungeduldig impatient OT 5

ungeeignet unfit OT 2

ungefähr about OT 1; roughly OT 3; approximately OT 5

ungenau inaccurate OT 4

Ungenauigkeit inaccuracy **WS 2**, 73

ungenießbar unpalatable **WS 1**, 12

ungerecht unjust **WS 2**, 60

Ungerechtigkeit injustice **WS 2**, 58

ungeschickt clumsy OT 2

ungestört undisturbed **WS 2**, 53

ungewöhnlich unusual OT 2; uncommon OT 5

ungezogen naughty OT 2

unglaublich incredible OT 2; unbelievable OT 4

unglaubwürdig untrustworthy **WS 3**, 105

Ungleichheit inequality **WS 2**, 62

ungleichmäßig patchy OT 4

unglücklich unhappy OT 1; miserable OT 1

unheimlich scary OT 2; sinister **WS 1**, 35

unhöflich rude OT 2

Uni uni OT 3

Uniform uniform OT 1

Union union OT 4

Unisex… unisex OT 5

Universität university OT 1; college OT 5

Universum universe OT 4

unklar obscure **WS 1**, 43

unkonventionell unconventional OT 5

Unkraut weed OT 5

unmittelbar immediate OT 5

unmöglich impossible OT 2

unnatürlich unnatural OT 5

unnötig unnecessary OT 5

Unordnung mess OT 2

in Unordnung bringen to mess up OT 2

Unrecht injustice **WS 2**, 58; wrong **WS 2**, 76

unrechtmäßig illegitimate **WS 3**, 114

unregelmäßig irregular OT 1

unreif immature **WS 3**, 97

Unruhe(n) unrest **WS 1**, 18; riot **WS 2**, 58

unruhig turbulent **WS 3**, 94

uns us OT 1; ourselves OT 3

unsere(r, -s) our, ours OT 1

unsicher insecure OT 5

Unsicherheit uncertainty OT 5; insecurity **WS 4**, 146

unsichtbar invisible OT 5

Unsinn nonsense OT 1

unten beneath OT 3

unter under OT 1; below OT 2; among OT 3

unterbrechen to interrupt OT 2

Unterbrechung disruption OT 4

unterbringen to accommodate **WS 1**, 15

unterdrücken to oppress **WS 2**, 63

Unterdrücker(in) oppressor **WS 2**, 60

Unterdrückung oppression OT 5; suppression **WS 2**, 56

untergeordnet menial OT 5

Untergruppe subgroup **WS 3**, 96

unterhalb underneath OT 5

unterhalten to entertain OT 4

Unterhaltung entertainment OT 2

Unterkühlung hypothermia OT 2

Unterkunft accommodation OT 4

Unternehmen company OT 1; venture OT 5; enterprise OT 5; corporation **WS 2**, 66

Unternehmer(in) entrepreneur OT 5

Unternehmertum entrepreneurship OT 4

Unterricht lesson OT 1

unterrichten to teach OT 1; to tutor OT 5; to educate **WS 2**, 57

unterscheiden to distinguish **WS 2**, 83

sich unterscheiden to differ **WS 1**, 27

Unterschied difference OT 1; distinction **WS 1**, 27

unterschiedlich different OT 1; varied OT 4

unterschiedlich behandeln to discriminate OT 5

Unterschlupf shelter OT 2

unterschreiben to sign OT 2

Unterschrift signature **WS 2**, 78

unterstützen to support OT 1; to assist OT 4

unterstützend supportive OT 5

Unterstützung backing OT 4; assistance OT 5; aid OT 5

untersuchen to investigate OT 3; to examine OT 4

Untersuchung study OT 1; analysis OT 5

Unterwelt underworld OT 5

untrinkbar undrinkable OT 5

unvergesslich memorable OT 3; unforgettable OT 5

unverheiratet unmarried OT 5

unvermeidlich unavoidable **WS 2**, 54

unvernünftig foolishly OT 5

unverwechselbar distinctive OT 5; unmistakeable **WS 2**, 66

unvollständig incomplete OT 5

unwahrscheinlich improbable **WS 2**, 69

unzerbrechlich unbreakable **WS 1**, 20

Unzufriedenheit dissatisfaction OT 5

unzugänglich inaccessible OT 3

urban urban OT 4

Urkunde diploma OT 4; deed OT 5

Urlaub holiday OT 1; vacation OT 2

Urlaubsort resort OT 3

ursächlich causal **WS 4**, 142

Ursprung origin OT 3

ursprünglich original OT 3; inital OT 5

Urteil verdict **WS 2**, 70

Urvater forefather OT 4

usw. etc. OT 3

Utopie utopia **WS 4**, 146

V

vage vague OT 5

valid valid **WS 2**, 68

Vampir vampire OT 2

Vanille vanilla OT 1

Vanillesoße custard OT 1

Variante variation OT 5; variant **WS 2**, 68

Variation variation OT 5

variieren to vary OT 5

Vater father OT 1

väterlich paternal **WS 2**, 54

vegan vegan OT 4

Veganer(in) vegan OT 4

vegetarisch veggie OT 2; vegetarian OT 2

Vegetation vegetation **WS 1**, 22

Venusmuschel clam OT 3

Verabredung date OT 3

verabscheuen to loath OT 5

verachten to scorn **WS 3**, 101

verändern to transform OT 4; to shift OT 5; to alter **WS 3**, 117

Veränderung shift OT 5

verängstigt scared OT 1; frightened OT 1; terrified OT 3

verankern to embed **WS 1**, 12

veranschaulichen to visualize OT 4

veranstalten to put on OT 1; to stage **WS 2**, 53

Veranstaltungsort venue **WS 1**, 29

verantwortlich responsible OT 3

  verantwortlich machen to hold accountable **WS 4**, 136

Verantwortung responsibility OT 3

verärgert upset OT 2; cross OT 2; annoyed OT 3

Verb verb OT 1

verbal verbal OT 5

Verband bandage OT 2

verbergen to conceal OT 5

verbessern to correct OT 1; to enhance OT 4; to enrich OT 4

  sich verbessern to improve OT 3

Verbesserung improvement OT 3

verbieten to ban OT 3

verbinden to join up OT 2; to connect OT 2

Verbindung linkage **WS 2**, 73

Verbindung connection OT 2; link OT 2; tie OT 5; bond **WS 3**, 94

  in Verbindung in touch OT 2

  in Verbindung bringen (mit) to associate (with) OT 5

Verbindung bond **WS 3**, 94

verbissen fiercely **WS 1**, 15

verblüffen to baffle **WS 3**, 119

verblüfft puzzled OT 5

Verbot ban OT 5

Verbrauch consumption **WS 1**, 36

verbrauchen to consume OT 4

Verbraucher(in) consumer OT 5

Verbrechen crime OT 4

verbreiten to spread OT 4

verbreitet diffused **WS 3**, 122

Verbreitung proliferation **WS 3**, 110

Verbrennungs… internal combustion OT 4

verbringen to spend OT 1

verbunden linked OT 2; devoted OT 4; affiliated **WS 2**, 71

Verbundenheit solidarity **WS 2**, 77

Verbündete(r) ally **WS 2**, 70

sich verbürgen to vouch **WS 3**, 93

verdächtig suspicious OT 3

verdammen to doom **WS 3**, 96

verdammt damned **WS 3**, 105

Verderben spoilage OT 4

verderben to spoil OT 2

verdeutlichen to illustrate OT 4

verdienen to deserve OT 2; to earn OT 3

(sich) verdoppeln to double OT 5

verehren to worship OT 5

Verein club OT 1

vereinbaren to arrange OT 2

Vereinbarung agreement OT 3; arrangement OT 5

vereinfachen to simplify **WS 2**, 68

vereinigen to unite OT 5; to unify **WS 2**, 66

Verfahren operation OT 4; procedure OT 4

verfallen to decline OT 5

verfallen ruined OT 3

Verfassung constitution OT 4

Verfassungs… constitutional OT 4

verfassungswidrig unconstitutional **WS 2**, 59

verfaulen to rot OT 5

verfechten to champion **WS 2**, 54

verfeinern to refine OT 4

verflechten to entwine **WS 1**, 17

verflochten intertwined **WS 1**, 35

verfolgen to pursue OT 4

Verfolgung pursuit OT 4

verfügbar available OT 4; disposable **WS 1**, 12

Verfügbarkeit availability OT 4

Verfügung disposal **WS 1**, 34; ordinance **WS 2**, 54

vergeben to forgive OT 2; to award OT 4

vergeigen to mess up OT 2

vergessen to forget OT 1

Vergleich comparison OT 5

vergleichbar (mit) comparable (to) OT 5

vergleichen to compare OT 1; to contrast **WS 2**, 77

Vergnügen treat OT 5

verhaften to arrest OT 4

Verhalten behavior OT 3

sich verhalten to act OT 1

Verhaltens… behavioural **WS 3**, 122

Verhältnis relation OT 5

Verhältniswort preposition OT 1

verhängen to impose **WS 1**, 30

verheerend devastating OT 5; disastrous **WS 4**, 136

verherrlichen to glorify **WS 2**, 56

verhindern to prevent OT 4

verhungern to starve OT 1

Verhütung prevention OT 2

verkalkt calcified **WS 1**, 12

Verkauf sale OT 3

verkaufen to sell OT 1

Verkäufer(in) sales assistant OT 2

Verkehr traffic OT 1

verkleinern to minimize **WS 3**, 95

verklemmt uptight OT 5

verknallt: in jmdn. verknallt sein
to have a crush on OT 4

verkünden to declare OT 4

verlagern to relocate **WS 1**, 24;
to shift **WS 2**, 66

Verlangen demand OT 5

verlangen nach to yearn for **WS 1**, 13

verlängert prolonged OT 5

verlangsamen to slow down OT 4

verlassen to leave OT 1; to evacuate OT 4
sich verlassen auf to rely on OT 4

verlässlich reliable OT 4

verlegen to misplace **WS 1**, 22;
to relocate **WS 1**, 24

verlegen to relocate **WS 1**, 24

Verleger(in) publisher OT 5

verleihen to award OT 4

verletzen to injure OT 2; to hurt OT 2;
to insult OT 5

verletzend hurtful **WS 2**, 72

verletzlich vulnerable **WS 2**, 73

verletzt hurt OT 1

Verletzung injury OT 2

sich verlieben to fall in love OT 5

verlieren to lose OT 1

Verlust loss OT 4

Vermächtnis legacy OT 4

Vermarkter(in) marketer **WS 3**, 114

vermeiden to avoid OT 4

vermissen to miss OT 2

vermitteln to impart OT 4; to
communicate OT 4; to convey OT 5

vermuten to suppose OT 1; to suspect
WS 1, 25; to assume **WS 2**, 57

Vernachlässigung neglect **WS 2**, 70

Verneinung negative OT 1

Vernetzung interconnectedness
WS 3, 97; connectivity **WS 3**, 110

vernichten to wipe out OT 5; to
annihilate **WS 4**, 138

vernünftig sensible OT 2; reasonable
WS 2, 84

veröffentlichen to release OT 4;
to publish OT 4

Veröffentlichung publication OT 4

Verordnung act OT 5

Verpächter landlord **WS 1**, 19

Verpackung packaging OT 3

verpflichtend mandatory OT 4;
compulsory **WS 3**, 115

verpflichtet sein to be obliged (to) OT 5

Verpflichtung commitment **WS 1**, 30

Verputz plaster OT 1

verräterisch treacherous **WS 1**, 18

verringern to reduce OT 4; to diminish
WS 2, 73

Verringerung reduction **WS 3**, 93

verrückt crazy OT 2; mad OT 2;
insane **WS 3**, 117

Verrückte(r) nut OT 5

Vers verse OT 3

sich versammeln to rally **WS 2**, 58

Versammlung assembly OT 1

verschieden various OT 4; divers OT 4

verschlafen to oversleep OT 4

verschlimmern to compound **WS 4**, 135

verschlüsselt in code OT 2

verschmelzen to merge **WS 2**, 60

verschmutzen to foul OT 5; to pollute
OT 5

Verschmutzung pollution OT 3

verschneit snowy OT 4

verschrotten to scrap **WS 2**, 53

verschütten to spill OT 2

verschwenden to waste OT 3

verschwinden to disappear OT 3;
to vanish OT 4

versehentlich by accident OT 2;
by mistake OT 2; accidentally OT 3

verseuchen to foul OT 5; to pollute OT 5

versichern to assure **WS 1**, 23

Version version OT 2

versklaven to enslave **WS 2**, 54

versöhnlich conciliatory **WS 2**, 57

Versöhnung reconciliation **WS 3**, 112

versorgen mit to provide OT 4

Versorgung catering OT 3

Verspätung delay OT 4

verspotten to mock **WS 2**, 64

Versprechen promise OT 2

versprechen to promise OT 2

Verstand mind OT 1

verstärken to reinforce OT 5; to amplify
WS 4, 135

verstaubt dusty OT 4

verstauchen to sprain OT 2

Verstauchung sprain OT 2

(sich) verstecken to hide OT 3

versteckt ulterior **WS 3**, 116

verstehen to understand OT 1

verstopfen to plug in OT 1; to clog OT 4

verstreuen to scatter **WS 1**, 35

Versuch attempt OT 2

versuchen to try OT 1; to attempt
WS 1, 12

Versuchung temptation **WS 3**, 108

vertäuen to moor OT 3

verteidigen to defend OT 5

Verteidigung defence OT 5

verteilen to distribute OT 4

Verteilung distribution **WS 2**, 62

sich vertiefen to delve into **WS 3**, 111

Vertrag treaty OT 4; contract OT 4

Vertrauen faith OT 3

vertrauen to trust OT 2

vertrauenswürdig trustworthy **WS 4**, 140

vertraut familiar OT 2; intimate **WS 1**, 29

Vertrautheit familiarity OT 4

vertreiben to dispel **WS 2**, 82

vertreten to represent OT 3

Vertreter(in) representative OT 4

vertrödeln to muck around OT 5

verunreinigen to contaminate OT 5

verursachen to cause OT 2

verurteilen to sentence OT 5; to convict
OT 5

Verurteilte(r) convict OT 5

Verurteilung sentence OT 5; conviction
OT 5

vervielfachen to multiply **WS 4**, 136

vervielfältigen to reproduce **WS 4**, 135

vervollständigen to complete OT 1

Vervollständigung completion OT 4

Verwahrung custody OT 5

Verwaltung administration **WS 1**, 30

verwandt related OT 3

Verwandte(r) relative OT 3; kinsman
OT 4

Verwarnung caution OT 5

Verweigerung denial **WS 3**, 105

Verweilzeit dwell time **WS 4**, 135

verwendbar usable OT 5

verwenden to utilize **WS 2**, 77

verwirrend confusing OT 2

verwirrt confused OT 2; puzzled OT 5;
bewildered **WS 3**, 119

verwöhnen to indulge **WS 3**, 110

Verzögerung delay OT 4

verzweifelt desperate OT 3

vice versa vice versa **WS 2**, 70

Video video OT 1

Video-Blog vlog OT 3

Videokassette video OT 1

Videospiel video game OT 2

Vieh livestock OT 5

Viehbestand livestock OT 5

viel lots, a lot OT 1
viele many OT 1

vielfach multiple OT 2
Vielfalt variety OT 4
vielfältig diverse OT 4
Vielfältigkeit diversity OT 4
vielleicht maybe OT 1; perhaps OT 3
vier four OT 1
Viertel quarter OT 1
   viertel vor quarter to OT 1
vierzehn fourteen OT 1
vierzig forty OT 1
Vintage vintage OT 5
violett violet OT 2
violett purple WS 1, 13
viral viral OT 4
virtuell virtual OT 5
   virtuelle Realität VR, virtual reality
     WS 3, 99
Virus virus WS 4, 140
Visualisierung visualization OT 3
visuell visual OT 2
Vizepräsident(in) vice-president OT 4
Vlog vlog OT 3
vloggen to vlog OT 3
Vlogger(in) vlogger OT 3
Vogel bird OT 1
Vokal vowel OT 1
Volks... folk OT 2
Volksabstimmung referendum WW, 11
voll full OT 1
Vollendung accomplishment WS 1, 37
Volleyball volleyball OT 5
völlig totally OT 3; thoroughly OT 5
völlig absolute WS 1, 29
Vollkorn... wholegrain WS 1, 36
vollständig exhaustive WS 3, 114
Vollstreckung enforcement OT 5
vollzeit full time OT 2
Volontär(in) intern OT 5
von by OT 1; of from OT 1; off OT 1
vor before OT 1; ago OT 1
voranbringen to further WS 2, 62
vorangehen to precede WS 2, 65
Voraussetzung requirement OT 5
vorbereiten to prepare OT 1; to get
   ready OT 1
Vorbereitung preparation OT 2
Vordergrund foreground OT 4
Vorderseite front OT 1
vordringen to encroach WS 3, 112
voreingenommen biased OT 5
Voreingenommenheit bias OT 5
Vorfahr(in) ancestor OT 3
Vorfall incident OT 5
Vorfreude anticipation WS 1, 29
vorführen to demonstrate OT 5

Vorgang operation OT 4
Vorgänger(in) predecessor WS 3, 111
vorgeben to pretend OT 1
vorgehen approach OT 5
vorgehen: hart vorgehen gegen
   to crack down on **WS 2**, 73
vorgesehen destined WS 2, 76
Vorhang curtain OT 2
vorher previously OT 4
Vorhersage prediction OT 2
vorhersagen to predict OT 2;
   to presage **WS 2**, 69
vorhersehbar predictable OT 5
vorhersehen to anticipate WS 1, 37
Vorlage template OT 4
Vorlesung lecture OT 4
Vorliebe preference OT 4
vorn(e) at the front OT 1
   nach vorne bringen to elevate
     WS 2, 68
vorrangig paramount WS 2, 55
Vorrat supply OT 3
Vorreiter(in) trailblazer WS 2, 74
Vorschlag suggestion OT 1; proposition
   WS 4, 134
vorschlagen to suggest OT 1; to propose
   WS 1, 30
vorschreiben to prescribe OT 5
vorschulisch preschool OT 5
vorsichtig careful OT 1; cautious
   WS 3, 97; tentative **WS 3**, 107
vorsichtig sein to be aware OT 4
vorsingen to audition OT 3
Vorsitzende chairwoman WS 2, 62
Vorsitzende(r) chairperson WS 2, 62
Vorsitzender chairman WS 2, 62
Vorspeise starter OT 1
Vorsprechen audition OT 3
vorsprechen to audition OT 3
vorstellen to present OT 1; to introduce
   OT 2
   sich etwas vorstellen to imagine OT 1
Vorstellung introduction OT 2; notion
   WS 3, 101
Vorstrafregister criminal record OT 5
Vorteil pro OT 2; advantage OT 3;
   benefit OT 4
vorteilhaft beneficial OT 2
vortreten to step up OT 5
Vorurteil preconception WS 3, 105;
   prejudice **WS 3**, 116
vorwärts forwards OT 2
Vorwurf blame OT 4
vorziehen to prefer OT 1
VR VR, virtual reality **WS 3**, 99

Vulkan volcano OT 2
vulkanisch volcanic WS 1, 25

W
wach awake OT 2
Wacholder juniper WS 1, 22
wachsam watchful WS 3, 114
wachsen to grow OT 1; to expand OT 5
Wachstum growth OT 5
Wächter(in) guard OT 5
Waffe weapon OT 3
Waffel waffle OT 3
Wagen trolley OT 2; carriage OT 2;
   wagon OT 4
wagen to dare OT 2
Wahl choice OT 1; option OT 2; election
   OT 3
Wahl... electoral OT 4
Wahlbezirk constituency OT 4
wählen to elect OT 4; to select OT 4
Wähler(in) voter OT 4; constituent OT 4
Wählerschaft electorate WS 1, 30
Wahlmann elector OT 4
Wahlrecht vote OT 5
Wahlstimme vote OT 5
Wahn craze WS 3, 108
wahr true OT 1
während while OT 2; whereas OT 5
Wahrheit truth OT 3
wahrnehmen to perceive WS 2, 68
Wahrnehmung perception WS 3, 95
wahrscheinlich probably OT 2;
   likely OT 2
Wahrscheinlichkeit probability
   WS 3, 106; likelihood **WS 3**, 108
Währung currency WS 1, 31
Wahrzeichen landmark OT 3
Wal whale OT 2
Wald forest OT 1; woods OT 2;
   woodland OT 4
Walfang whaling OT 2
walisisch Welsh OT 1
Walross walrus OT 4
Walspeck blubber OT 2
Walzer waltz WS 1, 26
Wams doublet OT 3
Wand wall OT 1
Wanderer, Wanderin walker WS 1, 12
Wandern hillwalking WS 1, 12
wandern to hike OT 1; to wander WS 1, 16
Wandgemälde mural OT 2
Wange jowl WS 3, 119
wann when OT 1
warm warm OT 1
Wärme warmth OT 4

warnen to warn OT 2
Warnung warning OT 2; caution OT 5
warten to wait OT 1; to hang on OT 2
Warteschlange queue OT 1
Wartung maintenance OT 3
warum why OT 1
was what OT 1
Waschbär racoon OT 4
Wäsche laundry OT 3
waschen to wash OT 2
Wäscherei laundry OT 3
Wäscher(in) washer OT 4
Wasser water OT 1
wasserdicht waterproof OT 2
Wasserfall fall OT 1; waterfall OT 1
Wasserhahn tap OT 3
Wasserkraft hydro-electric OT 4
Wasserloch waterhole OT 5
Wasserscheide watershed **WS 1**, 34
Wasserschildkröte turtle OT 2
Wasserstelle watering hole OT 5
Wasserwaage spirit level OT 5
weben to weave **WS 1**, 17
Wechsel transition OT 5
Wechselgeld change OT 1
wechseln to change OT 1; to exchange OT 5
Wecker alarm OT 2
weder … noch neither … nor OT 4
Weg way OT 1; path OT 1; track OT 2; avenue **WS 3**, 97
weg off OT 1; away OT 2
Wegbereiter(in) groundbreaker **WS 4**, 140
Wegbeschreibungen directions OT 2
wegen due to OT 5
Wegmarkierung waymarking **WS 1**, 15
Wegweiser signpost OT 5
wegwerfen to discard **WS 3**, 104
wehen to blow OT 2
Wehr brigade **WS 1**, 38
wehtun to hurt OT 1
weiblich female OT 2
weich soft OT 1
Weide pasture **WS 1**, 36
sich weigern to refuse OT 4
Weigerung refusal **WS 2**, 60
weil because OT 1
weinen to cry OT 1
Weinrebe vine OT 4
weise wise **WW**, 11
Weisheit wisdom **WS 3**, 105
weiß white OT 1
Weißkopfseeadler bald eagle **WS 1**, 38
weit far OT 1; wide OT 2

weit entfernt distant OT 4
weiter further OT 4
weiter vorn ahead OT 2
weiterführend secondary OT 1
weiterführende Schule secondary school OT 1
weitermachen to continue OT 2; to go ahead
weitverbreitet widespread **WS 1**, 36
Weizen wheat OT 5
welche(r, -s) which OT 1
Welle wave OT 1; ripple **WW**, 11
Wellensittich budgie OT 1
Welpe puppy OT 2
Wels catfish **WS 1**, 12
Welt world OT 1
Weltraum space OT 1; outer space OT 5
Weltstadt cosmopolitan city OT 4
weltweit worldwide OT 3; global OT 4
Wendung phrase OT 1
wenige few OT 1
weniger less OT 2
wenn whilst **WS 1**, 17
wer, wen, wem who OT 1
Werbung advertisement OT 1; ad, advert OT 2; avdvertising OT 2
Werbung machen für to advertise OT 2
werden to become OT 2; to get OT 2
werfen to throw OT 1; to toss OT 1
werfen to hurl **WS 3**, 119
Werkstatt workshop OT 1; garage OT 4
Werkzeug tool OT 2
Werkzeugkiste toolkit OT 5
Wert value OT 4; merit OT 5
wert worth OT 4; worthy **WS 3**, 97
wertschätzen to value OT 5
wertvoll valuable OT 2
Wesen being OT 4
Wesen essence **WS 1**, 13
wesentlich essential OT 4; crucial **WS 3**, 96
im Wesentlichen in essence OT 4
Wesentliche essence **WS 1**, 13
Wespe wasp OT 3
wessen whose OT 1
Westen west OT 1
Wettbewerb competition OT 1
Wettbewerber(in) competitor OT 4
wetteifernd competitively OT 4
wetten to bet OT 1
Wetter weather OT 1
Wettkampf match OT 1
Wettkämpfer(in) contestant OT 4
Whisky whisky **WS 1**, 17

wichtig important OT 1; major OT 3; relevant OT 4; essential OT 4; dominant OT 4
Wichtigkeit importance OT 3; significance OT 5
Widder tup OT 2
widerlegen to debunk **WS 1**, 12
sich widersetzen to defy **WS 1**, 21; to oppose **WS 2**, 60
widersprechen to contradict **WS 3**, 94
Widerspruch contradiction **WS 3**, 111
Widerstand resistance OT 5
Widerstandsfähigkeit resilience **WS 1**, 14
widerstehen to resist OT 5
widerwillig unwilling OT 4
Widrigkeit adversity **WS 1**, 16
Widrigkeiten odds **WS 1**, 17
wie how OT 1; as OT 1
wieder again OT 1
wieder annehmen to resume OT 5
Wiederaufbau reconstruction **WS 2**, 58
Wiederbelebung revival OT 5
wiedergutmachen to right **WS 2**, 76
Wiedergutmachung amends OT 5
wiederherstellen to restore OT 3; to recreate **WS 3**, 119
Wiederherstellung recovery OT 3
wiederholen to repeat OT 1
sich wiederholend repetitive OT 5
Wiederholung repetition OT 5
Wiederverheiratung remarriage OT 5
wiederverwendbar reusable OT 3
wiederverwenden to reuse OT 4
wiederverwerten to recycle OT 2
Wiederverwerter(in) recycler OT 3
Wiederverwertung upcycling OT 4
Wiege cradle OT 3
wiegen to weigh OT 3
Wiese meadow OT 2
wild wild OT 2; feral OT 5
Wildfang tomboy OT 5
Wildnis wilderness OT 2
Willkommen! welcome OT 1
willkürlich random OT 5
Wind wind OT 2
Winde winch OT 3
Windel nappy OT 3; diaper (AE) OT 3
windig windy OT 2
Windrad wind turbine OT 4
windsurfen to windsurf OT 1
winken to wave **WS 2**, 53
Winsch windlass OT 3
Winter winter OT 1
winzig tiny OT 1; mini OT 5
wir us, we OT 1

wirklich really OT 1; truly OT 4; actual OT 4
wirksam effective OT 3; efficient OT 5
Wirkung effect OT 3
Wirtschaft economy OT 5
wirtschaftlich economic OT 5
Wirtschaftswissenschaftler(in) economist WS 4, 144
Wissen knowledge OT 4
wissen to know OT 1
Wissenschaft studies OT 1
wissenschaftlich scientific OT 3
Witz joke OT 2; pun OT 4
   Witze machen to joke OT 2
wo where OT 1
   wo (auch) immer wherever OT 3
woanders elsewhere WS 3, 117
Woche week OT 1
Wochenende weekend OT 1
wöchentlich weekly OT 4
wogen to surge WS 1, 36
Wohlbefinden wellness OT 5; wellbeing OT 5
Wohlfahrt welfare WS 1, 31
Wohlfahrtsorganisation charity OT 2
Wohlstand prosperity WS 4, 136
Wohltätigkeits... charitable WS 1, 14
Wohltätigkeitsveranstaltung fundraiser OT 2
Wohn... residential OT 4; housing OT 5
wohnen to live OT 1
Wohnsitz residence WS 1, 25
Wohnung flat OT 1; apartment OT 1
Wohnungs... housing OT 5
Wohnwagen caravan OT 1
Wohnzimmer living room OT 1
Wolf wolf OT 4
Wolke cloud OT 1
Wolkenkratzer skyscraper OT 3
wolkig cloudy OT 1
Wolle wool OT 3
wollen to want OT 1
wollig woolly OT 2
Wombat wombat OT 5
Wort word OT 1
Wortart part of speech OT 2
Wörterbuch dictionary OT 2
Wortliste wordlist OT 2
Wortschatz lexicon OT 5
Wortspiel pun OT 4
Wrack wreck OT 3
Wunder wonder OT 4
wunderbar wonderful OT 1
sich wundern to wonder OT 4
wunderschön gorgeous WS 3, 117

Wunsch desire OT 5
wünschen to wish OT 2
wünschenswert desirable WS 4, 144
würdig worthy WS 3, 97
Würfel dice OT 1
   in Würfel schneiden to dice WS 2, 69
würfeln to dice WS 2, 69
Wurm worm OT 1
Wurst sausage OT 1
Wurzel root OT 3
würzen to spice OT 4
Wüste desert OT 3
Wüstenbildung desertification WS 4, 138
Wut anger WS 2, 60
wütend enraged WS 2, 59; furious WS 3, 113

Y

Yacht yacht OT 5
Yoga yoga OT 5

Z

zaghaft tentative WS 3, 107
Zahl number OT 1; figure OT 3
zählbar countable OT 1
zählen to count OT 2
zahlreich numerous WS 1, 39
Zahn tooth OT 2
Zahnbürste toothbrush OT 4
zart tender WS 1, 31; delicate WS 3, 119
Zauber magic OT 1
Zauberer, Zauberin magician OT 1
Zaun fence OT 1
Zebra zebra OT 1
Zehe toe OT 1
zehn ten OT 1
Zeichensetzung punctuation OT 3
zeichnen to draw OT 1
Zeichnung drawing OT 4
zeigen to show OT 1; to point OT 1; to indicate OT 4; to reveal OT 4
Zeit time OT 1; period OT 3
Zeitachse timeline OT 2
Zeitform tense OT 1
zeitgenössisch contemporary OT 4
Zeitpunkt timing OT 3
Zeitschrift magazine OT 1
Zeituhr timer OT 5
Zeitung newspaper OT 1
Zeitwort verb OT 1
Zelle cell WS 1, 37
Zelt tent OT 1
zelten to camp OT 1

Zeltplatz campsite OT 2; campground OT 2
zementieren to cement WS 2, 58
Zentimeter centimetre OT 2
zentral crucial WS 3, 96
Zentral... central OT 1
Zentralheizung central heating OT 2
Zentrum center OT 2
zerbrechen to snap OT 3
zerebrale Kinderlähmung cerebral palsy OT 5
zeremoniell ceremonial OT 3
zerfetzen to shred OT 2
zerkleinert shredded OT 2
zerklüftet ragged WS 1, 15
zerlegen to take apart OT 4
zermürbend gruelling WS 1, 22
zerschlagen to crush WS 1, 32
zerschneiden to slash WS 1, 36
zerstören to destroy OT 2
Zerstörung destruction OT 4
Zertifikat certificate OT 2
zertrümmern to batter OT 4
Zeug stuff OT 2
Zeuge, Zeugin witness OT 3
   Zeuge sein von to witness OT 3
Zeugnis certificate OT 2
Ziege goat OT 3
ziehen to draw OT 1; to pull OT 1
Ziel aim OT 4; target OT 4; finish WS 2, 76
zielen to aim OT 4
   zielen auf to target OT 5
zielgerichtet purposeful WS 3, 116
ziemlich rather OT 3; quite OT 3; relatively OT 4
zieren to grace WS 1, 17
Ziffer digit OT 2
Zimmermann carpenter OT 3
Zinn tin OT 2
zirkulieren to circulate OT 4
Zirkus circus WS 1, 43
zischen to whizz OT 2
Zitat quotation OT 2
zitieren to quote OT 2
Zitronenlimonade lemonade OT 1
Zittern tremor OT 3
zittern to shiver OT 3
Zivilisation civilization WS 1, 15
zivilisieren to civilize WS 2, 54
zivilisiert civilized OT 5
zögerlich hesitantly OT 4
Zögern hesitation OT 3
zögern to hesitate OT 3
Zoll customs OT 2; toll WS 3, 119
Zoll toll WS 3, 119

Zoll (2,54 cm) inch OT 2
zollfrei duty free OT 2
Zone zone OT 2
Zoo zoo OT 1
zu to OT 1; too OT 1
Zubehör accessory OT 3
zubinden to tie OT 5
Zucchini zucchini OT 3
züchten to breed OT 5
Zucker sugar OT 1
zuckerhaltig sugary WS 1, 36
zuerst at first OT 2; firstly OT 3
Zufahrt driveway OT 4
Zufall chance OT 2
zufällig accidentally OT 3; random OT 5
   zufällig entdecken to happen upon OT 4
zufrieden pleased OT 1
Zug train OT 1
Zugang access OT 2; gateway OT 5
zugänglich accessible OT 2
zugeben to admit OT 5
zügig brisk WS 1, 37
zugreifen to access OT 4
zugunsten in favour OT 4
Zuhause home OT 1
zuhören to listen OT 1; to hark WS 1, 13
Zukunft future OT 2
zukünftig prospective WS 3, 105
zulässig acceptable WS 3, 96
zumachen to shut OT 2
zunächst initially OT 5
Zunahme increase OT 3
Zunder tinder OT 2
zunehmend increasingly OT 5
Zuneigung affection WS 1, 13
Zunge tongue OT 3
zuordnen to allocate OT 4
zurechtkommen to cope OT 5

zurück back OT 1
zurückfordern to reclaim WS 2, 69
zurückgehen to decrease OT 5
zurückgewinnen to reclaim WS 2, 69
Zurückhaltung aloofness WS 3, 95
zurückkehren to return OT 2
zurücktreten to resign OT 4
zurückverfolgen to trace OT 3; to backtrack WS 4, 135
zurückweichen to retreat WS 1, 18
Zurückweisung rejection WS 2, 60
zurückziehen to recant WS 2, 58
   sich zurückziehen to withdraw WS 1, 18
zusammen together OT 1
Zusammenarbeit collaboration OT 4; cooperation OT 5
zusammenarbeiten to collaborate WS 4, 146
zusammenfassen to summarize OT 2; to outline OT 4
Zusammenfassung summary OT 1; abstract OT 4
Zusammenhang context OT 4
   mit etw. in Zusammenhang stehen to relate to OT 5
zusammenlaufen to converge WS 2, 58
zusammenlegen to fold WS 2, 69
zusammensacken to slump OT 5
zusammenstoßen to clash WS 2, 59
Zusammenströmen confluence WS 3, 114
zusammentragen to collate WS 1, 22
Zusatz addition OT 4
zusätzlich spare OT 3; additional OT 5
Zuschauer(in) spectator OT 2; viewer OT 3; bystander WS 4, 138
zuschlagen to strike WS 1, 19
Zuschuss grant OT 4

zuspielen to pass OT 2
Zustand condition OT 2
zuständig in charge OT 1; competent OT 4
zusteigen to get on OT 2
Zustellung delivery OT 5
zustimmen to agree OT 1; to approve OT 4
zustimmend affirmative OT 3
Zustimmung approval WS 2, 71
Zutat ingredient OT 2
zuteilen to allocate WS 1, 22
zutreffend applicable WS 2, 82
Zuverlässigkeit reliability WS 3, 106
Zwang compulsion WS 3, 101
zwanzig twenty OT 1
Zweck purpose OT 5
zwei two OT 1
zweifach dual OT 4
Zweifel doubt OT 5
Zweig stick OT 2; twig OT 2
zweimal twice OT 2
zweisprachig bilingual OT 3
Zweisprachigkeit bilingualism OT 4
zweitens secondly OT 2
Zweite(r, -s) second OT 1
Zwiebel onion OT 2
Zwilling twin OT 1
zwingen to force OT 5; to compel WS 3, 108
zwischen between OT 1; among OT 3
zwischenmenschlich interpersonal OT 5
Zwischenstation waypoint OT 2
Zwischenzeit meantime WS 3, 119
zwölf twelve OT 1
Zyklon cyclone OT 5
Zyklus cycle OT 4
Zynismus cynicism WS 2, 69

Dictionary: Names

A
Agra [ˈɑːgrə] city in India WS 1, 39
Alaska [əˈlæskə] most northern and largest US state by area WS 1, 21
Ali Smith [ˌæli ˈsmɪθ] Scottish author, playwright, academic, and journalist, born 24th August, 1962 WS 1, 35
Alicia Garza [əˌliːsiə ˈgɑːrzɑː] American civil rights activist, cofounder of Black Lives Matter, born 4th January, 1981 WS 2, 70

Angles [ˈæŋglz] Germanic invaders who settled in Britain during the post-Roman period WS 1, 21
Arran [ˈærən] island in western Scotland WS 1, 40
Aretha Franklin [əˌriːθə ˈfræŋklɪn] American singer and songwriter (1942 – 2018) WS 2, 53
Ayrshire [ˈeəʃə] former county of south-east Scotland WS 1, 31

B
B. B. King [biː biː ˈkɪŋ] American blues singer and songwriter (1925 – 2015) WS 2, 67
Beatles [ˈbiːtlz] British pop group of the 1960s WS 3, 103
Bill Clinton [bɪl ˈklɪntən] 42nd President of the US, born 19th August, 1946 WS 2, 79
Black Lives Matter [blæk laɪvz ˈmætə] (BLM) political and social movement which highlights and opposes racism,

discrimination and racial inequality experienced by black people **WS 2**, 70

Black Panther Party [blæk ˈpænθə pɑːti] political organization founded in the 1980s by African Americans as a way of fighting against discrimination and racism, using violence if necessary **WS 2**, 62

Blind Willie McTell [ˌblaɪnd wɪli mækˈtel] American blues and ragtime singer (1898 – 1959) **WS 2**, 66

Bobby Seale [ˌbɒbi ˈsiːl] American political activist and author, cofounder of the Black Panther Party **WS 2**, 62

Bonny Prince Charlie [ˌbɒni prɪns ˈtʃɑːli] Prince Charles Edward Stuart (1720 – 1788) **WS 1**, 18

Brazil [brəˈzɪl] country in South America **WS 3**, 95

Breonna Taylor [briːˈænə ˈteɪlə] African American woman killed by police officers, her death led to numerous protests against police brutality (1993-2020) **WS 2**, 78

Brexit [ˈbreksɪt] Britain's "exit" from the European Union in 2020 **WS 1**, 30

C

Cairngorms [ˈkeəngɔːmz] mountain range in central Scotland **WS 1**, 22

Caledonia [ˌkæləˈdəʊniə] old name used for Scotland **WS 1**, 18

Capitol [ˈkæpɪtl] building in Washington D. C. where the US congress is located **WS 2**, 83

Cèilidh [ˈkeɪli] social occasion with music and dancing, particularly in Ireland and Scotland **WS 1**, 28

Charles Macintosh [ˌtʃɑːlz ˈmækɪntɒʃ] Scottish chemist who developed a method of making waterproof fabric (1766 – 1823) **WS 1**, 38

Colin Kaepernick [ˈkɒlɪn ˈkæpərnɪk] American football player and civil rights activist, born 3rd November, 1987 **WS 2**, 71

Corona [kəˈrəʊnə] infection caused by coronavirus **WS 3**, 111

Czech Republic [ˌtʃek rɪˈpʌblɪk] country in central Europe **WS 3**, 95

D

Denmark [ˈdenmɑːk] country in northern Europe **WS 1**, 18

Duke of Edinburgh's Award [djuːk əv ˈedɪnbrəz əwɔːd] (DofE) award comprising various programmes for young people between the ages of 14 and 24 **WS 1**, 14

E

Edinburgh [ˈedɪnbrə] capital city of Scotland **WS 1**, 12

Edward II [ˌedwəd ðə ˈsekənd] king of England (1284 – 1327) **WS 1**, 18

Elizabeth I [ɪˌlɪzəbəθ ðə ˈfɜːst] queen of England and Ireland, she is generally regarded as one of England's greatest rulers (1533 – 1603) **WS 1**, 18

F

Frederick Douglass [ˌfredrɪk ˈdʌgləs] African American abolitionist who escaped slavery and became a leading figure working to end slavery (1817 – 1895) **WS 2**, 57

G

Ghana [ˈgɑːnə] country in West Africa **WS 3**, 95

Gen-Z [ˌdʒen ˈzed] generation born between 1996 and 2012 **WS 3**, 99

George Floyd [ˌdʒɔːdʒ ˈflɔɪd] African American man who was murdered by a police officer. His death became a symbol for police brutality against black people and lead to global portests (1973 – 2020) **WS 3**, 56

Gandhi [ˈgændi] Indian lawyer, writer and social activist known for his nonviolent protest (1896 – 1948) **WS 2**, 58

Glasgow [ˈglɑːzgəʊ] Scotland's largest city **WS 1**, 12

H

Harlem [ˈhɑːləm] district in Manhattan, New York **WS 2**, 60

Harper Lee [hɑːpə ˈliː] American author best known for her 1960 novel To Kill a Mockingbird (1926-2016) **WS 2**, 64

Harriet Tubman [ˌhæriət ˈtʌbmən] African American woman who escaped from enslavement and became a leading activist in the campaign to end slavery (1821 – 1913) **WS 2**, 57

Hawaii [həˈwaɪi] last state to join the US in 1959, located in the Pacific Ocean **WS 2**, 79

Highlands [ˈhaɪləndz] high mountain region of Scotland **WS 1**, 12

Huey Newton [ˌhjuːi ˈnjuːtən] American political activist and cofounder of the Black Panther Party (1942 – 1989) **WS 2**, 62

I

Iceland [ˈaɪslənd] country in the northern Atlantic Ocean **WS 1**, 21

Indiana [ˌɪndiˈænə] state in the midwest of the US **WS 2**, 57

Ireland [ˈaɪələnd] second largest Island of the British Isles, divided into the Republic of Ireland and Northern Ireland **WS 1**, 17

Irvine [ˈɜːvɪn] town in Ayrshire, Scotland **WS 1**, 31

Isobel Wylie Hutchison [ɪzəbel ˈwaɪli ˈhʌtʃɪnsn] Scottish Arctic traveller (1889 – 1982) **WS 1**, 21

J

J. K. Rowling [ˌdʒeɪ ˌkeɪ ˈrəʊlɪŋ] British author, best known for the Harry Potter book series, born 31st July, 1965 **WS 3**, 103

Jackie Kay [ˌdʒæki ˈkeɪ] Scottish poet, playwright, and novelist, born 9th November 1961 **WS 1**, 46

Jackie Robinson [ˌdʒæki ˈrɒbɪnsən] first African American to play in Major League Baseball (1919 – 1972) **WS 2**, 75

James Brown [ˌdʒeɪmz ˈbraʊn] American singer and songwriter of soul music (1933 – 2006) **WS 2**, 67

James Robertson [dʒeɪmz ˈrɒbətsn] Scottish author, born 14th March, 1958 **WS 1**, 35

Jefferson Davis [ˌdʒefəsən ˈdeɪvɪs] American politician who served from 1861 to 1865 as President of the Confederate States (1808 – 1889) **WS 2**, 55

Jesse Owens [ˌdʒesi ˈəʊənz] African American Athlete who won four gold medals at the 1936 Olympic Games in Berlin (1913 – 1980) **WS 2**, 74

Jim Crow [ˌdʒɪm ˈkrəʊ] 'Jim Crow' was a racist term for a black person. The Jim Crow laws were enforced in different US states between 1876 and 1965 and provided a systematic legal basis for segregating and discriminating against African Americans. **WS 2**, 76

Joe Biden [ˌdʒəʊ ˈbaɪdn] 46th President of the United States, born 20th November 1942 **WS 2**, 83

John Wilkes Booth [ˌdʒɒn wɪlks ˈbuːð] man who killed Abraham Lincoln (1838 – 1865) **WS** , 57

Juneteenth [ˌdʒuːnˈtiːnθ] holiday on 19 June to celebrate the end of slavery **WS 2**, 78

K

Kamala Harris [ˌkɑːmələ ˈhærɪs] 49th Vice-President of the US and the first African American and woman to be in office, born 20th October, 1964 **WS 2**, 70

Kentucky [kenˈtʌki] state in the south of the US **WS 2**, 57

Ku Klux Klan [ˌkuː ˌklʌks ˈklæn] (KKK) hate organization in southern US states, opposes equal rights for black people and uses violence and terror **WS 2**, 60

L

Loch Ness [lɒk ˈnes] deep lake in the Highlands of Scotland, famous for its myth of the monster "Nessie" **WS 1**, 20

Louis Braille [luːɪs ˈbreɪl] French educator and developer of the Braille system of printing and writing used by the blind (1809 – 1852) **WS 3**, 123

Louise Welsh [luˈiːz ˈwelʃ] English author, born 1st February, 1965 **WS 1**, 35

Louisiana [luˌiːziˈænə] southern US state **WS 2**, 75

M

Macbeth [məkˈbeθ] play by William Shakespeare **WS 1**, 18

Malcolm X [ˌmælkəm ˈeks] African American leader and activist (1925 – 1965) **WS 2**, 60

Margaret Thatcher [ˌmɑːgrət ˈθætʃə] British conservative politician and Britain's first female prime minister (1925 – 2013) **WS 1**, 31

Martin Luther King Jr. [ˌmɑːtɪn ˌluːθə ˈkɪŋ dʒuːniə] most important leader of the US civil rights movement, his speech "I have a dream" is by many regarded as a masterpiece of rhetoric (1929 – 1968) **WS 2**, 52

Mary Queen of Scots [ˌmeəri ˌkwiːn əv ˈskɒts] Mary Stuart, served as queen of Scotland (1542 – 1587) **WS 1**, 18

Maya Angelou [ˌmaɪə ˈændʒəluː] American poet, memoirist, and actress (1928 – 2014) **WS 2**, 75

Mecca [ˈmekə] city in Saudi Arabia, visited by many Muslims every year for religious reasons **WS 2**, 61

Michigan [ˈmɪʃɪgən] state in north central US **WS 2**, 60

Muhammad Ali [məˌhæmɪd æˈliː] American boxer and activist (1942 – 2016) **WS 2**, 60

N

New Delhi [njuː ˈdɛli] capitol city of India **WS 4**, 134

Nicola Sturgeon [ˌnɪkələ ˈstɜːdʒən] Scottish politician, first minister of Scotland and first female leader of the Scottish National Party, born 19th July, 1970 **WS 1**, 31

Nobel Prize [ˌnəʊbel ˈpraɪz] prize given in six categories for outstanding work, named after founder Alfred Nobel **WS 2**, 58

Norway [ˈnɔːweɪ] country in northern Europe **WS 1**, 18

O

Oakland [ˈəʊklənd] city in the US state of California **WS 2**, 62

Omaha [ˈəʊməhɑː] city in the US state of Nebraska **WS 2**, 60

Opal Tometi [ˌəʊpl təˈmeɪti] human rights activist and cofounder of Black Lives Matter, born 15th August, 1984 **WS 2**, 70

Orkney Islands [ˈɔːkni aɪləndz] group of more than 70 islands in Scotland **WS 1**, 13

P

Patrisse Cullors [ˌpætrɪs ˈkʌləz] American Activist and cofounder of Black Lives Matter, born 20th June, 1983 **WS 2**, 70

Pennsylvania [ˌpenslˈveɪniə] state in the north-east of the US **WS 2**, 57

Prague [prɑːg] capital city of the Czech Republic **WS 3** , 95

Prince Philip [prɪns ˈfɪlɪp] Duke of Edinburgh (1921 – 2021) **WS 1**, 14

R

Robert Burns [ˌrɒbət ˈbɜːnz] Scottish poet (1759 – 1796) **WS 1**, 28

Robert E. Lee [ˌrɒbət iː ˈliː] leader of the Confederate States' armies during the American Civil War (1807 – 1870) **WS 2**, 56

Robert the Bruce [ˌrɒbət ðə ˈbruːs] king of Scotland (1274 – 1329) **WS 1**, 18

Rosa Parks [ˌrəʊzə ˈpɑːks] American civil rights activist (1913 – 2005) **WS 2**, 53

Ruby Bridges [ˌruːbi ˈbrɪdʒɪz] American civil rights activist, born 8th September, 1954 **WS 2**, 75

S

Sao Paulo [saʊm ˈpaʊləʊ] largest city in south-east Brazil **WS 3**, 95

Seattle [siˈætl] city in the north-western US **WS 2**, 62

Skye [skaɪ] Scottish island **WS 1**, 18

Springfield [ˈsprɪŋfiːld] city in the US state of Illinois **WS 2**, 57

Sutherland [ˈsʌðələnd] county in northern Scotland **WS 1**, 34

Sweden [ˈswiːdn] country in northern Europe **WS 3**, 108

T

Thailand [ˈtaɪlænd] country in south-east Asia **WS 3**, 95

Toni Morrison [ˌtəʊni ˈmɒrɪsən] American author (1931 – 2019) **WS 2**, 75

Tony Blair [ˌtəʊni ˈbleə] prime minister of the United Kingdom from 1997 to 2007, born 6th May, 1953 **WS 1**, 35

V

Val McDermid [ˌvæl mækˈdɜːmɪt] Scottish crime writer, born 4th June, 1955 **WS 1**, 34

Vesna Main [ˌveznə ˈmeɪn] Croatian writer **Ws 3**, 124

W

Westray [ˈwestriː] one of the Orkney Islands in Scotland **WS 1**, 13

William Shakespeare [ˈwɪljəmˈʃeɪkspɪə] English writer of poems and plays, regarded by many as the greatest writer of all time (1564 – 1616) **WS 1**, 18

William Wallace [ˌwɪljəm ˈwɒlɪs] Scottish soldier who led an army against the English forces of King Edward I (1270 – 1305) **WS 1**, 18

Acknowledgements

Text credits

Individual text credits can be found under or next to the respective texts on the page.

Picture credits

|akg-images GmbH, Berlin: 59.1, 74.3. |Alamy Stock Photo, Abingdon/Oxfordshire: AFF 79.2; agefotostock 52.3; allan wright 41.1; allOver images 17.6; Antonio Guillem Fernandez 137.1; Atkinson, Neil 70.2; Avpics 92.3; B Christopher 118.1; Barton, William 71.3; Berg, Georg 28.1; Berkut, Anna 134.1; Cal Sport Media 74.1; Cavendish, Alex 71.2; Chalabala, Jaromir 23.3; ClassicStock 115.1, 115.2; Cole, David 31.3; Contraband Collection 62.1, 62.2; Croft, Richard 25.3; Daemmrich, Bob 9.1, 143.1; Dagnall, Ian 66.2; Dalberto, Lorenzo 46.1; Danita Delimont Creative 11.1; Dimitris K. 92.4; DisobeyArt 71.4; Donaldson, Dave 29.1; DragonImages 111.1; Drinkwater, Ros 43.2; Evans, Robert 134.2; Findlay 30.1, 43.1; GARY DOAK 34.1, 35.3, 35.4; Gilbert, Jeff 32.1; GL Archive 57.1; Glasshouse Images 53.1, 102.2; GM/Current Affairs 79.1; gotravel 39.1; Gras, Philippe 67.1; Hager fotografie 102.6; Hale-Sutton, Duncan 18.3; Hamblin, Mark 40.1; Housden, Nigel 20.6; Hyderabad 140.3; ibreakmedia 59.4; Imagebroker 13.1; imageBROKER 38.1, 109.1; Islandstock 82.2; JOHN BRACEGIRDLE 17.4; Jones, Tim 22.1; keith morris 101.1; keith morris news 112.1; KGPA Ltd 19.1; lakshmiprasad S 132.1; Lenscap 67.2; Loop Images Ltd 41.2; Lou-Foto 132.2; Lukassek, Thomas 12.1; Lund, Jacob 123.3; Masterton, Iain 17.2, 26.1, 31.1; McDermott, Jarlath 102.5; MediaPunch Inc 52.4; Michael DeFreitas North America 10.1; Mint Images Limited 109.2; Molloy, Michael 42.4; Nick Scott plaques/sign photos 42.1; Northern Wild 22.3; Oeler, Christian 40.2; Olivers, Michael 35.1; Oreolife 118.4; PA Images 12.3, 14.1; Patti McConville/Stockimo 141.2; Perc, Franz 26.2; Pictorial Press Ltd 66.1, 66.3, 102.1; PjrNews 126.1; Powered by Light/Alan Spencer 32.2; Pritchard, Stan 34.2; public domain sourced / access rights from American Photo Archive 78.1; public domain sourced / access rights from World of Triss 102.3; Rann, Kelly 67.3; Rawpixel Ltd 92.2; Reddy, Simon 45.2; robertharding 26.4, 136.1; Rodgers, Gina 86.1; Roxby, Kay 17.3; Sally Anderson Archive Photos 124.2; samuel wordley 109.3; Schreck, Carrie 83.1; Sermulis, Edgars 72.2; SeventyFour Images 109.4; Shawshots 54.1; Stirling, Charles 126.2; Stocktrek Images, Inc. 54.2; Strelow, Marcel 5.1, 12.4; Sukapan, Thiti 95.2; Sutherland, Lynne 32.3; Sykes, Homer 42.3; Sykes; Homer 42.2; Szymczyk, Dorota 112.2; Tack, Jochen 118.3; Trinity Mirror/Mirrorpix 47.1, 53.2, 103.1, 150.6; Turrill, Keith 70.1; UPI 56.1, 69.1; viviana loza 93.1; VL 118.2; WENN Rights Ltd 26.3, 35.2; West, Jim 77.1; Westend61 GmbH 16.1; ZUMA Press, Inc. 79.3. |Alamy Stock Photo (RMB), Abingdon/Oxfordshire: Ammentorp Photography 37.1; Bailey-Cooper Photography 25.1; incamerastock 55.1; Stocktrek Images, Inc. 82.1; Sybille Reuter 10.2; Utomo, Hermin 106.1; WENN Ltd 103.2, 150.4. |Bridgeman Images, Berlin: © Look and Learn 12.2. |CartoonStock.com, Bath: 84.1. |deutsche presse agentur, Frankfurt/M.: 74.2. |Domke, Franz-Josef, Wunstorf: 3.1. |Donnelly, Karen, Brighton: 13.2, 20.1, 20.2, 20.3, 20.4, 20.5, 23.1, 23.2, 33.1, 39.2, 39.3, 39.4, 39.5, 39.6, 39.7, 72.1, 94.1, 96.1, 108.1, 113.1, 139.1, 139.2, 140.1, 140.2, 143.2, 144.1. |fotolia.com, New York: Dolgopiatov, Igor 17.1; Jakub Krechowicz 123.2; Monkey Business 115.3; rupbilde 133.1. |Getty Images, München: Bettmann 63.1; Henderson, Thearon W. 71.1; Sengstacke, Robert Abbott 5.2, 59.3; © Bettmann/CORBIS 53.3. |Himmelstoß, Julie, München: 80.1. |iStockphoto.com, Calgary: Abulkhanov, Ildar 98.1; AdrianHancu 25.2; AzmanL 100.3, 150.3; chrisboy2004 114.1; Digital Vision Vectors 45.1; DragonImages 98.2; FG Trade 68.1, 95.1; gorodenkoff 98.3; Horree, Peter 119.1; kyolshin 17.5; MarijaRadovic 92.1; mariusz_prusaczyk 122.1; Mary981 124.1; Nikitina, Viktoria 95.4; peeterv 95.3; Prostock-Studio 121.1; Rohappy 27.1; Vallenari, Flavio 47.2; xavierarnau 11.2; zeljkosantrac 7.1, 93.2. |Picture-Alliance GmbH, Frankfurt a.M.: AP Photo 75.1; AP Photo/Brekken, Isaac 52.1; AP Photo/GENE HERRICK 59.2; dpa / UPI 102.4; dpa/Zinken, Paul 103.3, 150.5; Everett Collection 61.2; New China News/zReportage.com/Hou Jun 74.4; Photoshot 95.5; PictureLux/The Hollywood Archive Fotograf: Marion S. Trikosko 61.1; united archives/91020 123.1. |Royal Scottish Geographical Society, Perth: 21.1. |Shutterstock.com, New York: Ink Drop 31.2; McCann, Josh 138.1; Stuart, Pete 15.1. |Shutterstock.com (RM), New York: Liam Daniel/Focus Features/Kobal 18.2; Photo by Icon/Ladd Co/Paramount/Kobal 18.1. |stock.adobe.com, Dublin: Dietl, Jeanette 100.1, 150.1; donatas1205 141.1; Feodora 73.1; Marco 22.2; Viktoriia 100.2, 150.2. |Süddeutsche Zeitung - Photo, München: KPA 52.2. |ullstein bild, Berlin: The Granger Collection 57.2. |United Nations, New York, NY: https://www.un.org/sustainabledevelopment/wp-content/uploads/2019/01/SDG_Guidelines_AUG_2019_Final.pdf), "The content of this publication has not been approved by the United Nations and does not reflect the views of the United Nations or its officials or Member States". 135.1. |Williamson, Pete, Kent, Southorough, Tunbridge Wells: 48.1, 49.1, 50.1, 50.2, 50.3, 88.1, 89.1, 89.2, 90.1, 90.2, 91.1, 91.2, 128.1, 129.1, 130.1, 131.1, 131.2.

Audio credits

|Audio 19 uses music from: The Banshee. Gravel Walks. The Old Copperplate by Sláinte | https://freemusicarchive.org/music/Slinte, Music promoted by https://www.chosic.com/free-music/all/, Creative Commons CC BY-SA 3.0, https://creativecommons.org/licenses/by-sa/3.0/. |Audio 23: Mein Schottland: Der Podcast: Folge 1: Die Insel Arran, 18.11.2017, Henning Rolapp, https://www.meinschottland.de/podlove/file/1/s/download/c/select-show/MSC001-Die_Insel_Arran.mp3. |Audios 32, 39, 44 produced by Wildfang Video- und Audioproduktion, Berlin. |Audio 47: Common and John Legend. Glory. Selma: Music from the Motion Picture.

Columbia Records, 2014. |All other dialogues and words and phrases produced by Anne Rosenfeld for RBA Productions (rbaproductions.co.uk). Recording engineer Mark Smith.

Video credits

Videos 6 and 12 produced by Creative Listening (https://www.creativelistening.co.uk). Producers Rachel Booth, Jackaby Barsby.